CHILD DEVELOPMENT
IN NORMALITY
AND PSYCHOPATHOLOGY

Child Development in Normality and Psychopathology

Edited by

JULES R. BEMPORAD, M.D.

Director of Children's Services
Associate Professor of Psychiatry
Massachusetts Mental Health Center
Harvard Medical School
Boston, Massachuetts

BRUNNER/MAZEL, *Publishers* • New York

Library of Congress Cataloging in Publication Data
main entry under title:

Child development in normality and psychopathology.
   Includes bibliographical references and index.
   1. Child psychopathology—Congresses.   2. Child
psychology—Congresses. I. Bemporad, Jules.
RJ499.C4833   618.9'28'9   79-24086
ISBN 0-87630-210-X

Copyright © 1980 by Jules R. Bemporad

Published by
BRUNNER/MAZEL, INC.
19 Union Square
New York, New York 10003

MANUFACTURED IN THE UNITED STATES OF AMERICA

Preface

The motivation to produce this book evolved as a result of teaching professionals at various stages of training and of different backgrounds who were involved in supplying care for children. During classes or rounds, I would be frequently asked for a reference that would serve as a guide to normal development, as well as describing how the growth process could be altered by certain conditions. While I was able to distribute a "reading list" and hope that the students would go to the library and consult the specific articles, I felt there was a need for this information to be easily available between two covers, a need which hopefully this book will fulfill.

This volume is intended to serve as an introduction to the development and psychopathology of the child for the clinical practitioner. Toward this end, I have asked the contributors to stress practical considerations with extensive clinical illustrations rather than theoretical issues. However, beyond the pure dissemination of clinical or factual knowledge, it is hoped that the following pages will impart a broader theoretical viewpoint, namely that the psychopathology of childhood is best studied and understood against the framework of normal development.

JULES R. BEMPORAD, M.D.

Contents

Contributors

JULES R. BEMPORAD, M.D.
Director of Children's Services, Associate Professor of Psychiatry, Massachusetts Mental Health Center, Harvard Medical School, Boston, Massachusetts.

STEPHEN L. BENNETT, M.D.
Associate Professor of Psychiatry, Columbia University College of Physicians & Surgeons, New York, New York.

PENELOPE BUSCHMAN, R.N., C.S., M.S.
Clinical Specialist in Child Psychiatric Nursing, Babies Hospital; Instructor in Clinical Nursing, School of Nursing, Faculty of Medicine, Columbia University, New York, New York.

STELLA CHESS, M.D.
Professor of Child Psychiatry, New York University School of Medicine; Director of Child and Adolescent Psychiatric Services, New York University Medical Center, New York, New York.

RICHARD A. GARDNER, M.D.
Clinical Associate Professor of Psychiatry, Columbia University College of Physicians & Surgeons, New York, New York.

RODMAN GILDER, M.D.
Clinical Associate Professor of Psychiatry, Columbia University College of Physicians & Surgeons, New York, New York.

MARY B. HAGAMEN, M.D.
Director, Child and Adolescent Psychiatry, Nassau County Medical Center, East Meadow, New York.

MAHIN HASSIBI, M.D.
Clinical Associate Professor of Psychiatry, New York University School of Medicine, Assistant Director of Children's Service; Bellevue Hospital, New York, New York.

BRUCE HAUPTMAN, M.D.
Director, Preschool Programs, Instructor in Psychiatry, Massachusetts Mental Health Center, Harvard Medical School, Boston, Massachusetts.

JEANETTE JEFFERSON JANSKY, Ph.D.
Educational Director, Robinson Reading Clinic, Babies Hospital; Clinical Assistant Professor of Pediatrics, Columbia University College of Physicians & Surgeons, New York, New York.

CLARICE J. KESTENBAUM, M.D.
Director of Child and Adolescent Psychiatry, St. Luke's Hospital; Associate Professor of Psychiatry, Columbia University College of Physicians & Surgeons, New York, New York.

ALAN M. LEVY, M.D.
Chief, Child and Adolescent Psychiatric Services, Beth Israel Medical Center; Associate Clinical Professor of Psychiatry, Mount Sinai School of Medicine, New York, New York.

NINA R. LIEF, M.D.
Director, Early Childhood Development Center, Associate Professor of Clinical Psychiatry, New York Medical College, New York, New York.

ROBERT D. MEHLMAN, M.D.
Training and Supervising Analyst, Boston Psychoanalytic Society and Institute; Assistant Clinical Professor of Psychiatry, Harvard Medical School, Boston, Massachusetts.

YEHUDA NIR, M.D.
Director of Pediatric Psychiatry, Memorial Sloan-Kettering Cancer Center; Associate Clinical Professor of Psychiatry, Cornell University Medical Center, New York.

LETTY J. POGUL, Ph.D.
> Assistant Clinical Professor of Medical Psychology in Psychiatry, Columbia University College of Physicians & Surgeons, New York, New York.

CHARLES A. SARNOFF, M.D.
> Author of *Latency*; Full Time Private Practice, New York, New York.

VERNON SHARP, M.D.
> Lecturer, Adolescent Psychiatry, Columbia University School of Social Work, New York, New York; Private Practice, Scarsdale, New York.

JOHN A. SOURS, M.D.
> Clinical Assistant Professor of Psychiatry, Cornell University College of Physicians & Surgeons; Training and Supervising Adult and Child Analyst, Columbia Psychoanalytic Clinic for Training and Research, New York, New York.

JUDITH ZARIN-ACKERMAN, Ph.D.
> Coordinator of Intervention Programs, Early Childhood Development Center, New York Medical College, New York, New York.

CHILD DEVELOPMENT
IN NORMALITY
AND PSYCHOPATHOLOGY

Part I

INTRODUCTION

1

Theories of Development

JULES R. BEMPORAD, M.D.

For, of all the wonders which life presents to us in such plenty, that of development is surely the greatest. Let us recall what it means: on the one hand we have this little drop of jelly which, as a fertilized ovum, represents the germ of an organism; on the other is the wonderful edifice of the complete living creature, with its myriad of cells, its endlessly complicated organs, character, instincts. When we compare the beginning with the end of this process it is easy to understand why it is that in all attempts to solve the great riddle of life, scientifically or philosophically, this cardinal problem of development has been preferred as the starting point.
Ludwig von Bertalanffy,
Modern Theories of Development, 1933

INTRODUCTION

An assumption which will appear again and again in the following pages of this book is that a knowledge of basic normal development is necessary for appropriate diagnosis and treatment of childhood psychopathology. The relative normalcy or deviance of any behavior must be viewed against a developmental framework. What is a normal response at one age can be a grossly pathological reaction at another. The evaluation of any given child must take into account the dynamic process of development both in terms of the specific child's own developmental path and how he compares with others at his particular stage of growth. We have to view the child in the context of where he has been and where he is apt to be going in his life history. Therefore much of our diagnostic assessment and therapeutic intervention will be based on the belief that the child is involved in the process of change in response to both external

3

shaping influences and internal biological forces. Despite the importance of this process, current knowledge of the totality of development is still rudimentary and incomplete.

The major theoretical systems which have yielded an understanding of the developmental process have been the psychoanalytic, the cognitive and the behavioral perspectives. Each of these systems approaches the child from differing points of view and usually studies different aspects of the totality of the child's experience so that there has been little integration of their findings. However, each system has uncovered certain basic questions about the psychological growth of the child, although often expressed in a different jargon and derived from different methodologies. Some of these recurring themes will be enumerated at the end of this chapter.

The Concept of Development

We all know that children change as they grow older, that eight-year-olds are capable of tasks beyond four-year-olds who in turn are superior to infants. With each successive stage of development, the child appears to increase his abilities in various areas; but this does not answer questions regarding the nature of development itself. Is development simply realized by increasing complexity of similar behavior, or does it involve qualitative leaps with the appearance of novel behaviors? Is development smoothly continuous or can it be divided into stages or periods of rapid progress and periods of stagnation and/or consolidation? Are certain times in a child's development more sensitive to stress in certain areas than other times and does improper environmental reaction during these periods uniformly result in later aberrations? Finally, what are the causes of development? Is a child's increasing complexity the inevitable manifestation of an innate blueprint or is change merely the response to external stimulation or demands?

These are difficult questions which do not lend themselves to facile answers. What is somewhat surprising is that these questions have been seriously studied only in the fairly recent past. The study of child development appears to have had to wait for a more global change to occur in the intellectual climate of Western culture. This alteration of thought was brought about by Darwin's revolutionary doctrine that the species had developed, thus that we live in a changing world. Before Darwin, man and the world were seen as static and unchanging (24). One need only look at some pre-Darwinian medical texts with the pictures of a complete homunculus, snug within the sperm cell, to appreciate the change in thought that followed evolutionary theory. For the homunculus did not develop; being already formed, it merely grew bigger. The idea that the structure actually went through a complete change in development had to await the intellectual assimilation of Darwin's provocative thesis.

The earliest theories attempting to explain development were, in fact, blatant and gross applications of evolutionary theory. In terms of embryology, Haeckel's dictum that "ontogeny recapitulates phylogeny" indicated that the human fetus went through all of the anatomic stages of animal evolution. In the field of child psychology, G. Stanley Hall's famous "recapitulation theory" similarly attempted to explain development as a reliving of evolutionary stages. For example, the young child's proclivity for swinging on branches was seen as an atavistic recapitulation of our apelike ancestors' arboreal life. Similarly, the latency age child's tendency to form groups was seen as a revival of primitive man's tribal existence. This heavy handed application of evolutionary theory to all aspects of life reached its most extreme form in the political theories that regarded certain peoples as insufficiently "evolved" and thus suitable only for inferior social and economic status. Regardless of misapplications, the overall impact of this way of thinking was that man has a history which, in some way, he carries with himself and that, in the course of both evolution and development, organisms go through profound qualitative changes.

It was in this spirit that the great neurologist, Hughlings Jackson, began to study seriously the human nervous system and its pathology within the framework of evolution. In his Croonian lectures, given in 1884, Jackson (20) suggested that neurological symptoms may, in some cases, represent a return to a less evolved state, a process which he called "dissolution," meaning a process of dedifferentiation, a taking to pieces, which produced negative and positive symptoms. By negative symptoms, Jackson meant the loss of normal functioning due to destruction of brain tissue. The positive symptoms resulted from the liberated expression of older structures that had been formerly controlled by the intact higher, more evolved, structures. These positive symptoms, which included such psychiatric aberrations as hallucinations and illusions, were seen as the manifestation of the releasing of primitive areas of the brain secondary to injury.

By considering the nervous system and human behavior in an evolutionary framework, Jackson presented a truly novel concept of disease:

the reemergence of intact older phylogenetic modes of integration, released by the destruction or malfunction of later evolutionary structures. Jackson's theorizing did not go unnoticed by Sigmund Freud who, prior to his momentous contributions to psychiatry, had been a student of neurology. Freud supported Jackson's theories in his early book on aphasia (9) and was equally stimulated by the Darwinian approach to psychology. Freud's early theories also postulated a phylogenetic "layered" model of the mind. As early as 1896 (9), Freud described, in a letter, a picture of the psyche which had evolved "by a process of stratification" into a series of transcription mechanisms, each representing "the psychical achievement of successive epochs of life." Thus the major thrust of the Freudian, and therefore the psychoanalytic, investigation into the basis of human behavior was to search into the past which each adult carries within himself and unconsciously repeats in his everyday behavior.

However, while Freud speculated that in severe mental illness there may be a reemergence of more primitive forms of mentation, he believed that most individuals regressed back to earlier stages of their own lives rather than back to archaic stages of mankind. It was through his clinical experience with patients who exhibited "libidinal" regressions, back to childhood, that Freud reconstructed a model of child development. In this manner, the speculations of Darwin about the evolution of one species from another eventually influenced a powerful theory of the formation of human personality. This model, expressed in many of Freud's works but most fully elaborated in his *Three Essays on the Theory of Sexuality* (12), has had tremendous impact on our current thinking, not only in psychology but in virtually every social science.

THE PSYCHOANALYTIC APPROACH

The psychoanalytic theory of child development is but one part of a much larger theoretical structure and cannot be comprehended without some rudimentary exposition of the system as a whole. Therefore, before dealing with this particular approach to child development, some basic formulations of psychoanalysis will be presented:

The Topographic Hypothesis: Freud's first comprehensive statement on the structure of the psyche appeared in the last chapter of *The Interpretation of Dreams* (11). This early model is roughly an adaptation of a stimulus-response mechanism in which incoming stimuli increase levels of tension in the organism which are in turn discharged by motor activity.

Therefore, the basis of behavior is the discharge of internal tension. Freud, however, also postulates inner generators of tension as a result of instincts which need expression. These instincts are tied up with fundamental life processes such as eating, etc. However, the expression of two instinctual drives, sexuality and aggression, are in direct opposition to social organization and thus their pure expression must somehow be blocked or at least modified to fit socially acceptable mores. This inner conflict, between the need for instinctual gratification and the need for social acceptance and communal existence, forms the cornerstone of the psychoanalytic theory of mind. Freud postulated that most of human behavior, including not only pathological symptoms but such normal phenomena as dreams, hobbies, jokes and slips of the tongue, were the result of a compromise in the great battle between the instincts and society. Much of this conflict, however, occurs outside of our awareness, in the unconscious, and it is only through a painstaking examination of bits of behavior that the unconscious meaning of that behavior (i.e., the hidden gratification of instinct) can be discerned. These unacceptable thoughts and wishes are repressed, that is, actively kept out of conscious awareness and forced into the unconscious, and are expressed only in a symbolic guise, as in the nightly dramas of dream life. Here, the stratified theory of mind is plainly evident: There is a conscious stratum which is awareness, a preconscious stratum which contains the repositories of the past (memories) which can gain awareness, and last, an unconscious stratum whose antisocial contents are denied access to awareness by an active censor who juggles the amount of instinctual gratification that can be safely gained at any given time. This division of the mind into three strata described the topography of psyche and so has been called the "Topographic Hypothesis." Later, Freud was to further define the logical characteristics of the unconscious vis-à-vis consciousness. Unconscious mentation is said to follow primary process thinking, meaning that gratification is always avidly sought without regard for logic or consequences. Conscious mentation follows secondary process thinking which is characterized by logical and verbal organization, inhibition of impulses and social responsiveness. It was postulated that the young child manifests primary process thought which is gradually submerged into the unconscious with increasing maturation, although it reappears in the dreams or psychiatric symptoms of adults. Another, less technical, description of the levels of mentation can be found in Freud's differentiation of the pleasure and reality principles. The former is dominated by gratification at any cost, even the correct interpretation of reality, while the latter is concerned with an appreciation of things as they really are in the surrounding world. It was postulated that the infant gives up the pleasure principle through maturation (possibly because hallucinations or distortions do not afford true gratification) and gradually adjusts to reality in the never ending search for instinctual gratification.

Dynamic Theory: The real impact of Freud's theory of mind is that there is always conflict or at least tension between the socially unacceptable biological urges and the inhibiting and regulating forces of society. According to this model, there is ceaseless mental activity with defenses against instincts and environmental stimulation provoking increased surges of instinctual pressures. The actual mechanisms of defense came under increased scrutiny as simple repression became but one of many possibilities for keeping unconscious contents out of awareness.

The Structural Theory: As the agency responsible for defense against the expression of instinct became more important, it also became clear that this sophisticated process transpired outside of consciousness. Therefore, a revised theory of mind was needed in order to account for unconscious processes that were not in the service of instinctual gratification. This model of mind was formally presented in *The Ego and the Id* (13), published in 1923. In this work, Freud described the now familiar tripartite division of the psyche into id, ego and superego. Since this model stresses mental structures it has become known as the "Structural Theory" and is Freud's last thorough description of the psyche.

Briefly, the id mentally represents all that is inherently biological in man. It is the repository of the primitive and childhood past and the source of instinctual and psychic energy. It follows the laws of primary process mentation and is not accessible to consciousness but ceaselessly pushes for the gratification of wishes. The ego is the structure that represents external reality within the psyche. The ego must find ways of preventing the blatant expression of id impulses yet also allow some discharge of tension. It accomplishes this task by the various mechanisms of defense which permit wishes to be gratified in symbolic or disguised ways. The chief weapon of the ego appears to be anxiety (14). When the id urges threaten to be expressed in a situation which might cause eventual damage to the individual, the ego mentally portrays the consequences of such expression which results in a feeling of dread and apprehension, called "signal anxiety." This experience serves as a warning and usually suffices to repress the unacceptable urges. In contrast, pathological anxiety results when the ego is unable to stop the repression or modification of instinctual urges, that is, a failure of the signal technique.

In this later theory, great emphasis was placed on the ego as the regulator of the expression of the id and as the tester of reality. It was believed that the ego, in fact, derived from the id as the infant came into increasing conflict with its environment. Additional support for the ego later derives from the superego, which is essentially the intrapsychic structure that represents learned cultural standards. The superego develops in later childhood as a form of identification with the same sex parent, with the internalization of the parent's moral values. Whenever the ego permits id expressions that are counter to the social norms that have been internalized into the superego, a feeling of guilt results, causing further inhibition of instinctual expression. The presence of the superego, however, can be a mixed blessing. While assuring that the individual will conform to social mores, the attitudes internalized into this agency can be so inhibiting and punitive that too little gratification is obtained, so that psychiatric illness may also result.

Psychosexual Development

With this brief and obviously cursory outline of psychoanalytic theory, we can now proceed to that aspect of the theory that specifically pertains to development (12). As is characteristic of adult mental life, the psychological experience of the child is also best described as one of conflict between instincts and society. Freud postulated a series of different instinctual forces that become active at sequential stages of development as a result of biological maturation. The gratification of these instincts resulted in the sensation of pleasure (since there was a concurrent decrease in tension) and so were termed erotic, as forerunners of later sexual experience. In fact, these early instincts were not extinguished in later life but their gratification was relegated to the foreplay that preceded gential intercourse, which defined adult eroticism. In certain cases, an overly strong persistence of these childhood instincts was said to result in certain perversions. In still other individuals, the early instincts had not received sufficient gratification during the appropriate childhood stage so that an unconscious need for satisfaction persisted, or too much gratification of a particular instinctual mode may have occurred so that, again unconsciously, the individual continued to desire childhood gratification in adult life. This excessive persistence of childhood instinctual pressures was termed *fixation* and this led to a propensity for *regression* to that particular form of drive satisfaction at times of stress. Much of adult psychopathology was explained as a regression to a childhood state of gratification with the expression of early instincts. However, as discussed above, the ego and superego did not permit the open expression of these unacceptable instincts but forced a compromise by disguising the partial expression into symptoms or other more socially acceptable behaviors.

The important concepts which were stressed by this theory are the following: Symptoms are not random behaviors but have a psychological meaning which can be understood if we know the life history of the individual; childhood wishes persist into adult life and greatly determine the everyday behavior of adults; and child development can be defined as a sequential series of stages with a defect in gratification at any stage affecting the successful passage of the child through subsequent stages.

Only a cursory description of each stage will be given here as the subsequent chapters deal with psychosexual development in much more detail. Briefly, the oral stage is defined by the infant's deriving pleasure through sucking, feeding and later through biting. While the drive toward oral gratification initially serves the life-sustaining process of feeding, gradually oral activity becomes pleasurable in itself. Later character traits associated with fixation at the oral stage include excessive passivity and dependency.

The anal stage begins with the innate maturation of the sphincters and the shift of the child's interest from sucking and eating to eliminatory functions. The child is said to obtain pleasure from holding in or letting go of feces. During this stage, the child must learn to time his elimination to conform to the mother's demands, resulting in the conflict of pleasing the self by expelling wastes at will. Eventually, the child does control his sphincters in order to insure the continuation of the mother's love. Later characteristics thought to represent unresolved anal conflicts include possessiveness, obstinacy and stinginess.

The phallic stage results from the child's shift of interest to the genitals. This fascination with external genitalia is said to occur in both genders, leading to a recognition of the anatomical differences between the sexes. According to traditional psychoanalytic theory, the girl feels that her external genital (the clitoris) is inferior to the boy's penis, leading to a sense of inadequacy that is to haunt her the rest of her life. As a result of her awareness of this organ inferiority, the girl blames her "castration" on the mother and turns her affection to the father, who possesses the prized penis, and focuses on her vagina as an erotic zone. This formulation has been severely attacked by feminists who view it as frankly deprecatory of women. Freud was, in fact, somewhat tentative about his theories of female development, admitting that, in the last analysis, this subject remained a mystery.

The sexual development of the male gained larger acceptance and was put forward with greater assurance. It was postulated that during the phallic stage, the male child wishes exclusive possession of the mother and becomes jealous of the father, initiating the familiar Oedipal complex. The child expects retaliation from the father for his erotic desires for the mother and eventually gives up the mother for fear of his physical integrity. The successful resolution of the Oedipal conflict occurs when the son models himself after father and receives vicarious gratification through this identification. The internalization of the latter's values and morals via identification becomes the nucleus for the superego, which represents cultural norms intrapsychically. Later difficulties resulting from an unresolved Oedipal complex are believed to be problems in heterosexual relationships, among other neurotic symptoms.

The latency period is a time of relative quiescence, which Freud believed to be the aftermath of the violent upheaval of the Oedipal drama. The fear of retaliatory bodily harm (i.e. castration) causes a repression of all erotic drives and a shifting of interest to cognitive and social tasks. The child detaches himself emotionally from the mother and widens his scope to include school, peers and others outside the nuclear family orbit.

This period of relative stability is interrupted by the biolgoical changes that herald puberty. Under the influence of biochemical changes, the instincts reassert themselves with a push toward erotic gratification. During this period of adolescence, the healthy individual, having discarded the mother as a sexual object, will choose a partner among his peers. Similarly, other same sex adults will be selected as ideal figures, fostering the final giving way of the child's tie to parents. At this stage, the erotic instincts are truly genital, with intercourse as the major objective which, Freud reasoned, serves to propagate the species.

This early statement of psychoanalytic theory clearly stressed the biological (i.e. instinctual) aspects of mental life. It would appear that the mode of erotic discharge determined the characteristics of the rest of the personality. While aware of cultural and social factors in child development, it seems as though Freud centered on the biological substrate of the personality in his effort to integrate his view of child development with the larger theory of mind which emphasized the continued conflict between instincts and culture.

Not long after Freud had outlined this theory of development in order to explain the aberrant behavior of his adult patients, the conceptual range of these libidinal stages was greatly enlarged, especially by Karl Abraham.

While Abraham (1) restated much of Freud's original thinking about the psychosexual stages, and even supplied confirmatory clinical material, he broadened the scope of these stages and emphasized a different aspect in their development. Freud had stressed the biological mode of release at each stage but Abraham added the type of human interaction (so-called object relations) that occurs during each stage. This was an important addition that continues to influence psychoanalysis today, for it switched the major concern of the theory from a semi-physiological to a predominantly psychological view of development. Abraham also interpreted the occurrence of psychopathology as the result of fixations at childhood stages but mainly in terms of modes of relating. As a result of his work, the psychoanalytic view of development included in its scope the progression of types of relationships from infancy through adolescence. For example, the oral phase was characterized by a specific mode of infant-mother interaction as well as the predominant use of the mouth in obtaining gratification.

Ego Psychology

This was essentially the status of the psychoanalytic theory of development for roughly two decades when the growing influence of the so-called "ego psychology" asserted its influence on developmental theory. This movement within psychoanalysis reaffirmed the importance of the ego in everyday behavior. Briefly, this meant that overt behavior was not only the direct result of unconscious forces but that consciousness and the learned defenses against these forces greatly affected one's activity. Ego psychologists gave the environment a greater role in the shaping of personality which, at times, had been seen as the result of the unalterable unfolding of innate forces. At the same time, ego psychologists postulated that this central mental structure did not originate from the id but had its own autonomous development, especially in so-called "conflict-free" spheres of the ego (15).

Ego psychology appears to have derived mainly from changes in therapeutic techniques, shifting the focus of attention to the ego defenses against instinctual forces rather than centering only on the expression of id contents. This alteration of emphasis was also reflected in the theoretical approach to child development. The child's own defensive capabilities at different stages were appreciated, as were the environmental forces that could strengthen or weaken the ego's mechanism of defense.

The logical sequence of this appreciation of external forces in development was to study the effect of culture on child-rearing. It was felt that while the parents are obviously significant in the rearing of a child, they are part of a specific society with particular values and expectations. In addition, much of childhood is spent in interaction with non-familial individuals such as teachers and friends who also shape the character of the child by expressing the mores of their culture.

ERIKSON'S PSYCHOSOCIAL THEORY

An attempt to integrate the traditional framework of psychosexual stages with the contributions of cultural anthropology was made by Erikson (7) in his "epigenetic" theory of personality. Erikson agrees with Freud and Abraham that at specific stages in ontogeny some particular function reaches special importance for the child and that an appropriate environmental response is necessary for normal growth. For Freud, the developmental stage was defined by an erogenous zone and for Abraham it was expanded to emphasize parental relations; Erikson defines such stages as times of crisis in which the individual's innate maturation encounters and conflicts with social mores. He defines each stage as consisting of a task which should be mastered if adequate development is to continue. Therefore each stage is a choice point that leads either to continued growth along healthy lines or an aberrant deviation in the course of development. Erikson reinterprets the basic stages against a sociological framework, noting differences in the ease or difficulty encountered by children of different cultures. Erikson also attempts to describe the child's actual conscious experience at each stage, describing development in terms of how the child is viewed by himself and others. At the same time, Erikson also acknowledges the fundamental psychoanalytic concept of innate maturational stages with the sequential unfolding of unconscious instinctual forces.

The traditional oral period is described by Erikson as the stage of "basic trust versus mistrust" where the infant gains a fundamental attitude of security in his surroundings and in himself. The prevalent mode for this stage is "incorporation" exemplified by the infant's comfort in developing the ability to receive and to accept. By "getting what is given" and by "learning to get somebody to do for him what he wishes to have done," the infant develops the basic groundwork for his later capacity to be the giver to others. During this period, Erikson hypothesizes that the infant forms a rudimentary sense of identity from the awareness of "I am what I am given." Obviously, the successful progression through this stage is greatly dependent on the quality of maternal care.

Erikson characterizes the anal stage as the stage of "autonomy versus shame and doubt." The increasing maturation of the child's musculature allows him to control his body and, with this feat, gain a sense of autonomy. He develops his own sense of self and, no longer a passive recipient, he forms an identity on the basis of "I am what I will." The crisis of this stage revolves over the control of one's body and with it the freedom of self-expression versus suppression, the balance between willfulness and cooperation with parental wishes. Erikson notes that many of the problems of this stage are secondary to the mores of Western civilization that idealize a mechanically trained, faultlessly functioning and always clean, deodorized body, as well as maintain an obsession with orderliness, punctuality and thrift. Toilet training appears to be but one of the many skirmishes in the battle for autonomy. If the child's budding will is squashed, he may experience the pain of shame, that he is visible to others while in the process of an unacceptable activity. Ultimately, this self-inhibition may culminate in an over-control of the will, a fear of self-expression and a strict adherence to law and order. Similarly, the child may doubt his own impulses, forever requiring the reassurance of an external structure which allows a certainty he does not feel within himself.

The phallic stage is characterized by Erikson as concerning "initiative versus guilt." The previous stage may have convinced the child that he is a worthwhile person; now he has to decide what kind of person he will be. Erikson states that in his choice, the child hitches his wagon to nothing less than a star. He wants to be like his parents who appear to him to be very powerful and very beautiful. He plays with the idea of how it would be to be them. The child's identity at this stage is centered around "I am what I will be." His newly developed cognitive, linguistic and imaginative powers allow him to fantasize and compare himself with the parental ideal. For Erikson, it is this comparative mode that sets the scene for the Oedipal conflict and the painful recognition for the child that, in the gential sphere, he is not yet an adult. Throughout this stage of sexual curiosity and concomitant fear, the child must maintain a sense of initiative or self-motivated activity. Ideally, the child balances his dangerous fantasies and his guilt with the acquisition of a sense of moral responsibility, i.e. the creation of the Freudian superego. The danger is that the intrusive acts and the even more intrusive fantasies will lead to a deep sense of guilt which will paralyze his future zest for learning and doing. Here again cultural and parental attitudes are of prime importance. Successful mastery of this stage depends largely on the parents allowing the child to feel himself to be of equal worth while different in age and capabilities and allowing a peaceful cultivation of his initiative.

The next stage, corresponding to the Freudian latency period, is characterized by Erikson as dealing with "industry versus inferiority." At this stage, the child's sense of identity rests on the dictum "I am what I learn." Rather than focusing on sexual repression, Erikson stresses the burgeoning cognitive abilities and the extra-familial contact with society as characteristic of this age. This is the era of industry in making things, collecting things, and in participating in cooperative efforts with others. The conflict of this stage is whether the child feels that his labors will be adequately valued by society or whether he will be deemed as inferior in the eyes of others (and as a result by himself). If the latter unfortunate resolution occurs, there is a danger that the child will limit his further endeavors to solitary pursuits and fear public exposure of his efforts except when these endeavors conform to cultural mores so as to insure acceptance. The continued usage of newly acquired cognitive or social skills will be stifled for fear of humiliation. If, on the other hand, the child feels his productions to be valued by others, he will internalize a sense of competence and adequacy and a positive feeling toward an adventurous use of his skills.

The culmination of all the prior stages for Freudian theory is the genital stage when the previous component instincts are submerged into genital procreative contact with a suitable partner. Here again, while acknowledging the biological changes implicit in puberty, Erikson stresses the sociocultural tasks of adolescence. For Erikson, this is the stage of "identity versus identity diffusions," implying that the prime object of the young adolescent is the consolidation of a personal sense of self, of an inner sameness and continuity which will be maintained despite varied life experiences. Implicit in this achievement of identity is the acceptance of a social role and the creation of a certain ideological perspective that will guide behavior. This coalescence of a personal identity is dependent on the successful passage through all the previous stages which allowed a partial integration of self-identity in circumscribed areas. The threat of this stage is "identity diffusion," meaning the inability to maintain an independent sense of self but rather to rely on cliques, organizations, or identification with hero-figures to supply one's identity. Here again, Erikson believes that American culture with its adulation of successful self-made men and its belief in upward social mobility makes the acceptance of a stable identity especially difficult for the youngster who has to face the world alone for the first time.

Erikson has described further developmental crises throughout adult life which are beyond the scope of this work and the reader is referred to the original sources for their exposition. It is noteworthy, however, that Erikson, while accepting the psychoanalytic doctrine of repeating childhood experiences in adult life, also portrays the individual as facing further crises beyond childhood as a result of his internal maturation coming into conflict with social demands. In this sense, Erikson believes that development actually continues through old age, with each stage bringing its own problems and opportunities.

Other Contributions

In more recent years, two theorists have made further significant contributions to the psychoanalytic theory of child development. These influential writers are Anna Freud in England and Margaret Mahler in the United States.* Anna Freud was one of the first psychoanalytically oriented researchers to actually engage in the direct study of children. Throughout her long career, she has contributed greatly to the study of various aspects of childhood. Of her many innovations, her concept of "developmental lines"(8) is most germane to the overall theory of development. By developmental lines, she refers to the tracing through childhood of the interaction between the id (innate biological forces) and the ego (forces of acculturation and of mastery). To quote Anna Freud, "What we are looking for are the basic interactions between id and ego and their various developmental levels, and also age related sequences of them which, in importance, frequency, and regularity, are comparable to the maturational sequence of libidinal stages or the gradual unfolding of the ego functions." Therefore, Anna Freud intends to show how the previously described libidinal stages are, at each step, in constant relationship with the ego's own maturational scheme.

---

*Melanie Klein has also contributed a great deal to the psychoanalytic theory of child development. Her views, long thought to be out of the mainstream of theory, have recently experienced popular revival in this country but mainly in reference to adult psychopathology.

While based on the classical psychosexual stages, the landmarks described in the various developmental lines are more elaborate and clinically richer. The most reliable and well established developmental line, which most closely approximates the classical stages, and serves as the prototype for the other developmental lines, is that of dependency to emotional self-reliance and adult relationships. This line represents the gradual evolution of the child's significant attachments to others from birth to adolescence. However, Anna Freud also considers developmental vectors that were of only peripheral interest in the original formulations. For example, she documents the significant milestones involved in the child's progress from interest in his body to play with toys or from play to work.

Another helpful aspect of Anna Freud's careful documentation is that her stages along the developmental lines are easily applied to concrete everyday situations, allowing theoretical support for practical decisions concerning real life activities, such as the readiness for nursery school, when to expect certain attitudes from a child, when adoption is least successful, etc.

However, the most significant contribution of this description of stages may be the relationship between progress along the developmental lines and psychopathology. The latter is seen as a blockage of one or several developmental lines, usually by the environment at first, but later by the child himself. Much of therapy should be aimed at removing the blockage—so that the child, unhampered, will grow naturally along healthy lines. There is an emphasis on health rather than pathology as a natural state if the child is unaffected by organic or environmental deterrents. Anna Freud's writings have done much to shape classical psychoanalytic theory so that it is directly usable by clinicians dealing with normal and disturbed children. Her work, while of the highest theoretical caliber, also contains much practical value.

Like most psychoanalysts, Mahler evolved a theory of normal development on the basis of clinical experience with pathological states, in her case with severely disturbed young children. Over 40 years ago, Mahler had noted that certain psychotic children decompensated when they were seeparated from their mothers. These children did not appear to have developed an independent state of self, but relied on the mother to serve as an auxiliary ego. From her experience with such children, Mahler described a specific childhood entity, symbiotic psychosis, and her interest in problems of separation led her further to a general theory of the normal psychological development of the young child (25).

She describes three major phases in early development: the autistic, the symbiotic, and that of separation-individuation. The first psychological state of life, for Mahler, can be called that of "normal autism," meaning that the young infant does not actually relate to reality but is in a state of "primitive hallucinatory disorientation." The neonate is asleep much of the time and when awake it is believed that he has little notion of where the self ends and the environment begins. The task of this early stage is for the infant to achieve homeostatic equilibrium in his new extra-uterine environment.

The symbiotic stage begins around the second month of life when the infant, according to Mahler, develops a dim awareness of an external other who satisfies his needs. The infant absorbs this other into his own personal sense of oneness so that there is "a dual unity with one common boundary." Thus begins a symbiotic fusion with the mother in which the "I" and the "not-I" are not yet clearly differentiated. Gradually, the infant begins to attend more and more to external stimuli and to explore the mother as an external object. In this manner, he begins to separate himself psychologically from the mother. The child should, however, begin the slow separation process with a confident expectation that his needs will continue to be met as well as a positive curiosity about the environment. This is essentially the beginning of separation-individuation and involves the child's differentiating himself from the mother. While still needing close physical proximity to the mother, the infant begins to look beyond her for pleasure and stimulation. He also takes pleasure in using and exploring his own body.

At about 10 months, the child begins what Mahler calls the practicing subphase of the separation-individuation stage, which continues until roughly 15 months of age. This period is characterized by the child's growing autonomy, his exercising his new locomotor skills, and the shift of interest from the mother to toys and other objects. Also, the child's increasing use of distance sense modalities, such as sight and hearing, allows him to be physically distant from the mother although still secure if he can see or hear her. The mother's reactions during this period are crucial in that she must read the child's cues to be emotionally held or let go. Some mothers refuse to let their children separate, while others push them into independent behavior prematurely. In general, this early toddler period is marked by the child's "love affair with the world," in which he appears intoxicated by his new abilities and impervious to the knocks, falls and frustrations that he encounters. Mahler believes that the young toddler feels omnipotent and that this feeling still derives from his sharing in what he perceives as his mother's omnipotence.

The third subphase of the separation-individuation process, called "rapprochement," indicating the child's return to the mother, begins at about 16 months of age. At this age, the child is more interested in mastery than locomotion and begins to realize his own limited ability to adapt successfully to his environment. The child will then return to the mother for support and help. During this subphase, the child is believed to be emotionally vulnerable, for he is beginning to form a realistic assessment of his capabilities and liabilities. The parents must be acutely aware of the child's needs and be able to give help yet still allow the child to master certain experiences on his own. Mahler indicates that this subphase may be the most crucial for later adjustment, as individuals may withdraw from the real world to the safety of their parents or may internalize grossly distorted views of the world if the problems of this subphase are not adequately resolved.

The last subphase, which begins around the third year, is concerned with consolidation of individuality and a decreased reliance on the parents. This latter achievement is thought to result from a secure inner image of the mother so that her brief absences in reality can be tolerated since her internalized image can offer reassurance and comfort when she is not physically present. At this time, the child renews his interest in the external world and enjoys contact with peers and adult strangers. The confidence experienced during this final subphase obviously depends largely on the successful resolution of the previous rapprochement subphase.

Mahler believes that there is a natural order to the progression of the stages and subphases, although she acknowledges possible differences and overlapping in specific individuals.

Summary

In tracing the historical course of the psychoanalytic approach to child development, some major changes in emphasis may be observed. There appears to be a definite broadening of interest from sexuality to other areas of the personality. In defense of Freud's initial stress on sexual behavior, it must be conceded that he was well aware of the importance of non-libidinal aspects of the personality. However, he stressed erotic development because it was essentially ignored by others of his generation and because he attempted to include child development under his overall biologically oriented theory of human nature. Today, much of what Freud called sexual energy is considered by many to encompass the general instinctual, biological forces in the personality. These forces are now thought to play a less significant role, with a greater appreciation of cultural factors and of the primary importance of the ego, implying adaptation, mastery and conscious thought. Finally, the whole process of growth seems to lay much more stress on the healthy aspects of development rather than the pathological aspects. Erikson's epigenetic system as well as Anna Freud's concept of developmental lines describes the evolution of emotional health rather than the inevitable production of neurosis because culture must by its very civilizing forces restrain the primitive urges of the id.

THE ORGANISMIC APPROACH

The psychoanalytic approach to child development appears to have been influenced by the revolution in thought brought about by Darwin's theory of evolution which added a historical dimension to the human psyche. The organismic approach also seems to be derived from theoretical biology, especially in regard to the organization of living beings.

In the early part of the 20th century, Spemann began experimenting with newt embryos, exchanging pieces of embryonic tissue from one anatomical location to another. He found that if the transference of tissue took place before a certain time of embryological growth, the grafted piece of tissue took on the characteristics of the tissue area where it was placed. What the transplanted tissue eventually became appeared to depend on its location. However, the results were quite different at a later stage of embryonic development. At a later time the grafted tissue kept its original characteristics, regardless of where it was transplanted. It appeared that at this later stage, the fate of the embryonic tissue was already determined. Spemann (35) postulated the presence of a "developmental organizer" in order to account for the difference in these results. Once this organization of tissue had taken place, environmental effects could not alter its eventual development.

Spemann's work was extremely influential in that it showed that through development, tissue is intrinsically organized and that this organization persists despite external changes. He further concluded that this organization was intimately linked with differentiation, in that once the tissue had differentiated into a specific organ type, it could no longer revert to another anatomical form. These, and similar experiments by others, led to the idea that development of cells, as well as of other biological structures, followed a lawful scheme of organization which orders the eventual fate of all living matter.

The biological interest in anatomical differentiation soon stimulated similar speculative studies in the area of psychological development. Koffka, one of the first Gestalt psychologists, wrote a book called *The Growth of the Mind* (23), early in this century, attempting to describe the organismic principles of child development. In this work, Koffka emphasized the need to delineate the laws that govern the various levels of organization. Koffka wrote, "We must therefore try to envisage the problems of mental growth as they really are: We must seek to understand the peculiarities of mental evolution, and must try to discover its laws" (p. 1). To these ends, Koffka applied the holistic principles of Gestalt psychology to the growth of children, showing how the mind reflects different levels of organizational complexity at various stages of maturity. The organismic approach to the child as a complex whole representing an evolving system of varying modes of integration has been used primarily to assess cognitive development. The disordering forces of emotions or drives were acknowledged by adherents of this approach but their major concern was the manner in which experience is integrated at different stages of life.

Werner's Concept of Development

Following in the holistic tradition of Koffka, Heinz Werner set out to more accurately define the stages of mental development. His lifelong effort was to articulate the basic laws that could account for the changes in any evolving system. As such, his studies included investigations into the formal aspects of psychopathology, the particular structure of primitive society, the growth of language, as well as the mental development of the child (37). Werner stated that developmental psychology has two major goals: 1) to grasp the characteristic pattern of each developmental level and its own special organization; and 2) to determine the relationship between these levels in terms of increasing complexity so that any general tendencies in the developmental process may be discovered. Werner believed that development is a creative, fluid process with novel abilities emerging at each new stage, which cannot be adequately explained by mechanistic theories that either view new abilities as only more sophisticated, but basically of the same form as existing processes, or as new abilities being simply added on to the unchanged organism. For Werner, each advance involved a transformation of the entire organism. Each new stage represented a totally new organizational synthesis which is comprehensible by different criteria than the previous or later stages. Therefore, development is innovative, all pervasive, with each stage representing relatively closed, self-subsisting totality.

In order to measure the progression of development, Werner relied on two major standards which he clearly assimilated from biology. He formulated these standards into basic principles as follows: 1) Development proceeds from a state of relative globality to a differentiation of parts; and 2) there is an integration of these parts into a hierarchical arrangement. Therefore, the two major criteria for measuring progression were differentiation and hierarchization. The biological roots of these concepts are clearly evident in the studies of cellular morphology and embryology as mentioned above. For example, primitive embryonic cells are undifferentiated and equipotential. Each has the capacity to develop into various types of organ cells. As these cells mature, they differentiate and become able to perform specific functions as liver cells, or neurones, etc. In addition to the differentiation into the various organ systems, there occurs a "hierarchization" so that one group of cells is able to control the activities of others. In this manner, a complex organism can function adequately and coherently.

In order to assess experimentally these two major dimensions of development (differentiation and hierarchization), Werner formulated five parameters, which may be measured through ontogenesis. The first parameter, that of *syncretic* and *discrete* functioning, applies to abilities or functions which are separate in the adult but fused in the child. For example, young children often cannot differentiate between inner and outer experience. Piaget found that up to a certain age children believe that other people can see their dreams or certain rooms are full of dreams (26). The child cannot separate out his internally generated psychic experiences from his perception of the external world. Another illustration of syncretic functioning is the child's fusing together the emotional and cognitive aspects of a situation. Werner states that the child attributes emotions to inert objects or ascribes purposeful causality to material events. A child may state that a flower is happy or a rock is sad or that nighttime or rain were caused by human wishes. Some of these descriptions are retained by adults in aesthetic works (i.e. an angry sea or a lonely tree) but for the adult, the syncretic usage is metaphorical, while for the child it is quite real.

The second parameter is that of *diffusion* versus *articulation* and describes the progress from an early global appreciation of experience to the ability to separate out parts in relation to the whole. For example, when a young child is asked to copy geometric figures, he will tend to omit details and create a symmetrical global pattern. A square or the letter "C" was found to be reproduced as circular, demonstrating a lack of appreciation for articulated parts such as corners or breaks in contour.

Another example of the diffuse nature of the child's functioning is his confusion of a part of an object or sequence with the whole object or sequence. Werner reports a boy who was afraid of spiders becoming upset when a hair stuck to his fingers. When the hair was removed, the child asked, "Didn't the hair bite you?", showing that he equated qualities (biting) of the part (hair) with the whole (spider).

The other three parameters are: 1) the *indefinite* versus *definite*, which refers to the increasing ability to direct behavior toward a desired goal; 2) the *rigid* versus *flexible*, which describes the transition from stereotyped, repetitive behavior to more varied and appropriate action sequences; and 3) the *labile* versus *stabile*, which deals with the gradual change from distractibility in the young child to the persistent behavior of the adult which continues despite interruptions.

It may have become apparent that Werner was more concerned with grasping the essence of the developmental process and with formulating basic laws by which to describe it, than in a detailed study of the concrete behavior of children at different stages of ontogenesis. His experiments and clinical studies were secondary to theoretical pursuits and were mainly used to illustrate his major concept of development as a whole.

While not specifically interested in exhaustively describing individual stages of ontogenesis, Werner did sketch out some levels of organization which characterize the child's thinking processes as he grows from infancy to adolescence. The first level of organization is the *biological-organismic*, which consists mainly of physiological events and innate reflexes. The next level is the *perceptual*, during which experience is organized by the appearance of the surrounding world. The last level is the *conceptual*, during which behavior is directed by symbolic representations of reality. Werner stressed that as the newer levels of organization are reached, the older modes of behavior are not lost but rather are relegated to a lower hierarchical status. Such primitive modes of experience and action could reemerge during stress or illness. Although Werner sketched out these developmental levels of organization, his major contribution was in describing the laws of development and not its specific stages. This more detailed task has been actualized by Jean Piaget and his coworkers who have meticulously studied the intellectual growth of children for over half a century and have revolutionized the field of cognitive development.

Piaget's Genetic Epistemology

Piaget has called his work "genetic epistemology," thus stressing that he is concerned with the way the mind structures reality as well as the developmental origins of this ability (27). He believes that at every stage of development the world is experienced in an age-appropriate manner, with the earlier forms of cognition laying the foundation for the later stages, eventually leading to the abstract concepts of adult thought.

Before describing these epistemological stages, it may be worthwhile to review some of Piaget's more general concepts as well as his overall philosophy of child development. For Piaget, intelligence is essentially successful adaptation to one's environment. Our cognitive abilities are seen as biologically useful ways of relating to the external world which emerged during the evolution of mankind. As such, cognition is closely linked to action, and thought may be considered as a form of internalized action. Furthermore, since intelligence may be defined as adaptive action, the primitive reflexes of the newborn are as intelligent as the abstract formulations of an adult mathematician. Therefore, there is an inherent continuity in development as it exemplifies different forms of intelligent behavior.

Although intelligence is basically adaptation, the latter term is more complex than a simple equilibrium between the child and his surrounding world. According to Piaget, adaptation consists of two complementary processes: assimilation and accommodation. Assimilation describes the process through which reality is broken down or modified in such a way as to be incorporated by the existing mental structure of the child. Accommodation, on the other hand, represents the manner in which the child has to alter his own mental structures to handle reality. In assimilation, the environment is modified to insure adaptation; in accommodation, the organism modifies itself to adapt to new situations. It is the interplay between these two basic processes that determines the progressive development of mental structures. These fundamental cognitive structures that underlie intelligent behavior are called schemas. Piaget's major interest has been to define and describe these schemas at different stages of development. For it is ultimately the organizing schemas that can explain the observable behavior and the changes seen in the behavior of the growing child are actually a reflection of the progression of the cognitive schemas.

This interest in the basic organizational structures that exist beneath surface behavior helps to explain Piaget's particular manner of investigation, called the "clinical method." Piaget asks children of different ages to solve the same problem, noting the performance of each child. Of greater importance than the final answer is the child's explanation of his particular mode of solution, for this yields the types of mental processes and the level of understanding that are responsible for the end result. Through a large series of these investigations, Piaget has been able to document a series of specific stages describing the cognitive modes (i.e. the schemas) that are utilized during the various phases of childhood. For Piaget, it is the schema, the mode of organizing and constructing experience, that significantly changes through ontogenesis.

The earliest schemas are exemplified by pure action sequences without true mental representation. These are characteristic of the *sensorimotor period* which extends from birth to roughly two years of age. Although devoid of conceptual representation, these action schemas are adaptive and thus "intelligent." At first, the sensorimotor period is characterized by innate reflexes to environmental stimuli such as sucking, grasping, etc. This stage of reflexes gives rise to the stage of acquired habits in which the infant actively manipualtes and changes objects in his environment. During the sensorimotor period, the child progresses through specific "circular reactions," meaning action sequences in which the result of a behavior serves as a stimulus for the behavior to be repeated. The primary circular reactions, seen during the first four months of life, do not noticeably change the environment except to make the innate behavior more adaptive. Thus, after a few days, the newborn nurses with more assurance and is better able to locate the nipple. The result of more efficient feeding is the repetition of the sucking response. In this manner, an innate response sequence becomes stabilized and may be transferred to other environmental objects, as in the case of thumb sucking.

The secondary circular reaction, which occurs from four to eight months of age, is characterized by the infant repeating a response which fortuitously caused a pleasant change in the environment. Piaget describes how a child at this age will repeatedly pull a string attached to a rattle in order to hear the sound of the rattle. In this manner, the infant begins to separate internal actions from external results and to demonstrate intentional acts. The tertiary circular reactions do not occur until after one year of age and demonstrate the cognitive progress that has transpired. In these action sequences, the behavior is no longer repetitive and stereotyped but rather reflects the infant's ability to vary his activities in order to produce novel results in the environment. Alternative solutions are attempted to specific problems and the infant is no longer locked into a monotonous action-response repetition.

Other cognitive achievements of the sensorimotor period concern the structuring of space and the gradual understanding that objects in the environment have a permanent and independent existence. Through a series of ingenious experiments, Piaget has demonstrated that at first the infant appears to be interested in objects only when they are directly in visual range. Later, the child will search for objects when they are removed from view but only in the place where they first disappeared. Thus, as a ball is placed behind pillow A and then in full view of the child placed behind pillow B, the child will reach for it behind pillow A. After a year of age, the child begins to understand multiple displacements and search behind pillow B. Toward the end of the sensorimotor period, the child can even cope with "invisible movements." This means that the child can search for an object even when he did not directly see it put in a set place. For example, if a ball is put into a clenched fist and then the fist put behind a pillow and the ball released, the young infant will persistently search the hand for the ball. At about 18 months, the child will look behind the pillow where the ball was released, even though he did not witness the ball being put there.

Therefore, in the sensorimotor period, the child learns about intentional actions and achieving desired results by various willed activities. He also structures his physical world so that he recognizes the permanence of objects existing in three-dimensional space. The end of the sensorimotor period is characterized by the beginning of an internal representation of the external world. The child can now begin to picture objects within his mind and carry out sequences mentally rather than in actual behavior.

The true ability to reproduce the world internally initiates the second major period of development in Piaget's system. This is called the *Preoperational* stage and spans the time from roughly two to seven years of age. Although internal conceptualization is possible at this stage, the internal world is still a concrete mirror of reality. In the early part of this period, the child does begin to substitute symbols for objects in his acquisition of language but his thinking cannot transcend the possibilities of the real world. It is only when the child reaches the operational period that reason overcomes appearance and the child is able to mentally perform operations that would be impossible in the real world. Despite the concreteness of the preoperational stage, however, the young child's thinking is far from objective or accurate. The child will distort reality to comply with his elementary understanding and will remain oblivious to obvious logical contradictions. Assimilation is much more prevalent than accommodation as evidenced by the frequent use of fantasy by the young child.

A particularly significant characteristic of the preoperational period is what Piaget calls "egocentric" thinking. This term means that the child believes everyone else sees the world as he sees it, that he cannot put himself in the epistemological place of others. For example, when asked to describe the view of a model of mountains from positions other than his own, the child repeats what he perceives from his own specific vantage point. Coupled with this egocentricity is animistic thinking, meaning that material events have intentional causes. Young children are reported as believing that night comes so we can sleep or that rain is caused by putting on a raincoat. The emotional impact of these distorted modes of thought can only be speculated upon. It may be that much of the childhood phobias and adult neurotic behavior reflect the primacy of this primitive attempt to make sense of the environment. What is apparently lacking is a central criterion by which to structure reality and the child seems to project his own sense of willfulness, causality, and teleological reasoning onto most of his life experiences.

At about four years of age, the child begins to utilize an objective standard to organize experience and becomes able to group objects into separate classes. However, this classification is on the basis of perception rather than logic. The child is "centered" on the most conspicuous perceptual aspect of an event and utilizes that aspect in relating events or objects or experiences. For example, Piaget presented children with a box containing 20 wooden beads, 18 of which were brown and two of which were white. The children were then asked whether a necklace made from brown beads would be longer, shorter, or equal in length to a necklace made from wooden beads. Children at this stage mostly replied the brown beads would make the longer necklace. From this and similar experiments, Piaget concluded that the child at this stage is incapable of thinking of two subordinate classes, that is, white and brown beads, at the same time as he is thinking of the whole class, that is, the total number of wooden beads. The child's attention is centered on the preponderance of brown beads in relation to white beads, the most conspicuous property, and he cannot simultaneously switch from the relation of "brown beads to white beads" to the relation of "brown beads to the total number of beads." The child's thought is guided by the perceptual aspect of reality. Children continue to conclude that a brown bead necklace would be longer even after they acknowledge that there are more wooden beads than brown beads. The point is that these two aspects of the same situation cannot be integrated at this level. At the level of concrete operations, stretching from roughly age seven to age 11, however, the child immediately answers that the wooden bead necklace would be longer because "there are more wooden beads than brown beads." Here the child can simultaneously take into consideration the relation of brown beads to white beads (part to part) and brown beads to wooden beads (part to whole). Piaget asserts that at this later stage the child's thought is "decentered," that is, no longer exclusively focused on the perceptual, and is "reversible," that is, can move back and forth through a logical, relational thought sequence.

A similar example of the preoperational child being centered on the perceptual qualities of his world can be found in Piaget's experiments on conservation. One such experiment involved an equal amount of liquid in two identical beakers, A-1 and A-2, which the child acknowledged as the same. The liquid from beaker A-1 was then poured into two smaller beakers, B-1 and B-2, directly in front of the child. The child is then asked if the liquid in the beakers B-1 and B-2 was equal to the amount in the original beaker A-2. Children at the preoperational level of intelligence believe that the quantity of liquid has been altered when poured into the two smaller beakers. Similar alterations in quantity are ascribed to when the liquid is poured into different shaped beakers, although here again the liquid is poured directly in view of the child. Piaget concludes that these interpretations are due to the child's lack of the schemas of reversibility and conservation; the child centers on what he sees and cannot disengage his thoughts from his perceptions so that he can mentally reverse the process and conclude that the amounts of water were originally the same. Because of this perception-bound set the child cannot consider two aspects of one situation simultaneously, but can only examine one aspect at the expense of all the others. For example, when the child at this stage is shown a ball of clay that is rolled into a sausage shape, he will say that there is either more clay because the sausage is longer than the ball or less clay because the sausage is thinner than the ball. The child cannot conceive of the ball simultaneously becoming both longer, thus having more clay, and thinner, thus having less clay. It is this ability to attend to two aspects of the environment and to relate them in a coherent fashion that leads to the schema of conservation and marks the beginning of the operational stage. Similarly, with the bead experiment described above, the child in the preoperational stage cannot conceive that white beads and brown beads equal wooden beads. He is centered on the color and cannot conceptualize the two aspects of color and total number simultaneously.

With the onset of the *operational* period, at about age seven, perception loses its primary position as a means of structuring reality and gradually thought becomes dominated by reason rather than appearance. The immediate consequence of this evolution is that the child can conceive of events which would be impossible in the real world. He can go back in time or reverse the directions of a sequence. He can also consider more than one aspect of any given situation. Concurrent with this "de-centering," the child becomes less egocentric. He can truly begin to order the world around him by logical rather than perceptual categories. The exercise of these newly formed schemas may account for the latency child's obsession with collecting objects and labeling them. The child at this age is very interested in classifying and ordering his surroundings. This surface behavior may demonstrate the forming of mental structures which can deal with hierarchical classes based on logical consistency.

Yet during this first part of the operational period, the child can only use logical classification with concrete, tangible objects. He cannot yet classify intangible concepts such as laws, or mathematical formulas. Therefore, this phase is called "concrete operations" by Piaget, since operational thought is possible only with concrete objects. Furthermore, Piaget speculates that the actual content of the objects of the child's experience affects his use of judgment and logical organization. There-fore, a child may be able to successfully solve a problem using beads (a discontinuous medium) yet fail at the same problem using water (a continuous medium). The form of thought thus largely depends on the concrete contents of experience.

It is in the final phase of development, called "formal operations," that thought is freed from the concrete world. This stage, which begins about age 11, is the culmination of cognitive development in man and represents the particularly human ability to reason abstractly. The pre-adolescent becomes able to deal with intangible abstractions which can-not be represented in reality. He begins to see relationships between relations rather than relationships between objects. He can appreciate the possible alternatives of any given situation. These advances lead to an "experimental spirit" in which one factor is kept constant while all others are systematically varied.

One of Piaget's and Inhelder's experiments (28) demonstrates the difference between concrete and formal operations quite clearly. They arranged a series of jars of colorless liquids and then showed the child that by adding a few drops from the last jar to an unknown mixture of the liquids a yellow color could be produced. The significant aspect of this problem was that there was no way for the child to figure out ahead of time which mixture of liquids would produce the yellow color once the indicator was added. Inhelder and Piaget then observed the manner by which children tried to combine liquids to arrive at the yellow color. The younger child attacked the problem by adding a few drops from the last jar to each of the others and then felt essentially defeated. From here on he proceeded in no particular order and usually did not think of mixing various liquids and then adding the drop from the last jar. The child at the stage of formal operations, however, solved the problem by systematically going through all combinations of liquids, often keeping notes to be sure that he could keep track of his experimentations. Eventually, he not only solved the problem but also identified the different liquids as to their relationships. For example, one jar contained a substance that prevented the color from appearing. Therefore, in the stage of formal operations a person can generate theories about relationships and derive laws that will explain occurrences in the environment. These laws are not limited to their immediate content and can be applied to analogous events. To quote Piaget, "Indeed the essential difference between formal thought and concrete operations is that the latter are centered on reality whereas the former grasps transformations and assimilates reality only in terms of imagined or deduced events" (28, p. 149). This appreciation of the possible and the intangible also allows the adolescent to become concerned with his future and with his own thinking. This may partially explain some adolescents' fascination with abstract concepts and intellectualization.

This brief review of the work of Werner and Piaget reveals their emphasis on cognition at the expense of emotional development. For many years, their work was ignored by clinicians who saw little applicability of the study of cognition to the everyday problems children presented in their offices. In more recent times, there has been a growing appreciation of the importance of cognitive development by educators and practitioners. While the reasons for this current interest are many, one overwhelming factor has been the realization that a child's behavior largely reflects the way in which he perceives the world. Therefore, if we are to understand the behavior of children, both normal and abnormal, we must grasp the manner by which the child structures his environment. As will become evident in the following chapters, the cognitive level of the child is all important to an understanding of his actions, whether one is an educator, a psychoanalyst or a behaviorist. Werner and Piaget, among others, have made enormous strides in helping us get a glimpse of how the child constructs his phenomenological world.

Some preliminary attempts have been made to integrate the cognitive and psychodynamic theories of development, however, with only limited success. The difficulty appears to be that traditional psychoanalytic theory views cognition as merely the ego's way of handling unconscious drives which are believed to be the real determinants of behavior. Piaget, while acknowledging the existence of emotions, ignores affective development except as a general motivator of cognitive development. In fact, Anthony, in a paper comparing the Piagetian and Freudian approach to development (2), comments on one such attempt to integrate these two schools and states that it should serve as warning to those who would try to concoct the same indigestible mixture. Despite this grim prophesy of the ultimate inability to synthesize the two systems, it is still worthwhile to briefly mention some attempts which have been made to integrate psychoanalytic and cognitive approaches.

Anna Freud (8) has described basic characteristics of childhood experience which closely fit Werner's and Piaget's findings although she does not specifically refer to their work. Anna Freud refers to the child's *egocentricity,* by which she means his misinterpreting all events as having special relevance for him, that the child perceives events only in terms of his own needs and wishes. Anna Freud also mentions the child's relative *weakness of the secondary process* so that fantasy often supervenes over reality and behavior is directed by magical beliefs and a lack of logical analysis. One instance of this distortion, according to her, is the translation of sexual events into nonsexual terms, such as interpreting sex as violent or believing that insemination occurs orally or anally. Finally, Freud mentions the *impaired evaluation of time* in the child who measures the passage of time by the pleasure or pain of its duration rather than by a clock or calendar.

Arieti (3), a psychoanalyst with an extensive knowledge of cognitive theory, has proposed an original theory which utilizes both psychodynamic and cognitive approachs. Arieti has tried to reconstruct the inner experience of the developing child as he deals with emotionally laden experiences. Along these lines, Arieti proposes that not all emotions are at the same level of sophistication but rather that there are three levels of felt emotions. Simple states such as fear, rage or satisfaction are primary emotions which are global and elicited directly by environmental stimuli. Toward the end of the first year of life the child experiences "second order emotions," which are not set off directly by external events but by the anticipation of an event. A still higher "third order" of emotions is experienced after the child realizes that he can affect feeling states in others and that, reciprocally, others can alter his own mood state. Examples of such third order emotions are depression, hate, joy and love. This contribution of Arieti may have important ramifications for it shows how cognitive growth dovetails with emotional development and that different emotions may require varying intellectual abilities to be experienced.

Arieti has also discussed the inner perceptions of others during development and how these stage-specific modes of cognition may recur in pathological states. His work is an impressive beginning in bridging the gap between logical and emotional growth, which are actually but two sides of the same coin. It may be hoped that with renewed interest in each other's work the psychoanalysts and the cognitive theorists will enrich each other's formulations toward a fuller and more realistic account of human ontogenesis.

THE SOCIAL-BEHAVIORAL APPROACH

Just as the psychoanalytic and the cognitive approaches have their roots in specific larger philosophic doctrines, the social-behavioral view of child development is a modern application of the philosophic tradition of empiricism. This theory proposes that all cognitive contents are derived directly from experience and that child development can be accounted for by the growing child's accumulation and transformation of sense data. For example, the British philosopher John Locke assumed that at birth the mind was a *tabula rasa*, a blank tablet, lacking any inherent content, upon which the sensation of sense data made impressions. The growth of the mind was conceived of as a sort of mirroring of reality, copying what it experienced and organizing its experience by certain physicalistic laws. The important process was getting sensation to the brain to insure proper input of information.

This theory was put to a peculiar experimental test after the French Revolution when a French educator, Itard, attempted to civilize the "wild boy" of Aveyron (19). This child, assumed to be about 12 years of age, had been found in the forest and had apparently been living a feral existence. Itard reasoned that he could educate the child if he supplied him with the proper sensory input. In his two monographs, describing his efforts to educate the wild boy, Itard frequently cites Condillac, one of the most extreme empiricist philosophers, demonstrating Itard's fundamental belief in this theoretical position. Itard did succeed in teaching the boy a great deal about social behavior, and it seems that the two became close friends, but the boy was never able to master language. Itard concluded that this failure was probably due to the child being basically defective, and not to the possibility that after certain mental structures have crystallized further sensory input is without effect. Itard's works have remained classics as early experiments in child psychology and also because of the ingenious methods that Itard devised in order to educate the boy, which have subsequently become standard remedial techniques.

The empiricist approach gained notoriety in this country in the work of John Watson (36) who founded the "behaviorist" school of psychology. In an historical context, behaviorism appears to have been a reaction against the emphasis on introspection and mental phenomena that was the then prevalent interest of academic psychology. Watson proposed to do away with consciousness in his theories and, instead, to concentrate on overt behavior which could be observed and measured; thus the term "behaviorist." The underlying principles of Watson's theory were simply that psychic events are actual behaviors and not mental phenomena and that behavior is always a response to either an internal or external stimulus. The infant is said to be born with certain innate reactions to specific stimuli. As he matures, other stimuli become associated with the innate ones and can also elicit basic responses. Concurrently, as the brain matures, responses become more complex and varied. However, the basic "reflex arc" of a stimulus eliciting a response remains the fundamental process in development.

Watson demonstrated his concepts in the famous experiments on "Albert," a young infant whom Watson had observed since birth. Albert had shown a fear response to loud noises. On the other hand, Albert demonstrated a lively interest in small furry animals seen at a zoo. In the experiment, Albert was presented with a white rat which he immediately reached for in an exploratory manner. As soon as his hand touched the rat's fur, a steel bar was struck behind him, creating a loud noise. At this sound, Albert reacted with fear and withdrew his hand from the rat. This sequence was repeated several times; each time Albert touched the animal, the noise was produced. After awhile, Albert markedly changed his behavior toward the rat; the mere sight of the animal was enough to produce avoidance and fear. Albert developed similar responses to other white fuzzy objects, such as cotton wool.

Watson's experiment was an application of Pavlov's previous work on "conditioning" in dogs. In Pavlov's experiment, a novel stimulus was also paired with a natural simulus so that, in time, the former will elicit the same response as the latter. Pavlov showed that if he rang a bell each time he presented food to a dog, eventually the sound of the bell without the food would cause the dog to salivate. In both Watson's and Pavlov's experiments one stimulus is substituted for another to elicit the same response. By this process of association of stimuli, Watson hoped to explain the increasing variety of childhood behaviors.

This method of conditioning also led to one of the first systematic attempts at therapy of children. In 1924, Mary Cover Jones (21) used Watson's method to cure "conditioned fears" in children by associating a pleasure stimulus with the fear stimulus. Jones was able to "uncondition" a child's fear to other furry animals by pairing a rabbit with reassuring experiences. This early study may be seen as a prototype for "behavior modification" therapies which, despite superficial differences, fundamentally utilize the same methodology.

Classical conditioning, as was utilized by Pavlov and Watson, may partially explain the evocation of a same response by a number of stimuli. However, the theory has difficulty in accounting for the tremendous increase in the variety and novelty of responses that chidren demonstrate as they grow up. Skinner (32) presented a more complex model of conditioning which attempted to show how new responses are generated and then maintained. Skinner termed this type of learning "operant" conditioning, to stress the notion that a behavior (i.e. an operant) is being conditioned rather than a stimulus. Briefly, operant conditioning implies that an organism normally makes a variety of random movements and, if one of these movements results in a reward, it will then be repeated. For example, a pigeon may peck randomly in its cage. If, however, pecking at a lever causes a pellet of food to drop into the cage, the pigeon, in time, will learn to selectively peck at the lever which brings a reward. By rewarding successive acts that proceed in a desired direction, behavior can gradually be "shaped" to reach new goals. For example, Skinner has trained pigeons to play ping-pong by selectively rewarding behavior that will culminate in ping-pong playing. Skinner has used the same formulation to account for the stabilization of all types of behavior. He applies the same basic principles to as complex an activity as the development of speech in babies, insisting that the parents' automatically repeating the infant's primitive speech is rewarding so that further efforts at speech continue. In the manner that pigeons were taught to play ping-pong, the child's verbal productions are "shaped" by parental rewards.

Watson and Skinner may be classified as extreme behaviorists and their formulations have been increasingly attacked by critics who believe that this form of behaviorism does not do justice to the complexities of the developing psyche. No one can doubt that reward and punishment alter the course of specific aspects of behavior but questions arise as to whether the whole process and content of development can be adequately encompassed by negative and positive conditioning. One major illustration is Chomsky's criticism of Skinner's theory of language acquisition (5). Chomsky contends that reinforcement may alter the superficial aspects of the way words are put together but that an operant conditioning theory does not explain the development of the "deep structures" of language, that is, the child's discovery that words have meaning. Chomsky asserts that language essentially reflects a more profound mental acitivty than vocal behavior. In general, critics have partially accepted the behaviorist position to account for the acquisition of primitive or motor skills but have rejected it as too simplistic to account for complex, cognitive and voluntary abilities.

On the other hand, behaviorists have also modified their extreme stand and have accepted "internal mediators" of behavior that are not always observable as are environmental stimuli. For example, the memory trace of an event may serve as a stimulus for a response, although the existence of the memory trace is as empirically undemonstrable as Freud's libido or Piaget's schema.

Bandura and Walters (4) have continued the behaviorist approach to child development but in a much more sophisticated and comprehensive manner. While they adhere to the basic postulates that most behavior is acquired and the principles of learning theory can account for the changes seen in development, they object to their predecessors' viewing the learning organism in isolation, outside of his social setting. Bandura and Walters stress the social context of development by focusing on imitation as a major source of new responses. In a series of experiments, Bandura showed that children can learn a novel behavior merely by observing others and without having to actually produce the response themselves. In an analogous study, Bandura and Walters pointed out the importance of "vicarious reinforcement," which means that a child will imitate responses for which a model was rewarded and avoid responses for which a model was punished. Therefore, conditioning and unconditioning of behavior can occur vicariously, without the child ever performing the act. All this is to demonstrate how important models (adult, peers, fictional characters) are in the eliciting of new behaviors and the stabilization of successful activities.

While most of this work is relevant in terms of the effect of the environment (such as T.V. violence or the way parents behave toward each other, etc.) on the development of the child, there appears to be a lack of appreciation for the cognitive complexity of the actual activity of imitation. It would appear that the act of imitation involves, at least, the formation of an internal image of the model, a realization of the consequences of acting like the model, and a putting of oneself in the place of the model. These mental events appear to contradict the pristine dictates of strict behaviorism which allows for only observable stimuli and responses to have any validity. Here again, when experimentation is carried out on higher levels of behavior, it becomes impossible to exclude mentalistic and nonobservable constructs.

The social-behaviorist approach has its merits in that it carefully spells out its basic postulates and attempts to validate its hypotheses through experimentation. This approach has been a constructive balance to some of the highly questionable theories that were prompted by armchair speculation rather than rigorous thinking and laboratory proof. This approach has also shown the importance of experience in development and argued against a nativistic view which considered development as only the autonomous unfolding of innate predispositions. One link to clinical theory has been the efforts of some social behaviorists to validate psychoanalytic concepts experimentally or to restate psychoanalytic propositions in learning theory terms which are less mystical and more operational. R. R. Sears (31) has made various attempts to objectively verify psychoanalytic concepts such as identification and dependency with varying success. Dollard and Miller (6) recast much of the psychoanalytic theory of instinct gratification in terms of innate (primary) and learned (secondary) drives. They would describe a transaction as follows: The infant satisfies his hunger (a primary drive) at the mother's breast but her smile or bodily contact, by its association with feeding, becomes the object of a learned secondary drive. In this manner, Dollard and Miller account for the occurrence of many acquired drives, such as shame, anxiety or love, which determine much of our adult behavior but may have their roots in the satisfaction of more basic biological drives.

In summary, the social-behavioral approach, while valid in clarifying some aspects of development, has not been able to present a consistent theory which accounts for the richness of the human personality. Some parts of development have been extensively studied but outside of the context of the whole person. When forced to account for the complexities of the whole child or the higher levels of functioning, it has also had to postulate mystical hypothetical variables that it originally set out to extricate from theory. In its own way, however, this tough-minded approach has served as a needed corrective to a tendency to speculate too freely; it has brought the field of child development into the laboratory and has created the viable and successful treatment modality of behavior modification.

CURRENT ISSUES IN DEVELOPMENT

These three major approaches to child development have been presented in order to give the reader a basic orientation to the chapters that follow. No one of the approaches is all encompassing and, perhaps, all three should be viewed as complementing each other. The psychoanalytic model is mostly concerned with the child's emotional development, the organismic approach centers on cognition, while the behaviorist-learning theory approach seems to focus on overt action. All three areas must be kept in mind when one is confronted with a living child in the office or in the classroom.

As disparate or disconnected as these theories may appear to be from each other, each grapples with some basic problems of development which recur whenever one studies the psychological growth of the child, regardless of theoretical origin. In closing this introductory chapter, it might be worthwhile to examine these recurring questions which transcend theoretical bias.

Nature-Nurture

One crucial question of development has always been the relative effect of heredity versus experience, the old "nature-nurture" controversy. The social-behaviorists clearly try to account for all development as determined by the environment while the early psychoanalytic theories, and, at times, Piaget seemed to view the child's surroundings as merely a stage on which the innate patterns could be played out. Certainly the mind requires external stimulation for continued growth; yet this stimulation must be filtered through an innate psychic organization that seems to be relatively independent of experience. Today, no one would take as extreme a position as stating that development is either totally reliant on or completely independent of the environment. Both innate and experiential factors play a role; the question is rather how they may interact for an optimal effect.

The more contemporary question would be what aspects of behavior are most or least modified by experience. Thomas, Chess and Birch

(34), in an extensive longitudinal study, have demonstrated that a person's temperament is in all probability inborn. On the other hand, a man's attitude toward authority figures is just as probably a result of past experience. While these examples may seem obvious, the origins of certain key functions such as verbal intelligence or abstract abilities are still in doubt.

D. O. Hebb (17) has approached the question of innate versus learned effects on development from the standpoint of comparative neuroanatomy. He found that the higher an organism is ranked in phylogenesis, the more that organism appears to require a prolonged period of learning during childhood. For example, insects appear to be able to perform adult functions almost at birth, while higher animals, such as primates, may take years until even rudimentary mature behavior is evident. Hebb explains this difference by noting that higher animals have much larger areas of the brain devoted to "association" functions in contrast to areas of the brain that are concerned with direct sensory or motor functions. Hebb calls the amount of association area tissue to the amount of pure sensory-motor tissue the A/S ratio. Species with low A/S ratios show rapid maturity since there is little association tissue to be organized. However, this same paucity of association areas limits the amount of flexibility in behavior once the relatively few association neuronal connections have been established. In contrast, organisms with high A/S ratios require a good deal of time for their massive association areas to be organized. Once this is accomplished, however, the organism is capable of highly versatile and autonomous behavior that is beyond simpler animals. Therefore, the role of innate versus learned factors may vary greatly across species. In man, with his huge association cortex, the role of learning must be great and indeed there is a prolonged childhood during which the brain is "programmed" by experience. However, the basic organization of how this experience is registered may ultimately be innate. The categories of thought seem to be genetically fixed but the contents of thoughts within these categories may reflect what one has experienced.

Critical Periods

There is yet a further ramification of this concept of the brain being programmed by experience and that is that the central nervous system appears to need adequate stimulation in order to mature. Riesen's (29) work with monkeys reared in darkness showed that the retina degenerates unless it is stimulated by light. On a behavioral level, Harlow's studies of infant monkeys showed that primates require adequate mothering in order to become normal adults (16). The organism's apparent requirement for specific environmental input at a set time in order for normal development to occur has given rise to the concept of "critical periods." This theory evolved from the early studies of Lorenz on new hatched geese (18). In normal development, goslings follow their mother in a straight line, but if Lorenz presented himself instead of the mother, the goslings followed him and formed a bond to him that continued to maturity. This attachment occurred only if Lorenz presented himself to the goslings at a specific time during their infancy. This specific time was termed a "critical period" and the formation of a lasting bond after one presentation was called "imprinting." Scott's (30) work on the relationship between a puppy and its trainer showed that there were critical periods for the formation of an emotional bond in higher species as well.

The crucial questions raised by the critical period theory are whether such periods occur in human development and, if so, can the deprivation of such specific environment-organism interaction be overcome due to the human brain's greater plasticity. Spitz (33) had proposed such a critical period for the formation of an emotional tie between an infant and the mother in the later half of the first year of the infant's life, stating that emotional separation for over five months results in irrevocable emotional damage. Later studies, however, have questioned the permanent effects of maternal deprivation. Similarly, deprivation of cognitive stimulation now appears to be remediable. Wolff (38) has suggested that as a result of the resiliency of the human brain and the large amount of association tissue, there may be "optimal periods" when certain tasks are more easily mastered if the environment supplies the proper stimulation, but that irrevocable "critical periods" as seen in lower animals do not exist in man.

While the issue remains unresolved, there may be a few generalizations about critical periods which can be cautiously formulated. Critical periods are more apt to occur in primitive global behaviors and less in highly sophisticated functions. This concept seems to best explain the emotional behavior of neonates or the bonding behavior of lower animals. It has not been useful in accounting for higher cognitive deficits in the adult. A very significant series of studies by Kagan (22), for example, concluded that children raised in a stimulus-poor rural atmosphere in Guatemala later caught up intellectually with children raised under more ideal urban circumstances.

Epigenesis

Related to the problem of critical periods is the concept of epigenesis. The psychoanalysts and the organismic theorists postulate that certain abilities or needs gain ascendency at set stages of development. This assumption is evidenced in both the Freudian psychosexual stages as well as Piaget's levels of cognition. There is the further inference that the child cannot properly proceed to the next stage without having successfully mastered the task of the preceding one, so that each stage represents a sort of "critical period." While most developmental theorists agree that the child's needs and abilities vary with increasing age, there is little consensus on the actual character of abilities themselves, the order of their appearance and the reasons for their presence. For the psychoanalysts, the causes of this unfolding are tied to biological development; for Piaget, the stages form an invariant logical order; while the social behaviorists do not recognize stages at all but a continuously increasing accumulation of stimulus-response chains. The current thinking might be summarized as assuming that there is an innate pattern of abilities that unfold through development but that it requires appropriate environmental stimulation to properly express itself.

The same question arises as to the sources of novel behaviors in development. As we have seen above, some theorists believe these arise through an innate genetic program while others believe that most behavior is copied from the environment. Here again, both nature and nurture appear necessary and the real problem is to decipher the optimal match of organism-environmental interaction. Even if novelty in development is genetically programmed, there is little doubt that environmental conditions have a great effect in the realization or stunting of growth potential.

Developmental Goal

Whatever the approach to ontogeny, however, most theorists would agree on the goal of development. This ultimate realization is the independence of the adult from automatically responding to either internal or external stimulation, that is, to be able to direct behavior after considering the multiplicity of impending urges and choosing the most fruitful response. Whether this ability is couched in psychoanalytic terms such as ego maturity, organismic terms such as self-regulatory systems, or behaviorist terms such as internal mediational response hierarchies, this capacity to contemplate one's options and choose one's future is the ability which may most truly characterize adult functioning.

REFERENCES

1. Abraham, K.: A short study on the development of libido, viewed in the light of mental disorders. In *Selected Papers on Psycho-Analysis*. New York: Brunner/Mazel, 1979.
2. Anthony, E.J.: The significance of Jean Piaget for child psychiatry. *Brit. J. Med. Psychol.* 29: 20-34, 1956.
3. Arieti, S.: *The Intrapsychic Self*. New York: Basic Books, 1967.
4. Bandura, A. and Walters, R.: *Social Learning and Personality Development*. New York: Holt, Rinehart & Winston, 1963.
5. Chomsky, N.: Review of B. F. Skinner's Verbal Behavior. *Language*, 25: 26-58, 1959.
6. Dollard, J. and Miller, N.E.: *Personality and Psychotherapy*. New York: McGraw-Hill, 1950.
7. Erikson, E.: *Childhood and Society*. New York: Norton, 1963.
8. Freud, A.: *Normality and Pathology in Childhood*. New York: International Universities Press, 1965.
9. Freud, S.: *On Aphasia*. New York: International Universities Press, 1953.
10. Freud, S.: *Origins of Psychoanalysis*. New York: Basic Books, 1954.
11. Freud, S.: The interpretation of dreams (1900). *Standard Edition*, 4-5, London: Hogarth, 1953.
12. Freud, S.: Three essays on the theory of sexuality (1905). *Standard Edition*, 7, London: Hogarth, 1953.
13. Freud, S.: The ego and the id (1923). *Standard Edition*, 19, London: Hogarth, 1961.
14. Freud, S.: Inhibitions, symptoms and anxiety (1926). *Standard Edition*, 20, London: Hogarth, 1959.
15. Hartmann, H.: *Ego Psychology and the Problems of Adaptation*. New York: International Universities Press, 1958.
16. Harlow, H. F. and Harlow, M. K.: Social Deprivation in Monkeys. *Sci. Amer.*, 207: 136-146, 1962.
17. Hebb, D. O.: *The Organization of Behavior*. New York: Wiley, 1961.
18. Hess, E.: Imprinting in Birds. *Science*, 146, 1964.
19. Itard, J. M. G.: *The Wild Boy of Aveyron*. New York: Appleton-Century-Croft, 1962.
20. Jackson, J. H.: *Selected Writings*. New York: Basic Books, 1958.
21. Jones, M. C.: The Conditioning of Children's Emotions. In C. Murchison (Ed.). *A Handbook of Child Psychology*, Worcester: Clark University Press, 1933.
22. Kagan, J: New Views on Cognitive Development. *Journal of Youth and Adolescence*, 5: 113-129, 1976.
23. Koffka, K.: *The Growth of the Mind*. Paterson, Littlefield, Adams, 1959.
24. Lovejoy, A.: *The Great Chain of Being*. New York: Harper, 1960.
25. Mahler, M.: *On Human Symbiosis and the Vicissitudes of Individuation*. New York: International Universities Press, 1968.
26. Piaget, J.: *Play, Dreams and Imitation in Childhood*. New York: Norton, 1962.
27. Piaget, J.: *Genetic Epistemology*. New York: Columbia University Press, 1970.
28. Piaget, J. and Inhelder, B.: *The Psychology of the Child*. New York: Basic Books, 1969.
29. Riesen, A. H.: The Development of Visual Perception in Man and Chimpanzee. *Science*, 106: 107-108, 1947.
30. Scott, J. P.: Critical Periods in Behavior Development. *Science*, 138: 949-958, 1962.
31. Sears, R. R., Rav, L., and Alpert, R.: *Identification and Child Rearing*. Stanford: Stanford University Press, 1965.
32. Skinner, B. F.: *Science and Human Behavior*. New York: Macmillan, 1953.
33. Spitz, R.: *The First Year of Life*. New York: International Universities Press, 1966.
34. Thomas, A., Chess, S., and Birch, H. G.: *Temperament and Behavior Disorders in Children*. New York: New York University Press, 1968.
35. Von Bertalanffy, L.: *Modern Theories of Development*. London: Oxford University Press, 1933.

36. Watson, J. B.: *Behaviorism.* Chicago: University of Chicago Press, 1924.
37. Werner, H.: *The Comparative Psychology of Mental Development.* New York: International Universities Press, 1948.
38. Wolff, P. and Fienbloom, R. I.: Critical periods in cognitive development. *Pediatrics,* 44: 999-1007, 1969.

Part II

STAGES OF DEVELOPMENT

2

Infancy

STEPHEN L. BENNETT, M.D.

In this chapter, a search of our current understanding of early developmental processes will be made to determine what can be reconstructed and turned to practical use. The view to be discussed is that the skills necessary for work with infants and parents follow the same principles as with other stages, that is, a blending of developmental knowledge with clinical practice. This chapter will focus on the problems of the individual clinician rather than those of larger organizations such as therapeutic nurseries or day-care centers. My stress on the solo practitioner will include not only the pediatrician and child psychiatrist in private practice but also the resident doing ward consultations.

There are two philosophic approaches to the assessment of infants that are somewhat in opposition. The first is that the clinical observations and skills required for work with infant-mother pairs are the traditional ones of a thorough history and examination, with special background and training being unnecessary for the majority of problems. The second view is that it would not hurt to read a few books. Continued clinical practice brings complex and difficult problems which require back-up help. The literature is, of course, one source, but it is also beneficial to have someone to talk to who enjoys discussing the issues of early development. These people are not often available within the usual medical circuit, but, rather, are to be found in some off-beat places, such as a psychoanalyst's office or some obscure part of the local teacher's college.

The child development literature is scattered, often turgid, and is with a few exceptions not noted for its felicity of style. *Child Development* and *The Psychoanalytic Study of the Child* can be equally tedious. The emphasis in this chapter will be on those papers that are not only utilitarian but also possess clarity and charm. Our emphasis on concepts which can be put to practical use will lead us away from some traditional subjects.

The more mystical concepts, such as infant state, affectual development, and mother-infant interaction, will be examined because our model for clinical approach will be the mother playing with the infant on her lap. We will try to mirror the mother by being aware of the infant's signals, and responding empathically to them, and also be in touch with our own fantasies. This approach is to be contrasted with that of placing an infant on a table and then doing something to this creature, such as poking for reflexes.

One powerful motive for examining infancy is the ontogenic fantasy of early intervention and rescue. The damaged egos found in some children in day-care centers lead to the rediscovery that Headstart programs are often too late. An irritable three-month-old infant, squirmily arching his back, gripped by a frantic mother battling to make contact, stirs the wish to have been there when the first interactional difficulties began. An addict mother, eager to escape the hospital, barely glancing at her trembly, small, and often premature newborn, arouses the desire to have seen her during pregnancy. Therapeutic frustrations lead to the hope for some magic critical period when intervention comes easily. This does not exist. The real issue is that one can only start when one sees the trouble, early or late, and tries in honest and good faith to relieve suffering when one sees it. Experience demonstrates quickly that earlier is not easier or more important, although it may be more interesting.

A VISIT TO A NEWBORN NURSERY

For our beginning, let us make a direct approach to infancy by entering a newborn nursery. I mean this not just as a literary device to enliven the imagination but as a necessary concrete first step. Observe there the aseptic tiles glistening under fluorescent lights, the cribs in tidy rows, and the baby nurses tending with impersonal efficiency to the feeding and bathing except for occasional whoops of banter and play.

As our guide book we will use Wolff's 1959 paper (132). Instead of wandering about and making observations on a variety of infants, we will sit by one crib and observe for at least four to five hours one feeding-sleep-wakefulness cycle. Wolff studied four infants for 18-hour stretches. In the stream of behavior observed, we will be able to pick out distinct segments—states such as wide-eyed wakefulness, drowsiness and crying. But let us concentrate now on that period which has been ignored until recently, sleep. When the nurses' chores are over, the nursery emptied of adults, we can distinguish in the quiet of our long watch two types of sleep. One is regular sleep; respirations are even, the infant is in sweet repose except for spontaneous startles every several minutes. The other type of sleep is irregular; breathing is uneven, the body jumps with odd little twitches and the quick small jerks pull the face into grimacing smiles, frowns, and other subtle expressions. Erections occur during this time. Of special interest in this latter phase of sleep is the fluttering of the eyelids. Here we can identify with ease the rapid eye movements and for the next several months distinguish the REM state without equipment. The witnessing of the REM state for the first time arouses a powerful sense of strangeness. What is going on? Is this small creature dreaming?

Those behavioral observations were confirmed, even overshadowed, by the explosion of neurophysiological research. Aserinsky and Kleitman in 1955 (4) described a motility cycle in sleeping infants which was manifested by ocular and body activity. In 1966, Roffwarg, Muzio and Dement (104), using electroencephalograms and electrooculograms, demonstrated that newborns spend half of their sleep time in the REM state in contrast to the 18% for adults. Premature infants can show 60 to 70% of REM sleep. The hypothesis offered at that time was that the REM state represented endogenous stimulation prior to and shortly after birth before exogenous stimulation was available.

STATES

The concept of state has been already mentioned but we need to define it better. Wolff (134) points out two definitions: The first refers to a state as a stable structure and the second defines state as a quantitative continuum. It is the first that has been implied in our observations so far. The existence of a cohesive organization has its roots in the genetic field theory of Werner (127) as well as in the implications of the REM state. The latter definition follows from activation and arousal theory which is usually based on autonomic measures such as heart rate or skin resistance. The discovery of the ascending reticular activating system demonstrated the brain wave patterns of arousal and activation, as well as their behavioral correlates in the sleep-wakefulness cycle. A relevant concept for this second view of state is the Law of Initial Value, which asserts that response to stimulation is a function of the prestimulus level (130). This law implies that it is not enough to consider the stimulus, but we must also know the condition of the organism that receives it.

For example, a tone will provoke a rise in a low level heart rate but there will be a decrease when stimulation is offered when the heart rate is high. Rather than choose one definition of state, both are clinically useful. State as an integrated structure helps us order the large segments of behavior while activation theory aids in considering the small states within a state.

These ideas concerning state can be best understood if concrete observations are made. A rewarding experience would be to witness the recording of the electroencephalogram of an infant and then review it with an experienced interpreter. Also, a feel for sleep and wakefulness in the newborn can be obtained by looking over the criteria used for the scoring of these states (3). An instructional film is available (77).

State and Individual Differences

Let us approach the nursery once again but move now from crib to crib. We will attempt a favorite type of study—the investigation of the variations in response to stimulation—part of the study of individual differences. The interest here has been two-fold: a curiosity concerning the role that the intrinsic variations of response, say to sound, have in personality development; and whether response extremes signal pathology. The start of such a study would be to ring a bell or offer a tone of a specific decibel level (17). There will be a variety of responses. Some infants will startle or offer a discrete twitch or eye blink. Other infants will become quiet and widen their eyes or become alert and turn their heads to the source of the sound in a searching movement. Many will give no response at all. The delight in discovering these striking individual differences and that you have come upon Freud's "primary congenital variations in the ego" (62) will be dampened when you apply to the N.I.M.H. for a million dollars to do a long-term follow-up study. A number of questions will be raised as to your controls. Questioned will be whether you have considered parity, sex, maternal medication, bottle versus breast feeding, Apgar score, time since the last feeding, and maturational level. All of these factors have an effect on response to stimulation and we will consider some of them. However, more than anything the question will be asked: What was done about state? Escalona (40) points out the important relationship between how the problem of state is handled and the kind of research results which are obtained. State can be ignored, randomized, controlled or investigated in its own right. Birns (17), for example, carefully considered and controlled for state before any stimulation. We will continue now with our appraisal of state in its own right.

Alertness

In our search through the organized periods of behavior, let us move on now to that state which, though lasting only a few weeks, is powerful in its impact. This is the alert inactive state. We will concentrate on this state because it is closest to what could be considered as conscious awareness in adults (133). A comment should be made here about "adultomorphizing." The scientific literature abounds with cautions that this is not a proper thing to do. From a clinical standpoint, not to do so is crippling because this would cut us off from our fantasies; those empathic elaborations, that spinning of stories that is vital for a rich sense of an infant. From the standpoint of a theoretical view of infancy, most mothers are Kleinians in the sense that they attribute to the newborn qualities of sexuality, rage, greed, and sophisticated object ties. It is these fantasies, the imagined beginnings of a unique individual, that create the framework within which subtle engagements can be made. If there are no fantasies then there is no infant "personality" and the care offered can only be rigid and routine (14). Hartmann, Kris, and Loewenstein (67) point out the human tendency to anthropomorphize and consider it a necessary process in language and thought without which feeling and vitality are lost.

Wolff (134) has described the alert inactive state as follows: The infant is inactive and the eyes are open, wide and bright. This brightness of the eyes is real, as is dullness, and with experience is readily apparent. The most striking feature of this state is that the infant will fix and follow a moving object. One method of observing this is to play with a newborn. Pick up this creature, get your hands on it. Best is to sit down, place the infant on your lap, cradle it with your hands and position your head about eight to nine inches from the infant's face. That there is a vis-à-vis can be determined be seeing your reflection in the infant's pupil. Then move your head in a slow arc and if contact has been made the infant will follow with his eyes and as well by jerky head turning.

The developmental course of this state is that it is present right after birth when the infant is highly aroused and can last then for several hours. We will see later the implications of this for human attachment. The alert inactive state is variable in its presence in the nursery but increases in the first week to about 10% of the time. By three-and-a-half weeks the infant can sustain alertness during activity, that is, attend to the environment while remaining active (133). It is about this time that a responsive mother ought to be able to engage a bright-eyed and active baby in enthusiastic, fast-moving, visual play.

One important aspect of alertness is that it is the infant's window to the world. An assumption made by Wolff (133) is that alertness is necessary for a true assessment of the environment. The infant experiences the world insofar as he/she is alert. If in another state, say drowsiness or crying, there would be experienced a different world. Of great importance is the observation that maternal medication decreases the time of alertness in the newborn (117). The implications of this are that a drowsy, dopey infant is not available for human interaction.

Visual pursuit can be used as an indicator of attention (136). In the first several days, such pursuit is accomplished by eye movements alone and by the fourth day is coordinated with head movements. The degree of pursuit movement is closely related to internal factors, organismic states within alertness such as activity, inactivity, hunger, fatigue and sucking.

Of practical importance is a maneuver that brings about alertness. Crying infants when picked up and held on the shoulder not only stop crying—most parents are aware of this type of soothing—but the majority of times, the infant opens his eyes, alerts, and visually scans (80). The prior state, as we see again, is crucial in that picking up a sleeping infant has no such effect. The implications of this are that a picked up infant, experiencing vestibular stimulation and not just cuddling, receives an enlarged visual experience at a time in the early weeks when spontaneous alertness is infrequent. Korner and Thoman (80) point out in their paper that in institutions crying babies are rarely picked up. This can be readily observed in any large nursery. Any baby nurse who makes a habit of picking up infants would be cautioned that she is spoiling the babies. Also, it can be observed that mothers vary considerably as to whether they use this type of soothing.

The various expressions of arousal are one category of individual differences that can affect the caretaker's response to the infant. Korner has investigated this issue (79) and found that there are individual differences in frequency and length of crying in newborns. Crying has a powerful impact on the caretaker and an irritable infant provokes involvement which can take the form of either soothing or fury. Conversely, an excessively placid infant can receive little stimulation. In histories taken of autistic children, all of us have heard or will hear the statement that the baby was "so good, never fussed." Not as dramatic as crying, but still potent in effect on the caretaker, is the duration of alertness and restlessness. Also, there are differences in the infant's capacity for visual pursuit. Distinctness and clarity of state can determine how easy an infant is to read. Korner states (78): "Babies whose need states are clear-cut and predictable can convey their needs more readily to their caretakers than babies who are not" (p. 65).

WHAT DO INFANTS LEARN?

Basic to alertness is that the infant is taking in the environment, that is, learning. Can this be demonstrated? This question whether newborn infants are capable of learning must be rephrased into the question whether classical and operant conditioning as well as habituation can be shown (86). The early Russian studies and the work of Marquis in the 30s (92) indicated that conditioning did indeed take place but these findings provoked little interest until recently. Lipsitt (85) points out the bias against early learning in the concept of maturational unfolding. Gesell timetables of development were dominant in previous decades and child neurologists are still more comfortable with this idea. In the past 15 years there has been renewed interest and considerable work done in this area although this is not easy literature to read and possesses its own technical jargon. Lipsett and Kaye (87), and Papousek (93) have demonstrated classical conditioning in the newborn. It has been felt that the old idea that the infant was too young and unformed and hence not capable of learning was due as much to "the use of ineffective experimental techniques as to chronological or neurophysiological deficiencies" (87, p. 30).

For example, habituation can be demonstrated (39). If an infant is exposed to a strong odor several times, the infant will startle at first and then not respond. Change the odor and the infant will react again and then again stop. This is a simple form of learning in which the organism learns not to respond. Is this a precursor of denial?

Operant conditioning, the technique whereby ongoing behavior is rewarded, has the most interest for us clinically. I do not mean allegiance to any exclusive behavioral control approach but rather we will look, especially in somewhat older infants, at what behaviors are susceptible to reinforcement. Kron (81) has demonstrated that on the first day of life, the sucking rate increases when rewarded with milk.

Lipsett (85) comments on what he calls pellet reinforcement, that is, if you do the right thing you get candy. Closer to real life instances would be a situation which is under the infant's control, such as the harder he sucks, the more milk he gets. Or, when the child turns his head and looks, he controls the visual input from his surroundings. For example, if you tie a baby's arm to a mobile, there will be an increase in his movement to receive the more interesting visual experience. The infant has control over his own stimulus input.

Visual reinforcement is most interesting, for if there is a channel of learning dominant in the newborn, it is visual. Wide open eyes signal alertness, but are these only empty states? If mothers are surveyed, some will feel that their babies see them but many will not feel a recognition until there is cooing or the social smile.

WHAT DO INFANTS SEE?

What are the visual capabilities of the infant? The evidence indicates a remarkable degree of development of the visual structures at birth. By the third or fourth month, the infant's visual system is almost functionally mature (128).

The work of Fantz has tangled directly with the problem of whether the infant actually perceives anything visually. He has written many articles and it would be best to start with an early one (43) and then sample his recent thoughts (45). Besides offering a clear presentation of the data, he has a way with words, a gift for aphorism. Starting in the 50s with just-hatched chickens, he tested whether they pecked at round or triangular shapes and found they preferred the former. Then Fantz extended his research to monkeys and to human infants using the visual preference method. For example, you place before an infant a checker board or a plain square and see which design the infant looks at longer. You will find that the infant looks longer at patterns. The conclusion is that there is some degree of visual perception which is unlearned at birth.

These experiments caught a different view of the infant. The testing done earlier was of the infant doing something, the visually-directed reach, for example. Piaget felt that the first mental structures are internalizations of overt actions (94) but Fantz's idea was that the infant acquired mental representations only by looking or listening. "The acquisition of knowledge about the environment begins with his first look" (44, p. 218). The relative amount of time the infant looks at targets is largely a function of stimulus properties. More basic than color and size are degree of patterning and the form. A quick view of what an infant learns would be obtained from just looking around yourself. Could it be that "the infant's future prospects as well as past experiences and present interests are reflected in his eyes?" (p. 53) This is not a passive experience. The selection and preference for certain characteristics of the world are like putting him in an enriched environment—this visual exploration gives him a headstart (46).

The use of fixation time and the visual preference technique alone still leave open the question as to whether the stares are cognitively empty or that information is being processed. Researchers are happier with multiple response measures. One favorite addition is heart rate, in that cardiac deceleration has been shown to accompany attention (84).

INDIVIDUAL DIFFERENCES

Let us return to our consideration of individual differences and examine the variations of inborn capacities other than states and visual behavior. One interest has been in those extremes which signal pathology. Bergman and Escalona (15) in a classic paper described a group of young children who were unusually sensitive to sensory stimulation. The outcome in later childhood was severe developmental deviations. It was suggested that they were insufficiently protected by a "stimulus barrier" (a construct we will discuss soon) and were overwhelmed by ordinary stimulation and developed a defensive "shutting out" of stimuli needed for development.

Individual differences in activity level have long been thought to be a crucial behavior characteristic. Fries (63) pioneered the study of activity level and its role in the mother-child relationship and personality development. Escalona in *The Roots of Individuality* (41) describes and compares active and inactive infants and relates their characteristics to other dimensions of early behavior. One is perceptual sensitivity, here not the extreme but the variations within the normal range. This and activity level are considered to be two independent organismic characteristics. Another dimension is spontaneous activity, that is, the capacity to sustain wakeful animation. Escalona's book is rewarding reading, especially in obtaining a sense of the complex and quirky fits and starts of development. The numerous descriptions of infant development can serve as useful case studies. These would be of special interest if any of us have prolonged involvement with a child characterized by a high or low activity level.

The theoretical stance taken by Escalona toward the process of development and the method of integrating the research material is of great practical use to us in enlarging what we see and helping us pull together our clinical impressions. So far, we have tried to maintain a view of development that it is not just an inexorable growth spurt of genetically programmed nervous tissue, implacably determined, nor do we wish to float on the gusty whims of the reinforcers blown by the world's winds. We have assumed that constitution and environment each bring and do something which influences developmental outcome. An individual's fortune is a mix of the genetic hand dealt and the player's skill and courage. This view is useful but not good enough. We need not give it up but rather save it for a quick understanding of the extremes—how crude deprivation or perinatal damage results in pathology. However, this view is not too helpful in responding to the surprises—why some institutional children survive and some handicapped babies prevail—nor does it help us navigate the mainstream of developmental flow. Escalona believes that the actual experience of the infant is the crucial variable in development. The important event, as Escalona has related in discussions, is not what is done to the infant but rather how the infant reacts, behaves and, by inference, experiences. An infant with a low threshold to tactile stimulation would respond adversely to a rough and tumble joyful family where children are tossed about, while a stolid, flabby infant could be vitalized by such an involvement. Another example offered is of the colicky infant whose distress cannot be relieved easily by a responsive mother and who would share the same experience of frustration with a sturdy and vigorous infant whose mother is austere and delaying in her feeding and comforting. "Thus, the same kind of actual experience may occur as the result of widely different combinations of environmental and intrinsic factors" (41, p. 62).

Another clinical and theoretical approach to early uniqueness is offered by Weil in her writings and teaching. Her concept of "the basic core" represents an integration of endowment and experience which continues as a fundamental theme as it intermingles in the flow of separation-individuation and psychosexual development (126).

Temperament

The best known presentation of the impact of early characteristics upon the caretaker has been put forth by Thomas, Chess and Birch in their book *Behavioral Individuality in Early Childhood* (124). In a longitudinal study of early individual differences, they found the persistence of the infant's early traits and style into late childhood. On this basis, they concluded that basic, inborn factors in development had been sorely neglected. The apt term used to characterize these innate traits is "temperament" and it is a useful word to borrow when questioning parents about the early style of their infants. The authors are quite unhappy with a unique triumvirate—Freud, Pavlov, and Watson—whom they feel to be environmentalists who have led untold numbers of mothers to believe that their children's troubles were all their fault. Their message is that parents need not suffer this guilt because no one is to blame. This view is well expressed in the subtitle of their popular work *Your Child is a Person* (30), which is *A Psychological Approach to Parenthood Without Guilt!*

Cuddlers and Non-cuddlers

One individual difference requires specific mention. A frequent complaint heard from mothers who have had difficulties from early on with a child is that the infant would not cuddle, in fact, recoiled from physical contact. There are often vivid descriptions of the infant practically throwing itself out of comforting arms, of a disagreeable arching of the back, and of a squirmy inconsolability. Schaffer and Emerson (109) have studied the response of infants to physical contact and were able to separate out two groups: those who readily accepted physical contact and those who resisted it. The authors believed that there was evidence of a congenital response tendency to avoid physical contact; in other words, variation in parental handling was not seen as the important variable. The authors felt that by itself the non-cuddling in infants was not a worrisome prognostic signal. There was difficulty only when the mother was unable to discover alternate ways to involve the infant, such as visual contact or rough play. This situation is similar to the more urgent demand on the parents of blind children to find an alternative to visual sensory channels.

MOTHER-INFANT INTERACTION

So far we have considered inborn capacities, the neat tricks the infant possesses, and have only flirted with the idea that the environment brought in by the caretaker makes its mark. We will review now some provocative new answers that have appeared over the last decade to the question of how early in life does the involvement of the caretaker make a difference.

A Look At Our Language

The work of John Bowlby has had immense impact on child workers because, beyond its theoretical statements, it possesses rich clinical observations with great practical consequences. His paper "The Nature of the Child's Tie to His Mother" (19) is a classic and is highly recommended reading. It was the major introduction into the analytic literature of ethological concepts and language. Bowlby emphasized that the infant's inborn biological equipment provided it with powerful signaling and control devices, such as sucking, crying, smiling, clinging and following, which made the early ties to the mother possible. This attachment behavior and the consequence of its interruption will be picked up later. As we look again at the early interactions between mother and infant, it becomes necessary to review our images and wonder whether we become trapped within the tightness of any conceptual scheme, the confinements of one vocabulary. The most elegant statement as to the confusion of language—how the same observations lead to disparate views—appears in the criticism of Bowlby's paper "Grief and Mourning in Infancy and Early Childhood" (20). In this work, Bowlby questions the traditional analytic concepts of orality and infantile narcissism. Anna Freud, in her critique, describes the confusions of language with a telling simplicity. "There is no other point where the clash between metapsychological and descriptive thinking becomes as obvious as it is here. It leads to the apparently paradoxical result that what in terms of the libido theory is the apex of infantile narcissism, appears in Dr. Bowlby's descriptive terms as the height of 'attachment behavior.' But we agree with him, of course, that never again in his life will the child be found to be more clinging to the mother or more dependent on her presence (60, p. 56).

Regulation of Rhythms

A powerful description of the process by which the mother-infant relationship is established has been presented by Louis Sander and his associates at the Boston University Medical Center. The theoretical underpinnings are a rigorous exegesis of the view that the focus must be on the organization of the infant-environment field, the baby and surrounding world as all of a piece. Though this is presented as a way of putting together research, we will draw on it as necessary for our clinical approach. The concept of adaptation is invoked to describe the interactions between the two uniquely different partners within the organization of the field. The language used and references offered are not only from developmental psychology and psychoanalysis but from contemporary biology as well, especially as it concerns temporal organization, circadian rhythms, and cybernetics.

This work allows us to return to the early cycle of sleep and wakefulness. Although by all rights one should read all of the many stately papers that offer rich details, the ideas required for our clinical view can be found in one review article—"Primary prevention and some aspects of temporal organization in early infant-caretaker interaction" (107, p. 190). The infant and caretaker are seen as becoming joined by recurrent encounters which are at first irregular and then take place with a greater regularity which results in a meshing of the two individuals into a "regulatory system." The methodology is precise and detailed—a feel for this is necessary and here there is no shortcut (106)—requiring around-the-clock data from on-the-spot observations as well as equipment that records the infant activity and all encounters with the caretaker.

Three groups of infants were studied who were raised under different caretaking conditions. One group of boarder babies received over the first 10 days the standard nursery care of feeding every four hours (and it can be assumed the usual brief impersonal contacts). A second group of boarder babies each received 24-hour-a-day contact with one surrogate mother during the first 10 days. A third group of infants was cared for by the natural mother with demand feeding (rooming in), an experience similar to the second group for the first five days except that after this initial period the babies were cared for at home. At the end of the first 10 days, the first group was given individual surrogate mothers and the second group was switched to a different caretaker. These two groups received this care from 10 to 28 days when they were transferred to a foster home.

The investigation attempted to assess the long-term effect of different caretaking methods during the first 10 days in later weeks. Following their first 10 days' experience, the infants received similar care from surrogate mothers. A second task was to assess the effect of changing the caretaker on the second group of infants. Two experienced caretakers were used who possessed different styles and personalities. The investigation wanted to determine if an infant is able to pick up these differences in the earliest days of life.

One finding was that infants' active states were longer in duration during the first several days. This is counter to the view of the drugged and exhausted baby who during the first days is unavailable for interaction. To quote—"What might be the adaptive significance of the longer time each day in states of relatively greater arousal during the first few days of life? Is there a reason for a relatively greater readiness for interaction with the caretaking environment at the outset?" (107, p. 193). One answer is that the unique behaviors of the infant—"his changing state, especially in the transitional segments, become clues for the experienced caretaker to guide her decisions. They constitute the configurations which identify the unique qualities of a particular infant. It is just these individual differences which are being learned by the caretaker and are being modified by the infant as they establish adaptation through mutual coordinations" (107, p. 193). Restated, it is those unique and subtle qualities of the states that serve as cues for the mother and make it possible for her to establish an interaction with the child. For example, it it likely that infant and caretaker establish signals that allow an easy transition between wakefulness and sleep. The mother may be able to put the infant to sleep in the first week while a stranger such as a father has a harder time of it.

The second finding was that the shifts to the daytime distribution of the aroused states were under some environmental control. This occurred in the caretaker-raised infants and was apparent in the first three days. Here an extrinsic temporal ordering of the day as made by the caretaker modified the intrinsic rhythms. This shift is of crucial importance to the mother's well-being. For example, a good question to ask the mother of a newborn would be how many times she had to get up at night.

A third finding was that the first 10 days of caretaking made a difference. In the first group of infants who were transferred to caretakers on day 11, there was a sharp change in sleep distribution over the next several weeks. A question posed but not as yet answered is—"How could something or some things that had happened in the first days of life be exerting such a continuing effect on the time in the day of sleeping over the rest of the first month?" (107, p. 196). Also, there was a reaction on the part of the infants in the second group when there was a change from one caretaker to another. An additional finding was that there were sex differences in the effect of the first 10 days of caretaking experience.

One major conclusion follows from this work—"the significance of the first 10 days of life may be greater than we have realized in the establishing of a basis for temporal organization of infant-caretaker interaction. The nonchalant separation of infant and mother in the first five days of life, which we have accepted unquestioningly as part of the standard maternity care, needs a thorough reappraisal" (107, p. 202).

How Early Is Early?

So far our interest has been in the remarkable capacities of the young infant. It needs to be questioned, however, whether these behaviors are any more than curiosities or the presaging of abilities that are only functional later on. Much of current infant research evokes the response of "Wow, can a little baby really do all of that?" There also follows the feeling of, "So what, does it matter that an infant can fix and follow visually the first minute rather than the first month?" The significance of the early behaviors we have been examining, specifically the infant's early alert state and visual abilities, becomes clearer when we consider a parallel research theme: the other side of attachment, the behaviors shown by mothers and any other involved party towards newly born infants.

Klaus and his associates at the Case Western Reserve University Medical School have investigated the process by which the parent becomes attached to the infant, not the traditional other way around (74). They feel that without this attachment to the infant the parent will not make the sacrifices necessary for the infant's survival. Their work began with observations made on premature infants in an intensive care unit where they, as had others, noted that these infants would leave the hospital in sturdy good health but that from this group came a strikingly high incidence of battering, accidents and failure to thrive. It was felt that the institutionally enforced separation between parents and infant contributed to a failure in the development of attachment, familiarity, caring, love, call it what you will, and this led to the greater likelihood of abuse.

From these beginnings followed an investigation of early maternal attachment, specifically the mother's first responses to premature and newborn infants when allowed extended contact (73). Observed was a predictable sequence of behaviors shown by mothers of full-term infants when they first saw their babies. First there was hesitant finger tip contact with the extremities, then in four to eight minutes a caressing of the trunk with the palm. With this exploration and handling there was rapidly increasing maternal excitement. Mothers of premature infants showed the same sequence but their behaviors were attenuated and sparse. There was a great interest in the eyes by the mothers of both the premature and full-term infants; 80% of the verbalizations concerned the eyes. There was in the first minutes an attempt to make eye contact and a rapid increase in the "en face" position between mother and full-term infant.

Right after delivery, the mother is in a highly emotional state. There is a greater level of excitement during home delivery than in the hospital. It was observed that in the former situation, mothers talked in a high-pitched voice and frequently reported experiences similar to orgasm.

Klaus catches this best in discussions of the experience as a border psychotic state where the top of the mother's head is coming off. They are then in a "state of ekstasis," using the Greek word for ecstasy.

Of great interest to us is that the mother's overpowering interest in the eyes and her attempts to make visual contact come in the first minutes when the infant is most likely to be alert and able to fix and follow visually. This early vis-à-vis appears to be an interaction of utmost importance in the development of affectional ties (73). Important as well is the finding of Condon and Sander (32) that the infant's body moves in rhythm with the mother's speech, whatever her language, as early as the first day. Klaus catches the meaning of this early, active, and reciprocal response of the infant to the mother thus—"You can't love a dishrag" (74, p. 120) and "you cannot make love to anyone who does not make love to you." (74, p. 117)

A question raised is whether this early time is a sensitive period for the development of human attachment behavior. This is so for goats and sheep. Kids and lambs separated from their mothers will be rejected or subject to aberrant mothering when returned. The occurrence of this seemingly species-specific maternal behavior was studied in humans. Two groups were compared. One group of mothers received the usual hospital procedure of a brief glance at the infant shortly after birth and then the 30-minute or less contact for feeding every four hours. A second group, matched for family background and infant characteristics, was allowed extended contact—16 extra hours. Especially important was the chance to play with their naked infant for an hour immediately after birth. At one month, the maternal behavior of each group was studied (72). The extended-contact mothers stayed with their infants for longer periods during the examination and engaged in more fondling, soothing and eye-to-eye contact while feeding. The conclusion of this study is stunningly simple—"These studies suggest that simple modification of care shortly after delivery may alter subsequent maternal behavior" (72, p.461). At one year, similar distinct differences were shown between the two groups. The differences continued for two years as shown in the linguistic behavior of the extended-contact mothers, who gave fewer commands and asked twice as many questions in more complex sentences that encouraged a response (23).

What are we to do with these striking results? One possibility is that we can ignore them, which is the fate of most developmental data. Another is that we can run with them in either of two directions. Since this chapter is addressed to the individual clinician, let us imagine situations where consultation is sought concerning the soon-to-deliver woman, where these findings could cause us to influence what happens immediately after delivery. For example, advice is often sought concerning women considered to be at high risk for future difficulties with their infant—the addict, the psychotic, or the very young teenager. These are all situations where the mother is likely to be separated from her infant more than usual. It would seem that there is some urgency in seeing that this does not happen but that, rather, the contact be prolonged. A milder situation is the woman with overt psychiatric symptoms who is likely to scare and bother an obstetrical floor and lose out on time with her infant. A not infrequent occurrence in a general hospital is the pregnant woman on a locked psychiatric ward. If she is unable to stay on the ward, a specific task would be to make arrangements that she return with aides at each feeding to care for her infant.

The other direction we can go is toward massive changes in the way our institutions are organized. Fortunately, many of the researchers who are providing the data, T. Berry Brazelton is a good example, are persuasive educators and popular writers as well. A theme that does not get across in the professional prose but is strikingly present when Marshall Klaus speaks directly to an audience—of course this is a highly personal reaction—is an evangelistic spell and a proselytizing force. I have observed a large audience of tough professionals respond to these ideas with emotion. The only other time this mood has been experienced by me in a scientific meeting is when the thanatology people get going. I am not sure that this passion is entirely a blessing. The so-called natural childbirth or lying-in movement has had in the past a cultist flavor that was never appealing to hospital administrators. However, now the doctrine is preached by establishment professors from classy places documented by tight developmental studies and rides the powerful tide of the consumer and women's movements. It will be interesting to see what happens.

Reciprocity

The work of T. Berry Brazelton demonstrates for us again the importance of the infant's early abilities. These infant talents, especially those engaged by the parents, have been translated into a practical clinical tool. This is to be found in his Neonatal Behavioral Assessment Scale (23). If there is one concrete experience that would aid anyone interested in young infants, it would be the training in the administration of this exam. Almost every point we have made about infants so far is vividly demonstrated there. The most direct way to arrange this training would be to call the man up and, depending on the part of the country, find out who nearby knows how to administer the scale. Let me emphasize that the intention of this suggestion is as an educational experience which, as we will discuss, has turned out to be an important fringe benefit for the parents of the infants tested. This, more than the other exams, fits into the needs of the clinician.

We are now well prepared for the central theme of this assessment scale. "The baby's state of consciousness is perhaps the single most important element in the behavioral examination. His reactions to all stimulation are dependent upon his ongoing state of consciousness and any interpretation of them must be made with this in mind" (23, p. 2). Starting with sleep, the infant is brought "through an entire spectrum of states." When the infant begins to fuss and cry, the activities necessary to soothe and console are rated. Besides the usual appraisal of reflexes and motor ability such as tone and response to being pulled to sit, there is an evaluation of interactive resources by means of the response to social stimuli. We have discussed the newborn's ability to orient to visual stimuli but most infants can track the source of auditory stimuli such as the human voice as well. The organization of states, their build up, peaking, stability, and self quieting can be assessed. The ability to shut out disturbing stimuli during sleep—habituation—can be evaluated.

This scale has been used to examine differences in full-term and premature infants and in cross-cultural studies as well. Of most interest for our purposes are its educational uses. If parents watch the exam, they gain a sense of the infant's repertoire of skills and interpret these as strengths and from this results increased attachment. Let us take this comment and restate it. Whatever the exam, most likely for us it will be talking to a mother while she has her infant on her lap; an acknowledgment of the baby's abilities can have important consequences. The spirit of this is a low-key fostering of awareness which permits the parents to look at and learn to read their infant.

The same theme from another line of research is the infant's interactional behavior (24). If the infant is shown an inanimate object, there is an intense build up of attention, then an abrupt turn off, a flailing, a turning down or shutting of the eyes, and then a return to the object with again a "hooked" attention. This attentional curve is jagged. The infant's behavior and attention span with the mother, compared to an inanimate object, are seen to be different by two to three weeks and clearly so by four weeks. With the mother, there is a smooth and rhythmic sequence of approach and withdrawal behavior. The average cycle of attention and withdrawal is four times per minute. The parent moves in the cycle as well, the two parties engaging in a rhythmic exchange—"playing a kind of swan's mating dance, as he or she moved in to pass on information or behavior when the infant was looking, and withdrew slightly to let up intensity when the infant withdrew" (25, p. 135).

Fathers seemed to be wired differently than mothers in that they would come in high and try to rev up the infant whereas the mother would come in low. It seemed that fathers expected a more jazzed up response from their babies and were able to get it. "Amazingly enough, an infant by two or three weeks displays an entirely different attitude (more wide-eyed, playful and bright faced) toward his father than his mother" (25, p. 138).

As early as four weeks, there was a clear difference in response to strangers who were not able to tune into the infant's rhythms. What is seen is the jagged curve of approach and withdrawal, as with objects, which does not result in long periods of attention. "It seems to be a behavioral precursor to the awareness of strangers seen at five months and anxiety toward strangers seen at eight months" (25, p. 138). The conviction of the researchers is that they can tell from observing any part of the infant's body whether he is interacting with parent, stranger, or object.

Fascinating is the consequence of teaching the mother to violate reciprocity by offering the infant a flat and expressionless face. As early as two to three weeks but clearly by seven weeks, the infant reacts strongly, first with attempts to make contact, then sobering, and finally with pulling away and a hopeless demeanor (125).

The spirit of this reciprocity, this rhythmic in and out movement and attention, is an aroused and playful pleasure. A view we will develop soon is the importance of sensing the shared affect in the infant-mother pair. Absolutely vital to our clinical approach and evaluation is that this performance is seen as early as two weeks and certainly by four weeks. Brazelton and his associates are investigating methods of identifying the failures to develop this synchronous rhythm—extremes would be the infant bombarded by stimuli or not receiving any—this possibly leading to such early pathology as failure to thrive. With our own increasing experience, we can use these observations ourselves as we examine the interaction between mother and infant. Again, an essential issue for clinical appraisal is the affectual interplay, the emotional exchange between the dyadic partners (1).

Critical Periods

In addition to our awareness that mother and infant are capable of bonding, attachment, caring, call it what you will, in the first seconds, days or weeks, and that there may be unhappy consequences if this does not occur, we are faced with the concepts of critical periods and imprinting. This began with Lorenz' paper in 1935 (88). The view presented was that the attachment process took place within a restricted time period and there was, crudely stated, a one-shot, now or never, process of learning called imprinting. Scott has been the clearest spokesman on this process—"The concept of critical periods is a highly important one for human and animal welfare. Once the dangers and potential benefits for each period are known, it should be possible to avoid the former and take advantage of the latter" (110, p. 957).

The application of the critical period idea to human children enjoyed wild popularity in the 60s during the heyday of Headstart, the national effort to solve all problems by getting in early. As part of the early intervention idea were cries of doom if there was early difficulty. We must now take a more discrete look and wonder about critical periods. Wolff (135) has considered thoughtfully the concept of critical periods as it applies to human cognitive development. "Available evidence does not support the view that there are 'critical periods' during which children must be exposed to a given learning opportunity or forever suffer some degree of intellectual deficit" (135, p. 155). Following from this, it can be questioned whether the "imprinting" model of infant-mother attachment offered by Bowlby and Klaus is not too simple and forgets what comes later: the continual interactional realignment, the shifting and relearning of the rules by each member of the mother-infant dyad. However, my impression is that, rather than being overdone, when it comes to institutions that care for infants these concepts have never gotten across. It takes but a few hours or so of sitting in a newborn nursery, pediatric ward, or foster care facility to see whether the babies are bright-eyed and alert, inquisitive, and emotionally responsive. The prevailing view, however, seems to be that as long as infants gain weight and are afebrile things are going well. Life is sustained but the result is a fat, dead-faced baby. For our clinical purposes we should take a moderate view of these concepts—whatever the developmental scheme we fancy, that of Freud, Piaget, Erikson, or Werner—they all have a concept of ideal levels, stages, periods and that what does or does not happen at that stage affects the future.

WHAT ARE THE BEST INTERESTS OF THE CHILD?

The work reviewed so far augments the classic studies of Anna Freud (59), Spitz (113), and Bowlby (18), who years before demonstrated the primacy and importance of the child's early tie to the caretaker. There is a slim powerful volume which takes this knowledge and translates it into direct and clear principles regarding children. This is *Beyond the Best Interests of the Child* by Goldstein, Solnit and Freud (65). They begin with the crucial distinction between the relationship of the child with the biological parent and the psychological parent and emphasize that though they are often one and the same it is only the latter that means anything to the child. From this they formulate principles. One is—"Placement decisions should safeguard the child's need for continuity of relations" (p. 31). It should be expected that if child placements are necessary they be as permanent as the handing over of a newborn to its biological parents. The second principle is that—"Placement decisions should reflect the child's, not the adult's, sense of time" (65, p. 34). Their stricture is that placement should proceed with "all deliberate speed," and that there is the same urgency as if the infant were in physical danger. Other issues concern strengthening the psychological parents by giving them the power to determine visitation by the non-custodial parent. Also recommended is that adoption be made final the day it takes place.

These ideas would seem to be non-controversial. This has not been so. It is instructive to listen to a presentation by one of the authors and hear the disgracefully niggling criticisms. The one objection that deserves consideration is that most of the infants concerned come from poverty and minority groups and are in danger of professionals intruding and violating their rights. The specter thrown up is of babies being stolen away. It is, however, precisely these infants who lie listlessly for months awaiting placement and then are shunted from one foster home to another. It takes months to reach decisions that should be made in days. The authors in their commentaries urge that every effort be made to assist troubled families and help them raise their own children. Society has not encouraged this. Solnit comments on the puritanism that recoils from paying families to care for their children. Another amazing experience is to listen when it is decided that the biological parent is not able to care for the infant and hear to whom it is then considered that the infant belongs—The Bureau of Child Welfare, the community, or various racial and religious groups? A point made by the authors is that child placement follows the emotional needs of the parent—whoever that may be at the time—and rarely the needs of the infant. A conclusion is the recommendation that those interested in infants maintain an uncompromising, even rigid, advocacy because it is unlikely that anyone else will.

THE USES OF INTERACTION

With the background acquired so far we can now place an increasing emphasis on practical clinical application. A question arising from our interest in interaction is just whom do you treat—mother or child? Neither. If the time chosen for intervention is the earliest months, then the therapautic unit is the mother-infant dyad. I mean this in the most literal sense of mother with babe in arms, infant on the lap, or right in front of her in a carrier. Evaluation and treatment during this early time should resemble research on mutual gaze behavior in that it would be a strange thing to do with one party missing. Although the interactional approach is a currently accepted concept, especially for research, it has not been developed clinically. Discussions of couple and family therapy stress the mystic unity that is supposed to occur in these groupings and, while this is questionable, it would seem important to examine the situation where two really are one.

The issue can be raised as to whether the interactional approach fits if there is severe deviance from normality in either nature or nurture. This concept of interaction, specifically in the work of Sander and Brazelton, refers to a normal developmental progression. Assumed is an average expected environment, rephrased as the good enough mother with the good enough baby. Some of the examples of pathology that we may see are so deviant that the more familiar scheme of one side doing something to the other may be more adequate. However, the position taken here is that whatever the pathology, the interactional approach in its concrete sense, mother and child together, is most useful. For example, recently a psychotic mother who was an inpatient on a psychiatric ward was seen together with her one-month-old hydrocephalic child. The infant did not fix visually and the mother had vivid fantasies about her baby's independence, his dislike of having people make funny faces at him, as well as his native love of music. It was striking to watch their mutual accommodation. By touch and with the mother's singing hymns and pop songs, there developed a rich synchrony and rhythm in spite of the serious difficulties which blocked many interactive channels.

One approach to the problem of describing this early interaction lies in looking again at the language we use. If we are to attempt this in a clinical setting, then the bare scientific prose which expands on feedback and systems theory with diagrams of many arrows does not help us much. One way to look at interaction is to consider the images used and try to choose a central metaphor. There are just so many ways that catch what happens between two people. If Klaus favors the images of erotic love, flavored with ethology, then we can say perhaps that Brazelton is describing two people dancing. Many of the images come from ordered systems. The words of music are particularly apt in that issues of time, rhythm, and the blending of many voices are caught with precision. The playful concept of games is a favorite—they have rules. Analytic explanations borrow heavily from warfare with the ideas of defenses, barriers, attacking and breaking through.

Games Infants Play

Our interactional interests are met splendidly by the games played between mother and infant. They have been considered from a cognitive point of view in Piaget's *The Origin of Intelligence in Children* (94); however, the playful interaction of mother and infant can also be studied as a guide for affective or motor development. Infant-mother games can start from the very beginning and draw upon the infant's reflex repertoire and the mother's style of engaging such basic processes as feeding (29). One clinical question is whether the games exist at all and, if so, what is their frequency? After exposure to Brazelton, we will be interested in the movements of both bodies, the ingenuity and rhythms, how well they dance together, do the two hearts beat in the three-quarter-time of reciprocity? The mother's patter, her running reportage of the game, and her verbal projections as to the baby's reactions catch the fantasy being played out as well as the affectual theme (14). One function of play is the encouragement and regulation of arousal. For example, the mother of a three-month-old will zoom in with delight and score by the response of a big gummy smile (7). The affect is not only shared pleasure; other feelings are expressed by games. An intrusive looming of the mother's head can be met by the infant's head turning, avoidance, apathy, or tears. These interpersonal events catch for us the spirit of the relationship. Call and Marschak describe this with elegance—these games "since they develop spontaneously between mother and infant, . . . can be regarded as a precipitant, a condensation, or the essence of that relationship" (29, p. 207).

Fraiberg enlarges our clinical view by her description of games as "a valuable diagnostic instrument for assessment of infant-parent relationships" (54, p. 219). In play, adults can express to their infants the entire range of feelings: sensuality and sadness, tenderness and rage. But these games need to be understood in a dynamic sense because they function to "regulate, through ritual and through the conventional disguises of play, the discharge of forbidden impulses" (p. 205). The defensive function of games results for the most part in a defusing of the parent's conflictual impulses but they can also serve as channels for the harmful acting out of these impulses.

THE ORIGIN OF AFFECT

We will now return again to the first days and trace affectual development. As was done with states of arousal, the emphasis will be interactional. Affect at this early time has usually meant the ontogenesis of the smile, which, although an interesting theme, represents a rather narrow view of affect. Knapp (76) offers a clear orientation to the study of emotions in the outlining of three component areas of affectual experience. The *first* area is that of private states of experience. It is only the adult partner in the dyad who can offer verbal expression to feelings and by verbal projections as well assign the infant an emotional state. The *second* area is the physiological processes which accompany these states. Rather than read the beat-by-beat heart rate or the EEG as in a proper physiological study, these processes are perceived intuitively by the mother and help her in what can be considered her most important task in the first months, which is the monitoring and regulation of arousal. The mother calms the infant from crying and soothes it to sleep, but for social engagement she stimulates the infant and then modulates this arousal, avoiding lows and overloading. Restated, the mother is in constant touch with the rhythms of arousal. The *third* area is expressive behavior, which we will examine further in the next few pages. The vocal, motor, and autonomic signals associated with these affective states and processes permit communication about them to the environment.

The seminal source for an explanation of expressive behavior was Darwin's *The Expression of the Emotions in Man and Animals* (33). In his attempt to explain expressive behavior, Darwin was the first to introduce the comparative phylogenetic method to the study of emotion. For example, a show of bared teeth meant all the better to bite with, and later derived into the sneer. Tinbergen and Lorenz took these early speculations and enlarged upon them in the development of the field of ethology, which is defined as the biology of behavior (34). It was found that some behavior was organized into innate motor patterns which were released by key stimuli in the environment. Our interest is in a special class of stimuli or signals called social releasers that mediate the social behavior within a species. Behavior patterns can have a communicative function, serving as signals if they are clear and conspicuous. They evolved in phylogenesis as a means of coordinating social behaviors. Just as the spots on the bill of a gull serve as releasers, so can these behaviors. These expressive movements can be learned or innate and their richness varies from species to species. For example, the fox, a solitary hunter, has sparse expressions compared to wolves who hunt in a pack. The evolutionary process by which a behavior is transformed into a precise and conspicuous signal and modified to serve communication is called ritualization (34).

With this background, let us review the past work on the most studied piece of expressive behavior in infants: the smile. Kaila in 1932 investigated the basic elements in the mother's face which led to the infant's smile. Used were cardboard diagrams and human faces (69). The two essentials postulated were the eyes and full face position. Spitz and Wolff in 1946 added a third essential which was movement (116). Their paper is a classic, easily available, and highly recommended. Ahrens in 1954 used a variety of diagrams and found that greater detail was demanded as the infant grew older (2).

These studies focused on the smiling occurring in response to visual stimuli. Recent work has examined stimuli from other sensory channels, including those from an endogenous source. The work of Robert Emde and his associates (37) has offered a view of the early smile that integrates neurophysiological and behavioral observations. His EEG studies which were reviewed earlier give an understanding of the ontogenesis of states and present a solid foundation for our look at affectual development.

The Endogenous Smile

If we return now to our vigil in the newborn nursery we can observe a fascinating piece of behavior during REM sleep. This is a brief, grimacing smile. It is endogenous in that it is not elicited by an external stimulus. This smiling is associated with rapid eye movements and occurs in bursts. It has been found not only in REM sleep but during a special phase of drowsiness where there were REMs. This state, called drowsy REM, is unique to the first two months of life. The infant's eyes can be open but glassy and there are endogenous smiles and sucking. Oftentimes the infant is considered to be awake and this pulls in the caretaker (35).

Additional studies showed that endogenous smiles occurred four to five times more often in the premature infant than in the full-term infant (37). Study of a microcephalic infant showed that the REM-induced smiling occurred at rates similar to those of normal newborns. This led to the conclusion that the seat of REM and NREM was in the brain stem (66) since essentially decorticated infants showed similar patterns to normals.

The Social Smile

In a longitudinal study of the development of the social smile (35), it was found that between the ages of one-and-a-half and two-and-a-half months, smiling occurred in response to a variety of stimuli—visual, auditory, tactile and kinesthetic. This smile was unpredictable, in contrast to the later predictable social smile in response to the human face. A conclusion reached was that there is "a sensory equivalence for smiling" (p. 185). We will pick this up again shortly in our consideration of blind infants. Any of these stimuli elicit a smile but this equivalence disappears when the social smile emerges and at this time visual stimuli are dominant. An interesting consideration is the relationship between these exogenous smiles and the endogenous smile. They appear to come from two separate maturational systems which use the same motor channels for expression. The endogenous smile drops out between the fifth and sixth month and this is most likely because of inhibition by the maturing cerebral cortex (36).

Another expresion of affect occurring in the first months which is important clinically is early fussiness. It is best known in its extreme form, which is infantile colic. In their longitudinal study, Emde, Gaensbauer and Harmon found that all of the infants showed periods of unexplained fussiness which was manifested by crying. This dysphoria was present in every infant and was not in response to hunger or pain and appeared to be endogenous (36).

The theoretical underpinnings of this work lie in the field theory of Spitz (114) and in Werner's concepts (127). These are explored fully by Emde, Gaensbauer, and Harmon(36). This monograph is a deliberately dispassionate look at emotional development. For our clinical purposes, it represents a bedrock blending of physiology and behavior. One of Spitz's concepts is that the pace of development in infancy is uneven—there are discontinuities. Another idea is that emotional behavior is a useful signal for times of rapid maturational change. This is supported by EEG shifts in organization that occur at the time of two dramatic affectual events. To describe these, Spitz borrows from embryology and uses the term "organizer." The flowering of the social smile is considered as "the first organizer of the psyche." The anxiety that occurs on confrontation with a stranger at eight months is the "second organizer of the psyche."

The Smile of Blind Infants

The study of blind infants offers us an understanding of the role of vision in development. This work is also particularly rewarding for us because out of it has come thoughtful ideas for treatment of high risk and vulnerable children.

The smile is a major guidepost on the developmental path of object relations and longitudinal studies of blind infants have indicated the role of vision in its formation (52). At 10 to 14 weeks, blind infants show the same irregular smiling to various nonvisual sensory modalities as do sighted infants. The human voice is one stimulus for the smile at this time and there is good equivalence between the blind baby's smiling response and that of the sighted baby. However, while at this time the human face elicits an automatic smile regularly in sighted infants, there is no counterpart in the blind baby. By two-and-a-half to three months there is in blind infants an increased frequency of smiling to touch and sound, but even though there is increased selectivity in favor of the mother, her voice will not regularly elicit a smile. Selma Fraiberg, who has performed most of the clinical research on blind infants states: "There is no stimulus in the third month or later (for the blind child) that has true equivalence for the human face gestalt in the experience of the sighted child" (53 p. 115). It is only the visual modality which elicits an automatic response at three months.

From three to six months, the smile of blind babies is selective to the parent's voice but it is not automatic. However, at this time what was most likely to evoke a smile was handling, tickling, jouncing, and hugging. The parent's desire for emotional response led to these effective alternate routes for stimulation.

Another difference was that even with a rewarding relationship with the mother, the blind infant's smile was muted. The full blown and joyful smile seen in sighted babies is rare in blind babies. The conclusion was that reinforcement by the mother's smile is necessary for the full smile in infancy.

Other Infant Expressions

The literature on early facial expressions has focused on the smile to the virtual exclusion of other facial displays. However, long before the social smile, the infant is capable of many complex, subtle, and fleeting expressions which can engage the caretaker. These expressions in the three-week-old infant were carefully described by Stechler and Latz (118). They can be observed easily by watching the mother respond to the split second transformations of the infant's face during early play. Special conditions of arousal are necessary to elicit the expressions in the first days and this is the playful visual engagement between infant and mother during the infant's alert state. Of interest is that in observations made on a group of boarder infants in a situation of deprivation, these expressions were not seen. An excellent example of one such expression can be found in the picture of the infant on the cover of the volume *Infant Psychiatry* (97). Here can be seen the bright eyes, the full face with an animated contour of the cheeks and the provocative upper lip curl. The latter, next to the crinkle under the eyes which is not seen there, is almost as powerful as the smile.

FREE PLAY AT THREE MONTHS

The themes developed so far—attentional and affectual development, and the interactional and regulatory capacities of the dyad—are all dramatized in the free play that occurs at three months. Stern (121), on the basis of a microanalysis of filmed interaction between mother and infant, points out that free play is a unique and early social event where the object for both parties is to amuse and enjoy each other, or restated, the goal is "the mutual maintenance of a level of attention and arousal within some optimal range in which the infant is likely to manifest affectively positive social behaviors such as smiles and coos" (p. 404). Selected issues will be chosen from Stern's work for discussion: the method of analysis; a look at the fine structure of mother-infant interaction, especially when it miscarries; a scrutiny of some unique maternal behaviors; and a thought about the clinical uses of all this. These ideas are elaborated with clarity and grace in his small volume "The First Relationship" (122a).

The method of microanalysis relies on film or selected segments of videotapes converted into film—24 frames a second—and thus permits an analysis of split second behaviors. The interactional behavior of a mother with her three-and-a-half-month-old twin boys was analyzed by Stern (120), using this technique. Gaze behavior of both mother and infants was chosen for analysis because of its maturity at three months and its existence as the principal communication in the dyad. Observation of the free play led to the conclusion that it was successful and mutually satisfying with one infant but that it was unsuccessful with the other and that this infant was left distraught. The first clinical impression was that the mother was overstimulating and controlling with the latter infant. What this meant on analysis was that, rather than something done to the infant by the mother, it was rather a mutual event which occurred repetitiously. The mother would approach and the infant would look away, and as the mother pulled back the infant turned back to her. A vicious cycle ensued with sparse mutual gaze and little mutual enjoyment. What needs to be stressed is that this was a fixed and endless interaction which crystallized, as does play, the essence of the relationship which was antagonistic and unsatisfying. Although the mother would more often initiate the sequence, they both could lead and would often act simultaneously. To return to our images—"A waltz serves as an analogy. Certain steps and turns will be cued by one partner—in between those cues both know the program well enough to move synchronously for short periods" (120, p. 513). A striking difference between the twins was the ability of one and the inability of the other to terminate contact with the mother. The latter was not able to stay away and was unable to resist responding to her movements. The theme of getting out is of great importance—"For some infants establishing mother-infant contact may prove less of a developmental issue than acquiring the ability to terminate successfully the contact. This may be especially true with controlling and overstimulating mothers" (120, p. 514).

Another issue, neglected in our attention to the abilities of infants, is the strange things mothers, in fact anyone from older children on up, do with young infants. These are infant-elicited maternal behaviors (122). Speech is offered in the singsong rhythms of baby talk with exaggerations of time and degree. Facial expressions are also enlarged in time and space. One characteristic expression is that of mock surprise where the eyes and mouth open as the eyebrows raise and the head is thrown up. Also exaggerated are other maternal expressions such as pouts and smiles. Maternal hand and body movements are dramatic and gaze is prolonged. These behaviors would be bizarre if offered to another adult and appear to be set off by the specific stimulus of a baby's face. It is possible that this exaggeration of time and degree fits the infant's timing and ability to process information. A clinical example is given of a mother with a richly versatile repertoire of low key vocalizations but who offered little in the way of touch, movement, and expressiveness. Her style was most effective with her infant at three months but it did not connect at four months. When higher intensity behaviors were used as well as other sensory modalities, the interaction was revitalized. An extreme example of this can be seen in some psychotic mothers who are heavily medicated. There is a paucity of maternal movement, expressiveness and vocalizations.

One clinical consequence of observing free play is that the game catches the spirit of the relationship and it is possible "to identify specific repetitive interactive events which appear to miscarry" (121, p. 419). As in any other evaluation, the behavioral observations must be integrated with the mother's history and complaints and her intrapsychic conflicts as well. A second clinical issue which we will return to is whether mothers are capable of readjusting their games and interaction. The impression is that as long as the behaviors were conflict-free, most mothers were capable of rapid learning. The use of videotapes is most valuable here in that they permit the mother to learn from self observation (121).

EARLY INFANT SEPARATION AND CONTROL

The picture we have sketched so far represents the current view of the young infant as an active seeker of stimuli rather than a passive lump. This idea requires enlargement. The fact that there are powerful signaling devices such as the cry and smile can be just a more bouncy statement that the infant takes some initiative in merging into the sticky glue of symbiosis. We have stressed so far the infant's capacity from the first seconds to attract and attach but just as important as the ability to get involved in interaction is the ability to get out. This capacity to detach, withdraw and separate is a neglected issue and has fascinating implications.

First, let us look at this from the mother's side. Brazelton has pointed out in discussions that we must attend to both sides of the mother's ambivalence. Bibring (16) has described the turmoil and the raw drives of pregnancy that resemble a pre-psychotic state. Rage and rejection appear in fantasies that the baby will be born dead or defective. Brazelton feels that this is a rehearsal for the possibility that this may happen. When, with birth, it does not, the positive side of ambivalence explodes and allows an instantaneous attachment to the infant. However, the negative side, the capacity to withdraw and detach, remains and is as important as attachment if both infant and mother are to achieve separateness.

The infant possesses the ability to detach as well by limiting and controlling the input of stimuli. He/she can do this by the use of the visual system which is functionally mature by three months. Robson (103) states—"Vision is the only modality which, by closure of the eyelids, gaze aversion, and pupillary constriction and dilation is constructed as an 'on-off' system which can easily modulate or eliminate external sensory input, sometimes at will, within the first months of life" (p. 13).

Gaze aversion can occur as early as the second week (118). This turning away of the head and eyes is an active act of avoidance. It can be seen as such by mothers who may interpret it as a rejection just as vis-à-vis is seen as a look of love. Persistent gaze aversion and failure to establish eye contact are characteristic of autistic children (68) and can serve as an early warning signal. This was a striking phenomenon when witnessed recently in a three-month-old infant. Not only could eye contact not be established but there was a tightening of the body and a turning of the head when this was attempted. Combined with institutional deprivation, this seemed a grim prognostic sign. Stimulation was offered but of a specific kind which avoided intrusiveness and explored other sensory channels, allowing eye contact to be finally established.

In our description of the reciprocal and rhythmic interaction between mother and infant, the emphasis was on the early tie. However, detachment is a basic part of this cycle of attention and non-attention which is indicated by looking and not looking. The in and out sequence occurs about four to five times a minute and, though it occurs by the fourth week, it is seen episodically at two to three weeks. The devices of withdrawal include looking away or down or glazing of the eyes but all the time the mother is kept in peripheral vision. Added later are brief looks away to other objects but the infant is able to return to the mother. One technique can be substituted for another but all fit smoothly into the negative part of the curve. This is thought to be a recovery phase from the intense stimulation of the positive phase and offers as well an opportunity to process the information received (24). This could be seen as a precursor of separation-individuation, whether it is seen as intrapsychic or as a behavioral event because the infant is able to engage in visual behaviors long before the achievement of their motoric counterparts.

The infant's ability to sort, gate, avoid and defend against external stimuli requires an awareness of the neglected concomitant of internal control. We have described the most important task of the mother, aside from the obvious feeding, which is to serve as regulator of the infant's states. However, the behavior we have just described allows the infant to exercise control over his own internal states of arousal.

The Pleasure Principle and the Stimulus Barrier

There are two psychoanalytic concepts which have particular relevance for infancy. One is the pleasure principle, which Freud (61) described as a fundamental regulatory process whereby the organism moves toward the goal of lowering drive tension. Actually, Escalona has commented in discussions that this idea is at odds with the current view that the infant seeks out stimuli and tries to maintain a mid-range of arousal where the most mature behaviors occur.

Also, in order to protect the organism against the assault of external stimuli, Freud (61) felt it necessary for the infant to develop a stimulus barrier. (See Pribram (95) for a discussion of the origin of this idea within the scientific project.) Benjamin (13) and Spitz (115) sponsored the idea of a passive and rigid stimulus barrier which served as a shield that prevented the transmission of stimuli. Spitz says it best: "The perceptual apparatus of the newborn is shielded from the outside world by an extremely high stimulus barrier" and "protects the infant during the first weeks and months of life from perceiving environmental stimuli" and so "the outside world is practically nonexistent for the infant" (115, p. 36). This is a fascinating concept which attempts to describe the beginnings of ego and defense, as well as the sense of inside and outside, and these two writers still have more to say about it than anyone else. Currently accepted, however, is the idea of an active stimulus barrier whereby the infant is able to sort, gate, avoid, and defend himself against external stimuli. This ability is based on gaze aversion, eye closure, staring through, going limp, and state changes such as crying and drowsiness.

OBJECT RELATIONS, SEPARATION-INDIVIDUATION AND INNER REPRESENTATIONS

One method for the study of attachment or object relations is observation of the effects of separation. At about seven months there is a clear shift in reactions to hospitalization with the classic separation sequence of protest and despair appearing at this time (108). This has been used as a guide to the timing of elective hospitalizations and separations from the mother in infancy. However, in institutions the fate of this idea unfortunately is that it is felt that it doesn't matter too much what happens to infants as long as they are fat.

Somewhere between six and 10 months there is the emergence of a reaction to strangers. This has been variously named "eight month anxiety," "stranger anxiety," or "negative reaction to the stranger." It is considered by Spitz (115) to result from the fear of the loss of the mother and to represent a form of separation anxiety. Benjamin (12) feels, however, that it comes from a separate theme of reactions to strange things that begins in earlier months and then emerges as a specifically human interaction. "At this age a stranger is best defined as one who does things differently" (p. 12).

Stranger anxiety is a major milestone in the development of human attachment and means that mother and strangers are no longer interchangeable. Provence and Lipton (96) describe an absence of such anxiety in institutional infants. There appears to be a longer stage of equivalence in the reactions to strangers in blind as compared to sighted infants, with the age of onset of stranger anxiety postponed until 13 to 15 months (53).

Another stage in the development of attachment is that of object constancy (91). Object constancy refers to the ability to understand the stability and permanence of the human object so that brief separations can be tolerated. Views of object constancy depend on inferences about mental representations or schema. Piaget's observations of the infant's response to objects placed out of sight are valuable here. If the infant searches and makes attempts to regain the lost object—this would depend on some kind of memory and picture of the object in space—then some sort of object permanence is considered to have developed (94).* The inanimate object concept has a developmental course similar to that of the animate object concept. Babies are more advanced in their concept of persons as permanent than in their conception of the permanence of inanimate objects. The most important factor in the growth of the concept of object is a satisfying relationship with the mother (10).

The work of Margaret Mahler tangles with this theme of the development of inner representation and structure, and needs to be put to practical use if we are to attempt an infant therapy of any sophistication (89). One way we could describe this approach is to say that we must closely observe the infant and maternal behavior and then make inferences about the inner world of the infant. However, this does not really catch it. The emphasis, if there is to be an analytic scrutiny of behavior, must be first of all on the intrapsychic. Here is a quote from Mahler that illustrates this view—"The behavioral surface phenomena of the process of separation-individuation can be observed in countless subtle variations as the accompaniment of the 'intrapsychic' onward development" (90, p. 49). These ideas have found their principal current use by analysts to explain their psychotherapy of borderline patients. One

---

*See the discussion of Piaget's system in Chapter 1.

might wonder whether it is not time for child workers to rescue and use them with infants and toddlers where they originated.

The psychological as opposed to the biological birth of the human infant occurs through the development of intrapsychic structucs during the first three years of life (90). There are two developmental tracks in this process. One is the ability to tolerate separation which is seen as the development of intrapsychic boundaries which allow the infant to distance himself from the mother. The other is individuation which is the development of intrapsychic uniqueness and autonomy. After a period of normal symbiosis—by which is meant an intrapsychic fusion with the mother which reaches its peak at four to five months—there is a gradual "hatching process" during which the infant begins to see himself as separate from the mother. Behavioral events which suggest an inner distancing and autonomy signal the first subphase of separation-individuation which is "differentiation." This is made possible by the increased locomotor ability as is seen in scanning, increased hand-mouth coordination, interest in objects, an exploration of the world, especially of the mother's face, and an interest in games such as peek-a-boo.

At the end of the first year, there is an overlapping of the phase of differentiation with the practicing period which is characterized by the infant's use of motor ability to get away from the mother first by crawling, then by toddling. This physical ability allows the infant to practice his new skills and to explore the world with careening enthusiasm. There is an imperviousness to the knocks and hurts that are part of exploration and the infant is able to regain enthusiasm by "emotional refueling" through the mother. However, there is a long process remaining before true object constancy based on a stable internal representation of the mother is reached in later years (90).

While considering motor ability, we should also examine its manifestations in blind babies. For the first nine months, the motor skills of blind infants parallel those of the sighted, but by the last months of the first year, the blind infant comes to a halt quite literally and is unable to crawl. This was felt to be related to the basic difficulty of the blind child not being able to reach objects by sound alone. At five months, when the sighted infant possesses the visually directed reach, the blind baby does not. "There is no adaptive substitution of sound for vision at this age" (52, p. 281). A program of early intervention taught infants the use of their hands through games and objects with the goal of teaching them how to reach toward sound. Also, mothers were taught how to read their baby's hands which served as an expressive language in the absence of differentiated facial signs (55). It was only with these skills that the infant learned to crawl. "No baby learned to creep until he first gave evidence he could reach on sound alone" (56, p. 392). This work with blind infants can be applied to other problems. Fraiberg speaks of acting as an interpreter of the blind infant's language and feels that this may be expanded to other groups of disadvantaged infants. For example, there are parents with no experience with child-rearing who could be helped to read their baby's messages (56).

There are two other areas of infant behavior in the first year which are linked to the development of object relations and are important to clinically scrutinize. An interactional milestone is the infant's ability to engage in on and off visual play with a human partner. This is the peek-a-boo game (75). It begins in a passive form at about five to six months when the partner takes the initiative. In the active form, the infant leads the alternating visual play. This occurs between six and 11 months and is tied in with Mahler's differentiation subphase, Spitz's stranger anxiety, and Piaget's stage IV of sensory motor development. It is associated also with the related play of dropping and tossing objects. Another observation to be made concerns transitional objects. The infant's "first not me possession" represents an intermediate area of experience which can be traced back to finger sucking and forward to solid toys, "between the thumb and the teddy bear," "between oral eroticism and true object relationship" (131, p. 89). Winnicott (131) offers a fascinating exposition of this intermediate area existing between inner and outer reality. It is the realm of illusion which occupies much of the infant's experience and is the source of religious and creative experience.

SEPARATION AND DEPRIVATION

The effects of the separation of the infant from the mother have been one source of ideas about infant development of great practical consequences clinically. Separation can be a murky concept and often confused with the results of absence from, deprivation of, or skewed relationships with the mother, as well as the effect of institutional care.

Deprivation

The damaging, even lethal effects of institutions have been known a long time. The mortality rate in orphanages and foundling homes at the turn of the century was described in the pediatric literature as being as high as 90%. At first, this was passed off as a result of bad hygiene but then came the awareness of something more when, in spite of the aseptic handling of children at a time when people really believed in germs, the mortality rate remained high. However, as more of these children survived, the long-term and damaging consequences of deprivation became known, especially in the child's inability to engage emotionally, control impulses, and to form a conscience. Our specific interest here is in the effects of separation and deprivation in the first year and this is caught with brutal and stark clarity by Spitz in his classic paper on hospitalism (112). He examined infants raised in an institution where they had little human contact or stimulation compared with a similarly aged group of children raised by their own mothers in a penal institution for delinquent girls. He found a tremendous developmental retardation in the first group as compared to the second. Anyone who has watched his movies—seen the hollow-eyed, wasted, blank faces—knows the impact of this. Thirty-seven percent of these children died after two years while none of the adequately mothered children from the penal institution died. Spitz pointed out that most authorities stressed two factors: lack of stimulation and the absence of the mother. He put his money on the absence of mother, but child development types during the peak time of interest in deprivation a decade or so ago recoiled against such mystical concepts as mother, and so attempted to describe deprivation and its remedy in terms of impersonal stimulation. American ingenuity stepped in with gadgets to do all of this, from a device to simulate maternal heartbeat to entire catalogues of neat equipment such as an Inquarium—"A true departure from conventional crib toys. Live fish swim before the infant's eyes introducing him to the visual pleasure of color and random motion. Heavy vinyl leakproof pouch attached securely to crib containing iridescent nuggets. Fish not included. Price $5.00." We can reject this indiscriminate stimulation because we have learned so far that stimulation and excitement, unless there has been gross deprivation, are not the organism's major needs but rather that the needed maintenance of a mid-range of arousal can only come from an empathic human source.

The clinical picture of infancy which results from institutional life has also been described in detail by Provence and Lipton in their book, *Infants in Institutions* (96). However, deprivation due to conditions of isolation, paucity of human contact, and automatic care such as propped-up bottles can occur as well in home situations (31), as we shall see in some cases of failure to thrive. Some of the more striking characteristics of what was considered to be a remarkably uniform pattern of deficits in all the infants studied are as follows. Apparent as early as the second month was the infant's failure to respond to being held. Other signs were lack of vocalizations and great intensity of looking. This latter vigilant scrutiny of the available adults is rather spooky when experienced. This staring does not indicate a developed visual discrimination which is actually delayed—the infant not distinguishing strangers from caretakers, faces from masks. This high level of eye contact and visual awareness has been called "vigilance" and "radar gaze" (5). There were no signs of attachment to a particular person and an absence of play and games such as peek-a-boo. There was blandness and barrenness of the affective repertoire. The poor development of speech was the most severely retarded of the functions that could be measured. For the first three to four months, the visual response to toys as well as the approach and grasp of them was normal, but by four to five months, there was decreased involvement with them. There was an inhibited development of the mental concept of the inanimate object as described by Piaget. We have seen already that inanimate object permanence is related to animate object permanence. There was no attachment to a toy as a transitional object. There was much less touching, playing, and exploring of the body than in home-raised infants. The one self-stimulating activity that was prominent was rocking. Of particular interest, since we have stressed the importance of affectual responses, was that the first dramatic indication of improvement (aside from weight gain) was that the infants' faces showed animation rather than the frozen, flat deadness of before.

Infant Response to Maternal Separation

It has been observed that young children separated from their mothers and admitted to institutions respond with acute distress followed by a slow and difficult period of adaptation. Spitz (113) in his classic paper on anaclitic depression described this syndrome as occurring in the second half on the first year and characterized by weepiness and withdrawal. A sequence of specific phases which follow separation has been described by Bowlby (20) and Robertson (101). First of all, there is the immediate response of *protest,* which is a period of tearful and unconsolable screaming. Following upon this is *despair,* which consists of apathy and unresponsiveness, and then last comes *detachment,* wherein the infant calms down and accommodates to the new people and environment. Bowlby considered that the phase of protest represented separation anxiety, that of despair signified grief and mourning, and that detachment represented defense. His thesis was that all these reactions were part of a single process which was the response of the child to the loss of the mother, and that adults engaged in a similar process upon the loss of a loved object. One specific objection to Bowlby's hypothesis was concern with his idea that protest and despair were the invariable responses of children to maternal separation. Anna Freud (60) pointed out that the children studied not only had to adapt to the loss of the mother but to the change to institutional life. Also, she did not feel that the separation responses of young children could be equated with the bereavement responses of adults. Another objection was theoretical in that the capacity to mourn was felt to be a function of object constancy and ego maturity. Robertson and Robertson (102) have attempted to study the response to maternal separation under pure conditions. They tried to get closer to the effects of separation by eliminating many of the factors that complicate institutional care and so they provided for a full-time substitute mother who would meet the child's emotional needs. None of the children given such care was considered to have responded with protest and despair and it was concluded that such responses followed upon separation from the mother only when aggravated by stress, multiple caretakers, and the strange environment associated with institutions. Bowlby's rejoinder was that study of the case histories showed that protest and despair were indeed present, albeit in an attenuated form. There is, however, an agreement among everyone that sensitive care will lessen harmful reactions.

SOME PSYCHOSOMATIC SYNDROMES OF INFANCY

This is an area with a sparse and scattered literature and there is still a need for single but full case reports, whether exploring theoretical concepts, such as in Kaplan's description of Daphne (70), or treatment. The most famous case was Engle and Reichsman's Monica which in the 50s and 60s was a unique contribution to the concepts of depression and psychosomatic medicine (38).

Julis Richmond in the 60s described in lectures a classification of the psychosomatic disorders of infancy, but this is only available in a short summary (99). Recently, Greenspan, Lourie and Nover (65) have offered a developmental approach to the classification of the psychopathology in infancy which promises to be useful. They emphasize, as has been done here, the need to consider the structure and organization of the infant's developmental level, because this influences the impact of the etiologic factors and the consequence of symptoms.

Besides the common consequences of loss and deprivation there do exist several syndromes of infancy which have been considered to result from a lack of stimulation. Failure to thrive would be the problem most frequently recognized but some of the less common entities are important in that they give us some idea of the varieties of responses and an orientation by which we can evaluate the borderline situations. In this survey we can begin to pull together some principles of treatment.

Failure to Thrive

Failure to thrive is a condition of infancy where the weight has dropped below the third percentile with no evidence of systemic disease. There may be developmental retardation along with many of the signs of deprivation and starvation, and an associated battered child syndrome as well (5).

All reports describe the central issue as arising from the family's difficulty in providing emotional and nutritional nourishment.Whitten et al. (129) argue against the idea that maternally deprived infants are underweight because of some psychologically induced defect in absorption or metabolism. Careful scrutiny of food intake has shown that lack of weight gain was secondary to not being offered enough food or not accepting it. My impression from observing infants who board in an environment of scarce stimulation is that in these days there is considerable emphasis on feeding and so the babies are fat but listless. Some deprived infants with a potential for serious emotional and mental sequelae are not detected because deprivation is only suspected if there is severe failure of the infant to gain weight. In follow-up evaluations of these infants the recovery of growth may mean only that there has been adequate nutrition rather than any improvement in respect to emotional and mental development.

The terms "maternal deprivation" and "neglect" are either not useful or must be used in the broadesst sense. In many cases, there is not neglect but some variety of deviance in the infant-maternal interaction. Not only deprivation but over-stimulation such as jostling and patting can be factors (28). The parents of these infants have had to cope with multiple stresses such as poverty, alcoholism and serious emotional illness. The mothers as well as the fathers were lacking in self-esteem and were themselves failing to thrive. None of the mothers had experienced loving and nurturing support in their own childhood (82). All reports describe these families as particularly difficult to reach.

There are principles of treatment that can be gleaned from the brief case reports in the literature. Beyond the obvious pediatric work-up and care, it is crucial that the mother, best the entire family, be engaged in therapy. Unfortunately, parental involvement is usually only obtained when the fancy tests all come back negative. The parents must not be scared off but must be made active participants in the treatment. Of greatest importance is that the mothers be extended a warm, supportive and nonjudgmental assistance. Through this relationship, the mother can be encouraged to talk about her feelings and problems with her baby. A case presentation which describes in detail the treatment of a five-month-old infant who was found to be starving is described by Shapiro, Fraiberg, and Adelson (111). We will review shortly some of the dynamic issues that are of particular importance in such a treatment.

Spasmus Nutans

Spasmus nutans is an uncommon and strange looking syndrome which consists of rhythmic head rolling and nodding accompanied by nystagmus. Fineman et al. (48) report a study of twins who developed this syndrome. From the very beginning, there was a limited emotional interaction between mother and child and rare tactile contact. The only involvement was visual and this was random and discontinuous because of the mother's abrupt departures. It was felt that these infants did not have the usual avenues of tension reduction and interaction with the mother, and so used a primitive mode of visual and motor self-arousal. Cases such as this can give us by hindsight an explanation for some of the unusual behaviors of infancy and help us begin to figure out why this syndrome appeared rather than some other maladaptive behavior such as rumination or failure to thrive. What was felt to be important in this instance was the centering of the interaction on one particular sensory channel, as well as the intermittent and partial deprivation.

Rumination

Rumination is an active bringing up of food into the mouth which is then sucked on, reswallowed, and often expelled. The image of a ruminant is apt in that there is regurgitation and chewing again of what has already been taken in. In this chewing of the cud, there is a tuned-out expression of pleasure on the face. However, this cow-like image is too bucolic and pretty because these infants are unattractive to look at. They slobber with vomity smelling food, are emaciated, and are isolated in their rumination. Hospitalization is often required because of malnutrition. The usual explanation is that this is a response to maternal depression and deprivation and represents a form of self-stimulation. However, rumination can serve as well as a self-pacification to handle over-stimulation. Stein et al. (119) report the psychotherapy of a case of rumination which was lifesaving in that the infant did not respond to the usual routine of hospitalization. A full-time caretaker was necessary as well as active therapy with the mother. A crucial issue, in this as in other pathological mother-infant pairs, was that the mother herself had had a deprived and damaged childhood.

Psychophysiological Vomiting

Ferholt and Provence (47) describe an infant with severe vomiting which they point out is a frequent psychophysiological symptom of infancy compared with the rarer rumination. In their treatment, they call upon Sander's view of the skill of the caretaker in synchronizing with the infant's innate biological rhythms. They emphasize that it is necessary to obtain detailed observations as to how the infant actually reacts in daily interaction with the mother. Therapeutic change requires first an understanding of the infant's tension, his bodily affectual states, as they are influenced by the experience of daily care. A complementary idea that comes from Escalona (41) concerns the linkage between sensory channels, specific events, and affectual states. For example, sounds can be used by the mother to convey a scolding anger during feeding or touches used when the child is in distress from a wet diaper. These are ideas that we are prepared to accept intellectually but are hard to translate into a treatment regimen. With certainty, we can agree that mother and child must be seen together and that home visits are of particular value in obtaining a sense of the routine interaction. However, therapeutic intervention must mean ultimately *a change in the infant's experience.* This requires a dynamic approach to the members of the family and, as in the case discussed by Ferholt and Provence (47), a lifesaving admission of the limited time available. Arrangements had to be made for adoption because treatment through the parents was not successful.

Childhood Schizophrenia and Developmental Deviations

It should be possible for us, if we see large numbers of infant-mother pairs, to identify some infants who are not only at risk for schizophrenia but who already show actual symptoms of this disorder (51). Fish (49) has been able to identify the developmental deficits of pre-schizophrenia as early as one month and to begin a preventive treatment. She espouses the view that repeated tests of infants of schizophrenic mothers show a "pandevelopmental retardation" that occurred in about half of her sample and was characterized by "a widespread disorganization of maturation which involved deviation in physical growth, postural-motor and visual-motor development, state behavior, and vestibular responses" (p. 62). This pattern of disturbances was felt to be different than that seen usually in chronic brain syndrome. These early deficits could be used as target symptoms for treatment and it was felt possible that the course of the deviations could be modified by such early identification and therapy. Of particular interest to us is Fish's description of the disturbance in the maturation of arousal and attention with extremes of irritability or apathy (50). Brody (27) also describes how mother-infant pairs can end in pathology due in part to deviant handling of arousal systems.

Brazelton et al. (26) report on an infant who showed early developmental pathology. This case is instructive in that it demonstrates how the early impairment of mother-infant interaction, here a paucity of mutual gratification, came across as a severe neurological disturbance.

Freedman, Fox-Kolenda and Brown (58) describe the development of a rubella baby with multiple handicaps first seen at three weeks. A consequence of the physical defects, sickliness, and irritability is that such an infant receives lessened environmental stimulation and so ends up unresponsive and autistic. In an imaginative therapeutic program, they assisted the mother in providing stimulation that fit this infant's particular needs and, as well, constructed a device that offered increased visual stimulation. They used Spitz's concept of the coenesthetic mode of sensation which predominates during the first six months and is to be contrasted with the later discrete and localized diacritic mode. According to Spitz, "Signs and signals that reach and are received by the infant in the first months of life belong to the following categories: equilibrium, tension (muscular or otherwise), posture, temperature, vibration, skin and body contact, rhythm, tempo, duration, pitch, tone resonance, clang, and probably a number of others of which the adult is hardly aware and which he certainly cannot verbalize" (115, p. 135).

Other groups of infants at high risk—each with a unique pattern of behavior which would affect interaction with the caretaker—are the premature, small for gestational age, and the narcotics-addicted infant. The Brazelton Scale is particularly useful as its results can give the direction for a treatment approach. For example, addicted infants are less able to sustain alertness or to orient to visual and auditory stimuli than normals. However, they are able to quiet themselves and respond to soothing even though they are irritable. They are also resistant to cuddling. These characteristics have their major impact on how the caretaker perceives and responds to them (123). Recognition of the difficulties would permit assistance of the caretaker in making a rewarding contact rather than rejection and rage.

Crying and Fussing

Conditioning techniques should be part of our bag of tricks. Unless ideologically stuck with one system, we can use conditioning within our approach, which is an amalgam of behavioral and dynamic views. Conditioning would seem to be of special use with nonverbal creatures such as infants. Etzel and Gewirtz (42) describe the modification of high-rate crying in two infants which they aptly term "infans tyrannotearus." They emphasize the need for careful observation to determine the reinforcers which maintain the crying. Besides removing these reinforcers and so extinguishing the crying, this technique is made more powerful by rewarding those behaviors that are incompatible with crying. Smiling can be conditioned (22), as well as vocalizations (98). Another behavior that can be reinforced is eye contact. Gewirtz (64) has suggested that infants in foster care should be taught "charm," i.e., that positive social responses should be conditioned. Also stressed by Gewirtz is that the reinforcers must be selected on the basis of what stimuli actually do act as reinforcers for the individual child. A dissenting note is offered by Bell and Ainsworth (11), who feel that those infants with conspicuous fussing and crying, who seem spoiled, have had mothers who have ignored their cues or have delayed in responding to them. "Thus, infants whose mothers are responsive to their signals have less occasion to cry—not only in the first months but throughout infancy" (p. 65). From what we have learned about reciprocity, we would agree with this statement and feel as well that the best reinforcer of smiles and looks would be the mother who reads clearly and responds to these signals.

TREATMENT OF THE INFANT-MOTHER PAIR

So far we have catalogued various instances of infant pathology utilizing the traditional model of conceptualizing the infant alone, artificially existing outside the mother-infant dyad. Sameroff (105), among others, has cautioned against the use of this approach, warning against making predictions only on the basis of constitutional factors or specific

environmental problems. If we were to be so one-sided as to conceptualize the infant as a separate entity, then we should also accord the
mother the same hypothetical status, and compile a series of pathological
states, such as addiction or psychosis, in our compendium of disease
entities of the child. The point is that we must always consider the infant
and mother together in any investigation of psychopathology. Restated,
a mother with a post-partum depression indicates the need for evaluation and perhaps treatment of the pair just as much as failure to thrive
in the infant. These difficulties are hardly subtle, any passerby could
sense something wrong, and we would wish to concern ourselves as well
with more commonplace distress such as anxiety and sadness, questioning whether the pair is growing and having fun, finding pleasure and
progress. Time and again a child psychiatrist hears something like
this—and it may be a retrospective falsification—"I was frantic about my
baby but my pediatrician said he was healthy and I thought I was a crazy
lady." Difficulty in the dyad can be reported verbally only by the mother
and can be signaled by complaints about herself as well as about the
infant. An idea that a year ago seemed extreme but now seems less so
is that indication of worry or concern about the infant or the mother
herself, even though both are in good physical health, warrants investigation of both members of the pair and perhaps referral to a child
psychiatrist. As with older children, distress on either side is enough to
indicate evaluation. I am not sure how many parents would go along
with this—or how useful such an interactive scrutiny would be—but it
is time we tried it out.

The remaining thoughts will attempt to add to what we have learned
so far and so fashion an approach to treatment. The beginning of evaluation and therapy is observation and verbal engagement with the
mother holding the infant. It is as important to obtain a developmental
history of the mother as it is of the infant because the baby's dynamic
meaning to the mother can have as much significance as any fact about
feeding or elimination. Although only an impression as yet, my experience has been that initial negative transference reactions are apt to be
severe. The usual fantasies of the therapist as interloper, child robber,
or blaming judge would seem intensified with infants. Another thought
is that a male physician posing as an authority on mothering is culturally
out of place and is perceived as such by the parents.

The maternal defenses and fantasies which become fluid and later
stabilize during the crisis of pregnancy have been described by Bibring
et al. (16). They suggest special therapeutic possibilities during this time

in that the acute disequilibrium present may allow an integration to occur successfully with only brief therapy. It would take longer experience than I possess to verify this but an impression can be offered. Just as negative reactions occur, so I have experienced when making home visits a special receptivity, an eagerness to talk and learn, and yet a loneliness on the part of the mothers.

Videotapes of the communicative system that develops between mother and infant have been used by Brazelton et al. (24) to help give parents an understanding of their infant's rhythms. Here we must meet head on the question of who is able to learn by these methods. Good enough parents appear to be capable of rapid learning by means of instruction, demonstration, and modeling. We need to look again at Stern's observation concerning the ease with which mothers pick up new games but wait a moment on his question as to whether learning can take place only in areas free of conflict. Let us take first the issue of learning in areas where there is no neurotic involvement. Our approach of seeing mother and infant together allows us to observe and comment on actual behavior. Most observers have felt that, rather than advice or criticism, it is most effective to underscore rewarding interactions such as "Did you see how baby brightened when you did that?" It is possible, however, within a responsive relationship to be instructional and comment on issues such as more rewarding ways of visual engagement or holding. But it can be wondered whether it is possible to modify any more than crude pieces of behavior. Some of the most interesting behaviors of both parties, such as mother-infant play at three months, consist of adjustments so rapid that they cannot be seen with the naked eye. They represent split second behaviors which are partially out of the mother's awareness, not under her conscious control (9). This is one level of relatedness that would need to be engaged for attempts at repair to take place. It is to be wondered whether the mother's flow of associations, her stream of affects and shifts of attention during therapy, this for the most part out of awareness as well, would touch this system. This is something that could be tested out by frame-by-frame analysis.

The next problem is how you tangle with conflict-laden areas. One answer is: Perhaps, you don't. The case of early developmental pathology described by Brazelton et al. (24) illustrates these problems with difficult situations. During the period the infant had the most trouble, the suggestions offered to the parents were disregarded but advice was sought when the child had shown spontaneous improvement. The parents of the infant with psycho-physiological vomiting described by Ferholt and Provence (47) had conflicts so resistant to intervention that the only solution to a life-threatening situation was the arrangement for alternative care. This bold step was in itself a major accomplishment.

One attempt at therapy with parents where the infant had a meaning imbedded in their most basic and pervasive conflicts and fantasies is described by Fraiberg, Adelson and Shapiro (57) in their elegantly written paper "Ghosts in the Nursery: A Psychoanalytic Approach to the Problems of Impaired Infant-Mother Relationships." The key issue in the therapy with the mother was help in touching the affective experiences of her own damaged childhood, which then allowed her to stop the repetition of this injury with her own baby. Fraiberg, Adelson and Shapiro point out that "identification with the aggressor" was the real ghost in the nursery. It was not the details of the childhood abandonment and brutality that were repressed but rather "what was not remembered was the associated affective experience" (57, p. 419). What is clear in the case presentation is that what is required is a demanding and sophisticated therapy. Although this is described as a psychoanalytic approach, and it is, the technique includes treating the mother and infant together and multiple home visits. It is interesting that the mother rejected the therapist who offered office psychotherapy for her alone and would only engage with the therapist assigned to treat the interaction.

My colleague Beatrice Beebe was involved with a case that illustrates many treatment issues (8). The reason for referral was the crisis created by a mother's sudden decision to adopt a child, which led swiftly to increasing disorganization and mutilation fantasies with the real possibility of their being acted out. Her analyst, who had seen her for a number of years and had assisted her through many difficult periods, requested assistance because he felt that the infant was in real danger and that both infant and mother required help and protection. From the very beginning of therapy, the suggestion was made to the mother that she bring the child along whenever convenient. At first, this was initiated with hesitancy but it was found that both of them appeared at almost every session. The infant was three months old when treatment began and the pair were seen three times a week in private office visits. The mother was a highly educated woman who was borderline with strong paranoid trends. A treatment problem which her previous therapist had described, but which was acutely intensified with a growing child and the need for swift intervention, was that every interpretation, suggestion, comment, or gesture was seen as criticism and attack, an avowal of her lack of worth and hatefulness. This then led to anxiety, rage and disorganization. There was considerable interactive difficulty between mother and child. One issue was the mother's intrusive play—harsh looming, abrupt rhythms, and staccato screeches—which led to an antagonistic response on the part of the child. This interaction was modified only after months of work because it was so embedded in issues of the mother's relationship with her own mother. By the age of nine months the child was brought with decreasing frequency. A toddler is hard to handle in an office and this sponsored a hoped-for beginning of the issues of separation-individuation.

A treatment such as this makes extraordinary demands, pulling on all of our knowledge of infancy and facing us with all the problems of a stormy adult therapy. It must be emphasized that though referral was made because of the association with a group doing infant research, that aside from videotapes taken twice, the therapy was in a little office miles from a medical center. This is not a boost for private practice but rather an awareness that aside from a few early intervention projects in a time of diminishing funds, private practice is the area where this type of therapy will most easily flourish. The problems are most certainly there and for the most part they are untreated.

Engagement with the concrete events of daily care and handling is of most importance (47) and home visits can be helpful in accomplishing this. Fraiberg, Adelson and Shapiro (57) call this kitchen therapy and this group has put together a powerful team approach (56). Home visits may not always be a good idea and in the case just described would not have been appropriate. The presence of infant and mother together is the essential, whether in the office or kitchen. Fortunately, at this age it is easier for mothers to bring their babies than to leave them home. As the focus shifts, the infant will be allowed to sleep in the corner or will be brought forth to complain about, play with, or fondle.

SUMMARY

In this review of current ideas about infancy, we have taken the infant-mother pair as our unit for clinical scrutiny. The earliness of attachment from both sides is impressive, often occurring in the first seconds. The process whereby, in the first days, the infant's inborn flow of states is integrated with the mother's rhythms is fascinating. One of these states, alertness, is the infant's window to the world and draws on a visual apparatus that is functionally mature by three months. We viewed the infant not as a passive and helpless partner but rather as an active, stimulus-seeking member of the dyad, able to learn and respond to social stimuli, and possessing powerful control and signaling devices. In the first weeks and months, infant and mother practice a reciprocal dance, in and out, and so by three months, with the flowering of the smile, their game has affectual force. Both partners connect, weave, dodge, and turn away—engage and disengage. The infant possesses then the ability to defend himself against an overload of stimuli from without and, by inference, from those within. A major role of the mother is to help regulate arousal and so provide a mid-range of excitation wherein the most mature behaviors can take place. With increasing exposure to the infant, caretakers demonstrate the infant-elicited behaviors which are exaggerations in time and space and so fit the infant's capacity to process information. All of these mutual abilities and behaviors flower in the early games that catch the spirit of the communication. Our clinical appraisal requires not only observation of behavior but a sense of the affectual interplay as well. We will pay attention to the commonplace routine of infant care and be aware of the clustering of events, sensory channel, use of excitation or soothing, and affect. The observer's fantasies will be encouraged through deliberate "adultomorphizing." By means of an appraisal of an infant's cognitive level, guesses can be made of the intrapsychic state or inner representation. The developmental history and the fantasies of the mother can offer us an idea of the crucial issues and the particular meaning of the infant. Out of this knowledge of the pair can come the understanding whereby we can offer help when it is necessary.

REFERENCES

1. Adamson, A., Als, H., Tronick, E., and Brazelton, T.B.: The development of social reciprocity between a sighted infant and her blind parents: A case study. *J. Amer. Acad. of Child Psychiatry*, 16:194-207, 1977.
2. Ahrens, R.: Beitrag zur Entwicklung der physignomie und Mimikerkennens. *Zeit für exp. und ang. Psychol.*, 2, 1954.
3. Anders, T., Emde, R., and Parmalee, A. (Eds.): *A Manuel of Standardized Terminology, Technique and Criteria for Scoring of States of Sleep and Wakefulness in Newborn Infants,* UCLA Brain Info. Serv., NINDS Neurolog. Info. Network, 1971.
4. Aserinsky, E. and Kleitman, N.: A motility cycle in sleeping infants as manifested by ocular and gross body activity. *J. Applied Physiol.*, 8:11-19, 1955.
5. Babero, G. and Shaheen, E.: Environmental failure to thrive: A clinical view. *J. of Pediatrics*, 71:639-644, 1967.
6. Barten, S., Birns, B. and Ronch, J.: Individual differences in the visual pusuit behavior of neonates. *Child Development*, 42:313-319, 1971.
7. Beebe, B.: Ontogeny of Positive Affect in the Third and Fourth Month of Life of One Infant, Unpublished Doctoral Dissertation, 1973.

8. Beebe, B.: Personal communication, 1977.
9. Beebe, B. and Stern, D.: Engagement-disengagement and early object experiences. In N. Freedman and S. Grand (Eds.), *Communicative Structures and Psychic Structures,* New York: Plenum, p. 35-55, 1977.
10. Bell, S.: The development of the concept of object as related to infant-mother attachment, *Child Development,* 4:291-311, 1970.
11. Bell, S. and Ainsworth, M.: Infant crying and maternal responsiveness. *Child Development,* 43:1171-1190, 1972.
12. Benjamin, J.: Further comments on some developmental aspects of anxiety. In H. S. Gaskill (Ed.), *Counterpoint: Libidinal object and subject. A Tribute to Rene Spitz on His 75th Birthday* New York: International Universities Press, 121-153, 1963.
13. Benjamin, J.: Developmental biology and psychoanalysis. In N. S. Greenfield and W. C. Lewis (Eds.), *Psychoanalysis and Current Biological Thought.* Madison: University of Wisconsin Press, 57-80, 1965.
14. Bennett, S.: Infant-caretaker interactions. *J. of Amer. Acad. of Child Psychiatry,* 10:321-335, 1971.
15. Bergman, P. and Escalona, S.: Unusual sensitivities in very young children. *The Psychoanalytic Study of the Child.* New York: International Universities Press, 3/4:333-352, 1949.
16. Bibring, G., Dwyer, T., Huntington, D. and Valentine, A.: A study of the psychological processes in pregnancy and of the earliest mother-child relationship. *The Psychoanalytic Study of the Child.* New York: International Universities Press, 1961.
17. Birns, B.: Individual differences in human neonates' responses to stimulation. *Child Development,* 36:249-256, 1965.
18. Bowlby, J.: *Maternal Care and Mental Health.* Geneva: World Health Organization Monograph, 1951.
19. Bowlby, J.: The nature of the child's tie to his mother. *International Journal of Psychoanalysis,* 39:350-373, 1960.
20. Bowlby, J.: Grief and mourning in infancy and early childhood. *The Psychoanalytic Study of the Child.* New York: International Universities Press, 15:9-52, 1960.
21. Bowlby, J.: *Attachment and Loss.* London: Hogarth Press, New York: Basic Books, 1969.
22. Brackbill, Y.: Extinction of the smiling response in infants as a function of reinforcement schedule. *Child Development,* 29:115-124, 1958.
23. Brazelton, T. B.: *Neonatal Behavioral Assessment Scale* (Clinics in Developmental Medicine, No. 50), London: William Heinemann Medical Books Ltd., Philadelphia: J. B. Lippincott Company, 1973.
24. Brazelton, T. B., Koslowski, B. and Main, M.: The origins of reciprocity: The early infant interaction. In M. Lewis and L. Rosenbaum (Eds.), *The Effect of the Infant on its Caregiver,* New York: John Wiley and Sons, 49-76, 1974.
25. Brazelton, T. B.: Early parent-infant reciprocity. In V. Vaughan and T. Brazelton (Eds.), *The Family—Can It Be Saved?* Chicago: Year Book Medical Publishers, 133-141, 1976.
26. Brazelton, T. B., Young, G. and Bullowa, M.: Inception and resolution of early developmental pathology. *J. of Amer. Acad. of Child Psychiatry,* 10:124-135, 1971.
27. Brody, S.: Some infantile sources of childhood disturbance. *J. of Amer. Acad. of Child Psychiatry,* 6:615-643, 1967.
28. Bullard, D., Glaser, H., Heagarty, M. and Pivchik, E.: Failure to thrive in the "neglected" child. *Amer. J. of Orthopsychiatry,* 37:680-690, 1967.
29. Call, J. and Marschak, M.: Styles and games in infancy. *J. of Amer. Acad. of Child Psychiatry,* 5:193-209, 1966.
30. Chess, S., Thomas, A. and Birch, H.: *Your Child is a Person—A Psychological Approach to Parenthood Without Guilt.* New York: The Viking Press, 1972.

31. Coleman, R. and Provence, S.: Environmental retardation (hospitalism) in infants living in families. *Pediatrics,* 19:285-292, 1957.
32. Condon, W. and Sander, L.: Neonate movement is synchronized with adult speech: Interactional participation and language acquistition, *Science,* 182: 99-101, 1974.
33. Darwin, C.: *The Expression of the Emotions in Man and Animals.* Chicago: University of Chicago Press, (1873), 1963.
34. Eibl-Eibesfeldt, I.: *Ethology—The Biology of Behavior,* New York: Holt, 1970.
35. Emde, R. and Harmon, R.: Endogenous and exogenous systems in early infancy. *J. of Amer. Acad. of Child Psychiatry,* 11:177-200, 1972.
36. Emde, R., Gaensbauer, T. and Harmon, R.: *Emotional Expression in Infancy—A Biobehavioral Study. Psychological Issues.* New York: International Universities Press, 1976.
37. Emde. R., McCartney, R. and Harmon, R.: Neonatal smiling in REM states: IV. Premature Study, *Child Development,* 42:1657-1661, 1971.
38. Engle, G. and Reichsman, F.: Spontaneous and experimentally induced depressions in an infant with a gastric fistula. *J. Amer. Psychoanal. Assn.,* 4:428-452, 1956.
39. Engen, T. and Lipsitt, L.: Decrement and recovery of responses to olfactory stimuli in the human neonate. *J. of Comparative and Physiological Psychology,* 59:312-316, 1965.
40. Escalona, S.: The study of individual differences and the problem of state. *J. Amer. Acad. of Child Psychiatry,* 1:11-37, 1962.
41. Escalona, S.: *The Roots of Individuality,* Chicago: Aldine, 1968.
42. Etzel, B. and Gewirtz, J.: Experimental modification of caretaker-maintained high-rate operant crying in a 6-and a 20-week old infant (Infans Tyrannotearus): Extinction of crying with reinforcement of eye contact and smiling, *J. of Experimental Child Psychology,* 5:303-317, 1967.
43. Fantz, R.: The origin of form perception, *Scientific American,* 204:66-72, 1961.
44. Fantz, R.: Visual perception and experience in early infancy. In H. Stevenson, E. Hess and H. Rheingold (Eds.), *Early Behavior,* New York: Wiley, 181-224, 1967.
45. Fantz, R. and Fagan, J.: Visual attention to size and number of pattern details by term and preterm infants during the first six months. *Child Development,* 46:3-18, 1975.
46. Fantz, R. and Nevis, S.: Pattern preferences and perceptual-cognitive development in early infancy. *Merrill-Palmer Quarterly of Behavior and Development,* 13:77-108, 1967.
47. Ferholt, J. and Provence, S.: Diagnosis and treatment of an infant with psychological vomiting. *Psychoanalytic Study of the Child,* New Haven: Yale, University Press, 31:439-459, 1976.
48. Fineman, J., Kuniholm, P. and Sheridan, S.: Spasmus nutans: A syndrome of auto-arousal. *J. of the Amer. Acad. of Child Psychiatry,* 10:136-155, 1971.
49. Fish, B.: The detection of schizophrenia in infancy. *J. Nervous and Mental Diseases,* 125:1-24, 1957.
50. Fish, B.: The maturation of arousal and attention in the first months of life. *J. Amer. Acad. Child psychiatry,* 2:253-270, 1963.
51. Fish, B.: Infants at risk for schizophrenia. *J. of Amer. Acad. of Child Psychiatry,* 15:62-82, 1976.
52. Fraiberg, S.: Parallel and divergent patterns in blind and sighted infants. *Psychoanalytic Study of the Child,* New York: International Universities Press, 23:264-300, 1968.
53. Fraiberg, S.: Smiling and stranger reaction in blind infants. In J. Hellmuth (Ed.), *Exceptional Infant, Vol. 2,* New York: Brunner/Mazel, 110-127, 1971.
54. Fraiberg, S.: The clinical dimensions of baby games. *J. of Amer. Acad of Child Psychiatry,* 13:202-220, 1974.
55. Fraiberg, S.: Blind infants and their mothers: An examination of the sign system. In M. Lewis and L. Rosenbaum (Eds.) *The Effect of the Infant on its Caregiver,* New York: John Wiley and Sons, 215-232, 1974.
56. Fraiberg, S.: Intervention in infancy—A program for blind infants, *J. of Amer. Acad. of Child Psychiatry,* 10:381-405, 1971.

57. Fraiberg, S., Adelson, E. and Shapiro, V.: Ghosts in the nursery: A psychoanalytic approach to the problems of impaired infant-mother relationships. *J. Amer. Acad Child Psychiatry,* 14:387-421, 1975.
58. Freedman, D., Fox-Kolenda, B. and Brown, S.: A multihandicapped rubella baby—The first 18 months. *J. of Amer Acad. of Child Psychiatry,* 9:298-317, 1970.
59. Freud, A. and Burlingham, D.: *War and Children.* New York: International Universities Press, 1942.
60. Freud, A.: Discussion of Dr. John Bowlby's paper. *Psychoanalytic Study of the Child,* New York: International Universities Press, 15:53-62, 1960.
61. Freud, S.: Beyond the Pleasure Principle. *Standard Edition,* 8:7-64, 1920. London: Hogarth.
62. Freud, S.: Analysis terminable and interminable. *S.E.,* 23:209-253, 1937.
63. Fries, M. and Woolf, P.: Some hypotheses on the role of congenital activity type in personality development. *Psychoanalytic Study of the Child,* New York: International Universities Pres, 8:48-62. 1953.
64. Gewirtz, J.: On designing the functional environment of the child to facilitate behavioral development. In L. Dittman (Ed.), *Early Child Care: The New Perspectives,* New York: Atherton Press, 169-213, 1968.
65. Goldstein, J., Solnit, A. and Freud, A.: *Beyond the Best Interests of the Child,* New York: The Free Press, 1973.
65a. Greenspan, S. Lourie. R. and Nover, R.: A developmental approach to the classification of psychopathology in infancy and early childhood. In J. Noshpitz (Ed.), *Handbook of Child Psychiatry* (Vol. II), New York, Basic Books, 157-164, 1979.
66. Harmon, R. and Emde, R.: Spontaneous REM behaviors in a microcephalic infant. *Perceptual and Motor Skills.* 34:827-833, 1972.
67. Hartmann, H., Kris, E. and Loewenstein, R.: Comments on the formation of psychic structure. *Psychoanalytic Study of the Child,* New York: International Universities Press, 2:11-38, 1946.
68. Hutt, C. and Ounsted, C.: The biological significance of gaze aversion with particular reference to the syndrome of infantile autism. *Behavioral Science,* 11:346-356, 1966.
69. Kaila, E.: Die Reactionen des Säglings auf das menschliche Gesicht. *Ann. Univ. Aboensis,* 17, 1932.
70. Kaplan, S.: A clinical contribution to the study of narcissism in infancy. *Psychoanalytic Study of the Child,* New York: International Universities press, 19:398-420. 1964.
71. Kennell, J., Jerauld, R., Wolfe, H., Chesier, D. Kreger, N., McAlpine, W., Steffa, M., and Klaus, M.: Maternal behavior one year after early and extended post-partum contact. *Developmental Medicine and Child Neurology,* 16:172-179. 1974.
72. Klaus, M., Jerauld, R., Kreger, N., McAlpine, W., Steffa, M. and Kennell, J.: Maternal attachment: Importance of the first post-partum days. *New England Journal of Medicine,* 286:460-463, 1972.
73. Klaus, M., Kennell, J., Plumb, N., and Zuelkhe, S.: Human maternal behavior at first contact with her young. *Pediatrics,* 46:187-192, 1970.
74. Klaus, M., and Kennell, J.: Parent-to-infant attachment. In V. Vaughan and T. Brazelton (Eds.), *The Family—Can It Be Saved?* Chicago: Year Book Medical Publishers, 115-121, 1976.
75. Kleeman, J.: The peek-a-boo game: Part I: Its origins, meanings, and related phenomena in the first year. *Psychoanalytic Study of the Child,* New York: International Universities Press, 22:239-273, 1967.
76. Knapp, P.: Introduction: Emotional expression—past and present. In P. Knapp (Ed.), *Expression of the Emotions in Man.* New York: International Universities Press, 3-19, 1963.
77. Koenig, K., Emde, R., and Metcalf, D. *States of Infancy: Polygraph and Behavior.* This film is available for rental from Brain Information Service, U.C.L.A. Center for the Health Sciences, Los Angeles, Calif. 90024.

78. Korner, A.: Some hypotheses regarding the significance of individual differences at birth for later development. *Psychoanalytic Study of the Child.* New York: International Universities Press, 19:58-72. 1964.
79. Korner, A.: The effect of the infant's state, level of arousal, sex, and ontogenetic stage on the caretaker. In M. Lewis and L. Rosenbaum (Eds.), *The Effect of the Infant on its Caregiver.* New York: John Wiley and Sons, 1973.
80. Korner, A., and Thoman, E.: Visual alertness in neonates as evoked by maternal care. *J. of Exper. Child Psych.* 10:67-78, 1970.
81. Kron, R.: Instrumental conditioning of nutritive sucking behavior in the newborn. *Recent Advances in Biological Psychiatry*, 9:295-300, 1966.
82. Leonard, M., Phymes, J. and Solnit, A.: Failure to thrive in infants. *Amer. J. Dis. Child,* 111:600-612. 1966.
83. Lewis, M.: The meaning of a response or why researchers in infant behavior should be oriental metaphysicians. *Merrill-Palmer Quarterly,* 13:7-18, 1967.
84. Lewis, M., Kagan, J., Campbell, H. and Kalafat, J.: The cardiac response as a correlate of attention in infants. *Child Development,* 37:63-71, 1966.
85. Lipsitt, L.: Learning processes of human newborns. *Merrill-Palmer Quarterly of Behavior and Development,* 12:45-71, 1966.
86. Lipsitt, L.: Learning in the human infant. In H. W. Stevenson, F. H. Hess and H. L. Rheingold (Eds.), *Early Behavior,* New York: John Wiley and Sons, 225-247, 1967.
87. Lipsitt, L. and Kaye, H.: Conditioned sucking in the human newborn. *Psychonomic Science,* 1:29-30, 1964.
88. Lorenz, K.: Der Kumpan in der Umwelt des Vogers, *J. Ornithol.,* 83:137-413, 1935.
89. Mahler, M.: *On Human Symbiosis and the Vicissitudes of the Individuation.* New York: International Universities Press, 1968.
90. Mahler, M., Pine, F. and Bergman, A.: *The Psychological Birth of the Human Infant: Symbiosis and Individuation.* New York: Basic Books, 1975.
91. McDevitt, J.: Separation-individuation and object constancy. *J. of the Amer. Psychoanal. Assn.,* 23:713-744, 1975.
92. Marquis, D.: Can conditioned responses be established in the newborn infant? *J. Genet. Psychol.,* 39:479-492, 1931.
93. Papousek, H.: The course of conditioning in newborns. In Y. Brackbill and G. Thompson (Eds.), *Behavior in Infancy and Early Childhood.* New York: Free Press, 259-274, 1967.
94. Piaget, J.: *The Origin of Intelligence in Children.* New York: International Universities Press, 1952.
95. Pribram, K.: The neuropsychology of Sigmund Freud. In A.J. Bachrach (Ed.), *Experimental Foundations of Clinical Neurology.* New York: Basic Books, 442-468, 1962.
96. Provence, S. and Lipton, R.: *Infants in Institutions,* New York: International Universities Press, 1962.
97. Rexford, E., Sander, L. and Shapiro, T.: *Infant Psychiatry,* New Haven: Yale University Press, 1976.
98. Rheingold, H., Gewirtz, J. and Ross, H.: Social conditioning of vocalizations in the infant. *J. Comp. Physiol. Psychol.,* 52:68-73, 1959.
99. Richmond, J.: Some direct observations of disordered behavior in infants. *J. Amer. Psychoanal. Assn.,* 10:571-578, 1962.
100. Ringler, N., Kennell, J., Jarvella, R., Navojosky, B. and Klaus, M.: Mother-to-child speech at 2 years—effects of early postnatal contact. *J. of Pediatrics,* 86:141-144, 1975.
101. Robertson, J.: *Young Children in Hospitals.* Second Edition with a Postscript. London: Tavistock Publications; New York: Barnes and Noble, 1970.
102. Robertson, J. and Robertson, J.: Young children in brief separation—A fresh look. *Psychoanalytic Study of the Child,* New York: Quadrangle Books, 26:264-315, 1971.
103. Robson, K.: The role of eye-to-eye contact in maternal-infant attachment. *J. Child Psychol. Psychiatry,* 8:13-25, 1967.

104. Roffwarg, H., Muzio, J. and Dement, W.: Ontogenetic development of the human sleep-dream, cycle. *Science*, 152:604-619, 1966.
105. Sameroff, A.: Early influences on development: Fact or fancy? *Merrill-Palmer Quarterly of Behavior and Development*, 21, 1975.
106. Sander, L., Julia, H., Stechler, G. and Burns, P.: Continuous 24-hour interactional monitoring in infants reared in two caretaking environments. *Psychosomatic Medicine*, 34:270-282, 1972.
107. Sander, L., Stechler, G., Julia, H. and Burns, P.: Primary prevention and some some aspects of temporal organization in early infant-caretaker interaction. In E. Rexford, L. Sander and T. Shapiro (Eds.), *Infant Psychiatry*, New Haven: Yale University Press, 187-204, 1971.
108. Schaffer, H. and Callender, W.: Psychological effects of hospitalization in infancy. *Pediatrics*, 24:528-539, 1959.
109. Schaffer, H. and Emerson, P.: Patterns of response to physical contact in early human development. *J. Child Psychol. Psychiat.*, 5:1-13, 1964.
110. Scott, J.: Critical periods in behavioral development, *Science*, 138:949-958, 1962.
111. Shapiro, V., Fraiberg, S. and Adelson, E.: Infant-parent psychotherapy on behalf of a child in a critical nutritional state. *Psychoanalytic Study of the Child*, New York: International Universities Press 31:461-491, 1976.
112. Spitz, R.: Hospitalism. An inquiry into the genesis of psychiatric conditions in early childhood. *Psychoanalytic Study of the Child*, New York: International Universities Press, 1:53-74, 1945.
113. Spitz, R.: Anaclitic depression. *Psychoanalytic Study of the Child*. New York: International Universities Press, 2:313-342, 1946.
114. Spitz, R.: *A Genetic Field Theory of Ego Formation*, New York: International Universities Press, 1959.
115. Spitz, R.: *The First Year of Life*. New York: International Universities Press, 1965.
116. Spitz, R. and Wolff, K.: The smiling response. *Genet. Psychol, Monogr.*, 34: 57-125, 1946.
117. Stechler, G.: Newborn attention as affected by medication during labor. *Science*, 144:315-317, 1964.
118. Stechler, G. and Latz, E.: Some observations on attention and arousal in the human infant. *J. Amer. Acad. of Child Psychiatry*, 5:517-525, 1966.
119. Stein, M., Rausen, A. and Blau, A.: Psychotherapy of an infant with rumination. *J.A.M.A.*, 171:2309-2312, 1959.
120. Stern, D.: A micro-analysis of mother-infant interaction—Behavior regulating social contact between a mother and her 3½ month-old twins. *J. of Amer. Acad. of Child Psychiatry*, 10:501-517, 1971.
121. Stern, D.: The goal and structure of mother-infant play. *J. Amer. Acad. of Child Psychiatry*, 13:402-421, 1974.
122. Stern, D.: Mother and infant at play: The dyadic interaction involving facial, vocal, and gaze behaviors. In M. Lewis and L. Rosenbaum (Eds.), *The Effect of the Infant on its Caregiver*. New York: John Wiley and Sons, 1974.
122a. Stern, D.: *The First Relationship: Mother and Infant*. Cambridge: Harvard University Press, 1977.
123. Strauss, M., Lessen-Firestone, S., Starr, R. and Ostrea, L.: Behavior of narcotics-addicted newborns. *Child Development*, 46:887-893, 1975.
124. Thomas, A., Chess, S., Birch, H., Hertzig, M. and Korn, S.: *Behavioral Individuality in Early Childhood*. New York: New York University Press, 1963.
125. Tronick, E., Als, H., and Adamson, L.: The communicative structure of face to face interaction. In M. Bullowd (Ed.) *Before Speech: The Beginnings of Human Communication*. Cambridge: Cambridge University Press, 349-370, 1979.
126. Weil, A.: The basic core. *Psychoanalytic Study of the Child*, New York: International Universities Press, 25:442-460, 1970.

127. Werner, H.: *Comparative Psychology of Mental Development,* New York: International Universities Press, 1948, rev. ed., 1957.
128. White, B., Castle, P. and Held, R.: Observations on the development of visually directed reaching. *Child Development,* 35:349-364, 1964.
129. Whitten, C., Pettit, M. and Fischoff, J.: Evidence that growth failure from maternal deprivation is secondary to undereating. *J.A.M.A.,* 209:1675-1682, 1969.
130. Wilder, J.: The law of initial value in psychiatry, *Proc. 3rd Internat. Congr. Psychiat.,* Toronto: U. of Toronto Press, 1:341-345, 1961.
131. Winnicott, D.W.: Transitional objects and transitional phenomena: A study of the first not-me possession, *Int. J. Psycho-anal.,* 34:89-97, 1953.
132. Wolff, P.: Observations on newborn infants. *Psychosomatic Medicine,* 21: 110-118, 1959.
133. Wolff, P.: The development of attention in young infants. *Annuals of N.Y. Acad. of Sciences,* 118:815-830, 1965.
134. Wolff, P.: The cause, controls, and organization of behavior in the neonate, *Psychological Issues, Monograph #17.* New York: International Universities Press, 5, 1966.
135. Wolff, P.: "Critical periods" in human cognitive development. *Hospital Practice,* 77-87, 1970.
136. Wolff, P., and White, B.: Visual pursuit and attention in young infants. *J. of American Academy of Child Psychiatry,* 4:473-484, 1965.

3

Early Childhood:
The Toddler Years

CLARICE J. KESTENBAUM, M.D.

THE TODDLER YEARS

"Doctor, I don't know what's happened to Alexander. He used to be so cuddly, so *easy*. Now he is constantly running from me. I can barely catch up with him in the park. He understands the word 'No'; in fact, it's his favorite word. Yet I found him climbing up the ladder of the highest slide—the one for older kids—saying 'No Alex' every step on the way up. He has a fit when he doesn't get his way—yelling and stomping his feet. When we go out at night and leave him with a babysitter, he clings to me the next day as if I went on a world cruise—and he won't eat a thing. Is something wrong?"

Words similar to these have been spoken countless times by countless distraught mothers to their pediatricians. The wise physician should probably prescribe two aspirins with the admonition "Yes Madam, there is indeed something wrong. Your child is two. Take a vacation and come back when he's three." Not for nothing is the expression, "terrible twos." One word to describe the parents of two years olds is "tired!" Yet for those parents able to withstand the ordeal with a modicum of patience and a sense of humor, the rewards are immeasurable.

The timetable for the period I shall describe is roughly from 18 months to three years. It is variable, as are all such developmental stages, and in no way implies an absolute norm.

This period encompasses what are also known as the *toddler years*, a phrase which describes the attempts of the crawling infant to become a biped—at first with a wide-based gait and frequent spills. By age two, however, most children can manage even stairs without falling.

To the Freudian, this is the *anal* stage of psychosexual development, following the oral, and preceding the phallic and oedipal periods (10). Freud focused on the importance of the anal zone as a source of sensory pleasure and on the child's increasing interest in the control of his own body. Erik Erikson labeled this period "autonomy versus self doubt," drawing attention to the toddler's wish to "do it myself" (7). Erikson's focus, therefore, is on the developing sense of self.

Margaret Mahler emphasized the importance of separating from the mother (15). Clearly, if the infant's task is to *attach* himself to the mothering figure, the two-year-old must learn to *detach* himself. This process is paramount in shaping a true sense of the self as a person distinct and separate from the mother. Mahler believes that the separation-individuation process is a crucial developmental task and a truly landmark achievement. The normal child gradually "hatches" from the "symbiotic common membrane." In contrast, the psychotic child remains fused with the mother and never attains a feeling of wholeness nor a differentiation of "self" from "non-self."

The mother's task during this phase centers around allowing the child to explore his surroundings, while at the same time setting limits on this exploration to protect him from harm. Learning the limits and knowing the boundaries go hand in hand with the meaning of "no."

The enormous growth spurt during the first year (when an infant triples his birthweight) slows down considerably by age two; the average weight of a two-year-old is 26 to 30 pounds (18). Parents who complain that their two-year-olds "eat nothing" should be reassured that the child does eat relatively less than before, but that he or she will not starve to death.

The toddler is close to 36 inches in height, and most of the deciduous teeth have appeared; by 15 months most children are walking; some are even running, bypassing creeping and crawling altogether. For a mother whose "lap-baby" is suddenly climbing over the crib railing and running out the door it is imperative to "baby-proof" the house immediately. All low-lying art objects, lamps, bottles, cleansers, medicines must be put out of reach and someone must keep a watchful eye every minute. These restrictions are all the more necessary insofar as the toddler has not yet acquired language skills sufficient to permit limit-setting through purely verbal admonitions.

Exploration of the child's ever-expanding world is accompanied by practice: practice in perfecting the art of building block towers, in throwing balls, in handling crayons etc. (19). Gross manipulations are better than fine ones at this age. The toddler's attempt to eat with utensils, for example, results in most of the food landing on the floor. Practice sessions of whatever sort can go on indefinitely, depending on the mother's ability to tolerate mess.

To many parents, the two-year-old seems intensely negativistic, resisting any attempt of mother (or other adults) to control him. The house becomes a battlefield. David Levy understood this "oppositional behavior" as the child's attempt to see himself as separate from his parents—and to establish his own set of rules (13). Freud had, of course, been well aware of this period of oppositionalism when he coined the phrase "anal stage."

It is interesting that Freud used the term "anal" to denote the developmental phase when negativism is at a peak; actually the power struggle between mother and child begins much earlier. The so-called battle-of-the-pot is preceded by the battle-of-the-spoon. The intrusive mother who behaves as though she needs total control could, if she so chooses, force open the infant's jaws and insert the spoon. The baby can at best turn his head away or spit out the food, but can otherwise do little else to fight off his mother. By 18 months, myelinization of the anal sphincter is complete. By this time, the child is in control of a bodily function with profound social implications. No matter how the mother may cajole or threaten, she cannot force him to "let go." Because of the child's new ability to control a part of the body whose normal functioning is so important to the parents, he can exert a measure of control over them (especially over mother). Partly for this reason toilet training has been viewed as a natural arena in which to study developing character formation and interpersonal relationships. Karl Abraham, a psychoanalytic pioneer and contemporary of Freud, wrote in his classic papers on the origins of a character traits, that the triad of *parsimony, obstinacy* and *orderliness* was derived from the anal period (1). Forcing a child, as with frequent enemas or other coercive measures, often leads to bitter memories of childhood experiences which set the tone for adult patterns of behavior.

Selma Fraiberg considers the parents as missionaries coming to socialize the little heathen (8). The socialization process depends on multiple factors: maternal *style* ("authoritarian" versus "democratic"), the child's own temperamental characteristics, and the matter of timing (viz., whether or not a child is ready for training). The child can either *give in* (submissive behavior) to his mother's demands or *hold out* (oppositional behavior). The mother's attitude toward the feces plays a key role in the child's own attitude. The child is unaware that his body products are objects of disgust or shame. More confusing is the fact that while mother applauds his act, she flushes away the product as it is produced.

The child may wish to please his mother, to win her smile or approval—or fight her for taking away his body-product. Often enough, he believes it is still a part of himself. He may want to keep the prize for himself—inside himself, or outside. He may have at one time played happily in his crib smearing feces on the railings and walls—suddenly he is told that his stool is messy and bad. Again, a child can react either by being overly orderly or stubbornly messy. One will frequently encounter a recently-trained child of two and a half or three who refuses to play with sand or fingerpaints in the nursey, walking around with hands outstretched, afraid to get dirty. This particular way of handling anxiety about displeasing the mother is termed a reaction formation and refers to a specific defense mechanism—in this case, denying the *wish* to be messy (9).

I was once asked to see a child in my practice who was causing his parents alarm. Bobby was a very bright two-and-a-half-year-old, articulate and outgoing. His mother was a rather rigid woman who hated bowel movements, used gloves to diaper him, and started training him as soon as Bobby could sit up. "He refuses to use the potty," she would complain; "he insists on leaving a B.M. anywhere else—the sofa, the piano bench, the kitchen table! Anywhere but the toilet."

I took Bobby to the playroom for an exploration play session using a dollhouse and minidolls. He immediately arranged the tiny bathroom fixtures and picked up the father doll. "Daddy stand up and make pee—now sit down for doody." He reached for the mother doll—"Mommy sit for pee *and* doody." "Jimmy make doody too," he said, as he handled the designated brother-doll. "What about this boy?" I asked, pointing to the obvious toddler-doll. "Oh, he go on here," he laughed, placing the doll on the dining room table. "Why does this boy make doody on the table?" I then asked him. "Oh, he go here and his mommy get so so mad and makes a face like this!" (he made a rage-filled expression and laughed gleefully).

There are other reasons a two-year-old might not be ready to use the toilet. A painful anal fissure followed by prolonged potty-sitting, might, for example, set the stage for a feared repetition of the painful experience. Other children have expressed fears that their feces are snakes or monsters about to invade their bodies. Fear of the "B.M. Monster" is reported rather frequently from children in this stage. The sensitive mother who knows how to avoid a struggle will work around a strong-willed child (one who has a particularly strong need to do it himself and at his own time) and will wait a few weeks or even months, until the child becomes ready on his own. Most two-and-a-half-year-old children want to become social creatures. Having older siblings (who use the toilet as a matter of course) helps, as does language acquisition. The patient mother will turn the training sessions into lessons in growing up. There need be no explanation for obeying the social customs other than those set forth by Donald Dunton: "Those are the rules. B. M.'s belong in the toilet and not in the diapers." 'Why, Daddy?" "That's the way it is" (6).

ACQUISITION OF LANGUAGE

Besides mastery of certain motor functions, the most significant maturational step for the two-year-old is the acquisition of language (16). All infants, whatever their cultural background, make babbling sounds. Infants seem to derive pleasure from these sounds independent of their effect on others. The universal sounds are the consonants p, m, b, t and the vowels a and e, a fact which might explain why "Ma-ma" is often the first word spoken in many unrelated languages.

By 10 months. the infant's pleasure is greatly enhanced by his being able to repeat the sounds his mother makes in response to his productions. The following vignette is illustrative:

> Marcy is 11 months and for some time has been gurgling and cooing to herself. Her mother walks in to change her diaper and Marcy says "Ma—ma." The mother shrieks with delight, hugs her and repeats "Yes—Mama! I'm ma-ma. Marcy's Ma-ma!" The baby picks up her mother's enthusiasm and again says "Mama."

The baby does not yet understand that she is actually labeling this woman—her own designated, all-important and all loving caretaker—"mother," although her mother imagines her baby has done just that, and reacts accordingly.

The child's biological ability to "speak" is unique. Language is the means by which a human being intentionally contacts another and is mutually understood. Lenneberg, a pioneer in the field of language development, believes that the ability to substitute verbal symbols for concrete perceptions lies in the mind of every normal infant (12). Moreover, the parents' words become the substrate of the child's thought processes which, in turn, immeasurably enhance the child's ability to master the environment. The average child knows three words by age one; by two, he has acquired close to 300 words and by age three, approximately 1000 words. Between the ages of 12 to 18 months, the child enters the stage of repetition of phrases. These phrases are not usually understood, but are merely words that the child has just heard (echolalia). "No touch," says Billy to his mother, touching the telephone cord. "No touch," he repeats, slapping his own hand. Three weeks afterward, he may grasp the meaning of the prohibition, although he will still probably grab the telephone cord when his mother is not looking. This is in contrast to the four-year-old, who has a rudimentary conscience and may have begun to internalize this prohibition. If development is arrested in the echolalia stage, language will not be used for communication. This abnormality is often seen in psychotic children (23).

By 18 months, the child shifts from audible thought to covert or *inner* speech. He is able to integrate his perceptions. Symbol formation begins and soon leads to complex learning. The child can begin to conceptualize and solve problems. Children's ability to comprehend language is greater than their ability to express what they mean. The first "speech" consists of naming things and people (holophrasic speech).

The 15-month-old who says "bottle" might be saying, in effect: "There is my bottle in the refrigerator," or "It is time for my lunch which is long overdue." An interpreter who knows the child is still very much needed at this stage to fill in the gaps and reduce the imprecision.

The 18-month-old child begins to use short sentences. These sentences follow syntactical and grammatical rules so perfectly that the renowned linguist Noam Chomsky has been led to postulate that the structure of language is biologically determined (5). Two-year-olds sound as if they are sending telegrams: "Daddy go bye," "Ball fall down." The sentences soon become more complex as adjectives and prepositions are added to embellish the children's productions.

Children with neurological handicaps or "developmental lags" often develop speech late. It is wise to send a child who has not spoken at all by age three for a full language-developmental evaluation. Neurological impairment is not the only reason for speech delay. In families where children are spoken to, read to (even before they are able to understand the meaning of the adult's words), language will develop earlier than with children from culturally deprived homes (16). Deprived children are spoken to mainly in phrases used to convey prohibitions or punishments from their harassed mothers: "Come here," "put that down," and "shut up!" are examples. These children are offered fewer explanations by their parents and less time is spent together for the enhancement of communication. Such parents are poor models for language transmission.

Most toddlers will eventually acquire enough language so that their dependency on their mothers is significantly reduced. Mother is no longer needed to interpret the countless gesticulations and grunts which only she can understand. At this stage fathers, siblings, or even strangers can understand the child's messages, though they may not always be perfectly clear. The child delights in his new language acquisition as if it were a new toy; he confronts strangers on the bus or in the park with "Look, birdie fly!" and will often start a conversation with the neighbor's dog.

With the toddler's acquisition of language, the mother can now explain the difference between a "stranger" and the "babysitter" who will remain with him for an evening. His frustration at not understanding or not being understood becomes minimal. Temper tantrums often disappear as speech develops, partly because of the enhanced capacity of the toddler to dissipate frustration via vocal interchange.

It is difficult for an adult to put himself empathically in the position of a bright, physically active and well-developed three-year-old with a serious communication problem.

Clinical Example

Gregory, age four, was referred to me by a speech pathologist who was treating him for an articulation problem. Gregory's I.Q. was in the superior range; neurological findings, apart from his inability to pronounce most consonants, were negative. He clung to his mother's skirts, refused to separate from her, and was extremely shy with adults and children alike. His mother was his constant companion who interpreted his needs to the world. She remained with him for the first 10 sessions, not only because Gregory would not allow her to leave, but also because I could not understand him. "Ii ee aa ook" he said, for example, pointing to a Dr. Seuss story. "Gregory wants you to give him that book," his mother translated. Gregory was furious when he was not understood or when anyone, including children, asked him to repeat himself. He would either become sullen and petulant or would fling himself onto the floor in spasms of rage. His speech therapist worked patiently with him and in a few months, Gregory progressed to the point where he was almost always understood. He would not allow his mother to give up her role as interpreter, however, and became furious when she tried to spend more time with his younger brother. Gregory's therapy sessions utilized doll play extensively. He was an imaginative child who invented a kingdom where Prince No-No ruled supreme, never allowing anyone to oppose his most simple request. In fact, No-No did not have to ask to have his wishes obeyed. His omnipotence was such that whatever he wished for simply happened, without his having to speak at all. Gregory needed help for his basic speech problem but also for his emotional reaction to being different, unable to express himself as others did. It is impossible to know whether or not those very factors which produced the speech pathology to begin with also played a role in Gregory's more than ordinary fear of new situations, in the degree of his rage outbursts, or in the lability of his mood. Nonetheless, Gregory's distress about not being able to communicate created such a problem with his developing self-concept, such lowered self-esteem, that psychotherapeutic intervention was necessary. He was later able to achieve a sense of mastery over his handicap.

THE DEVELOPMENT OF COGNITION AND SEXUAL IDENTITY

Accompanying the rapid strides in language development is the equally rapid progress in cognition. According to the Piagetian model, the 18- to 24-month-old child has an internal representation of actions in the external world (21). He has a mental image of an object and will search for it, even if he has *not* just seen it being hidden by someone (whereas at 12 months, he will search only for objects someone has hidden moments earlier). The ability to hold a mental representation is called *object permanence* and refers to the fact that objects exist in time and space. The child can now perform mental experiments, remember past actions and consider alternatives. He experiments with objects and discovers that a pot can make a noise, can carry sand, can hit the cat which can then cause his mother to yell "no" in a very loud voice. He also has a mental representation of himself. He can explore his own body and name his body's parts as being different from anyone else's.

"Johnny's nose, Mommy's nose," the toddler says, pointing first to his face, then to his mother's. By 18 months, gender-identity is fully established: the sense of being either male or female is now fixed (24). In cases of ambiguous sexual assignment, as with hermaphrodites, parents are advised not to change the assigned sexual role by surgical intervention after 18 months.

There are, of course, obvious biological differences between boys and girls and subtle social role differences. These are ordinarily established quite firmly by the child-rearing practices of any particular culture. Two-year-old children identify with the same-sexed parent. A boy knows he has a penis "like daddy" and it is impossible for him to imagine that there exists a race of people who lack this organ. The first time a little boy sees a naked girl, he can only imagine that she once had a penis which, for some reason, disappeared, or he may deny its absence entirely. "She has a penis but it's very small," three-year-old David told his mother as she was diapering his infant sister. "But don't worry, it will grow."

Even if the toddler is told "boys and men have penises and girls and woman have another organ called the vagina *inside* their bodies, he may still ask, "Mommy, may I see your penis, the one you keep inside?"

Two-year-old girls who grow up without brothers may have a similar experience and believe that all human beings have vaginas like theirs. One two-and-a-half-year-old girl took a shower with her father and ran out giggling, "Oh, mommy, look what a funny vagina Daddy has!" In most instances, however, there is a time (usually between two and three) when a girl will be exposed to a naked boy and can see all the things he can do with his organ: water the flowers and make designs in the snow. It's no use trying to convince her that she has a special organ inside or will grow up to have breasts or make babies. She regrets not having that organ *now* and will say so (22). Sensible mothers who have a good feeling about their own womanhood accept their daughter's complaints with ease. The disappointment is usually short-lived, depending on the mother's attitude. On the other hand, I have known instances where envy of the male was so great and apparently dealt with so poorly, the little girl insisted (over several years) on urinating into the toilet bowl standing up.

In our current society, same-sex dressing is not an issue since both boys and girls are used to wearing overalls and jeans. When a three-year-old boy insists on wearing his mother's high-heeled shoes and makeup, however, he is clearly identifying with her and not with the father. Therapeutic intervention is indicated in this case. Occasionally, a woman, usually separated, expresses such contempt for her husband that her son, afraid of incurring her wrath through being like daddy, begins to exhibit transvestite behavior.

In most cases, the two- to three-year-old is busily imitating the adults around him. Imitation is a precursor to true identification with parents which occurs later in the preschool years. The little boy puts on his daddy's hat and glasses "to be like daddy" and a girl shadows her mother's every action, trying to be just like her, playing "grown up" at every opportunity.

Play, in the two-year-old, is essentially solitary, even if it is in the presence of another child. The three- to five-year-old, on the other hand, tends to engage in more social activity, practicing roles in well-structured games of "play-house," "dress-up," and other imitative games (25).

As the child approaches three, he is well into the Piagetian stage of *pre-operational thought* (21). Concepts are expanding rapidly. The child is developing a sense of time and space. He can now postpone gratification, for a little while, at least. The sense of the future may only be "tomorrow" and the past "yesterday," but these are giant steps away from living only in the here and now.

The representational world is constantly changing. It is not strange for a two-year-old to have spatial distortions of such magnitude that he fears he might be sucked into the bathtub drain along with the soap bubbles. A plane receding into the distance (and becoming therefore increasingly more difficult to see) brought forth a torrent of tears from a little girl who wailed, "Daddy is on that plane getting smaller and smaller so that now he'll disappear." "Are there really small people in the television set?" asked two-year-old Billy. Or, "Why is the telephone talking to me with daddy's voice?"

The toddler's eye view of the world becomes more clear to adults when they happen to see a photograph taken by a three-year-old at a garden party: huge imposing adults loom up, seemingly oblivious of the small creatures below. No wonder the world seems peopled by giants!

Fantasy becomes increasingly important by age two and a half, but it is often difficult for a child to separate fantasy from reality. The child's world, to our way of thinking, is a magical place. Wishes might come true; monsters might be real. Three-year-old Betsy told me, "A monster came to my house and ate my plate." "Did that really happen, or is that a make believe?" I asked. "A make believe," she admitted, *"but it was just the same as a real one."*

For the toddler, concepts of growth and maturation are as difficult to grasp as percepts. For example, three-year-old Billy was angry with his father who had just disciplined the child for misbehavior. "When I grow big and you grow small, then I'll spank you," he said.

Birth and death are abstract concepts totally beyond toddlers' scope; nevertheless they are facts of life with which many children have to deal before they are able to fully comprehend their meaning. Death is understood as a permanent "going away." A three-year-old from a religious home visited his grandfather's fresh grave. He expressed the belief that his grandfather was living in a little house under the ground, hidden from view. "He comes out at night when nobody is looking since God doesn't want him to visit us anymore." Birth is an equally confusing concept. The toddler whose mother is pregnant notices she is getting rounder; she tells him a new baby is coming. The toddler reasons that the baby must have gotten inside in one of two ways, either his mother ate one up or babies are body products much like his own bowel movements.

The sophisticated mother may describe certain events of prenatal life—that there is a special place for the baby inside her uterus—where the baby can float in comfort until he is big enough to enter the outside world. Three-year-old Jenny described her understanding of the situation: "When I was in mommy's tummy I had my own swimming pool. I would swim up to her eyes and look out every night at my new room and my toys. Then I would swim back down and pretend to be asleep."

The fantasies of toddlers seem to be filled with cannibalistic wishes and fears, much like fairy tales and folklore throughout the ages (2). Hansel and Gretel who escaped being eaten by the wicked witch and Jack who slew the man-eating giant are but two examples of this universal theme. Relatives who embrace the tiny toddler with cries of "you look so sweet I could eat you up" provide additional fuel for fantasy-formation of this sort!

Children's dreams in the preoedipal period are fairly simple and straightforward. Repetition of daily events or simple wish-fulfillments are frequent (i.e., "I dreamed I ate an ice-cream cone"). Cartoon-like Mickey Mouse animal symbols are common. There is, however, still confusion about whether the nightly event is a dream or reality. Chukovsky, the Russian poet, in his book on the preschool child *From Two to Five** gives examples of this confusion. "Marina said to her mother one morning, 'Mother, why don't you ever appear in my dreams?' And in the evening of the same day she said: 'Lie down on my pillow, mommie. We'll look at my dream together.'"

The conceptual world of the child is rapidly changing. It is a totally egocentric world which the child believes revolves around him alone. Sharing is a foreign concept at two. If a companion tugs at a toy he may

---

*From Two to Five, Los Angeles: University of Calif. Press, 1968, page 23.

be greeted with a push or a loud "no." Taking turns with the truck, waiting five minutes for the next turn, as his mother suggests, falls on deaf ears. Only after repeated "trials" at sharing (under the careful supervision of an adult) is this early lesson in socialization mastered.

At two, there is no empathy. If a playmate falls down and begins to howl, the two-year-old might gaze at his friend with interest and say "Billy go boom." After he, himself, has had repeated spills and is cuddled and comforted by his mother, he may, the next time Billy falls, pat the head of the crying child, as he has seen his mother do, and say "All gone—hurt." This imitation of mother's behavior is empathy in its embryonic stage. Despite such forays into altruism, however, he firmly believes the world is still there to serve him. For example, Joey was two and a half and very attached to his mother. She had spent many happy hours playing with her generally good-natured son. One morning she was feeling ill and was too exhausted to go to the park. Joey pulled at her robe, saying "Bad mommy! I don't love you anymore, I want my good mommy again."

To the two-year-old, it is a black and white world with never a shade of grey. Mother is either seen as all good or all bad. She is the Fairy Godmother in Cinderella or the Wicked Witch in Snow White—no in-between.

To have both feelings invested in the same person seems to be impossible at this stage; they must be separate. The toddler thus struggles with ambivalent feelings but cannot yet integrate them. By age three, however, he has an internal representation of mother as a whole person. He begins to recognize that the mother, whom he loves one minute and with whom he is so furious the next, can indeed be one and the same person. He has, moreover, achieved a sense of her as separate from himself; when she is absent from him she still exists somewhere in the world and he trusts that she will return. With this step, he has achieved what we call *object constancy*.

SEPARATION ANXIETY

For the child under three, fear of separation from the mother is the strongest stimulus for anxiety. (When I speak of the mother, I do not necessarily mean the biological mother, but the mothering figure, the primary caretaker.) The two-year-old is still very dependent on his mother; the totality of his dependence is lessened by his developing motor skills as well as by the acquisition of communicative speech.

In the playground, the toddler of two and a half is able to spend increasing amounts of time away from his mother, as long as she remains close enough for him to yell for help. Under these circumstances, the child may become happily absorbed with his shovel and pail, seldom even glancing at his mother on the bench at the opposite side of the park. Winnicott writes of the child's ability "to be alone in the presence of mother" (28). If mother were to depart unannounced for a brief period, the child would become inordinately frightened and would cling to her for the rest of the day, not daring to leave her side.

Interestingly enough, children of two and a half are able to leave their mothers at home and go off with a familiar adult, but the reverse (when mother leaves him) is not true. It is as if mother remaining at home in a familiar spot makes the environment "safe" while he goes off exploring. But if *she* leaves him in the care of an unfamiliar babysitter or drops him off at a neighbor's house, he may protest. This does not mean mothers should never leave their children or put them in novel situations. The only way that the child can become able to master "normal" anxiety is to experience these everyday situations periodically and in a (semi-) protected setting. Eventually he learns that the danger (viz., mother's brief absence) is more imagined than real. It is important to understand the child's reaction, however, from the vantage point of the child's cognitive level. Until he has been left and *rejoined* a number of times, he will feel one degree or another of anxiety. This point is tellingly made in A. A. Milne's poem "Disobedience."

> James James
> Morrison Morrison
> Weatherby George Dupree
> Took Great
> Care of his Mother,
> Though he was only three.
> James James
> Said to his Mother,
> "Mother," he said, said he:
> "You must never go down to the end of the town,
> if you don't go down with me."
>
> James James
> Morrison's Mother
> Put on a golden gown,
> James James
> Morrison's Mother
> Drove to the end of the town.
> James James

Morrison's Mother
Said to herself, said she:
"I can get right down to the end of the town and
be back in time for tea."

King John
Put up a notice,
"LOST or STOLEN or STRAYED!
JAMES JAMES
MORRISON'S MOTHER
SEEMS TO HAVE BEEN MISLAID
LAST SEEN
WANDERING VAGUELY:
QUITE OF HER OWN ACCORD,
SHE TRIED TO GET DOWN TO THE END
OF THE TOWN—FORTY SHILLINGS
REWARD!"

James James
Morrison Morrison
(Commonly known as Jim)
Told his
Other relations
Not to go blaming him.
James James
Said to his mother
"Mother," he said, said he:
"You must *never* go down to the end of the town
without consulting me."*

The ability to trust that mother will indeed return when she leaves becomes an important step in the mastery of the environment and is a necessary prelude to entering nursery school. Most children will be able to take this step comfortably by age three or three and a half.

Precipitous separations from parental figures can be devastating to the two-year-old, particularly when the surrogate caretaker is unknown to him. Parents are well advised not to take long vacations away from a child who is between the ages of two and three. The following vignette illustrates this point:

> I once was asked to see a four-year-old girl (from a day-care center) who was described to me as apathetic and withdrawn. Her teacher was a sensitive woman, who tried in a dozen ways to engage her,

---

*A. A. Milne *When We Were Very Young*, E. P. Dutton and Co., New York, 1924, pp. 32-51. Reprinted by permission of Elsevier-Dutton Publishing Co., New York, Methuen Children's Books Ltd., London, and McClelland and Stewart Ltd., Toronto.

and felt she was just not "getting through." The little girl's mother, Mrs. S, was a depressed young woman from the Dominican Republic who sadly told me Maria didn't love her anymore. She described Maria as having been happy and outgoing as an infant. When Maria was two years old, Mrs. S, who was pregnant again, sent her to live with her grandmother in Santo Domingo. She felt the grandmother would be better able to care for her during her confinement as life was very difficult in New York City, and she did not want to leave her little girl with strangers. The first few days in a strange land were hard for Maria. First she cried bitterly; then she refused to eat. Soon, however, she was "her old self" and became attached to the grandmother. Unfortunately, the grandmother became ill several months later, and Maria was sent to live in a nearby town. Again, the traumatic scene of grieving and resignation repeated itself. At age three and a half, Maria returned to her mother in New York "but she didn't know me anymore," Mrs. S reported, weeping. "She didn't cry but nothing I could do made her happy and she just ignored me."

Maria's reaction to the repeated separation was typical. She behaved, as every mother will testify after a vacation, with a "who needs you?" attitude. It is as if she said "I trusted you and you abandoned me. I'll never allow myself to get close to you—or anyone—again." It was Mrs. S's own feeling of rejection and her own subsequent depression which prevented her from reaching out to Maria despite the little girl's aloofness.*

This story, because of the teacher's intervention, had a happy outcome. Unfortunately, many other children who experience similar separations—even with the kindest of caretakers—do not fare so well.

John Bowlby has written extensively on the phenomenon of mourning in childhood (3). He states that there is a causal relationship between loss of maternal care in early life and disturbed personality development. The pathogenic factor is, he believes, loss of the mother figure during the period between six months and three years. Ordinarily in this period, the child becomes closely attached to his mother. He will be content in her company and unhappy in her absence. Most children, of course, do not suffer serious disruption of the primary attachment in the early years. But if 1) the mother should die, or 2) a series of short-term caretakers are employed as a substitute for the one stable figure, or 3) the child is hospitalized for long periods of time in the absence of a mothering figure, clinical pictures which resemble mourning may indeed result.

Bowlby's own research involved the behavior of healthy children aged

*Kestenbaum in Brusilov and Witenburg—Introductory Chapter in *The Emerging Child* page XX, New York: Aronson, 1974.

two to three who had to be removed from their homes (briefly) and placed in a hospital environment. Together with James Robertson, he demonstrated young children's reactions to separation from their mothers. He described three definite phases, predictable in their sequence: protest, despair, and detachment. At first, the child demands, with tears and vociferous protest, that his mother be returned to him. This phase of protest may last several days. Later he becomes quiet, yet he is clearly preoccupied with thoughts of his mother. He has the appearance of a man who has lost all hope, who is in the depths of despair. The final phase, detachment, seems curious at first glance. The child, upon finding the lost mother returned to him at last, often does not seem to recognize her. When he returns home, he may be unresponsive for hours or days. In Bowlby's opinion, the detachment, if not rectified, can have deep significance evidenced in failure to attach to objects later in life. Bowlby believes that the three phases represent true mourning states and can lead to pathologic modes of adaptation. Specifically, these modes may predispose to depressive illness later in life, or aggravate any preexisting tendency toward a major depressive disorder.

THE TODDLER YEARS: SOME COMMON DEVELOPMENTAL PROBLEMS

It is apparent from the foregoing discussion that a knowledge of developmental stages may help a parent understand the various complexities of his or her child's behavior. The parent will then be in a better position to handle effectively whatever deviations from normal behavior may occur.

For example, temper tantrums are frequent occurrences during this time period. The parent should attempt to ascertain whether the rage outburst is a symptom of fear or of anger. The child, we have seen, is particularly prone to fears of abandonment. Not only may he lose mother, but if he is not "good," he may lose mother's love as well. On the other hand, the two-year-old is working very hard at learning to control his body and to obey parental commands (use the toilet! don't hit! stay dry! wait!). He is confronted daily with hundreds of such "orders," perhaps not verbalized in so many words but conveying the same strong messages nonetheless. The child's frustration at not being able to meet all the demands, coupled with his ambivalent feelings toward the beloved yet demanding parent, may provoke the episodes of losing control we call tantrums.

Parents should never allow a child to hurt himself (e.g. bang his own head) or hurt anyone else. They should wait for the outburst to end, remain with the child, and then quietly but firmly explain to the child their own understanding of the event. "You don't want to go to bed, but it is bedtime, so you have to go; I will stay here with you for a while, outside the door." In this example, the parent is communicating his awareness that the outburst was prompted by either fatigue or fear of separation.

Some children exhibit breathholding spells which can be very frightening to a parent. The child may turn blue and even lose consciousness. Most pediatricians, after ruling out possible cardiac or central nervous system illness, will reassure the parents that such "spells" are due to neurophysiological immaturity and will disappear by age three.

Sleep disturbances are frequently reported during the toddler years. A child who has slept through the night for two years may suddenly begin appearing in his parents' room night after night. If the child is verbal, he may express a fear that "noises" bother him, that a "monster" is in his room, or that he is afraid of the dark (14). These kinds of fears are universal among children of this age; they tend to decrease as the child gets progressively older. Between the ages of two and four, fear of the dark and fear of being alone are commonly reported.

The child of this age is attempting to achieve a separateness from his mother, yet separation anxiety is one of his chief stumbling blocks. It is not surprising, therefore, to find him frequently "checking up" to make certain she is nearby at night. Moreover, the child may be having frightening dreams, without yet being at the stage where he can differentiate real events from dream events. If a child is able to report dream content, the nightmares described commonly involve *falling, getting lost,* or being *attacked* by an *animal* (26). Since the child is in the process of resolving ambivalent feelings toward authority figures, again, it is not surprising that the threatening animal may symbolize his own angry feelings. The child may *project* his own feelings onto the dream-beast, feelings which would make him anxious if they were acknowledged as his own. Three-year-old Kevin came to his parents' bed one night and reported "I dreamed a lion was going to eat up John (the baby) but I punched him and wouldn't let him do it." Kevin had been demonstrating a good deal of hostility toward John and was not encouraged to express his anger at being (in his eyes) displaced by his little brother. In the dream, he projected the rage onto the lion and turned his wish to get rid of John into its opposite, i.e., he dreamed of "saving his brother's life."

Another sleep disturbance common between ages two and three is *pavor nocturnus* (night terror). This symptom must be differentiated from a nightmare. Night terror is a state of "dreaming while awake", or so it seems to the concerned parent. The child may cry out or walk in his sleep and seems to be experiencing great fear. His eyes may be wide open but he will not respond to his name or note the presence of his parents. The episodes last from a few seconds to ten minutes. Unlike the nightmare, the child has no recollection of the episode the morning after. In actual fact, the condition is, according to Broughton, a disorder of arousal, occurring in Stage IV of the sleep cycle, and is often associated with somnambulism and enuresis (4). Unless the occurrences are very frequent, most pediatricians would not recommend any further evaluation for very young children. They advise the parents not to awaken the child but remain with him for the duration of the episode and to then return him to his own bed.

Children who are prone to nighttime difficulties are often reassured by having a bedtime ritual with a parent, such as a bedtime story. Keeping a nightlight on or leaving the door ajar may help to dispel anxiety. If the child should appear in the parents' bed, it is usually best for the parent to return him to his own bed and to remain with him a short while. This represents the intelligent middle course. On either side of this are methods that are much less likely to succeed. Allowing the child to remain in the parents' room, for example, may create a very unwelcome pattern; but forcing the child to return to his room, alone, may lead to uncontrollable anxiety (and endless howling).

The child having difficulty sleeping alone may need his mother's voice to reassure him that she is there from time to time. Many children take a soft blanket or stuffed animal to bed; this "security blanket" becomes an important source of comfort in the absence of mother. Winnicott refers to such articles as "transitional objects"— a kind of talisman, a symbolic reminder of the absent mothers (27). Some children's beds resemble a menagerie, stacked high with dozens of toy friends or "imaginary" companions (17). The "make-believe" friend can serve a number of purposes; he can keep the child company when he is alone; he can bear the blame for the child's own misconduct ("Barbar did it") or, as with Binker in A. A. Milne's poem of the same name, he can accomplish tasks still difficult for the child.

> Binker's brave as lions when we're running in the park;
> Binker's brave as tigers when we're lying in the dark;

Binker's brave as elephants, he never never cries . . .
Except like other people when the soap gets in his eyes.*

Habits, such as thumbsucking and earpulling, are frequently observed as the child is falling asleep. These habits usually disappear as the child matures. Forcibly fighting the habit by dipping the fingers in foul-smelling medicine or by taping the thumbs is, of course, experienced as punitive. These methods rarely succeed in breaking such habits anyway. Shaming the child publicly has the effect of focusing attention on an innocuous but nevertheless socially undesirable trait. It serves to reduce the self-esteem of the compliant child and to strengthen the resolve of an obstinate one *not* to relinquish the habit.

There are a number of normative "crises" of early childhood which will ordinarily elicit a notable regression in behavior. For example, the birth of a sibling can cause a toilet-trained "dry all night" three-year-old to begin wetting the bed nightly as he did at two. These regressive symptoms are usually transient. Nocturnal enuresis is so common in early childhood that I do not consider it a problem for any child under four unless it is accompanied by a multitude of other symptoms.

Parents often ask how best to prepare a toddler for the birth of a sibling. How much the child will understand the explanations, of course, depends in part on his cognitive level. Nevertheless, no matter how carefully the parents have prepared a child, the three-year-old is still going to feel displaced by the new arrival. Bringing home a new baby is a bit like a sheik's telling wife number one that she is now to be shared with a new, younger wife who will remain in the palace forever: It doesn't help the displaced wife to hear from the sheik: "I will love you both the same."

For example, three-year-old Tony was well prepared for his brother Ted's birth. His mother had let him feel the baby kicking inside her; he was given presents before and after the event; his room was carefully kept the same as it had been before the birth. Tony was allowed to touch and hold the baby He spent as much time alone with his mother as he did before, since mother had a baby-nurse and was able to divide her time between the two boys. Nevertheless, on the third day after the homecoming, Tony tearfully approached his mother: "I don't like Ted. Throw him in the garbage. Give him to a lady in the park who *wants* him." His mother, somewhat taken aback after all her careful prepa-

---

* A.A. Milne *Now We Are Six*, New York: E.P. Dutton & Co., 1927.

ration, held her ground. "You don't have to love Ted," she said. "He is so little and can't talk or play now. He can't be much fun for you yet. But Ted is here to stay and you can *say* or *think* anything you like about him. You don't have to love him. But you will not ever be allowed to hurt him." Very soon afterwards, Tony began telling everyone who would listen how JoJo (the dog) didn't like Ted and how much JoJo wanted him to be gone. It was not long before the negative statements stopped altogether and in actual fact the boys eventually became quite close. Sibling rivalry, in this instance, was held to a minimum.

Another "normative crisis" of early childhood is hospitalization (whether for a routine surgical procedure or illness) (20). Preparation with doll play or picture books, along with careful description of events to follow, is important in helping the child prepare for the unknown. Nothing is more important for a child under three than to have a parent with him during his hospitalization. Psychoanalysts are all familiar with adult patients who report that the most traumatic event of their childhood was a hospitalization and the attendant separation from the parents. Many modern hospitals are aware of the important child developmental stages and the need for the parental presence. It cannot be emphasized strongly enough that the effects of transient pain from surgery for a child of two are minor compared with the emotional pain of isolation from the parent.

Some life crises are unavoidably traumatic, such as the death of a parent. It is important that a caretaker (viz., "mother-surrogate") replace the missing parent as soon as possible. The dead parent should not be ignored and quickly forgotten. The child should have the opportunity of talking about the dead parent, looking at photographs, and such. All this will facilitate the work of mourning, to whatever extent this is possible in so young a child.

CONCLUSION

I have attempted to outline here the main developmental tasks that confront the two- to three-year-old "toddler."

It is well to keep in mind the following principle: The child should be able to love, work and play at levels consonant with his age. In the case of the toddler, no real work is expected of him. Instead there are a number of developmental tasks crucial to this epoch in which he must show some degree of mastery. The main task relates to the need to achieve a sense of separateness from the mothering figure. His readiness, or lack of it, for nursery school and for age-appropriate social relationships will be the measure of his progress with the task of individuation. The toddler must be able, as well, to express affection for parents and siblings. Ideally, he should be able to communicate in words many of his needs and thoughts; he must be able to perform a number of motor tasks with skill. He must be able to listen attentively, to postpone gratification for a short while, at least, and to have a sense of pride in his new accomplishments. Finally, he should have a sense of pleasure in exploring his ever-widening world so that one could say that the child at three is becoming a truly social being.

REFERENCES

1. Abraham, K.: Contributions to the theory of anal character: *Selected Papers on Psychoanalysis*, London: Hogarth, pp. 370-393, 1927.
2. Bettelheim, B.: *The Uses of Enchantment: The Meaning and Importance of Fairy Tales*. New York: Knopf (Random) House, 1976.
3. Bowlby, J.: Grief and mourning in infancy and childhood. *Psychoanalytic Study of the Child*. New York: International Universities Press, 15:9-52, 1960.
4. Broughton, R. J.: Sleep disorders: Disorders of arousal. *Science*: 159, 1070-1078, 1968.
5. Chomsky, N.: The formal nature of language. In E. Lenneberg (Ed.), *Biological Foundations of Language*. New York: Wiley, 1967, 397-442.
6. Dunton, D.: *Lectures in Child Development*. Columbia Psychoanalytic Institute for Research and Training (unpublished), 1965.
7. Erikson, E. H.: *Childhood and Society:* New York: W. W. Norton, 1950. 2nd Ed., pp. 247-274, 1963.
8. Fraiberg, S.: *The Magic Years*. New York: Scribners, 1959.
9. Freud, A.: *The Ego and The Mechanism of Defense*. London: Hogarth, 1936.
10. Freud, S.: Three essays on the theory of sexuality (1905). *Standard Edition of the Complete Psychological Works of Sigmund Freud, Vol. 7*, London: Hogarth Press, 1953, pp. 123-243.
11. Harms, E. (Ed.): Problems of sleep and dreams in children. *Monographs on Child Psychiatry, No. II*, New York: Pergamon Press, 1964, pp. 73-75.
12. Lenneberg, E. H. (Ed.).: *Biological Foundation of Language*. New York: Wiley, 1967, pp. 127-142.
13. Levy, D.: The early development of independent and oppositional behavior. In G. Grinker (Ed.), *Midcentury Psychiatry*, Springfield, Ill: Charles C Thomas, 1953, pp. 113-122.
14. Mack, J. E.: Nightmares, conflict and ego development in children. *International Journal of Psychoanalysis*, 46: 1965, 403-428.
15. Mahler, M.: Thoughts about development and individuation. *The Psychoanalytic Study of the Child*. New York: International Universities Press, 1963, 18: 307-314.
16. Mussen, P. H., Conger, J. J., and Kagan, J.: The development of language. In *Child Development and Personality*. Fourth Edition. New York: Harper and Row, 1974.
17. Nagera, H.: The imaginary companion: Its significance for ego development and conflict solution. *Psychoanalytic Study of the Child*, New York: International Universities Press, 24: 165-196, 1969.
18. Nelson, W. E.: Physical growth and development. *Textbook of Pediatrics* (1933). 6th Edition. Philadelphia: W. B. Saunders, 1957, pp. 10-66.

19. Nelson, W. E.: Mental and emotional development. *Textbook of Pediatrics* (1933). 6th Edition, Philadelphia: W. B. Saunders, 1957, pp. 67-78.
20. Petrillo, N. and Sanger, S.: *Emotional Care of Hospitalized Children*. Philadelphia: J. B. Lippincott, 1972.
21. Piaget, J.: The origins of intelligence in children. In *The Stages of Intellectual Development of the Child*, New York: International Universities Press, 1962 pp. 157-166.
22. Roiphe, H. and Galenson, E.: Early genital activity and the castration complex. *Psychoanalytic Quarterly*, 41: 334-347, 1972.
23. Shapiro, T.: Language behavior as a prognostic indicator in schizophrenic children under 42 months. In E. Rexford, L. W. Sander and T. Shapiro (Eds.), *Infant Psychiatry*. New Haven: Yale University Press, 1976, pp. 227-238.
24. Stoller, R. J.: A contribution to the study of gender identity. *International Journal of Psychoanalysis*, 45: 220-226, 1964.
25. Walder, R.: Psychoanalytic theory of play. In C. Schaefer (Ed.), *Therapeutic Use of Child's Play*, pp. 79-94, New York: Aronson, 1976.
26. Van de Castle, R. L.: Animal figures in dreams: Age, sex and cultural differences. *American Psychology*, 21:623, 1966.
27. Winnicott, D. W.: Transitional objects and transitional phenomena: A study of the first not-me possession. *International Journal of Psychoanalysis* 34: 89-97, 1953.
28. Winnicott, D. W.: The capacity to be alone. (1958). *The Maturational Processes and the Facilitating Environment*, New York: International Universities Press, 1965.

4

Lines of Maturation and Development through the Phallic-Oedipal Years of Childhood

JOHN A. SOURS, M.D.

My mother died
unrocked, unrocked
    Ann Sexton, *The Death Baby* (16)

Daddy, daddy, you bastard, I'm through.
    Sylvia Plath, *Ariel* (13)

The phallic-oedipal phase of maturation and development is known by a number of terms. Educators refer to it as the nursery school years or the preschool years, whereas in psychoanalytic terminology it is also known as the stage of initiative versus guilt. This phase of maturation and development usually occurs between the ages of three and six years, although the actual onset and offset of this phase are not clearly demarcated.

The lines of maturation and development through the phallic-oedipal years of childhood include changes in many instinctual life and ego functions: 1) the shift from dependency toward adult object relationships; 2) the transition from suckling to eating; 3) going from wetting and soiling to bladder and bowel control; 4) irresponsibility changing to responsibility in body management; 5) growth from egocentricity to companionship; 6) the transitions from body concentration to the toy world, and from play to work; and changes in the structure and function

121

of 7) dreams, and 8) fantasies. These lines will be traced through the phallic-oedipal years until latency, and then later carried forward into adolescence in subsequent chapters. Some of these lines are better understood than others, and, in the case of phallic-oedipal development, more completely understood in the male child.

Many developmental issues during this phase of development extend beyond the age span of three to six years. Central to all development is psychosexual progression and personality formation. The vicissitudes, influences and transformations of the phallic-oedipal stage of psychosexuality affect every part of the developmental continuum and contribute enormously to the genesis of psychopathology.

Psychosexual development, in general, entails many more preadolescent changes than those seen in connection with physical development. This is especially true for the phallic-oedipal phase in which children become aware of genital differences, are more inclined toward masturbatory activity and genital explorations, are preoccupied with making up theories of reproduction and begin to manifest an attraction toward the opposite-sex parent. The phallic-oedipal period is, of course, the phase in which the Oedipus complex comes into full bloom, and at the same time it is the stage at which boys and girls experience intense castration anxiety. All the associated vicissitudes of this stage of psychosexual development occur independently of hormonal changes. During this stage of human development there are no significant primary or secondary changes in physical sexuality. The production of sexual hormones is limited to very small quantities of estrogen and androgen. Androgen production, however, increases in both sexes, more so in boys, after the phallic-oedipal stage when children enter late latency, after which there is a subsequently sharp rise in adolescence. Androgen production is somewhat different from that of estrogen excretion which increases gradually in both sexes starting at about age seven.

There are a number of components to the phallic-oedipal phase of development. The undercurrent of this phase is infantile sexuality which entails erotic-genital interest and exploration, sexual play, the discovery of sexual differences, the attraction to the opposite-sex parent with the eventual sense of loss of love, as well as the sense of injury and retaliation from the same-sex parent, along with the experience, for both sexes, of castration anxiety. In many respects, the pivotal force of this phase of development is castration anxiety, which is central to the creation and dissolution of the oedipal situation.

In order for the child to reach this stage of development, it is essential that he has completed many aspects of development in the anal-muscular phase which precedes phallic-oedipal development. The former phase of development starts between 10 and 14 months, at which time creeping, crawling movements occur, and extends to the third year when the child has attained libidinal object constancy. In order to proceed ahead, it is essential that the child during the toddler years develop motor skills, language, ego defenses and cognitive capacities preparatory for separation-individuation and autonomy. It is during this time that the child grows from cooperative babyhood to toddlerhood, a period which Erikson has labeled "autonomy versus shame and doubt." During this time, the erogenous zone shifts from the mouth to the anus-rectum, marking the beginning of anal eroticism and the associated conflictual, biological mode of fecal retention and elimination. Now the toddler shows self-assertion which is aimed at the furtherance of separation-individuation and autonomy. Through autonomy, the toddler can combat his sense of doubt and shame. Nevertheless, psychological, physical and social dependency, frustrations and disappointments foster serious doubts about his ability and freedom in asserting himself. At this time, the toddler experiences self and object images with blurring and confusion of the percepts. He wants to fall down and let go, not only with his hands, but also with his mouth, eyes and sphincters. Now the mother begins to give increasingly more prohibitions to prevent him from hurting himself.

Oppositional behavior at this time is common and should not be confused with negativism. The latter appears when the toddler believes he must protect the anal-muscular developmental process by turning his oppositional behavior into mutism, bowel and bladder incontinence, willfulness in food refusal and outright battles with mother. The toddler reaches separation-individuation through ego stages which are determined in part by the rate of neuromuscular and language maturation. In language development, maturation and learning go hand in hand, but the maturation of motor functions appears to be independent of learning. Language increases the child's sense of belonging to the family and allows him to use secondary process thinking and expressions.

The two-year-old toddler shows little interest in reciprocal play and contacts with peers. He is interested in building materials for the purpose of construction and destruction. It is not until later, during the preschool years, that the child learns to play cooperatively. Before that, play is mainly exploratory and is aimed at learning a safe range of autonomy. As he enters the phallic stage, the child expresses masculine and feminine trends in solitary role playing, often with toys displaying oedipal objects and phallic exhibitionism. Later, the child stages the Oedipus complex in group play.

When the toddler enters the phallic-oedipal phase of development, he experiences once again a burst of energy, initiative and curiosity. As Erikson has put it, the phallic child seems to be "on the make," likes "making," and displays great pleasure in the "conquest" of his mother. This intrusive quality is more apparent in boys, but yet it has its parallel in girls insofar as they, as Erikson says, are out for "a catch," giving the appearance of "being on the make" and clearly wishing to be attractive and endearing to the opposite sex.

At this point in development, the child shows his capacity to imagine his place in the family and his relationship to people in his immediate environment. Mahler has demonstrated that at the end of the fourth subphase of separation-individuation, the child has reached the level of libidinal object constancy and is capable of establishing mental images of the parents and his own self. He sees himself as having a social role in his group which helps him in defining his self-object representations. Ever since the age of three, the phallic child has been reminded that he is no longer a baby. He hopes to meet this challenge but quickly finds that his energy and intrusiveness lead him to experience frustration and pain when he discovers that he is incapable of doing what adults do. As a result, narcissistic defeat and humiliation are commonplace in his life in the family, nursery school and his peer group.

During separation and individuation, the genital zone becomes increasingly important as a source of endogenous pleasure and thereby enhances a sense of sexual identity and object relatedness and affects basic mood states as part of the early genital phase which, according to Galenson and Roiphe, is a preoedipal antecedent to oedipal development (5).

Prior to the phallic-oedipal years, the male and female child have an undifferentiated primary identification with the mother. In the ensuing months, however, the child internalizes parts of both mother and father. Before she is two years old, a girl imitates her mother and starts having a flirtation with her father. Then the little girl is mostly involved with her mother, and in a sense her investment with the mother is basically the negative Oedipus complex. At the time of separation-individuation, the little girl moves toward the positive Oedipus complex and then reaches out more affectionately and aggressively to the father. She devalues the mother. For the boy aged two to three and a half, the psychosexual identification begins to shift from the mother to the father. Likewise, the boy experiences a negative Oedipal complex whereby aggressive feelings are attached to the mother whom he regards as overprotective, nongiving and potentially engulfing. Ideally, in a few months the boy is able to make a shift in his allegiance to his mother whereby he then transfers his aggression to his father, thereby permitting the mother to be overvalued and desired. Now the father is seen as a competitor for the mother.

The phenomena of infantile sexuality are clearly apparent during child treatment. The phenomena are also apparent in the direct observation of children, sexual perversions, sexual foreplay, florid psychosis and states of regression. Adult psychoanalytic reconstructions of infantile sexuality are also helpful to our appreciation of the early years. But child analytic work provides the most convincing evidence for infantile sexuality. The child analyst has the unique opportunity of observing the child over a period of time. He is able to see the variations and transformations of instinctual drive and ego development, as well as the importance of core gender-identity, learning experiences, cognitive styles and functions, and language.

Infantile sexuality is the keystone not only of clinical psychoanalytic theory but also of concepts of human development in general. When Freud first published his *Three Essays,* in which he reviewed the past contributions to the subject of infantile sexuality as well as his own clinical experience, his work was considered a sacrilegious attack against the innocence of children (3). His view was also questioned because of his belief that infantile sexuality had a great effect on an individual's subsequent personality development. What was particularly upsetting to people at the turn of the century was that infantile sexuality was said to leave an affective residue in childhood experience which continued to express itself outside of awareness throughout the individual's life. Freud also suggested that disturbances in the development of sexuality led to neurosis, "the negative of a perversion." In addition, Freud formulated developmental psychosexual stages (oral, anal, phallic-oedipal, latency and genital) through which a child passes toward the completion of his development. Freud pointed out the universal oedipal constellation and the role of the incest taboo. His view of infantile sexuality suggested a mechanistic-biological concept which excluded environmental influences. With the development of ego psychology, however, the role of environment, as well as the development of the ego (perception, cognition, motility, defensive organization and adaptive-coping skills) took on more important roles. Infantile sexuality, therefore, acquired a more general meaning, including both internal and external influences and vicissitudes.

Freud was able to show that the sexual wishes of the adult's unconscious can not only lead to psychoneurosis but can also play a part in many of the normal everyday aspects of adult life such as play, superstition, dream, fantasy, wit and religion. These wishes, either ungratified or gratified during childhood, continue in the unconscious of the adult and motivate him. Clinical observations of children confirm Freud's views of infantile sexuality. Infantile masturbation, erections, genital and oral play in infancy and the toddler's curiosity about his excrement are all phenomena of infantile sexuality. In addition, normal nongenital lovemaking of adults satisfies many infantile sexual needs. The kiss demonstrates the importance of the mouth in lovemaking as do many endearments such as "sweetie" and "honey." Playful spanking and biting as part of foreplay are other examples. Likewise, obscenity has a universal meaning to people because it is unambiguous in its connection to infantile modes of pleasure. Another proof of infantile sexuality is sexual perversions. Psychoanalytic studies of perverts demonstrate that they experience what is desired unconsciously by adults and openly by infants. On another level, sexual fantasies are the wishes of infantile sexuality, especially apparent when they are floridly manifested in psychotic delusions and manifest content of dreams. Another type of evidence for infantile sexuality is the fact that amnesia for childhood events prior to six years is extremely common. Yet we know in watching young children that this is a time of intense emotional experience and excitement.

Historical study of the discovery of child sexuality has revealed that Freud's concepts in *Three Essays* were hardly his own observations. His theories of child sexuality were a composite of numerous observations of children. In 1867, the English psychiatrist Henry Maudsley pointed out examples of child sexuality. Later, before the turn of the century, Perez, Pross and Lindner wrote extensively about infantile sexuality. It is apparent from the historical study of Stephen Kern that it remained for Freud to synthesize the earlier data, through his extensive clinical experience, into a consistent theory of infantile sexuality (7).

In everyday life, we see in boys various manifestations of infantile sexuality as they enter and pass through the phallic-oedipal years. They are increasingly aware of the triadic relationship of family life, and, even without the birth of a sibling, wonder about pregnancy and delivery and how they came to be born. Even in the most sophisticated families, where sexuality is not a forbidden subject for discussion, the child must create his own theories of intercourse, pregnancy and birth. He wonders whether his mother will have more children and even thinks about his own ability to make a baby. Often, he will openly tell his mother that he wants to marry her. Maybe they could have their own baby, he thinks, and go off someplace and live wherever his fantasies and wishes take him. He may suspect babies are made by oral impregnation, are delivered *per annum*; he may view coitus as sadistic especially if he has witnessed his parents making love, and he is convinced of the universality of the penis—all views equally held by the oedipal girl (4).

He is soon confronted by the reality of his own being and the world in which he lives. There is no escape from his sense of inferiority and increasing anxiety and guilt about his wishes. He simply knows that he cannot do the many things that father does handily each day. Furthermore, in a healthy family, the son realizes that the quality of the mother's affection for father is something that he will never share, much less her sexual love with the father. However strong the denial of his smallness is, it cannot save him at that time from the awareness that he is smaller than his father in every respect. Consequently, the phallic-oedipal child, much like the toddler in his toilet training experience, meets with frustration and defeat.

The little girl in the phallic-oedipal period has no happier time of it. Failure and frustration are her everyday experiences. She can help her mother with chores but never is she able to equal or excel the mother in this capacity. If she is lucky, she is told to take care of her little brother or sister whom she resents and would like to hurt. By way of identification with the mother, she demonstrates her first interest in having a baby. At the same time, she fancies herself as a better mother, not to mention a better wife and lover than her mother. It is hard for the little girl to imagine why father stays with this woman who happened to have given birth to her a few years before. She dresses up for her father, scrambles to meet him at the door and tries in every way to make him feel important. Instead, she quickly realizes that during the evening, if not within a few minutes, the father's interest will be directed to the mother.

Direct observation of children, as well as our clinical experience, indicates that for the phallic child to reach this level of psychosexual development and to complete resolution of the Oedipus complex, a considerable degree of maturation and learning is necessary. This maturation and development cut right across all levels of ego development at a time when the development of the ego has reached a point where some degree of synthesis and consolidation is possible.

From about age three to five years, physical growth rapidly increases. The average boy grows about five inches and gains 10 pounds. The girl tends to be somewhat shorter and lighter. The organ that develops most rapidly is the central nervous system; by the time the child is five-years-old, over 90% of the nervous system tissue has attained an adult level of maturation, with myelin now deposited in the higher brain centers, particularly cortical and subcortical structures. Genitally, neurobiological organization is sufficiently developed to allow erotic excitation and orgasm although, of course, ejaculation and menstruation cannot yet occur. It is not until puberty that genital functions are possible. Also during this time, psychomotor coordination and digital dexterity are greatly increased. Language development has progressed beyond basic phonemes to morphemes. The child is now increasingly able to understand logical rules and syntactical structures. The phallic child is able to use language as a means for classifying, describing and comparing the objects that he encounters every day in his world. Nuances of language by age five are possible, and words can now be differentiated into meanings which are applicable to specific objects and events.

In object relations, the child continues to be egocentric up to the age of five. It is hard for him to empathize with other individuals, but as he passes through the phallic-oedipal period, his relationships become more sociocentric. Imaginary companions are no longer needed and, likewise, there is less need for dramatization of different roles. Perceptual capacities of the phallic-oedipal child increase as he enters this phase of development. Now he is able to differentiate stimuli in his environment in that he is capable of using specific language labels for them, attending to both the whole and its parts. Spatial organization, however, still remains not a particularly relevant dimension for the child. The phallic-oedipal child has now formed, to use Piaget's term, a representational world. Because of acquisition of language, increased memory capacity, especially evocative memory, his heightened ability to differentiate perceptual experiences and his increasing knowledge of the rules of arithmetic and logic, he is capable of increased intellectual performance. By the time the child has left the toddler stage, he is no longer in what Piaget calls the sensorimotor stage of intelligence and is at the level of true conceptual intelligence. He is now capable of symbolizations. Simple representations or intuitions begin to occur at ages four to five, later followed by articulated representations or intuitions which occur between the ages of five and seven. At the age of seven, the child has entered the stage of concrete operations, at which time he is able to conceptualize coherence, groupings and serializations. Later, from ages 11 to 15, he enters a period of formal operations when new structures, visuomorphic groups and lattices of logical algebra are possible. What must be kept in mind, however, during the phallic-oedipal stage is that the child's understanding of concepts is still partly colored by the perceptual aspect of the stimulus. For instance, at age four his concept of quality is dependent upon conceptual aspects of the stimulus. Piaget's famous experiment with beads in a tall cylinder jar illustrates this fact quite concretely. The phallic child is apt to consider beads in a tall cylinder as greater in quantity than beads in a short, squat jar which actually contains the same number of beads. From the ages of five to seven, however, as the child passes through the phallic-oedipal years into the middle childhood years, he begins to understand that the amount of beads is constant regardless of the change in the shape of the container in which they are held. Consequently, one can see that the phallic-oedipal child has added thought to his perception and is, in general, more thoughtful about the world in which he is living.

Dreams of children in the early phallic years demonstrate a tendency toward narration of events in very simple concrete terms. It is hard for a child of this age to tell the difference between a dream as a private experience and a dream as a shared experience. Furthermore, dreams are often depersonalized; dream images are iconic, usually involving monsters and threatening animals. Death is everywhere in these dreams, as the happy wish-fulfilling dreams of the earlier years are replaced by images of anxiety and guilt. Dreams of nakedness and embarrassment are their concern, as well as those of failing examinations, falling, flying, swimming and having teeth pulled.

Likewise, play during these years also changes. Children now want to play out various roles such as doctor, cowboy, ship captain, nurse and jet pilot. The play fantasy often aims at denying the anxiety associated with the child's smallness and relative overall inability to perform adult tasks. He wants to be big and do what big people do. Oedipal play is dramatic, often grandiose, filled with feelings of invulnerability, invincibility, triumph and eternal happiness.

Oedipal fantasies are universal and contain elements of the oedipal myth. The central figure of such fantasies is a hero, rescued from abandonment by someone from a lowly station in life, raised to adulthood when he follows a prophecy leading him to a rival whom he vanquishes and kills, only to realize his mistake and live forever with his guilt. These images can be transformed in fantasies into ones of monsters, attacking animals, castration by a father and self-castration. The fantasies make up for an unpleasant oedipal reality, allow wish fulfillment, blind terror and provide punishment for oedipal strivings.

The phallic-oedipal years of development are also important for psychosocial development. The phallic child's relationships with peers begin to change as he enters this stage. Up to the end of his toddler life, his peers were not particularly important to him. Reciprocal play seldom was enjoyed. As he enters nursery school, he becomes more aware of the external world, particularly the fact that teachers and peers are not so readily accepting of his behavior, nor do they tend to view him as quite as special as his parents. He is encouraged to mix with the other children, to go from solitary to parallel play and then to cooperative play. Finally, at the end of the phallic years, he is capable of reciprocal play in which there is greater opportunity for the discharge of instinctual drive and motor energy but also for the chance to try out new roles and skills.

The phenomena of the phallic-oedipal years demonstrate the change in erotic pleasures of the young child. Bowel-bladder pleasure and its transformations into personality development have already taken place. Anal erotism has been experienced during defecation and is connected with anal masturbation and anal retention. It is the stimulation of the mucous membrane lining the anus and the anal canal which leads to this kind of erotism. The pleasure is autoerotic although, of course, it may be enhanced by external sources. During bowel and bladder training, the child must negotiate with the mother, and it is by this kind of interaction that the erotism becomes related to the object. Ideally, at the end of the anal phase, the child repudiates anal wishes and sublimates this energy into activities such as playing with sand, painting and staying clean. At this stage of development, if erotic development is interfered with, the child is apt to excessively use mechanisms of reaction formation and repression to ward off these impulses, thereby jeopardizing his entry into the phallic-oedipal phase of development. Erotic interest shifts at the time of change to the phallic phase from the anus to the penis and clitoris.

The phallic child is now in a second phase of infantile masturbation. In this second phase, the boy's specific aims are penetration and procreation. This erotism is different from genital erotism of adolescence and adulthood as the phallic impulses are to penetrate but not to discharge semen. The impulses to hit, to press in, to knock to pieces, to tear open and to make a bull's eye are part of the male child's fantasy. Even if a child is sexually knowledgeable from discussions with his parents, as well as information obtained from the "street," he is still puzzled in the attempt to understand phallic penetration in intercourse. As a result, he must fall back on other ideas of sexual contact and pregnancy, ideas which have occurred to him in his everyday childhood experiences and feelings. Phallic wishes lead him to want to penetrate through the mouth, the anus, the navel and in this manner create a baby. This is the act of phallic erotism; on the other hand, the passive aim is to be penetrated and to bear a baby, a feeling that little boys are apt to have in the early phase of phallic development as part of the negative Oedipus complex in which the wish to be castrated becomes a necessary condition for being penetrated and is usually fantasied as anal penetration.

Under the impetus of wishes, sexual knowledge comes to the young child through perceptions and fantasies. Initially, the child believes there is only one sexual organ, namely, the penis, but later the child must face the perception that the female has no penis. Since this perception is not acceptable, he must disavow it, something which he cannot later do because of a reality sense which prevents him from maintaining the belief that there is no perceptual difference between the sexes. In order to maintain this belief, he then has to elaborate a series of fantasies along the lines that the girl's penis will later grow back. Consequently, as a defense, the male child may develop fantasies and neurotic symptoms related to the female genitalia as a way of avoiding anxiety. These fantasies are usually repressed at the phallic-oedipal stage as the child enters latency. This is, however, not the case with perverts who find no solution to the Oedipus complex. They are stopped short between disavowal of the perception and the denial through fantasy. As Freud put it, the pervert is confronted with the fact that his mother has no penis and in order to fill this gap, he must create a fetish or face a phobia.

Early in the male phallic psychosexual development, he becomes cognizant of his anatomical gender differences. His awareness of the male genitalia enhances his identification with his father and encourages him in this competititve direction. Furthermore, he begins to have fantasies of parental lovemaking which can be reinforced by either hearing or seeing the parents making love, as well as by whatever fantasies that the boy may have of his parents. Parens suggests that a "primary heterosexuality" in boys, as well as girls, pushes the boy toward the mother and starts the Oedipus complex (11). At this point, the boy wants to show his mother his penis and at the same time look at her breasts and genitals. His innate sense of the penis as a penetrating instrument and its source of great pleasure are manifested in masturbation, exhibitionism and sexual role playing. He may play games in which he is protective of his mother and in other respects imitates his father. He will make up stories and fantasies about larger rivals who are easily vanquished by him as in "Jack and the Beanstalk." Soon his view of his father is so threatening that he lives in dread of injury by the hand of his father. This threat forms the basis of castration anxiety which brings into his development a new theme, a theme which usually exists only in the child's fantasies but is reinforced by parental punishment and by the strength of his oedipal fantasies. The anxiety coming from the castration threat eventually leads to repudiation of the boy's oedipal wishes through suppression and repression which shifts the ego defensive organization. Evidence for this developmental shift is found in the everyday play of children as well as fairytales and fantasies. In addition, children's graphic productions, anthropological studies of totemic animals and the data from child analysis and psychoanalytic adult reconstructions are also supportive of these developmental trends.

Soon the mother indicates her unwillingness to respond to the boy's wishes, sending him perhaps into a jealous rage which may lead to a wish to kill her and to be loved by the father in her place. This is the negative type of Oedipus complex which also leads to a dread of injury and castration because of the passive wishes involved. Fear of castration is a universal fear among young boys because of the erogenous quality of the phallus itself, namely, pleasure and phallic tumescence which enhance fears that erotic fantasies will be revealed. Earlier experiences in losing the breast in weaning and later losing feces in defecation are antecedents to the overall sense of castration anxiety and body fragmentation. Because of castration anxiety, the boy finally relinquishes the maternal object and replaces the mother in the ego by way of an identification with her. At the same time, there is an introjection of the father into the boy's representational world and concomitantly an identification is made with this introjection, an identification which strengthens masculinity in the boy's character. Thus the boy's libidinal wishes for the mother are in part desexualized and sublimated and partly inhibited and transformed into impulses of affection for her.

Female phallic psychosexual development is much more complicated than male development and less well understood. Although Freud initially assumed that sexual development in both boys and girls proceeded in a similar manner, a view which he later modified after realizing that the little girl not only has to change her primary sexual object from the mother to the father, but also eventually her erogenous zone, from the clitoris to the vagina. In the beginning, however, the girl, much like the boy, starts off with the mother as the main libidinal object. Again like the boy, her earliest erotic fantasies are directed toward the mother. Between the ages of two and three years, however, she begins showing a preference for the father. Masturbation using the clitoris in lieu of the penis increases at this time as it does with masturbation for the boy. It is at this time, however, that gender differences in psychosexual development emerge. Her desire to play the man is not brought to an end by castration anxiety. It is, in fact, castration fear that propels the little girl toward the Oedipus complex. For now she blames her mother for the genital difference and looks to her father with the hope that he will repair her body damage and allow her to become a man like him. Even if she is aware of her vagina at this time, the clitoris remains the erogenous zone through phallic-oedipal development and usually the adolescent years when a switch from the clitoris to the vagina is made. It is during the time when the girl shifts her libidinal interest from the first object, the mother, to the father that she becomes aware of genital differences. At first, she wishes to repudiate her recognition of sexual difference. She tries to deny her fantasy of having been deprived of a penis. If successful, this denial increases her antagonism toward the mother and likewise enhances her fear of more retaliation from the mother. Likewise, the wish for a penis increases interest in the father and any brothers. It is at this time that penis envy and its manifestations (inferiority, jealousy, shame and rage) are evident. Castration anxiety is manifested by negative affects, like sadness, worry, anguish and despondence, connected with comments and comparisons of the external genitalia, as well as anxiety evidenced by phobias, sadism, rage and anxious preoccupations. The girl's passive wish is then turned toward the father's penis as he becomes the principal object. The rivalry with the mother, however, may be interrupted by brief negative oedipal erotic feelings toward the mother. Soon, however, she is rebuffed by the father and is forced to renounce her oedipal wishes. Thus, she is thrown back on her mother with whom she must emotionally remain until adolescence when she starts to move toward heterosexual objects.

The child's awareness and observations of the parents' sexuality play an important part in psychosexual development. Awareness of parental intercourse (so-called primal scene experiences) are stimulating and often very exciting and frequently lead to fear, dread and disgust. These experiences are ubiquitous but often not remembered in later life by the adult and frequently not recalled at all by the parents even after their occurrences. The repression of primal scene experiences occurs both for the parents and for the child. All children experience at least auditory primal scenes. They hear the parents' movement in bed, changes in breathing rate which suggest excitement or struggle, sounds of the mother's giggles, father's heavy breathing as well as various noises emitted at the time of orgasm. All these sounds are very stimulating to the child's fantasies, of course, and become even more graphic if the child has visually witnessed the parents having sex. In general, primal scenes are confusing for the child because he does not know who is doing what to whom. The younger child is particularly upset by the separation experience he feels as he witnesses the primal scene. Because his cognitive equipment is confused by what he perceives, parental intercourse is viewed as an act of aggression. Also connected with primal scene experiences is a child's fear that the mother will become pregnant. Pregnancy is another difficult fantasy during this stage of development because it stirs up old sibling rivalry feelings.

The Oedipus complex was considered by Freud to be the "cornerstone" of psychoanalysis, the central core of psychosexual theory of development and, in some respects, the phenomenological nucleus to his theories of infantile sexuality. It is a theory which is substantiated by a great deal of clinical and anthropological data. Rutter's critique of infantile sexuality, an objective overview of the literature, reviews empirical data supporting Freud's phallic-oedipal formulations (14). The Oedipus tragedy, from which Freud drew much of his view of the Oedipus complex, is found in the *Odyssey* which leads us to suspect that the legend is older than the seventh century, the time when the Homeric epics were being written down. It is an ancient and universal myth.

The Oedipus complex is basically a triadic developmental family phenomenon which involves a child's sexual strivings for the same-sex parent bringing him face to face with his erotic feelings and phallic wishes toward the parent of the opposite sex. The Oedipus-complex further differentiates the object-relatedness of the child. The desire for affection and stimulation from the parent of the opposite sex pushes the child into a competitive relationship with the parent of the same sex. For the boy, this competition leads to fear of castration; for the girl, castration anxiety intensifies her hostility and ambivalent feelings towards the mother, magnifies her romantic inclinations toward her father, stimulates her wish to own or have her own baby, and heightens her desire to be like her father and be a member of the male world. Thus, the Oedipus complex is an apprenticeship for heterosexuality and an essential developmental step for male and female psychosexual identity. In girls, the wish to have a baby, often evident at the beginning of the third year, marks the "awakening protogenital sexuality that gives rise to the Oedipus complex," an early sensuality that suggests an innate primary feminine disposition which appears at the end of senior toddlerhood as an early form of genitality. Thus, at this age the girl's psychic activity is dominated by a heterosexual genital drive which is preprogrammed to appear at this time. Parens, Pollock, Stern and Kramer suggest that the heterosexual genital drive pressure may be a stronger factor than castration anxiety for the girl's entry into the Oedipus complex (11).

The incest taboo, a strong deterrent to acting out of the Oedipus complex, is universal. No society has ever allowed an individual to mate with members of his or her family for procreation. The reason why it is universal has been debated over the years. The resolution of the Oedipus complex, therefore, takes place with changes in both the aims and objects of the instinctual drives. Love-dependent and erotic aspects of objects are dissociated, and new object relations develop with people, such as teachers and friends who are free of the incestuous taboo. The child identifies with the authority of the father who is introjected into the ego as the authority of the superego, thereby perpetuating the incest taboo and preventing the ego from returning to an earlier libidinal position with the parents. The libidinal components of the Oedipus complex are thus desexualized and sublimated and partly inhibited in their aims and partly transmuted into impulses of affection The overall outcome of this psychosexual phase and the resolution of the Oedipus complex is the structural formation of "precipitates" in the ego which consist of true identifications in some way united with each other, a combination which gives rise to the ego-ideal and the superego. Freud was quick to point out that because of the gender differences in the resolution of the Oedipus complex, the little girl's superego formation is quite different. For the girl, the breakup of the infantile genital organization comes from her increasing awareness during later development that her wish to have a child with the father can never be fulfilled. Consequently, Freud believed that the woman's superego is never impersonal or independent of its emotional origin as in the resolution of the male Oedipus complex.

The triadic interaction of the Oedipus complex does not only occur in the phallic-oedipal period of development. In adolescence, there is a resurgence of many aspects of the Oedipus complex as the adolescent tries to rework previous developmental issues. Often, in adulthood prior to a son's marriage there is an upsurge of oedipal feelings on the part of the father toward his future daughter-in-law. The same response, of course, can occur for a mother in her feelings for her newfound son-in-law. And in later life, grandparents may also have a return of their rivalrous feelings towards a son-in-law or daughter-in-law after the birth of a grandchild. Toward the end of the life, if aging has been complicated by brain deterioration resulting in loss of cognitive control and instinctual delay, a man may give vent to long repressed oedipal urges and make sexual advances toward young girls.

There is a variety of reasons why the Oedipus complex may not be resolved and the child may be unable to develop in latency. The child may not be able to enter latency because he lacks the capacity to form symbols and use fantasies. Or the child may regress in his ego latency structure so that he acts out impulses rather than discharging them by way of fantasies. The child may also simply regress to prelatency behavior whereby pregenital fantasies dominate behavior interfering with impulse control, learning and peer relationships (15). If a child has had multiple deprivations in his childhood and a poor relationship with parents, these experiences may very well lead to tenuousness in his relationship with parental objects leading to a limited control of aggressive and sexual impulses along with little capacity for sexual pleasure. Oedipal attachment may also be hindered if the child has been through extreme frustration or extreme overindulgence at the time of this phase of psychosexual development. If a parent of the opposite sex has been out of the home at the time of the child's phallic development, the child's relationship with the parent of the opposite sex may be affected. The child may be overly involved with the parent of the same sex, a situation which will make it difficult for him to be sufficiently free of this parent to form a heterosexual object choice later in life. If the opposite-sex parent is seductive toward the child and overstimulates him with unresolved oedipal feelings, the child's oedipal situation may never be tempered. If the parent of the same sex dies or deserts the family during the oedipal period, this may be the soil for conflict since the event coincides with the child's oedipal aggression toward this parent. It is best for the resolution of the Oedipus complex if the parent of the same sex be attractive, non-punitive and a satisfactory model for identification. At the same time, the opposite-sex parent should not be emotionally unpredictable, seductive or unduly punitive, so that the child will be able to place confidence in objects of the opposite sex. It is also important that the parents do not indicate any rejection of the child's genetic sex. It is best for the resolution of the Oedipus complex that the child identify with a happy concept of marriage seeing his parents' marriage in terms of pleasure, security and comfort.

Between the ages of three and five, the child struggles with his oedipal relationship and his competitive dependency vis-à-vis siblings and parents. During this time, he enjoys a happy illusion of being a miniature adult, but from age five to seven, he must come to terms with the illusion, often using fantasies which substitute for the primary objects in his family. Then he enters the stage of middle childhood, the latency years or, in Erikson's terms, the stage of "industry versus inferiority." The physical onset of this stage is marked by the shedding of the first deciduous teeth at which time the child ideally enters a period of repressive calm. At this point, if development has proceeded normally, the Oedipus complex has been resolved; narcissistic investment in the body, its various orifices and functions, is diminished until the prepubertal growth spurt of adolescence when instinctual drives are markedly heightened under the influence of increased androgenic production.

In the latency years, the child is not satisfied with merely "playing around" and doing "make-believe." This is a time when he turns to people outside the home with whom he hopes to identify. People that appeal to him for identificatory purposes are those who seem to have a great deal of competence and strength. The latency child's own feeling of competence and achievement is often seen as illusory; he cannot yet trust himself to his wishes. He increasingly turns to industry with the idea that workmanship is now most important. Less time is spent with the family, and now there is more concentration on tools, objects and work. Unlike his attitude during the phallic-oedipal years, he now emphasizes real goals which he wants to take to completion. He also at this time begins to learn to read and write with a sense of competence.

Differentiation of male and female gender roles is furthered during the middle childhood years. Children are encouraged to develop skills and show interest in gender-appropriate achievement. Nevertheless, some children want to retreat to the earlier years because they are unable to enjoy the work situation and feel inadequate. They long to return to the comfort of mother. The sense of failure and tendency toward regression are particularly marked if the child's mastery during the phallic-oedipal years was marginal. Furthermore, he misses out in developing his identity if work is something that he cannot be comfortable with. The latency child knows in his own way that part of what he will be in the future is determined by what he does now. It is at this level of development that work becomes a motivational force in the development of identity. Harry Stack Sullivan (17) was well aware of this when he referred to the latency period as the juvenile era, a time when the child is concerned with competition and compromise and is bent on the achievement of social competence.

Peer group participation and school activities further the differentiation of sexual identification. Peers help the latency child learn his role in society, ease his way into associative-cooperative play, teach him to subordinate his individual needs and wishes to the group, give him a new idea of his value relative to other people and help him learn his role in society. It is at this time that the latency child develops his academic skills, and it is also during these years that superego and ego-ideals are strengthened. The superego authority is invested in the introjection of the parents and occurs at the oedipal resolution. Now during the latency years, its power is available to help the ego in controlling id impulses. The structures of the superego and ego-ideal are further modified and amended as the child passes through middle childhood years into adolescence.

There has been much confusion about the instinctual life of the latency child. Freud in 1896 considered latency a time in which repression first appeared. Freud believed that latency lasted from age eight to age 10. He felt that sexuality was quiescent in the latency years. Further, he thought that the resolution of the Oedipus complex led to repression as a typical latency defense. Reaction formation, sublimation and the furtherance of superego development were important outcomes during that period. In addition, he believed that sexual energy was displaced in its gratification since its aims were inhibited. Later, in 1905, Freud indicated a change in his view. He thought that latency started at age six, but he continued to adhere to the belief that sexual quiescence was present between the resolution of the Oedipus complex and the time of puberty. Sarnoff (15) has pointed out in his review of latency that Freud continued to believe that phylogenesis resulted in the ego functions of latency. In other words, Freud continued to adhere to a biological view of latency throughout his career. Subsequent child developmentalists have questioned this view. They conclude that sexuality during the latency years is simply less observable, often repressed but more commonly suppressed because of the child's increasing social awareness. They also believe that masturbation in girls continues by way of indirect stimulation of the clitoris.

During latency, the child constantly has to fight against regression to a period in his life before the phallic-oedipal years. These pregenital impulses that haunt him are much more troublesome for boys. The child has to work out defenses against such drives and these defenses are a large part of the psychological work of latency. It is a time when secondary process thinking is consolidated, and the reality principle is firmly established. Positive object relations and identifications are now established. Personality is in large part formed during latency; but contrary to Freud's view, personality development continues through life, as long as a person is not bound by rigid fixations and pathological defenses.

Latency is not characteristic of mammals. Man is the only mammalian that has a latency period. Apes and monkeys, for instance, show nothing like latency in their development. Consequently, latency is now viewed as a cultural phenomenon. Sexual quiescence does not exist; libidinal drive strengths are maintained but not increased until prepubertal hormonal changes occur. Nevertheless, clinical data, as well as Kinsey's research data, show that sexual experimentation and curiosity continue through the latency years. Masturbation and sexually colored play are quite common in these years. The sexuality of latency is also characterized by increased social awareness of sexuality and by increased circumspection about sexual behavior, especially in the presence of adults. The only latency children who openly masterbate and exhibit their sexuality in public are mentally defective children or psychotic children.

Fantasies change during the early latency years when children defensively show dissatisfaction with parents. Often adoption fantasies appear, especially if there were deprivations early in childhood, and they are precursors to the "family romance," as are fantasies of having a twin, imaginary companions, and animal fantasies, all containing objects that love the child more than the parents. These fantasies soon change in latency into "family romance" fantasies granting a new origin to the child, making him into a hero whereby he gains strength and a refurbished identity.

There are two subphases during the latency years (1). In a sense, they are somewhat different. The first subphase occurs between the ages of six and eight years, when the child is especially fearful. It is a time when repression, suppression and aggression are most apparent. The child makes an attempt to control masturbation. He is vulnerable to regression to pregenitality, with the reaction formations of disgust, shame and guilt. The superego is very strict, and often it feels like a foreign body haunting him. In relationships with others, the superego is ambivalent and crude, especially in relationships with the same-sex parent. Sexual impulses must be controlled by the superego. The child does not want to view his parents as sexual objects although he is well aware of sexuality in general. He hopes to restrict the discharge of his sexual drive to fantasy and masturbation. And it is best that he continue masturbation; this provides him with an easy outlet for sexual feelings. At this time we see masturbatory equivalents, particularly in children who are fearful of masturbating. They appear as scratching, head-banging, nail biting and sadomasochistic behavior in varying degrees. Castration anxiety can continue, especially for girls, during this time. Penis envy frequently is prominent during this phase of latency. Secondary process thinking does not show any consistency. Often the child dips back into primary process thinking.

The second subphase of latency, ages eight to 10, is a period of increasing cognitive control and reality testing. Sublimation now is fuller and more successful, and the child suffers less over masturbation. His external world is more gratifying, and he tends to rely less on his fantasies. The superego is less severe and alien. In this phase, the child's sense of omnipotence is decreased, and his defenses and affects are more ego-syntonic and less involved in simple impulse control. Sexuality is more prominent and pressing and, from ages eight to 11, the latency child is apt to flee from sexual and heterosexual curiosity and interests.

Six- to nine-year-old children spend a great deal of time learning how to get along with others and competing with peers. Rules in this regard are viewed as absolute and immutable partly because of the severity of the superego and partly because of cognitive immaturity. By age nine, however, the child has some notion of reciprocity with other people. Now he can change the rules. These new rules apply to everybody. Between the ages of 11 and 12, children develop feelings of equity and fairness; they may even give concessions to handicapped players, realizing that other children's needs may be different from their own. Thus, they are able to transcend egocentrism, shift perspective and be emphatic with peers. The child is now more involved with his peer relationships, dependent on them to impart and point out external reality to him, help him control inappropriate impulses, show him new ways of coping and developing skills, as well as means for repairing damage to self-esteem and mitigating the sting of narcissistic injuries. The group helps one another through maintaining its own controls. In a sense, the peer group provides an auxiliary ego to the late latency child.

At about age eight, the child develops a sense of time. Death is now seen as something permanent around which he will build, depending on family and culture, an ideology of afterlife. He tries to trust in the future and be objective with himself. To some extent, he can detach from himself and other people so that he no longer narcissistically equates himself with others. Cause and effect are now less magical. Trust, autonomy initiative and industry are all part of his expanding cognitive awareness and strengthen his position vis-à-vis his identity and role in the culture.

In latency years, there is a deceleration in physical growth. Boys surpass girls at this time in that they are slightly taller and heavier than girls, are stronger, better coordinated and have a faster reaction time. This gender differential in growth usually ceases at pubescence when girls become slightly taller than boys and continue to be so until they are about 15 years old.

As boys and girls enter school in the latency years, there is a difference in their behavior, attitudes and accomplishments. Girls are frequently fearful. Initially very tearful about being in school, they show more motor inhibition, less inclination to activity in school and tend to stay closer to their mothers. In the toddler years, the female central nervous system develops faster than that of boys. Accelerated growth and deposition of myelin occur several years earlier in girls. Girls show a left hemispheric dominance manifested by better language arts skills which, however, are only a temporary advantage until mid-latency years. Girls are more alert to new situations with schematic differences and discrepancies. This alertness is partly responsible for their cautiousness and greater need for conformity.

Boys, on the other hand, are more given to activity which buffers their fearfulness. They are less skilled in the language arts, better able to see spatial relationships and do mechanical tasks. They evidence right hemispheric dominance in the early latency years. Male aggression is more prominent because it is displayed through physical activities and less so through words. In the early school years, boys often shun the school situation because they associate many of the activities such as drawing, cutting out, pasting, etc. with femininity. These activities are encouraged by teachers who, of course, are usually women. Unfortunately, in our culture few men teach in the lower grades. This is one reason why gender stereotyping is so readily maintained. Coeducation helps to remove gender stereotyping. It is clearly evident that coeducation helps to neutralize the biological gender differences of the classroom, dampens the aggressive potential of boys, encourages girls to compete in sports, and fosters gender equality.

The socialization that occurs in school confronts a child with the fact that he is just another child in the school and neighborhood. He is forced by circumstances into an associative-cooperative mode of play where new patterns of aggressive behavior as well as techniques for self-control are learned. The child must subordinate his individual needs and goals to the group. At home, the child must strike a balance between the values and activities of his parents and those of his peer group. The peer group puts the child in a situation in which he has to reevaluate internalized values. With a partial transfer of parental roles to teachers and members of the peer group, the latency child is more critical of his parents and retracts the omnipotence which he delegated to them in earlier years.

As a child passes through the latency years, his fears change from concrete, symbolic representations like ghosts, dangerous animals and monsters, to more generalized and less symbolic substitutes for his fears of parents. His anxieties now focus more on his everyday performance, although he still tries to create a balance between his old magical world and the new world of reality. For this reason, he may temporarily regress to an earlier stage where he can utilize old behavior in the service of controlling emotional conflicts. In doing so, he intensifies reaction formations such as guilt, disgust and shame against those infantile impulses stirred up by regressive shifts. Reaction formations now are more integrated into his developing character. In his sexual development, he must look outside of the home for new models for identification. The girl looks for idealized, romantic, prestigious identificatory figures although the early latency girl may still play out the role of mother and daughter. On the other hand, boys look for men who have status in society, people who are strong and assertive.

The peer group clustering is largely determined on the basis of sex differences which results in a cleavage between the sexes. And, in fact, the popularity of the child in the peer group has a lot to do with the clarity of the child's sex-type activities and attitudes. Girls tend to be more obsessive, boys, more compulsive in staying within the acceptable modes of behavior of the peer group. We find that latency children pick models for identification on the basis of not only cultural factors but also the child's own personality traits and skills. In other words, he tries to imitate a prestigious figure toward whom he feels he has kinship. For instance, a boy who is well-coordinated, outgoing and strong may choose an athletic star for his model. But these gender criteria break down in late latency and early adolescence when both girls and boys consider the male as much more competent in problem solving and adapting to the world. Unfortunately, this dichotomous distinction continues through adulthood, leaving the female with a negative self-concept which our society does little to dispel.

The games of the culture are vital to the latency child. For instance, games with rules (Piaget's third category of play) come into prominence during the latency years. Hobbies which are halfway between play and work are now selected; some lead to ego-mastery and a sense of productive competence. In latency years, there is a special culture with its own rules, rhymes, riddles—games which grownups are not permitted to enter. Latency rites include peculiar little superstitions, excessive counting, tongue-twisters, repetitive jokes which make fun of adults and odd collections of objects which serve as talismen. Hobbies appear early and frequently are precursors of later work. Brief coded messages are part of the clubs, packs and gangs of latency children, all of whom pride themselves on their group solidarity and individuality. Latency play, in general, is more realistic and frequently based on rules which now are not immutable. But there is an upholding of one rule which is unchanging; namely, the exclusion of those children from the group who do not fit into the social identity of the latency group. For instance, girls organize their clubs for the purpose of keeping other girls out, especially girls who like boys, and, of course, all boys. On the other hand, boys are greatly involved in games, projects and trips; their group concentrates on trading and gathering prize objects. In the group, there is a great deal of bartering which is another way of comparing strength and assets of members.

Toward the end of latency, children enter pubescence, which is generally regarded as a two-year interval preceding the onset of full puberty. Psychologically, pubescence is closer to the middle school years than it is to adolescence. Its onset is characterized by a spurt in physical growth which includes physical changes in both primary and secondary sexuality. For some children, pubescence can be very short-lived, hardly observable by even the child and his parents. But usually rapid spurts in the growth of the arms, legs and neck occur with, of course, changes in height, increase in weight and increased sexual impulses, along with growth of the genitalia. The triggers for pubescent growth are neuroendocrinological. After several years, at the time of actual puberty, these biological changes reach a peak characterized in the female by menarche and in the male by spermatogenesis. This is the time of development called preadolescence which is a misnomer as it is also used to designate the middle school years; in this respect it is not specific or meaningful enough to be a useful term. Pubescence, although it is close to late latency, should be regarded as part of early adolescence because of instinctual drive increases. At that time, sexuality blossoms and physical growth pushes forward at a rapid speed. Aggressive and sexual drives intensify, body concepts change, narcissistic body investment is augmented, and the pubescent child completes his cognitive shift from the concrete to the abstract. In some ways, there is a kind of irony to this change in that developmentally he is capable of greater rationality; but at the same time, he is overwhelmed with physical discomfort from his growth, emotional uneasiness about his body and, of course, he is bombarded with sexual feelings. At this time, the pubescent boy and girl are vulnerable to regressive shifts to phallic and preoedipal fixation points. For instance, attitudes of tidiness and cleanliness slip back to dirtiness; neatness is reversed to disorder and chaos, sociability to outright boorishness; relatively stable mood swings to euphoria and depression. The adaptive calm with the parents is shattered by aggression and alienation from them. In general, there is a resurgence of dependency conflict with surface ambivalence, more markedly in boys. Boys are at this time more mature and prone to regression. Girls tend to maintain a sophisticated facade, making boys feel even more inferior. At the same time, boys dread any trace of femininity in themselves and organize ego defenses around passive-active and masculine-feminine conflicts.

Thus, there occurs in latency a complicated reorganization of the defensive structures of the ego, enabling a balance between defense and drive, appropriate to the culture of the child and family, a balance which facilitates calm behavior and educability. The child now uses fantasy defensively to play out conflicts and discharge drives in thought rather than in action, thereby maintaining the balance of ego and id during latency.

REFERENCES

1. Bornstein, B.: On latency, *Psychoanalytic Study of the Child.* New York: International Universities Press, 1951, 8:279-285.
2. Erikson, E. H.: Identity and the life cycle. *Psychol. Issues*, 1: 50-100, 1959.

3. Freud, S.: Three essays on the theory of sexuality (1905). *Standard Edition.* Vol. 7. London: Hogarth Press.
4. Freud, S.: On the sexual theories of children (1905). *Standard Edition.* Vol. 7. London: Hogarth Press.
5. Galenson, E., and Roiphe, H.: Some suggested versions concerning early female development. *J. Amer. Psychoanal. Assn.*, 24: 19-58, 1976.
6. Hughes, T.: *Tom Brown's School Days.* London: J. M. Dent & Son, Ltd., 1949.
7. Kern, S.: Freud and the discovery of child sexuality. *History Childhood Quart.*, 1:118-141, 1973.
8. Kinsey, A. C., Pomeroy, W. B., and Martin, C. E.: *Sexual Behavior in the Human Male.* Philadelphia: Saunders, 1948.
9. Kinsey, A. C., Pomeroy, W. B., Martin, C. E., and Gebhard, P.H.: *Sexual Behavior in the Human Female,* Philadelphia: Saunders, 1953.
10. Mahler, M. S.: On the first three subphases of the separation-individuation process, *Int. J. Psychoanal.*, 53: 333-338, 1972.
11. Parens, H., Pollock, L., Stern, J., and Kramer, S.: On the girl's entry into the Oedipus complex. *J. Amer. Psychoanal. Assn.*, 24: 79-108, 1976.
12. Piaget, J. and Inhelder, R.: *The Psychology of the Child.* New York: Basic Books, 1969.
13. Plath, S.: *Ariel.* New York: Harper & Row, 1981, p. 51.
14. Rutter, M.: Normal psychosexual development, paper presented at the British Psychological Society Meeting, Leeds, Nov. 6, 1970.
15. Sarnoff, C.: *Latency.* New York: Aronson, 1976, pp. 382-386.
16. Sexton, A.: *The Death Notebooks.* Boston: Houghton Mifflin, 1974, p. 14.
17. Sullivan, H. S.: *Collected Works of Harry Stack Sullivan, Vol. 1.* New York: Norton, 1953.

5

Normal and Pathological Psychological Development During the Latency Age Period

Charles A. Sarnoff, M.D.

INTRODUCTION

The age period from six to 12 years is commonly designated in child psychiatric and psychoanalytic parlance as "latency." This term has a number of connotations. Often, the word "latency" connotes a period of diminished sexual drive. At other times, "latency" merely refers to the time period between six and 12 years of age. Scientific support for the concept that there is a diminished sexual drive during these years is lacking. If anything, latency children can manifest a good deal of sexually excited behavior, alternating with the ability to settle down in suitable settings, even in the face of highly stimulating and otherwise overwhelming situations. The supervening ability to settle down is a product of the strengthening of those areas of the personality that control drives and the excitement that uncontrolled drives produce.

The term "latency" retains value if used in the following context: Between six and 12 years of age a specific personality structure develops which is capable of producing a state of calm, pliability, and educability, which can be used as the basis for the transmission of culture in a school setting. A child in a state of latency is able to evaluate a given setting and control his drives to the point that he can cooperate and participate in a learning situation. Within this context, "latency" refers to the age period in which this specific personality structure places its imprint on the behavior of growing children. For heuristic purposes, I like to call this specific personality structure, "the structure of latency."

The specific form that clinically observable behavior takes during the latency age period is influenced by at least three factors. These are: behavioral expectations of the environment (situations, caretakers and peers), normal maturational unfolding, and the capacity to enter into a state of latency. The last factor itself experiences internal developmental changes between six and 12 years of age. During the latency age period, therefore, developmental clinical features reflect the influence of an amalgam of maturational steps, as well as the status of the capacity to enter into a state of latency.

It will be the purpose of this chapter to describe the normal and pathological manifestations of the ongoing interplay between the defensive personality structure that characterizes the latency age period and the contributions to behavior of the development of cognition, physical maturation, and the social organization in which the child lives.

The Role of Latency in Socialization

The time period of latency denotes an important phase in the socialization of the individual. The primary emphasis is on a shift in attention cathexes which subordinates parental admonitions and inner needs to the pressures of the social group. Developmental shifts in cognition support this process. The shift between the ages of six and seven to the use of words as the primary medium for the codification of experiences to be retained in memory and the shift, greatest at about eight years, in the symbolic forms used in the creation of adaptive fantasies from phantasmagoric to realistic forms are the cognitive thrusts most involved.

In early latency, the structure of latency is implemented for the mastery of current stresses. This is an organization of ego mechanisms that helps to master current stresses by evoking threatening associated fantasies in masked and symbolized form. The fantasies evoked have origins in the past experiences of the child and are usually recalled in terms of affecto-motor dominated memory patterns. Thus, oedipal feelings and overwhelmingly intense feelings of desertion become the daily experience of the early latency child. A shift to affect-binding, verbal and conceptual memory organizations is helpful in taking the child's early experiences out of action as immediate determinants of behavior. This leaves the child free to deal with reality. At this time in the child's life, parents and caretakers usually are presenting the child with religious stories, mythic tales and other verbal carriers of the principles of socially acceptable behavior in the particular society. The child seizes upon these stories as tools for expressing early personal fantasies which had hitherto found inadequate means for expression. Societies can be defined by the specific myths and tales through which socially acceptable behavior is codified and transmitted. Through the acquisition of those culturally homogeneous fantasies, which bind the individual's disruptive inner excitements, individuality is lost. The child is bound to the group with which he comes to share these "truths."

In early latency, the parents pick the myths and inputs of socialization. In late latency, the attention cathexes of the child shift from the parents to peer groups. At this point, parental choice becomes less important in determining the ethics of the child. The shift from fantastic to realistic elements as symbols for the expression and mastery of disturbing fantasies leads the child away from the need for parental help in finding binding fantasies. The child can find these elements himself in the world around him. Adaptive fantasy becomes "future planning." Where does this shift in cognition lead the child? In societies that permit some social flexibility to the late latency child, the attention cathexes go to the world outside the home, to an exploration of sources for the memory contents from which ethical decisions will be drawn. The beginning of an ethical individuation from the parents is set in motion at this point.

Thus, in the period of latency, two opposing processes are set in motion. At first, there is an incorporation and formalization of parental social attitudes, making possible the continuity of culture. Social flexibility, in the form of opening of the mind to social forces at odds with the family ethics, becomes available in late latency. Adaptability of cultures to changing environmental and technological conditions is made possible by this latter mechanism of adjustment. Thus, the events of latency should be studied by those with interest and concern for matters dealing with conformity to society's demands on the part of the individual, as well as the adaptability of societies as whole units to the stringent demands made by changes in environmental, political and religious climates.

ROLE OF FANTASY FORMATION IN LATENCY AGE CHILDREN

We turn first to the characteristic defensive personality structure that produces the state of latency in the latency age child (six-12 years of age).* This personality structure is made up of a consistent organization

---

*For a more extended study of this, the reader is referred to the author's book *Latency*, which deals extensively with the subject (8).

of those defenses which deal with anxiety-causing fantasies. Such anxiety-causing fantasies are expressions of drives which demand fulfillment in areas of function in which fulfillment is socially proscribed or biologically impossible.

The child who has the fantasy of wanting to have a bicycle, or anything else that is well within his grasp, need use no defenses. On the other hand, when confronted with intense fantasy wishes for those things which are impossible, he must defend himself from his own fantasies, in order to control the anxiety that is stirred up by frustration of, or the fear of punishment for, forbidden wishes.

For instance, it is really not possible for a latency age child to act on a wish to beat up a much bigger person, especially if the person that the child is angry at happens to be the father. No matter how intensely sexual excitements may be felt, it is not possible for these children to achieve any completely satisfying gratification of their sexual drives. Most are not orgastic. The children become overwhelmed by these realistically inexpressible fantasies and have to deal with them intrapsychically. If the defenses are not sufficiently developed or, if developed, not well implemented, the child's excitement reaches the point at which behavior becomes hectic, impulsive, and disruptive. When this happens, the child can be described clinically as either unable to enter a state of latency or experiencing an interruption of his capacity for latency.

By and large, fantasies that have to do with the relationship between the child and parents or other adults in the environment are those which are least likely to be fulfilled. Jealous, sexual, and aggressive interrelationships with adults, and siblings, provide the basic fantasy contents around which most of the defensive activity becomes involved. If one wishes to become more specific in describing the fantasies against which the child's defenses are mobilized, one finds a march of fantasies, associated with each passing year.

Each fantasy in its turn is based upon the new and unfolding problems that the child is brought to ponder by the expanding awareness that is the product of cognitive and social maturation. Thus, certain fantasies and types of fantasy activity characteristically begin at a specific phase of maturation. Their control relates to universally experienced phenomena. For instance, at the point at which the prelatency child is able to differentiate himself from the outside world and from his parents, his emotional reactions revolve about problems of separation and loss. When the child reaches the age of three, he is able to differentiate sexes. His thoughts turn to sexual differences. When he reaches the age of toilet training, his thoughts become involved with bowel and urinary control.

There are typical thought preoccupations and fantasies, which are processed during the latency age period as well. At the beginning of the latency period (five to six years of age), thought processes and fantasies revolve around certain experiences that the child has been dealing with since the age of three. At that age, he recognized that there was a couple in his life (his parents) who were leaving him out of things. They had activities of their own, in which he played no part. After this recognition, the child begins to develop fantasies about what the couple is doing. He begins to have fantasies of taking the role of one of the parents in whatever it is that the parents are doing without him. Whether these activities be sexual, going out together, or entertaining people, the child assumes the role of first one parent, then another, in a fantasy molded by his own interpretive recapitulation of the parental actions. This forms the basis of the well-known Oedipus complex. When a child reaches six, the capacity to experience guilt develops (with which we'll deal further) and fantasies of taking the role of either of the parents can become associated with guilty discomfort. The fantasy itself can no longer be experienced directly. Rather, it has to be dealt with through the use of certain defenses. Specifically, symbolic distortions help to hide the meaning of the original fantasy by creating a new, seemingly less dangerous fantasy upon which the mind of the child can dwell. It is characteristic of children in early latency to develop a much more masked way of thinking and fantasizing about the experiences and observations they are trying to master.

In a child younger than six, ideas are presented directly as in the following example. A four-year-old girl looked at her grandmother. She admired aloud a beautiful pin that the grandmother was wearing. The grandmother stated in a rather direct and matter-of-fact fashion, "When I die, I'll leave it to you." The child responded in equally direct fashion, in a manner typical of the prelatency child, "Oh Grandma, I know it's wrong to say, but I can hardly wait!" On the other hand, the latency age child, when confronted with such a thought, will activate defensive processes that will hide it from his own sight. The following vignette will illustrate. A boy of nine was in treatment for disruptive behavior in school. His mother had reported that his father had scolded and slapped the boy on the day of the session here described. When the child arrived for his session, I had expected that he would tell of his experience and of his anger at his father. Instead, the youngster spoke proudly of his father's new car, emphasizing its technical advances (e.g., wide track). None of the father's scolding or beating was discussed. The youngster eventually turned the content of his session to a description of a fantasy of a war in which he killed the general.

Characteristically, the unmodified (latent) fantasies that reflect the child's response to stress during the early latency years deal with taking one parent's place in the relationship between the parents (the Oedipus complex). The fantasies are modified to produce the form manifested in the clinical situation (the manifest fantasy). The child is constantly exploring identifications with each parent and living out the roles he has chosen in fantasy. When the fantasy is pleasant, it can be expressed in unmodified form.

When fantasy thought leads to fear of harm to self or to parents, it has to be distorted and modified if it is to continue as conscious fantasy. "Harm to self" means physical harm and the pain of uncomfortable affects. During the latency age period, children experience any situation which is humiliating or overwhelming as potentially harmful and something to be mastered. What are the possible techniques that a child can use to master overwhelming stresses? First, the child can do to another what has been done to him. When a child comes into a therapy session and attacks the therapist, it's worthwhile to ask the child when he himself has been so attacked. Second, the child can talk about the experience directly. Third, the child can develop a fantasy to master the circumstances of the situation that stressed him. The last of the three techniques takes emotional pressure off of the child without affecting the environment or involving other people. With it, the child can appear to be unaffected by stress and uninvolved with drives. The third technique provides support for the quiet, calm pliability that characterizes the child in the state of latency.

Oedipal fantasies, which combine elements of replacing the parents in their various roles (including sexual) with fear of retribution, reach a high level of intensity during early latency. They continue to populate the fantasy life of the individual thereafter. However, with passing years, additional fantasy contents appear. The contents relate to the problems the child encounters at a given stage of development. Their pertinence to the immediate problem at hand pushes them into prominence. This results in a deemphasis of Oedipal fantasy in the middle and late latency years.

From a clinical standpoint, one must be able to differentiate fantasies which are age-appropriate from these which are inappropriate in the evaluation of normality. For instance, when a child begins to feel a sense of independence from the parents at about seven or eight years of age, fear fantasies of being small, vulnerable, and all alone in the big world appear. This is reflected in fear of monsters. The monsters are symbols. They are masked representations of the fears. Beyond the age of nine or 10, the problem of passivity becomes a major point of issue. These children, who, unlike Peter Pan, want to grow up, would like to be able to take over and run their own lives. They object very much to parental interference. Of course, this becomes much more intense as they reach adolescence. However, one can see clear evidence of this independence in late latency. The child begins to defy the parent, and confronts the parent with a desire to make his own decisions. Often they say angrily, "Don't treat me like a baby!" When this happens, the child oftens finds himself threatened by the loss of the parents' love, since the parents want the child to continue to behave like that healthy, happy youngster who did everything he was told in early latency. At this point the child is readying himself in fantasy to confront his parents and to turn his adaptive energies from fantasies towards demands and actions that will have an effect on the world. Some children who are conflicted about confronting their parents in this way deflect the challenge into the form of a fantasy of defiance, with accompanying guilt and doubt. As a compromise to resolve this conflict these children actually develop symptoms (this will be discussed below), such as urticaria, paranoid ideation, and obsessional symptomatology. Therefore, if these symptoms are present in a late latency child, it is wise to look for conflicts with parents or the parent in the child's "mind's eye" over passivity, stealing, sexual play, greater freedom of movement and smoking. As the child masters the problem of independence from his parents, this symptomatology clears. These symptoms are usually transient manifestations which mark the period from about nine to 12 or 13 years of age.

The late latency child who is struggling for independence usually deals with a harsh, limiting, and condemning parent in his fantasies as well as the real parent. The limitation placed on the child by this fantasy evokes hostility in the child. This hostility toward the parent causes the child to distort the real parent, usually the mother, into a stick-wielding disciplinarian (the phallic mother). Direct confrontations between the child's wishes and the parent's wishes often generate a great deal of hostility. In the child who cannot articulate his demands in words, that hostility would change his world; symbols and fantasies are developed to produce a comforting inner world. Such fantasies find the defeated child in the role of a powerful baseball player or a famous movie star.

There are other characteristic fantasies which mark the latency period. These are related to the awakening of concern about sexual identity, which intensifies at the point that children begin a growth spurt, about nine years of age. Pinching in of the waist and evidences of sexual dimorphism create concern in a child who hasn't fully decided to be comfortable with the sex to which he or she has been assigned biologically. They worry about what they'll look like as adults. They ask whether they really are boys or girls. Boys wonder if they can turn into girls and girls wonder if they can turn into boys. These are all quite definite fantasies that can be detected in interviews with children in late latency. In addition, dawning sexuality brings concerns, curiosity, and worries about what sex feels like, what's right, what's wrong, how babies are born, and which of all the theories they know describes the real means of procreation.

Throughout the latency period the child does not have the realistic curbs on fantasy which would challenge his potential for being anything he wishes to be. Therefore, there is very little in the way of the hopelessness and depression that appears in the adolescent. By and large, as will be described later, depression in the latency age child is manifested more in terms of listlessness and somatic symptomatology than it is in hopelessness and depression.

Up to this point, we have dealt with the definition of latency and the fantasies that predominate in the responses of latency age children to the different tasks with which they are confronted. New experiences stir up preoccupations, thoughts and questions. Observation, understanding parents and teachers, and confidences shared with older children can often put the child's concerns to rest. Some of the preoccupations, thoughts and questions do not have ready answers and some bring the child into confrontation and conflict with parents. This leads to the requirement that these thoughts not be dealt with directly, but rather through fantasy. Often these thoughts, when dealt with directly, are disorganizing, and as such, they require either defensive maneuvers on the part of the ego of the child, or reassurance through direct communication with an adult. The basic approach in psychotherapy with these children relates to this process. The therapist may help the child to elaborate fantasies so as to master disorganizing experiences, awarenesses, or thoughts. The therapist may help the child to verbalize his concerns and then help the child to clarify his ideas or give reassurance that the child will learn to cope with these situations as he grows and matures. The therapist may help the child by strengthening those mechanisms of defense that are appropriate for his or her age.

Awareness, appreciation, and understanding of the typical fantasies that have been presented in the paragraphs above are necessary before pursuing an investigation of the defenses which are used by the child in coping with them. The clinically apparent personality structures of the latency age child are integrated systems of drives, thought preoccupations, and defenses. Manifest fantasies and symptoms are the products of the interaction between age-appropriate preoccupations and associated defenses. As noted above, once a typical preoccupation or forbidden wish has been defended against and has become unconscious, it is referred to as a latent fantasy. The conscious fantasy, which has been produced by the action of modifying defenses on typical preoccupations and wishes, is called a manifest fantasy. A child begins to develop feelings of guilt, feelings of fear, feelings of concern with loss of love, or even injury at the hands of the parents, when the child reaches the developmental level (four to seven years of age) at which he begins fantasying himself in one of the roles of the parents as a couple who relate to each other (the Oedipus complex). This is especially so should one of these thoughts appear directly in consciousness. The child therefore must deal defensively with the appearance of such fantasy or be overwhelmed with uncomfortable affect.

Typically, the latency age child defends by regressing to an earlier level. This earlier level is one in which fantasying about taking one of the parents' roles in the couple relationship is replaced by urges to enjoy messing, smearing, and the expression of anger. Once the child has regressed to this level (anal-sadistic), the child has a different set of mechanisms for dealing with his urges. When the child was two years old he could barely do much more than mess and smear or hold back his stool to get at his parents. During the latency age, he has more mature techniques for dealing with the urge to mess. One we call "reaction formation." With this mechanism, the child turns his urges into their opposites. Cleanliness, calm, and good behavior replace rage and messing. The calm and good behavior can further be supported by obsessional activities such as collecting. Latency children are famous for collecting. They collect stamps, pebbles (which are sometimes lined up and glued onto boards), and baseball cards.

Fantasy formation also serves as a defense. The fantasy forms are dictated by the attacking messing urges produced by the stage of regression. Children fantasy being attacked by others or cleaning things up and being the mommy who cleans up the house. These mechanisms bind the child's urges to such a degree that a period of calm and pliancy is produced, that is so marked that these children are described clinically as pliable, cooperative, and educable. Indeed, it is as a result of such latency mechanisms of restraint that the highly excited children that one sees playing in the playgrounds at recess can settle down so quickly in the school room to learn and study.

For a child to complete the work of the latency age period, these episodes of calm and educability are necessary. The work of the latency age period is the transmission of culture through the formal verbal syntaxes that are acquired through reading, school and parents. Parent-child interaction has an intense effect on the progress of the work of latency. The parent who spends time with his child and involves him in verbalizations that require increasingly complex levels of abstraction and memory organization increases his child's potential to acquire the knowledge and mental attitudes of his culture. Verbal neglect and intense interpersonal involvements which overstimulate the child tend to blunt the cognitive skills of the child or to limit the time and energies that the child has available for applying his full cognitive potential to the work of latency. A parental involvement that in actuality helps a child to live out the fantasy of being one of the parents (e.g., walking around nude, stimulating the child, taking the child into bed, or fighting, yelling and screaming as may happen between parents) can result in the child becoming too stimulated. A great deal of drive energy gets stirred up in the child of the sort that makes Oedipal fantasies extremely uncomfortable and mandates regression.

When regression occurs, drive, affect, and excitement intensify. The content of the fantasy involved with the drive, affect and excitement shifts to emphasize a minor element in the thought preoccupations. This usually involves the anal-sadistic (messing, teasing, stubbornness, negativism) elements. Alternatively, where these components are not readily detectable in the Oedipal fantasy, already available fantasy structures of the anal-sadistic sort are called into play or intensified. Such a regression can produce so great an intensification of the urge to mess and to misbehave and be negative, that the mechanisms of restraint are overwhelmed. Many children have no way of defending themselves against this, and a specific type of pathology appears which is the overwhelming of the latency state and a regression out of the state of latency. When this happens, the child becomes ill-behaved, hyperactive, and unmanageable within the classroom.

Children who are able to avoid this outcome are those who have a set of defense mechanisms which will buffer them against the need to regress. I like to call this ability the "structure of latency." This structure includes a set of mechanisms which shift the thought preoccupations of the child, who is being over-stimulated, into a substitute fantasy on an Oedipal level in which the child masters the stressful situation while masking the meaning of fantasy through the formation of symbols. In children who have an impairment in the ability to form symbols, there is a resulting impairment in the ability to enter upon and maintain states of latency.

The special organization of ego mechanisms that I call the "structure of latency" consists of repression (when ideas are pushed out of consciousness) followed by fragmentation of the fantasy in the unconscious area so that the fantasy, if it were to reappear, would be difficult to recognize. This process of masking is enhanced by symbolization of the fragmented elements so that the original contents would be even less recognizable and anxiety-provoking. This is followed by the development of a series of fantasies which are the manifest fantasies which represent the original latent Oedipal fantasies. These become the ordinary fantasies of playing cops and robbers, of playing house, and the rich and unique fantasies of the latency age child: trips to distant planets, battles with monsters, and robbers coming into the house at night when the child is going off to sleep. All have their origins in these mechanisms and form the normal neurotic fantasy activity of the latency age child who, in spite of the extraordinary degree to which he immerses himself in fantasy, is able to maintain a very realistic way of dealing with the pressures of school and his teachers when in the classroom situation. This is the normal condition.

There are three pathological conditions which arise as a result of impairments in the development and function of the "structure of latency" and the associated pathways for regression and displacement which have been described above. First, one can be confronted with the child who fails to enter latency at all because of a failure to symbolize. This prevents him from being able to attain the kind of defensive fantasy structures that are necessary to maintain a state of latency. Second, there is the condition of over-stimulation. At times, the energies conveyed through regression to the urge to express smearing, messing, aggressive, stubborn, negative attitudes are so strong that the structure of latency and the mechanisms of restraint are overwhelmed. Clinically, the child becomes ill-behaved and a creature of impulse.

In some children, failure to adjust at the level of anal regression using the mechanisms of restraint can produce further regressive responses.

These children may become involved in jumping rhythmically, tearfulness, depression, thumbsucking, hair twirling, television watching and overeating.

Third, one finds youngsters who have been able to develop the defensive fantasies of the structure of latency and to maintain them without resorting to regression when over-stimulated. However, the fantasies are insufficient to master the situation if left as fantasy alone. The child is impelled to act on the fantasy by using displaced gestures aimed at solving a seemingly unrelated problem.

The typical clinical picture which emerges for each of these states can be used to differentiate them. The child who has not entered into a state of latency usually has difficulty with verbalization and tends to be a quiet child who, when confronted with stresses, tends to become extremely anxious, reports no dreams, is able to participate passively in the dreams or fantasies of others, tends to spend a lot of time in front of the television set, and may do such things as awakening the parents at four o'clock in the morning to get reassurance about something that is disquieting or discomforting for him. He has very little capacity for delay. The second type of child, who cannot deal with over-stimulation through the fantasies produced by the "structure of latency," will tend to act out in an impulsive manner with destructive hostility, breaking things belonging to other children, often getting into fights. There is no formed fantasy guiding their misbehavior. One never knows from which direction the misbehavior will come. The third type usually becomes involved in actions which have fantasy form. An example would be the youngster who invited friends to his farm while his father was absent on a long trip and ordered his mother to hook the horses up to the buckboard so that all the children could go on a hayride. When the mother refused, the child hit the mother with a whip. The child had been moved too much into the parental role and couldn't handle it. A second example would be the child who had noticed that his peers all had their own bank accounts, and who took the bank book of a friend, signed out most of the money of his friend's bank account in his own name, and then deposited it in his name.

The developmentally correlated fantasies of the latency age period make their first appearance at times when developmental factors expose the child to reality situations which need to be mastered. In attempting to deal with reality situations which cannot be mastered in reality, the child must use fantasy formation or regression and restraint. The goal is to master intrapsychically what is otherwise impossible to master in reality. The child finds himself in a very frustrating situation. School work and athletics provide otherwise denied gratifications in reality. Therefore, a good deal of a normal child's energy and attention is devoted to these areas. The child pursues those areas which physically and mentally he is capable of mastering and avoids those that he is not capable of mastering. The healthy child deals with that which he cannot master through the mechanisms of restraint and the structure of latency.

Children who are on constant guard against being put in passive situations cannot pursue the reality goals of the latency age child. This is especially so when the late latency life situation and cognitive development introduce desires for independence and peer dominated pursuits and choices of activity. The children seek freedom from parental control. In addition, they are painfully aware of the inroads of a reality made of people more than twice their size. The angry affects engendered by this painful awareness fuel the creation of an intense fantasy life which may encompass most of their waking time. This diminishes their already meager capacity to deal with reality.

Those children who devote most of their time to trying to master situations which cannot be mastered in reality, and who put most of their energy and time into fantasy, produce a pathological state. The degree of their involvement in fantasy can reach a pathological level on a par with breakdowns in fantasy formation (see above). They become preoccupied with fantasy. They are constantly confronted with the blow to self-esteem that a youngster faces when he cannot master something in reality. Such children attempt mastery through comments such as, "Who's the boss around here?" or, "Nobody can tell me what to do, I know what to do," and, "You're not me, therefore you can't tell me what to do."

COGNITIVE DEVELOPMENT IN THE LATENCY AGE CHILD

Before we will be able to pursue more of what the latency psychic life is like in normality and pathology, it will be necessary to develop yet another theme. Our first section explained the ways in which fantasy is used to deal with reality situations; this section focuses on the ways in which reality is perceived, remembered, and understood. It is an error to believe that a child has an adult intellect, but has not yet achieved adult size. Most informed experts in the field of child development recognize that the development of awareness is far from complete as a child reaches the age of six. Nowhere is this developmental actuality more easily seen than in the drawings of children in the latency age, where the unfolding of concept and motor skill becomes undeniably clear. These developmental events have been amply documented by DiLeo (3) and Fine (4).

By the time the child is five years old, his motor skills have reached the point that he is able to copy a circle, a cross, a square, and a triangle. It is not until seven years of age that a child is able to copy a diamond. Copying is not the only area where maturational growth can be seen. If a six-year-old child is asked to draw a picture of a man in a boat (spontaneous recall), it is not unusual or pathological for the child to draw a picture of a boat which is transparent so that the entire body and legs of the man in the boat can be seen. This sort of transparency is usually acceptable until nine years of age. Beyond the age of nine, this type of production becomes quite rare and it is, if found in an adult, considered to be an indication of psychosis. In drawing the human figure, by the time the child reaches the age of six he is able to draw eyes and hands and legs by combining circles and vertical and horizontal lines. A certain amount of movement can be imparted to a drawing with the use of lines drawn in diagonals, as the child approaches the age of latency. The entire body of an animal or person is contained within a single outlining line at this age. From six to seven years of age, children begin to draw pictures in which figures are involved in an interaction with other figures. In effect, fantasy content with movement is introduced. At about eight and a half years, depth is introduced. For instance, when drawing a horse, overlapping of parts of a figure without transparencies begins to appear (4). Details, enrichment, and adornment become characteristic of the drawings. Depth through shading first appears at about nine and half years and becomes an important element in the drawings of 11-year-old children.

Cognitive growth can also be seen in other areas of development. For example, there is also maturation in the symbolizing function. The child at the age of six has been capable for quite awhile of producing his own symbols, with unconscious meanings. He is fully able to participate passively in the symbolic productions of others, as occurs in TV watching. Passive participation relieves the child of the responsibility and "guilt" for having thought up some of the ideas he is enjoying, which coincide with his own.

By and large, the symbols of the young child (aged six to eight and a half) are amorphous and distorted. From six to eight and a half, the latency age child fantasizes about amorphous, distorted, highly symbolized characters who are coming after him. From eight until about 12 years of age, the child's fantasies, especially persecutory fantasies, contain thoughts about real people. It is not until the child enters adolescence that real people in the real world dominate his fear fantasies.

Although figure drawings can be used as evidence of the ongoing development of cognition during the latency years, there is too much variability between one child and another for a timetable to be established which can be used for the differentiation of normal from pathological states. Fortunately, there are more reliable developmental indicators. Piaget has described the unfolding cognition of the child in terms of the child's ability to understand and explain natural phenomena (11). He has noted that before the age of seven, children have a tendency to explain phenomena on the basis of intuition, giving highly personalized kinds of explanations. At seven, a type of thinking which he calls "concrete operational thinking" begins. This is a form of abstract thinking in which the abstract operations of the mind can be brought to bear upon concretely present items of experience. This type of thinking predominates until about 12 years of age. It is characterized by the ability of the child to explain, on the basis of realistic considerations, a natural phenomenon. Thus, the child (aged seven to 12) will be able to recognize that a shadow is produced because a stick stands between the light and the place where there is no light. This is in contrast to the intuitive concept of the younger child that the shadow is hiding from the light because it's afraid. At 12 years of age, at the very tail end of latency, Piaget described a change in the explanation of phenomena. He called this new state "abstract operational" thinking. At this age, abstract thought processes can be applied to other abstractions. Ideas can be used to understand other ideas in the absence of concrete representations of these ideas.

The organization of the process of memory also undergoes developmental changes by which normality can be judged during the latency age period. From the first year of life, the content of a child's memory has been dominated by affects, motor experiences, and sensations. The very young child can remember what has happened in terms of the total experience (visual, kinesthetic, auditory, haptic), without the interposition of words. Words are only gradually introduced, about the end of the second year, through the child's ability to recognize that a word that a parent has used represents a certain pattern of action which is required of the child. The pattern of action is remembered, the recognized word merely being a signifier of the action. As the child matures, he is able to add more words. The sensory-motor modality remains predominant, however, in the memory for experiences. This is similar to the modality used when an adult learns to dance by being shown the steps without verbal communication. In spite of the absence of words, the adult remembers where and how to move.

By the time the child reaches the age of 26 months, words have become more efficient memory agents than the totality of sensory experiences. However, the words and ideas they represent may become associated with anxiety. Repression comes into play. This results in a split between the words and the anxiety-loaded ideas. This repression is supported by the substitution of less affect-charged words for the original words. In this way, psychoanalytic symbols are introduced during the development of the child. These are the symbolic forms which permit the child to develop the kind of fantasies that I have described as typical of latency. These more advanced language skills are not organized in such a way that they can be used as the predominant media for carrying memory into consciousness until six years of age. DiLeo, in his study of the drawings of children, has pointed out that a six-year-old child can draw far more than he can describe in words (3). Schachtel had noted this limitation in the prelatency child (9). There is an apparent shift to greater use of verbalization as a medium for memory at the onset of the latency years. Affecto-motor memory is deemphasized. If an observer considers memory and consciousness to be defined only in terms of verbal recollection of events, then the latency age child must be considered to have amnesia for the period before the age of latency.

It is, therefore, within the range of normality for a latency age child to have an apparent diminution in the acuity of his ability to remember global experiences and the prelatency events which have been limned in memory in sensory and affecto-motor, rather than verbal, terms. Yet another factor in this apparent amnesia for experiences before latency is related to the repression of the actual recall of events in words accompanied by the substitution of symbols which represent the original event. A major portion of the appearance of memory loss is associated with the shift away from the recognition of nonverbal memory as a valid medium for the recall of events. In essence, at about six years of age there is a shift in the predominant media for memory from the affecto-motor memory organization to an organization of memory which is dependent upon a rote verbal description of what has been heard or what has been seen.

Obviously, a great deal of detail is lost but a great deal of efficiency is gained. This permits a child to enter school and to learn by rote times tables, and such things as simple poems, spelling, writing and reading. It is not until the child reaches the age of seven and a half to eight that the ability to remember abstract aspects of experiences develops and becomes available for use at the behest of the society. Such abstract aspects of experience and understandings of the intrinsic nature of things and events then can be expressed on a motor level (modeling in clay), a verbal level (verbal description of events), or an abstract level (metaphors, poems, and theoretical interpretations). Any one of these expressions can then be examined by the subject or the observer and processed further to be reduced to a verbal concept or formula. Abstract conceptual memory (which entails the ability to perceive an intrinsic characteristic and to represent it in memory) can be applied subsequently to concrete things (Piaget's "concrete operational thinking").

This is important clinically. It is necessary in making interpretations or talking to a child to be sure that one approaches the child with abstractions which relate specifically to concrete events or affects. Directions for taking medication, for instance, which contain any kind of abstraction or thought process in which it is necessary to apply principles of judgment should relate to concrete situations and should be illustrated with examples. The application of the understanding and memory of intrinsic characteristics cannot be applied to abstractions until 12 years of age (formal operational thinking).

The development of the abstract conceptual memory organization is necessary for adjustment to the changing environment of an industrial society. It can lead to estrangement from one's fellows in a magically oriented "mythologically educated society." Therefore, the encouragement or discouragement of the maturation of the developmentally available potentials related to abstract conceptual memory is an important element in the evolution of cultures in the mass and the adaptation to culture in the individual. The development of this skill depends on the handling of the child during the latency years.

It should be kept in mind that a child can recognize the abstract similarities that help to identify many breeds as one animal in the very earliest years of life. Abstraction is not something that first develops during latency. What develops in latency is a refinement of the ability to perceive the abstract intrinsic nature of an object and then to recall the abstract concept spontaneously for later use. This characteristic first appears at approximately seven and a half to eight years of age.

Primitive societies tend to develop educational techniques which direct children away from the fulfillment of such capacities. In highly technical and industrial societies, such a memory organization is required for the proper handling of money, future planning, and an individual life style. Failure to achieve this psychological developmental level is a matter of pathological importance if progress in child development is judged from the standpoint of a cultural relativism which holds in high regard success in areas of endeavor which produce scientific knowledge, technical proficiency, material rewards, and life-preserving public health measures. Leadership qualities for such a society are lacking in those who do not have the ability to conceptualize, organize, and carry out plans and programs. The capacity to understand theoretical concepts, acquire a college education (as differentiated from a college degree), and the abstract principles upon which professions and businesses are based, also becomes unattainable. It is for this reason that many individuals who have been brought up in a more primitive social setting, who attempt to enter an industrialized society during adolescence, find great difficulty in adjusting. Only supportive and menial activities are available for them as employment when they attempt to become members of that society. Nurcombe has pointed out the failure of Australian Aborigines to achieve in this regard (7). Therefore, all cases of school failure or deflection from school activities which are brought to the clinician's attention should be examined, using tests for concrete thinking as well as tests to see whether there has been a failure to achieve the ability to comprehend the abstract kernel of that which is characteristic within a given situation.

SEXUAL DEVELOPMENT DURING LATENCY

It is a rare child in our culture who is involved in open heterosexual activities during the latency age period (6, 8). Most six- to eight-year-old children are involved in masturbatory equivalents. Direct masturbatory activity appears from age eight on. When a latency age child is fantasying and acting out the fantasy, using his entire body to express it, this is a masturbatory equivalent. In carrying this out, the masturbatory fantasy is hidden by high degrees of symbolization. The symbolization makes it difficult to see that there is a direct sexual content in the latent content of the fantasy. There are youngsters during the period of transition from latency to adolescence who lose the capacity for masking. They act out fantasies which have direct sexual and perverse components. For instance, a youngster made slashes in his back and experienced a sensation which he later was able to describe as similar to the sensation associated with ejaculation, when he could feel the blood flow. This would occur at times when he saw himself or another man dressed in an undershirt. Typically, in the shift to adolescence, the child goes from involving the whole body in acting out symbolized masturbatory fantasies to sitting quietly while thinking about sexual fantasies and directly stimulating the genitals.

THE DEVELOPMENT OF THE CONSCIENCE

There is a major developmentally guided reorganization of conscience during the latency age period. As a child enters the latency age period at about six, he normally becomes aware of the meaning of guilt. A child can be asked directly, "What is guilt?" and be expected to answer correctly. If the child does not answer correctly, the nature of the answer is important. Varying degrees of internalization of social demands and guilt (conscience) can be delineated by a study of the answers. The child, for instance, who says, "Guilt means that when you take something, you're afraid someone's going to punish you," still is experiencing an externalized conscience. The child who says that guilt means that you take something and you feel bad when you get caught, is a person who shows a corrupt conscience with a great deal of externalization. This is quite different from the normal sensation of guilt which first begins to be experienced at about six years of age, and which is described as follows: "When you feel like you want to do something, you feel bad because it's wrong."

The state of latency is ushered in when the child has the ability to know right from wrong and guide his behavior accordingly. This underlies the ability of a child to size up a situation and to appreciate when certain kinds of behavior patterns are expected. For instance, if a child sees a balloon in the classroom, he knows that the likelihood is that he can be more active and noisy. He can be on his party behavior. If there's no balloon and the teacher is standing there with a book in her hand, then that requires calm classroom behavior. The uproarious loosening of all restrictions that occurs in recess behavior is activated only at recess time, by the child who has the capacity to have in his "mind's eye," a behavior pattern appropriate for that given situation. The child who is consistent in his capacity to apply appropriate behavior to appropriate situations has what is called "behavioral constancy." Behavioral constancy is a necessary prerequisite for being able to attend school. It guides a child's mechanisms of restraint toward limiting acting out behavior. Piaget has carefully studied the development of conscience in latency children and has noted a shift from a "morality of restraint" to a "morality of cooperation." Under the "morality of restraint," the child shifts away from a world view in which he does only what he is ordered to do by his parents. Discussion with a child is seldom effective until he is about six or seven years of age. The parent has to tell the child to do what is expected of him, or the child does not respond properly. The child does not have sufficient behavioral constancy to be put on his own. Once the child is capable of latency, a morality of cooperation can be set up in which the child is informed on the basis of guilt and his capacity to judge right from wrong behavior, that there is a problem to be solved, that others before him have had to face and solve such a problem, and that the child, now entering into the more grown-up phase of latency, must be able to make decisions and solve problems in cooperation with the parents rather than in response to the parents' demands.

As the child approaches eight years of age, the conscience of the child is guided by a tendency to move away from parental influence and begins to seek influences from outside. At this point the individuation from the parent, which had taken the form in the first years of life of being able to recognize himself as different from the parent, now begins to move into a form which can be conceived of as relating to personal identity in terms of morality and moral entities. At about eight and a half to nine years of age, children enter into the phase of ethical individuation. They begin to establish a content for the part of conscience, that guides behavior, which is derived from sources other than the parents. These sources are primarily teachers and peers in school. The earliest appearance of this takes the form of the child who wants to wear something similar to what the other children are wearing or who wants to see a movie that the other children have seen, or to get some bubble gum that the other children are getting when his parents insist that these activities are not necessary or required, or for that matter, are even bad for him. The child begins to reflect influence of peers in his expectations and comes into conflict with his parents. There is likely to be inner conflict, anyway. The child is not only in conflict with the parent of the nine-year-old but also with the parent he remembers when he was six and seven or younger, the parent of the morality of constraint. The influence of these images of the parent of the young child is derived from the fact that they have a multitude of sources. In addition to conscious memory of admonitions, there are internalized images of the parent as an object for identification. These images are established in the following way. As the child begins to regress away from, and to repress as a means of dealing with, the Oedipus complex, there is a loss of the objects involved (parents). What results is the precipitation of an identification with the parents which becomes a very important part of the superego. To many, this is the strongest element in the superego. Certainly it serves to guide behavior during the return to conservatism that succeeds the period of adolescent rebellion which in turn was the product of ethical individuation. Challenges to the authority of these internalized early parental images are usually accompanied by a great sense of guilt and doubt. Children often resolve this through the development of symptoms. The symptoms are paranoid persecutory fantasies of robbers coming to hurt, urticaria, nausea, abdominal complaints, obsessive-compulsive patterns or tics, to mention the primary ones. These are usually transient. I consider it important to differentiate between early and late latency on the basis of the fact that in early latency, the child uses the latency mechanisms of defense to deal with conflicts with parents in terms of a wish not to cooperate. The late latency child's conflicts relate to a challenge of parental wishes by his own wishes which are based not merely upon negation of the parents' wishes, but on the positive contribution from outsiders (e.g., peers and teachers).

The essential paradigm of the shift from early to late latency is the transition in the fantasy structures of the child from fantastic fears of amorphous persecutors to fantastic fears of realistic persecutors. It is in the early moments of late latency that the child begins to be influenced more strongly by the real world. This shift marks the appearance of a momentum in maturation which will increase in impact as peer pressure and ever-increasing sexual drive energies lend their weight to a call that will carry the child away from the unfulfillable fantasies of early latency. This culminates in the ability of the maturing body to seek out objects in reality for sexual purposes and for the expression of aggression. It is during this characteristic late latency process that the structure of latency and its attempts to deal with reality through the development of fantasy are transformed into "future planning." In the transition to "future planning," the fantasy resolution of problems becomes planning upon which future actions can be patterned in place of fantasy as a primary private means of discharge. This replaces fantasy which could only serve as an autochthonous means of discharge.

During the late latency-early adolescent period, there is a shift in the symbolic forms used. The transition encompasses a move away from the use of symbols which express an inner feeling and are only slightly modified to entertain or communicate to others. In their place, there appear symbols and associated fantasies which are selected not only on the basis of their ability to evoke feelings and memory elements and resolve conflicts in the individual isolated from the world, but also on their ability to communicate and to entertain. Such communicative symbols are developed during late latency or early adolescence.

PSYCHOPATHOLOGY IN THE LATENCY AGE PERIOD

Psychoses and the Latency Age Period

Up to this point we have dealt with normal developmental stages during the latency age period as well as variations from the norm which can be considered to be subclinical pathology. Within the latency age period there are clinical manifestations of specific syndromes of symptoms which are recognizable as psychoses, neuroses and depressions. We therefore shall turn our attention at this point to the characteristics of these conditions as they occur in this age group.

Childhood psychoses will be dealt with in another chapter and will be only briefly mentioned here. By and large, these are either endogenous phenomena or manifestations of massive psychic trauma which have an existence of their own independent of the psychodynamic forces that produce the state of latency. Therefore, we are going to concentrate only on the differential diagnosis of states related to latency defensive structure and psychotic states.

The major time period in which difficulties occur in differential diagnosis is late latency (from 11 to 13 years of age). It is during this period (as noted above) that children begin to develop paranoid persecutory episodes in response to conflicts related to ethical individuation. This time period is also the age at which adult forms of schizophrenia (especially paranoid forms) first begin to be recognized, and at which prepubescent schizophrenia, the last appearing form of childhood schizophrenia, begins to be manifest. Differential diagnosis is difficult in identifying these conditions.

The paranoid episodes associated with ethical individuation are relatively transient, although they point toward the development of a borderline personality in adulthood. They do not point toward a major disorganization within the few months following onset of symptoms, which is characteristic of true schizophrenia. In all three pathologies paranoid persecutory episodes can occur.

In the paranoid persecutory episodes associated with ethical individuation, the child and the parent may report night fears and phobias
occurring from five to seven years of age. The child usually has a history
of a rich fantasy life and the persecutory beliefs can be seen as specific
fantasies of the latency age child, like those described when we spoke
of the structure of latency. Close history reveals a direct temporal association to conflicts accompanied by doubt or fear. For instance, a child
was told by her friends that she had to steal if she wanted to be a member
of their group. She didn't want to do this, became frightened, and
developed a fear that there were people in a gray van outside my office
who were going to kidnap her. When she was able to verbalize her
concern about being forced to steal and was able to talk about the fact
that she had taken something and then put it back, the episode cleared
completely.

The childhood schizophrenic manifesting his illness in prepubescent
schizophrenia also may develop paranoid persecutory delusions at this
time. This is characteristic of the natural development of the disease.
The normal child begins to project introjects at about four years of age
and so develops fear fantasies at that time (1). The childhood schizophrenic does not begin to project introjects until 11 years of age, so that
most of the persecutors are internal: voices from within, straw coming
from their joints, salamanders talking to them from within their throats.
It is not until they reach the age of 11 or so and begin to project out
their introjects that fear fantasies involving objects outside themselves,
external persecutors, begin to be perceived. These youngsters usually
have poor peer relations and difficulty in school. They are picked on
and differentiated from the others. Specifically, they have no history of
persecutory fantasies during the age period from six to eight years of
age. The adult form schizophrenia of early onset with paranoid features
is particularly difficult to differentiate from persecutory delusions associated with ethical individuation. History of adjustment during the
latency years gives little help. They may or may not have friends.

Adult schizophrenia of early onset is diagnosed on the basis of poor
relatedness, decline in or poor peer relationships, and a thinking disorder associated with predicate identifications supporting bizarre content. It is difficult to elicit a specific precipitating event, conflict or doubt
in temporal or demonstrated causal relationship to the appearance of
the persecutory fantasy. The temporal onset of these conditions seems
to be correlated more to the beginning of hormonal activity than to
ethical individuation. Cognitive maturation in the latency age child pro-

duces the ability to use abstract thinking in proverb interpretation at about 11 years of age. The application of abstract abilities to appropriate problems begins to differentiate normals from those who are going to have concrete thinking. Since the child with adult schizophrenia of early onset may have impaired abstract thinking, while the child with the persecutory delusions associated with an overwhelming of the structure of latency and ethical individuation has good abstract thinking, and develops abstract thinking along normal lines, it is wise to ask children with persecutory fantasies to interpret proverbs. Concrete responses are only equivocal indicators, while the presence of good capacity to abstract points strongly to a regressed structure of latency as the source of difficulty.

If there is any doubt, a child psychiatrist should be called into consultation on these cases. Prepubescent schizophrenia and the adult schizophrenia of early onset usually produce catastrophic intrusions on the person's life and development which can be modified to some extent by management, medication, and psychotherapy. On the other hand, regression in the structure of latency is a transient state reflecting ego weaknesses and/or adjustment difficulties.

Neuroses Associated with Latency

There are "normal" neuroses in latency which are characterized by the transient development of neurotic symptoms associated with periods of adjustment to expanding awareness and the appearance of new modalities of defense or the modification of well-established defenses. These have been covered in the above. They will be recapitulated here briefly.

As a child enters into early latency, the persecutory fantasies that develop contain amorphous monsters who haunt and threaten the child. These usually clear by the time the child is eight or nine years of age, but may persist, especially exaggerated during the period of ethical individuation. Although obsessional mechanisms are very much a part of latency it is not considered to be a pathological sign for a child to avoid stepping on a crack in the sidewalk for fear he'll break his mother's back. This is so even though there is a clear-cut obsessional thought involved. Compulsive touching, touching three times, or counting in three's are very often seen during the period of ethical individuation. These sometimes reach proportions which are so uncomfortable for the child and the parent that professional advice is sought. Fortunately these symptoms usually clear spontaneously. The availability of the mechanisms of defense that support such symptom formation presages the mobilization of obsessional defenses later on in life in certain cases. One should be on the lookout for this.

Hysterical symptomatologies are subtle in this age range, the most common being anesthesias of the genitals. Children who have experienced overwhelming sensations during masturbatory activities develop the inability to feel. This process may lead towards becoming ascetic as the child moves into adolescence. Since these phenomena do resolve in most cases, if they are discovered they should be followed, with a psychotherapeutic intervention called for if an ascetic, markedly inhibited character is detected developing as the child enters adolescence. To attempt to treat or to shatter this defense during latency would undermine the whole process of latency. Therefore therapy should not be undertaken unless the defense is associated in some way with an anxiety in and of itself which is disorganizing in the child.

Depression

Depression in latency has characteristics different from those seen in adults and smaller children. For the sake of this discussion, the symptomatology of depression can be divided into three groups. These consist of affects (severe depressive feelings, feelings of low self-worth, a sense of helplessness, depressed facies, crying and sadness), somatic symptoms (psychosomatic disorders and vegetative symptoms such as psychomotor retardation) and motivational impairments (listlessness, and loss of will to work). A latency age child who becomes depressed has far fewer of the symptoms associated with depressive affects than is usual with smaller children, adolescents and adults. Therefore, the diagnosis of depression is often bypassed in favor of a diagnostic nosology that takes into account the predominance of the other aspects of the symptomatology. The negative affects are not as strong in the latency age child who is depressed. Therefore the depression appears to be masked.

Depression during latency is usually manifested in somatic symptomatology (10). Affects do not dominate because the latency age child has the ego mechanisms of latency to deal with affects. Depressive states involve the evocation of affecto-motor experience associated with object loss and marked variations in sensory stimulation during the early years of life. The three differentiated components described above appear together as part of this process. Usually there are associated latent fantasies which are responses to object loss and experiences of humiliation. These are dealt with through the defenses associated with the structure of latency. This results in a lessening of the strength of the affective component in the depressive process. The fantasies that occupy the child during latency cause regression or repression because they are associated with affects which are uncomfortable such as anxiety, fear of loss of love, and castration fears. Affects activate the mechanisms of restraint and the structure of latency. The affect of depression has a similar effect. Therefore, affects of sadness and depression are experienced by a child only briefly. (An exception is mourning, when reality is so over-whelmingly strong.) Depressive affects are experienced only briefly, and then are processed by the structure of latency to the point that they become unavailable to consciousness. However, the other differentiated components of depression persist. Therefore, it is wise to be suspicious of depression in a latency age child whenever symptoms and signs appear clinically which relate to the motivational or somatic components of depression. The characteristic symptoms and signs that accompany depression in latency are generalized pruritus, sleep disturbances, eating disturbances, intestinal disturbances such as vomiting and diarrhea, a fall-off in school work, malaise, listlessness, and, to a much lesser extent, crying, sadness, sad facies, and an affect of depression; low self-worth and hopelessness are typically not found. The absence of hopelessness relates to the fact that the child's sense of reality does not develop strongly enough until age 11 or 12 for the child to feel that there cannot be a correction or turning around of disappointing processes or events. The latency age child usually has hope.

The events that precipitate and support depression during latency are primarily object losses. This usually involves loss of a parent or a friend. Loss is the key element. This is another factor that differentiates latency depressions from adult depressions. In adult depressions, the precipitating cause is often not detected. The severe depressions of childhood (i.e., those lasting more than three months) are usually specifically related to an event which can be detected merely by talking to the child and asking him about what has happened, or by getting a history from the family which then can be confirmed by the child.

CONCLUSIONS

In spite of a certain degree of neglect in recent years, the concept of "latency" as a stage in child development has persisted. I believe this relates to the fact that the term "latency" describes a discrete clinical phenomenon which has to be taken into account if the nature of child-hood is to be comprehended in its entirety.

The latency state has always intruded into the awareness of scientists in the form of unexpected findings which call for an explanation. The explanations for these findings have resulted in the various theories of latency. At first, it was noticed that adults in analysis did not bring to their sessions associations which reflect on the latency time period. This caused the pioneers of psychoanalysis to observe children of this age to see if the factors that accounted for this specificity could be discovered. At first, explanations of latency emphasized ego functions. Observations of the behavior of children soon revealed periods of calm, quiet, pliability and educability to which the term latency, originally associated with the fact that memories from this period remained "latent" in adult analyses, was then transferred. Calm was then equated with latency. At one point, a diminution of sexual drive was incorporated into this concept, markedly changing the meaning of the term "latency."

Recently, I have described a cognitive disparity between the memory organizations of the latency child and the adult. This disparity has resulted in difficulty in recalling the affecto-motor (recall through feeling and action) and symbolically distorted (recall through fantasy distortion) memory organizations, to which the latency child resorts in time of trouble, in the analyses of adults (8). Through the creation of fantasies embodying symbols and whole body activities (memory in action in latency age fantasy play) the child is able to maintain "latency calm, quiet, and educability" in the face of stress. There is thus an intrinsic link between the paucity of verbal memories of the latency period in adult analyses and the quiet of the latency state. The tendency to maintain calm by turning uncomfortable memories into symbols and play activities creates problems in associative retrieval of memories from this period.

The existence of a process during the latency years with consistent intrinsic characteristics defined in terms of ego functions (e.g. the mechanisms of restraint and the "structure of latency") can no longer be denied or ignored. This process of ongoing development can be defined in terms of normal and pathological aspects of both function and maturational elements. Clinically, normal and pathological characteristics can be delineated and can be of use to the therapist in evaluating the underpinnings of aberrant behavior. Explication and organization of these characteristics have been the purpose of this chapter.

REFERENCES

1. Bender, L.: Childhood schizophrenia. *Journal of the American Academy of Orthopsychiatry,* 1947, 17: 40-56.

2. Connell, H.: Depression in childhood. *Child Psychiatry and Human Development,* IV, 2. Winter, 1973, pp. 71-85.
3. DiLeo, J.: *Young Children and Their Drawings.* New York: Brunner/Mazel, 1970.
4. Fine, S.: *Heidi's Horse,* Pleasant Hill, California: Axelrod Press, 1976.
5. Hippler, A.: Latency and Cultural Evolution. *Journal of Psychohistory.* Spring 1977, pp. 419-439.
6. Kinsey, A. C., Pomeroy, W. B. and Martin, C. E.: *Sexual Behavior in the Human Male.* Philadelphia: Saunders, 1948.
7. Nurcombe, B.: *Children of the Dispossessed.* Honolulu: University of Hawaii Press, 1976.
8. Sarnoff, C. A.: *Latency.* New York: Aronson, 1976.
9. Schachtel, E.: *Metamorphosis.* New York: Basic Books, 1959.
10. Sperling, M.: Equivalents of depression in children. In: M. Sperling, *The Major Neuroses and Behavior Disorders in Children,* New York: Aronson, 1974.
11. Woodward, M.: Piaget's theory. In J. G. Howells (Ed.), *Modern Perspectives in Child Psychiatry.* New York: Brunner/Mazel, Inc., 1971.

6

Adolescence

VERNON SHARP, M.D.

Adolescence is nature's great second chance (7). In adolescence, every previous developmental issue reemerges from the quietude of latency. These developmental issues were not settled previously. During latency they simply went underground along with most external signs of conflict. However, when adolescence appears, the lid comes off. Everything again comes up for a vote . . . this time in spades.

Each child's total sum of previous experience now passes in review again. The previous pains of growing up are broadcast anew in all directions. The myriad lessons learned from traumatic and beneficial experiences with parents and siblings are reworked and reshaped into new configurations of coping skills. Instinctual forces from the oral, anal, and phallic-oedipal periods of development are all reactivated and reexperienced in thought, feeling, or action. The resulting collisions with the real world at home and at school, with parents, teachers, and peers, subject the adolescent to many new experiences. As adolescence progresses, the slag-heap of discarded childhood skills, values, attitudes, and aspirations grows larger, to be left behind permanently as adulthood is approached. Adolescence is a time of continuous learning, unlearning and relearning.

Viewed a different way, the ego of the adolescent becomes like a general who, besieged in battle, divides his forces for many different functions. Some of these are defensive, others adaptive, and still others restitutive in their results. Defensive functions such as denial and displacement of affect serve to protect the young person from an overwhelming flood of feelings. For example, in one moment he* may be

---

*In this chapter "he" and "his" will be used to denote "he/she" and "his/hers".

engulfed in a storm of despair. In the next, all is serene, although the presenting problem remains a festering sore. Fury at the parents may be displaced onto the classroom. The hapless teacher finds himself catching it in the neck . . . and in wholesale quantities at that. Those in the environment may suffer, but the adolescent gains a temporary respite from inner explosions.

Adaptive functions such as sublimation and neutralization of drive energies redirect these energies into more effective and socially acceptable channels and achieve more mature gratifications for the youngster. For example, the adolescent who last week was ready to murder his younger brother for the slightest transgression may suddenly manifest a burst of altruism and offer to babysit the next weekend—for free!

The restitutive functions serve to repair losses sustained in the battle to grow up. For example, adaptive "regression in the service of the ego," (20) serves periodically to slow and reverse the march toward adulthood so that the adolescent's ego may slide back to earlier modes of gratification and "take a breather" for a while.

The fluctuating interplay of ego functions and aspirations can be seen on the one hand in the hyper-independence of the young adolescent who distances himself from his family and has nothing but contempt for any offers of help. He insists on doing everything for himself. Yet, the next day or the next week, he may abruptly allow his longings for tenderness, comfort, closeness, and fusion with mother to erupt suddenly and acceptably where they are then lived out in a "return to the fold." Neither the adolescents themselves, nor their parents and teachers, know the next direction the adolescent's behavior will take.

For many young people, the crucial years of adolescence provide, perhaps, the richest opportunity for: 1) learning to feel fully and vibrantly; and 2) learning to speak and hear the language of self-acceptance (if restrictive and nonaffirming patterns of upbringing have thwarted these lively capacities). During adolescence each individual has a vital second chance to understand and integrate his emotions.

A TIME OF EXTREMES

Adolescence is a time of extreme behaviors. The excesses can include: drug abuse, social and sexual exploitation, violence, school failure, vandalism, isolation, alienation, and despair. On the other hand, adolescence is equally a time of great promise and joy. It's a time of optimism and eagerness, anticipation and ecstasy, new discoveries and high ideals. These extremes of personal experience are often hard to cope with.

However, with the inexorable unfolding of sexual maturation, explosive physical growth, new capacities for abstract reasoning and an unprecedented panorama of feeling states, the normal adolescent must surrender forever the ways of childhood for better or worse.

The adolescent has to cope daily with pressures and expectations across the entire spectrum of growth and development. These include all realms of human potential: social, cognitive, physical, emotional, sexual, athletic, recreational, occupational, cultural, and avocational . . . and I may have left out a few. Adolescents have to keep all these balls of fire juggled in the air at once. Is it any wonder we sometimes find them knocked-out? When an adolescent in therapy comes to a session depleted and exhausted, I may review this list with him. It's a helpful reference point from which to review his expectations of himself in each area and evaluate more precisely where the pressures of that day may be originating.

THE TRANSITION PROCESS

In order to move through the crossroads of adolescence, the young person must overhaul his outlook on life, his view of himself, and his entire personality. Everything he has built psychologically during the previous decade of his life must be demolished and reassembled. This process is essential before he can progress to normal adult status.

Pain accompanies all growth. Every step forward means the loss of past securities (35). The safety of the present must be abandoned for the unknown pitfalls and opportunities of the future. Previously established psychic structures, identifications, and modes of coping must decay and a new adult status must develop (5). With this deterioration, the adolescent experiences a sense of emptiness, sadness, and even despair. At times, he feels completely lost as though his life has no direction. His ideal self-image vanishes. The guiding principles of his earlier conscience evaporate. With the onslaught of inner turmoil and outer stimulation, his ability to cope disappears. Such losses must be followed by the healing process of grief and mourning. This "work of mourning" consumes his energy (15). He may feel drained and depleted, but successfully completed, his grieving becomes a healing balm. It lays the foundation for new identifications, feelings, and ways of experiencing his world. This process is painful and normal.

NORMAL DEVELOPMENT

Normal adolescence has been studied by Daniel and Judith Offer, using the concept of "normality as average" in selecting subjects (33).

Middle-class, suburban, high school males were studied. They represented the full range of adolescent functioning, from sickness to superior adjustment. The students comprising the middle of that range were designated as "normal." They were followed through high school and for four years or more afterwards.

Among normal adolescents in the study, the psychological transition to adulthood followed one of three patterns: continuous, surgent, or tumultuous.

The Continuous Growth Group

The continuous growth group grew continuously and easily through the formative teenage years. In the Offers' study, this group represented one-fifth of the total sample. They were purposeful and self-assured as they moved toward a sound adulthood. Their families had been stable throughout their lives. Their childhoods were unscarred by death or serious illness among their siblings and parents. Their genetic backgrounds and environmental surroundings were excellent.

Significantly, these young people had built a firm foundation for adolescence by mastering each previous developmental stage without apparent setbacks. They handled external events and inner feelings with flexibility, good sense, and a free flow of emotional expression. They felt comfortable with themselves and society. They had a clear-cut sense of identity; they could combine diverse experiences as stimuli for growth.

The parents of these youngsters encouraged their children's independence. As the adolescents were changing, the parents themselves were flexible in their responses to growth and change. Throughout their sons' adolescent years, these parents could alter their outlook and actions to meet the shifting needs of their children. They turned from the more protective modes of parenting used previously in their sons' childhoods. They displayed a resilience in letting go which facilitated grown-up behavior in their sons. The young men gratified their mothers and fathers in following parental behavior and standards. Both parties freely shared their satisfaction. The parents' pleasure with the sons benefited the youngsters in many ways. Chiefly, the sons were free to create their individual life-styles outside the family unit.

At home, the behavior in these families included much affection, respect and exchanging of values. Away from home, the young men lived lives similar to their parents' lives, but increasingly separate from them.

These young men related well to other people. They had close male friends and could talk easily with them. Relationships with girls became more important during high school and subsequent years. By the end of the four-year follow-up period, they had strong pictures of themselves as involved and sharing human beings. With few blindspots or limitations, they could engage in a trusting give-and-take association with young women.

They related well to themselves. A full sense of conscience guided their decisions; conflict was minimal. Their goals and ideals were distinct. In the family and community at large, they comfortably identified with older people of both sexes.

The Offers' subjects experienced many emotions, freely and easily. They knew and accepted their inner encounters with feelings such as shame and guilt. The young men acknowledged the events provoking these feelings and knew how to handle them.

These adolescents were actively attuned to their inner worlds of fantasy. Frequently, they would translate these fantasies into action. Their daydreams often portrayed their high self-esteem. With pleasure and anticipation, they would daydream about success in athletic, sexual, academic, social and other realms. Realistic judgment and an awareness of their limitations guided their subsequent actions. Repeated disappointments rarely occurred.

This group had its problems. They experienced a full range of life's blows, unexpected traumas, and an occasional conspicuous failure. Yet, as these challenges arose, their patterns of coping and problem solving approached the ideal. Their responses were active and open. To prevent an overload of affect, they used the ego defenses of denial and isolation of feeling. They could plan and wait for future satisfaction without undue pain and frustration. They felt fear, anxiety and depression, but not for long. As a result, emotional pressures were channeled into successful action. The young males appropriately expressed their aggressive and sexual impulses without self-destructive action. Aggressive feelings were accepted readily as healthy emotions and were clearly distinguished from hostility.

This group was composed of relatively happy human beings. Overt symptoms or chaotic behavior rarely disrupted their lives. They never sought treatment nor did the researchers suggest it. They represented that portion of the adolescent population least likely to seek out the helping professions. Thus, the patterns of their lives have been underrepresented in much of the research and writing about adolescent development.

The Surgent Growth Group

This group fits the typical adolescent image described in the professional and popular lay literature. They comprised one-third of the study sample.

The surgent growth group showed a cycle of ups and downs. "Three steps forward and two steps backward" (sometimes four or five steps backward) typify this group. The public image of adolescents stems from the emotional turmoil, mixed feelings and uncertainties of this group. At times, these adolescent males looked like the young men they were capable of being; at other points, they became the children they used to be. At times, this sliding backward looked as if it might be permanent.

These young people could not let themselves count on anything, either in themselves or from others. Their sense of value and self-worth wavered constantly. At times they tried to reach for sustaining contact and relationships with family and friends. Yet under stress, their self-destructive behavior cut off these vital sources of feedback. At these moments, they were unable to cope with their loneliness and despair.

Self-defeating actions were conspicuous but limited. These young men would defeat themselves by getting angry and blaming others. At the same time, they would ignore the problems they created. They were temporarily blind in seeking answers. Their families had suffered moderate degrees of severe illness, death or separation. Their genetic background and environmental surroundings contributed to their troubles. Within this group the study found slight birth injuries, learning disabilities, and mild physical limitations. Family financial hardships, neighborhood crowding and shifting family standards added to environmental stress.

These young men were more passive than the continuous growth group. They took less action. In swallowing their anger and assertiveness, they became depressed. At times, however, strong anger, fear or anxiety could be transformed into flexible action. Yet at other times, confronted by a crisis, such as the death of a close relative, they would repress their feelings and rigidly control their conduct. Following bouts of despair, inaction would spread into other areas of their lives.

These subjects had good friends. Yet the friendships were less constant than in the smooth growth group and they required more energy to maintain. Some of these young people found relationships with male friends more rewarding than contact with girls. Their increasing sexual thoughts and feelings frightened them. These males related to young women at a later time in their development than did the continuous growth group. As an exception, a small number experimented with sex early in high school. Possibly, this pursuit was an attempt to master anxiety. These sexual experiments sometimes led to increased self-confidence, but never lasted.

Divergent values, standards and opinions marked relations with and between their parents. Their fathers and mothers often disagreed on discipline, religion, and school work. Open conflict between parents and children was frequent but not overpowering. In some cases, the mothers could not admit their sons' independence. They had difficulty letting them grow and separate from home.

The boys had conflicting self-images, but they kept their long-range actions pointed toward their goals. Lack of enthusiasm, work inhibition and self-defeating action often blocked their paths. They expressed angry disappointment by repudiating parents, rebelling against teachers, and ignoring their own ambitions.

This group was moderately aware of their inner feelings, but they controlled self-expression tightly. Strong emotions could produce purposeful actions, but these adolescents retarded their own growth in various areas and for varying lengths of time during the study.

The Tumultuous Growth Group

The tumultuous growth group displayed more of the typical chaotic view of adolescence and represented one-fifth of the study population. (Another one-fifth of the study sample did not fit clearly into any one of the three main categories.) Openly exhibiting pain and anguish, the tumultuous group appeared troubled and overwhelmed by internal disorder. These youngsters have filled the mind of the public via the media. Whether in the depths of despair or bragging about their latest triumph, these teenagers were consistently in turmoil. On the one hand, they needed support for fragile attempts at creative actions, yet on the other, they defied and renounced every source of help. These young men desperately needed new ways to cope with inner and outer surprises; yet new strategies evaded them. The tumultuous growth group entered adolescence with the following impediments and deficiencies. Genetic and environmental backgrounds were profoundly more deficient than those of the previous two groups. Family turmoil was conspicuous. Some subjects had parents coping with painful marital conflicts. Others had mental illness in the family. In contrast to the study's primarily middle-class origins, the chaotic growth group had some subjects from the lower middle class. This class difference may have caused additional stress in

the school setting of the study.
rious problems outweighted satisfactions for them. They did not develop
sound methods for solving problems or relating to people. A high percentage displayed clinical symptoms and had received psychotherapy.
The young men had unclear self-images and experienced frequent disappointment.

Confusion, turmoil and distress were integral parts of this group's
emotional separation from their parents. Separation from their sons was
painful to the parents and evoked much conflict. The young men had
to fight to break away. Those who did not experience this strife of
breaking away were observed not to grow emotionally.

Parental values were vague or contradictory. Parents attempted to
impose their unclear values in arbitrary or authoritarian ways. To get
a sense of individuality, these young men would repudiate their parents'
values. A painful and humiliating power struggle would result. Mis-
trustful of adults, the adolescents turned to peer relationships with intensity. They depended on peer feedback for their self-image. Peer
associations could be sustaining briefly, but they invariably broke up. As
they did so, deep despair evolved. Unable to turn to their parents for
affirmation and feedback, these youngsters seemed lost. However, on
the positive side, they rarely resorted to severely destructive ways of
handling their feelings. In addition, they were able to experience a wide
range of intense pleasures as well as pains.

The subjects in this group dated at a younger age than those in the
first two groups. Their girl friends were mothering figures during the
boys' early adolescence. The boys themselves were more immature,
clinging and dependent, and some of them did not develop beyond this
stage during the study. Others developed their sense of independence
much later than the other two groups. At that point, they finally were
able to appreciate the individuality of their female friends as whole
people, not simple nurturing objects.

Many subjects in the tumultuous group were introspective and sensitive. In school, they shunned medicine, law and engineering. They
preferred the social and psychological sciences, humanities or the arts.
They had more work paralysis and psychological pain than others. However, they fell within the normal range as defined in the study population. They were almost as well adjusted in overall functioning as were
the other groups. In spite of their chaotic patterns, this group included
honor students and humane young people. They were simply more
conflicted at home, less happy with themselves, more critical of society,
and skeptical about their own futures.

The tumultuous growth pattern may be visualized as the continuous repetition of a cycle, a series of variations on the themes of dependence and independence (Figure 1). These themes are the central core of all growth and development (32) and begin with the child's inherent thrust toward maturity. This is always experienced by the child as the unfolding of new skills, inclinations, and urgings.

In adolescence, the explosion of independent strivings is conspicuous. This quest for independence has occurred repeatedly during previous growth surges and is certainly not new in the child's development. How-

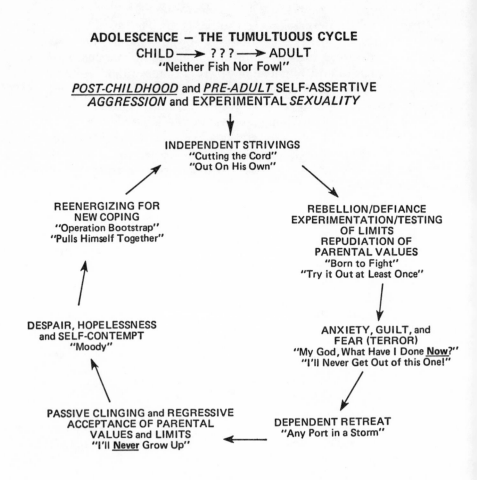

ADOLESCENCE – THE TUMULTUOUS CYCLE

CHILD ——➤ ? ? ? ——➤ ADULT

"Neither Fish Nor Fowl"

POST-CHILDHOOD and *PRE-ADULT* SELF-ASSERTIVE *AGGRESSION* and EXPERIMENTAL *SEXUALITY*

INDEPENDENT STRIVINGS
"Cutting the Cord"
"Out On His Own"

REENERGIZING FOR
NEW COPING
"Operation Bootstrap"
"Pulls Himself Together"

REBELLION/DEFIANCE
EXPERIMENTATION/TESTING
OF LIMITS
REPUDIATION OF
PARENTAL VALUES
"Born to Fight"
"Try it Out at Least Once"

DESPAIR, HOPELESSNESS
and SELF-CONTEMPT
"Moody"

ANXIETY, GUILT, and
FEAR (TERROR)
"My God, What Have I Done **Now**?"
"I'll Never Get Out of this One!"

PASSIVE CLINGING and REGRESSIVE
ACCEPTANCE OF PARENTAL
VALUES and LIMITS
"I'll **Never** Grow Up"

DEPENDENT RETREAT
"Any Port in a Storm"

Figure 1

ever, the degree of urgency and intensity *is* new, fueled as it is by the appearance of self-assertive, normal aggression and the new appearance of sexuality in all of its experimental forms. The new quest for independence supersedes all that parents and teachers have previously meant to the young person: nurturance, constraint, direction, rules, guidance, caring and warmth. The adolescent seems determined to do battle at any cost with the "cold, cruel world," the colder and crueler the better. This is accomplished by launching into a variety of risk-taking and challenge-seeking activities. The entire spectrum of defiance, rebellion, repudiation, and experimentation then ensues. However, it should be noted—and this is vital—the rebellion is *not* against the parents themselves, but against the nonaffirming, nonvalidating things they do. Rebelliousness, repudiation and defiance are *not* essential for normal adolescence, certainly in their destructive forms. The smooth patterns of parent-child interactions seen in the Offers' continuous growth group clearly demonstrate this. In each child, there is an irreducible core of fundamental human need which, when met by affirming (perhaps gifted!) parents, results in smooth patterns of unfolding development. The patterns of excessive stress and coping failure as seen in the surgent and tumultuous growth groups emerge only when parents are not fortunate enough to be the beneficiaries of ideal parenting themselves. They then manifest the strictures, deficits, and emptiness of their own lives. It is these elements against which their adolescent youngsters must rebel. This repudiation is vital indeed, if the adolescent is to find a fresh start for himself. Sadly, the less endowed adolescent is immersed in the social, environmental and genetic limitations which surround his parents. Likewise, his building blocks for his fresh start are limited to those coping skills and attitudes which he has learned from his parents by imitation and identification with them. If our society is to thrive we must provide adolescents with new options and access to novel coping strategies. Innovative and creative projects such as Outward Bound and high school peer counseling programs have succeeded admirably, but more are needed.

Proceeding with the cycle in Figure 1, we observe a variety of defiant, risk-taking behaviors. These in turn lead to increasing levels of guilt and fear, sometimes amounting to terror as the young person moves further out on the limb. As he finds himself further from the warm nest of home and its certainties, he may turn increasingly to the peer group for its support and whatever assets or delinquent and destructive standards it may have. Often, the pain of fear is masked by angry feelings and a face-saving return to repudiation and defiance.

Sooner or later, unless home is particularly barren, the adolescent will stage a dependent retreat, returning to the nest either willingly or unwillingly. He may figuratively wander in the back door as much as to say, "Well, here I am!" or he may be forced or dragged back after acting out in some self-defeating way. Typical of these latter maneuvers are school failure and truancy which involve the school administration as a reentry vehicle—or there may be acts of delinquency which involve the police and youth officers. Either way, the adolescent who is testing for a limit to his rebellion will utilize the authorities with which he clashes for an eventual return to the fold. However, this return to the fold, since it represents dependency, is anathema to such young people. It stands for "babyishness," childhood needs, and frightening regressive wishes for comfort and warmth—in short, all of the most feared levels of their own inner vulnerability.

Since dependency is abhorred and despised, returning to its expression represents a major loss, defeat, and failure of nerve in attaining cherished goals. These losses are accompanied understandably by feelings of depression, discouragement and despair. Here the young person is totally down and dissatisfied; everything is either wrong or not enough. There's grumbling, grousing and griping. Blame is laid in every direction. All this griping serves as a smoke screen hiding the innate need to experience dependency in order to charge his batteries before returning to the fray. As the adolescent becomes rejuvenated and reenergized, sooner or later "Operation Bootstrap" occurs, the adolescent picks himself up off the floor (that's what home is—a foundation, a springboard toward the future) and launches himself into the mainstream of his independent strivings. Thus the tumultuous cycle continues until adulthood supervenes.

The results of the Offers' study cannot be applied to all adolescents. The researchers studied only middle-class, suburban males. They made no attempt to study adolescent females or those in other cultural and socioeconomic groups. However, the study is detailed in this chapter in order to highlight two of its findings. First, the continuous growth group clearly demonstrates the presence in this country of a core of adolescent young people who do not have to experience patterns of painful adolescent turmoil in order to grow and develop normally. Second, there is a remarkable correlation between patterns of parenting and patterns of adolescent growth. In other words, for each of the three groups, the study demonstrates a striking correlation between, on the one hand, the degree of ease and effectiveness with which each group makes its journey through adolescence and, on the other hand, the presence or absence of healthy, skillful patterns of parenting and growth-facilitating hereditary and environmental factors.

Adolescence has a biological beginning in puberty and a social ending with the onset of early adulthood. The conspicuous physical changes of puberty thus define this epoch more dramatically than in any other phase of the human life cycle.

The age of onset of puberty varies over a normal range. Onset at 12 to 13 is average for girls, 13 to 14 average for boys. Late onset may occur normally at 15 or 16 years of age. This extremely wide variation in the normal is cause for great apprehension and self-doubt among adolescents. Witness the genuine agonies of the early-blooming girl who towers over her classmates in stature and whose curves and interests contrast starkly with those of her girl friends. Recall also the vitiating pain of the late-blooming boy who seems always to be saying, "Hey, wait for me!" Girls mature one or two years earlier than boys. This is easily observed in seventh-grade classes, where the girls have begun to blossom into young women and the boys all look and act like children, more interested in T.V. and touch football than in the girls.

Puberty is preceded by a sudden growth spurt of pubescence, roughly two years prior to puberty itself. This is followed by the characteristic physical developments of adolescence which unfold in an orderly sequence. For girls, this sequence starts with breast budding and is followed by the growth of straight pigmented pubic hair. Next, the preceding spurt of physical growth peaks and slows down, to be followed by the growth of kinky pubic hair. Then menstruation occurs and is followed by the appearance of mature axillary hair.

For boys, puberty begins with testicular enlargement and is followed by the appearance of straight pigmented pubic hair. This is followed by enlargement of the penis, early changes in the voice, the occurrence of first ejaculation, and the growth of kinky pubic hair. Next the rate of physical growth peaks and slows down, axillary hair appears, and the voice undergoes a more marked change. The final development is usually the appearance of hair on the chest.

The process of puberty takes about two years in both sexes. The climax of sexual development, marked by the first menses in girls, and the production of live sperm in boys, occurs somewhere between the start and finish of the process. Shortly after puberty, boys may have spontaneous ejaculations of semen during sleep (nocturnal emissions) often accompanied by erotic dreams. Depending on the emotional climate in the home, these "wet dreams" may or may not be the focus of concern for the young man. In girls, menstrual periods are usually irregular at first and fertility does not begin until about one year later. During this first year, adolescent girls who experiment with early sexual activity while ignoring birth control take a major risk. They can be lulled into a false sense of security about pregnancy before fertility arrives.

The onset of menses can be a time of rich fulfillment for the young woman. It signifies her arrival at the long awaited threshold of full womanhood and is an occasion for joy. On the other hand, depending on the emotional climate in her family, it can be a time of doubt and fear; this, in spite of the increasing availability of sexual information and acceptance of sexuality in contemporary society (38).

A noteworthy feature of adolescent physical development is asynchrony ("split growth"). This is defined as the tendency of the body's separate parts to grow at widely different rates. At various times, arms, legs, nose, chin, neck and other body parts may suddenly sprout individually with no regard for proportion or harmony. From this emerges the typical awkwardness and gawky appearance so especially noticeable in adolescent boys. In fact, the two sides of the body may grow at entirely different rates, although by the end of puberty they end up in balance.

In view of the great distress experienced by young people who fall into the "too early" and "too late" categories, it's often helpful to know that every adolescent belongs to one of several specific growth patterns, each of which follows a fixed curve. In fact, by assessing an individual's skeletal development, body build, sexual development and age, quite accurate predictions can be made of how tall a person will be and when he will get there. It can be reassuring to know that eventual adult stature can be predicted and that, unless endocrine abnormalities are present, the adolescent young person will sooner or later "arrive." However, for most adolescents at one time or another, everything will be totally "out of step" (37).

THE THREE PHASES OF ADOLESCENCE

Adolescence is divided into three separate parts, each with its major developmental tasks. Early adolescence begins with puberty and ends at age 15 or 16. Middle adolescence begins then and blends into late adolescence by 18 or 19 years of age. Late adolescence blends into early adulthood and as such has an indefinite termination depending on factors related to education, occupation, marriage, social expectations, and intrapsychic development. Each phase has a particular cluster of psychological features and developmental issues.

Early adolescence is the time of greatest upheaval. The relative tranquility of latency is fractured by the appearance of edgy discomfort, uncontrolled tension and inner turmoil not seen since the preschool years. Gone is the pleasantly compliant youngster who was easily taught and took suggestions readily. Suddenly present are the unpredictable explosions of temper, unexplained spasms of tears and hurt feelings, quixotic shifts of mood from the darkly sullen to the ecstatic and back. Emotions are everywhere and nowhere for very long. Neither the parents, the teachers, nor the young adolescent himself knows where he will be next. This is a time of deep-seated inner turmoil, of essential "Sturm und Drang" (19).

Early adolescence is also a time when the skill of the therapist is most sorely taxed. The young person's capacity for sustaining his human relationships is globally altered. Indeed, at this phase, therapy is adequate if the therapist can manage to maintain a continuous human contact, preparing the way for more fruitful work in later stages.

During early adolescence, the rejection of parents and other adults can be particularly violent. This corresponds with the adolescent's view of these adults as representatives of society's codes, values and constraints. All of these restrictions are summarily dismissed along with the devalued and "irrelevant" parents. More to the point, this wholesale saddling of the parents represents the adolescent's projection onto the outer world of the painful *inner* restraints of his own childhood conscience, with which he is having increasing trouble. When inner forces are bewilderingly at war, the vision of restrictions as coming only from outside persecutors is easier to cope with.

As the early adolescent turns from adults, there occurs at times a fanatic devotion to the peer group as a substitute source of values, security, and input. This can apply especially to peers of the same sex, whose views and advice are eagerly sought and whose manners of speech and dress are readily copied. At the same time, the struggle for peer acceptance can lead to increased loneliness, until relating skills are acquired and social connectedness is experienced.

Middle adolescence is a relief, both for the youngster himself and those around him. There is a greater sense of composure, a greater toleration for the differences and uncertainties of life, and a greater willingness to adopt a live-and-let-live philosophy. The middle adolescent becomes preoccupied and absorbed in himself. There is more energy available for work and relationships, especially of the try-it-on-for-size, maybe-the-new-one-will-fit kind. This applies equally to new relationships and to new ways of coping with the outside world. At this time, the young person becomes more available to himself, to his family, to his teachers, to his therapist. Although the peer group remains important, there is less slavish devotion to it. There is an increased capacity to step outside the peer group and see oneself as a separate individual. There's a new emphasis on the youngster's own growing sense of autonomy and individuality. Even so, something is missing. Relationships still tend to be impermanent, with a tenuous lack of depth, in spite of all the vitality and fervor which may flow temporarily.

Late adolescence is a time for "getting it together." It is a time of synthesis and harmony, of commitment and definite choices, of forcefulness and independence, and, most of all, of an abiding sense of "ego identity," as opposed to ego diffusion, to use Erikson's bipolar perspective (12). Many questions, such as, "Who am I?" and "Where am I going?" and "Who will be the boy/girl for me?" with all of their underlying loneliness and emptiness, are now supplanted with a different and more complete view of the self and the world.

The late adolescent by now is in college or pursuing an occupation. By necessity he has made definitive choices, though they may not be permanent. These include commitment to a future course of work or study and, implicitly, to a course for his life. Likewise, there are commitments to same-sex and opposite-sex relationships. They may be platonic or sexual, but they are based on a greater sense of self-certainty, self-awareness, and self-worth. This increasing ability to sustain patterns of love and work draws together the many strands of ego identity.

The developmental outline sketched above can be further illuminated by the "structural view" of psychoanalytic dynamics: namely, the interplay of energies from the three structures of the mental apparatus, the id, ego, and superego. During latency, the instinctual forces of the id are relatively quiet and the stable structures of the ego and superego efficiently direct the behavior and thoughts of the young person. With the onset of puberty a revolution occurs. The hormones governing growth and sexual development seemingly defy measurement. Their effects on the regulatory centers of the central nervous system are explosive. Sexual and aggressive impulses threaten to exceed available ego resources and superego controls. The balance between ego and id shifts.

The id takes over and takes off, as it were. The ego is left running behind while the contortions and turbulence of early adolescence errupt.

By middle adolescence, the turmoil subsides. The more mature and skilled ego catches up and becomes able to mediate successfully between id forces and superego restrictions. There is a global settling down, a process which is deepened and carried forward through the years of late adolescence. Individual defensive maneuvers, conflict resolutions, and coping mechanisms become shaped into more stable patterns. By late adolescence further learning of new (and unlearning of old) coping skills has progressed to the preadult stage of ego development. Except for minor alterations, these will serve the adolescent for the remainder of his life.

SEXUAL DEVELOPMENT

Sexual development in boys begins with the physical changes in pre-puberty and builds through the phases of normal growth toward that transition from boyhood to young manhood embodied in the first ejaculation. In the data collected by Kinsey and his group, this occurs through masturbation approximately two-thirds of the time and by a nocturnal emission (wet dream) in the remaining one-third (27). Where sexuality or body image is subject to severe conflict or if the wet dream is reminiscent of an unresolved issue around bedwetting, this can be a source of major distress. However, this does not usually constitute a problem since the first ejaculation is usually deliberately sought and since there is a growing social acceptance of the normal phenomena of masturbation in our culture.

Similarly, sexual development in girls begins with the physical changes of prepuberty, and builds through the stages of growth to the dramatic transition of menarche. This marks the physical achievement of the ability to have a baby and is an event of supreme psychologic importance.

During the twentieth century the onset of menstruation in Western societies has been occurring earlier by approximately four months per decade. As a result, a girl in the United States today is likely to have her first period almost a year earlier than her mother. Menarche occurs on the average at about 12½ years of age. This is probably due to improved diet and medical care. In most well-educated, middle-class homes today, menstruation is anticipated in advance. In addition, there is much discussion in peer groups. However, in spite of this openness on the surface, at other levels there are major reverberations in feeling and fantasy.

First, there is the entire spectrum of romantic and erotic themes of rebirth and awakening to womanhood, as symbolized in the myth of Sleeping Beauty. The possibilities of romantic attachment, blissful union, and feminine affirmation by giving birth to a baby in her own image are universal dreams of young girlhood. Then, too, there are the fears of pain and injury in childbirth, anxiety over loss of control of body functions, and the heightened symbolism of blood. In early adolescence, all of these elements combine in a turbulent mixture which requires continual reworking and synthesis as the young girl grows and develops toward a lasting sense of femininity and a secure identity as a mature woman.

In both sexes, the combination of physical development and positive life experiences builds steadily toward orgasmic capacity and a readiness for sexual intercourse. According to the Kinsey surveys, first intercourse has been experienced by about 50% of young people by late adolescence (28). Young men experience first intercourse at a younger age than women. Prior to late adolescence, most adolescent sexual activity is masturbatory. In boys, masturbation begins in early or middle adolescence and by late adolescence 90% of young men have masturbated. Failure to do so at this time is indicative of severe conflict over body image and sexuality. The average frequency of masturbation among males is one to three times per week, although the normal range is quite broad and variable. Compulsive masturbation is accompanied by a frequency higher than normal and is experienced with little pleasure. It serves to relieve pervasive anxiety which may have its roots in many areas of adolescent conflict.

Among adolescent girls, masturbation occurs in about 20% of the normal population during early adolescence, increasing to approximately 60% by late adolescence. The reported average frequency is once per week or less. Cultural expectations and pressures play a major role in encouraging or inhibiting masturbatory activity and there is wide individual variation. There is generally less gratification of sexual impulses through masturbation in girls than in boys. It is not unusual for women who have never masturbated to experience a full capacity for heterosexual pleasure in adult intercourse. It is highly unusual for a man to do so.

In therapy with adolescent boys, concern over homosexuality arises frequently, either as a presenting complaint or in the course of therapy. After exploring the origin and meaning of these feelings, one usually finds such boys having the same struggles with heterosexual fears as their peers, only more so. The more these strong heterosexual feelings are blocked in their expression through fantasy and sexual contact, the more they will revert to expression in homosexual fantasies and urges, particularly during masturbation. It is often quite difficult to determine whether homosexual feelings have their origin in heterosexual conflict or are truly indicative of an emerging homosexual identity. The best approach is usually a wait-and-see attitude. In the meantime, I often discuss with adolescent patients the fact that human beings are inherently bisexual. I remind them that during adolescence sexual feelings rub off on all relationships: male and female, past and present. Therefore homosexual feelings will have to be experienced at some level (either in or out of conscious awareness) by every young man who ever loved his father during childhood, and similarly, by every young woman who loved her mother in childhood. This does not mean that these young people will become lesbian women or gay men: It indicates that adolescent global feelings of sexuality are flowing in nonspecific channels.

At this point the psychoanalytic concept of genital primacy should be discussed. This is the last in the sequence of unfolding psychosexual stages organized around the erogenous zones, with its onset in early infancy and its development and consolidation through the course of childhood, adolescence and young adulthood. When genital primacy is achieved, the pregenital impulses (oral, anal, oedipal-phallic) find expression and satisfaction in adulthood with their original aims sublimated and now organized in the service of genital activity, pleasure, and function. Genital love is mature love, in which an overriding concern for the satisfaction and well-being of the love object becomes as important as self-satisfaction. Balint (2) has commented, however, that the mere presence of satisfactory genital activity does not ensure the existence of mature genital love in the fullest sense of the term. Achievement of mature genital love remains to be attained often throughout the remainder of the entire life cycle.

THREE PERSPECTIVES ON ADOLESCENCE

Adolescence may be viewed from three different viewpoints, the psychosexual (5, 13), the psychosocial (11), and the cognitive (34).

The psychosexual perspective views adolescence as a continuation of the evolutionary development of the instinctual drives. Sexuality and healthy aggression take a vital turn toward adult maturity. The inborn psychologic time clock now ticks at a more rapid, exciting pace. The struggle of the ego against the powerful emergence of new instincts forms the rich tapestry of adolescence in the literature and life of this period. We can appreciate the powerful forces, the stark drama, and even the foreboding of tragedy as seen in such classics as *Romeo and Juliet, Catcher in the Rye* and *Rebel Without a Cause.* The adolescent must traverse a wide expanse of unmapped and even dangerous psychological territory as he leaves the security of home and parents, surrenders his oedipal strivings, and moves into the world of his peers and its promise of genital sexuality and adult responsibility. The painful mixtures of feeling at this time are sometimes impossible to bear. The promises of womanhood and manhood are equally desired and dreaded. The goals of the future—vague, indistinct, and confusing—both beckon and repel. Repeatedly, mature adulthood seems both essential for survival and impossible to attain. However, with the passage of time and increasing experience, the young woman and man move steadily into adult life, hopefully armed with the consolidated coping achievements of adolescence.

Another perspective, the psychosocial, has been richly elaborated by Erik Erikson. This viewpoint comes from the tenets of ego psychology (as opposed to id psychology). As a result, Erikson's formulations are closer to the everyday conscious experience of educated people in Western society. His insights have become a valued part of our educational heritage. His overview of the "Eight Stages of Man" (11) pictures the crucial developmental tasks at each stage of the human life cycle from birth to late life. The stage of identity formation in adolescence is a crucial turning point in his view of human growth and development. Identity will be discussed later in the chapter.

The third perspective, that of cognitive development in adolescents, conveys another powerful force in the changing panoply of preadult development. Jean Piaget (34), the Swiss psychologist, has described the years of adolescence in terms of a vast expansion of the capacity for abstract thinking. This occurs within a specific framework: the sequence of cognitive stages he has described from infancy to adulthood. In adolescence, a shift occurs from the limited dimensions of the concrete stage of mental operations to the vastly more powerful stage of formal thought. The concrete stage, generally overlapping the years of latency, is logic of a very limited scope, relating to specific, concrete objects, which can be mentally manipulated. This makes it impossible to reason on assumptions, abstract propositions, and hypotheses.

Beginning in early adolescence, there is a dramatic shift to the formal stage in which the young person suddenly finds himself able to manipulate ideas in themselves and finds his thoughts no longer chained to the manipulation of concrete objects. He begins to understand abstract theories and concepts and is suddenly able to build ideal projects for the future. Unlike the child who is content to live in the present and the domain of everyday reality, the adolescent is capable of a passion for ideas, ideals, and ideologies. Suddenly, an endless variety of hypotheses can be made and from these, infinite conjectures become possible and further stimulate the intelligence of the adult-to-be. These intellectual transformations allow the adolescent: 1) to delay immediate action in favor of mental visualization and planning; 2) to achieve his integration into the complex world of adult interaction, which depends on formal thought; and 3) to conquer the fundamental intellectual operations which are the basis for education at the high school and college level. This literally is a "heady" introduction to the systems of thought and the flights of delirious fancy that become possible in adolescence.

However, the full capacity for the richness of formal thought is achieved by only one-third of the population. Many adolescents develop only partial access to formal stage modes and develop other strategies of mental coping. They rely primarily on developing a spectrum of standard methods for solving problems. A lifelong pattern of seeking to match new problems with the patterns of their standard thinking repertoire develops. Obviously, this method of reasoning in a complex and ever-changing society lacks the coping power of full formal stage functioning in solving the problems of living, but can be adequate for an average range of functioning which requires little creativity.

Two different styles of formal thinking emerge in adolescence: convergent and divergent. Getzels and Jackson (16) and Hudson (22) have described these dimensions of adolescent reasoning. Convergers tend to think in exclusive terms, seeking to find one common path, a single correct answer. Divergers tend to think inclusively, bringing in many possibilities and a broad range of elaborations starting with a given theme. Convergent thinkers tend to seek careers in the sciences: engineering, physics, and mathematics. Divergent thinkers lean toward the humanities and the arts. Effective thinking includes both modes but for most youngsters (and adults) one predominates. Because conventional intelligence tests and much of traditional education tend to favor convergent modes, divergent thinkers can have a hard time in conventional schools.

The pathology of thought in adolescent development deserves special emphasis. Let's look at schizophrenia and delinquency. Dulit (9) has observed:

> The special quality of *abstraction* is a prominent feature of thought disorder in schizophrenia. Because flights and excesses are so commonly seen among normal adolescents greatly caught up in but not yet adequately in control of this new cognitive capacity, one of the recurrent challenges for the therapist is to try to distinguish normal adolescent "irregularities" of thought from seriously pathological thought disorder. This can be a difficult distinction even for the expert. A diametrically opposed trend can be seen in delinquent adolescents where the capacity for abstraction is commonly greatly underdeveloped, in large measure a casualty of their overinvestment in direct concrete action: Thought is something one does while counting to ten. Delinquent adolescents rarely take that much time before acting on their impulses. As a consequence, they rarely find themselves troubled by second thoughts—usually, not even by first thoughts—about the probable consequences of the next move they're about to take (p. 200).

Therapy with such patients may very well be directed, in part, at trying to reverse that trend. This can be done by helping the young patient recognize the self-limiting consequences of his thinking style, then patiently reminding him of these insights when he encounters further obstacles. At the same time, cautious interpretations of underlying dynamic themes can aid him in his efforts to replace his impulsiveness with thoughtful problem solving.

CONSCIENCE

The word "conscience" is not used technically in the language of psychodynamics. However, since it is a familiar concept in the daily life of the adolescent and contains many elements vital to his understanding of himself, it is worth consideration and definition. The conscience may be viewed as a combination of two psychic structures: the superego (with its critical, punitive "right and wrong" restrictions on behavior—like the Ten Commandments: "Thou Shalt Not. . .") and the ego ideal (with its benevolent praise, rewards, and compliments—like the Beatitudes: "Blessed is he that. . ."). Whereas the superego has its roots in the earliest stages of development and assumes a definite form prior to latency, the ego ideal does not assume its definitive dimensions until after adolescence (5). However, its component parts are also present from infancy onward. All of the affirming, validating and approving experiences felt with other human beings merge to form the ego ideal. These are remembered consciously and unconsciously and are experienced inwardly as the actions and voices of crucial nurturing figures, notably the child's parents and especially the parent of the same sex. For example, in the normal development of a young girl, the major characteristics of her ego ideal are made up of her mother's characteristics, aptitudes, attitudes, and views of herself (both positive and negative). For boys, the ego ideal consists of the same internalized characteristics of the father. A tremendous amount of emotional energy is invested in the formation of the ego ideal during adolescence. This formation takes place via a growth sequence which recapitulates the prelatency sequence of parental ties. The sequence is similar in boys and girls. Let's consider the young girl.

In early adolescence, there is a return to the early stage of yearning for an exclusive relationship with her mother. Sexuality is now in the picture and rubs off on everything. Her yearning for her mother is no exception. Her internal longings are often kept at a very dim level of consciousness and may be accompanied by a jealous rivalry with her father. When this happens, he may be quite taken aback by a sudden explosion of anger from his young daughter when he and her mother are sitting alone on the sofa minding their own business.

However, no matter how close her ties with mother, the young girl's yearning for exclusive love cannot be permanently satisfied. As a way out of this predicament the young girl typically "chums" in her peer group among her same-sex friends. Indeed, at this particular time she seems constitutionally "allergic" to boys and may have no opposite-sex friends at all. This stepping-stone process moves from an erotically-tinged love of mother to an intensely energized love of other girls in her peer group and is referred to as the "homosexual stage" of early adolescent development. At the same time, for the typical young adolescent girl, the father is a much more practical object of her love and her wishes for exclusive possession. Indeed, in our culture, very intense father-daughter relationships at this stage are vastly better tolerated than mother-son relationships of a similar kind. Therefore, the young girl is able to transfer her love to her father while committing herself to an irreversible surrender of her wishes for exclusive possession of her mother. As middle adolescence approaches, the young girl moves beyond the stepping-stones of father-love and chum-love to unify her erotic strivings in a search among her peers for boys who appeal to her.

At this time, her unconscious admiration for an idealized image of her mother condenses to form her ego ideal. Subsequently, she will unwittingly use this idealized image of her mother as a point of reference when she makes significant choices among available boys with whom to experience her newfound inner standards and expectations.

The superego undergoes a parallel sequence of development. An "average expectable environment" of childhood has already shaped the superego of the latency age child. Established at the close of the oedipal stage of development, it becomes a stable code of conduct during the early school years. However, with the approach of adolescence the superego of childhood is doomed. The child's system of restraints and rewards cannot accommodate the new realities. These new realities consist of a rapidly maturing body, entirely new ways of thinking and feeling, and the growing potential for adult sexual behavior. The old superego has served its purpose and now must be dismantled. Its components must dissolve in order to create a new form, smoothly or otherwise. From new feelings and experiences the adolescent designs a new conscience for the future. He literally goes "back to the drawing board."

In early adolescence the powerful emergence of new thoughts and feelings brings with it a full spectrum of newly reactivated forbidden unconscious oedipal feelings and fantasies: in the young boy, desire for the mother and jealous resentment of the father. There is a similar evolution in the young girl. This combined assault by sexual and aggressive feelings upon the old superego standards, values, and restraints is too much for the ego to bear. The adolescent seeks distance from his parents in a defensive retreat from them. At the same time, his old values become fair game for his own scornful questioning and abrupt repudiation. As representatives of those old values, the parents come in for equal scorn and repudiation, to be replaced for a time by the standards of the peer group. Clearly the old childhood prohibitions against sexuality in all its forms and against many forms of aggression have got to go. However, this process is a severe strain on parents. It is difficult for them to maintain sufficient perspective to realize that the old values of childhood must be repudiated during the adolescent years to permit a full rich adulthood.

The parents often are aware of a real risk for the child at this time. They worry that the influences of peer group and culture will be destructive of reasonable and beneficial parental standards. Although the term is overused by frightened parents and teachers, there is such a thing as "bad company." Nevertheless, for the majority of youngsters, the best of what the parents represent tends to be preserved and self-destructiveness is kept to a minimum. Most young people, given the advantages of education and a stable unbringing, are wise and self-protecting in their choice of friends over the long haul. On the other hand, when environmental advantages are lacking and intrapsychic forces are predominantly destructive, major disintegration of values, standards and behavior will follow.

Deficient superego function results in a variety of pathological pictures. Johnson (23) has described the ways in which some parents unconsciously promote specific kinds of destructive behavior in their children in order to gratify their own repressed impulses. For example, the parent may harbor hidden wishes to steal or harm other people. When these behaviors are expressed by the child, they are silently reinforced when the parent fails to correct them. This parent-child interaction creates what she calls "lacunae" in the superegos of the children. These were children who in other areas appeared normal and law-abiding. This is but one facet of the broad spectrum of delinquency, but throughout that spectrum, which so plagues modern society, there runs a common red thread of superego depletion and deficiency.

Anna Freud (14) described the severe asceticism and the affectless intellectuality some adolescents may manifest. These are youngsters who are severely over-controlled . . . indeed, "conscience-ridden." They rigidly ignore, deny and vitiate their own instinctual evolution. These youngsters appear dreadfully afraid of the power and intensity of their erotic and aggressive wishes. As a consequence, superego restrictions get powerfully reinforced—so much so that if allowed to go unchecked, this process will block the development of entire realms of adult sexual feeling and self-assertion. Too much superego can be as destructive as too little.

In addition to the dangers of delinquency and asceticism, there exist the full range of neurotic inhibitions representing misplaced superego blockage of normal id and ego growth. Although the foundations for these disorders are laid down in early childhood, the potential for profound restructuring of the superego in adolescence is loaded with hope. However, the youngster will be denied his rightful opportunity for a full and rich adult life if the natural forces of growth or educational and therapeutic forces do not bring about the restructuring process.

IDENTITY

In *Childhood and Society*, Erik Erikson (11) formulates his "epigenetic" principle of growth and development in the human life cycle. He describes a psychobiologically predetermined ground plan which he terms epigenesis. This plan unfolds in each person's life in distinct, successive phases. In each phase of childhood, the parents transmit to their children the values, viewpoints, and predominant coping methods of the society in which they live. The parents, in turn, have learned the values and skills of a past society from their own parents. As the individual grows through childhood, his teachers, peers, and the media further affect his preordained psychic evolution. In due time, the epigenetic time clock confronts the young person with the developmental tasks of adolescence. It requires the adolescent to rearrange his genetic endowment, societal input, and life experiences. He reworks these building blocks to form a unique personal configuration: his ego identity. This global reworking constitutes the "identity crisis" of adolescence.

As the individual progresses through childhood and the teenage years, he encounters a wide variety of life experiences which may either promote or defeat his identity formation. Erikson conceptualizes five variants of identity formation. Hauser (21) lists these in outline form:

I. *Progressive Adolescent Identity Formation*
Continual increase in synthesis and integration of "constitutional givens, idiosyncratic libidinal needs, favored capacities, significant identifictions, effective defenses, successful sublimations and consistent roles."

II. *Identity Diffusion*
Continual decline in synthesis of identifications and ego functions. Diminishing senses of wholeness and continuity with self and community. Fragmentation.

III. *Identity Foreclosure*
Rigid self-definition. Lack of change in syntheses. Premature aborting of identity development. (Superficially resembles successful identity formation.)

IV. *Negative Identity*
Premature self-definition based on *repudiated*, scorned roles and identifications. Commitment to what is personally despised. (This approach to life seems to say, "It's better to be a bad somebody than a well-behaved nobody" (9).)

V. *Psychosocial Moratorium*
"Experimental" state. No firm commitments made. "Trying on" of roles and integrations. Characterized by flexibility, flux, but *not* disintegration.

Erikson (12) proposes this overview of the final dimensions of identity:

> Man, to take his place in society, must acquire a *"conflict-free,"* habitual use of a dominant *faculty,* to be elaborated in an *occupation:* a limitless *resource,* a feedback, as it were, from the immediate exercise of this occupation, from the *companionship* it provides, and from its *tradition;* and finally, an intelligible *theory* of the processes of life.

In the above, Erikson implies that the young person, in establishing his identity, has acquired both an all-encompassing world view and an inner, microcosmic awareness of a unique self. The latter includes all the individual's aptitudes and blind spots, strengths and weaknesses. Resolved and in focus, they are essential foundations for a dominant faculty or talent and its expression in the life work of the individual. Erikson further suggests complementary social, sexual, and age roles as support for the work identity. This achievement occurs only after the sweeping riptides of adolescence subside into the smoother flow of adulthood.

FAMILY REGRESSION AT ADOLESCENCE

In contrast to the relative stability of the family with a normal latency age child, the entire family of an early adolescent normally enters into a period of disequilibrium. An important aspect of this family instability is a temporary regression in sibling, marital and family functioning. This change reflects a creative return to earlier modes of personal experience and interpersonal behavior. Stage-specific for adolescence, this regression, when falling within the normal range, is circumscribed, temporary and centered around the adolescent. By mid-adolescence, this regression is resolved and leads to growth and development in family and adolescent alike. In normal families, this regression provides the empathic interpersonal framework within which family members can recognize, share and facilitate adolescent development. This sequence of shifting empathic interactions revolves around the adolescent's own regression. The sequence constitutes a family developmental crisis. Often it repeats in a creative way earlier stages within the life cycle of the family and its members.

Ravenscroft and his colleagues (36) studied hospitalized adolescents in a small, open door adolescent unit at the National Institute for Mental Health. They worked closely with the patients and their families in once- or twice-weekly, dynamically-oriented family therapy sessions. In addition, the parents had couple therapy weekly while the adolescent had individual therapy three times a week.

Siblings of the index patient were also observed as they approached, entered or outgrew their own adolescence. Some families repeatedly experienced severe difficulties with each new adolescent. This observation revealed a stage-specific family vulnerability for raising any child during the adolescent phase of the child rearing life cycle. Each new adolescent, in turn, found himself the center of the family's painful blind spots and unresolved conflicts. Other families had trouble exclusively with male or female adolescents, while still others had problems with only their first or last adolescent. Finally, some familes characteristically displayed a weakness when coping with either the early or late phase of adolescence; they did well with their teenage children otherwise. Throughout the NIMH study, several points were made clear. The adolescent's growth depended greatly on the entire family. The family provided a vital opportunity for full reawakening and reworking of his infantile dyadic and triadic conflicts. The family, with its individual and collective capacities and limitations, affected the constructive resolution of normal conflicts. The adolescent, too, was equally responsible for the outcome of these processes.

The parents were observed to undergo a personal reawakening and reworking of their own childhood and early adolescent conflicts. Clearly, the direction and degree of the parents' regression were dramatically shaped by their own previous adolescent experience. Regression was also influenced by their present position in the different stages of their own life cycles. For instance, a father's physical strength and his effectiveness in his career might be on the decline just as his son is discovering his own vigor and virility; a mother might be nearing menopause while helping her daughter as she enters her menarche. These crucial transitions set powerful feelings into motion.

The parents, responding out of their past experiences with their own parents, are forced to reexamine their current balance of coping maneuvers for sexual and aggressive issues in their own marriage. For example, the son might turn to his father for support and protection should his mother react negatively to his new sexuality. However, the mother's troubled feelings might also put a strain upon her husband and affect their relationship too. Then, the feelings of both parents become amplified throughout the family system, creating further disequilibrium. If the father also begins to regress, still more reverberations arise.

Under this strain, marital partners were often observed to shift in their degree of closeness to each other. They either moved further into or out of the marriage. Older and younger children were drawn into the vortex. The changes in family relations often reawakened the children's previously resolved jealousies and rivalries.

Often, within the changing tides of emotional balance in the family, new coalitions were formed as family members banded together. In these situations, the vulnerable, disruptive adolescent was at times scapegoated. At other points, he was teased back into latency life pursuits or pushed into premature adultlike behavior. Or, forced out of the family, he sought peer group relationships for their comfort and support.

Even the extended family was affected. Boundaries became indistinct between marital partners and their own parents. To their family of origin, they became either more rebellious, distant and independent, or closer and more dependent. This shift depended on the intensity and direction of their own reawakened and unresolved parental dependency needs. Grandparents were observed to become more involved or more removed. In either case, the changes reflected widespread disequilibrium and disruption of established family dynamics.

ADOLESCENT OBJECT RELATIONS

Kernberg has recently summarized the psychoanalytic theories of human object relations (26). This viewpoint offers new perspectives on the many-faceted world of adolescence. The bi-personal fields which provide the emotional nurture for all human beings are composed of the self and another person, a complementary human object. From the instant of birth onward, the quality of self and object interactions determines first the survival of the infant and later the fullness and richness of human existence. Kohut (29), in a related development, has formulated a psychology of the self in which healthy narcissism (self-love) is seen to exist throughout the human life cycle and to follow a line of development all its own, independent from but interacting with the lines of development of each other structure in the psychic apparatus. Central to his formulation is the concept that in order to thrive, the human being needs from earliest infancy onward a continuing input of emphatic affirming and validating experiences from the vital human objects in his life, most notably his parents. This implies, as well, that both parents be able to provide the infant and, later, the growing child with well-timed and optimum amounts of the nourishing frustration which serves as a stimulus to further growth. Further, each parent must have matured sufficiently by having his own healthy narcissism affirmed and validated to have developed a sense of separate individuality. From this follows the ability of the parents to affirm one another in a sustaining, loving relationship which allows the acceptance and affirmation of each offspring in turn. Kohut places great emphasis on the function of empathic mirroring (29), in both the parenting and treatment situations, as an essential modality for promoting optimal growth of the self.

What can these approaches bring to our understanding of adolescence? First, recall that the latency age child is firmly rooted at home, in spite of his many activities at school and with peers. In early adolescence, he begins to need distance from his parents since they serve as constant reminders of childhood and its now-disparaged wishes. He needs to move toward a supportive, like-minded peer group. This is a crucial transition point, during which deep emotional ties with age-mates can evolve—especially with one or two "chums" of the same sex. The ability to "open up" and share feelings and experiences, which this special protected relationship can foster, is of vital importance. On this phase can hinge the adolescent's development of subsequent capacities for closeness and true intimacy with others throughout his life. Because this budding new capacity is fragile it is painfully vulnerable. If it meets with callous or indifferent responses, it is susceptible to immediate regression, whereupon it may be covered over by protective, sullen withdrawal or superficial, shallow states of relatedness. The empathic, validating responses of understanding parents and receptive peers are vital if the bipolar fields of interaction in early adolescence are to generate sufficient nurturance for the emerging new aspects of personality. For this "reaching out" to continue it must be affirmed and acknowledged.

Same-sex peer group and chum relationships are typically followed by a phase of mixed peer group interaction, then dating in a group, and finally dating as a couple separate from the group. As the adolescent grows, parent-child relations gradually evolve to adult-adult relations. The young person permits himself to remain related to, but not bound to or emotionally dependent upon his parents. Concurrently, his capacities for sensuality, sexuality, sharing, and commitment all flow into the central stream of early adulthood intimacy. The ability to take risks, confident that empathic, affirming intimacy is likely to follow (and yet able to remain strong if it doesn't) is the promise waiting at the end of the stage of young adulthood. It can be approached with confidence only if the fullest possible sense of identity has been previously achieved.

The years of middle and late adolescence with their panoply of object relationships, conflicts, talents, defenses and changing character structures must coalesce to form a sound ego identity with an inner sense of cohesion and continuity.

Such an identity, fully realized, like most aspects of psychological maturity, is partly achieved by many, fully achieved by only a few. This winnowing-out process continues throughout the life cycle, defeated or enhanced by the quality of object relations in each successive stage. Those who reach the final stage, that of integrity versus despair (12) (when "one does not fear death because one does not fear life itself") . . . are few indeed.

ACTING OUT

The phenomena of adolescence include a variety of behaviors in which the dramas of human anguish and irreconcilable opposites are literally acted out on life's stage. The concept of acting out includes a variety of syndromes (3, 6). Two types will be discussed here. In the first, there is a search for immediate discharge of feelings via ill-considered and impulsive action. It's as though the id says, "go," the superego says, "no," and the ego is too weak to mediate between the two, so the id wins out. For example, repeated overeating in adolescence ("munching out") may be simply an unspoken statement that: "Nobody cares about me. Nobody feeds me. I feel empty and must feed myself, no matter what." In this instance, the actions may express feelings of boredom or unbearable loneliness. The anxiety which accompanies these feelings is then relieved in the action.

The second type of acting out is more complex. It combines fantasies from the past with frustrating or painful aspects of present reality. This type of acting out has deep personal significance and dynamic meaning. It contains more than the impulsive drive discharge of the moment. Often it is highly characteristic and predictable for a given youngster. It may involve feelings of omnipotence and magic. Specifically it is like a neurotic symptom: The behavior contains both the underlying needs *and* their prohibition. Both are expressed together at the same time and in the same act. An example is the boy who gets caught while shoplifting. On the one hand, let's say he feels empty, depleted, and cheated. He wishes in a childlike, magical way to get something for nothing. At the same time there is a desire to repudiate parental restraints, to experience excitement with peers, and to get relief from painful tension. On the other hand, he knows it's wrong, feels guilty, and expects punishment. This all gets expressed when he manages to steal impulsively in front of two clerks and three adult bystanders. They see it. He gets caught. The defiant thief becomes the hapless victim. Thus, he accomplishes both the expression of the forbidden wishes and their punishment at the same time.

All self-destructive adolescent behavior may be viewed as acting out. Experimenting with lethal drugs, seeking physical danger, provoking the police, and committing acts of destructiveness are all cases in point. In each instance, the actual consequences and dangers are denied or only dimly perceived. Intense pressure to express feelings and wishes without the action-delay which is typical of more adult behavior is experienced. The electrified tensions of the adolescent's inner world are denied and his outer world bears the brunt of his short-circuit.

In therapy, acting out is often used to get a message across to the therapist. For example, during a therapeutic crisis, resentful feelings about childhood restrictions or prohibitions may rub off on the therapist. The therapist is experienced as the restricting, nonaffirming parent. Painful disappointment and rage edge toward conscious awareness, but they're too hot to handle directly. They then get lived out in defiant rebellion against the therapist in the form of missed appointments. In actions, the missed appointment says, "You don't care about me and I'm mad! You never do what *I* want . . . I won't do what *you* want (i.e., come to my therapy session). I'm leaving and I'm never coming back! So there!" If a good relationship exists (and both the youngster and the therapist are blessed with that indispensable element of good fortune), the therapy continues eventually and the troublesome feelings can be explored so the young person can gradually come to terms with them. The ever-increasing mastery of the inner and outer worlds of adolescence may thus proceed.

DELINQUENCY

Action is the positive thrust of adolescence. The adolescent spans the entire action-spectrum from constructive risk-taking in new and more mature ventures to self-destructive and antisocial acting out. Either way, for good or evil, the adolescent is attempting to maintain his balance and find himself through action. We will now consider the destructive end of the spectrum.

Delinquency may be considered from two points of view: the social and the individual. The social perspective is the most obvious, since delinquency and criminality are defined by the society in which they occur. This concept of definition is important, because the scope of delinquency is relative to the culture and subculture in which it occurs. For example, delinquent behavior in a middle-class suburban subculture might be highly adaptive for survival in a war-torn country or a ghetto subculture.

The earliest studies of delinquency attempted to correlate antisocial behavior with such gross factors as constitutional body-type, mental retardation, brain damage, poverty, traumatic environments and delinquent companions. Although these correlations appealed to common sense, they never developed predictive power because for every delinquent found to have a significant constellation of these factors there always existed many other nondelinquents with exactly the same factors in their background. As the search for social factors became more explicit, researchers turned their attention increasingly to the family of the delinquent. The Gluecks (17) constructed an effective prediction table from a factor analysis of family background developed through sampling a large group of delinquent boys. By scoring five separate family factors they were able to predict the chances of delinquency with a high degree of accuracy. The five factors were:

1. Overstrict or erratic discipline of the boy by his father
2. Unsuitable supervision of the boy by his mother
3. Indifferent or hostile attitudes of the father for the boy
4. Indifferent or hostile attitudes of the mother for the boy
5. Unintegrated patterns of family cohesiveness.

These factors had not only predictive but also heuristic value. They could be used as specific foci for treatment intervention by institutions and individual therapists. Nevertheless, these factors, although highly predictive in a statistical sense, failed to account for individual patterns of delinquency and the occurrence of specific delinquent acts. For a fuller understanding of these dimensions of delinquency, consideration of individual dynamics is essential.

Among early workers with delinquent youth, August Aichhorn (1) stands above the rest. This gifted man evolved an approach to the understanding and treatment of delinquents which still serves as a model. He viewed delinquent acting out as a protective cover for painful underlying feelings of emptiness, loneliness and fear. In his treatment center in Vienna, he envisioned the bricks and mortar as a restraining physical environment peopled by a caring network of staff members constantly attuned to the fluctuating needs and self-destructiveness of the young patients there. He saw the delinquent strategies of young adolescents as essential to their balance and impossible to give up unless these youths were forced to do so in the presence of better and more humane alternatives. In this setting of caring confrontation, the delinquents' antisocial strategies could no longer operate. As these strategies fell by the wayside the underlying painful deficiencies of self-image and coping skills were laid bare. Aichhorn and his co-workers could then help these troubled youngsters cope with their core feelings and develop less self-defeating ways of living. This all took place in a firmly structured atmosphere. In other words, Aichhorn recognized that attacking the delinquent behavior directly was futile. To the adolescents in his care, giving up the delinquent behavior too soon would have meant unmitigated disaster. Why return to home and society, and the intolerable inner agonies experienced there, when these could be avoided by an array of delinquent solutions? Aichhorn was able to circumvent this logic by removing the effectiveness of the delinquent behavior and providing alternate models in the form of staff actions and decisions. In essence, he enabled these youngsters to resume the normal processes of ego and superego development. They were able to accept self-restraint and conform to more socially-approved behavior standards out of affection for the caring and emotionally-available members of the staff. These new motivations flowed from a desire to retain give-and-take relationships with these life-sustaining workers.

Patterns of delinquency are often diagnostic of the underlying areas of conflict. Sexual and aggressive acting out bears on hidden conflicts about masculinity and femininity. Chronic running away bears on the coexisting struggles for independence and recognition. Death-defying actions may betray underlying feelings of weakness, self-hate or despair.

In middle-class communities, certain delinquent adolescents bring major intellectual and emotional deficiencies to the school and peer group. Limited in their abilities to compete effectively with the more "with it" youngsters, they band together to seek excitement and to experience a uniqueness which is denied them otherwise. Defeating people (including themselves) and destroying property become prominent as they search for a sense of power. These particular youngsters often come from "hopeless homes" which are dominated by sterile, nonaffirming rules and regulations to be followed by rote. Here, the adolescent's words and actions are not viewed as information to be understood, but as errors to be eliminated and "straightened out" in order for the young person to fit a procrustean mold of preconceived behaviors. This type of devaluing interaction wreaks havoc with the developing self-awareness and self-esteem of these children. In such homes the parent-child interactions are found to be very similar to the Gluecks' five factors.

SCHIZOPHRENIA

Acute schizophrenic decompensation in adolescence occurs in vulnerable individuals with predisposing ego weaknesses. These young people simply are unable to surmount the major adaptive challenges of this period. The ego weaknesses seem to evolve from a complex mixture of inborn constitutional factors and peculiar patterns of family upbringing. For example, many of these youngsters from an early age seem unusually fragile, sensitive and shy. When such children are fortunate enough to experience an upbringing which is sensitive and solid, they then can become gifted adults. On the other hand, when their vulnerabilities meet child rearing patterns that are confusing, nonaffirming, overstimulating, or illogical, then the stage is set for later trouble.

The clinical picture varies, but often is characterized by ominous anxiety, panic states, sleep disturbance, violent nightmares, and the breaking down of barriers between the person's inside and outside worlds. There may be a dreaded sense of fragmentation of the self, a dissolving of personal meaning and significance, and a feeling that one should take action immediately about a problem of overwhelming proportions —without knowing the nature of the problem or the appropriateness of any actions. This clinical picture may emerge in two ways. It may represent an acute deterioration in the chronic course of "process schizophrenia," starting in early childhood or infancy, or it may represent a sudden personality deterioration in a youngster whose inner weakness and family pathology have remained masked behind a facade of normality.

When symptoms are acute and clearly psychotic, the possibility of drug ingestion of either hallucinogens or stimulants must be considered. However, when these are ruled out, the diagnosis of schizophrenia becomes clear and appropriate management is obvious. Often, however, one sees a much more vague and confusing clinical picture. The question then arises: Is it incipient schizophrenia or simply a transient manifestation of intense but normal adolescent disorganization?

The schizophrenic process can be detected among the following clinical components: a thinking disorder which seems deeper and more pervasive than normal adolescent illogic; flattened affect and the wooden rigidity which often accompanies it; global malfunctioning across a wide range of ego functions; persistence of malfunctioning over an extended period of time, beyond the normal ups and downs of adolescence; aimless and nonsensical behavior which doesn't "fit" within the adolescent's own frame of reference; extreme preoccupations which may be expressed in remote, bizarre or highly idiosyncratic terms; highly inappropriate feelings of fear, hostility, resentment or suspiciousness; and, finally, a feeling of fragmentedness, emptiness, or unrelatedness which often comes across as an "uncanny" or "spooky" feeling experienced by the examiner. Such young people are often impaled on the horns of the "need-fear dilemma" (8). In this state, the schizophrenic youngster experiences an inordinate need for other people or for institutional structures which will provide him with the regulation and organization that his own inner resources cannot provide. At the same time, the young person has an inordinate fear, even terror, of being influenced and malignantly controlled by the very people and structures which he needs so desperately. This bind can be accompanied by states of extreme withdrawal, which if unattended can progress to chronic isolation.

An Ego Function Assessment can be done in the office to clearly elucidate the clinical status of these patients (4). In this assessment, the micropathology of schizophrenia can be clearly viewed by observing the intactness or fragmentation of the person's functioning across a spectrum of 12 distinct ego functions. For example, such ego functions as reality testing, judgment, control of drives and impulses, capacity for object relations, formal thought processes, the intactness of the stimulus barrier, and the operations of autonomous and synthetic ego functions can all be quantified with precision.

What about the causes of schizophrenia? Lidz (31) has studied the central schizophrenic pathology of language and thought. In his research, schizophrenic patients invariably grew up in disturbing families. In these families, profound distortions in communication and expectation were learned by the children. From infancy, their growth seemed thwarted; their separateness and individuality of thought and feeling were ignored. Distorted patterns of thinking and coping resulted and were the only ways these children could survive. Lidz summarizes the emotional climate in which these youngsters became schizophrenic as follows:

The brain permits thinking but does not guarantee its rationality. Meanings alter in the service of emotional needs; and when a person's acceptability to himself and others is threatened, when no way out of an irreconcilable dilemma can be found, and when all paths into the future seem blocked, there is still a way. One can simply alter his perceptions of his own needs and motivations and those of others; one can abandon causal logic or change the meanings of events; one can regress, retreating to a period of childhood when reality gave way before the wish, when one felt central to the parents' care, or even to a time when one was not fully separated from the mother—and thus regain a type of omnipotence and self-sufficiency. In short, one can become schizophrenic (31, p. 10)

One of the irreconcilable dilemmas referred to above can be observed in the unbearable tensions created by the "double-bind" type of illogical communication seen in many of the families of youngsters who later become schizophrenic. For example, while in military service, I worked with a young service man in his late teens who had experienced a florid schizophrenic breakdown. He was an amiable young man who reconstituted quickly in the stress-free atmosphere of a naval hospital. Yet he would experience the process described by Lidz each time his parents would visit. His father was a remote, ineffective man and was often unemployed. His mother was an attractive, but childlike and seductive woman. She had experienced a barren and depleting upbringing herself and was quite over-attached to the patient, her only child. He had joined the Navy in a desperate effort to find a sense of himself away from home. On visits to the hospital his mother would coo over him in an infantilizing way, exhorting him to get well quickly, return to his cozy room at home, and resume his overprotected role with her. At the same time she repeatedly emphasized her expectation that he enter a nearby competitive college and accomplish great things. She seemed totally unaware that he had had extreme academic and social difficulties in high school and had been unable to graduate. Her mutually exclusive expectations were that he return to a state of infantile passivity with her and at the same time become an active achiever. This was his double bind and it drove him to complete distraction. For several days after each of her visits he would revert to states of babbling incoherency, interspersed with loud proclamations that he was a famous comedian well-known throughout the world. He would alternate between states of extreme agitation requring medication and nonstop monologues consisting of one-liners and sarcastic jokes, often told about himself. These were frequently truly engaging . . . except, tragically, the joke always seemed to be on him. In spite of the distressing clinical picture, the prognostic outlook for this young man was good as it developed. Treatment efforts were aimed at helping him see his mother's double-binding expectations as a severe disorder of attitudes and logical thinking. Its locus was entirely within *her* life-space, not his. A complementary therapeutic goal consisted of helping him to develop a sense of personal integrity and autonomy, entirely separate from home and parents. As his own individuality began to evolve, he was able to separate his picture of his parents from his core sense of himself. As he did so, he realized that he was not responsible for satisfying his mother's impossible dream nor was his life restricted to the limiting images of his father.

This case illustrates a type of family pattern from which schizophrenic ego weakness can grow. There are others in this complex field but they will not be considered here.

DRUGS: RITES OF PASSAGE VERSUS PATTERNS OF ABUSE

Drug use in adolescence may serve the psychodynamic purpose of avoiding unbearable inner conflict and painful feeling-states. As such, drug use is similar to delinquency and schizophrenia. That is, drugs temporarily can protect vulnerable adolescents from the tasks of growing up and can soften their sometimes overwhelming feelings of fear, despair, and loneliness.

For a full understanding of adolescent drug use, it must be remembered that drugs today are constantly available, easy to use, and serve many purposes. For example, in the face of fears of closeness and terrors of rejection, drugs may be "social lubricants" and vehicles of social acceptance. They can make up for a lack of mature self-confidence and independence. In these instances, drug use constitutes an important adolescent rite of passage to adulthood, and falls in the category of temporary experimental behavior which may be discarded easily, sooner or later. The use of drugs in these ways by adolescents does not necessarily imply that they are being *mis*used, any more than the use of alcohol by adults at cocktail parties necessarily implies its misuse in that context. The concept of abusive use will be discussed later.

In another context, drug use is a logical response to seductive media messages proclaiming "chemical cures" for the pressures and tensions so rife in contemporary culture. Advertisements of pleasure and happiness are seen as representative of the culture to which young people soon will belong. Youth buys the message and plays it to the hilt . . . unfortunately, with little knowledge or experience of the risks involved. The resulting questions logically go something like this: "If TV says just one of those nice pills brings such easy relief, what would happen if I took ten . . . or twenty? That might *really* be nice!" Or: "If cigarette smoking produces as much happiness as I see in the magazine pictures, why not smoke marijuana or something stronger? At least nobody says it causes lung cancer yet!"

At this point, a clear distinction should be made between the young people who may periodically experiment with the major drugs and those who gravitate repeatedly to them in their efforts to cope with the pressures of growing up. The casual users are to be found in many normal subcultures and are psychologically healthy for the most part. Those who depend on drugs to maintain their balance may be viewed as abusers. Further, drug abuse may be defined behaviorally as any drug use which causes adverse effects to the physical, intellectual or emotional well-being of the user. Physical and intellectual ill-effects are usually easy to define. Emotional ill-effects may be defined as any interference in the familial, interpersonal, economic or political spheres of the user's life. For example, interference in the familial sphere refers to any loss of respect, status, or privileges at home stemming from drug use. Interpersonal interference refers to loss of friendship or love relations. Economic interference occurs, for example, when allowance money is all used up for drugs instead of for food or school supplies. Interference in the political sphere of the user's life involves conflict with established community authorities such as the police or school administration. The crucial emphasis in the foregoing definitions is not on drugs per se, but on the detrimental *effects* of their use, a vital dimension which parents and others may fail to emphasize. However, if these effects are kept in the foreground, healing (as opposed to criticizing) dialogues become possible with drug-abusing youths, as in the following conversation with a youngster who's using marijuana destructively during school hours. Parent or therapist: "Look, you know I don't agree with your use of pot, but I could accept it as a difference of opinion between us, except for one thing, and that's the business of what's been happening to you lately. It's the *effects* of your using it at school that bother me most. I know lots of kids are into it but I hate to see you being hassled by your dean about your grades and cutting class. That makes you feel lousy and that is a big part of why I'm upset." Usually the young person confronted in this way immediately will minimize the effects, negate their importance to him/her, and repudiate the authorities involved. However, at least a nonjudgmental and task-oriented dialogue can start. Later on, this might lead to, "Look, I don't object to your getting good feelings, and lots of them at that. But, I *do* object to the self-defeating effects of your getting your good feelings from smoking pot in school. I've got to believe there are other ways to get them." Such confrontations tend to focus the adolescent's attention not on drugs, but on his self-defeating behavior as stemming from his own decisions and judgments about the risks and costs involved. These approaches have been used with increasing effects by parents, youth workers, and therapists.

Let's turn now to a consideration of the drugs themselves and how they may be abused. A detailed discussion of all the major drugs available to adolescents is beyond the scope of this chapter. Instead, it will be enough to say that they include the following: 1) the Sedatives/Hypnotics, including alcohol, the barbiturates and similar sedatives (Dalmane, Quaalude), and the minor tranquilizers (Librium, Valium); 2) the Narcotics (Codeine, Methadone, Heroin and others); 3) the Analgesics/Anesthetics (Glue Solvents, Chloroform, Phencyclidine ("PCP" or "Angel Dust"), Darvon and others); 4) the Stimulants, including the amphetamines ("speed"), cocaine, caffeine; 5) the Psychedelic/Hallucinogenic drugs, including LSD, MDA, Mescaline, peyote, psilocybin; 6) Nicotine; and 7) Cannabis, including marijuana, hashish, THC. This classification is based on the differing pharmacology of these substances rather than on such characteristics as degree of risk, frequency of use, or legal versus illegal status.

Let's look first at the psychedelic/hallucinogenic drugs. Early studies of these substances revealed a frequent "nothing to lose" attitude among chronic abusers (30). These young people often described a history of great conflict and anxiety accompanied by equally great feelings of hopelessness about ever getting free from anxiety. Sophisticated users of "acid" knew the possible risks—namely, prolonged psychosis, acting out of destructive tendencies including homosexual impulses and suicidal inclinations, overt expression of previously latent psychosis, and the occurrence of "flashbacks" defined as the reappearance of drug manifestations weeks or months later. Nevertheless, there was a "can't wait" drive to seek immediate relief. In the oral consumption of powerful, potentially lethal, mind-altering chemicals, many elements coexisted at the same time. An attempt at self-nurture, an illusion of autonomy and self-sufficiency ("I can take this trip all by myself") and an omnipotent grandiosity in tempting fate and defying death were all present. In addition, there was a repudiation of physical limitations and social restraints. Finally, there was a distorted exaggeration of the normal risk-taking urges of adolescence.

Many psychedelic/halucinogenic drug abusers experience specific con-
stellations of feelings between trips. They often feel a sense of inertia,
alienation, deadness and loneliness. There are patterns of fragmented
relatedness to peers and older adults, intense egocentricity, and a kind
of isolated, empty pride. The high of the trip serves to temporarily
relieve these feelings. It produces either a state of excitement, togetherness and relatedness, or a state of euphoria or sublime transcendence
in which negative feelings don't exist.

Adolescents with specific unmet needs, hungry yearnings, and coping
deficits seek specific types of drugs to fill their emptiness (39). The final
drug choice often is determined by a process of experimental trial and
error. For example, young people who feel small, inadequate and helpless will gravitate toward amphetamines, seeking the euphoriant effects
of "speed." Youngsters who feel lonely, isolated and cut off from other
people will move toward marijuana and related drugs which produce
subjective experiences of fusion and merger. Other adolescents in states
of chronic tension produced by the heightened sexuality and aggression
of adolescence may seek to "nod out" in a state of heroin intoxication.
This state produces a feeling of blissful satiation, a decreased involvement with external reality, and a profound reduction in the appetites
for sex and self-assertion. Acute heroin intoxication recreates an early
infantile narcissistic state. Phencyclidine (PCP) and its easily-synthesized
analogs produce an obtunded, "zonked out" state of diminished awareness with a variety of unpredictable consequences. Chronic users experience a complete range of feelings from rage or pleasant euphoria
to depression and hallucinations. Defensive ego structures change and
result in diminished capacities for managing feeling states. With higher
doses, behavior often becomes completely unpredictable and anything
may emerge.

In the abuse of drugs there is always an element of risk-taking. This
derives from the normal adolescent need to experiment with new challenges. However, active risk-taking must be clearly distinguished from
passive risk-taking. The experience of drug consumption is passive in
its motivation and outcome. This passivity reveals an underlying sense
of emptiness and absence of autonomy. It is thus directly opposed to
the active industrious independence and initiative of more adaptive
adolescent states.

Marijuana and alcohol are intimate parts of the youth culture. They
both produce a "mellow" mood of relaxed tranquility and loosening of
inhibitions. Both may act as mild euphoriants and produce an illusion
of control over feelings. Although they are frequently lumped together,

they are quite different. Alcohol is the more dangerous of the two. Its immediate toxic effects are more serious, it is specifically addicting, and its long-range ill-effects on health are proven. It tends to dull sensations and have a depressing effect in higher doses. Finally, its toxic effects on mentation and coordintion can of course be fatal.

"Pot" tends to have an alerting effect, making sensations sharper and more poignantly perceived. Its short- and long-range effects are less dangerous than those of alcohol. Although it can produce toxic states and become habituating for susceptible individuals, it is not addicting. It has become a part of the normal socialization process in various sub-cultures.

Controversies prevail over the physical and psychologic dangers of marijuana use. However, its use does not automatically lead to the abuse of the major substances. Youngsters who are psychologically predis-posed to major drug abuse will usually find their way there with or without the use of other substances.

LOVE

The love relationships of adolescence gradually unfold as the young person moves beyond puberty and into the subsequent phases of new relationships with himself and other people. These relationships are marked at first by passionate, intense, narcissistic preoccupation. That is, they are largely self-centered and reflect an urgent quest for need-satisfying objects of the moment. (10) A mirror-reflection of a major aspect of the self-image is eagerly sought. The young person responds eagerly to another who is sublimely similar. At other times, there is a passionate search for someone who can fill a particular emptiness or self-deficiency of the moment. Physical beauty, athletic prowess, and artistic skill are intensely admired and desired. These relationships are fleeting and temporary. They are based on the transient need of the moment. An entire spectrum of desires is represented. There are needs for input (affirmation and recognition as a person); for sharing of self through sameness of feelings; for output and release of sexual tension; for a target for aggressive urges; for stability and support either in the peer group or the adult world. There may be a quest for power and domination over a weaker partner who is less developed, emotionally or intellectually. Paradoxically, the young adolescent desperately searches for a kindred spirit one minute, only to drop him or her like a hot potato the next. This is then followed a week later by the voice of astonishment,

"I don't know what I *ever* saw in her!" Well, if the truth be known, he saw an aspect of himself which he needed to have mirrored at the time, but with which he no longer needs to identify. The astonishment over the intensity of a past relationship can be quickly followed by a sense of disdain for a discarded aspect of the self—a used-up, burned-out cinder of an old identification. The "old flame" is now a repudiated aspect of the self in the passing parade of adolescent attachments. The old friend, once the recipient of good self-images, now becomes a target for projected bad images and thus the object of contempt.

The present love object, male or female, can become too tempting because of intense sexual or dependency yearnings. There then follows a frightened or angry rejection of the present object. The feelings of warmth, excitement and attraction that accompanied the relationship are denied. As the rejection proceeds, feelings of inner vitality and richness are lost, to be replaced by a heartsick sense of emptiness at the core. This then followed by a period of withdrawn isolation until the sparks of yearning are ignited once more.

In some individuals, the transient "fickleness" of early adolescent love relationships is not outgrown. These young people do not progress to the more committed constancy of late adolescence and early adulthood (18). In their early years, they have experienced deficiencies in the development of their own self-image. They seem to lack a sense of inner wholeness and continuity ("healthy narcissism") (29). They often feel great distress when they perceive their use of other people to fill their empty spaces. It's as though pieces of their own inner world were missing and other people are used as replacement parts rather than loved for their own separate qualities. These young people feel an inability to fall in love or an incapacity to love anyone else but themselves. The long-range outlook for them is hopeful with appropriate therapies, but these will not be considered here.

Josselyn (24) has studied the love relations of late adolescence. She has observed the increasing frequency with which young people in their late teens have begun a type of relationship new in her experience. A couple will form a pair relationship in which there appears to be genuine love and commitment. There is sharing of financial responsibility and other obligations. Sexual relationships are monogamous and fulfilling. The young people behave to all appearances as though they were married and they appear to be happy.

However, in her clinical work with these adolescents Josselyn has observed a disquieting fact. Namely, the underlying motivations seem to represent developmental arrests. She observes repeated themes of fear of being alone, childlike wishes to be protected, and a willingness to give up sexual relationships or seek them from others if that would insure the protective aspects of the relationship for the future. Josselyn feels that these relationships are more symbiotic than mature and therefore serve to thwart growth toward self-realization and mutual autonomy. In these ways she feels these young people bring more liabilities than assets to their relationships. To what extent this will prove to be the case in long-term follow-up remains to be seen.

I would like to end this chapter where it began—with the theme of Nature's Great Second Chance—this time in the context of adult love relationships. The painful tasks and the exciting promises of adolescence carry with them the capacity to create a new adult with vast and creative potentials. In this newness lies the hope for rich and sustaining relationships, particularly the potential for love relations of the deepest sort.

The capacity to fall in love and remain in love represents the culmination of all prior developmental struggles. Falling and remaining in love require a union of full genital sexuality with the capacity to maintain a mature, deep, and lasting relationship—rare items indeed if the popular music and literature of every age are to be believed. Before this union can occur, the critical hurdles of each developmental epoch must be surmounted with sufficient resulting strength to serve as a foundation for all the stages to come. Adolescence is a vital keystone upon which rests the full range of adult capacities to sustain loving relations.

Kernberg (25) has postulated the evolution of these adult capacities through two essential stages. The first stage has its roots in the earliest months and years of life. It requires that the adult have a profound sense of basic comfort with the sensuality and body-closeness of infancy . . . that is, a capacity for trust and tenderness. This basic tenderness must then be intimately blended with the ability to see the loved one as a whole person . . . that is, a separate individual possessing a unique combination of good and not-so-good attributes (32). This vision of the loved person must be far more than the collection of transient, need-satisfying images characteristic of early adolescent loves.

In the second stage, the trusting body-pleasures of tenderness must expand into the capacity for full genital sexual expression. This expansion completely depends on the successful resolution of the crucial mother-father-child triadic conflicts of prelatency. From this success can flow that abiding sense of confidence, initiative, and self-worth so apparent in effective women and men and so fundamental to integrity in human contacts. Finally, the second stage reaches fruition (if all has gone well) when the capacity for genital love finds itself increasingly in harmony with an evolving inner capacity for deep, passionate and lasting attachment with another person—equally endowed and whole in his or her own right.

And that's not all. Balancing the joys and satisfaction of total relationships, there must be an ever-ready capacity to feel sadness for the relationships which don't endure and for the inevitable disappointments that punctuate the ones that do . . . an ability to experience and tolerate guilt, longing, and despair, plus the healing grief which must follow them; all of this without losing sight of one's wholeness and life perspective.

It's not an easy task. Adolescents need and deserve our patience and forbearance, our good humor (while trying to understand them better) and our good wishes for the long voyage ahead. With faith, hope, and love (plus a healthy dose of good luck) most of them will make it.

REFERENCES

1. Aichhorn, A.: *Wayward Youth.* New York: Viking, 1948.
2. Balint, M.: *Primary Love and Psychoanalytic Technique (On Genital Love).* New York: Liveright, 1965.
3. Bellak, L.: Acting out: Some conceptual and therapeutic considerations, *Am. J. Psychotherapy,* 1963, 17, 375-389.
4. Bellak, L., Hurvich, M., and Gediman, H.K.: *Ego Functions in Schizophrenics, Neurotics, and Normals,* New York: Wiley-Interscience, 1973.
5. Blos, P.: *On Adolescence: A Psychoanalytic Interpretation.* New York: The Free Press, 1962.
6. Blos, P.: On the concept of acting out in relation to the adolescent process, *J. Am. Acad. Child Psych.,* 1963, 2, 118-136.
7. Blos, P.: The second individuation process in adolescence, *The Psychoanalytic Study of the Child,* New York: International Universities Press, 1967, 22, 162-186.
8. Burnham, D.L., Gladstone, A.I., and Gibson, R.W.: *Schizophrenia and the Need-Fear Dilemma,* New York: International Universities Press, 1969.
9. Dulit, E.P.: Adolescence, In G. H. Wiedeman (Ed.), *Personality Deviation and Development.* New York: International Universities Press, 1975.
10. Eisnitz, A.J.: Narcissistic object choice, self representation. *Int. J. Psychoanal.,* 1963, 50, 15-25.
11. Erikson, E.H.: *Childhood and Society.* New York: Norton, 1950.
12. Erikson, E.H.: The problem of ego identity. *J. Am. Psychoanalytic Assn.,* 1956, 4, 56-121.
13. Freud, A.: Adolescence. *The Psychoanalytic Study of the Child,* New York: International Universities Press, 1958, 13, 255-278.
14. Freud, A., Instinctual anxiety during puberty, In *The Writings of Anna Freud,* Vol. II, Revised Edition, New York: International Universities Press, 1966.
15. Freud, S.: Mourning and melancholia. *Standard Edition,* 14: 243-258. London: Hogarth Press, 1957.

17. Glueck, S. and Glueck, S.T.: Prediction of delinquency. In S. Glueck (Ed.), *The Problem of Delinquency,* Boston: Houghton Mifflin, 1959.
18. Goldberg, A.: On the incapacity to love: A psychotherapeutic approach to the problem in adolescence. *Arch. Gen. Psych.,* 1972, 26, 3-7.
19. Hall, G.S.: *Adolescence: Its Psychology and Its Relation to Physiology, Anthropology, Sociology, Sex, Crime, Religion, and Education,* New York: Appleton, 1904.
20. Hartmann, H.: *Ego Psychology and the Problem of Adaptation,* New York: International Universities Press, 1958.
21. Hauser, S.T.: Self-image complexity and identity formation in adolescence: Longitudinal studies. *J. of Youth and Adolescence,* 1976, 5, 161-177.
22. Hudson, L.: *Contrary Imaginations,* New York: Schocken Books, 1966.
23. Johnson, A.: Sanctions for superego lacunae of adolescents. In: K.R. Eissler (Ed.), *Searchlights on Delinquency.* New York: International Universities Press, 1949.
24. Josselyn, I.: Implications of current sexual patterns: An hypothesis. In: S.C. Feinstein and P.L. Giovacchini (Eds.), *Adolescent Psychiatry,* Vol. 3. New York: Basic Books, 1974.
25. Kernberg, O.: Barriers to falling and remaining in love, *J. Am. Psychoanal. Assoc.* 1974, 22, 486-511.
26. Kernberg, O.: *Object Relations Theory and Clinical Psychoanalysis,* New York: Aronson, 1976.
27. Kinsey, A.C., Pomeroy, W.B., and Martin, C.E.: *Sexual Behavior in the Human Male,* Philadelphia: Saunders, 1948.
28. Kinsey, A.C., Pomeroy, W.B., Martin, C.E., and Gebhard, P.H.: *Sexual Behavior in the Human Female,* Philadephia: Saunders, 1953.
29. Kohut, H.: *The Restoration of the Self,* New York: International Universities Press, 1977.
30. Levy, N.J.: The use of drugs by teenagers for sanctuary and illusion, *Am. J. Psychoanal.,* 1968, 28, 48-56.
31. Lidz, T.: *The Origins and Treatment of Schizophrenic Disorders,* New York: Basic Books, 1973.
32. Mahler, M.S., Pine, F., and Bergman, A.: *The Psychological Birth of the Human Infant: Symbiosis and Individuation,* New York: Basic Books, 1975.
33. Offer, D., and Offer, J.: Three developmental routes through normal male adolescence, In S.C. Feinstein and P.L. Giovacchini, *Adolescent Psychiatry,* Vol. 4, New York: Aronson, 1975.
34. Piaget, J.: *Six Psychological Studies,* New York: Random House, 1967.
35. Pollock, G.H.: Mourning and adaptation. *Internat. J. Psychoanal.,* 1961, 42, 341-361.
36. Ravenscroft, K.: Normal family regression at adolescence, *Am. J. Psych.* 1974, 131, 31-35.
37. Stone, L.J. and Church, J.: *Childhood and Adolescence,* New York: Random House, 1957.
38. Weideger, P.: *Menstruation and Menopause: The Physiology and Psychology, the Myth and the Reality,* New York: Knopf, 1976.
39. Weider, H., and Kaplan, E.H.: Drug use in adolescence: psychodynamic meaning and pharmacogenic effect. *The Psychoanalytic Study of the Child,* New York: International Universities Press, 1969, 24, 399-431.

Part III

CONDITIONS AFFECTING THE COURSE OF DEVELOPMENT

7

Mental Retardation

MAHIN HASSIBI, M.D. *and* STELLA CHESS, M.D.

From an historical perspective, severe and profound retardation has always been in the province of medical concern, while mild and moderate retardation came into general awareness only after educators focused their attention on children who did not seem to perform according to the expectations of academic institutions. Tests of intelligence (or, more accurately, measures of intellectual potential) were first devised to help identify and track these students.

This dual background has made it necessary to keep the definition of mental retardation on the broadest possible basis, omitting from the clinical descriptive definition any reference to etiology, course and prognosis of this heterogeneous entity. One of the most serious drawbacks of this type of labeling is the degree to which information and misinformation about any one subgroup of retardates tend to be generalized and applied to the entire population of retarded individuals. For example, while a percentage of retardates will remain dependent into adulthood, financially and otherwise, on their families or on public facilities, others do become productive members of society and function independently. Furthermore, while some cases of retarded development are genetically determined, the majority of retarded individuals do not transmit their low intellectual ability to their offspring via genetic route. The mistaken idea that they do is evidenced by legislation mandating sterilization of retardates in several states.

DEFINITION

The American Association on Mental Deficiency (9) gives the following definition: *"Mental Retardation refers to significantly subaverage general*

221

intellectual functioning existing concurrently with deficits in adaptive behavior and manifested during developmental period."

Average intellectual functioning is reflected in I.Q. scores obtained by 50% of a random population on standardized tests such as the Stanford-Binet or the Wechsler Intelligence Scale for Children (WISC). When scores on such tests are below two standard deviations, "significantly subaverage general intellectual functioning" is said to exist. The standard deviation on WISC is 15 points and on Stanford-Binet 16 points. "Developmental period" covers from infancy to 18 years of age. Standard measures of "adaptive" behavior are based on items related to development of motor behavior, language acquisition and self-care. As the child approaches school age, he is expected to have control over his sphincters, to be able to feed himself independently, to use most of the utensils designed for eating, such as a fork, glass and spoon, and to dress and undress with minimum assistance. The age-appropriate level of "social maturity" is thus a reflection of maturation and learning. In school-age children, "adaptive behavior" is more loosely defined. However, self-direction, independent functioning and social abilities are important parameters and their level is indicative of the child's ability to comprehend language, to communicate with others and to have acquired skills necessary for social interaction.

CLASSIFICATION

Mental retardation, as reflected in the scores on the I.Q. tests, is divided into four categories:

	I.Q. on Binet	*I.Q. on WISC*
Mild	52-67	55-69
Moderate	36-51	40-54
Severe	20-35	25-39
Profound	11 and below	24 and below

Degrees of impairment in adaptive functioning also vary from mild to the extreme lower limit; thus, a child may exhibit only some degree of lag and limitation or, conversely, he may be totally dependent on his caretakers. Although the retarded child with higher intellectual functioning may be expected to acquire more social skills, the relationship between the I.Q. and the degree of impairment or attainment in adaptive behavior is not a linear one. Hence, the incorporation of the adaptive dimension into the definition of mental retardation is necessary to broaden the concept. The measured intelligence, on the other hand, has a fairly good predictive value as to the maximum educational attainment of the child. Consequently, children who are mildly retarded (educable) are expected to learn the basic skills of reading, writing and computation up to 5th-6th grade levels while the moderately retarded individuals (trainable) may learn to distinguish some written signs and do simple counting of numbers. With severe and profound retardation, expectation for academic learning is totally unjustified.

ETIOLOGICAL CONSIDERATIONS

Except for cases in which identifiable damage to the central nervous system can be held accountable for mental deficiency, the etiological factors in mental retardation are of associative and correlative natures. Causative links are postulated on the assumption that generalized impairment and dysfunction of the nervous system will limit the ability of the organism to select, order and incorporate appropriate stimuli from the environment; conversely, an improverished environment will fail to provide the type and degree of stimulation needed for the optimal functioning of the brain and its higher order activities. Among the associative findings with mental retardation, the loose category of "sociocultural and familial factors" heads the list, since it is known that a substantial majority (70-80%) of children with mild to moderate retardation belong to this group.

1) Sociocultural and Familial Factors

Low socioeconomic status has been long associated with a high proportion of mental retardation (1). In those countries in which a disadvantaged minority belongs for the most part to the low socioeconomic class, at times the finding of low intelligence has been attributed to racial genetic factors. However, such views have been largely discredited (15) and the relation between genetics of intelligence and genetics of mental retardation are independent of each other.

Among disadvantaged families, social pathology such as poverty, substandard housing and joblessness is coexistent with chronic medical and emotional ill-health of parents and children. Impoverished homes hardly provide a suitable ground for fostering children's intellectual growth because of circumstances of financial dependence upon social agencies, insecure occupations of parents, and/or emotional atmospheres replete with hopelessness, depression and frustration. Furthermore, as will be noted later, a variety of factors which contribute to causation of mental retardation are more prevalent among this group than among the general population. Some medical conditions such as lead poisoning are predominantly found among children who live in poverty; thus, impairment in intellectual functioning as a sequela of plumbism is more often noticed when the child comes from a disadvantaged background. Other conditions such as prematurity and low birth weight are more likely to produce neurobehavioral impairment when combined with impoverished socioeconomic status (20). Even though all factors involved in genesis of mental retardation in this sociocultural group have not been identified and studied, it seems logical to assume that the interaction between a mildly dysfunctional organism and the unsupportive, unhealthy and damaging environment is likely to cause an overall impairment in intellectual functioning.

2) Genetic Factors

This group of causation may be divided into two categories: chromosomal abnormalities and those abnormalities due to inborn deficiencies in necessary enzymes.

A) Chromosomal abnormalities:

Anomalies in chromosomes may involve the sex or the somatic chromosomes. Although cases of mental retardation associated with sex chromosome aberrations such as Turner's syndrome (XO) or Kleinfelter's syndrome (XXY) have been reported in the literature, low intellectual functioning does not always seem to be a part of the clinical picture. Aberrations of the somatic chromosomes, on the other hand, are frequently associated with moderate to severe degress of retardation. The best known example of this group of anomalies is Down's syndrome, or mongolism.

Down's Syndrome: The syndrome was first described in 1866 by Langdon Down, a British physician (7). Because certain facial features of these patients resembled the mongolian ethnic group, the terms "mongolism" and "mongoloid" were used to identify these patients. Current workers in the field prefer Down's syndrome as designation for this condition and previous terms have fallen into disuse.

The etiology of Down's syndrome was the subject of intense interest and speculation until 1959 when Lejeune and co-workers (13) noticed that cells from the tissue cultures of these patients showed 47 chromosomes instead of the normal 46 chromosomes. The extra chromosome was morphologically similar to the two pairs of group G chromosomes and thus the term trisomy 21 was coined. However, further investigations indicated that this was not the only type of chromosomal aberration to be found in karyotypes of these patients. In some cases of Down's syndrome, the extra genetic material is translocated to another autosome, for example translocation from #21 to #13, #14 or #15 autosomes. Furthermore, while in some patients all cells show the same chromosomal configurations, in other patients only a portion of cells in the culture are abnormal. This is termed mosaicism. The majority of children with Down's syndrome show a trisomic picture, with a very small portion revealing translocation and mosaics. There has been as yet no explanation as to why additional genetic material or translocation with loss of some portion of chromosomes has an adverse effect on the intellectual functioning of the afflicted individuals.

The incidence of Down's syndrome is one in every 700 live births. Maternal age is a contributing factor in trisomy 21 in that after age 35 the likelihood of a mother giving birth to a child with Down's syndrome increases until age 45, when the risk approximates one in every 40 births (11). Children with translocation usually have one parent with abnormal karyotype who is phenotypically normal. The incidence of Down's syndrome in the offspring of such families is about one in every four pregnancies. With present knowledge and medical technology, elimination of Down's syndrome or a major decrease in the incidence of this disorder is at least theoretically possible.

Diagnosis of Down's syndrome can usually be made on clinical grounds. These children show such characteristic features as hypotonia, slanted eyes, epicanthal folds, saddle-like low-bridged nose and a large protruding tongue. Retarded development becomes more apparent as the infant grows older. Language acquisition is particularly slow and speech, if it develops, is usually unclear. Chromosomal studies verify the clinical diagnosis and have a high rate of accuracy. Prenatal diagnosis can be made through amniocentesis.

B) Gene defects resulting in inborn deficiencies of enzymes:

In this group of disorders, absence or malfunction of a necessary enzyme results in abnormal metabolism with subsequent retardation in growth and intellectual deficiency. Parents of these children are usually heterozygotic carriers of the defective gene and the condition is not clinically apparent in them. However, for a recessive gene to be inherited a homozygous state is necessary which requires that the affected child inherit the defective gene from both parents. Under these circumstances, the risk of such combination is one in every four pregnancies. Although a large number of single gene defects have been identified, the most common one among this group is phenylketonuria (PKU).

Phenylketonuria: Phenylketonuria is caused by the absence of the enzyme phenylalanine hydroxylase which is responsible for transformation of phenylalanine into tyrosine. The condition occurs at the rate of one in every 10,000 to 15,000 live births (2). Because up to now these patients have not reproduced, these defective genes are lost from the population; however, it is estimated that 10 to 12 persons in every 1000 are carriers of the gene and, therefore, sources of future PKU in the population.

Because of tyrosine deficiency, these children usually have blond hair and blue eyes. The condition must be suspected and a diagnostic workup embarked upon in any mentally retarded child with blue eyes and blond hair. Laboratory tests include presence of abnormal metabolites in the urine and an elevated blood level of phenylalanine. Development of Guthrie Inhibition Assay for phenylalanine has made it possible for newborn infants to be screened for PKU; this mass screening has been mandated in some states. Although it has been shown that other clinical conditions may be associated with elevated blood level of phenylalanine, early diagnosis and institution of dietary measures have helped prevent the development of mental retardation. In general, children develop normally when the disease is recognized during the first few weeks of life and good dietary control achieved. Children who are diagnosed after six years of age do not seem to show any increment in I.Q. even after good dietary control has been instituted. Even though the restricted regimen of these children is not without the danger of creating hypoproteinemia, at the present time special diet is the only effective method of treatment for PKU as well as for some of the other disorders in this category of enzymatic deficiency impairing normal metabolism.

3) Prenatal Factors as Cause of Mental Retardation

These factors may be of a general nature such as maternal malnutrition, drug ingestion or toxemia of pregnancy, or they may be of a more specific nature such as viral infections, particularly during the first two trimesters. Prematurity of whatever etiology is shown to increase the risk of mental retardation in infants. Birth weight under 2000 grams, especially in the small-for-date newborn, increases the possibilities of damage to the central nervous system with subsequent retardation in intellectual development. When premature infants or those with low birth weight are born into deprived and disadvantaged families, the risk of retardation is appreciably increased.

Viral infections during pregnancy may cause direct infection of the fetal tissues with such consequences as congenital malformation, cerebral palsy, mental retardation, or fetal mortality. A number of viral diseases of the mother have been tentatively associated with various abnormalities in newborns. The deleterious influences of maternal rubella and cytomegalic inclusion disease have been clearly demonstrated (5). Congenital anomalies, including mental retardation, have been reported in 50% of children whose mothers contracted German measles during the first month of pregnancy, 22% during the second month and 6% during the third month. The retardation may be combined with other handicaps such as deafness and/or blindness, or it may appear in a child who is otherwise normal. Because infants with congenital rubella excrete the virus from urine and the pharynx for many months after birth, the possibility of continuous damage to the brain following birth cannot be excluded. At the present time a vaccine is available and future mothers can be immunized against rubella. Studies have shown that gamma globulin can prevent the manifestation of rubella in pregnant mothers. However, viremia persists after injection of gamma globulin and it is not yet known whether infants born to such mothers are completely free from the effects of rubella infection.

Cytomegalic inclusion disease remains clinically silent in the mother, but causes serious consequences for the fetus. Some infants are born with microcephaly, others show radiographic findings of paraventricular intracerebral calcifications. Hepatosplenomegaly and jaundice may be present. The virus, as well as inclusion-bearing cells, may be found in urinalysis. Although some infants with cytomegalic inclusion disease may totally recover, others show signs of neurologic involvement, including mental retardation and convulsive disorders.

4) Perinatal Factors

Prolonged labor and complicated delivery, whatever the cause, may result in fetal distress and anoxia and thus cause damage to the nervous system. Non-cephalic presentation and delivery such as breech or transverse presentation prolong the labor and may cause fetal distress. Anomalies of the pelvis, uterus or placenta are other factors which complicate the delivery. When the placenta covers the cervical opening (placenta previa), the infant cannot be born without prior tearing or removal of the placenta, and loss of blood may interfere with sufficient flow of oxygen to the baby, resulting in anoxia. Hazards associated with an umbilical cord which is too long or too short are well known. When the cord is too short, rupture and hemorrhage cause anoxia, while long cords may prolapse and be compressed between the pelvis and the head during passage through the birth canal and cause cessation of blood flow to the fetus (17).

5) Factors during the Neonatal Period

Newborn babies may exhibit signs of ill health immediately after birth. The general state of an infant's health can be detected by observation of his pulse, breathing, color, movement, etc. These observations were organized by Apgar (3) in a systematic way. Babies are expected to have an Apgar score of 4-10 immediately after birth. When the score is less than 4, emergency measures such as administration of oxygen are required in order to prevent anoxia of the brain.

Rh Blood Incompatibility:

Rh incompatibility between maternal blood and the blood of the fetus, if not treated upon birth, causes breakdown of the red blood cells of the infant and high level of blood bilirubin which results in damage to the nervous system (kernicterus). Exchange transfusion for bilirubin of more than 20 mg percent has lessened the risk of CNS damage and subsequent mental retardation for these infants.

Advances in obstetrics have reduced the risk of birth injury and anoxia and routine pediatric examinations of the newborn are of utmost importance in early detection and correction of neonatal conditions causing brain damage. However, intrapartum and neonatal factors are still contributing causes to the development of mental retardation.

6) Postnatal Factors

Infection: Infections of the central nervous system due to various agents may leave neurologic sequelae causing mental retardation. The most common organisms responsible for meningitis during infancy and childhood are Hemophilus influenza, meningococcus, and type B pneumo-coccus. Prompt and adequate antibacterial treatment is necessary to prevent permanent damage to the nervous system. Depending on factors related to the virulence of the bacteria, the adequacy of treatment, host conditions, and the severity of the disease, sequelae may be present or absent. In about 10 to 20% of cases, these children will suffer from residual symptoms such as mental retardation and/or convulsive disor-ders and behavior symptoms associated with chronic brain syndrome.

Trauma: Injury to the skull may range from minor episodes without any lasting consequence to major damage causing retardation and other neurologic symptoms. After a depressed fracture of the skull, the extent of the brain tissue destruction will determine the rate and the final outcome of recovery. A condition which has recently attracted much attention is chronic subdural hematoma associated with the battered child syndrome. In cases of child abuse, repeated trauma to the head, combined with parental neglect and reluctance to seek medical help for the child, or the physician's negligence, may allow subdural hematoma to develop and go undetected. Mental retardation, blindness and con-vulsive disorders may follow (16).

Poison: Although various poisons may cause damage to the nervous system, lead poisoning is by far the leading cause of such damage in this country. The source of lead toxicity is usually ingestion of lead-containing paint or inhalation of pollutants with high level of lead. Chronic toxicity and lead deposits in various organs, including the brain, cause retardation, convulsions and other symptoms of brain damage.

Endocrine: The major endocrine disorder causing mental retardation is hypothyroidism. Symptoms include lethargy, dry skin, sparse hair, and weight gain in spite of poor intake of food. Clinical diagnosis is verified by presence of anemia, elevated blood cholesterol and decreased protein-bound iodine in the blood. The stunted physical growth and concomitant mental retardation are preventable when hypothyroidism is identified early and necessary hormonal replacement is administered.

Anomalies of bony structures: Whenever the flow of cerebrospinal fluid between the ventricles and the spinal canal or its absorption into the bloodstream is obstructed, hydrocephalus will develop. In hydroceph-alus, mental retardation is due to atrophy of the cortex caused by the pressure of the excessive fluid within the ventricles of the brain. Hy-drocephalus may be caused by meningitis or space-occupying lesions, or it may result from congenital anomalies such as spina bifida and myelomeningocele. Early operative procedure is necessary in order to prevent brain atrophy. Another condition giving rise to such atrophy is craniosynostosis in which premature closure of sutures between various cranial bones causes the skull to exert pressure on the developing brain with damage to the cortex. The causes of craniosynostosis are not known. Although some operative procedures have been devised to remedy the situation, the results so far are not encouraging.

Metabolic disorders: Metabolic diseases which cause mental retardation are usually not recognizable during the first few months of infancy. It is estimated that about 5% of children with retardation suffer from diseases of metabolism which are usually genetically determined. Disorders such as various forms of leukodystrophies have remained essentially untreatable and lethal. When the condition can be identified before birth, therapeutic abortion remains the only solution.

7) Psychiatric Factors in Causation of Mental Retardation

Psychiatric and psychological factors may accompany mental retardation of various etiologies or be a contributing cause of low intellectual functioning. During the preschool years, psychosis of childhood is an important cause of low adaptive functioning and below average performance on tests of intelligence. Some researchers (19) consider early infantile autism to be a condition which may or may not be accompanied by mental retardation. Others, such as Kanner, view uneven performance on intelligence tests to be a primary symptom of early infantile autism. Whatever the underlying cause, the disorganization of behavior in early childhood psychosis will adversely affect the child's normal intellectual growth.

Other conditions such as disorders of central language function and communication, with their concomitant behavioral problems, may seriously influence the child's cognitive ability and present a picture resembling mental retardation. Behavioral disorders of varying severity are quite common among mentally retarded populations; they complicate the clinical picture and lower the child's limited capacity still further.

DIAGNOSTIC ASSESSMENT IN MENTAL RETARDATION

As is the case with all diseases of childhood, the diagnostic workup in mental retardation consists of a detailed history of the child's pre-, peri- and post-natal life, an investigation of the family background, and the clinician's assessment of the child-patient. While psychological testing is a mandatory part of a diagnostic evaluation if mental retardation is suspected, laboratory studies must be initiated only when the clinician finds signs and symptoms compatible with certain diagnostic entities.

The first step in evaluation is an interview with parents or other caretakers of the child. Presence of both parents gives valuable data as to the nature of parental interactions, their agreement or dissonance about child-rearing practices, the quality of the emotional support or affective distancing which the child receives within his family. Finally, any special needs of each parent in regard to the physician's role and function are usually indicated or inferred by the astute clinician. Furthermore, each parent may be more knowledgeable about his or her own family background and thus contribute to a more accurate picture of the child's genetic heritage. Parents' ages, as well as the ages of siblings and their level of academic and occupational achievements, are among the identifying data which must be collected on every child. Maternal age at the time of pregnancy and number of pregnancies and live births before and after the patient's birth may give important clues as to the nature of causative factors. Prenatal history and conditions of labor and delivery may ascertain or rule out certain causations.

Since the patient's developmental history begins with birth, the weight of the infant and/or his Apgar score may be of relevance to his subsequent growth. A detailed description of the infant's style of reactivity and temperamental qualities is necessary, as well as the age at which various milestones have been acquired, in order for the clinician to make inferences as to the relative contribution of organic and environmental factors in the presenting picture. While psychological testings are required to delineate the child's comparative weaknesses and strengths in cognitive functioning, the level of adaptation can be judged only from the description provided by parents and caretakers and from the clinician's own observation. Children who attend school are also observed by non-family members and their social interactions and educational attainments are reflected in reports obtained from their teachers.

History of medical illnesses and surgical operations may be obtained from the patient's pediatrician or from the clinic or hospital which he has attended. However, parents' description of the child in health and sickness and their perception of his behavior during and after hospitalization are important supplements to the history. Finally, it is during this initial interview with the parents that the clinician will have an opportunity to assess parental grasp and understanding of the problem and their attitudes toward the child. While only cautious inferences can be made at this stage as to the degree of parental ability or deficiency in their parenting function, it is important for the clinican to make a determination as to the most effective way of imparting the diagnostic information and intervention strategy to them.

Observation and Evaluation of the Child

Behavioral observation of the child must be directed toward elucidation of the child's style of interactions with his human and inanimate environment as well as of his emotional state, predominant mood and activity level. The ease with which a child is willing to enter the playroom without his parents and his response to their encouragement and to the child psychiatrist's invitation reflect the degree of freedom from anxiety and sense of trust in adults that he has achieved. Once in the playroom, the child's level of verbalization and his comprehension of language are noted. For most younger children, the spectacle of numerous colorful toys may be distracting to the point that the child may be unable to choose any toy. For purpose of evaluation of a retarded child, a combination of a few simple toys and one or two games or puzzles is sufficient.

When the child chooses a particular object for play, his understanding of the function of the toy and the use to which it is put is noted. If the child has difficulty in utilizing a toy, it is important for the psychiatrist to wait and see whether the patient can realistically judge his need for adult help, whether this request is clearly articulated by the child, or if he is willing to accept help if offered. Furthermore, in demonstrating an activity to the child, the clinician can determine the child's interest and his rate of learning of a new task.

Some children throw only a cursory glance at various toys and move from one activity to the next even when capable of manipulating an object or carrying on with an activity. These children's short attention span will severely hamper their learning. Others may be content to engage in stereotyped repetitive acts for a long period of time. When the psychiatrist makes an attempt to introduce a new activity, these children are resistant and may withdraw or react with intense frustration and anger. An extreme perseverative tendency places a limitation on the quality and quantity of new stimuli which the child can recognize. Other children may repeat an activity because they are proud of their mastery over the particular task and have received encouragement and approval for their demonstrated skills. However, because these children are clearly responsive to adult approval, it is possible to motivate them to engage in other activities and to judge their ability to master different tasks. Because learning by imitation plays an important part in young children's acquisition of skills and knowledge, the patient's willingness and ability to imitate the psychiatrist must be observed.

In summary, whether interactions and activities are initiated by the child or directed and encouraged by the psychiatrist, the goal of a diagnostic interview remains the same: to elicit behavioral responses and describe observations which, put together, will give a picture of the child's abilities and deficiencies in dealing with his environment and the demands placed upon him. When the child is capable of verbalization of his own wishes, apprehensions and feelings, such information must be elicited by sympathetic questioning. The experienced examiner usually adjusts the complexity of his own language to the level of a child's comprehension (21). This must be of prime concern when the child's mental age is far below his chronological age. With children who are mildly or moderately retarded, a simplified mental status examination includes statement about the child's orientation, coherence of his thinking processes, and subjective report of his moods. Questions regarding hallucination must be carefully worded and the child's suggestibility and his desire to please adults kept in mind. Misinformation, ignorance and concreteness of children may come together and create explanations which are clearly illogical. Interpretation of such illogical statements is a task which requires careful consideration of the child's ability to grasp the meaning of his experiences and the type of adult explanation available to him.

The child's fund of general information may be tapped by direct questioning or indirect inferences. The more immediate environment and the more relevant experiences are the logical point of departure. Names of colors, days of the week, or the name of a school teacher may be all the information that the child can produce in response to questions. Other children may know the name or the time of their favorite T.V. program. Children who attend school are asked to write their names or give their date of birth. In evaluating the child's fund of knowledge, it is important to begin on the simplest level and progress into more complex issues until the child has exhausted his resources.

Children's drawings of a person, tree and house can provide information about their level of perceptual organization, their body image, a rough estimate of their intelligence, and a quick glance at their fine motor coordination as revealed in grasping the pencil.

Neurological examination with special focus on non-focal signs may be performed as a part of psychiatric interview. Besides the level of motor activity, the child's fine and gross motor coordination and his sense of balance can be noted by observing the child during various play activities or elicited by engaging the child in tasks which reveal any anomalies in the particular area. For example, hopping on one foot may be a part of a game of hopscotch, or fine motor coordination may be detected when the child tries to open a box or grasp a pencil.

The child's physical appearance may give important clues as to the cause of mental retardation. For example, in Down's syndrome the majority of patients are diagnosed on clinical basis alone. On the other hand, children whose weight and height are below the 3rd percentile of the growth curve may or may not be intellectually retarded.

Deviant behavior such as mannerisms, rituals or primitive responses must be noted. Some retarded children smell all objects, others put toys in their mouth for exploration or try to chew on them (6). Some show fear upon encountering certain objects or are intensely reactive to others. Self-destructive activities or destruction of objects characterize some children's behavior, while others may show unpredictable changes in mood, impulsive activities, or aggressive behavior toward the examiner. Some children show pleasure in receiving praise, others are happier when a piece of candy is offered, and yet other patients are oblivious to any attempts to attract their attention.

Upon the termination of the psychiatric evaluation, a short exchange with parents may be necessary in order to ascertain whether the child's behavioral responses are his habitual mode of interaction or special circumstances have occurred before the evaluative sessions. A child with a minor cold or in state of hunger or sleepiness may be more irritable and disorganized than is his wont. At times it may not be possible to complete an evaluation during one session or special circumstances may require that the child be seen for further observation. For example, a psychiatrist may want to observe a child without any prior sedation; conversely, sedation may be necessary before one can judge the child's maximum level of functioning.

Psychological Testing

Psychological tests are procedures by which the psychologist attempts to obtain a sample of a person's behavior in a systematic manner which would allow comparison between different individuals. Tests of intelligence and their scoring systems are standardized so that established norms are available for the comparison and the outcome is more objective (8).

The most commonly utilized test of intelligence is the Wechsler Intelligence Scale for Children (WISC). The test is composed of a verbal and a performance part. The verbal portion requires verbal reasoning, vocabulary definition, and comprehension of the basic principles involved in social judgment. The performance part consists of evaluation of the child's ability to observe, to identify missing elements in a picture, to provide the correct sequence to a pictoral story, and to construct certain configurations with designated blocks. The accumulated and weighted scores on the verbal and performance parts are calculated according to a standardized table and the Intelligence Quotient (I.Q.) is thus obtained.

Another test with wide popularity is the Stanford-Binet test which was originally constructed by Binet and subsequently revised by Terman at Stanford. The test in its present form covers from age two to adulthood. At each age level there are six subtests which are designed to tap such areas as vocabulary, comprehension, abstraction, and numerical concepts. The level at which a child can successfully complete all the six subtests is called the "basal age" and the level at which none of the answers is correct is the "ceiling age." Normative tables provide the I.Q. scores that the child has thus obtained.

Another important concept in psychological testing is that of mental age. The mental age on the Stanford-Binet is calculated by adding all the credits that the child received above his "basal age" to the scores given for completing all items on the base level. For example, if a child of nine obtains the number of credits that an average child of four years of age would have ordinarily obtained, then he is said to have a mental age of four. In studies of cognitive functioning of mentally retarded individuals, the retardate is usually matched with a control mate of the same mental age, since the chronological age would be of little value in such tests.

In psychological assessments of mentally retarded children, motivational and experiential factors play an important role (22). The failure orientation based on a long background of unsuccessful attempts at problem solving may hamper the child in his performance, or his preference for interpersonal interaction may detract from his ability to be goal directed.

During infancy or when the child's retardation is of considerable proportion, the tests used are scales of developmental status and the result is expressed as developmental quotient (D.Q.). The earliest standardized test is Gesell's Developmental Schedule, which provides normative data in four areas of motor, adaptive, language and personal-social development. The test is utilized from four months to five years of age, but is particularly useful up to about three-four years. Other scales such as Bayley Scales of Infant Development are constructed along the same lines as Gesell's, with some modification. D.Q. and I.Q. measures are not synonymous and they do not show a strong correlation with each other. Although the predictive value of D.Q. for future intellectual development has been disappointingly low, it has been noted that when D.Q. measures are obtained at regular intervals, the correlation with subsequent I.Q. is high. The most important use of Development Scales in infancy is for the study of presence or absence of physical and sensory handicap as well as of the intactness of the infant's neurological apparatus. In infants in whom mental retardation is suspected or confirmed at an early age, periodic assessment of developmental status is necessary in order to monitor the rate and progress of development and to implement intervention strategies for remediation and experiential enrichment.

Speech and Language Evaluation

While it is well known that profound and severe retardation have a serious impact on language development, the degree of language disability may vary in children with mild and moderate retardation. Associated defects such as hearing loss, emotional disturbance and lack of proper environmental stimulation may limit the language development of a retarded child to a greater extent than the level expected from the severity of cognitive deficit alone. Although clinical observation and psychological tests provide information about the child's speech and his comprehension of language, at times it is necessary to obtain formal evaluation of speech and hearing in order to identify defects which may be corrected and to plan for specific remediation. History of delayed speech and slow rate of language acquisition is a common finding in mental retardation. However, depending on the cause of retardation, hearing defect of various degrees may complicate the picture. Furthermore, parents of retarded children may often fail to encourage verbal interaction and expression by the child and thus hamper the child's language development.

Laboratory Studies

Searching for the etiology of mental retardation may require certain laboratory procedures, the nature of which can be determined by historical information and/or clinical suspicion of the possible causative factors. For example, x-ray of the skull is of prime importance when the family history reveals presence of pregnancies terminating in miscarriages or still births, or it may be indicated when microcephaly or hydrocephalus are observed. Chromosomal studies are to be requested when other members of the immediate family have been diagnosed as mentally retarded or the clinical features raise the possiblity that genetic factors may account for the retaration. Electroencephalogram, on the other hand, is a useful procedure only when seizure disorders have been suspected. Unless a complete laboratory workup is a part of a research protocol, indiscriminate use of medical resources and ordering of all laboratory studies is of highly questionable value, even though the majority of the tests are harmless to the patient.

The most common laboratory procedures in investigation of mental retardation are as follows:

1) Blood and urine tests for metabolic by-products and chemical substances which are known to have deleterious influence on the nervous system. Among these are screening tests for aminoaciduria and for level of lead in blood of children with history of pica or clinical picture of acute lead poisoning.
2) Chromosomal studies in such conditions as Down's syndrome, Cri du Chat, or ovarian agenesis (Turner's syndrome).
3) X-ray studies of the skull when space occupying lesions or deformities of bony structure are suspected. Skeletal series is necessary if the child's bone age is in question, as is the case with hypothyroidism.
4) E.E.G. brain scan, pneumoencephalogram, and other specialized studies are used for differential diagnosis when the results of some procedures necessitate further investigation.
5) Chromosomal studies of parents and siblings may be needed when the child's retardation is found to be due to genetic causes.
6) Amniocentesis in pregnant mothers is indicated when maternal age, history of blood incompatibility, or genetic disorders in the family make an intrauterine determination of the fetal status desirable.

CLINICAL PICTURES IN MENTAL RETARDATION

The clinical picture in mental retardation which is not complicated by behavioral disorders depends on the chronological and mental age of the patient at the time of evaluation. The most uniform findings are manifestations of limited intelligence and adaptive functioning. Intellectual limitation is reflected in small vocabulary, short and simple sentences, below average fund of knowledge, constricted imagination, and difficulty in solving age-appropriate problems. Low level of adaptive functioning is reported or observed in the child's need for assistance in those areas of self-care which children of his age are usually capable of performing independently. As a general empirical rule, when a child's behavior corresponds to his estimated mental age, the dissonance between the behavior and chronological age is not considered deviant. For example, repeated questioning or repetitious statements and activities of a child with a mental age of three-four is explainable on the basis of the mental age, regardless of the child's chronological age, since children of average intelligence engage in such behavior at that age.

However, it must be noted that both earlier reports from institutionalized retardates and the more recent literature on non-institutionalized retarded children have indicated a high percentage of psychiatric disorders associated with mental retardation. In a six-year follow-up study of 44 mildly and moderately retarded children who lived with their middle-class familes, Chess (4) found 18 children with some degee of psychiatric disorder ranging from reactive behavior disorder (2.3%) to psychosis (6.9%), with a sizable percentage (27.3%) showing behavior disorder due to neurological damage. In a study of 100 consecutive admissions to the Mental Retardation Training program of the Langley Porter Neuropsychiatric Institute, Philips and Williams (18) found only 13 children diagnosed as retardation without any behavior disorder.

CAUSES OF BEHAVIOR DISORDERS IN MENTAL RETARDATION

Behavioral problems associated with mental retardation do not significantly differ from those found among the non-retarded population; in reviewing the literature, it becomes clear that no particular personality characteristics can be attributed to retardation per se. Organismic and interactional factors which are responsible for the causation of behavioral pathology in normal children are no less deleterious to the emotional and mental health of the retarded children. On the contrary, the retarded child, by virtue of his limited intellectual resources, his meager coping ability, and his prolonged dependency, is more vulnerable than his normal peers to the vicissitudes of life events and, therefore, more at risk for development of deviant patterns of behavior.

The etiology of retardation may play a role in the type of psychiatric syndrome. For example, organic brain syndrome is more likely to be found in association with retardation due to damage to the central nervous system. However, among children in whom the cause of retardation is unknown, the prevalence of psychiatric disturbances is no less and may be even more than that found in children whose limited intellectual functioning is due to identifiable etiology (14). Disturbed social relationships, school problems and aggressivity are among the most common presenting complaints in school-age children, while preschoolers may present with severe temper tantrums, disorganized behavior and self-mutilating acts. In the mildly retarded group, dysphoric mood and anxiety or neurotic symptomatology may further limit the individual's functioning.

The interpersonal milieu of a mentally retarded child is another source of possible pathogenesis. Some parents are overprotective and thus do not allow the child the range of freedom necessary for his emotional growth. Other parents set unattainable goals for their children; as a result, they are chronically frustrated and, consequently, hostile toward the child. For some, the fact of retardation is totally unacceptable and the devastating influence of parental rejection and underprotection adds to the child's burden. Siblings may feel resentful of the special attention that the retarded child receives from the parents and thus feel justified in their overt or covert hostility toward the retardate, or they may find the presence of a retarded sibling a shameful event which deprives them of some normal activities which their peers can enjoy.

Lack of community support systems or the reluctance of a family in caring for a retarded child may result in the child's institutionalization for long periods of time (10). Overcrowding and frequent staff change-over in some institutions deprive the retardate of the opportunity for bond formation with adults and limits his ability for socialization. Peer interaction may be another source of stress for mentally retarded individuals in that most children of the same age find the slowness of the retarded child intolerable and some may be outright rejecting or cruel to him. Younger children who are normal soon outpace their retarded playmates and abandon them. Feelings of loneliness and alienation or fear of the more advanced unsympathetic peer group are other causative factors in the development of psychopathology in these patients.

Academic demands and class placements which do not make special provision for the limitations and disabilities of the retarded child may make school a continous source of unhappiness and frustration for the intellectually deficient youngster. Some children find such situations so unbearable that they become chronically truant and easy victims for delinquent youngsters who seek unquestioning followers. The natural desire of children for acceptance, the special dependency of a retardate, and his deficient judgment may combine to lead the retarded youth into imitation or passive participation in harmful activities of delinquent gangs. Psychosis in mental retardation may be due to the underlying neurological damage and be manifested by primitive, disorganized behavior and impulsive and explosive episodes. Clinical pictures resembling schizophrenia have been also reported.

Differential Diagnosis

The syndrome of retardation without concomitant behavioral disorder is relatively easy to identify. However, special attention must be paid to diagnostic errors caused by a clinician's neglect of sensory defects such as blindness and/or deafness which may go unrecognized or uncorrected. For example, a child with severe hearing loss and subsequent lack of speech may be incorrectly labeled as retarded, with the result that appropriate stimulation is not provided and cognitive functioning remains underdeveloped. Children with central language disorder or developmental speech lag must be carefully assessed in terms of their adaptive functioning in non-verbal areas and their performance on those tests of intellectual ability which do not require intact receptive and expressive language.

In very young children whose retarded development is complicated by manifestations of behavioral deviancy, the diagnosis of early infantile autism may be a source of confusion. While the classical picture of early infantile autism is clearly distinguishable from mental retardation, some mixed pictures with autistic features may present diagnostic confusion. In mental retardation the ability to relate to people remains intact, while cognitive malfunction and signs of deviancy such as ritualistic behavior may be present. On the other hand, the defect in human relatedness is one of the basic signs of autism and autistic-like psychosis.

MANAGEMENT AND TREATMENT IN MENTAL RETARDATION

Treatment planning for mental retardation begins with the informing interview with the parents. The ominous diagnosis of mental retardation, even if long suspected, cannot fail but to profoundly distress and disturb the parents. Some parents become so distraught by the information that they are not able to understand subsequent discussion with the physician and must be given several sessions to inquire and integrate all that is told them. Feelings of guilt, search for contrary viewpoints, protest, despair and depression, apprehension and financial worries are all part of the emotional reactions that are experienced by parents who are informed that their child is retarded. During this stage the clinician must maintain an attitude of sympathetic understanding without sharing the parents' hopelessness or forcing a premature closure of the expression of disbelief and wishful denial by them.

Discussion must include a description of the child's approximate mental age and its implications in terms of child-rearing practices of the parents and their expectations. For example, some parents are frustrated by the fact that their long, complicated explanations to the child about various subjects do not seem to terminate the child's repeated questioning or modify his behavior. The clinician's task is to analyze the components of such interactional processes, to clarify the meaning of the child's behavior based on the child's level of understanding, and to bring parental behavior in line with the child's need and capabilities.

When the degree of retardation is disclosed, the implication for schooling and the maximum level of academic achievement must also be described. Some parents make the assumption that a retarded child's problems will be overcome by time and therefore expect their child to learn with slower pace but without any upper limitation on the quantity or quality of academic tasks. Such misconceptions require patient clarification. However, undue pessimism may be as harmful to the child as unrealistic optimism and the clinician must try to strike a balance between the two extremes. Factors interfering with the child's optimum functioning are of particular import, since their removal and the subsequent improvement in the child's behavior not only benefit the child, but also have a motivating and hopeful influence on the attitude of his caretakers.

Intertwined with concerns and questions about the child are also apprehension and legitimate inquiries about the meaning for the rest of the family of having a retarded child. When the etiological investigation has clearly indicated that retardation is due to genetic causes, other members of the family must be apprised of the situation and the risk to future pregnancies must be spelled out for parents or those sibs who are of marriageable age. When special diets are prescribed, information regarding the diet, the necessity for its maintenance, and the special responsibility of other members of the family for monitoring the regimen must be stressed.

Having a retarded child imposes a special financial and social burden on the family. The clinician must be aware of the legitimate needs of other members of the household and avoid giving parents the impression that other needs and obligations must be continuously ignored or given scant attention. A normal pattern of social and interpersonal interaction and an atmosphere of relaxed contentment in the household cannot be achieved unless parents and sibs of the retarded child can engage in most, if not all, those functions and activities which are pleasurable to them.

When the severity of the child's problems or the inability of parents requires that the child be institutionalized, the clinician's task is to explain this recommendation on the basis of the needs of the child and to avoid generating feelings of excessive guilt and worthlessness on the part of the family. Finally, because of the chronic nature of retardation and the vicissitudes of life events and crises which can be expected to develop in the future, the family must be advised regarding the community resources which can provide necessary advice and help to the family and to the patient on the long-term basis.

EDUCATIONAL SERVICES

Depending upon age and the degree of retardation, the mentally retarded child is placed in special educational settings. Mainstreaming of mentally retarded children has been advocated as more to their advantage because it provides greater stimulation and appropriate social models. On the other side, it deprives the child of special teaching methods and exposes him to constant failure. To discuss these issues properly would require lengthier consideration than is appropriate here.

Preschool programs are of particular help for young retardates whose limitations have been discovered during early childhood. These programs are designed with the goal of providing an environment which encourages development of social and adaptive skills and tries to prevent the appearance and fixation of the behavioral styles and attitudes which hamper the child's future healthy interaction with his surroundings. Diagnosis and remediation of deficiencies in learning strategy, as well as training in perceptual and cognitive patterns which are needed for future school learning, are among other functions of such preschool programs. When the child's home environment is impoverished and developmental lags in communicative and social skills may be partly due to the disadvantaged background, the nursery school experience may, in fact, be of such compensatory value as to be regarded as a preventive measure in combatting future retardation (12).

Elementary school classes for educable children are usually designed for children between ages six and 13 years. These classes are small and ungraded and the emphasis in earlier years is on expansion of vocabulary, socialization, and the development of understanding of social and safety rules. Between ages nine and 13 the children are expected to acquire basic reading and computation skills. On secondary school levels, the ultimate goal is to prepare the retarded adolescents for vocational programs. The subjects to be studied are further advancement in reading, writing and mathematics, as well as developing work habits and understanding of the principles involved in relating to co-workers and supervisors. Some retarded youngsters exhibit special talent for certain manual skills. Others may be more interested in simple, routine jobs. It must be noted that temperamental and personality factors play a significant role in vocational adjustment of retarded individuals, as well as in their school performance. Children with low intensity of mood and high persistence are more likely to utilize their limited intellectual abilities to their fullest degree.

PSYCHIATRIC TREATMENT IN MENTAL RETARDATION

As has been repeatedly emphasized, presence of deviant behavior places a heavy burden on the limited intellectual and adaptational capacities of the retarded child. Psychiatric treatment of the behavioral disorder is, therefore, of utmost necessity in order to reduce the deleterious consequences for the child's functioning, as well as to help with his personal adjustment.

Treatment of behavioral disorder must be tailored to the needs of the child with special consideration given to cognitive disabilities. Children with reactive behavior disorder need an opportunity to unlearn their maladaptive patterns and acquire more realistic styles. However, part of the treatment in these cases must be directed toward environmental manipulation and removal of those factors which are either a source of continuous stress or help maintain undesirable behavior. For children with neurotic symptomatology, individual psychotherapy in the form of play therapy and simplified verbal interaction is helpful.

Children who exhibit disorganized disruptive behavior may need sedation in the form of tranquilizing medication if they are to take advantage of other remedial and instructional programs. In prescribing tranquilizing medication, it must be kept in mind that the quantity of medication which would totally control the child's disruptive behavior may at the same time make him non-responsive to all other stimuli. A balance must be established between the degree of sedation necessary for smooth management and the level of responsiveness and alertness necessary for interaction with the environment.

Various methods of behavior modification are used in treatment of self-mutilating activities. These methods may range from such simple procedures as withdrawal of attention when the behavior is manifested to more drastic measures such as administration of a weak electric current whenever the child is about to engage in such behavior. Principles of learning theory and behavior modification strategies have been of great value in teaching desired skills and extinguishing undesirable activities in children whose retardation is of severe to profound degree.

SERVICES FOR THE RETARDATES

Because mental retardation is a multifaceted problem requiring skills and expertise of various professions, community services for retarded individuals usually consist of a diagnostic team. Pediatricians, neurologists, child psychiatrists, psychologists, social workers, nutritionists, and representatives from the field of education are all called upon to provide answers for the following questions: Is this child retarded? What is the etiology of his cognitive disability? Is he in need of medical-psychiatric care or of various rehabilitative measures? What sort of educational and remedial program will be best suited to his needs? How can his family be helped to care and provide for him?

The multidisciplinary approach to diagnosis and treatment and management planning for the patient is designed to assure that every retarded child receives the optimal degree of stimulation, instruction and help necessary for his growth and development.

Furthermore, the chronic nature of the problem necessitates the long-term involvement of community services with the family and the child. Parental resources and special needs must be periodically evaluated in order to provide the family unit with the continuing support needed to cope with a retarded child. From the public health viewpoint, it is not only necessary to prevent an increase in the retarded population, but also important to be aware of the psychological damage to various members of a family unit which can result from the highly stressful situations.

For some families, the emotional support and guidance of professionals familiar with the unique needs of retarded children are sufficient; others may need short periods of respite from caring for their retarded child. Crises involving other family members may make it impossible for the parents to continue to devote special attention to their intellectually disabled offspring, or the child's behavior may present the family with a new set of concerns which they can no longer tolerate. In all these situations a reevaluation of the child's status and of the family's problem is required in order to plan the proper intervention. For some families it is sufficient to remove the child for a short period to special camps, institutions or foster homes, and to thus allow a reorganization and replenishment of the family's coping mechanisms and exhausted resources. Under other circumstances the child may need longer-term care away from the family.

Finally, such issues as sexual activities of retarded adolescents or their developing need for vocational programs are occasions which call for fresh assessment of the problem. While involvement of a psychiatrist may be unnecessary when the retarded child is within an appropriate educational setting and the parents are receiving the necessary counselling from other professionals, any reassessment or reevaluation calls for a renewed attempt to identify the emotional and interpersonal status of the patient and the appropriateness of the various contemplated plans for management and disposition.

REFERENCES

1. Adams, M.: *Mental Retardation and Its Social Dimensions.* New York: Columbia University Press, 1971.
2. Anderson, J.A. and Swaiman, K.F.: Phenylketonuria and allied metabolic disease. U.S. Department of Health, Education and Welfare, Social and Rehabilitation Service Children's Bureau, 1967.
3. Apgar, V.: A proposal for a new method of evaluations of the newborn infant. *Anesth. and Analg.,* 32: 260-267, 1953.
4. Chess, S.: Evolution of behavior disorder in a group of mentally retarded children. *J. of the Amer. Acad. of Child Psychiat.,* 16: 1, 1977.
5. Chess, S., Fernandez, P. and Korn, S.J.: *Psychiatric Disorders of Children with Congenital Rubella.* New York: Brunner/Mazel, 1971.
6. Chess, S. and Hassibi, M.: Behavior deviations in mentally retarded children. *J. of the Amer. Acad. of Child Psychiat.,* 9:2, 1970.
7. Down, L.: Observations on an ethnic classification of idiots. London Hospital, *Clinical Lectures and Reports,* 3: 259-62, 1866.
8. Fishler, K.: Psychological assessment services. In R. Koch and J. Dobson (Eds.), *The Mentally Retarded Child and His Family,* New York: Brunner/Mazel, 1976.
9. Grossman, (Ed.): *Manual on Terminology and Classification in Mental Retardation.* American Association on Mental Deficiency Special publication No. 2, 1973.

246   *Child Development in Normality and Psychopathology*

10. Hagaman, M.B.: Family-support systems: Their effect on long-term psychiatric hospitalization in children. *J. of the Amer. Acad. of Child Psychiat.* 16, 1, 1977.
11. Koch, R. and de la Cruz, F.F. (Eds.): *Down's Syndrome (Mongolism): Research, Prevention and Management.* New York: Brunner/Mazel, 1975.
12. LaCrosse, E.: The contribution of the nursery school. In R. Koch and J. Dobson (Eds.), *The Mentally Retarded Child and His Family.* New York: Brunner/Mazel, 1976.
13. Lejeune, J., Turpin R., Gauthier, M.: Chromosomic Diagnoses of Mongolism. *Archives Franc., Pediatrics,* 16: 962-3, 1959.
14. Menolascino, F. J.: Psychiatric aspects of retardation. In R. Koch and J. Dobson (Eds.), *The Mentally Retarded Child and His Family.* New York: Brunner/Mazel, 1976.
15. Mercer, J.R.: Sociocultural factors in educational labeling. In M.J. Begab and S.A. Richardson (Eds.), *The Mentally Retarded and Society: A Social Science Perspective.* Baltimore: University Park Press, 1975.
16. Morse, C., Sahler, O. and Friedman, S.: A three year follow-up study of abused and neglected children. *Amer. J. of Diseases of Children,* 120:439-446, 1970.
17. Niswander, K.R. and Gordon, M. (Eds.): *The Collaborative Perinatal Study of the National Institute of Neurological Diseases and Stroke: The Women and Their Pregnancies.* Philadelphia: Saunders, 1972.
18. Philips, I. and Williams, N.: Psychopathology of mental retardation, a study of 100 mentally retarded children. *Amer. J. of Psychiat.,* 132, 12, 1975.
19. Rutter, M.L.: Psychiatry. In J. Wortis (Ed.), *Mental Retardation,* Vol. 3, New York: Grune and Stratton, 1971.
20. Sameroff, A.: Early influence on development: Fact or fancy? *Merrill-Palmer Quarterly of Behavior and Development,* 21, 4, 1975.
21. Szymanski, L.S.: Psychiatric diagnostic evolution of mentally retarded individuals. *J. of the Amer. Acad. of Child Psychiat.,* 16, 1, 1977.
22. Zigler, E. and Balla, D.: Personality factors in the performance of the retarded: Implications for clinical assessment. *J. of the Amer. Acad. of Child Psychiat.,* 6, 1, 1977.

8

Autism and Childhood Schizophrenia

MARY B. HAGAMEN, M.D.

Autism and childhood schizophrenia are deviations in development that have been surrounded by mystique since they were described initially in the United States in the early 1940s. This is most likely due to confusion regarding their definition as diagnostic entities, as well as to the fact that, even today, after 35 years, we do not clearly understand their cause or what can be done to effectively treat such disorders.

HISTORY

In 1943 Leo Kanner (14), a child psychiatrist, described 11 children from the Johns Hopkins University Clinical Service who, despite normal appearance, did not relate to people in an ordinary way and were developing socially, emotionally and intellectually in a disorganized fashion. He spoke of their condition as *early infantile autism.*

For many years, developmental specialists such as Gesell had been aware of such children who were "oblivious to persons." In 1941, Gesell (11) commented on the fact that their bizarre behavior, coupled with an attractive countenance, tended to build up an impression of dormant or obscured normality—"a demeanor suggestive of unreleased potential." Gesell furthermore cautioned that if the physician yielded to such an impression and implied to the parents that the condition was a reactive response to the environment, they would be encouraged to feel that the child would "find himself" in time, which Gesell felt was not the case. In fact, he saw the condition as a fundamental mental deficit, a type of retardation.

In 1942, Lauretta Bender (2) described a smiliar clinical syndrome, as seen at Bellevue Hospital in New York City, which she felt was an

247

expression of schizophrenia in children. Like Dr. Bender, many experts have seen *early infantile autism* as the earliest form of schizophrenia, since severely disturbed relationships with people are a prominent symptom in both conditions.

Kolvin in England (15) and Makita in Japan (16) have reported on the age of onset of psychoses of childhood. Michael Rutter (20) pooled these findings in a most useful graph (Figure 1) which shows that, based on age of onset, there are two peaks of incidence of childhood psychoses. There is a relatively large group with onset prior to age three and a second group that occurs after a period of normal development, with peak frequency after the age of nine. These late onset psychoses appear to be a downward extension of adult schizophrenia, but are described

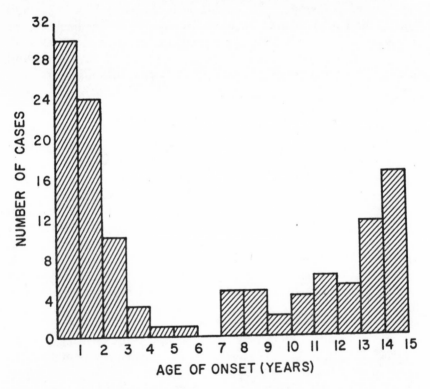

FIGURE 1. Distribution of cases of child psychosis by age of onset. Data from Makita (16) and Kolvin (15), as compiled by M. Rutter (20).

generally as *childhood schizophrenia*. A very small heterogenous group has an onset in middle childhood. They often represent organic conditions that can occur at almost any stage of development. Thus, when psychoses begin between three and eight, organic conditions are particularly suspect. (Tuberous sclerosis, hepato-lenticular degeneration, Huntington's chorea, lead encephalopathy, and Heller's disease are among the neurological disorders that must be investigated.)

The focus of this chapter will be on the two larger groups of psychoses seen in childhood: the early onset psychoses (autism) and the late onset psychoses (childhood schizophrenia).

The discussion will be approached through the following questions that are most frequently asked by parents:

> What is wrong?
> What is the cause?
> What can be done about it?
> What is the course of the disorder?

AUTISM

What Is Wrong?

Autistic children have a disorder which becomes manifest during the early developmental stages of childhood. Their behavior is characterized by failure to relate appropriately to people and by a selective impairment of cognitive and/or perceptual functioning which reduces the ability of the child to understand, communicate, learn and participate in social relationships.

The National Society for Autistic Children, a study group sponsored by parents of autistic children, has pioneered in the development of a better understanding of the disorder. They have described the specific characteristics of autistic children as outlined below (17).

Such children are typically multihandicapped in their abilities to receive and communicate information, resulting in behavior inappropriate to the physical and social demands of their environment. As in aphasia, the concomitant communication disorder or profound learning disability appears to be a severe central disorder in symbolic ability resulting from the incapacity to use and to understand language appropriately. There is apparently a particular inability to process language through auditory channels. The difficulty is often accompanied by impairment of motor, visual and auditory perception. The behavior of an autistic child is typically improved by appropriate educational procedures. A combination of some or all of the following idiosyncratic behaviors characterizes the autistic child. These behaviors vary from child to child and time to time in severity and manner, and include:

1) Severely impaired speech or complete lack of speech.
2) Impaired or complete lack of relatedness, and social inaccessibility to children, parents and adults; aloneness, withdrawal, seeming lack of desire for affection.
3) Extreme distress for no readily discernible reason.
4) Retardation or lack of intellectual development in certain areas, sometimes accompanied by normal or superior abilities in other areas.
5) Repetitive and peculiar (inappropriate) use of toys and objects and/or similar repetitive and peculiar body motions, such as incessant rocking, ritualism.
6) Unusual reaction to perceptual stimuli, such as seeming not to hear certain sounds and overreacting to others (e.g., "holding hands over ears," "looking through" objects, poor eye contact, inability to perform certain gross and/or fine motor activities appropriately, walking with a peculiar gait, limpness of the fingers, inability to hold a pencil appropriately).
7) Onset of disorder at birth, or else apparent normal early development followed by deterioration in functioning or decreased developmental rate within approximately the first three years of life.
8) Hyperactivity or passivity.
9) Apparent insensitivity to pain.

As the development of autistic children was studied further by Eisenberg and Kanner (6), these pioneering child psychiatrists described what they thought to be the primary deficits: a) extreme aloneness, and b) obsessive insistence on the preservation of sameness.

It was felt that the other characteristics of the syndrome, such as language deviation and disturbances of motility, were all secondary to the affective defect. As other investigators became interested in autistic children, attention was focused on their unusual speech development—an interest that soon extended to the more comprehensive phenomena of language. In England, Rutter (19) studied large numbers of such children and then proposed that the basic defect in autistic children was a communication disorder which occurred in different children with varying intensity. In some cases, the defect seemed to be so severe as to permeate every level of the child's existence.

Bender (3) had expressed a similar idea when she hypothesized that childhood schizophrenia was the result of a maturational lag at the embryonal level characterized by a primitive plasticity in all areas from which subsequent behavior results. Thus, when the disease began in early childhood, the impact in many cases was so widespread that the children appeared retarded. She felt such cases were a subtype of childhood schizophrenia best described as pseudo retardation.

If we look at the autistic child's inability to comprehend any aspect of his environment as a basic or primary problem, his aloneness is then logically seen as a secondary feature. Since he is more comfortable when the environment is the same, it stands to reason that preoccupation with sameness might also be a correlary of this lack of perceptual integration. It appears that the signals reaching the child's brain cannot be processed in a meaningful way to interpret the environment. Social interactions seem to be particularly baffling to the autistic child. Having been unable to register experiences of affective contact himself, he seems unable to comprehend the significance of emotional relationships. Therefore, young autistic children are isolated and unable to react appropriately to the people in their environment. Such children must be taught the significance of emotional and social relationships just as a blind or deaf child must be taught the significance of visual and auditory sensations in everyday life.

Ornitz and Ritvo (18), working at the University of California in Los Angeles, pioneered studies of the neurophysiologic characteristics of autistic children and proposed that the problem was one of perceptual inconstancy in that signals were processed in such an erratic manner that the child could not make sense of them.

As time passed and data increased, hypotheses have been modified. Rutter (20) now feels that the deficit is broader and deeper than a communication deficit and sees it as a defect in cognitive functioning. Ritvo (21) prefers to describe the deficit as a one of perceptual integration. Today there is an increasing and healthy trend to describe the significant areas of performance precisely. This is characterized best by the group at U.C.L.A. (21) where description of autistic children has been organized into defects of:

a) perceptual integration
b) motility
c) language
d) ability to relate
e) developmental rate.

The theories of Ritvo (21) are not incompatible with those of Rutter (20), nor do they contradict Bender's hypothesis (3) or Kanner's observations (14). The crucial question is: Which comes first—relatedness or language? If we go back to the experiment of the Emperor Philip Augustus, who tried to see what tongue children would speak if they were raised from birth without being spoken to, we remember that no child survived until the age of two. Supposedly, they succumbed to emotional deprivation. Is not the relationship between affect and language development so intertwined as to be inseparable in the infant? Can cognitive development proceed without language—receptive and expressive? Is it not necessary to receive and register affection from the environment before one even has a desire to communicate?

We know very little about the development of receptive language. Friedlander (9) has pointed out that receptive language function appears to involve processes and variables that lie at the very heart of mental development and the child's successful adaptation to the world of things, the world of people, and the world of action that surrounds him.

What is then wrong with the autistic child? Utilizing the observations of Kanner (14), Rutter (20), Ritvo (21), and Bender (3), we can theorize that autistic children have a deficit in perceptual integration that can vary in quality and intensity. Such a deficit inhibits the understanding of the environment by the affected child to such a degree that language development (necessary for cognition to progress past the level of a two-year-old) does not occur.

In the newborn, a prerequisite for comprehension of the environment is awareness of the human relationship. Perception of the world begins with the baby's interpretation of this first social cue. The primary caretaker who feeds the child provides pleasure. In normal babies, the social cues are comfort and satiation; after a few months of life, the infant is able not only to receive and register this information from the environment, but also to send back his own social cue—a smile.

Could it be that with autistic babies this capacity for interpretation is defective? If we can consider the effect of deficits in perceptual integration beginning at birth, this seems possible. The pleasure registry of the central nervous system is confused and performs in such an erratic manner that it disorganizes the normal way by which a baby learns.

Thus, the feedback system through which the average child interacts with his environment is inoperative. To establish the foundation for later cognitive development, an organized perception of everyday experiences is necessary in the early months of life. When the perception registry is faulty, the critical roots so necessary for the development of receptive language cannot be set down.

In highlighting the need to study receptive language development, Friedlander (9) points to the model of the computer that can process no information until it has been programmed; he then compares, by inference, the newborn human infant to the unprogrammed computer.

The normal baby begins to interact with the environment, creating a critical feedback loop, within the first 24 hours of life. However, in babies who later demonstrate autism, we can theorize that the capacity to organize early perception may be so defective as to make the environment meaningless. This results in the indifference of such children to outside stimuli.

Using the analogy of the simpler calculator instead of a computer, we might consider what happens when one circuit is defective. Although the calculator lights up and continues, ostensibly, to function, what is registered as input and what is retrieved are both distorted. Such might be the situation with the autistic child.

What Is the Cause?

The primary cause of autism is a poorly understood deficit of brain function. Bender (2) has always supported this view. Chess (4) provided increased evidence for a neurologic etiology in her report of the high incidence of autistic children born to mothers who had rubella in the first trimester of pregnancy. Follow-up studies have shown that nearly 25% of children diagnosed as autistic go on to develop seizures in later life (19).

The syndrome may be viewed as a final common pathway, a condition that can be caused by any one of a variety of insults to the central nervous system of the affected child, occurring sometime between conception and the third year of life.

Autism is not caused by faulty parenting—a myth that grew up around misinterpretation of some of the early observations of the parents of autistic children. This is not to say that parents do not play a critical role in the autistic child's development. As with all children, parents of autistics can create an environment that will enhance or inhibit their child's potential.

The effect of autistic children on their parents, as well as on others involved in their direct care, deserves much greater attention than it has received. Because autistic children are emotionally unresponsive and frequently difficult to manage, they create incomparable stress on those responsible for their care and training. This can result in odd behavior on the part of the parents which is a reaction to caring for the autistic child. Many children with autism require 24-hour supervision of the quality necessary for preschool children—a responsibility that calls for extraordinary adaptation on the part of other family members.

As mental health workers, we would be well advised to accept responsibility for the primary prevention of psychopathology by addressing ourselves to the needs of the families of autistics as a target population. They are a deserving group who have been frequently neglected.

What Can Be Done About It?

While a variety of treatments have been tried in the past 30 years, there is no one specific treatment that has produced major improvement in a large percentage of autistic children or has changed the long-range outcome of the disorder.

Psychotherapeutic, behavioral, medical and educational approaches have all been tried. Each has something to contribute to the management and understanding of the autistic child.

The best results can be expected when the deficit is identified as a developmental disorder by the second birthday and the parent is educated to understand the intricacies of the perceptual disorder, trained in behavior management, and put into a working relationship with a school or center that provides supportive structure with a focus on language development and training in socially acceptable behavior. Parents can then become partners with professionals in exploring their child's capacity for development (12). As with the mothers of blind or deaf infants, parents need expert professional help in order to understand and meet their child's special needs.

While individual psychotherapy is not recommended for the young child, supportive guidance for the family is essential. Parents may need psychotherapy to help them come to terms with the loss of the anticipated healthy child. In the majority of cases, autism is hard for parents to understand and almost impossible to accept. Parent groups such as the National Society for Autistic Children provide education, comfort and support. Parents of children with autism need to have a mental health professional who is experienced in the ways of autism, who is available at times of crises, and who can work with them to give them insight about their situation, as well as act as advocate for the autistic child in long-range planning.

Although total institutionalization is not recommended, some kind of family support system that provides respite from the 24-hour care of the autistic child is essential in order for other members of the family to maintain their emotional health and resilience. Such needs are highly variable, depending on the family composition, competence and life-style. Large extended families are apt to have more resources than small nuclear families to provide the kind of respite that allows parents worry-free breaks during which they can recharge their emotional batteries.

The birth order of the autistic child is a highly significant variable in the family's ability to manage independently. If the autistic child is the firstborn, the situation is frequently far more stressful than when such a child is the last to be born.

Allowance for the emotional needs of all family members should be part of treatment planning for the autistic child. Social agencies should be called on to provide babysitters, homemakers and other family support services when there is no one within the family to relieve the parents.

Some families cannot manage the autistic child at home even with training and support. If such is the case and an alternate home placement is not available, a boarding school often provides the best solution. It allows the child to maintain contact with the family during vacations and holidays, and does not have the permanence associated with institutionalization in a state facility (13).

With the forceful trend away from institutional care, it is hard to know what facilities will be receptive to autistics in the future.

It is likely that those who function in the retarded range with I.Q.s below 50 will become the responsibility of government agencies that provide service for the mentally retarded, since autism is now included in the federal guidelines defining developmental disabilities.

What Is the Course of the Disorder?

Although there is a wide variation in individual outcome among children who have been labeled autistic, it has become increasingly evident from follow-up studies that the prognosis is poor for most children so diagnosed.

Approximately two-thirds of autistic youngsters have deficits of cognition such that they remain retarded throughout their lives. Long-term follow-up studies show that about half of the remaining third (one-sixth of the total) find gainful employment, while the other half of this third attain but a fair social adjustment (1).

The best predictor of outcome appears to be the measured I.Q. done around the age of five. Initial reports by Kanner and Eisenberg that speech by age five is a critical marker in differentiating those who do well from those with the graver handicap appear to be a reflection of I.Q. (7).

In general, if the I.Q. is below 50, the outlook is poor, regardless of other factors. However, if the I.Q. is above 50, the prognosis is related to the degree of language impairment. If the latter is severe, the outlook is more guarded; with a lesser degree of language impairment, the outlook becomes brighter.

As yet we do not know how the course of the disorder will be affected by the combined efforts to provide:

   a) early intervention
   b) parent training
   c) specialized training in communication skills
   d) social and vocational training
   e) deinstitutionalized rearing.

Observations to date indicate that the child's level of functioning may be raised minimally. Autistic children of average or superior intelligence may be able to function in a routine job that utilizes their abilities and to live a well-organized life that is not subject to change. It is hoped that the intervention techniques described above will enable even the lower functioning autistic children to lead a sheltered life in a community group residence. As they grow older, the large majority of autistic young adults show a decrease in behavioral deviance and tend to have the same needs for lifetime supervision as the trainable retarded population. A small number, one to two percent of the lower functioning youngsters, retain aggressive and/or self-destructive habits. To date, no satisfactory alternatives to total institutionalization have been found for these children.

With a clearer understanding of the disorder, workers in the field are much more goal directed to find ways to help children compensate in specific areas of deficit. Improvement, though painfully slow, continues with most young people affected by autism who are given individual attention for as long as such interest and attention are available.

CHILDHOOD SCHIZOPHRENIA
(LATE ONSET PSYCHOSES)

What Is Wrong?

"Psychotic disorders are characterized by altered contact with reality.

The psychotic child is attempting to adapt to a subjectively distorted concept of the world. This is in contrast to the neuroses in which a child is adapting in a morbid fashion to his real life situation" (1).

The clinical features of late onset psychoses resemble those of adult schizophrenia. They can be divided into two groups that may have considerable overlap—those with an abrupt onset and those with a gradual, more insidious course. The behavior of the children in both groups may be similar. However, in those with an acute onset, the premorbid level of overall adjustment is usually superior to the child with a slowly evolving psychotic picture. As a group, parents of children with an insidious onset are apt to tolerate more deviation in their offspring than parents of youngsters with an acute onset.

Initially, schizophrenic children demonstrate a change of personality that appears as an overreaction to a minor stress. There tends to be withdrawal from contact with people, sometimes accompanied by a violent reaction if attempts are made to counter such withdrawal. The child remains aware at all times and, initially, is thought to be manipulating. Thinking tends to become distorted with illogical reasoning, schoolwork falls off, sleep is disturbed, and school refusal is not uncommon. In some cases there may be odd posturing that is related to the thought disorder (a nine-year-old boy walked about with his head on his left shoulder to keep his brains from running out of his leaky right ear). Disorders of motility may occur that resemble conversion hysteria (an 11-year-old girl displayed total inability to walk related to her delusion that she was walking into death). Such behaviors can be distinguished from neurotic disorders in that they are only a small component of the total picture; they do not appear as the isolated symptom seen in hysterics with "la belle indifférence." Hallucinations are common and are most frequently auditory. When visual hallucinations do occur, they are more apt to be seen in children who are functioning at a preoperational level according to Piaget (5).

It should be pointed out that childhood schizophrenia is a rare disorder. In Kolvin's study of late onset psychoses (15), he stated that 87% of children so diagnosed had been seen as shy, timid or sensitive before the development of their psychotic symptoms. Also, over half of the children with late onset psychoses had some delay in language development, but not the other characteristics of early onset psychoses.

What Is the Cause?

As with early onset psychoses, there is little understanding of the cause of late onset psychosis. Like adult schizophrenia, there appears to be a genetic predisposition to the disorder and a review of the family history of children presented for hospitalization is apt to yield the history of a relative who was institutionalized because of psychosis. Because no differentiation has been made between early and late onset psychoses in most studies, the significant variables that relate to their etiology and outcome are not available.

Bender (3) conceptualizes the entire group of childhood psychoses on a continuum with adult schizophrenia:

> Childhood schizophrenia is an early manifestation of schizophrenia as it appears in adolescents and adults. It is an endogenous disorder of the total organism. The inherited predisposition may remain latent or may develop into some form of schizophrenic illness. When such decompensation occurs in early childhood, it is the result of a combination of inherited tendencies and a noxious or traumatic event, intrauterine or perinatal.

Bender goes on to point out that many, but not all, schizophrenic children present some of the features of infantile autism as described by Kanner (14); this is in agreement with Kolvin's findings (15) that about half of the late onset psychoses have some developmental delays, particularly in the area of language. Thus, there is overlap in the symptomatology with early onset and late onset psychoses, but in the latter disorder there seems to be:

a) more evidence of a family history of mental illness;
b) a better ability to use language;
c) a higher level of cognitive functioning;
d) a greater capacity to utilize personal strengths.

The role played by the environment is invariably greater in the late onset psychoses, if only by virtue of the time across which it has been acting. Variations in the environment influence the child with a predisposition to schizophrenia in a poorly understood way. Insights regarding this are emerging from a series of longitudinal studies that deal with children who are at high risk for the development of psychoses because one or both of their parents have had a psychotic episode (8). Not all children who are at risk become psychotic, despite disturbing psychosocial experience. Garmezy (10) has pioneered in the study of children who are at risk for schizophrenia in order to understand what personal characteristics and subsequent life experiences provide protection against psychotic breakdown.

Whatever the cause, it is likely that there are many significant variables, both environmental and constitutional, that determine an individual's behavior. There is general agreement that psychoses are the result of very complex interplay between an individual's genetic endowment and his or her experiences within the environment.

What Can We Do About It?

Treatment of the late onset psychoses of childhood is comparable to the treatment of adult psychoses. If the onset is abrupt, patients benefit from short-term inpatient care where chemotherapy can be utilized in a carefully controlled manner and the patient can be observed away from the emotionally charged atmosphere of the family. Separation from the family often prompts a vivid demonstration of the critical psychodynamics, as well as some degree of insight on the part of both the child and the parent. With this material, psychotherapeutic interventions are expedited and a treatment plan involving whatever modalities are most appropriate can be developed.

In children where the onset has been insidious, the treatment situation is much more difficult and is in direct proportion to the length of time since atypical behavior was first noted. In such instances, chemotherapy directed at the target symptoms is helpful. Manipulation of the environment as it pertains to social and educational programs is mandatory. A receptive, well-organized school that provides the schizophrenic youngster with a chance to develop his strengths is ideal. Many such children are gifted intellectually and are able to adapt to the world largely via intellectual endeavors. Although remaining exquisitely sensitive to the comments of others, they often can be reached by an intuitive teacher who, after gaining their respect, can guide them through academic projects with gentle critiques that stimulate growth. Individual supportive psychotherapy can be helpful for both parent and child.

In some families, psychotic children create great stress when their condition becomes chronic. They are the source of perpetual annoyance because of their perseverative quality, their mannerisms and their inappropriate social behavior. Boarding school placement can often afford a chance for the child to mature in a setting with others who have similar problems, thus allowing the normal children in the family an opportunity to gain what attention they need from the parents who otherwise might be preoccupied with the psychotic child. As with early onset psychoses, families vary in their ability to live comfortable with the psychotic child and have varying needs for increased outside support.

What Is the Natural Course of the Disorder?

Because of the low incidence of the disorder, follow-up studies that deal exclusively with children who have experienced late onset psychoses are not available. Barker (1) reports that the condition is usually progressive and that the prognosis is considered poor, with many requiring institutional care. In the author's experience, this has not necessarily been the case. In those children with acute late onset psychoses, there is usually a good response to medication and reorganization of the milieu. Psychotherapeutic intervention is helpful and recovery can be expected in the majority of cases. In late onset psychoses of insidious origin, the picture is less optimistic. Success is often dependent on the ability of the child and his family to adapt to realistic lifetime goals. Many such children grow up to lead rather sheltered lives as conscientious adults who are able to adapt as long as they feel secure in their environment, but who are in the need of constant reassurance. They can blossom with an understanding employer who is willing to accept their diligence, dedication and good attendance record in lieu of speed and adaptability to change.

CASE HISTORY: AUTISM WITHOUT MARKED RETARDATION

H. was his mother's first pregnancy. Aside from a minor viral illness, pregnancy and labor were normal and the child was born after five hours of labor. He weighed 6 lbs., 4 oz. He was said to have had a high pitched cry and an expiratory moan at birth. At three days of age, H. developed jaundice and an exchange transfusion was done on the fifth day after bilirubin rose to 24.2 mgs. percent indirect because of OA incompatibility.

Growth and neuromuscular development appeared basically normal and milestones were appropriate; however, personality and response to his environment are described as far from normal relatedness. H. was hyperactive, a headbanger, and given to tantrums. He ate everything in sight indiscriminately: dirt, grass, stones. He appeared fearless and often wandered aimlessly amid hazardous circumstances. At age four, he was described as compulsive in his desire for sameness. He lined his toys up exactly the same way each time he played with them and became upset if they were changed. He showed little, if any, affection to people other than his mother, with whom he was inconsistently responsive. He was said to spin and twirl frequently.

At age five, H. entered a special preschool program for emotionally disturbed children where the emphasis was on language training and learning to trust the teacher. Although he was not a problem in school, he was increasingly hard to manage in his home, particularly because of the demands made on his mother by his new baby brother. Because of this, H. was admitted at age six to the state psychiatric hospital for children both for a comprehensive evaluation and to offer his family respite. He was discharged after one month. Testing at the time of hospitalization was as follows:

Stanford Binet	60
Peabody	67
Merrill Palmer	78 months

Three years later, at age nine, a review of his status via the framework set forth by Ritvo is as follows:

Perception

H. has the receptive language of an average three-year-old. He frequently wears a puzzled look and is often slow to interpret changes in his environment. His mother reports that he cannot focus on two things at once. Thus, if he is playing intently and she wants to tell him something, she must go to him, interrupt his play, hold his hand, and look him in the eye while she gives him her message. Otherwise, H. is apt to seem oblivious to her comments. He seems to be able to process a very limited set of facts at a time.

Developmental Rate

H. is rather small for his age and has the appearance of a child younger than his nine years. However, physical development has always been within standardized norms.

Relatedness

Although he was initially indifferent to his mother, at about age four he became quite attached when she began to work intensely with him on language development. Gradually, he began to acknowledge other significant people in his life: his father, his teacher, his doctor, etc.

Despite his progress with adults, he engaged only in parallel play with other youngsters until about age eight, when he began to notice and want to play with other children. At age nine he is beginning to develop friendships with classmates in his special public school.

Speech and Language

H. had erratic and unusual language development. His first words were repetitions of things he had heard (delayed echolalia). Although he had a large vocabulary of nouns, it was very hard for him to express his ideas. H. could conceptualize meanings from letters with greater ease than from words—for instance, he would not use the word "cookie" but would ask for a "c o o k i e." Because he was intrigued by the television program Sesame Street, it was assumed that his penchant for spelling was related to the impression this program made on him. He loved letters and on occasion seemed to communicate by spelling out his wants. Spontaneous syntax, i.e. putting an idea of his own into a sentence, did not occur until age seven. Gradually, between eight and nine years, his language has become more and more appropriate, but he continues to be very concrete. He has learned what is expected of him in ordinary social interactions and is capable of responding appropriately when questions are phrased the way he understands. For instance, when asked, "What is your name?" he quickly responds and can answer other direct and precise questions of identification, such as address, phone number, etc. However, if he is asked, "Who are you?" he seems to draw a complete blank and to a stranger might appear aloof and unresponsive.

Motility

At age nine, H. exhibits minimal excessive behaviors, such as hand-flapping. This occurs when he is thwarted and can progress to jumping, kicking, headbanging tantrums. Such tantrums have decreased in frequency over the past year.

Summary

Although H. is still reserved and shy at age nine, his behavior appears almost normal to a stranger. His relatedness continues to have an unusual quality, but he is not "alone" as he was at age five and he is beginning to tolerate change, though he has a preference for the sameness in surroundings and routine. If something out of the ordinary is anticipated in his life, he must have this explained to him if he is to not react with temper tantrums and hyperactivity. Although language is developing nicely, he remains at the level of an average three-and-a-half-year-old in expressive ability.

CASE HISTORY: AUTISM WITH MARKED RETARDATION

R. is the youngest of three sons of an engineer and his wife, who is full time in the home. He was born after a nine-month uncomplicated pregnancy and spontaneous labor with forceps delivery. He had a birth weight of 7 lbs., 5 oz. His mother received both cortisone and ACTH throughout her pregnancy for an exzematoid condition. R.'s neonatal period was uncomplicated; however, towards the end of the first year, his mother noticed that he was different than her other two children. He seemed awkward to hold because he did not mold to her body when he was picked up. R. did not give eye contact to his parents and was indifferent to their overtures. Milestones were delayed; he sat at 10 months, stood at 16 months, walked alone at 22 months. By age two, there was no evidence of either receptive or expressive language. He was seen by a variety of specialists who reported that he appeared to have normal hearing but seemed mentally retarded.

As an infant, R. preferred certain rooms in the house and screamed inconsolably when he was taken outside his own bedroom or the family kitchen. Although he was unresponsive to his parents and siblings, he showed an interest in things, but even then he seemed to have a very constricted sphere of awareness. At age one-and-a-half, R. seldom showed an interest in objects more than a few feet from his person, a characteristic of the normal five-month-old baby. He focused his interest on articles within his reach. In his third year, he became interested in puzzles and blocks which he lined up repeatedly in exactly the same way, rejecting attempts by his mother to engage him in tower building or other varieties of block play.

During the late preschool period he was a severe management problem as he began to tear in a perseverative fashion whatever was available to him—magazines, newspapers, wallpaper, clothes. He seemed to enjoy the noise of tearing. There was no evidence that he understood any words spoken to him. However, he did associate the noise of a car engine entering the driveway with his father's return from work, which he appeared to anticipate with pleasure at about age three. He could also recognize the sound of a candy wrapper being removed and would come to receive the candy. Both of these noises were associated with a visual image and a physical happening.

At age five, R. attended a special nursery program where he began to adapt to group activity. However, language progressed minimally and tearing increased in association with soiling and smearing. At age seven, he was admitted to a state psychiatric facility for children. At this center, his parents were trained in behavior modification techniques in an effort to stop his destructive activity. Through their joint efforts, the parents and staff were able to extinguish his most irritating habits and R. was phased back into his home to attend school in the community. Since he required 24-hour physical supervision, his care was a great strain on his family, frequently keeping them from engaging in normal family activities; thus, R. returned to the hospital on weekends (5a).

Toilet training progressed very slowly over the next six years; it was accomplished for the most part by age 13. Both at home and at school, from age seven onward, there was emphasis on communication using as many modalities of stimulation as possible to provide meaning. Eye contact was initially forced by holding his chin when speaking to him. After about age nine or 10 he began to use spontaneous eye contact with those in his immediate surroundings. At about the same time, he began to associate words with things—a phase that occurs in normal development just before one year. Ever so slowly, R. began to build a vocabulary primarily with nouns. Gradually, he began to associate sounds with happenings and developed a tiny amount of delayed echolalia that was useful and appropriate, if at times redundant.

If we review the status of this case at age 14 in light of the deficits of autism described by Ornitz and Ritvo (18), the effect of autism on development can be more readily understood.

Perceptual Integration

Although hearing is sensitive, R. has a minimal of receptive language compared to an average two-year-old. His major cues from the environment seem to be visual and must be associated with other sensory experiences to be effective. He still has a good bit of difficulty accepting changes in routine or personnel. For instance, if other than the regular staff appear in the hospital kitchen, he is apt to get up and try to push them out of the room since they do not fit with his understanding of what should be. R. has a remarkable sense of time and awareness of the sequence of routines, a characteristic that his parents have capitalized on in such a way as to normalize the appearance of his behavior. Although it is unlikely that he understands more than the anticipation of sequential events, he gets dressed, eats breakfast, rides the bus to school, goes to the appropriate room, and follows the class routine until time to go home. He is beginning to associate meaning to happenings as demonstrated by the following incident.

Because he was given to excessive behaviors on a school trip and became unmanageable when he tried to make other children conform by pushing them into line, straightening their clothes, etc., his teacher decided not to take him on a subsequent school outing. She therefore did not give him a permission slip on the day she passed them out to the other children. R. recognized this as a deviance that would affect him. When he came home, his mother prepared for the next day in her regular routine by putting his lunch money in an envelope. (This is the way R. would understand what will happen the following day.) R. then tore up the envelope and went to get a paper bag, since on field trip days the children take a bag lunch instead of eating at school. His mother gave him the bag lunch so that he could understand that bag lunch did not equal a field trip. Although he did not comprehend the whole thing, he did realize that he had missed something and requested a bag lunch for the next several days.

The aforegoing is an example of the very slow and tedious progress in comprehension made by such youngsters.

Motility Pattern

Bizarre and excessive behaviors, such as flapping, lunging and darting, that were very prominent from age four to age 12 have diminished. They do occur when R. is not occupied or when he is particularly excited, at which time they have the characteristics of neurologic overflow common to preschoolers with maturational lags. Also, at times of anxiety or boredom, R. will sit and rock as he waits for something to happen.

Capacity to Relate

From total indifference towards his parents, R. has become a child who is very attached, seeking them out, standing beside them at school meetings, never letting them out of his gaze. From a child with no eye contact, R. has become a boy who stands out because of his constant staring. He seems to be continuously exploring his environment through his eyes and looking for visual cues. This gives him a look of intelligence and sensitivity for at times he reflects the mood of the social experience by subtle changes in his own expression as he intently watches the faces of those near him who are in conversation. The observer cannot help but note the similarity of this phenomena to echolalia, where the child reflects by echoing what is said to him in an effort to elaborate on his understanding of the meaning of words. (It is interesting that Burton

White (22), in his discussion of normal babies, points out that staring behavior is a normal phenomenon in the second year of life, taking up from 15 to 20% of all waking time.)

Language

At age 14, R. has a receptive vocabulary of about 100 words, which is comparable to that of a normally developing child in the second year of life. He realizes that conversation is a part of social existence and at times tries to participate with jumble jargon that can occasionally be deciphered. Such phrases are repetitions of what others have said to him on previous similar occasions (delayed echolalia)—for instance, "Getcherjaketon" for, "Get your jacket on." This is apt to be said at a time when people are leaving to go home. Elaborate language is primitive at best and there is no spontaneous syntax.

Developmental Rate

At 14, although well developed and nicely proportioned, R. has a childish appearance. Secondary sex characteristics are just starting to emerge. Physical milestones were moderately delayed; toilet training was grossly delayed, most likely due to persistence of negativism rather than lack of physical control.

Summary

R. is a 14-year-old autistic boy with marked retardation who was noted to be different during his first year of life because of unrelatedness and delayed milestones. Language development has been minimal, and although he now understands approximately 100 words or phrases, his expressive speech is almost totally delayed echolalia. He attends special classes in the public school, where he is mainstreamed with trainable retardates for some part of each day. Social behavior has been effectively shaped by his parents so that he conforms well to the social norms at home, at school, and in the community. Yet he still needs the amount of supervision required for a toddler. He cannot be left alone and needs earshot surveillance at all times. His perceptions are frequently confusing and he continues to try to preserve sameness. He understands sequences and schedule and has adapted to his routine, but becomes upset if it is changed. His mother has a sensitivity to his perceptions and manages him skillfully; however, R. is still given to withdrawn or bizarre behavior with those who do not understand him. It is anticipated that he will be a candidate for some type of sheltered community living when he reaches young adulthood.

REFERENCES

1. Barker, P.: *Basic Child Psychiatry.* Baltimore: University Park Press, 1975, pp. 77-101.
2. Bender, L.: Childhood schizophrenia. *Nervous Child,* 1942, 1: 138.
3. Bender, L.: Schizophrenia in childhood—its recognition, description and treatment. *American Journal of Orthopsychiatry,* 1956, 26: 499-506.
4. Chess, S.: Autism in children with congenital rubella. *J. Autism Child. Schizo.,* 1971, 1: 33-47.
5. Christ, A.: Cognitive assessment of the psychotic child: A Piagetian framework. *Journal of Child Psychiatry,* 1977, 16: 2, 226-237.
5a. Drabman, R., Spitalnick, R. et al.: The Five-Two Program: An integrated approach to treating severely disturbed children. *Hosp. & Com. Psychiat.* 24: 1, 33-36, Jan., 1973.
6. Eisenberg, L. and Kanner, L.: Early infantile autism. *Am. Journal Orthopsychiatry,* 1956, 26: 556-566.
7. Eisenberg, L.: Psychiatric disorders of childhood. In A. Friedman and H. Kaplan (Eds). *Comprehensive Textbook of Psychiatry.* Baltimore: Williams & Wilkins, 1967.
8. Erlenmeyer Kimling, L.: Issues pertaining to prevention and intervention of genetic disorders affecting human behavior. *Primary prevention of psychopathology,* Vol. 1, 1977.
9. Freidlander, B.Z., Receptive language development in infancy: Issues and problems, *Merrill-Palmer Quarterly,* 1970, 16: 7-51.
10. Garmezy, N.: The nature of competence in normal and deviant children. Address given at Third Vermont Conference on the Primary Prevention of Psychopathology, June 23, 1977.
11. Gesell, A., and Amatruda, C.S.: Developmental diagnosis. The evaluation and management of normal and abnormal neuropsychologic development. Cited in H. Knoblock and B. Pasamanick (Eds.), *Infancy and Early Childhood.* New York: Harper and Row, 1974, p. 321-323.
12. Hagamen, M.: Family support systems. *Journal of the American Academy of Child Psychiatry,* 1977, 16; 1, 53-66.
13. Hagamen, M: Childhood psychoses: Residential treatment and its alternatives. In B. Wolman, A. Ross, and J. Eagan (Eds.), *Handbook of Treatment of Mental Disorders in Childhood and Adolescence.* Englewood Cliffs, N.J.: Prentice-Hall, 1978.
14. Kanner, L.: Autistic disturbance of affective contact. *Nervous Child,* 1943, 2: 217-250.
15. Kolvin, I.: Psychoses in childhood—a comparative study. In M. Rutter (Ed.), *Infantile Autism: Concepts, Characteristics and Treatment.* London: Churchill Livingstone, 1971, pp. 7-26.
16. Makita, K.: The age of onset of childhood schizophrenia, *Folia Psychiatrica Neurologica Jaeonica,* 1966, 20: 111-121.
17. National Society for Autistic Children: *Working Definition of Autistic Children.* Albany, New York: Jan. 14, 1973.
18. Ornitz, E.M. and Ritvo, E.R.: Perceptual inconstancy in early infantile autism. *Archives of General Psychiatry,* 1968, 18: 76-98.
19. Rutter, N.: Concepts of autism—a review of research. *Journal Child Psycho. and Psychiatry,* 1968, 2: 1-25.

20. Rutter, M.: The development of infantile autism. *Psychological Medicine,* 1974, 4: 147-163.
21. Ritvo, E.R.: *Autism—Diagnosis, Current Research, Management.* New York: Spectrum Publications, 1976, p. 5.
22. White, B. L.: *The First Three Years of Life.* Englewood Cliffs, N.J.: Prentice-Hall, 1975, p. 121.

9

Minimal Brain Dysfunction

RICHARD A. GARDNER, M.D.

From the early 1920s (when our present child psychotherapeutic approaches first began to be generally applied) until the middle-to-late 1950s, most children with behavioral and/or learning problems were considered to be suffering with psychogenic disorders. This view was especially common around the time of the Second World War when the influence of classical psychoanalysis was at its height.

With the recognition that many children with psychiatric disturbance were actually suffering with a neurophysiological disorder (commonly referred to as brain injury, hyperactivity and, more recently, minimal brain dysfunction), an ever increasing percentage of children are being diagnosed as "organic." The pendulum has shifted so far in the direction of viewing many children's psychiatric disturbances as neurologic in etiology that there are clinics in which the overwhelming majority of child patients are so diagnosed. One could say that, at the time of this writing, if the disease has not become pandemic, the diagnosis certainly has. Yet in spite of its vogue, there are still those "holdouts" who deny the existence of the disorder (or more accurately, group of disorders) and consider the dysfunction to be more in the heads of those who make the diagnosis than in the brains of the children being so labeled.

An important reason for this situation is the lack of well-defined criteria upon which the diagnosis is often made. The most subjective and impressionistic guidelines are often utilized when deciding that a child exhibits hyperactivity, distractibility, impulsivity, impaired attention span, and the host of other signs and symptoms that have been considered to be part of the syndrome. The problem has been further compounded by the looseness with which developmental data have been

269

utilized in making the diagnosis. Most agree that some, if not many, of the symptoms of minimal brain dysfunction (MBD) can be best understood as developmental lags and impairments. (Many MBD symptoms, e.g, some types of visual and auditory processing problems, as well as motor coordination deficits, are not primarily the result of developmental lags.) Yet conclusions regarding the developmental component are often made without the utilization of normative data—just the "clinical impression" that the child is too old to be exhibiting a given type of undesirable behavior, but that it is expectable performance in a younger child. Until such data are obtained and rigorously utilized, the field is bound to remain in a state of confusion (31).

In this chapter, I describe those aspects of the MBD syndrome that are generally considered to reflect developmental lags and disorders. I confine myself, however, to those developmental impairments for which there is good objective evidence available—evidence that will enable the examiner to quantitatively define the nature and extent of each developmental impairment. The rate of neurological maturation (for the purpose of this presentation I will use the terms *maturation* and *development* interchangeably) varies considerably among children. For example, some begin walking at 10 months and some not until 16 months. The crucial question confronting the examiner is where to draw the line between the normal and the abnormal. The best kinds of data provide percentiles and/or standard deviations. Accordingly, the examiner is able to state: "Ninety percent of children Robert's age can stand longer on one foot than he can," or "Joan's performance on the Raven's Coloured Matrices is in the 90th percentile." The examiner can then state what he considers to be the significance of such findings. It is only in this way that diagnostic confusion will be reduced and therapeutic efficacy enhanced.

The factors that can contribute to significant deviations in neurological development are multiple and there is much that we have yet to learn. Genetic factors are no doubt operative. But anything that can interfere with central nervous system functioning may result in developmental lags. Any entity that deleteriously affects nerve cells, central nervous system connective tissue, cerebral blood and spinal fluid, and brain and skull size may impair neurological development.

The nerve cell myelination process provides an example of the way in which developmental lags can result. Yakovlev and Lecours (57), in an excellent study, have demonstrated that there is great variation among the parts of the brain with regard to the age when the myelination process is completed. Myelinization begins during fetal life and terminates at different times in different parts of the brain. Although most nerve fibers in the brain are completely myelinated by the third to fourth year of life, certain sections of the brain do not complete the process until many years later. The reticular formation, for example, is not fully myelinated until the teens and many intracortical association fibers don't complete the process until *the fourth decade of life.* It is reasonable to assume that nerve fibers do not function optimally until completely myelinated and that children whose myelination process is particularly slow will manifest various types of neurological immaturity. Some children with such lags may represent only the lower end of the bell-shaped curve for myelinization rate. In others, disease processes may have caused the retarded myelin development. And in still others a combination of factors—myelination lag *and* exposure to detrimental extrinsic influences—may bring about developmental lag.

The list of disease processes that have been implicated as etiological factors in facilitating or causing developmental lags is extensive and it is beyond the scope of this article to discuss them in detail. Briefly, the following have been implicated with varying degrees of confirmation: 1) prenatal infection, intoxication, radiation, hemorrhage, dehydration, and cardiovascular disease; 2) perinatal infection, hemorrhage, trauma, cephalopelvic disproportion, umbilical cord complications, eclampsia, resuscitation problems, and prematurity; 3) postnatal infection, intoxication, trauma, nutritional deficiency; 4) early childhood seizures, trauma, and infection. For a more complete description of possible etiological factors in minimal brain dysfunction, the reader is referred to Kawi and Pasamanick (34), Ross and Ross (48) and Wender (54).

A discussion of minimal brain dysfunction and developmental lags must consider the concept of *soft neurological signs.* This somewhat controversial concept was first introduced, to the best of my knowledge, by Bender (3) in a discussion of minor neurological impairments seen in schizophrenic children. The term is generally used to refer to two classes of mild neurological impairment often seen in children with MBD. Denckla and Rudel (19) use the terms "soft developmental type" and "soft neurological type" to refer to these two classes.

The first type includes manifestations of developmental lags such as lateness in suppressing such primitive signs as the Babinski and tonic neck reflexes; significant lateness in such developmental milestones as standing, walking, talking, and bowel and bladder training; and persistence of immature speech patterns on a neurological (as opposed to a psychogenic) basis. Such signs have to be elicited during the period during which they should have disappeared, but *before* they belatedly do so. For example, the average child begins to walk during the 10-14 month period. A child who is still not walking at 19 months would be considered by most examiners to have a neurological developmental lag that many would label a soft neurological sign. If at 20 months the child begins to walk, the sign would no longer be present. If the child was first seen at 20 months, then one would have to make some judgment about the parents' reliability in order to decide whether or not such a sign *was* present. (Signs, by definition, are manifestations observed by the examiner.) This introduces a subjective element, at times, which may compromise the credibility of those who report such signs.

The second type comprises those mild abnormalities that one may find when conducting a traditional neurological examination. They include such findings as: reflex asymmetries; hypo- and hyperreflexia; mild tremors and choreiform movements; motor overflow; and mild coordination deficits. Again, subjective elements may enter when making such decisions. For example, one examiner may consider a child to have 2+ deep tendon reflexes (normal) and another may decide that they are 3+ (hyperreflexic).

Many, like Ingram (33), do not believe in the existence of such signs and consider use of the term a manifestation of "soft thinking" on the part of those examiners who believe in the concept. Schain (49) is also dubious about the existence of soft neurological signs because of the vague criteria upon which they are often based and the low inter-examiner agreement found when multiple examinations of the same patient are conducted. I personally am an adherent to the concept of soft signs. It seems reasonable to me that for many signs and symptoms there should be borderline and intermediate states, rather than just a yes or no situation. The best way to settle this conflict is to conduct objective studies of both normals and those with MBD—studies in which one *quantifies* the findings. In many areas, such data are already available (and will be presented in various parts of this chapter) and readily confirm, in my opinion, the existence of such intermediate states. For many other soft neurological signs, studies still need to be done to determine whether or not they in fact do exist (again, in various parts of this chapter I will define the types of studies still necessary for such clarification).

PHYSICAL GROWTH

Although the terms growth and development are often used interchangeably, growth, strictly speaking, refers to the increase in body size whereas development refers to advancement in function and complexity.

Height and Weight

In evaluating a child with MBD, one does well to measure *height* and *weight* and determine whether such dimensions are in the normal range. Most standard pediatric textbooks have charts of such data. However, the author has found useful the growth curves provided by the National Center for Health Statistics (40). The data for these charts may be the most comprehensive yet obtained and enable the examiner to quickly determine the child's percentile for height and weight. If one can get longer-term height and weight information from the child's pediatrician or previous medical examinations, one can plot a growth curve and determine whether the child is remaining within the same percentile band or shifting. (The causes of such shifts are particularly important to investigate as they may pinpoint the time of onset of pathological processes and thereby give information about the etiology of disorders affecting growth.)

When utilizing such charts, it is important for the examiner to consider certain factors which might affect the child's growth. Prematurity will often result in a child's being smaller. Calculating the child's age from the mother's expected date of delivery rather than from the actual date will make the child a few months younger and result in a shift to a higher percentile, but this may often still not place him or her in the average range. Racial factors must be considered; for example, orientals are usually shorter than caucasians. Nationality may be operative; for example, Scandinavians are often taller than Italians. Family factors must be considered; the shortness of a child whose father and grandfather were also short should be considered less pathological and less supportive of the MBD diagnosis than a short child with no such family history. Nutritional deficiency may not only reduce height and weight but serve as an etiological factor in MBD. Similarly, when physical diseases such as chronic nephritis, celiac disease, and congenital heart disease are present, not only may the child's height and weight be low, but these conditions may contribute to the child's organic brain syndrome. Lastly, one must consider the child who is not only small for his or her age with regard to height and weight, but whose entire neurological and emotional status may be below age level. Such children might do well being considered one or two years younger than they really are and treated as such in most areas of functioning. These are the children who might do quite well by repeating kindergarten. They are just one to two years behind in most areas of functioning and continue to progress in all areas in a consistent way. They are not the same as retarded children who, as the years go on, may remain fixated at early levels in various cognitive functions.

Head Circumference

In evaluating the MBD child, one does well to measure the *head circumference*. The aforementioned NCHS Growth Charts (40) provide good normative data and percentiles from birth to 36 months; Paine and Oppé (43) provide such norms from six months to 10 years of age. When measuring head size, it is important to appreciate that body growth occurs in a cephalo-caudad direction, so that the younger the child (infant, fetus, and embryo), the greater the size of the head compared to the rest of the body. One does well, therefore, to compare head size to the child's height before coming to any conclusions. Accordingly, a child whose head circumference is in the 15th percentile, for example, and whose height is also in that range should not necessarily be considered to have any abnormality of head size. If, however, such a child's height is in the 50th percentile, then his or her head should not be considered to be developing properly and the cause of his or her relatively small head circumference should be investigated.

Normally, the posterior fontanel and the cranial bone sutures should be closed by six to eight months and the anterior sutures by 16 to 18 months. The size of the skull is generally determined by the pressures placed on the bony plates by the skull contents, particularly the brain. Premature fusion of the cranial bones will result in various skull abnormalities, usually referred to as craniosynostoses. The diagnosis of such conditions requires detailed measurements of various skull dimensions and reontgenographic examination. When, however, cerebral a- or hypogenesis is present, there is a uniform diminution of pressure on all cranial plates and microcephaly results (the sutures may then remain open). Macrocephaly may also be seen on physical examination, a common cause of which is varying degrees of hydrocephalus. In my experience, the most common abnormalities in head size that are associated with MBD are mild microcephaly of unknown etiology (sometimes presumed to be associated with mild cerebral hypogenesis) and arrested hydrocephalus (again producing only mild to moderate enlargement of the head).

Bone Age

At times, one may want to determine the *bone age* of a child with MBD. Such a determination is probably more accurate than height, weight, and head circumference in evaluating for the presence of a lag in body development. The appearance and union of the various epiphysial centers of ossification follow a definite time schedule from birth to maturity. By comparing with norms, roentgenograms of the child's level of bone ossification and union, one can determine the child's "skeletal age" or "bone age." Most often the bones of the hand and wrist are used. Such evaluations, of course, must be done by those trained in these procedures. But the results can be useful for those evaluating a child for the presence of MBD.

PRIMITIVE REFLEXES

The appearance and disappearance of certain primitive reflexes provide an excellent example of the developmental type of soft neurological sign. These primitive reflexes can be divided into two categories: 1) those that disappear with age and 2) those that appear with age. A soft neurological sign is considered to be present when the reflex is still present a significant time after the overwhelming majority of children have lost it or when it fails to appear when most, if not all, normal children exhibit it.

Moro Reflex

An example of the first category of primitive reflex is the Moro reflex. If a newborn infant is placed on its back and one slams down sharply on its bed or table, the infant's arms extend and then abduct as if it were embracing someone, its fingers spread, and its femora become flexed on the pelvis. It is as if the infant were trying to climb up a pole. The same reaction can be elicited by maneuvers that cause a sudden extension of the infant's head on its spine. Accordingly, if the baby is pulled up by the arms from the supine position, while allowing the head to remain on the table, the reflex will be exhibited when the arms are dropped. Or if the child is held with the examiner's right hand supporting its head and the left hand supporting its trunk, the reflex will exhibit itself if the right hand is quickly dropped so that the infant's head can fall back 20-30 degrees. Paine and Oppé (43) provide data regarding the ages at which this reflex becomes suppressed by the infant's developing brain. According to their findings, about 93% of infants will still exhibit the reflex by one month, only 22% by five months, and by six months normal children should no longer manifest the sign. Its presence beyond that time is strongly suggestive of neurological impairment.

The Tonic Neck Reflex

This is a more complex mechanism that is of greater predictive value than the Moro with regard to neurological dysfunction. When the infant is placed in the supine position, and its neck sharply rotated along the long axis of its body, the extremities which the child faces become extended whereas those it turns away from become flexed. According to Paine and Oppé's data, this reflex may or may not be present at birth. If not, it should develop quickly so that by one month it is present in 67% of children. It reaches its peak frequency at two months, with 90% of children manifesting it. Its frequency then declines so that by six months only 11% exhibit it and by seven months it was not present in any of the children they studied. Its presence beyond that time is strongly suggestive of neurological impairment. The reflex is probably a residuum of the withdrawal reaction that lower animals exhibit when suddenly surprised by an enemy. Imagine, for example, an animal sleeping in the prone position, suddenly being awakened by a foe. It does well to face the source of alarm while recoiling away from the danger. This is best done by extending the limbs close to the foe which the animal is facing and flexing those that are most distant from the enemy. In this way the animal falls back and removes itself somewhat from the danger, while still maintaining itself in the best position to observe it.

Although Paine and Oppé consider the tonic neck reflex to be normally obliterated by seven months and Critchley (16) states that he has never seen it beyond eight months of age in normal children, Bender (3) believes that it can persist in modified form until the age of six years. She believes that when a normal child of four or five years of age is asked to stand erect with his or her arms extended, and the examiner twists the child's head, the arm which the child then faces will extend and the other arm flex slightly. Exhibiting such arm movements beyond six years she considers to be a sign of neurological impairment, and this is especially seen in schizophrenic children whom Bender believes to be suffering primarily with a neurophysiological disorder. She goes further and holds that the whirling that these children sometimes exhibit is an exaggeration of the tonic neck reflex, with the whole body moving on its longitudinal axis, rather than merely the extremities.

Babinski Reflex

The pattern of loss of the Babinski reflex provides another example of this type of soft neurological sign. Paine and Oppé (43) state that the Babinski sign is generally present at birth and is usually suppressed by the age of one year. However, Brain and Wilkinson's excellent study (9) reveals that things are not so simple. They found that a child may lose the Babinski sign as early as nine months and as late as 24 months. However, the period of diminution of the reflex is broad. Whereas in the newborn the reflex can be elicited from a wide variety of stimuli as high as the abdomen and the thighs, the area from which the Babinski can be evoked gradually narrows as the child grows older until it confines itself to the sole of the foot. In addition, during the period when the reflex is becoming obliterated, there are times when it may be elicited and times when it may not be. The only thing that one can say with certainty is that by 24 months it should no longer be present and that children who exhibit it beyond that time are strongly suspect for neurological dysfunction.

Pincer Grasp

The development of the ability to oppose the thumb to the forefinger (pincer grasp) is an example of a sign that appears with age. At birth the normal child will exhibit a grasp reflex, i.e., there is reflex grasping to palmar stimulation. By four-six months the child should develop the capacity to voluntarily (rather than reflexively) grasp an object by grossly clenching it (but not with forefinger-thumb opposition) (22). Around the sixth month some children will start to be able to grasp voluntarily, utilizing forefinger-thumb grasp. According to Paine and Oppé (43), 16% of children do this by seven months, 63% by nine months, 95% by 11 months, and 100% by the age of 12 months. Accordingly, a child who cannot utilize a pincer grasp after one year of age is probably suffering with a neurological impairment.

THE DEVELOPMENTAL MILESTONES

Although the preceding discussion covered phenomena that might justifiably be referred to as developmental milestones (and my subsequent discussion will include such material as well), the term is generally reserved for those landmarks that one usually inquires about in routine history-taking in pediatrics and child psychiatry. The milestones that I generally inquire about and the age ranges at which they take place are:

smiles, two months; crawls with abdomen on floor, six-seven months; sits for short periods without support, seven-eight months; creeping on hands and knees, eight-nine months; stands with support, 10 months; first words, nine to 12 months; walks with support, 12 months; walks without support, 13-15 months; bowel and bladder trained during waking hours, 24 months; and simple sentences, 18-24 months. Any pediatric textbook will provide the reader with similar tables.

It is important that the examiner appreciate that these milestones are rough averages and that children vary greatly with regard to the ages at which they accomplish these tasks. Most examiners appreciate that parents may be extremely unreliable regarding the dates at which the child reached each of the landmarks. In fact, it is probably only a rare parent who will be accurate regarding most of them. It is common for a parent to guess an answer rather than say that he or she doesn't recall the specific time when the child first exhibited the behavior inquired about. My experience has been that the age of the first words and the age when the child first walked unaided are best remembered. In addition, parents usually have better recall for their firstborn children than for those who came subsequently. By the time the third or fourth child appears, each step is no longer a unique event for the parents and so is less likely to be recalled years later.

Children with MBD are often late in reaching the various developmental milestones. Again, one must be cautious regarding what one designates as late. A child who does not walk until 18 or 19 months is late in acquiring this capability. However, the child who is not speaking sentences at 2½ may still be perfectly normal. Bernstein, Page, and Janicki (8) found that 62% of 413 hyperactive children they studied had lags in their developmental milestones.

SPEECH

It is important to differentiate between speech and language if one is to properly understand the difficulties of children with MBD. Language refers to the process by which one forms and processes the *symbols* for various entities. Speech refers to the articulation and verbalization of such symbols. For example, when a child is shown a pen and asked what it is, he must first have learned which linguistic symbols his particular society utilizes to refer to that particular object. If he speaks English and has no cerebral impairment, he will think of the word *pen.* If he is French he will think of *plume,* and if he is German the word *Feder* will come to mind. Each culture and society may devise its own linguistic symbol for an object. When the child then utters the word for the object, he uses speech, and it is this aspect of the sequence, the phase of articulation, that I will be focusing upon here. (I will subsequently discuss certain aspects of language development as well.)

Because of the great variability of speech development among normal children, a child's level of speech maturation may be a poor criterion upon which to base a diagnosis of MBD (12). In addition, psychological factors play an immensely important role in the rate at which a child will learn to speak and the level of maturity he will attain. Wyatt (56) and de Hirsch (17) have emphasized how the mother's feedback, her availability as a speech model, and her involvement with the child play a vital role in speech development. Furthermore, regression of speech and fixation at immature speech levels are common manifestations of psychogenic disorders of childhood. Accordingly, delineating the purely neurological factors in abnormal speech development may be especially difficult. Yet, there are normal sequences of speech development, sequences that are neurologically based, and it behooves the examiner to be familiar with them if he or she is to properly evaluate the child with MBD.

De Hirsch (17) describes the following stages in the normal development of speech: cooing, birth-three months; babbling, five to ten months; echolalia, 10-12 months; single words; two-word sentences; and more complex grammatical forms. Children with neurodevelopmental speech disorders may reveal speech patterns immature for their age. In addition, they may present with a history of sucking difficulties, chewing problems, excessive and prolonged drooling, a long history of nasality, and delayed onset of speech. With regard to the latter, most clinicians hold that a child should start utilizing meaningful speech by the age of three. If a child is not speaking by four, one must consider serious pathology, but it is possible that only minor psychogenic disturbance is present. However, most agree that if a child is not using meaningful speech by five, then he or she is suffering with a serious psychiatric disturbance and one must think of such disorders as schizophrenia, mental retardation, and autism.

The aforementioned speech difficulties are manifestations of the generalized developmental lag that is so often seen in children with MBD. The immature or slowly developing speech is one manifestation of the more generalized neurophysiological immaturity. In addition, one may see speech abnormalities that are related to more specific brain disorders. The child with cerebellar problems associated with coordination difficulties and intention tremors is likely to have an articulatory deficit. Just as the child's fingers may not move smoothly on the finger-to-nose test, the tongue does not move smoothly in the mouth and the other muscles of articulation do not function optimally. Extrapyramidal lesions producing resting tremors and choreoathetoid movements are likely to involve the articulatory musculature with similar motor difficulties.

Lastly, certain neurological impairments may result in the child's appearing to have a speech problem when there is none. For example, an auditory processing problem may interfere with the child's accuracy of hearing so that speech becomes impaired because the child is not likely to verbalize well if he or she cannot process auditory input well (10). And the dysnomic child, as well, may appear to have a speech problem when he or she really has difficulty in word finding, that is, in retrieving from memory the word he or she wishes to verbalize.

The clinician who is not trained in speech pathology may find useful the articulatory criteria proposed by Shank (50), who holds that children should have mastered the following sounds at each of the years listed below:

3.5 years: p,b,m,w,h
4.5 years: t,d,n,g,k,ng,y
5.5 years: f,v,s,z
6.5 years: sh,zh,l,th
8.0 years: s,z,r,wh

In this table s and z appear twice because the loss of the central incisors between six and seven causes the child to mispronounce these letters during this period. A four-year-old child, for example, is likely to have mastered the *b* sound but not the *v*. Accordingly, he or she may say *glub* instead of *glove*. Proper pronunciation of the *r* comes late and a *w* is often easier for the child to substitute. Accordingly, *rabbit* becomes *wabbit*, and *tree* becomes *twee*. Another useful test of speech development is that utilized by Peters et al. (44). The child is shown a series of 24 pictures of objects easily recognized by most children (e.g., dress, flag, clown, star, tree, dog, and thumb). The child is merely asked to name the pictures as the examiner points to them. Points are given for each correctly pronounced word and points deducted for each word that is not accurately articulated. Although the normative data are rough for each age bracket (2½-3½, 4-6, and 7+), the test does provide the examiner with a general level of the child's articulatory maturity.

Speech problems are common among children with MBD. They are related to the language difficulties so commonly seen in these children as well as other neurological impairments. Owen et al. (42) found that 42 percent of the educationally handicapped children in their study needed speech therapy, whereas only 20 percent of the normal control group required such treatment.

MOTOR COORDINATION

Problems in motor coordination are frequently described in children with MBD. It is in this area especially that the subjectivity of the examiner may cast doubt on the validity of the reported findings. For example, a child neurologist may state that his five-year-old patient exhibited poor coordination when serially opposing his thumb to each of the other four fingers. One can justifiably ask how one differentiates the normal from the abnormal when a certain amount of impaired coordination is to be expected of the five-year-old when performing this task. The examiner might reply that he has been observing children perform this maneuver for 30 years and can state with certainty that this particular child was slower and exhibited more slippage and opposition failure than the normal five-year-old.

There are two possibilities here. The examiner is correct or he is incorrect. If he is correct, it will be difficult, if not impossible, for him to explain to the novice examiner how he knows the exact degree of impairment that differentiates the normal from the abnormal. Must the novice observe children for 30 years before he or she can state with certainty where that point lies? Even then, his or her point of differentiation might be different from the predecessor. Or perhaps the experienced examiner is using inaccurate criteria for differentiation and therefore diagnosing an abnormality when the child's performance is normal—and for 30 years he has been making the same mistake. The utilization of such impressionistic diagnostic criteria has contributed to much confusion in the field. The examiner does well, therefore, to use only tests for which there have been well-defined criteria established and good normal and abnormal data collected. I will discuss here those tests that I have found most useful in evaluating for the presence of coordination deficits. I will comment as well on some commonly used tests that may be less useful.

Fine Motor Coordination

Denckla (20,21) has placed repetitive finger-to-thumb tapping coordination on a more objective foundation by measuring the speed with which children from ages five to 10 perform 20 repetitive thumb-to-index-finger taps (average of two trials with each hand). For example, a seven-year-old boy is found to perform such a maneuver with his right hand in six seconds on the first trial and five seconds on the second. His average is then 5.5 seconds. Referring to Denckla's normative data, one finds that the average seven-year-old boy (N = 39) performs this maneuver in 5.94 seconds with his right hand (S.D. = 0.81). Accordingly, this patient's score is in the normal range—suggesting no problem in fine motor hand coordination. Denckla has also obtained normative data for successive finger-to-thumb opposition by measuring the time it takes five-to-10-year-old children to perform five series of successive passages of the thumb (starting with opposition to the little finger) past each of the other four fingers (a total of 20 taps). Again, the average score of two trials with each hand is obtained. For example, a nine-year-old girl takes 13.5 seconds to perform 20 such taps on the first trial with her left hand and 14.0 seconds on the second trial. Her average score is 13.75 seconds. Denckla's normative data indicate that the average nine-year-old girl (N = 14) performs this maneuver in 9.84 seconds with her left hand (S.D. = 2.20). Accordingly, this patient's score is almost two standard deviations slower than the norm and strongly suggests the presence of a fine motor coordination problem.

Another useful test of fine motor coordination is Part I (Eye-Motor Coordination) of the *Frostig Test of Visual Perception* (25). Here the child is asked to draw lines within progressively narrower paths (without touching the sides). Elsewhere, he or she is asked to draw straight lines between points with as little deviation from the midline as possible. Normative data are available from ages four years 0 months to seven years 11 months. One can express the child's performance on this sub-test in terms of chronological and/or "perceptual age." For example, a girl six years and three months old obtains a raw score of six on this part, which corresponds to a scaled score of seven. The average girl her age obtains a scaled score of 10. To make the score more meaningful, one could say, after referring to the proper chart, that she is performing like the average child of four years three-to-five months. Although fine motor coordination impairment can result in a low score on the Frostig I subtest, children with dyspraxia and visual processing problems may also do poorly on this test.

The *Purdue Pegboard Test* (45) has excellent potential as a test for fine motor coordination in children. It was originally designed to test adult applicants for precision assembly-line work in factories and has proved itself to be a sensitive instrument for singling out those who would be particularly adept at industrial tasks requiring fine motor dexterity. There are four sections to the test. In the first, the examiner records the total number of metal pegs the subject can place in a row of holes with the preferred hand during a 30-second period. In the second section, the same procedure is repeated with the non-preferred hand. Next, the number of pegs the subject can fill with both hands simultaneously is recorded. In the fourth section, the subject is asked to perform the more complicated task of first placing the peg in the hole, then successively placing a washer, a short collar, and then a second washer on the peg. The total number of such assemblies accomplished during a one-minute period is recorded. This last section, in my opinion, is an extremely sensitive test of fine motor coordination.

The test material includes extensive normative data for adults. However, I only know of one study (15) in which normative data were collected on children. The total number of children utilized, however, for all age groups combined and both sexes was 183 and only the first three sections of the pegboard test were included in the study. Regrettably, the authors omitted the fourth section, the one I consider to be the most sensitive test of fine motor coordination. This author has collected data on all four sections of the Purdue Pegboard Test for both normal children and those with MBD. These findings are presented in other publications (26b, 26c). Rapin, Tourk, and Costa (46) found the Purdue Pegboard Test to be useful in differentiating normal children from those with brain damage. They found that 98% of normal school children performed at their expected level of competence, whereas only 22% of children with brain damage did so. Knights and Ogilvie (37), however, found no difference between brain damaged and normal children on their performance on the Purdue Pegboard. This examiner's initial data appear to support the findings of Rapin et al. that the test is useful in such differentiation (26b, 26c).

Knights and Moule (38) have used a standard hand tally counter mounted on a board as a very sensitive test of fine motor coordination. The child is simply asked to tap the lever of the mechanical counter as rapidly as he or she can during four 10-second trials. The counter itself records the total number of taps. The child's score is the mean of the best three of the four trials. The authors provide normative data for 169 children from CA five through 14.

The Denver Developmental Screening Test (24) has four sections, one of which is devoted to "fine motor-adaptive" development. A few of the tasks in this section test for fine motor coordination. The tasks are scored primarily on a pass-fail basis (for example, thumb-finger grasp, and neat pincer grasp of raisin). For every age level, one can determine approximately what percentage of children are capable of successfully performing the given task. Some of the subtests of the *Lincoln-Oseretsky Motor Development Scale* (51) are designed to evalute fine motor coordination. The author has found subtests 5 (touching fingertips), 17 (tapping), and 27 (tracing mazes) to be the most valuable in this regard. (The maze test here is not truly a maze in that the child is not required to select from among various paths; rather, he or she is asked to draw within the narrow path with many right-angled turns while avoiding pencil contact with the sides. Accordingly, this is primarily a test of fine motor coordination.) However, the scoring system is somewhat vague and not as quantitatively precise as most of the aforementioned tests.

Fine and Gross Motor Coordination

Many types of motor performance involve both gross and fine motor activity. An example is writing, which in the early years is primarily a gross motor act, but as the child matures it gradually progresses to a fine motor act. I know of no studies in which large amounts of normative data have been collected on pencil grasp at various ages. The author has conducted a preliminary study, the findings of which are reported in another publication (26b). Until more data are collected, we have to rely on somewhat impressionistic guidelines. Most examiners hold that from birth until the age of three the normal child will grasp a pencil with a closed fist. This is called the *simian grasp* because it is similar to the way apes will grasp a pencil or rod. It is also called the ulnar grasp, because the fingers on the ulnar aspect of the hand are used, whereas in more mature grasps (v.i.) only fingers on the radial side of the hand are utilized. The child holds the pencil in the clenched fist with the thumb usually covering the index finger. When writing (or scribbling, which is far more common prior to three) there is little movement of the muscles of the fingers, hand, or forearm. Rather, most of the pencil movement results from movements of the arm above the elbow. All muscles, distal to the elbow, are held quite rigidly. "Writing" at this age, then, is primarily a gross motor activity with little peripheral fine motor movement. Retention of the simian grasp beyond the age of three is generally considered by child neurologists to be a pathological sign and suggestive of a lag in neurological development. The longer beyond the age of three a child exhibits a simian grasp, the more pathological its significance.

Between the ages of three and five the normal child will exhibit a three-point pencil grasp. The pencil is held between the thumb, index, and third fingers. However, the second and third fingers are hyper-extended at the distal joints rather than flexed as is the case with the adult pencil grasp. Accordingly, the palmar surfaces of the first three fingers are in extensive contact with the pencil, whereas in the adult grasp only the tips of these three fingers are generally in contact with the pencil. The pencil is jammed into the webbed space between the thumb and the index finger or it may be pressed against the index finger. Because of the extensive contact between the surfaces of the pencil and the fingers, the pencil cannot be easily wiggled; rather, it is rigidly held. When writing, the primary movement is from the forearm, rather than from the utilization of the intrinsic muscles of the hand and fingers. In this grasp one can see a progression from the gross arm movements of the simian grasp to the more peripheral fine motor movements of the adult grasp. It is an intermediate development between the adult and the simian grasps. A child who exhibits this kind of grasp beyond the age of five and a half is probably suffering with some kind of neurodevelopmental lag; the older the child, the more serious its pathological implications.

After the age of five and a half, the normal child is capable of holding a pencil like an adult. The distal joints of the thumb, index, and third fingers are flexed. Accordingly, the point of contact between the hand and the pencil is primarily at the tips of the first three fingers and at the point where the pencil rests on the web between the thumb and the index finger. Accordingly, this way of holding the pencil is generally referred to as the *pincer grasp* or the *tripod grasp*. The primary movements of the pencil originate from the distal fingers, not the hand, and not the forearm. This represents the final step in the progression from the gross arm movements of the simian grasp to the highly sophisticated fine motor movements of the adult pincer grasp. However, the developmental changes do not stop here. Generally the pincer grasp of the five-year-old is rigid. It is not until eight or so that the pencil is held so loosely that it can be wiggled by the examiner. A child whose muscles are hypotonic may go through the above progressions; however, in no phase is the pencil held tightly. Rather, it is loosely held and often dangles. Furthermore, it can easily be removed from the hand and may often be dropped.

It is important also for the examiner to appreciate that psychological factors may play a role in pencil grasp, but when requested to write letters, the more mature tripod grasp may be used because the child has come to associate scribbling with the immature grasp and writing with the more mature. Or the psychologically regressed child may use an immature grasp as one manifestation of the regression. Lastly, it is important for the examiner to appreciate that these three grasps are the most common. There are other grasps that one may encounter that do not fit well into any of these categories.

On occasion, one will see an adult who is completely normal in the neurodevelopmental sense and yet he or she will hold a pencil with collapsed distal digital joints (extended rather than flexed). Such a phenomenon is most likely a result of the retention of an earlier habit on a psychogenic basis rather than a manifestation of a neurodevelopmental lag. Many forms of behavior manifest such habit retention. For example, we generally retain throughout life the accents of our childhood even though most of our adult years may be spent in another environment. We may retain the childhood names of our siblings when they themselves have long given up the name and others never use it.

The ability to oppose the thumb to the forefinger (and the other three fingers) is a uniquely human quality. The higher apes can use only a simian grasp. This capacity was not only useful for primitive man in the development of tools but, more recently, has been crucial to the progress of modern industrial society. This capacity, along with more complex and sophisticated cerebral functioning, is the primary differentiating factor between man and all lower animals and has enabled him to surpass all lower forms of life in adaptation and creativity.

The *Lincoln-Oseretsky Scale* (51) has a number of subtests that evaluate both fine and gross motor coordination. Subtest 12 attempts to quantitate the child's capacity to catch a ball. Catching a ball requires the child to accurately move his or her arm to the place where the ball is likely to be (a gross motor act) and to grasp it at exactly the right moment with one's fingers (a fine motor act). The subtest provides specific instructions regarding distance between examiner and child, method of throw, ball trajectory, etc. Because the child's success depends in part upon the examiner's accuracy (and he is not immune from coordination problems), the test results are not too reliable. In subtest 15 the child is asked to balance an 18-inch rod crosswise on the index finger for at least 10 seconds. Both fine and gross motor abilities are evaluated in this subtest. My own experience with it has been that most of my patients do not seem to be as facile with this task as those in the normative group and I am therefore a little suspicious of the norms. In subtest 18 the child's speed in placing pins and matchsticks into boxes is recorded. This is a good test of fine motor coordination and some gross motor activity is also called into play as the child moves his or her arms back and forth. (It is not, in my opinion, as good a test of fine motor coordination as the fourth section of the Purdue Pegboard.) As mentioned, my main objection to the Lincoln-Oseretsky Scale is the vagueness of the developmental norms, so even the best subtests on the scale become less credible because of them.

Gross Motor Coordination

Denckla (21) has provided some excellent normative data for a number of tests of gross motor coordination. In each of these tests the child is timed while performing a task involving repetitive movements. The child with gross motor impairment will perform the task more slowly than the normal child and so one can objectify the extent of the defect by measuring the amount of time it takes for the child to perform the task. The tasks for which she has collected normative data for boys and girls ages five to 10 are: 20 repetitive foot taps (with heel fixed on the floor the child is timed while executing, as rapidly as he or she can, 20 taps of the ball of the foot on the floor); 20 repetitive heel-toe alternating movements (starting with the heel touching the floor and the ball of the foot raised, the child is timed while executing as rapidly as he or she can 10 pairs of rocking movements in which the heel and the forefoot alternately touch the floor). Mean scores for each age are provided, as well as standard deviations so that the examiner can determine exactly how abnormal his or her patient is and at what age level the patient is functioning. The only drawback to Denckla's studies is that there are only 14 children in each age/sex group. Although statistical significance is claimed, a much larger group needs to be studied if one is to confidently apply these norms to all children.

Denckla (21) has also collected norms for hopping on one foot. For this activity the child is not timed; rather the examiner asks the child to try to hop 50 times on each foot and records the number of hops the child successfully performs before placing the other foot on the floor. Data are supplied indicating the percentage of children at each age level (from five to 10) who successfully perform 50 hops. For example, 85% of five-year-olds do 12 hops (the 50-hop criterion is not used for those below seven); 85% of six-year-olds do 25 hops; and 90% of seven-year-olds do 50 hops. Touwen and Prechtl (52) also present normative data for hopping. They merely state the number of hops children of different ages should be able to successfully perform. (The number of children upon which their data are based is not provided.) For example: the average four-year-old should be able to hop five to eight times, the five-year-old nine to 12 times, the six-year-old 13-16, and the seven-year-old 20 times. There are obvious discrepancies between the two sets of normative data, suggesting strongly that more definitive studies in this area need still be done.

Knights and Moule (38), using the same mounted digital counter utilized for measuring finger tapping (v.s.), have collective normative data on foot tapping speed on 169 children CA five through 14. The child is asked to see how rapidly he or she can tap the lever of the mechanical counter with his or her foot during four 10-second trials. The digital counter itself records the total number of times it is tapped during each trial period and the mean of the best three of the four trials is the child's score.

Subtest 22 of the *Lincoln-Oseretsky Scale* (51) attempts to objectively measure children's ball-throwing capacity at various ages. The child is asked to throw a ball at a 10″ square target from a distance of eight feet. Specific instructions are provided regarding positioning of the arms and feet before throwing. The previously described reservations about this scale's scoring criteria hold here. Lastly, the *Denver Developmental Screening Test* (24) has a section devoted to the evaluation of gross motor coordination. I consider it to be far superior to the previously discussed fine motor-adaptive section. A large number of normative gross motor activities can be examined and the child easily compared to his peers. In infancy, normative data are provided on sitting with the head steady, standing with support, walking with support, and walking without support. For later periods, data are provided on kicking a ball, throwing a ball, jumping in place, pedaling a tricycle, heel-to-toe walking forward, and heel-to-toe walking backwards. Unfortunately, the Denver Scale only goes to age six. An extension to upper ages would be useful.

Coordination deficits are among the more common signs and symptoms described for children with MBD. It is in this area that subjectivity is especially common. More complete data of the developmental norms are vital to obtain if we are to evaluate adequately children with such deficits.

MOTOR PERSISTENCE

Younger children cannot maintain a state of muscle contraction as long as older children. For example, they cannot stand on one foot, clench their fists, or keep their eyes shut as long as older ones. There is a developmental progression of the capacity to maintain muscle tension on a voluntary basis and children with MBD may exhibit lags in such progression. The term *motor impersistence* was first used by Fisher (23) to refer to the impairment in this function. The phenomenon was defined by Garfield, Benton, and MacQueen (27) as the "inability to sustain certain voluntary motor acts initiated on verbal command." They considered the impairment to be the result of a primary defect in sustaining attention. Benton (7) subsequently used the definition: "the inability to sustain an act that has been initiated on command."

One good test of motor persistence (or for the presence of motor impersistence) is the child's ability to stand on one foot. Denckla (21) has provided norms for the length of time that children from five to 10 can be expected to stand on one leg. For example, she has found that 85% of five-year-olds can balance themselves on the dominant foot for 10 seconds; 85% of six-year-olds can do so for 20 seconds; and 90% of seven-year-olds can do so 30 seconds. Touwen and Prechtl (52) have also provided such data, expressed in terms of the number of seconds that the average child at ages three to seven should be able to stand on one leg. For example, the average three-year-old cannot perform this task well, if at all. The average four-year-old should be able to stand on one leg for five to 10 seconds; the five-year-old 10-12 seconds, and the six-year-old 13-16 seconds. Subtest 32 of the *Lincoln-Oseretsky Scale* (51) also provides some normative data for standing on one foot, as does the *Denver Developmental Screening Test* (24).

Garfield (28) has provided some rough guidelines for detecting motor impersistence of the muscles of the eyes, mouth, and tongue. For example, he states that by seven a child should be able to keep the eyes shut for two 20-second trials; keep the mouth open for a similar period; and protrude the tongue for the same length of time. Recently, this author has been collecting data on a motor steadiness tester which, among other things, evaluates for the presence of motor impersistence. A more detailed description of this device will be presented in the section on hyperactivity.

MOTOR OVERFLOW

The term *motor overflow* refers to the involuntary movements that occur in association with and in addition to a specific act that the child has been requested to perform. They are unnecessary to the performance of the task at hand and generally serve no ostensibly useful purpose. For example, when the child is asked to oppose repetitiously his or her thumb to the index finger, the other fingers of the hand move repetitiously as well. At the same time, the child may stick his or her tongue out of the mouth, there may be movements of the arms and shoulder, twitches and grimacing may be observed, and the fingers on the other hand may go through the identical motions.

These other motions are generally referred to as *associated movements* or *adventitious movements*. The phenomenon is usually referred to as *motor overflow* or *motor spread*. The term *synkinesia* refers to the ipsilateral overflow of such movements and the term *mirror movements* is generally used when the overflow is contralateral in the homologous extremity or symmetrical part of the body. Most examiners agree that the younger the child the greater the number of adventitious movements one will observe and that by adolescence they are usually not present. Most examiners agree, as well, that such movements are likely to be more common in children with MBD than in their peers of the same age and that this relates to the failure of the brains of such children to have suppressed this primitive response.

Touwen and Prechtl (52) describe what they refer to as the *mouth-opening, finger-spreading phenomenon*. The examiner supports the child's relaxed arms on his or her forearm. The child is asked to close his or her eyes, open the mouth, and stick out the tongue. Up to the age of three or four there will be associated spreading and extension of the fingers. This phenomenon will be present with less frequency at ages five to six, and should no longer be present by seven to eight. Its presence beyond that age is suggestive of neurological impairment. In another test for the presence of adventitious movements, the child is asked to walk on tiptoe 20 continuous paces back and forth. Children up to seven will generally exhibit associated movements. Commonly the arms extend and clenched fists may be made. Lip and tongue movements may also be seen. The authors consider the presence of such movements beyond seven to eight years of age to be a sign of neurological impairment.

Kinsbourne (35) describes a *finger stick test* for the presence of associated movements. With arms extended, four light sticks or ball-point pens are placed between the fingers of each hand (a total of eight sticks). When all the sticks are securely held, the child is asked to drop *one stick only* from the dominant hand, while trying to hold on to the other seven. In each of six trials, the examiner counts the number of sticks dropped by the *non-dominant hand*. (Although sticks may be dropped by the dominant hand, these are not counted.) In six trials, the maximum number of sticks that might be dropped by the non-dominant hand is 24. According to Kinsbourne, the normal six-year-old should not drop more than a total of five sticks in the six trials. To do so is suggestive of neurological impairment.

Abercrombie, Lindon, and Tyson (1) describe what appears to have potential as a good test of motor overflow. The child places both hands on the table with the palmar surfaces down. The examiner points to each finger in succession and asks the child to raise that finger and *only* that finger. Observation is made of both homolateral and contralateral raising of other fingers. This tests appears to have merit in that one can readily objectify the observations. Unfortunately, the authors are not clear regarding the scoring system and they provide data on only six- and nine-year-olds (25 in each group).

Cohen, Taft, Mahadeviah, and Birch (13) have done the most extensive and objective work that I know of in providing objective normative data for motor overflow, as well as comparing normal children with those with MBD. In their examination, the child (with eyes closed) is asked to perform five tasks: 1) repetitive opposition of the thumb and forefinger for 15 seconds, 2) repetitive opposition of the thumb and fifth finger for 15 seconds, 3) successive opposition of the thumb to each of the other four fingers, 4) alternate squeezing and relaxing of a rubber toy which is held in the hand, and 5) rapid alternation and supination of the hand for 15 seconds. The presence of adventitious movements (on either side) is recorded for each of the sections on a scale of 0 to 3 (with 0 signifying no adventitious movements, and 3 representing maximum associated movements). The child, therefore, can obtain a maximum score of 15. The test is repeated for the other hand for which there is also a maximum score of 15 (total possible score is therefore 30). Normative data are provided for children from six through 12 (N varies from 31 to 72) as well as for children with signs of CNS impairment (N varies from 12 to 28). The authors found that there was no significant difference between the normal and neurologically impaired groups below the age of nine. After that, the organically impaired group exhibited significantly more adventitious movements.

EYE-HEAD DISSOCIATION

In the routine examination of the extraocular muscles of a five-year-old child, the examiner traditionally asks the child to keep his or her head still while the eyes follow an object which traverses the various visual fields. Typically, such a child will move his or her head in order to view the object, rather than just move the eyes while the head is still. If the examiner urges the child to keep the head still, he or she will usually still not "cooperate." Even when the child's head is held by a nurse or the mother, the child will attempt to move the head in order to view the moving object. Such a child is not being negativistic; he or she is generally not capable of dissociating head from eye movements at that age. It is only by age seven that most children can do this. The child over seven who cannot probably has some neurological impairment (44).

The normal five- and six-year-old may read a book with the whole head going back and forth in order for the eyes to properly scan the printed page. (This phenomenon is sometimes compared to the carriage on the typewriter which must shift back totally to the left with each new line.) Some MBD children still exhibit this phenomenon after the age of seven and may receive optometric treatment to correct this "deficiency." I believe that such treatment *for this condition* is unwarranted. It is generaly a manifestation of a developmental lag and usually corrects itself by eight or nine, in my experience. If after a year of such treatment the child is "cured," the parents will usually consider the improvement to be the result of the therapy. Actually, the therapy probably had absolutely no influence on the acquisition of this ability and the improvement would have occurred anyway. In addition, even if the impairment were to remain, it is not a particularly debilitating handicap and is certainly not worth the time and expense that its "treatment" often entails.

HYPERACTIVITY

Most adults could not possibly imitate continously the movements of a two-year-old for more than a few minutes. Even the athlete who is completely "in shape" would be worn down long before the toddler. Normal children often run rather than walk. Every kindergarten teacher knows how active her children are, especially the boys. Things gradually quiet down as the child grows older so that by the teens the youngster's activity starts approaching the adult level. Hyperactivity has generally been considered to be one of the hallmark signs of MBD—so much so that many refer to the entire disorder as *hyperactivity*. Considering how active normal children are, how does one differentiate the normal amount of hyperactivity from the abnormal degree that MBD children are alleged to have? It is only when good developmental norms have been established that we will be in a position to determine 1) whether

MBD children are indeed more active than normals and (if 1 is true) 2) whether a given child is hyperactive (that is, more active than normal) and, if so, to what degree.

A number of instruments have been devised which attempt to quantitatively measure a child's degree of activity. Devices which have been tried include: pedometers and actometers which are strapped to the child; special chairs and cushions which record activity level; cameras, photoelectric eyes, ultrasonic generators, and magnetic relay systems in grid rooms; and radio telemetry. (Space does not permit a detailed discussion of these instruments. The reader who wishes an excellent summary of their uses and drawbacks should refer to Ross and Ross [48].) To the best of my knowledge, normative data on large groups of children of different ages have not been obtained for these devices. Some of the studies have, however, compared normals with MBDs, regarding activity levels, with contradictory and equivocal results. More important, none of these instruments has enjoyed widespread utilization—generally because of the impracticality of their utilization outside of a laboratory setting.

Kløve (36) has described a Motor Steadiness Battery which includes an instrument that appears to be a sensitive indicator of activity level. The device consists of a metal plate with a series of nine progressively smaller holes into which a stylus is placed. Each time the stylus touches the side of the hole, a connecting clock records the duration of contact. In addition, the number of contacts with each hole made during the 10-second trial period is also recorded. Children ages five to eight are required to try only the four largest holes, those 9-14 complete all holes. Knights and Moule (39) have collected normative data on children ages five to 14 (N varies from 10 to 24 in each age group [males and females not separated]). Knights and Ogilvie (37) have found that children with brain damage do significantly more poorly on this graduated holes test than normal children.

This author considers this type of test to be an excellent way to quantitatively measure activity level, and specifically whether hyperactivity is present. However, I consider that there are certain drawbacks to the Kløve instrument. First, the child is required to place the stylus in each hole for only 10 seconds. Recent work (14) strongly suggests that the hyperactivity of MBD children is secondary to the impairment in concentration. It is not simply a problem with attention, but in *sustaining* attention. Accordingly, such children may be able to watch TV cartoons for hours at a time and remain quite still because the rapid turnover of stimuli does not require more than a fraction of a second of attention to each stimulus. However, such children often have great difficulty when reading because this activity requires them to attend for long periods of time to very few stimuli. Therefore, with reading they exhibit their poor concentration and distractibility. This results in the jumpiness that is viewed as hyperactivity.

This theory is further confirmed by the argument that stimulant medication reduces these children's hyperactivity by improving their concentration. Such a theory does not require the concept of a "paradoxical effect" by the stimulants; rather, one can simply assume that stimulants act in these children just as they do with normals, that is, they merely improve concentration. Accordingly, such a device would more sensitively test for hyperactivity if the child were required to maintain the stylus in the hole for a longer period of time. Furthermore, when using the device it is possible for the child to avoid contact between the stylus and hole by pulling it ever so slightly out of the hole. An instrument with a contact plate at the end of the stylus would guard against such "cheating." The above workers have not described the child's position and do not state whether it has been standardized in such a way that all children are the same with regard to hand and arm support, or lack of it. The authors do not differentiate between males and females, the assumption being that there are no differences. Lastly, the number of children used at each age level, although of possible statistical significance, is not large enough to allow one to confidently use such data as a standard for all children.

Recognizing the value of such a device, the author and his colleagues have recently developed a motor steadiness tester which attempts to rectify some of the drawbacks of the Klove-Knights-Moule instrument (26). In this device the child is asked to hold a stylus of 5/64" (.078") in diameter in a hole 9/32" (.281") in diameter. Three 60-second trials are required (providing, therefore, a prolonged period of concentration). Each time the stylus makes contact with the side of the hole, a buzzer sounds and the contact time is recorded. The stylus is 4" long with a plate placed at the tip so that attempts to pull it out will result in contact. In addition, a similar plate is placed 1" in from the tip to insure against pushing the stylus in too far. A third disc is placed 4" in from the tip, to serve as a shield, behind which the child holds the short handle of the stylus. In this way the distance between the child's hand and the hole is standardized. The child's position is standardized as well, so that no leaning of the arm or wrist on the table, leg, or body is permitted.

Furthermore, the child is not permitted to place his or her arm against the chest for extra support. In addition to hyperactivity and the ability to sustain attention, the instrument tests for motor impersistence, as well as the presence of resting tremors and choreaform movements. (It does not test for intention or kinetic tremors.)

The author has collected normative data on 500 children (IQ 90-110) ages five through 14. The number of children at each age level is at least 25 boys and 25 girls, and their data are dealt with separately. In addition, he has collected data on over 300 subjects with well defined diagnoses of MBD (only children in special classes were used). His data, which are presented in other publications (26b, 26d), indicate that there is a definite reduction of touch time with increasing age, that normal girls at every age level are less active than boys, and that there is a significant difference at all age levels between normals and those with neurological impairment.

BODY IMAGE

Space does not permit a detailed discussion of the concept of body image. I will, however, discuss two aspects of the development of the child's image of his or her own body that are of importance in the diagnosis of MBD.

Most examiners generally consider the drawing a child makes of a person to be a representation of him- or herself. It is considered to be a projection of the self as the child views him- or herself. Both neurological and psychological factors are generally considered to play a role in the formation of the body image, as well as the projection of it that one can observe in figure drawings. There is a normal progression in children's figure drawings from the primitive drawings of the three-four-year-old to the more sophisticated and adult-like figures drawn by the adolescent. Goodenough (30) was among the first to attempt to quantitate the degree of sophistication one could expect at different ages and Harris (32) elaborated her scoring system significantly. Using Harris' scales, one can score a child's drawing in accordance with its complexity and the number of details provided. The mental age so obtained correlates well with the MAs obtained on various standard tests of intelligence. The child with MBD may reveal a MA impairment through the person he or she draws. It is important for the examiner to appreciate that an immature drawing may be the result not only of neurological immaturity or developmental lag, but also of psychological immaturity and regression.

The ability to discriminate right from left also follows a definite developmental sequence that has been intensively studied by Benton (4, 5). According to Benton, one should not simply try to determine whether the child knows right from left; rather, one must concern oneself with a number of more sophisticated discriminations. By age six the average child should be able to point to his or her right and left body parts and should be able to respond correctly to questions such as: "Show me your left hand" and "Show me your right eye." By age seven he or she should be able to respond to double *uncrossed* commands like: "Touch your left ear with your left hand" and "Touch your right eye with your right hand." By age eight to nine the child should be able to successfully execute double *crossed* commands such as: "Touch your right eye with your left hand" and "Touch your left ear with your right hand." By age 11 the child should be able to accomplish the more difficult task of identifying a single lateral part on the confronting examiner: "Point to my (the examiner's) right eye" or "Point to my left ear." And by age 12 the child should be able to execute the even more complex commands involving combined orientation to his or her own body and that of the confronting examiner: "Put your right hand on my (the examiner's) left ear." "Put your left hand on my right shoulder."

VISUAL PROCESSING

The term "visual processing" is a rubric under which are subsumed a number of functions related to the ways in which the brain receives, scans, identifies, integrates, classifies, and utilizes visual information (11). Impairments in one or more of these functions are common in children with MBD. Because the terms denoting the various deficits in visual processing are often used in different ways, I will define each term and then describe how a deficiency of the particular function can contribute to problems in children with MBD.

Visual Discrimination

This refers to the process by which the individual differentiates one visual stimulus from another. A color-blind person has a problem in visual discrimination in that he or she may not be able to differentiate between hues that others may readily distinguish. Poor performance on the *Colored Progressive Matrices* (47) results from the difficulty in differentiating similar, but not identical, visual patterns from one another. Normative data are provided for children from ages five and a half to

11. They do poorly on the Form Constancy Subtest of the *Developmental Test of Visual Perception* (25) as they have difficulty differentiating between circles and ellipses, squares and rectangles. The Frostig test provides normative data from ages four years 0 months to seven years 11 months.

Many years ago Orton (41) noted that children with neurological learning disabilities may have trouble differentiating between letters that are reversals of one another. This deficiency may be one of the contributing factors (but certainly not the total cause) in the reading disability so common in these children. Examiners, as a general rule of thumb, usually consider reversals beyond the second grade to be suggestive of minimal brain dysfunction. However, the author knows of no collection of normative data on the reversal frequency of children of various ages which has been incorporated into a standardized testing instrument. Accordingly, he has recently devised such an instrument and has collected data on over 500 normal children (IQ 90-110) between the ages of five and 14. (There are approximately 25 boys and 25 girls at each age level.) The test is divided into two parts. The first evaluates for the presence of reversals when a child is asked to write numbers and letters. This is a task of *execution*. The second part evaluates the child's ability to recognize reverse letters when they are written as mirror images. This is a test of *recognition*. In part of the second test letters are presented in pairs with one of each pair oriented incorrectly. The child is asked to put a cross over the letter or number that is "pointing in the wrong direction." In another part of this test, the letters and numbers are presented singly. Some are correctly oriented and others are presented in mirror image orientation. Again, the child is asked to place a cross over the number or letter that is "pointing in the wrong direction." Data on over 300 children with MBD (ages five to 14) have also been collected. Early evaluation of the results indicates that children with MBD exhibit significantly more reversals than normals. In addition, reversals are seen among children who have gone beyond the second grade and this instrument should prove useful in differentiating the normal degree of such reversals from the abnormal. These findings are further described in other publications (26a, 26b, 26c).

Visual Perception

This term refers to the capacity to ascribe meaning to a visual sensation. The MBD child may readily be able to identify red from green and easily differentiate these from other colors. However, he or she may have trouble learning that a red light means *stop* and a green light means *go*. There is nothing intrinsic to these colors to suggest that they should mean *stop* and *go*. Social convention add special meanings to these sensations. The linkage between the color and its meaning may seem obvious and easily learned, but this is not the case for the children with MBD. They are puzzled by such associations and do not readily make them.

This problem may contribute to the reading disability so often seen in children with minimal brain dysfunction. They have trouble associating the written word with the object which it represents. For example, the word *knife* and the letters *k-n-i-f-e* that are used to refer to the object are not intrinsically a part of the object nor is there anything particular about these five letters that should warrant their being used to refer to the object knife. The Germans do quite well with the letters M-e-s-s-e-r and the French with c-o-u-t-e-a-u. Convention dictates the utilization of these particular letters for this purpose for social convenience, to enhance communication and to prevent the confusion that would result in the world if such labels were not employed.

Visual Agnosia

The impairment in understanding the meaning of visual symbols is also referred to as visual agnosia. The child with a neurological learning disability has trouble making these connections. When such a child sees the letters k-n-i-f-e, he or she has trouble associating them with the object that they signify. When viewing these letters, he or she does not readily envision a knife—clearly a severe handicap in understanding written language. Although children with minimal brain dysfunction who suffer with this particular deficit will do poorly on many standardized reading tests, there is no test that this examiner knows of which particularly focuses on this deficit. Rather, the poor performance that MBD children traditionally exhibit on standardized reading tests is the result of many neurological impairments that may interfere with their reading capacity. Hopefully, someone will devise a test which specifically evaluates for this capacity. Then, we will have norms that will help differentiate children with this impairment from those who are normal.

Visual Memory

This term refers to the capacity to store and retain visual stimuli. Things don't seem to "stick" in these children's minds as well as and as long as they do in normal children. De Hirsch (18) refers to this impairment as the "fluidity" problem that these children have. She compares the process of impressing material into the memories of these children with writing in the sand with a stick. Their impressions are transient—blown away as easily as letters in the sand by passing breezes.

Children with impairments in visual memory do poorly on Benton's *Revised Visual Retention Test* (6) in which the child is asked to reproduce from memory geometric designs that he or she was permitted to observe and study within a short time prior to being asked to reproduce them. Normative data are available from ages eight to 14. In addition, the Digit Symbol subtest of the *Wechsler Intelligence Scale for Children* (53) is a test of visual memory. Extensive normative data are available for ages five years 0 months through 15 years 11 months and the test has been quite useful in differentiating normal children from those with minimal brain dysfunction who suffer with visual memory problems.

Visual Distractibility

This refers to an impairment in which the child's capacity to focus on the most important stimulus is deficient because attention is too readily shifted to competing stimuli of less significance. When doing the traditional hidden-picture puzzle game, in which the child tries to find various figures camouflaged in a complex scene, visual distractibility interferes with the child's performance. Accordingly, MBD children do poorly on the *Southern California Figure-Ground Visual Perception Test* (2) which quantitates this capacity and provides normative data on children from ages four years 0 months through 10 years 11 months. More important, when reading, the child's eyes tend to wander away from the line being read to other words on the page. I know of no normative data on visual distractibility separated from figure-ground perception.

AUDITORY PROCESSING

The term *auditory processing* covers a number of functions related to the brain's utilization of auditory stimuli. These include: localization and identification of the sound source; discrimination among different sounds; differentiation between significant and insignificant auditory stimuli; understanding the meaning of sounds; reproduction of pitch, rhythm, and melody; and combining speech sounds into words (11).

Auditory Discrimination

This term refers to the process by which the individual differentiates between auditory stimuli. Wepman's *Auditory Discrimination Test* (55) is a well-known test for auditory discrimination. The child is presented with paired words such as *tub* and *tug, zest* and *zest, pat* and *pack,* and asked to state whether the words are the same or different. Forty word pairs are presented: In 30 of these the words are different and in 10 the words are identical. The most meaningful errors are those in which the child states that different words are the same to him. Of 30 such possible errors, a five-year-old should not make more than six, a six-year-old is allowed a maximum of five errors, a seven-year-old four errors, and an eight-year-old three. The child who exceeds the maximum number of allowed errors is considered to have an auditory discrimination problem.

Auditory Perception

This refers to the capacity to appreciate the meaning of auditory stimuli. The individual with an auditory perceptual defect has difficulty matching an auditory stimulus with the specific meaning that social convention has ascribed to it. There is nothing intrinsic in the ring of a classroom bell that means *recess,* nor in the schoolyard teacher's whistle that means *"give me your attention."* The impairment is also referred to as *auditory agnosia.* Probably, the area in which such a deficiency will produce the greatest difficulty is spoken language. If we cannot link the spoken word with the meaning assigned to it by society, we will have great difficulty relating properly to others. In learning to read, the child is usually exposed simultaneously to the visual symbol of an entity (the written word that denotes the entity) and the auditory symbol (the spoken word that represents it). The two processes complement and reinforce one another in the process of learning to read. Accordingly, the child with such an auditory perceptual deficit will generally have significant trouble learning to read.

Although there are many standardized tests of reading comprehension, in some of which the examiner reads material to the child and then tests his or her understanding, there are many factors that can produce poor performance on such a test. I know of no test that specifically focuses on the auditory perceptual problem as defined here. Normative data are certainly needed.

Auditory Memory Deficit

This term refers to the impairment in storing and retaining auditory stimuli. The child who does poorly on the Digit Span subtest of the WISC often has deficient auditory memory (although poor auditory attention and auditory distractibility can produce such results). In this test the examiner recites a series of numbers and the child is asked to repeat them. The sequences become longer and the examination of this subtest ends when the child fails to successfully repeat a second trial of numbers of equal length. Normative data are available for children from ages five years 0 months through 15 years 11 months.

Auditory Distractibility

The child with this problem tends to focus attention on auditory stimuli that may not be as important as those to which he or she had originally been attending. In the *Auditory Selective Attention Test* devised by Goldman, Fristoe, and Woodcock (29), normative data on auditory distractibility have been collected. In this test the child listens to a record which requests him or her to point to one of four presented pictures. Progressively louder distracting auditory stimuli interfere with the child's concentrating on the speaker. Normative data are available from ages three and up. Children with MBD may exhibit greater auditory distractibility than normals.

CONCLUDING COMMENTS

It has been my aim in this article to impress upon the reader the importance of normative data on the various neurodevelopmental processes in diagnosing minimal brain dysfunction. Minimal brain dysfunction is being overdiagnosed, in part, because such data are either not available or not utilized; diagnosis thus becomes subjective and capricious. The utilization of such data will place the diagnosis on a firmer foundation and do much to reduce the present state of confusion that exists regarding this important diagnostic entity.

REFERENCES

1. Abercrombie, M., Lindon, R., and Tyson, M: Associated movement in normal and physically handicapped children. *Dev. Med. and Child Neurology*, 6:573-580, 1964.
2. Ayres, A.: *Southern California Figure-Ground Visual Perception Test*. Los Angeles, Ca.: Western Psychological Services, 1966.

3. Bender, L.: Clinical study of 100 schizophrenic children. *Amer. J. Orthopsychiatry,* 17:40-56, 1947.
4. Benton, A.: *Right-Left Discrimination and Finger Localization.* New York: Harper & Brothers, 1959.
5. Benton, A.: Right-left discrimination. *Pediatric Clinics of North America,* 15:747-758, 1968.
6. Benton, A.: *The Revised Visual Retention Test: Clinical and Experimental Applications.* New York: Psychological Corporation, 1955.
7. Benton, A.: Neuropsychological aspects of mental retardation. *J. of Spec. Ed.,* 4:3-11, 1970.
8. Bernstein, J. E., Page, J.G., and Janicki, R.S.: Some characteristics of children with minimal brain dysfunction. In C. K. Conners (Ed.), *Clinical Use of Stimulant Drugs in Children.* Amsterdam: Excerpta Medica, 1974, pp. 24-35.
9. Brain, W., and Wilkinson, M.: Observations in the extensor plantar reflex and its relationship to the functions of the pyramidal tract. *Brain,* 82:297-320, 1959.
10. Brutten, M., Richardson, S., and Mangel, C.: *Something's Wrong With My Child.* New York: Harcourt, Brace, Jovanovich, Inc., 1973.
11. Chalfant, J., and Scheffelin, M.: *Central Processing Dysfunctions in Children: A Review of Research.* National Institute of Neurological Diseases and Stroke, Monograph No. 9. Washington, D.C.: U.S. Government Printing Office.
12. Charlton, M.: *Clinical Aspects of Minimal Brain Dysfunction,* Behavioral Sciences Tape Library, Teaneck, New Jersey: Sigma Information, Inc., 1973.
13. Cohen, H., Taft, L., Mahadeviah, M., and Birch, H.: Developmental changes in overflow in normal and aberrantly functioning children. *J. of Pediatrics,* 71:39-47, 1967.
14. Conners, C. (Ed.): *Clinical Use of Stimulant Drugs in Children.* The Hague: Excerpta Medica, 1974.
15. Costa, L., Scarola, L., and Rapin, I.: Purdue pegboard scores for normal grammar school children. *Perceptual and Motor Skills,* 18:748, 1964.
16. Critchley, M.: *The Dyslexic Child.* London: William Heinemann Medical Books Limited, 1970.
17. De Hirsch, K.: Early language development. In S. Arieti, (Ed.), *American Handbook of Psychiatry,* second edition, Vol. I, pp. 352-367. New York: Basic Books Inc., 1974.
18. De Hirsch, K.: *CIBA Medical Horizons Conference on Minimal Brain Dysfunction.* New York City, Nov. 6, 1976.
19. Denckla, M. B., and Rudel, R.: Anomalies of motor development in hyperactive boys without traditional neurological signs. (unpublished manuscript).
20. Denckla, M. B.: Development of speed in repetitive and successive finger-movements in normal children. *Dev. Med. and Child Neuorlogy,* 15(5):635-645, 1973.
21. Denckla, M.B.: Development of motor coordination in normal children. *Dev. Med. and Child Neurology,* 16:729-741, 1974.
22. Escalona, S., and Stone, L.: Normal development: Personality and behavior. In H. Barnett (Ed.), *Pediatrics.* New York: Appleton-Century-Crofts, 1968.
23. Fisher, M.: Left hemiplegia and motor impersistence. *J. of Nervous and Mental Disease,* 123:201-218, 1956.
24. Frankenburg, W., Dodds, J., and Fandal, A.: *Denver Developmental Screening Test,* Denver, Colorado: Project and Publishing Foundation, Inc. (Test forms may also be obtained from Mead Johnson Laboratories, Evansville, Indiana.)
25. Frostig, M.: *Developmental Test of Visual Perception.* Palo Alto, California: Consulting Psychologists Press, 1961.
26. Gardner, R.: *Motor Steadiness Tester,* Lafayette, Indiana: Lafayette Instrument Co., 1978.
26a. Gardner, R.A.: *The Reversals Frequency Test.* Cresskill, New Jersey: Creative Therapeutics, 1978.

26b. Gardner, R.A.: *The Objective Diagnosis of Minimal Brain Dysfunction*. Cresskill, New Jersey: Creative Therapeutics, 1979.

26c. Gardner, R.A. and Broman, M.: The Purdue Pegboard: Normative data on 1334 school children. *J. of Clin. Child Psychol.*, 8:156-162, 1979.

26d. Gardner, R.A., Gardner, A.K., Caemmerer, A. and Broman, M.: An instrument for measuring hyperactivity and other signs of MBD. *U. of Clin. Child Psychol.*, 8:173-179, 1979.

27. Garfield, J., Benton, A., and MacQueen, J.: Motor impersistence in brain-damaged and cultural-familial defectives. *J. of Nervous and Mental Disease*, 142:434-440, 1966.

28. Garfield, J.C.: Motor impersistence in normal and brain-damaged children, *Neurology.* 14:623-630, 1964.

29. Goldman, R., Fristoe, M., and Woodcock, W.: *Auditory Selective Attention Test.* Circle Pines, Minnesota: American Guidance Serivce, Inc.,

30. Goodenough, F.: *Measurement of Intelligence by Drawings*, New York: World Book Co., 1926.

31. Haller, J., and Axelrod, P.: Minimal brain dysfunction syndrome, *Amer. J. of Diseases of Children.* 129:1319-1324, 1975.

32. Harris, D.B.: *Children's Drawings as Measures of Intellectual Maturity*, New York: Harcourt, Brace and World, Inc., 1963.

33. Ingram, T.: Soft signs, *Dev. Med. and Child Neurology.* 15:527-530, 1973.

34. Kawi, A. A., and Pasamanick, B.: Prenatal and paranatal factors in the development of childhood reading disorders, *Monograph Soc. Res. Child. Dev.* 24(4):1-80, 1959.

35. Kinsbourne, M.: Minimal brain dysfunction as a neurodevelopmental lag, *Annals of the N.Y. Academy of Sciences.* 205:268-273, 1973.

36. Kløve, M.: Clinical neuropsychology. In F.M. Forster (Ed.), *Medical Clinics of North America*, pp. 1647-1658, New York: Saunders, 1963.

37. Knights, R., and Ogilvie, R.: A comparison of test results from normal and brain damaged children, Department of Psychology, University of Western Ontario, Research Bulletin No. 53, London, Canada 1967.

38. Knights, R. M., and Moule, A.: Normative and reliability data on finger and foot tapping in children, *Perceptual and Motor Skills.* 25:717-720, 1967.

39. Knights, R., and Moule, A.: Normative data on the Motor Steadiness Battery for children, *Perceptual and Motor Skills.* 26:643-650, 1968.

40. National Center for Health Statistics: *NCHS Growth Charts*, Monthly Vital Statistics Report, Vol. 25, No. 3, Suppl. (HRA) 76-1120, Rockville, Maryland: National Center for Health Statistics, 1976. (These charts may also be obtained from Ross Laboratories of Columbus, Ohio.)

41. Orton, S.: *Reading, Writing and Speech Problems in Children*, New York: W. W. Norton & Co., Inc., 1937.

42. Owen, F., Adams, P., Forrest, T., Stolz, L., and Fisher, S.: Learning disorders in children: sibling studies. *Monographs of the Society for Research in Child Development*, Serial No. 144, Vol. 36, No. 4, pp. 1-77, 1971.

43. Paine, R., and Oppé, T.: Neurological examination of children, *Clinics in Developmental Medicine*, Vol. 20/21, Spastics International Medical Publications, London: William Heinemann Medical Books Ltd.; Philadelphia: J.P. Lippincott Co., 1966.

44. Peters, J., Davis, J., Goolsby, C., Clements, S., and Hicks, T.: *Physician's Handbook: Screening for MBD*, Summit, New Jersey: CIBA Medical Horizons, 1973.

45. *Purdue Pegboard Test:* Lafayette, Indiana: Lafayette Instrument Co.

46. Rapin, I., Tourk, L., and Costa, L.: Evaluation of the Purdue Pegboard as a screening test for brain damage, *Dev. Med. and Child Neurology.* 8:45-54, 1966.

47. Raven, J.: *Colored Progressive Matrices*, revised edition, London: H. K. Lewis and Co., Ltd., 1956.

48. Ross, D., and Ross, S.: *Hyperactivity: Research, Theory, and Action*, New York: John Wiley

and Sons, 1976.
49. Schain, R. J.: *Minimal brain dysfunction, Current Problems in Pediatrics.* Vol. V. No. 10, Chicago: Year Book Medical Publishers, Inc., 1975.
50. Shank, K.: Recognition of articulatory disorders in children, *Clinical Pediatrics.* 3:333-334, 1964.
51. Sloan, W., The Lincoln-Oseretsky motor development scale, *Genetic Psychology Monographs.* 51:183-252, 1955.
52. Touwen, B., and Prechtl, H., The neurological examination of the child with minor nervous dysfunction, *Clinics in Developmental Medicine.* No. 38, Philadelphia: J. B. Lippincott Co., 1970.
53. Wechsler, D.: *Wechsler Intelligence Scale for Children,* New York: The Psychological Corp., 1949.
54. Wender, P.: *Minimal Brain Dysfunction in Children,* New York: Wiley-Interscience, 1971.
55. Wepman, J. M.: *Wepman Auditory Discrimination Test,* Palm Springs, California: Language Research Associates, 1958.
56. Wyatt, G.: *Language Learning and Communication Disorders in Children,* New York: Free Press, 1969.
57. Yakovlev, P., and Lecours, A.: The myelogenetic cycles of regional maturation of the brain, In A. Minkowski (Ed.), *Regional Development of the Brain in Early Life.* Oxford and Edinburgh: Blackwell Scientific Publications, 1967.

10

Specific Learning Disabilities: A Clinical View

JEANNETTE JEFFERSON JANSKY, Ph.D.

The term "learning disability" is used with increasing frequency to designate the academic difficulties of some children and young adults. Professionals differ in the way they characterize, diagnose, and treat children who have trouble learning at school. Moreover, the individuals who offer remediation come with job titles from such varied disciplines as clinical, education, or school psychology, special education, education of exceptional children, and remedial reading, as well as learning disabilities. Given the many vantage points from which academic problems are viewed, it is little wonder that those in allied professions, the parents, and the children themselves are confused as to what and how much is wrong.

The present discussion is limited to a specific category of learning problems in which the defining characteristic is the failure to learn in spite of average or better intelligence and in the absence of such primary contributing factors as emotional disorder, sensory impairment, and gross neurological dysfunction. The interference with learning appears to originate within the child and is not the result of poor teaching or cultural differences. It is not that learning difficulties do not occur in children with special disorders or dysfunctions; they do, but they are just one aspect, and not the major one, of a more global and pervasive pathology. Because the present discussion is limited to the learning disability that is the child's major complaint, the term "specific learning disability" will be used.

There is general agreement that the child with a specific learning disability may have trouble mastering some or all of the following school performances: reading, spelling, handwriting, composition writing, arithmetic, and foreign language.

The contributing components of these performances have been the subject of investigation (31,25), but have yet to be conclusively defined. The likelihood that the demands of these performances change somewhat as a function of level of advancement complicates the researcher's task. Put differently, we lack clear answers to such a basic question as: "Just what competences are we teaching when we teach beginning reading, or arithmetic?" A different question is that of *how* the subjects are to be taught (7). And still another issue is that of the attributes of successful students (as opposed to the nature of the subject they have mastered or how they have been taught). Rsearchers (36,12,2,33,8,3,42) have probably devoted most attention to the study of the characteristics of the poor learner, with the result that there is some consensus as to the kinds of non-academic performance deficits that accompany failure in the primary subjects. There is less agreement, however, as to the way these associated problems interact with printed language and arithmetic difficulties. Nor has it been determined whether learning disabilities constitute a single syndrome of deficits or several rather distinct clusters of deficits (40,24,34,32).

The cause or causes of these problems have not been clearly established. Investigation of the family history frequently reveals that several members have been similarly affected and so there appears to be a genetic factor. However, the mode of transmission and exactly what it is that is transmitted are not at all clear (46,22,35,37,18). In some instances, pregnancy, delivery, or the neonatal period may be somewhat burdened (24). While minimal brain dysfunction and maturational lag are frequently referred to as causal agents, unequivocal formal support for these conclusions is lacking. Therefore, however plausible such explanations may be, they are inferences and should be regarded as hypotheses until replicable evidence accumulates (16). Finally, the presence of such a history has little bearing on the severity of the learning disability and is of doubtful value in planning treatment (29,39).

Even if there were agreement as to these issues, it would be difficult to estimate the incidence of specific learning disability because there is no consensus as to the degree of difficulty, by age, that must be present for a performance to be considered deficient or failing. One approach to the problem has been suggested by Yule (48), who used a regression equation in which achievement was predicted on the basis of an established correlation between educational attainment, age, and I.Q. It appears likely that these disabilities are far more widespread than has been recognized. For generations (and before intelligence testing became routine), the children were simply regarded by their teachers and parents as being "slow."

In spite of the continuing elusiveness of hard data about specific learning disabilities, data that would explain the condition, it is a fact that most experienced diagnosticians and remedial specialists would agree on which child has this disability and which has not. And despite differences in opinion as to the nature of the reading process, for instance, and the use of markedly varied teaching methods, able therapists have helped many children to compensate for or largely overcome their problems with learning to read.

The discussion that follows draws on that consensus and on clinical experience in the attempt to describe the child with the learning problem. Some requirements for academic success will be postulated. The characteristics and deficits that accompany or appear to contribute to the child's difficulty with learning will be set off against these requirements for success. The observations must be considered as tentative for reasons set out above.

SUCCESS AT SCHOOL

What are some of the requirements for being successful at school? A basic prerequisite, by no means to be taken for granted, is that the student comes to school adequately fed and clothed (5). Hopefully, he or she will enter first grade with expectations and demands that match what is offered in the classroom. Either he will have been told what classroom life is like or he will have enough background information to find out rather quickly for himself. He will expect to be taught to read, to write and to work with numbers and will intuitively understand that mastery will not occur immediately (19). He will, if he is fortunate, have parents who have communicated to him that learning what is taught at school is valuable and worth the loss of the time spent playing and socializing that marked the preceding years (22). He will be mature enough or well enough motivated to be able to inhibit the impulse to move about; in other words, he will be able to sit without too much discomfort for an hour or longer. He will be interested in learning to master pencil use for writing, having had prior experience during kindergarten in drawing. He will be able to portray a somewhat detailed representation of a person (21) and to copy simple designs, such as circles, squares, and triangles.

The same child will be functioning reasonably comfortably at the verbal level, which is to say that he can extend his experience by listening to and processing spoken information. He will be able to follow directions (4), to understand many of the fine points of a story that is read to him, to find the absurdity in a joke, and to absorb what his peers tell him. Moreover, he has a reasonably good ear for sounds; while he may not be able to determine the number of sounds in a word (30), he can hear fine differences between sounds (45) and words, and he can repeat short sentences verbatim (25). He can also express himself through words. In spite of occasional lingering articulatory infantilisms, he can be readily understood (45). He has a wide vocabulary and can use words rather precisely. He can speak fluently in constructions that are reasonably mature (6). Although he may not be able to retell a complicated story, he can discern the line of a story depicted by a sequence of pictures and can use the pictures to tell the story (25).

The youngster who is ready for school will know the names of many letters and may be able to write a few to dictation. She will know how to write her first name and copy printed words recognizably (14). She will be able to find which two words match in a group of four or five words (14). She will be interested in printed words and will have asked questions at home about them; in fact, she may be able to read a few words. Even if she is unable to do so, she will be able to learn to read and spell a familiar word with a "strong" configuration (such as "boy") within about an hour (14).

Above all, she is curious: She wants to discover and to master. She is challenged by the work and is able to cope with it. She can work for short periods on her own. Although she may not be equally "ready" in all of the areas discussed, she will be ready in most and will sense how to deploy her strengths to cope with her shortcomings—and a few weaknesses will not deter her (14,25).

One could teach this child by virtually any well organized and closely supervised method and she would learn to read. It almost seems that all the teacher really has to do is to systematize practice.

When the successful student is nine or 10 or older, he is well oriented to the school routines. He knows the rules and usually chooses to follow them because he understands and identifies, up to a point, with the underlying rationale. He can keep track of his possessions and can make and carry out some plans without adult supervision. He is also relatively autonomous with regard to school assignments to be done at home. He has a number of interests outside school and, stimulated by his investment in them, has accumulated considerable information about them.

During class he pays fairly close attention. He reads not only at school but also outside of class; the amount varies widely, as does the selection. He may read books in a series, children's encyclopedias or newspapers, magazines, television schedules, comics or a history book—the point is that he is using reading to enlarge his world. It is no longer an end in itself; it has become a means to an end, a tool. Our student can also learn a spelling list in a relatively short time and can write brief stories and factual essays. He knows, roughly, when to use periods and capitals and his grammar is acceptable.

The able nine-year-old can apply some of the numerical operations learned at school to his daily experience outside. He is interested in and capable of managing small amounts of money. He can buy things and make change. He can tell time and work within short time limits. He knows the names of days, months, seasons and can read a calendar. He has some sense of the sequence of holidays.

In describing the able student we have described someone who demonstrates neurophysiological, emotional, and cognitive maturity. Expressed behaviorally, he is a coper, one who is able to manage much of what he is asked to do at school, one for whom academic success has value, and one who enjoys overcoming reasonable obstacles and the sense of accomplishment that follows. He welcomes praise, but in the main he works for the pleasure accruing to himself.

School may be the child's first formal indoctrination to his or her culture. The youngster who has himself in hand finds the process instructive: He has mastered certain academic skills, such as reading and manipulating numbers and non-verbal symbols, but he has also acquired a working knowledge of the functioning of a typical institution. He has discovered the way he is manipulated and he will have learned something of how to work through the system and how to get the system to work for him. It is to be hoped, of course, that through his experience at school he will be helped to learn to change aspects of the system that no longer serve adequately.

The child who cannot cope with the system by virtue of his difficulty in learning suffers not only the deprivation of mastery but also an estrangement from the mainstream of his culture. This is a fundamental estrangement. While in some cases this has been turned to creative advantage, it is more often the rule that repercussions of failure confirm or lead to a sense of low self-esteem, despair, dislocation, and, ultimately, rejection. As the child proceeds through the grades, his feeling that he has been cast off may become fixed and his school experience may actually be painful and destructive instead of being useful. In many children, the anger that accompanies failure is externalized in the form of destructive behavior, a response that may become a permanent pattern. The ultimate loss in human productivity is immeasurable.

SPECIFIC LEARNING DISABILITY

It behooves those who care for children to be aware of the characteristics that signal specific learning disability because recognition is the first step toward intervention. It must be emphasized again that children who present specific difficulties with reading, writing, and arithmetic *can* learn, given appropriate, timely intervention. When there is a suspicion of learning disability, children should be referred for evaluation immediately. Too often, physicians and teachers counsel the parents to wait in the expectation that the child will "catch up." The delay in providing treatment often results in the reverse: At the very least, delay may be the decisive factor in the child's slipping beyond easy reach of help; at worst, it may deprive him of the chance he had for just making it.

What are some of the characteristics of the child with specific learning disability?

The History

As mentioned, investigation of family history may show that one or several members of the family have trouble with some aspect of language or learning. It may be found that an uncle was late to speak and had trouble learning to read, that a sibling repeated a grade, or that mother is a poor speller.

Also, as indicated previously, pregnancy, delivery, or the neonatal period may have been somewhat complicated. For example, research by de Hirsch, Janksy, and Langford (14) showed that more than half of a sample of 53 children who had had low birth weight lagged behind controls in reading and spelling at the end of second grade. Other investigators have reported similar findings (28).

The developmental history may reveal that the child sat and took his first steps at about the expected times, but careful questioning of the mother may uncover delay in some aspect of language acquisition. Occasionally, the child was late in combining words to form short phrases. Denckla (17) found that many children who eventually have academic difficulties were slow to learn to use color names (although they were able to match colors). Many parents, however, are unaware that the child's expressive language is clumsy. Still more frequently overlooked by parents are spotty gaps in comprehension. The less verbal children in the group are little interested in listening to stories, preferring to run about. Their disinclination is often regarded as a simple matter of preference (which it is, of course), rather than as including elements of avoidance and a signal that may indicate questionable understanding. Occasionally, parents are aware when the children have trouble following directions; spatial concepts, especially "behind" and "backwards," are frequently misunderstood (19).

The Presenting Picture

Developmental and Emotional Immaturity

When the child comes for evaluation, he may strike the examiner as appearing younger than his chronological age mates. The face, arms, hands and torso may have the soft, rounded contours of a younger child. He may be overly active or, less frequently, underactive. He may find it hard to sit comfortably—though much of the time he seems compelled to run, he may suddenly slump inertly, with his head on the table. In sum, he is unable to relegate his physical self to the background where it should serve as a support and framework for cognition. Instead, his unpredictable motility interferes with attention and concentration (2).

Emotionally, the child seems immature (26). Even at six or seven years of age he may have trouble separating from his mother, begging her to accompany him into the examination room. The somewhat older child may not want her to leave the office to do some errands. Many children have strong oral needs; they may have their fingers in their mouths or eat candy voraciously, if given the opportunity. Often they have trouble working for long-range goals; they cannot postpone gratification (10). They may decide to avoid working at activities, such as reading or learning addition, because mastery is not immediate. If one asks the mother how the child amuses himself at home, she may state that he has trouble playing by himself and that he has few friends. Such a child may have little interest in the workings of the external world or in the views of others because of his preoccupation with his own needs and feelings.

Even if the child presented no further problems, he would be a risky candidate for school because learning requires an active, assertive approach and a reasonably high frustration threshold. The child with the learning disability has additional problems, however.

Handedness and Directionality

For years it was thought that poorly established handedness or left handedness was a correlate of trouble with learning, but reasearch has not necessarily supported this hypothesis. Actually, ambiguous laterality is not uncommon in young children (1). Some youngsters with specific learning problems are, however, late to learn to identify right and left sides of themselves and, afterward, many are slow to identify right and left on the person opposite them and to follow right-left directions (41). The same children may have trouble establishing the left to right sweep of printed words and sentences for reading and writing.

Coordination and Grapho-Motor Competence

The child may or may not show incoordination during large muscle activities, such as ball throwing. (Actually, many children in the group who fare poorly at ball play and team sports may do rather well at climbing, riding, skiing, sailing, and swimming.)

Many have trouble with small muscle coordination as required for writing. The problem by no means extends to all activities requiring fine muscle skill. Some children are proficient in making models and handling tools. Some even use the pencil well for drawing. Not infrequently, trouble managing a pencil is confined to the act of writing, which, as de Hirsch (13) has pointed out, is a verbal symbolic activity. They may find it hard to form letters, to pick out the essential features that make it possible to distinguish between them (20). They have trouble with layout—showing relative differences in size and orientation, maintaining letters on the line, and placing them correctly.

Not surprisingly, the child may be inept at copying printed designs (14,25). These problems are similar to those he encounters when he attempts to write. The lines may be clumsily drawn, the angles rounded. But his major difficulty is with placing *parts* in correct relationship and in locating the several *designs* on the page in satisfactory relation to one another and in terms of the page as a whole. Most children automatically anchor the configurations firmly on the page with little effort, but the child with a grapho-motor problem has to fight to keep them from flying wildly off the page or from tumbling together in a heap in the middle.

Older children attempt to maintain control by obsessionally counting dots, measuring angles, and generally worrying about accuracy. The tendency of the children to rotate, reverse, and invert designs has been commented upon frequently. If the examiner requests the child to draw the designs from memory, it is found that configurations may be forgotten or distorted (usually in the direction of simplification). Obviously, design copying is a task of considerable complexity. It requires not only an understanding of letter-like configurations and the interrelationship of parts, but also the ability to execute the configuration, to recreate the essence of the Gestalten. It is a measure of the individual's skill at managing abstract printed forms in a spatial field. It is also demanding in terms of fine muscle organization and it requires the ability to inhibit impulsivity.

Language Status

Rather mild but pervasive language deficits can almost be considered the hallmark of the group of poor readers among learning disabled children (13). The oral language concomitants are discussed extensively in two books by de Hirsch and Jansky (14,27). The following remarks are drawn from these sources, as well as from the work of Cazden (6) and ongoing clinical observation. Because the deficits are marginal, because the child is obviously alert and responsive, because he may be talkative, his gaps may pass unnoticed. It is quite possible, moreover, to have a rather high Verbal I.Q. in the presence of language gaps. Just because an individual has demonstrated verbal conceptual gifts, it is a mistake to conclude that all other aspects of language functioning are equally superior.

Sounds. Many of the children have problems with the management of phonemes, or sounds. On the receptive side, they may not be able to distinguish between words that differ only by a single sound (pat-pad). Usually, their problem is more apparent during conversation because they misunderstand words from time to time. In addition, children may have trouble blending parts of spoken words to form wholes, that is, with making the leap, as they listen, from the given word-components to the whole word formed when components are combined.

Some learning disabled youngsters have trouble pronouncing certain sounds: *r, l, s, z, sh, th, ch,* and *j* are among sounds most frequently misarticulated. It is far more common for children in this group to mispronounce words not because they find it hard to form the sounds, but because they do not recall their order. It may be that their recollection of the sound structure of the spoken word is blurred and their pronunciation reflects this. Sometimes the phonemic structure of the word becomes more primitive ("lettuce" becomes "less") and sometimes the sequence of sounds in the word is distorted or scrambled (a 16-year-old said *"poticks"* rather than *"depicts"*). Rate of speaking is usually rather fast.

Words. The children often have subtle difficulties with words. Many of them learn to isolate single words from the flow of speech far later than do their peers. They may, for example, hear *"have to"* as a single word: *"havta."* Words do not have an especially strong configuration and are not, individually, held especially well in memory. Children may be unfamiliar with the meaning of some specific words, a phenomenon often missed by parents and the child himself because the youngster gets the sense of the utterance from context. Not infrequently, he will interpret a sentence using the word correctly, yet will be unable to provide a definition.

Dysnomia is one of the most frequent verbal deficits of youngsters with learning problems. The dysnomic child knows the meaning of the word perfectly well and could define it if asked. His difficulty is his inability to evoke the word at the moment he needs it. Sometimes a related word will come out, and sometimes a description of function or a pronoun is substituted for the noun. There is an overuse of filler words, such as "like," and of pronouns and non-specific nouns, such as "thing." Occasionally, output is dysrhythmic, the flow having been interrupted by the child's groping for words. He may repeat sounds or whole words, a manifestation that has been confused with stuttering but is quite different (15). A special category of the problem is the child's difficulty remembering words that refer to time markers, specifically, his birth date, the names of days of the week, the seasons, and the months. He is slow to separate conceptually seasons and months and once he grasps the difference, it takes him a while to learn the names that belong to each category and to evoke them appropriately. His failure to remember his address belongs to the same category. A seven-year-old with learning disabilities may not even know what is expected when asked for his "address." When the question is rephrased, "Where do you live?" he is more likely to respond, but he may provide an incomplete answer. The difference between city and state will be lost to him for some time to come.

Sentences. The children have grammatical problems as well. Their difficulty repeating verbatim sentences that increase in complexity is probably partially related to their inability to incorporate into their own verbalizations more sophisticated syntactic constructions. Some young-sters also misunderstand sentence forms that are heard less frequently and those that reflect rather subtle distinctions in meaning. The difference between the declarative and the conditional is an example. ("You will go," and "You might go.") They also have problems when a more frequent ordering of parts of speech is changed to a less frequent sequence. The child would understand if asked to point to the picture in which the cat chases the dog. Were the same information expressed in the sentence, "Show me the dog the cat chased," he might misunderstand. He may not be able to follow more complicated clause patterns. When interpreting the sentence, "The fireman rushed to the burning house, picked up his fire hose, and, after smoking a cigar, put out the fire," such a child might say, "You can't put out a fire with a cigar!"

With regard to expression, the omission or misuse of sounds is a morphological rather than an articulatory error in some cases. The omission of the *s* from "cats" reflects as often the speaker's failure to incorporate the plural marker as it does the speaker's inability to pronounce the *s*. This youngster may have a more generalized difficulty formulating sentences. Having gotten off to a clumsy start, he may retreat and begin again. The constructions he uses may be primitive rather than elaborated. When quoting, he may simplify. The movie title "The Man Who Would be King" becomes "The Man Who Could be King." He may make grammatical errors. The younger children in the group have difficulty with the irregular past tense verb forms. Such a seven-year-old might say, "I hitted a ball." Occasionally, parts of speech may be confused: "The king couldn't war good." The sentences of older learning disabled children are frequently unwieldy. A lengthy utterance will be found to consist of fragments and of extended, awkwardly formed compound sentences linked by the connector "and."

Longer Units. The individual in question may also have trouble with longer language units. One youngster might be unable to answer correctly factual questions about a story read to him; another might have trouble drawing inferences from what was read and is always the last to answer questions about what will happen next in the story. Many are unable to find the absurdity in a statement read to them; the problem may be their difficulty sorting out essentials from nonessentials, a problem separating figure from ground. The adolescent with academic difficulties often has trouble interpreting proverbs because he cannot detach himself from the concrete example. He may not grasp the fact that in metaphor the instance given represents a general truth. In explaining, "You never know the worth of water until the well is dry," he might say, "Certainly. Anyone knows that you don't know how much you need water until you haven't got it."

There are also problems with larger units of expressive language. The learning disabled child's monotonous delivery reflects his failure to use emphasis and melodic change to underscore the meaning he is trying to convey. The stories he tells may be difficult to follow because he has trouble pulling out the story line from the morass of supporting detail, with the result that the story goes on indefinitely, often without reaching a conclusion. Moreover, the youngster makes little effort to show cause and effect, or the relationship between events he is describing. He does not use interpretative commentary to make the listener's task easier.

The above remarks about the language of the learning disabled child illustrate the tie between his language difficulty and his cognitive problems, for he demonstrates failures of memory, categorization, and the ability to generalize and to make inferences.

The child's language problems are often subtle, as mentioned before. It is rare that the untrained listener picks them up, because most of the children can follow the general classroom discussion reasonably well (though there will be an occasional report card comment to the effect that the child has trouble following directions). When attempting to interpret what the child has said, most listeners fill in from their own experience the gaps in the information that is being related. So long as the child speaks rather volubly, pronounces words correctly, and uses standard English, he will be regarded by most people as an adequate speaker. (Most listeners are far more aware of the different grammatical constructions used by speakers of non-standard English than they are of the kind of grammatical errors described here.) If the child's stories and anecdotes are rambling and a little difficult to follow, they are regarded as being dull rather than as inadequately told.

Academic Performances

The difficulties children have with reading, writing, and spelling have been described by de Hirsch (12), Orton (36), Silver and Hagin (43), and others.

Reading. In attempting to learn to read, some children have difficulty distinguishing between letter forms. Those that are most similar present the greatest challenge: *m, w, r, n, h, b, d, p, q, j, i,* and *l* may be hardest because difference rests on spatial orientation or in small variations in length of line. These children have great trouble stabilizing the forms; it may not be so much that they consistently reverse letters as that they experience them as shifting randomly—as much during recall as when they look at them on the page. A separate but often concomitant problem is the stabilization of letter sequence in printed words. The child with specific learning disability often begins to read words at the right rather than at the left side, and he may transpose letters within the word in a right to left sequence because he has not securely established the conventional tracking direction. Able readers probably do not read words in letter by letter fashion, either, but they do work across the page from left to right and they probably group frequent letter combinations, such as "th" in "this" or the "ou" in "shout." The child who has trouble learning to read is slow to build up an information bank of letter group probabilities. He also has trouble holding to a line of print, slipping from one line to the next and omitting phrases and whole lines.

This youngster's problems with memory and elicitation are also disabling. He finds it hard to learn the letter names and sounds, and to remember the names of whole printed words. He may find it hard, therefore, to learn phonics and to build a sight word vocabulary. He may recognize the letter or the printed word only to forget what it is called, or he may remember the spoken equivalent but forget the printed form to which it belongs. It is characteristic, but puzzling and frustrating to both the child and his teacher, that he will remember the letter sound or word one day but forget it the next. All these problems stem from the fragile linkage between the spoken and printed systems.

An additional difficulty may arise from poor "sentence sense." The child who is ready to learn to read anticipates from the way the sentence begins how it may end; the words he sees match his expectations and he "learns" them. The learning disabled youngster, whose grammatic sense may be uncertain, is less likely to guess correctly and thus this additional approach to reading may be unavailable to him.

Without assistance, he may not learn to read at all. What happens more often is that he reads ineffectively, so that the process is frustrating and infuriating. He reads slowly and fails to produce spoken equivalents for common sight words, such as "what" and "said." He has trouble sounding out the longer, less familiar words. He misreads easy words (reading "the" as "he"), inserts or substitutes words of his own, and omits words from the text. He may lose his place. His discomfort is readily apparent. Some children yawn the moment they are given something to read. Others ask for candy. Some become visibly anxious: They sweat and their hands and voices may shake, or they may cry. Others become angry and complain about reading, criticize the material or the examiner. Some refuse to try and a few simply walk out.

Even when this child develops some mastery over the printed word, his troubles may persist in the form of difficulty comprehending what he has read. These problems come to light quite readily in the course of one of the more advanced silent reading comprehension tests. Tests for the early grades usually include pictures that facilitate guessing, but the tests for fourth graders and older children are difficult for those who have comprehension problems. The small print and narrow spaces exacerbate early difficulties in managing spatial arrangement; the words and letters lose their distinctive quality so that the printed forms all look alike. The exercises demand familiarity with a wide variety of topics, many of them outside the child's experience or interests. This is an especially difficult problem for the learning disabled child, given his problems with the processing of information. The relative brevity of the exercises may put him at a disadvantage because there is little redundancy of information; on the contrary, the information is tightly packed and each sentence is part of a chain necessary for full comprehension. The child may manage a long story or a whole book more easily because of the greater opportunity for becoming familiar with the author's vocabulary and style, as well as with events and characters.

Additional problems in reading tests arise from sophisticated grammatical constructions, problems that are analogous to those that arise during processing of spoken language. (The difficulties he has understanding social studies and history texts, in which sentences may be extremely complex, are of the same order.) Or, he may have trouble using grammatical cues to follow the thread of information. Our reader may manage to read the text and to have some sense of what it says, yet have trouble manipulating the information. A question that asks him to go a step farther, that is, to select the best title for the passage or to make an inference from the text, may prove to be too demanding.

Lack of familiarity with the meaning of words is a complicating factor. Problems of this nature may show up either during the comprehension test or during the reading vocabulary section of the test. In some cases, an individual can infer what a word means from the way it is used in the sentence. His chances for survival decline as a function of the increase in number of unfamiliar words. He may falter when it comes to questions that probe his knack for sorting out shades of meaning. Thus, he might be posed the choice, "The word 'great' in line 7 means—'magnificent,' 'famous,' 'very large,' or 'worthy.' " The student's score on the vocabulary section may be low simply because he had difficulty deciphering the words. The examiner can determine whether this was the case simply by reading aloud the words, including the synonym choices. If the child responds correctly during this oral test of vocabulary, the problem is not with word meanings. The latter comes to light when the response choices are reviewed and it is found that he is unfamiliar with either the key words or the synonyms provided.

Parents and teachers lament the child's disinterest in reading and often complain that he would improve were he to read more. In view of the monumental obstacles to comfortable reading, as described above, it is the unusual child who finds the resources in himself not only to decide to struggle on, but also to make way against odds.

Spelling. The children in this group make characteristic spelling errors. These include orientation and sequencing mistakes—they reverse letters in words and transpose them. Sometimes, when an individual's memory of the printed word form is very poor, he simply makes up printed words out of whole cloth. The latter look not at all like the original and seem bizarre. If the child uses a letter sound approach to spelling, the frequency of letter transposals and strange spellings decreases. However, the youngster who has trouble with auditory discrimination and the ordering of the sequence of sounds makes mistakes when working by way of the sounds in the word. Voiced and voiceless phonemes may be confused (*v* and *f*, for example); the same is true for very similar sounds (*th* and *f*). Moreover, the individual's rendering of the sound pattern may be flawed; elements that are unstressed during pronunciation may be omitted ("hump" may be written as "hup"). The child who mispronounces words may incorporate his errors in written forms of words.

The lack of easy correspondence between spoken and printed English words has been discussed extensively. If all words were spelled the way they sound, "his" would be spelled "hiz" and "bitten" would be spelled "bitn." There are rules that specify the number of ways each speech sound may be spelled and rules for adding prefixes and suffixes to word roots, but these are cumbersome to learn and easily forgotten. In practice, no matter what his training, the child who approaches spelling by way of sounds usually selects the most frequently encountered options. His spelling of many words will be readable, but it will not be correct.

The fact that there is no correlation between spelling and intelligence suggests that the ability to spell well is simply a knack people have to varying degrees. It is very likely that this enables them to readily learn and remember the way the printed words look. The good speller may occasionally use the sound pattern of the word as an adjunct when in doubt, but for the most part he probably relies on his recall of the printed letter configuration, as well as on his knowledge of the printed markers that distinguish between parts of speech. Thus, he will instinctively select the correct spelling for the short *u* and for the *f* sounds in writing "tough" and he will intuitively express in written form his understanding that the *t* sound at the end of "hot" is written "t" because it represents a simple sound-letter correspondence at the end of an adjective, while he knows that the *t* sound at the end of "wished" must be spelled "ed" because the latter is the past tense ending for regular verbs in written English. This knowledge is so much a part of the fabric of a good speller that he does not need to make a conscious effort to work out the rule. And it is because the information has become so automatized that the adult who spells well underestimates the difficulties of the child who does not. The teacher and parent believe that the child is making careless errors and could spell correctly if he would only try harder.

Handwriting. The learning disabled child's compositions look disorganized. Poor handwriting was touched upon earlier. His problems with letter formation and management of relative size and of spacing were discussed in some detail. The compositions usually look messy. There are frequent crossings out, evidence of letters misformed and rewritten, of misspellings with attempts to correct. The spacing of words is usually erratic; the words may be crowded together or separated at irregular intervals. The individual's difficulty with grammar is reflected in his omission of sentence markers, that is to say, of periods and capitals. The way the child sets out a page of print is almost as much his signature as is his name.

Compositions. The compositions of the children frequently mirror their spoken language. Those who have trouble formulating what they say may experience writing blocks. They complain either that they cannot think what to say or that they can express what they have to say in a very few lines. The kinds of mistakes these children make when they try to express themselves in writing are very similar, regardless of the length of their productions. Their characteristic spelling errors appear, and in addition they frequently leave off suffixes that they might have included had they been writing a dictated spelling list and if they were less burdened by the more complex process of writing to communicate. One will find "The two boy ran for the ball," or "They struck at the ball and miss.

As suggested above, some compositions are so sterile and barren that they cannot be judged from the standpoint of organization of material. Others impress the reader as rambling and disjointed. It should be noted here that most learning disabled children find it easier to write stories and poems than to compose essays or a summary. The latter is more demanding because of the requirement of factual accuracy and the linking of arguments to form a logical chain that culminates in the conclusion. The individual who has a reading disability has trouble organizing information, with the result that certain small points are highlighted at the expense of the pertinent data. He often forgets to indicate cause and effect and he finds it hard to act as the interpreter for the reader. Many children write about themselves, their thoughts, feelings and reactions, rather than about their subject. It might be argued that most poorly written essays suffer from the above shortcomings. The similarity between manner of speaking and pattern of writing is a major characteristic that differentiates the learning disabled student from his peers. His poor writing is not primarily the result of poor teaching or of a disinclination to learn or to communicate.

Foreign Language. The youngster experiences the same kinds of difficulty in learning a foreign language that he had when learning to read and to write English. He has trouble amassing the vocabulary of a second language, in part because of his dysnomia and in part because of the necessity to make fine distinctions between word roots shared by so many of the romance languages. The child also has trouble learning the noun declensions and the instances when various forms apply, because his own internalized grammar is so shaky. It is equally hard for him to learn to conjugate verbs. He is not used to coping with accents, above all when his own delivery is monotonous and his sense of word parameters so uncertain. When he attempts to speak, he has trouble learning and pronouncing a new consonant and vowel sound system. When listening, he may find it hard to locate the word boundaries during the flow of speech. The strange language may remain a meaningless collection of sounds indefinitely.

Some preschool children who are high risks for learning disability are exposed to two languages at an early age. They do learn something of each language, but their mastery of both languages often lags behind that of peers who are better endowed linguistically. Neither language serves for precise verbal expression and the level of understanding of both languages is lower than it would have been had there been just one to contend with. Some learning disabled children do, eventually, master a second language, but usually only after their first is well established and when they are adolescents or older (28).

Arithmetic. Because deficits in symbolic functioning are basic to learning disabilities, children in this group often have trouble mastering numerical, as well as verbal tasks (44). Most, though not all, learn to recite numbers from 1 to 10 or 20 fairly easily, but this does not necessarily mean that they can count off. The child seems to be slow to grasp one-to-one correspondence, or the meshing of the spoken number name, in sequence, with the object that is being counted. He has difficulty adding and taking away, even when he is working with real objects, because he loses his place either when pointing or while counting. He may be slow to convert groupings of objects to a printed symbol, the written number, that stands for the size of the group. "4" is, for him, quite unrelated to a group of four objects. He has trouble learning to recognize and to remember the different printed numbers and he has the same problems writing numbers as writing letters. He forms the printed number symbols awkwardly and rotates and reverses them.

Once he has established the association between number symbol and the group it represents, he may fail to manipulate the symbols accurately for various reasons. It takes him longer than his classmates to learn addition and subtraction facts. In practice, when solving problems, he frequently resorts to counting on his fingers, an approach that is unsatisfactory because it is slow and limited. He is frequently asked to learn the multiplication tables before he is sure of his addition and subtraction facts, and sometimes in the process he forgets the underlying groupings and operations that the facts stand for. When he is confronted with written computational problems he is hampered by difficulty aligning columns and by messily written numbers. Part of the problem stems from poor spatial layout; part comes from not having mastered the significance of place, with attendant lack of regard for organization in setting out the numbers. He is inattentive to sign and may add when he should subtract, and he may rotate the plus sign which is then perceived as the signal for multiplication.

By and large, the child's chances for error rise with the number of steps required to complete the problem. While the latter is true for all children, the errors of the learning disabled child represent a much greater underlying confusion than do those of his classmates.

The impulsiveness of many children in this group exacerbates the problems with learning arithmetic. The individual who cannot inhibit the urge to move about does not take time to write out his computation neatly, to check procedures carefully, and to take a moment to reflect on the answer to determine whether or not it makes sense. The work sheets of this child show poorly controlled pencil marks with wildly written, almost illegible numbers which appear to be very poorly anchored to the page. The teacher may react to his paper almost as if it were an assault.

The same youngster usually has more trouble with word problems than he has with unadorned computation exercises. Casting problems to be solved in words may be a source of real confusion because some of the words that are keys to the appropriate procedure are common words with poorly defined printed characteristics. In the problem, "Six of the comics on Bob's shelf were his own and four had been borrowed from Martin; altogether, how many comics were on the shelf?" one key word is "and." As a printed configuration, "and" lacks a strong physiognomy (the other key word, "altogether," stands out more strongly) and the child is likely to miss it. The word "borrowed" might mislead him into thinking that subtraction is called for. Again, the more steps the problem demands, the harder the task is for the child. The observer who watches the struggle the youngster has simply to read the problem, can appreciate his difficulty in processing information. He finds it hard to pull out pertinent facts.

Outside of school he may be slow to learn to manage money. He has not learned the value of the various coins, does not understand prices, and does not know how to make change.

Some children seem to manage adequately in arithmetic once they have mastered the basic processes, that is to say, once they have the tools with which to work. Others may never safely establish the tools and will continue to encounter the kinds of problems described.

Emotional Status

De Hirsch (11) has discussed the interaction between emotional and learning difficulties. The child who fails at school may well have had doubts about his adequacy from his earliest years, doubts related to conflicts within the family constellation. The experience of failing upon entering school confirms his low opinion of himself. Attempts to reassure him verbally as to his basic intelligence fail because the roots of his doubt extend beyond the academic area into the period before he entered school. Failure at school may exacerbate the youngster's problems with his parents and siblings. He becomes marked by them as the low achiever, a status that may become fixed in family dynamics. When this occurs, the child's failure becomes necessary for the stability of the family unit, a situation that makes success at school threatening from a psychological standpoint to every member of the family. A somewhat closer look at the family mythology shows subtle exaggerations and distortions, so that the learning disability of one member becomes the focal point that "explains" and obscures difficulties of other family members. In a very real sense, the learning disabled child is vulnerable to becoming the scapegoat.

For the child himself, the day at school can be a harrowing experience. He finds he cannot escape from failure. He falls behind in many subjects because of his difficulty reading his assignments. The classroom teacher's response to the child may affect him adversely. It is not that she dislikes or rejects him (although it may seem so to the child and his parents), but rather that she feels she has failed. This may cloud her objectivity so that she seizes on the view that the failure is the child's. Actually, her training has probably not prepared her for the fact that it is unreasonable to expect this child to learn certain things at the time and pace that is appropriate for his classmates. Because he cannot do this, the teacher may conclude that he cannot learn at all. Of course, this is not true, but unfortunately her anxiety and doubts are communicated to the child and simply add to the burdens of the day at school.

If he is motorically clumsy, he may do poorly at sports; thus, success may elude him even in nonacademic areas. He sees the gap between himself and his peers widening and his belief that he is a failure is strengthened.

The child's struggle to keep up may weaken with the passing years and he may resort to a variety of avenues of escape from the anxiety attendant on being unable to cope. He may lose himself in wish fulfilling fantasy in which he is omnipotent and his detractors are destroyed. He may try to gain status with his peers through daring, antisocial exploits. He may try to hide the seriousness of his plight from himself and, by so doing, evolve a series of rationalizations about why he fails. Unfortunately, the methods he chooses for dealing with his anxiety tend to be counterproductive in that they take him farther away from addressing and resolving his problems. Clearly, he cannot resolve them by himself; he needs the backing of his parents and the school and technical guidance from professionals who understand him and know how to help him.

The Syndrome

Innumerable symptoms of specific learning disability have been set out in the foregoing pages. It was stated earlier that it is not known whether specific learning disability represents a single syndrome or several characteristic clusters of problems. Children who present most or all of the symptoms described do exist, but they are in the minority. Similarly, there are some children who present isolated but substantial deficits, yet function perfectly well in spite of them. The majority of children who are referred for evaluation present several of the signs and the severity of the accompanying problem and of the academic difficulties varies widely. The writer believes that certain symptoms do characteristically appear together, but would hesitate to take the position that the clusters are invariant for fear of missing important interactions that do not fit into prescribed groupings. Assigning cases to predetermined groupings may be hazardous because of the loss of data that enrich and refine the diagnostic picture and highlight, rather than blunt, the individuality of the case. A point can certainly be made for the desirability of relating therapeutic approaches to diagnostic patterns, but rigid grouping is not a necessary condition for tailoring remediation to the child's needs.

Although the locus of deficits varies from one child to the next, it should be emphasized that the deficits, wherever they appear, are remarkably similar in kind. The learning disabled child has problems with processing, storing, and retrieval of information, whether he is recalling a letter-like form, remembering how the letter *j* is shaped, attempting to retell a story, learn the sound for *ow*, or the printed form of the spoken word *what*, the sum of 9 and 6, or the third person singular ending of the Spanish verb *venir*. He finds it very hard to stabilize what he knows, with the result that he cannot count on material that he has been taught from one day to the next.

Vellutino (47) has collected extensive data to support the conviction, shared by Orton (36), de Hirsch (13), this writer, and others, that a dysfunction in one or more aspects of linguistic functioning may account substantially for the child's reading, writing and spelling disability. Because the youngster's hold on verbal data is so tenuous, he has difficulty automatizing performances that must become tools. Lacking the tools, he is locked in a morass of half-skills and his forward motion is seriously compromised.

Early Identification

Early identification is virtually a prerequisite for successful intervention (14,27). The preschool child who is delayed in learning to use language should be referred for evaluation by a specialist who is trained in that discipline. Too often, the pediatrician overlooks subtle problems with language, especially difficulties with language comprehension. He may reassure the mother of the child who has not yet started to talk at the age of two that he will use words when he is ready. The child may do so, but the judgment should be left to the professional who is thoroughly conversant with language development. Specialists in other areas are, understandably, far more likely to express concern over articulatory problems. These, however, do not necessarily reflect the child's general language status and they are poor predictors of academic success. It is emphasized, then, that referral for evaluation may appropriately be made the moment there is a suspicion that the child shows deficits in areas crucial for learning. For the preschooler, these would include questions as to language (as opposed to speech) development which might arise as early as the second year and problems managing pencil and paper (as seen at the end of the fourth or the beginning of the fifth year).

Diagnosis

The purpose of the diagnostic evaluation is to get an assessment of the child's weaknesses and strengths in the areas described in the foregoing pages. The questions the diagnostician must answer are: How widespread are the child's nonacademic difficulties? In what areas are his problems and how severe is each deficit? To what extent does he lag behind his peers in the several achievement areas? What are his resources for compensation—specifically, in which of the areas critical for success does he perform adequately or well? To what extent does he recognize that he has a problem and to what degree is his appraisal realistic? Is he aware that his problems are limited in scope, are remediable, and do not reflect negatively upon him personally? Is he aware of his strengths? Most children are far more eager to learn than some of their behavior may suggest. Critical considerations are the amount of effort the child will be able to invest in learning and an assessment of the extent to which his energy is bound to coping with his various conflicts. How well do the parents understand the child's difficulty? Will they be willing to back the remedial program, which may require adjustments in the academic schedule and changes in school? Are they prepared to invest considerable time in treatment? The remedial course is lengthy and most parents must be prepared for an involvement that will sometimes last several years. Parental anxiety is understandable and the question is, how is it managed? To what extent do principal and teachers understand the child's problems? Will they be able to devise programs that are not too difficult and allow for his ongoing problems, but that challenge the child sufficiently to stimulate learning? An accurate assessment of each of the above variables, and others, is part of the diagnostic process.

The evaluation will *not*, per se, tell the therapist how to treat the child. Hopefully, it will yield a picture of what the child brings to the learning process. It will provide information as to how he operates. The data will be considered in the light of each remedial specialist's view of the skills that are necessary for learning to read, spell and solve arithmetic problems. Hypotheses for treatment approaches will arise from the combined information.

CASE ILLUSTRATIONS

Two case discussions might serve to exemplify the diagnostic picture and the way the specific learning disability evolves in practice.

Billy

Billy was referred for language evaluation at the age of four years two months because his nursery school teachers could not understand what he said. They reported extensive mispronunciation of words.

We learned from Billy's mother that she herself reads slowly and is an indifferent speller. The boy is one of fraternal twins, the parents' only children. He was born at term, of average birth weight. The mother pointed out that Billy was being dominated by his twin sister, who was described as intelligent and aggressive. It was the sister who determined what games the two would play and made the decisions.

Billy presented as a silent, stolid child who had a little trouble separating from his mother but was persuaded to accompany the examiner into the playroom. He waited passively to be told what to do. He cooperated, but without much display of interest or enthusiasm.

His fine motor coordination when playing with toys was acceptable; indeed, the only time he came to life was when he was putting together puzzles. He held the pencil in the right hand, but had considerable difficulty using it. He could not draw a picture of a person and the only geometric shape he managed to copy was a circle. He did try, however. Billy misinterpreted pictured situations. Shown a drawing of a little girl standing precariously on a stool as she reached for cookies, with a dog jumping at the stool, Billy completely overlooked the fact that the child was reaching for something and had placed *herself* in an untenable position. He interpreted the the picture as showing that the dog was attempting to knock down the child.

There were spotty gaps in language comprehension. Billy scored at age level on a spoken vocabulary test, but he did not follow the line of the story told him and had trouble following verbal directions. He fended off responsibility for addressing difficult questions by responding, "I don't know," without attempting to push through.

A remedial program was initiated. At first, the aim was to stimulate language growth: to expand comprehension of spoken language and to work for more differentiated verbalizations and a larger vocabulary. The therapist postponed work on articulation. An additional aim was to help Billy to learn to use a pencil and to act out stories, an activity that he resisted.

Billy's progress in most areas has been slow but quite steady. It was found that he was eager for structure and would persevere when the work was rigidly organized. Although one would have wished for him to be able to cope with a more flexible approach, Billy's receptive and expressive language improved considerably during his kindergarten year. However, his speech was even harder to understand than it had been when he was first seen, because he talked more and spoke in longer units. His parents had been warned in advance that this would probably occur. Work on writing and letter recognition during the kindergarten year also went well. Billy labored at these structured tasks, but continued to be reluctant to engage in imaginative play. Just before he entered the first grade, he began to read and to write a few words.

The school, which is unusually flexible, made special provisions for the boy during his first three years. They assigned an assistant teacher to work with him individually. It was toward the end of his first grade year that treatment time was available for work on the child's articulation. Billy and the speech therapist worked both on correct pronunciation of sounds and on reading and writing activities. By the time he was eight, his articulatory difficulties had disappeared.

The school psychologist determined that Billy's I.Q. fell at the upper extreme of the average range, with Performance score higher than Verbal score. Billy slowly mastered arithmetic facts, but was unable to handle French and this course was dropped from his program.

He continued through the middle school years to receive help in the language areas; the emphasis has continued to be the expansion of linguistic skills, working through the medium of reading and writing.

Upon completion of his sixth grade, Billy scored at the 50th percentile by independent school standards in reading vocabulary and comprehension, spelling, and arithmetic tests. Recently Billy has begun to enjoy writing fanciful tales.

Billy can hardly be described as a voluble speaker. He continues to excel at nonverbal activities; he handles tools well and can make many household repairs. He has some good friends and exhibits a quiet competence. One no longer thinks of him in relation to his sister.

Billy's success is not dramatic; the noteworthy aspect of outcome is that he has reduced the gap between himself and his peers and is holding his own. His greatest therapeutic asset has been his tenacity and willingness to withstand frustration. He has had the full backing of his teachers, who appreciate him, and of his parents, who have worked with him at home, under direction, and have supported the therapeutic plan that has extended over a period of eight years.

Martha

Martha was referred for evaluation at age 10 and a half. She was reading and spelling poorly. Her performance in arithmetic also lagged behind expectation.

Her father reported his own long history of academic difficulties, eventually resolved by sheer willpower by the time he was in his third year of high school. A number of the father's cousins and their children also had trouble learning to read and spell. Parental standards for achievement and behavior were high.

Neonatal history, delivery, and early development had been uneventful, though Martha was considered to be somewhat clumsy. Language development had been a little delayed, but the parents stated that Martha had since become a voluble talker. They noted that she enjoyed sewing and cooking, but they were clearly concerned about Martha's intelligence. (The individual who referred the child commented beforehand that the parents considered Martha to be somewhat retarded.)

In continuing with the history, the mother contrasted Martha with her younger brother who was characterized as "a super boy," brilliant in school, successful at sports, responsible, and gregarious. Martha was, not surprisingly, said to be very jealous of her brother. There was, in addition, a younger sister. Described as clever and capable at the time, this child was eventually evaluated because she, too, had some trouble learning to read in first grade. (It was Martha who pushed for the investigation because she recognized the similarity between her younger sister's problems and her own.)

We learned that the first and second grade teachers had been demanding and critical of Martha's slowness to move ahead. The parents had transferred Martha to a less demanding school. She was happier there, but no one paid attention to her reading problems and Martha had no friends her own age at all, though she was well liked by adults.

Martha presented as a heavy, overly active, and extremely anxious child. She was pathetically eager to please and very relieved that her problems were finally being investigated. She was found to have a Full Scale I.Q. of 120, with a Verbal rating of 115 and a Performance score of 121. She was markedly impulsive, tending to respond precipitously and without reflection. On the positive side, she was willing and accepted every suggestion eagerly, though she often spoiled her work by going too fast.

She drew well but wrote poorly. By and large, she attained average scores on the receptive language tests and there were no significant gaps in comprehension. Evaluation of spoken language revealed that Martha was slightly dysnomic and had trouble expressing complex ideas in words; she told rambling, disorganized stories. She was also somewhat concrete.

She scored about two years below grade level in reading and spelling and about half a year behind in arithmetic. She reversed and transposed letters and numbers and had trouble with layout. Her compositions were childish and primitive.

Martha brought in impressive samples of her cooking, sewing and artwork; she played the guitar and sang well. Martha thus showed herself to be assertive, capable, and well organized in some nonacademic areas. An attempt was made to present a more favorable picture of Martha to her parents.

Although Martha, like Billy, has worked very hard, her impulsiveness stands in her way. Another problem has been her reluctance to translate her desire to improve into solid work on areas of special weakness, such as the writing of essays. She prefers to work at tasks that are easier for her. There has been very little support from the school. Martha was frequently given no homework at all, or else assignments that were inappropriately hard. The parents have been enthusiastic about Martha's progress, which has been modest. She has been coming for three years and scores presently at about the 40th percentile in arithmetic and reading. Spelling score now lags only a year behind grade expectation.

As we have gotten to know Martha, it has become clear that her failure has its place in family dynamics. The parents continue to stress her brother's accomplishments. However, it has since been learned that he repeated the first grade and was for years an indifferent reader. Moreover, some of his misbehavior away from home extends beyond childish pranks and, far from being a responsible worker, he avoids as many duties as he can. The brunt of household responsibility (among the children) falls on Martha, who is expected to cook and to care for her younger siblings when her parents go out, which is frequently. She is not paid for these chores, but does not complain. On the contrary, she goes out of her way to please her parents and when birthdays are celebrated she makes extensive arrangements for the party and bakes the cake. She gives her father expensive presents with money earned from babysitting.

Martha is a compulsive eater and she has grown obese. There have been several episodes of stealing. Martha used the money to buy gifts in an attempt to win friends, but she has continued to be the butt of ridicule at school. She was sent home recently for fighting with a girl who had tried to exclude her from a committee.

Her well-meaning parents were concerned and eventually agreed to a psychiatric evaluation and, subsequently, to treatment. They sincerely want to help Martha, they have faithfully supported the remedial program, and they love her, but they may not realize the extent to which family dynamics have contributed to her lagging self-esteem.

It should also be noted that Martha's problem was identified late. Had she received the attention she needed at the time she began to fail, she would doubtless be farther along the way to compensating for and overcoming her difficulties. (Martha's younger sister is progressing rapidly.) The case also illustrates the negative effects of indifferent schooling. Had Martha received the individual assistance afforded Billy, she might have progressed more rapidly. Parental demands for home service have been excessive in relation to the emotional nourishment Martha received (and her needs have probably been strong from the beginning). Her feeling that she has been deprived has made it hard for her to curb her impulsiveness.

The brief case illustrations have indicated the symptomatology sketchily. In both instances there was a positive family history of reading and spelling disorder, but this was much more striking in Martha's case than in Billy's. Both children evidenced language deficits, but they were more pronounced in the boy than in the girl. Even so, the referring adults had been aware only of Billy's articulatory problems. No one had identified his striking delays in other aspects of language functioning; Martha was actually described as a highly verbal child. Both had considerable grapho-motor difficulties, but Martha's problem with management of spatial arrangements was the more severe. Both youngsters had difficulty learning arithmetic facts. Billy was unable to learn a foreign language; Martha's performance in this area remains untested.

Both children showed signs of emotional difficulty. Billy was unusually passive and Martha was infantile and impulsive. Neither child could be considered to present a clearly defined "type" of specific learning disability, though spatial problems were somewhat more pronounced in Martha and verbal difficulties more inpressive in Billy. A variety of additional considerations determined the sort of treatment each received and the kind of progress each made. Both children are very representative of the kind of case that is referred for treatment.

It is apparent that Billy's early referral resulted in early progress and paved the way for a smooth entry into first grade. While not a top student, Billy never really experienced the impact of failure. Because he was passive and conforming, his academic problems might have been overlooked had the school not been advised about them from the outset. He might have slipped out of reach before anyone noticed that he was in trouble. Had he been picked up only in the third grade, there would have been no time for the kind of language stimulation experiences he had, in fact, been receiving for four years. Reading comprehension would surely have been a formidable obstacle at that point.

Martha, who came for help only after four years of failure, has made less progress. Her behavioral difficulties have interfered with progress and her social adjustment has been unsatisfactory. She might have advanced more in both respects had she been referred sooner. Martha was also less fortunate in the classroom teaching she received. In addition, her case illustrates the part one child's learning problems can play in family interaction. The parents eventually came to see Martha as a failure, not only in response to her academic situation, but to support the myth that her brother (unlike his father before him) is a "super boy." The burden has been heavy for both children. The educational therapist was neither willing nor equipped to cope with Martha's psychological problems; even if she were, it is felt that it would be a mistake for one therapist to undertake two kinds of treatment requiring quite different kinds of training. Moreover, in a combined treatment, the focus may become unclear. Time spent on emotional problems would have made inroads on time directed to essential remediation.

Finally, it is clear that both children progressed, in spite of differences in the age when remediation was initiated. Both are managing in a regular classroom and are expected to continue to improve, in spite of the fact that there continues to be ample evidence of accompanying deficits. Examples could be given of children who have made less progress and others who have made spectacular gains. The cases selected are more typical, however, in terms of symptomatology, course of treatment, and outcome.

CONCLUSION

No attempt has been made to discuss the various approaches to remediation for children with specific learning disabilities. These vary widely and can be roughly categorized by the size of the verbal unit that receives most attention: the phoneme, or sound; the word; the sentence; and longer units. Actually, each aspect must be attended to, the difference being the point of entry and the amount of time allotted to each unit.

There are several characteristics of effective therapy.

1. The approach is structured and well organized.
2. The child is always presented with relevant material in amounts that he can handle successfully.
3. He is provided with ample opportunity for practice and overlearning, so that his gains are firmly established.
4. The thrust of work at each session is to facilitate mastery of the performance as a whole. As he learns a part process, such as techniques for sounding out words, he is taught how to use them to facilitate reading in context. He learns to spell words so as to be able to communicate by writing. He learns to borrow, when subtracting, so that he can make change when he shops.
5. The therapist forms a therapeutic alliance with the child, who is seen not as the object of the teaching process, but as a participant.

The foregoing pages have attempted to describe the child with a learning disability. Although difficulties are subtle and not easy to discern upon superficial contact, they may be extensive and potentially disabling unless treament is initiated promptly. The prognosis for most children is excellent if they are provided with the help they need for as long as is necessary. While referral for neurological and psychiatric evaluation provides useful information, the most effective treatment, as of this writing, has been pedagogic. It is extremely important to work with parents and school, because their supportive involvement is crucial for a successful outcome.

There is no question but that the long treatment course is costly in time and money. However, the price of failure in both human and financial terms is much higher.

REFERENCES

1. Belmont, L. and Birch, H.: Lateral dominance, lateral awareness and reading disability. *Child Develop.*, 36: 56-71, 1965.
2. Bender, L.: Problems in conceptualization and communication in children with developmental alexia. In P. Hoch and J. Zubin (Eds.), *Psychopathology of Communication.* New York: Grune and Stratton, 1958.
3. Benton, A.: Developmental dyslexia: Neurological aspects. In W. Friedlander (Ed.), *Advances in Neurology*, 7 :1-47, 1975.
4. Berko, J.: The child's learning of English morphology. *Word*, 14: 150-177, 1958.
5. Birch, H.: Health and the education of socially disadvantaged children. *Develop. Med. and Child Neurol.*, 10: 580-599, 1968.
6. Cazden, C.: *Child Language and Education.* New York: Holt, Rinehart, and Winston, 1972.
7. Chall, J.: *Learning to Read: The Great Debate.* New York: McGraw-Hill, 1967.
8. Critchley, M.: *Developmental Dyslexia.* London: William Heinemann Medical Books, 1966.
9. De Hirsch, K.: Early language development. In S. Arieti (Ed.), *American Handbook of Psychiatry* (2nd Ed.), Vol. 1, New York: Basic Books, 1974.
10. De Hirsch, K.: Early language development and minimal brain dysfunction. *Ann. of N.Y. Acad. Sci.*, 205: 158-163, 1973.
11. De Hirsch, K.: Language deficits in children with developmental lags. In R. Eissler, A. Freud, M. Kris, and A. Solnit (Eds.), *The Psychoanalytic Study of the Child*, 30: 95-126. New Haven: Yale Universities Press, 1975.
12. De Hirsch, K.: Specific dyslexia or strephosymbolia. *Folia Phoniat.*, 4: 231-248, 1952.
13. De Hirsch, K.: Studies in tachyphemia: Diagnosis of developmental language disorders. *Logos*, 4: 3-9, 1961.
14. De Hirsch, K., Jansky, J., and Langford, W.: *Predicting Reading Failure.* New York: Harper and Row, 1966.
15. De Hirsch, K., and Langford, W.: Clinical note on stuttering and cluttering in young children. *Pediatrics*, June: 934-940, 1950.
16. Denckla, M.: Learning disability, Lecture presented to educators. Babies Hospital, Columbia-Presbyterian Medical Center, Spring 1973.
17. Denckla, M.: Performance on color tasks in kindergarten children. *Cortex*, 8: 164-176, 1972.
18. Finucci, J., Guthrie, J., Childs, A., Abbey, H., and Childs, B.: The genetics of specific reading disability. *Ann. of Human Gen.*, 40: 1-23, 1976.

19. Freud, A.: *Normality and Pathology in Childhood.* New York: International Universities Press, 1965.
20. Gibson, E., Gibson, J., Pick, A., and Osser, H.: A developmental study of discrimination of letter-like forms. *J. of Compar. and Physiol. Psychol.,* 55: 897-906, 1962.
21. Goodnenough, F.: *Measurement of Intelligence by Drawings,* Yonkers-on-Hudson: World Book, 1926.
22. Hallgren, B.: Specific dyslexia (congenital word blindness). *Act. Psychiat. et Neurol.,* Suppl. 65, 1950.
23. Hess, R.: Early education as socialization. In R. Hess and R. Bear (Eds.), *Early Education: Current Theory, Research and Action.* Chicago: Aldine, 1966.
24. Ingram, T., Mason, A., and Blackburn, K.: A retrospective study of 82 children with reading disability. *Develop. Med. Child Neurol.,* 12: 271-281, 1970.
25. Jansky, J.: The contribution of certain kindergarten abilities to second grade reading and spelling achievement. Unpublished Ph.D. thesis, Columbia University, 1970.
26. Jansky, J.: The marginally ready child. *Bull. Orton Soc.,* 25: 69-85, 1975.
27. Jansky, J., and de Hirsch, K.: *Preventing Reading Failure.* New York: Harper and Row, 1972.
28. Kawi, A., and Pasamanick, B.: Association of factors of pregnancy and reading disorders of childhood. *J.A.M.A.,* 166: 1420-1423, 1958.
29. Kenny, T., Clemmens, R., Cicci, R., Lentz, G., Nair, P., and Hudson, B.: The medical evaluation of children with reading problems. *Pediat.,* 49: 438-442, 1972.
30. Lieberman, I., and Shankweiler, D.: Speech, the alphabet, and teaching to read. Paper presented at the NIE conference on the theory and practise of beginning reading instruction, Learning Research and Development Center, University of Pittsburgh, May 1976.
31. Maliphant, R., Supramaniam, S., and Saraga, E.: Acquiring skill in reading: A review of experimental research. *J. Child Psychol. Psychiat.,* 15: 175-185, 1974.
32. Mattis, S., French, J., and Rapin, I.: Dyslexia in children and young adults: Three independent neuropsychological syndromes. *Develop. Med. Child Neurol.,* 17: 150-163, 1975.
33. Money, J.: *Reading Disability: Progress and Research Needs in Dyslexia.* Baltimore: Johns Hopkins Press, 1962.
34. Naidoo, S.: *Specific Dyslexia.* London: Pitman, 1972.
35. Norrie, E.: Ordblindheden. In L. Thompson (Ed.), *Reading Disability.* Springfield: Thomas, 1959.
36. Orton, S.: *Reading, Writing, and Speech Problems in Children.* New York: W.W. Norton, 1937.
37. Owen, F., Adams, P., Forrest, T., Stolz, L., and Fisher, S.: Learning disorders in children: Sibling studies. *Mon. of the Soc. for Res. in Child Develop.,* 36 (4, serial No. 144), 1971.
38. Rockefeller, N.: Don't accept anyone's verdict that you are lazy, stupid or retarded. *TV Guide,* October 16, 1976.
39. Rourke, B.: Minimal brain dysfunction: Is diagnosis necessary? *J. of Learn. Disabil.,* 1976.
40. Rutter, M.: The concept of "dyslexia." In P. Wolff and R. MacKeith (Eds.), *Planning for Better Learning, Clinics in Develop. Med.* No. 33, London: SIMP/Heinemann, 1969.
41. Rutter, M., Tizard, J., and Whitmore, K. (Eds.): *Education, Health and Behaviour.* London: Longman, 1970.
42. Rutter, M., and Yule, W.: The concept of specific reading retardation. *J. Child Psychol. Psychiat.,* 16: 181-197, 1975.
43. Silver, A. and Hagin, R.: Specific reading disability: Delineation of the syndrome and relationship to cerebral dominance. *Comprehensive Psychiat.,* 1: 126-134, 1960.
44. Slade, P. and Russell, G.: Developmental dyscalculia: A brief report on four cases. *Psychol. Med.,* 1: 292-298, 1971.

45. Templin, M.: The study of articulation and language development during the early school years. In F. Smith and G. Miller (Eds.), *The Genesis of Language*, Cambridge: M.I.T. Press, 1966.
46. Thomas, C.: Congenital "Word-blindness" and its treatment. *Ophthalmoscope*, 3: 380-385, 1905.
47. Vellutino, F.: Alternative conceptualizations of dyslexia: Evidence in support of a verbal-deficit hypothesis. *Harvard Educ. Rev.*, 47: 334-354, 1977.
48. Yule, W.: Predicting reading ages on Neale's analysis of reading ability. *Brit. J. Educ. Psychol.*, 37: 252-255, 1967.

11

Chronic Illness in Children

ALAN M. LEVY, M.D. and YEHUDA NIR, M.D.

INTRODUCTION

A long-term illness or disability in childhood, regardless of the diagnosis, poses serious problems to the child, the family, his physician and the general health services of the community. The impact of any long-term illness on a child is often more severe than on an adult since it is more likely to lead to distortions in physical, social, educational and emotional development. In addition to the problems which are specifically related to health care, there are a host of social, psychological, educational and economic problems which are associated with long-term conditions and which strain the resources of the community.

Dorland's Medical Dictionary defines chronic illness simply as one which persists over a long period of time (12). Webster's New International Dictionary defines a chronic disease as one of long duration or one characterized by slowly progressing symptoms (60). Mattsson's definition appears to be the most comprehensive and functional; he states, "long-term or chronic illness refers to a disorder with a protracted course which can be progressive and fatal, or associated with a relatively normal life span despite impaired physical and mental functioning. Such diseases frequently show periods of acute exacerbations requiring intensive medical care" (31, p. 801).

Modern advances in medicine have greatly changed the balance between acute and chronic illness. There has been a marked decline in the frequency and seriousness of infectious diseases as well as nutritional disorders (40). There is a presumed increase in the survival of many children with chronic conditions (24). Due to these relatively recent developments, children with life-endangering conditions like diabetes,

337

hemophilia, cardiac malformations, renal failure, asthma and many other serious ailments, remain alive having to face, however, an existence that is fraught with severe physiological and psychological complications which strain the child's and family's adaptational skills. An extreme example of this is the child raised in reverse isolation in a sterile environment so that he may stay alive. These new situations impose on mental health practitioners, social workers, educators, rehabilitation personnel and parents a need to develop both the theoretical framework and the practical tools to deal with this situation.

There seems to be some confusion about chronic childhood illnesses stemming in part from the plethora of terms used to describe these illnesses—labels which often reflect poorly defined terminology. The terms most commonly used are: hereditary, genetic, congenital, defective, handicapped, chronic illness, and long-term disorder. These are used interchangeably, despite their nonequivalence. Although not necessarily contradictory, these terms, in fact, focus on different aspects of a disease such as etiology, time of appearance, duration, disability, location and extent, and treatability.

For example, oral clefts can be described as congenital (time of appearance), hereditary (familial trait), genetic chromosomal (impairment), defective (structural impairment), handicapping (functional impairment), and long-term (duration). The description chronic, however, is not applicable. Another example, asthma, can be described as handicapping, long-term or chronic. The terms hereditary, genetic, congenital, and defective do not apply to the majority of cases.

To appreciate the enormity of the problem posed by chronic illness in childhood, one has only to look at the epidemiological studies which describe incidence, prevalence, mortality and hospital use. Sultz et al. have provided extensive epidemiological data on chronic illness in Erie County, New York, based on the years 1946-1961 (53). One out of every 76 children under age 16 had been diagnosed as having one long-term disease. Viewed another way, there was one newly diagnosed case of chronic illness in every 56 live births (53).

A National Health Survey for the year 1966-1967 reports that 23% of children under 17 years of age had one or more chronic conditions (21). In a Selective Service study (57) of 18-year-olds conducted in 1965, 15% were rejected because of chronic handicapping conditions. Between 20 and 40% of children in low income families suffer from chronic conditions according to a HEW report, August 1974, which was prepared in conjunction with the Medicaid Early Diagnosis and Periodic Screening Program (50).

In a study of Monroe County, New York, covering the years 1967-1971 (22), the overall rate of chronic illness was 137 per 1,000. These results are similar to those of a study by Pless (38), who suggests that the total cumulative prevalence of chronic illness in children under 18 years of age is between 10 and 20%. These figures apply only to children with physical disorders.

In a study of a 10-county region in Upstate New York, data gathered from 82 physicians indicated that an average of 7.4% of all children seen annually have one or more chronic conditions (39).

Below is a list of the more common chronic conditions of childhood.

Division of illnesses according to systems involved:

Nervous system and sense organs: Seizure disorders, spina bifida, cerebral palsy, deafness, blindness.

Respiratory system: Asthma

Cardiovascular system: Congenital deformations, rheumatic heart disease

Gastrointestinal system: Malabsorption syndromes, gastric and duodenal ulcers, ulcerative colitis, granulomatous colitis, megacolon, colostomy.

Genitourinary system: Nephritis, hypospadias, chronic urinary tract infection, genital ambiguity, kidney transplants.

Hematological system: Hemophilia, leukemias, hemoglobinopathies.

Immunological system: Allergies.

Collagen disease: rheumatoid arthritis, lupus erythematosus.

Endocrine system: Diabetes, thyroid disorders, obesity, adrenogenital syndrome.

Dermatological system: Albinism, neurodermatitis, psoriasis, eczema.

Skeletal-muscular system: Scoliosis.

Genetic disorders: Trisomies, cleft lip, cleft palate, Tay-Sachs disease.

Other conditions: Amputation, scarring due to burns, plastic reconstruction, cystic fibrosis, cancer, sequelae of accidents.

THE MIND AND THE BODY

The unitary concept that man is a total dynamic biopsychosocial entity relfects current thinking about illness. Earlier notions that considered the body and mind as totally separate entities have faded (57). In fact, Hippocrates said, "It is more important to know what sort of person has a disease than to know what sort of disease a person has."

In the 1940s and '50s, Alexander and Grinker (20) stressed the psychosomatic view which calls attention to the emotional components of physical diseases. This view seemed to imply that certain illnesses originate in the psyche and find expression in the soma. Grinker stated in 1953 that "psychosomatic connotes more than a kind of illness, it is a comprehensive approach to the totality of an integrated process of transactions among many systems—somatic, psychic, social and cultural" (20, p. 188). Noyes and Kolb described psychosomatic illness as: 1) physical symptoms without bodily disease; 2) physical disease whose cause was originally emotional; 3) organic disease is present but certain symptoms do not arise from it but from the emotions (35).

In 1956, Selye introduced his concept of the General Adaptation Syndrome based on his theory of stress (47). Since that time, stress has often been mentioned as a factor in psychosomatic conditions. The stress response is, by definition, not specific since it could be produced by virtually any agent. This implies that stress can originate from the psyche or from the soma. Indeed, Selye felt that while a great deal of attention has been given to bodily changes brought about by mental attitudes, almost no systematic research has been done on the opposite of this—the effects of bodily changes on mentality.

Paralleling the above concerns about the mind-body relationship has been the growth of psychological and psychoanalytic notions concerning body image, body ego and body identity. Schilder spoke of the psychological basis of the body image and the libidinous structure of the body image (46). He felt that the image of the human body referred to the picture of our own body which is formed in our mind—that is to say, the way in which the body appears to ourselves.

Hinsie's Psychiatric Dictionary defines both body image and body identity as "the conceptualization of the body's structure and functions that grows out of awareness of the self and one's body in intended action" (23, p. 379). The body ego is defined as consisting of "the psychic representations of one's body and self—memories and ideas connected with the body along with their cathexes" (23, p. 250).

We conceptualize a chronic disease as a stress, in Selye's terms, which affects the unitary mind-body equilibrium in a profound fashion. Physical disturbance (be it local or systemic, biochemical or traumatic, confined to an organ or to an entire organ system, etc.) will create an imbalance in the body's homeostasis and upset not only its equilibrium at that time, but also interfere with its maturational and growth processes. These disruptions will then have an effect on simultaneously evolving intrapsychic and psychosocial processes. Once interfered with, these systems will in turn influence the original disturbances, creating a feedback mechanism that often augments the original conflict. This may set up a vicious cycle which continues its back and forth effect. Finally, however, an equilibrium is attained, if only temporarily, often at a level which reflects a handicap or curtailment in physical and/or emotional functioning.

DEVELOPMENTAL CONSIDERATIONS

It is difficult to set forth a single and consistent formulation regarding the relationship of chronic illness and the psychobiological developmental process. One can definitely say, however, that chronic illness, regardless of the age of the child at the time of onset or the specific features of the disease itself, will affect the child's and family's developmental process in certain nonspecific ways simply by virtue of the fact that it exists in the child's life. Some of these effects include: the stigma of being chronically ill, accompanying physical limitations, increased dependency, potentially shorter life span, and the need to psychologically integrate an altered body image. Chronic illness is stressful for both the child and his or her family, creating a variety of psychological problems.

From a developmental point of view, the age of onset is an important factor in determining the impact of illness on the child. An illness, such as cleft palate, occurring as it does during the oral stage, will affect that developmental stage. It will also color subsequent developmental stages, attainment of which depends to a great extent on a successful negotiation of the preceding phase. The illness acts as a stress and its timing produces specific pathological responses according to the developmental periods it affects. Such a concept of chronic illness has led to descriptions of diseases relating to personality types, such as a cleft palate personality.

One may state that the very nature of the illness itself is of primary importance or at least as important as the age of onset. McDermott (32) reports that children with congenital handicaps such as blindness or crippling seem better able to accept their condition than diabetic, hemophiliac, or cardiac children who rebel against their illness. These latter children must live by rules they do not understand as they only vaguely sense their chronic illness and internal metabolic processes. The blind or crippled child, however, is aware and in touch with his handicap and deals with it actively on his own terms. Thus, the nature of the handicap will have a profound effect on personality development.

In sum then, the conceptualization of the relationship of chronic illness to psychopathological developmental processes is multifaceted. Time of onset, specific characteristics of the illness, as well as the general nature and the existence of an illness, all play a role. For each child and family, an individual formulation must be developed and considered.

To assist in this formulation, we can be guided by the work of Erikson (15), Solnit and Senn (48), and Anna Freud (18). Each has conceptualized a systematic way of following the developmental process and its related normal and abnormal personality development. Erikson (15) talks in terms of psychosocial phases of development and has labeled each with terminology that describes the central socialization process of the particular stage. For example, the oral period is called the oral sensory period and is equated with the development of trust versus mistrust. The anal period is labeled as the anal muscular period and is characterized by issues of autonomy versus shame and doubt. In total, Erikson conceptualizes eight stages in the psychosocial development of man (15).

Solnit and Senn (48) have provided a chronological outline of development (birth to six months, six months to 18 months, 18 months to five years, five years to 12 years, and 12 years to 18 years). For each of these age periods they list tasks in process for both the child and mother as well as the subsequent pathologies that can ensue if these mutual tasks are not well negotiated. They focus on the interaction between parent and child as the child progresses through various psychosexual phases. Anna Freud (18), on the other hand, has proposed the notion of developmental lines and follows each activity of the child in longitudinal fashion as it progresses from birth through successive psychosexual stages until it reaches its completion or maturation. The chronic illness, then, be it viewed from the perspective of general illness, age of onset, its specific characteristics, or all three together, can be evaluated based on these formulations.

According to the above three viewpoints, a chronic illness in the first six months of life (such as cleft palate) may be seen as having an impact on the development of trust (Erikson), the physiological adjustment to extra-uterine life (Solnit), and finally on the developmental line of rational eating (A. Freud).

By using the aforementioned perspectives, one could generalize that the earlier an illness appears, the greater the risk for emotional, social and educational problems, or the later a chronic illness appears (i.e. kidney disease), the fewer the opportunities for pervasive developmental problems and the greater the likelihood of more discrete psychological impact. For chronic illnesses of intermittent nature, such as asthma, that skip about developmental periods, there could be a patchwork interference on the phase-specific developmental processes.

It must be noted, however, that the existence of chronic illness in a certain developmental phase does not necessarily mean that it will seriously color each and every developmental task in progress. The extent of the effects of the illness will be mediated by such factors as its severity, family response to the illness, requirements for hospitalization, surgery, painful procedures and side effects from medication.

REVIEW OF LITERATURE

Until the late 1950s the pediatric and psychiatric literature devoted little attention to the emotional problems of the chronically ill child. The pioneering work of D. Levy (28), R. Spitz (51), and A. Freud (17), in the 40s and 50s dealt primarily with the child's reaction to acute illness, hospitalization, and separation. The issue of chronic illness as an intrinsic component of the child's developmental process was only alluded to but not explored in depth. In dealing with the problems facing the chronically ill child, one should examine three separate aspects of this experience—namely: 1) the physical symptoms, pain and malaise caused by the disease, 2) the hospital experience during the acute phase of the illness, the often painful diagnostic and treatment procedures which may include surgery followed by long periods of immobilization (these experiences might be repeated many times during acute exacerbations of the chronic illness), and 3) the quality of life for the child with chronic illness (4, 31).

The reaction to physical symptoms and pain may be significantly influenced by the child's and the family's knowledge and understanding of the nature and etiology of the condition and the degree to which they misinterpret or distort the facts. The child's response to pain may depend on "the manner in which the child invests bodily events with libidinal and aggressive cathexis" (17, p. 75). The psychological significance of the pain to the child will affect his reaction which can vary from total mastery of the experience to masochistic submission.

Hospitalization, diagnostic procedures, and surgery have been given a great deal of attention as the central traumatic experienes of both the acutely and the chronically ill child (17, 27, 36). Specific factors that have been considered pathogenic during hospitalization include: the change of emotional climate during illness, particularly through the shift of the mother's attitude, the experience of being nursed and its resultant pull toward passivity, as well as regression stimulated by dependence. D. Levy (28) stressed the importance of the child's age on admission while the issue of separation was dealt with by Bowlby (5). Another factor that has to be taken into consideration is the child's premorbid personality (52). Specific negative reactions such as depression and apathy, negativism, fears, night terrors, onset of neurotic symptomatology, and learning difficulties have been ascribed to hospitalization (28, 36, 52). Rothenberg gives his observations of negative reactions to hospitalization, the acronym FAGS—fear, anger, guilt and sadness (44).

In the examination of the psychological effects of various clinical conditions, it becomes evident that chronic ailments fall into categories which have one or several common denominators. Depending on the frame of reference, one can view chronic illness as:

Dangerous, life-threatening   *or*   Benign
    (asthma, renal insufficiency)   (scoliosis, cleft palate)

Congenital (cleft palate, cardiac   *or*   Acquired
    malformation)   (TB, rheumatic fever)

Symptoms at birth (hemophilia, .   *or*   Symptoms later in life
    cleft palate, hypospadias)   (diabetes, asthma, rheumatic
                                               fever, seizure disorders).

Conditions with visible   *or*   Conditions without perceptual
    dysfunction (scoliosis, cleft   localization (diabetes, renal
    palate, hypospadias)   insufficiency, seizure disorders)

The psychological reactions of children suffering from illness will depend heavily upon which one or more of the above mentioned categories fits the condition.

Recent psychiatric literature on the chronically ill child addresses itself both to general themes in chronic illness and to specific disease entities. One general theme which is often discussed is the emotional adjustment of chronically ill children. D. M. Bullard (6) states that the occurrence of emotional or personality difficulties contrasts with the superior adjustment that the body makes to physical handicap. These emotional difficulties seem to characterize the majority of chronically ill children. Other experiences shared by these children include: a sense of loss, a sense of being different, physical limitations, suffering, and mourning the loss of health.

In those papers dealing with the various handicaps as separate entities, one encounters frequent unanimity in the description of psychological syndromes as they relate to particular ailments. Children have been described in their psychological profiles as cardiacs, hemophiliacs, orthopedics, suggesting a predictable relationship between the type of physical ailment and the child's psychological reaction. The age of onset and the child's environment seem responsible for the observable variations from case to case. This is an important finding which also sheds light on the concept of symptom formation in general. In contrast to the traditional psychosomatic model, we are dealing with a much simpler somato-psychic reaction in which the stimulus being physiological or physical is easier to assess; its impact is often specific.

Children with oral and facial clefts provide a good example of the one-to-one, almost predictable relation between the physical handicap and the psychological reactions to it. These children are universally seen as good and compliant. Damage to the oral cavity creates excessive dependence on the mother and her ministrations, while at the same time the mother who blames herself for the damaged child does not permit any expression of anger. Such dynamics contribute to the development of complacency.

Fear of widespread brain damage and fear of sudden, unpredictable loss of control are seen as central issues for children with chronic seizure disorders. This condition, like diabetes and renal insufficiency, among others, is also characterized by an inability to localize perceptually the nature and extent of the illness, often producing serious distortions on the part of children about their diseases. This is in contrast to handicaps such as oral clefts, spina bifida or scoliosis where the damage can be visualized and understood with greater clarity (13).

The central themes of existence for children with nephropathies, on dialysis and with kidney transplants are: 1) the life-threatening aspects of the condition, and 2) the physical assault experienced by the child as a result of the frequent surgical and medical interventions. Side effects of corticosteroids and stunted growth are other important elements that confront the child with renal ailments.

Children with congenital heart disease are generally not seen as having a unique personality structure. However, a study of 28 randomly selected children with congenital heart disease revealed serious emotional disturbance in all the patients, similar in severity to a group of children in a psychiatric clinic (2).

Children with cystic fibrosis are a new entity in the chronically ill group since until the relatively recent past they did not survive their second year of life (8). Their lives seem to center around extensive treatment regimens which involve specific diets, antibiotics, daily postural drainage, etc. Their dependency on continuous parenting is therefore excessive and a pervasive factor in their psychological and emotional development. The cystic fibrosis children's reaction to illness lacks specificity except for excessive concern with flatulence and the smell of their feces. Otherwise, they have the same concerns as other chronically ill children: anxiety about body intactness, feelings of inadequacy, and the perception that their illness is a punishment (17, 19, 43).

Problems related to cryptorchidism have been described as unique due to the fact that the impairment is in the genital area. Castration anxiety, disappointment in the masculinity of the son, and secretiveness surrounding the condition are seen as major components in the development of psychological complications (10).

The fluctuating course of the illness seems to be an important factor in the psychological adaptation of the hemophiliac. Totally asymptomatic periods are followed by debilitating crises. This necessitates rapid shifts in adaptive and coping mechanisms. Other, non-specific features of hemophilia involve pain due to bleedings, immobilization, separation from family during hospitalization. As in asthma, seizure disorders, and other chronic illnesses with acute exacerbations, the danger of renewed bleedings looms continuously over the hemophiliac and his family, fostering persistently high levels of anxiety. In contrast to asthma and seizure disorders, the bleedings are inevitable while asthmatic attacks and seizures are unpredictable and unavoidable.

The psychological reactions of chronically ill children specifically affect aspects of their development and their parents' attitude toward them. Walker-Smith, Porteous and Gardiner (59) report on the effect of coeliac disease on the mother-child relationship. They found that there was a high incidence of emotional symptoms in these children and significant disturbances in the mother-child relationship, with maternal anxiety, depression and preoccupation often occurring. These symptoms in the mother and child either disappeared or greatly improved once the child had responded to a gluten-free diet, except when the mother was already emotionally disturbed before the onset of the child's illness.

In dealing with preschool children, Bentovim (3) pointed out that while we pay attention to the known responses of the infant to the warmth, empathy, efficiency and control shown by the mother, we must also pay attention to the quality of the response from the child. The child's activity, passivity, positive and negative moods, ease of stimulation, regularity or irregularity, all will affect mother's response.

There has been a great deal of discussion as to whether emotional problems exist prior to the onset of the disease and perhaps contribute to its occurrence, or whether they develop after the illness and can be considered part of the outcome of the disease. In a study of these above concerns, Sultz et al. have reported that, in general, chronically ill children exhibited more behavioral deviancy than control children (53). Among the chronically ill children, those with conditions classified as "somatic" were usually more seriously ill with greater residual physical disability. If emotional disorder is simply a consequence of childhood illness, it might be expected that these more severely ill children would be the more seriously disturbed. Actually, they were far less disturbed, according to the measures of behavioral deviation, than children with the less severe conditions classified as "psychosomatic." This finding suggests that behavior deviation indicative of emotional disorder may precede the onset of "psychosomatic" conditions.

There is a growing body of evidence which associates emotional and behavioral deviation and the etiological development and episodic recurrence of the chronic conditions classified as "psychosomatic." Correlations have been found between the onset or recurrence of rheumatoid arthritis and stressful situations such as grief, poverty and worry. It has been observed that arthritic children are emotionally depressed and uncooperative, and that they exhibit feeding problems. Evidence from research on childhood peptic ulcers and bronchial asthma suggests that children with psychophysiological illnesses often have emotional problems such as overdependence, insecurity and unchanneled hostility which predate the onset of the actual illness. Psychological factors such as suppression of anger, feelings of inadequacy and emotional immaturity have been mentioned as being associated with eczema.

The Erie County study of behavioral deviancy in chronically ill children provides a means for comparing the frequency of behavioral disorders among three random samples constituting normal children, children hospitalized with "psychosomatic" conditions, and children hospitalized with "somatic" conditions based on an objective measurement scale. Children with "psychosomatic" conditions experienced significantly more behavioral problems than control children in the specific areas of eating behavior, bedtime behavior, speech difficulty and temper loss. The finding that chronically ill children with conditions classified as "psychosomatic" experienced more behavioral deviancy than children with "somatic" conditions and control children has important implications in the treatment of children with certain conditions (53, p. 127).

APPLICATION OF THE DEVELOPMENTAL MODEL

Three conditions will be discussed in some detail in order to explore the various aspects of developmental interference resulting from chronic illness.

Cleft Palate

Cleft palate or cleft lip is a congenital defect with reported incidence ranging from 1 in 600 to 1 in 1200 births (42,56). The cause of the defect is uncertain with both genetic and nongenetic (intra-uterine) influences having been implicated. In addition to the visible disfiguration, this condition creates a serious impairment in the infant's ability to suck, interferes with normal eruption of teeth, can delay and impair speech development, and due to secondary ear infections, might cause partial loss of hearing.

Psychological studies of children with oral or palate clefts describe them as suffering from excessive drive inhibition, lack of confidence, noncompetitiveness and underachievement. These children are universally, throughout psychiatric and medical literature, described as "good," easy to deal with and uncomplaining patients. The most salient psychological features of the cleft palate condition are: 1) the mother's perception that her own imperfections caused her to have a damaged child (56) and the resulting narcissistic hurt. This experience leads to denial of these unacceptable feelings and pressure on the child not to express his dissatisfaction. Any complaints by the child are seen as an accusation and might result in the loss of the angered mother's love. 2) The fact that this condition is congenital and located in the oral sphere becomes an organizing factor, a central modality in the infant-mother relationship. The expected oral gratification is frustrated by the defective oral apparatus and sucking and feeding are experienced as unpleasurable or even life-threatening due to frequent regurgitation. This situation leads to excessive dependence on mother, feelings of maternal deprivation with a resulting desire to please the mother in order to improve her care.

If one examines this condition from a developmental point of view, it is easy to detect serious interferences in the tasks the newborn baby is expected to negotiate during his first year of life. Using the Senn-Solnit model (48), it becomes clear that the first task, namely the physiological adjustment to extra-uterine life, is made difficult for the child with a cleft palate because of the inability to suck comfortably and efficiently. This difficulty is augmented by the first surgical intervention that usually takes place around the third month of the child's life and is followed by dropper feeding and physical restraint of the child's hands.

These children do not become thumb suckers and are not especially interested in food in later life. The mother cannot sustain herself and the baby pleasurably during the first stage of the child's life and therefore experiences anxiety, lack of fulfillment and often becomes depressed as she does not receive emotional gratification from the baby.

Cleft lip and/or cleft palate will have a strong impact on a child's psychosexual development as conceptualized by Anna Freud. It will particularly interfere with oral development "from suckling to rational eating," and as a result of this, will have a negative impact on other psychosexual developmental sequences.

The inability of the mother to effectively care for the infant due to the congenital defect will, by necessity, also interfere with what Erikson considers to be the central issue of the first psychological stage of development, namely, basic trust versus basic mistrust. The experience of sucking as well as biting will be disrupted. Tensions, frustrations, and impaired drive control are some of the potential complications that the cleft palate can cause in this stage. This experience might interfere, according to Erikson, with the "sense of identity . . . a sense of being alright" (15).

The early interference with crucial developmental tasks places children with clefts in a special category among chronically ill children. It also causes uniformity in their psychological profiles as described in psychiatric literature. Despite the fact that the treatment of this condition, which includes surgery and extensive orthodontic procedures, is usually successful and completed early in their lives, the psychological effects of this condition are deeply anchored and become inseparable components of the child's personality. The general drive inhibition interferes with academic achievement and probably with achievement in other areas (42). Psychotherapy is almost universally indicated. However, due to the complex interaction between the narcissistically hurt mother and her passive dependent child, therapeutic intervention is perceived as a threat to the dyad and therefore avoided.

Other congenital conditions like spina bifida, despite their appearance at birth, do not have the same impact on the development of the child because motor impairment and possible interference with sphincter controls only become central in the child's life towards the end of the first year of life. The psychosexual development during the oral stage is not likely to be interfered with significantly. Later, however, the anal stage, and the issues of autonomy versus shame and doubt will bear the full brunt of the child's physical malformation.

Seizure Disorders

Children with seizure disorders react differently to their long-term illness (58). The fear that there is damage to the child's brain, a deficiency that will influence the child's intellectual and emotional functioning seems to be a central concern for both parents and children. This seems to reflect lack of understanding and confusion regarding the function of the brain. This confusion has historical antecedents, as far back as the Biblical times when epileptics were seen as either insane or prophets. Conditions which the child cannot localize perceptually, for example, epilepsy or diabetes, are an additional psychological burden as they do not allow the patient to test reality as to the seriousness, extent, and nature of the illness (25). One often encounters a child whose intellectual knowledge coexists along with idiosyncratic, encapsulated, primitive thought processes about his/her illness.

Another important issue in seizure disorders is the anticipated and feared sudden loss of control. This has both personal and social meaning. The former relates to a general inability to control impulses while the latter causes embarrassment, experienced when attacks occur in public places. Daily dependence on medication is another characteristic of this disorder. This, in addition to age of onset, will be an important component in the development of personality characteristics of the child with a seizure disorder. In the very young child, parental concern about the illness and overprotectiveness might interfere with the separation-individuation process (30). This interference, because it is based on a realistic concern, is different from the one created by a symbiotic mother. It also lacks specificity as the same attitude might be expected from parents of children with other chronic ailments.

Seizure disorders appearing in latency might interfere with the developmental achievements of that period, namely, social adaptation, sublimation of drives, and a lessening of dependency on parental figures. It is our impression that the impact of this disorder is most significant and psychologically most damaging in adolescence. Some researchers claim that the most serious hazards of the epileptic disorder do not lie in the seizures per se but in the associated emotional complications, the result of poor handling of the illness by the patient and his immediate and more distant environment (29, 41).

Social problems, academic underachievement, and serious psychiatric disorders have been noted in up to 40% of these children. The seizure disorder as experienced by the adolescent patient interferes with several important developmental tasks of adolescence, namely, acceptance by the peer group, definite separation from parental figures and reaching out for heterosexual relationships. By perceiving himself as "different" from his peers, the epileptic adolescent is forced to isolate himself from other teenagers and remains, therefore, dependent on his parents. These adolescents feel that they do not fit with other children of their age group and avoid contact primarily because of fear of a seizure in public and the resulting embarrassment. The dependence on parental figures is intensified by the daily intake of medication which reinforces the feeling of being controlled. Having to swallow the pills as often as three times a day makes it difficult for the child to even attempt to deny his illness. A particularly painful problem for the epileptic adolescent is the fact that he cannot obtain a driver's license, thereby increasing his already strong dependence on his parents.

Viewing seizure disorders developmentally leads one to conclude that although the condition will leave its imprint on the psychological development of the child at any age at which it appears, it is primarily during adolescence that the full impact of the disorder will be felt. There will be serious interference with the developmental tasks which are central to adolescence and the achievement of adulthood.

In Erikson's psychosocial terms, a major interference will take place during the stage of development generally negotiated during adolescence, which deals with issues of intimacy vs. isolation. This is a stage when "body and ego must now be masters of the organ modes and of nuclear conflicts in order to face the fear of ego loss in situations which call for self-abandon . . . in the solidarity of close affiliations, in orgasms and sexual unions, in close friendships and in physical combat . . . the avoidance of such experiences . . . may lead to a deep sense of isolation (15, pp. 263). It seems safe to assume that the adolescent with a seizure disorder will be preoccupied with fears of loss of ego control, fears of self-abandon and of physical contact. It is not surprising, therefore, that although not examined from this point of view, social isolation, avoidance of peers and avoidance of sexual relationships have been described in every one of the studies that deal with children who have suffered from seizure disorders.

Renal Failure, Hemodialysis, Kidney Transplants

This set of conditions which usually follow each other chronologically (some children experience only the first two) seems to combine the worst features of all acute, chronic, and even potentially fatal ailments and handicaps. Like children with acute medical illness, they are exposed to repeated hospitalizations, separation from home, dietary restrictions, and painful medical and surgical interventions, in addition to suffering from the illness itself (14). The chronicity of their illness causes continuous incapacitation, school absenteeism, social isolation, pain and depression—while the continuous struggle for survival places them psychologically in the category of children with life-threatening diseases such as leukemia and other forms of cancer. E.O. Poznanski (37) gives this state of affairs a proper perspective when she asks, "Has technology exceeded the limits of psychological adaptation?" This seems to be a very serious question which is applicable also to other medical entities, i.e. to children who have lived in a bubble for purposes of reverse isolation, for years devoid of human contact.

Due to the overwhelming nature of these conditions and the therapeutic procedures, there seems to be an almost unending list of negative psychological experiences and reactions that these children have to deal with.

Renal failure, the initial part of this chronic illness, primarily has a physiological impact. It causes varying degrees of physical discomfort, loss of appetite, and nausea due to increased BUN, painful catheterizations of the penis in the male child, and the unpleasant experience of having to wear a urine bag for periods of time. It can lead to apathy and depression, both on physiological and psychological bases and result in academic failure mostly due to reduced school attendance. Young children who suffer from this condition have been described as slipping into regressive behavior easily. The final determination that the kidneys are not functioning precipitates three major events: 1) nephrectomy, 2) hemodialysis, and 3) kidney transplant from either a living donor or a cadaver (37).

Nephrectomy is the first major trauma in this chain of events. It means a loss of a body part and an abdication of reliance on one's own body, overwhelmingly underscored by the cessation of urination. The child is given hardly any time to cope with those feelings, to mourn the loss as the next step, hemodialysis, follows immediately. The central experience of this period is pain, immobility for long stretches of time, dietary restrictions, and anxiety due to the uncertainty of the outcome of this procedure. Some children perceive dialysis as torture and submit passively to this procedure. The pathetic and dehumanizing aspects of this experience can be seen in the fact that children ask to be put on dialysis because they are allowed to eat more while they are hooked up to the machine. Again, while they have to cope with all of this, they are confronted with the new, possibly psychologically insurmountable problem—the kidney transplant.

Initially, this idea is perceived in totally unrealistic terms. The transplant is equated with total recovery, becoming healthy again, without any problems—a rebirth fantasy. Despite explanations to the contrary, the children cling to this fantasy for a long while. It is usually followed by increasing doubts, the "if" period. "If I get a transplant . . . . " "If my transplant works . . . . " This stage might lead to depression with total suspension of any plans for the future. The transplant itself often becomes a Catch-22 situation. Coming from a live donor, it is fraught with seemingly unending and serious psychological reactions, while coming from a cadaver, it has life-threatening physiological complications, namely, increased chances for rejection.

The usual reaction following a transplant from whatever source is depression, most probably due to the breakdown of denial and confrontation with the shattered fantasy of a problem-free existence. Psychiatric literature addresses itself extensively to the problem of the donor-recipient relationship. If the kidney came from a parent, it often creates an alliance between the donor and the child to the exclusion of the spouse. Some parent-recipient pairs get involved in a quasi-symbiotic relationship, the child fearing retaliation from the parent for the loss of the kidney. This, in turn, might result in submissiveness or rebellion—depending on the premorbid relationship of the dyad. The reception of a kidney from a parent of the opposite sex might lead to confusion as to sexual identity. Mothers who have donated a kidney have described this experience as having a baby, a rebirth of the sick child, with the reverse, the physiological rejection of the kidney by the child, being perceived as a personal rejection.

Children, independently of age, have serious distortions about the procedure in general. Many fear that the kidney will tear loose during strenuous exercise and, as a result of this distortion, restrict their daily activities.

What has been described above is a true Pandora's Box of potentially insurmountable difficulties affecting every area of the child's functioning and interfering with the developmental process. The older the child when he or she becomes ill, the better he or she can cope with this difficult situation as he or she can resort to ego skills and defenses attained during the premorbid years. The family's ability to cope with the multiple problems is also a significant factor in the child's adjustment. Families of children with renal failure have been described as living in a continuous emotional turmoil to a point of exhaustion, isolated from each other (26).

As in the child with seizure disorders, adolescence is the period when there is the greatest interference with developmental tasks. The battle for intimacy vs. isolation is usually lost. Adolescents with renal problems have very marginal social relationships. They act younger than their chronological age, lack autonomy and have a negative self-image. School participation may be seriously impaired.

Due to the overwhelming nature of the illness, the children and their families find themselves in a state of almost continuous crisis and are therefore available for psychiatric intervention. It is by now almost a rule that every renal hemodialysis-transplant team incorporate a psychiatrist. Psychotherapy is primarily supportive with stress on independence and self-reliance.

EFFECTS OF CHRONIC ILLNESS ON THE FAMILY

"Chronic illness not only causes ill health, but it depletes energy, costs a tremendous number of dollars and causes many people to require long periods of supervision, observation and care; it burdens the people who have to give the care" (61).

The emotional stress and burden for parents and siblings of the chronically ill child are considerable and varied. For instance, parents may feel guilty that their child is ill—especially if the illness has a genetic origin. A parent or sibling may feel rejected since so much time has been focused on the ill child. This can lead to anger and resentment toward the patient (33). Some parents, particularly mothers, become overprotective of the patient. They are fearful, avoid discipline, become frustrated and bring up a frightened, overprotected child. An entire family may act in this way. Other parents, especially the father, may abdicate family responsibility. Any or all family members may minimize the importance and meaning of the patient's illness in an attempt to deny the problem. Resentment is usually present. Repressed wishes to reject the ill child can lead to depression which can make the rejection permanent. The child senses the rejection, feels isolated and ignored. In turn he gets angry and depressed and may exhibit rebellious behavior. This may precipitate further rejection and isolation. The emotional pressure on the family can lead to a broken marriage. Short of a failing marriage, one also notes that parents can become physically fatigued and find that their ability to socialize has been greatly diminished. However, it is interesting to note that whenever a family copes effectively with the adversity and crisis, both the marriage and family life are strengthened.

It has been noted that the presence of a chronically ill child in some families leads to the wish to have another child as a replacement. More often, however, the ill child is integrated into the family along with the healthy children.

Haggerty et al., in a study of parental attitudes and knowledge about their chronically ill children, found that only one parent in five thought that they understood their child's condition well (22). Quite obviously, this fact can, in turn, influence the child's response to his own illness and the level of parental concern. Parental ignorance of the nature of the illness may be a function of low intelligence or inadequate medical assistance. More likely, however, these findings reflect psychological phenomena such as denial and depression.

The child's chronic illness may affect the family in a very tangible way (57). Rising medical costs, more often than not, will create financial problems—especially for families in lower income categories. The increased demand for money creates worry, concern and anxiety that is felt in òne way or another by each family member. The wage earner in the family may seek a second job, a nonwage earner may decide to go to work. The need for money may compete with the need for time to attend to the special requirements of the ill child. All of this may mean that the parents work harder and longer only to become more exhausted and irritable with each other and the children. Increasing competition for time may also result in the parents' having less time with each other or any of the children. The siblings of the ill child will resent this family disruption caused by the chronically ill family member. Finances must be a critical consideration in the treatment plan. Low income families clearly need assistance with the cost of chronic illness—while middle income families appear likely to need this help as many chronic illnesses soon exhaust their savings.

The daily life of a family with the chronically ill child is often disrupted. Any or all of the following may occur. There may be medications to be given—often as many as four to six times a day. There may be appointments to be kept with physicians, speech therapists, remedial educators, laboratory technicians, physiotherapists, etc. Each appointment may require special transportation arrangements. There may be special therapies to administer at home, such as physiotherapy, inhalation therapy, or exercise. In case of arthritis or spina bifida, the patient may need help in feeding and dressing or even need to be physically lifted from place to place. Home laundering requirements can increase dramatically as well as the need for special household cleaning as in cases of allergy or asthma. There can be a requirement for considerable purchases of medication, special supplies and appliances. Often a special diet— as in diabetes or chronic kidney disease—will multiply the time allocated for food preparation. In cases of arthritis or cord injuries, there may be a need to structurally modify the home living circumstances to include ramps, special beds, chairs, etc. In cases of asthma or seizure disorder, the sleep of the patient as well as the family may be interrupted many times during the night either to administer routine medication or to attend to the patient's emergency medical situation.

EFFECT OF CHRONIC ILLNESS ON SCHOOL LIFE

Chronic illness often creates interference with schoolwork as measured by the low grade level performance, high absenteeism and pupil-teacher problems. Chronically ill children may require special school transportation, special class groupings, and even physical modification in the school buildings. Haggerty found that seven percent of chronically ill children require special education and three percent special tutoring (22). He pointed out that when chronically ill children were matched with children of equal I.Q.'s, the chronically ill children were consistently and significantly overrepresented in the underachiever group. Twenty-six percent of the children in this study were below grade level. In families where the parent had less than a high school education, there was a higher incidence of underachievement and teacher-pupil problems. In another study, 26% of the chronically ill children missed at least six weeks of school during the year (53). Children from middle-class families had the highest rate of extended absences. Children without siblings had the greatest amount of absenteeism, whereas those with three or four siblings had the least. Twenty-seven percent had missed some school as a result of their illness, with the likelihood of school absence related to the severity of the illness. Just as chronically ill children will have special emotional hazards to face, so do their teachers. The teachers may be overconcerned, pamper these children or even reduce their expectations of the child's performance. This attitude has a negative effect on the child and could lower his self-esteem and ability to cope. On the other hand, teachers may be unsympathetic, critical and lack understanding of the child's situation. They may act harshly and be unforgiving towards the child. In a sense, teachers face all of the potential reactions to the chronically ill child faced by the child's parents. Many teachers of chronically ill or handicapped children have suffered an illness or handicap and are drawn to this area of teaching. It is interesting to note that in planning education for handicapped children, the planners often leave out the concepts the children themselves have of their school and education. Thomas and Yamamoto (62) demonstrated that the children reacted more differentially to the people involved rather than to the curricula.

PSYCHOLOGICAL INTERVENTION AND TREATMENT

Intervention and treatment considerations for the chronically ill child differ from those of other children insofar as they are multifaceted in nature, continue over a longer period of time, often are more difficult to put into effect, and have a lower rate of success.

We agree with Davis (11) that psychological reactions, adaptive or maladaptive, invariably accompany long-term illness and physical disability in child and family—so much so that routine psychological evaluation is essential for a comprehensive rehabilitation program.

It is important for both the psychiatrist and the pediatrician to be in charge of the overall evaluation process since the medical and psychological problems are so intertwined. The evaluation process should include the psychological developmental assessment of the individual child and family dynamics. Additionally, a careful assessment must be made of how the special needs of this child and family can be matched to the school, recreational, transportation, social welfare and general medical care system, etc. A special checklist for planning psychological evaluation, education and treatment of a child with a chronic physical illness and disability has been suggested by Davis (11).

While educationally supportive or counseling approaches suffice for some chronically ill children, individual or group psychotherapy is, however, indicated for most. Concomitantly, some form of group or individual treatment for the parents is almost always necessary to help them deal effectively with such problems as grief, anxiety, fear, and depression (9). Such interventions have been successfully utilized with parents of children with hemophilia, congenital heart disease and spina bifida (1, 7, 16, 45).

Davis (11) notes the degree of successful psychological adaptation by a child to a physical disability is related more often, but not solely, to parental coping and attitudes than to the type or extent of the disability. It has also been found that crisis intervention approaches are useful when both parents are seen during the crisis stage of their child's illness.

Therapy will frequently be needed for the siblings of the chronically ill child. A recent study of children with spina bifida showed a surprising incidence of psychopathological conditions in their siblings (54).

Since the care and treatment of a chronically ill child usually involves individuals other than the child's pediatrician or psychiatrist, some form of psychological support as well as education must be provided for nurses, teachers, and speech therapists.

There are few facilities or individuals prepared to take on this long, burdensome and demanding task. However, we know that when the task is addressed with understanding and the setting of realistic goals, a great deal can be accomplished for the child and his family.

CONCLUSION

The ever-increasing number of chronically ill children will produce a ripple effect beyond the family to the community at large. Since the management of the chronically ill child requires the coordinated efforts of physicians, nurses,. teachers, social workers, and rehabilitation personnel, there will be a concomitant need not only to augment the education of these individuals but also to increase their numbers. The greater awareness of the special problems of the chronically ill child will necessitate an expansion of existing health facilities, hospital beds, special care units such as rehabilitation centers, and convalescent homes (49). In addition, community programs, day care centers and foster care will be necessary. Changes in insurance coverage and federally financed health programs will be required. Volunteer services will be necessary to bolster programs either under public or private auspices. The civil rights of the chronically ill children must be protected. Only recently are organizations for this group (i.e. handicapped) demanding minority rights and fighting discrimination (55).

Such groups are bringing to the public and medical profession awareness of the societal and environmental obstacles faced by the chronically ill or handicapped. For example, it has not been publicly known that until recently no more than four blind individuals are allowed on an airline flight at any one time. Another major problem is the lack of accessibility to public facilities (school concerts, etc.) since there is often no provision for a wheelchair to enter the facility. There exists a general need for public education regarding the nature and extent of chronic illness. As pointed out by Mendelsohn, "the physician who is responsible for identification, screening, diagnosis and management of children with chronic disease is practicing community medicine whether he knows it or not. He becomes involved in major issues which face American medicine and American society today. These issues include such problems as the delivery of inpatient and outpatient health services, community and political action, parent organization and participation, manpower development, public health aspects of screening techniques and medical-ethical consideration" (34, p. 641).

REFERENCES

1. Agle, D., and Mattsson, A.: Group therapy with parents of hemophiliacs. *Journal of the American Academy of Child Psychiatry*, Vol. 11, 1972.
2. Auer, E.T., Senturia, A.G., Shopper, M., and Biddy, R.: Congenital heart diseases and childhood adjustment. *Psychiatry in Medicine*, 2:23-30, 1971.
3. Bentovim, A.: Handicapped pre-school children and their families—Effects on child's early emotional development. *British Medical Journal*, Sept. 9, 1972.
4. Bergman, T., and Freud, A.: *Children in the Hospital.* New York: International Universities Press, Inc., 1965.
5. Bowlby, J.: Childhood mourning and its implications for psychiatry. *Amer. Journal of Psychiatry*, 118:481-498, 1961.

6. Bullard, D.M.: The response of the child to chronic physical disability. *Physical Therapy,* 48:592-601, 1968.
7. Burke, C.: Working with the parents of children with hemophilia. *Nursing Clinics of North America,* 7, 1, December 1972.
8. Burton, L.: Caring for children with cystic fibrosis. *Practitioner,* 210:247-254, 1973.
9. Cofer, D.H., and Nir, Y.: Theme-focused group therapy on a pediatric ward. *International Journal of Psychiatry in Medicine,* 6:541-550, 1975.
10. Cytryn, L., Cytryn, E., and Rieger, R.E.: Psychological implications of chryptorchism. *Journal of the American Academy of Child Psychiatry,* 6:131-165, 1967.
11. Davis, R.: Family of physically disabled children. *New York State Journal of Medicine,* June 1975.
12. *Dorland's Illustrated Medical Dictionary.* Philadelphia: W.B. Saunders Co., 25th ed. 1974.
13. Dorner, S.: Adolescents with spina bifida: How do they see their situation? *Archives, Disease in Childhood,* 51:439-444, 1975.
14. Drotar D.: The treatment of severe anxiety reaction in an adolescent boy following renal transplantation. *American Journal of Child Psychiatry,* 14:451-461, 1975.
15. Erikson, E.H.: Eight stages of man. In *Childhood and Society,* New York: Norton, pp. 247-274, 1963.
16. Field, B.: The child with spina bifida. *Medical Journal of Australia,* 2:1284-1287, 1972.
17. Freud, A.: The role of bodily illness in the mental life of children. *Psychoanalytic Study of the Child,* 7:69, 1952.
18. Freud, A.: The concept of developmental lines. In *The Writings of Anna Freud. Vol. 6,* New York: International Universities Press, Inc., 1965, pp. 62-69.
19. Gayton, W.F., and Freidman, S.B.: Psychosical aspects of cystic fibrosis. *American Journal of Diseases of Childhood,* 126:856-859, 1973.
20. Grinker, R.: *Psychosomatic Research.* New York: Norton, 1953.
21. Goldstein, H.: Demographic information in maternal and child health. In H. M. Wallace et al. *Maternal and Child Health Practices,* Springfield, Il.: Thomas, 1973.
22. Haggerty, R., Roghmann, K., and Pless, I.: *Child Health in the Community.* New York: John Wiley & Sons, 1975.
23. Hinsie: *Psychiatric Dictionary.* 4th Edition, Oxford University Press, 1970.
24. Illingworth, R.S.: The increasing challenge of handicapped children. *Clinical Pediatrics,* 3:189-190, 1964.
25. Kaufman, R.: Body-image changes in physically ill teenagers. *Journal of the American Academy of Child Psychiatry,* 11, 1, Jan. 1972.
26. Khan, A.U., Herndon, C.H., and Ahmadian, S.Y.: Social and emotional adaptations of children with transplanted kidney and chronic dialysis. *American Journal of Psychiatry,* 127:114-118, 1971.
27. Langford, W.S.: The child in the pediatric hospital. *American Journal of Orthopsychiatry,* 31:667, 1961.
28. Levy, D.: Psychic trauma of operations in children. *American Journal of Diseases of Children,* 69:7-25, 1945.
29. Livingston, S.: *The Diagnosis and Treatment of Convulsive Disorders in Children.* Springfield, Il.: Charles C Thomas, 1954.
30. Mahler, M.S.: *On Human Symbiosis and the Vicissitudes of Individuation.* New York: International Universities Press, 1968.
31. Mattsson, A.: Long-term physical illness in childhood: A challenge to psychosocial adaptation. *Pediatrics,* 50:801-811, 1972.
32. McDermott, J., and Akina, E.: Understanding and improving the personality development of children with physical handicaps. *Clinical Pediatrics,* 2, 3, Mar. 1972.
33. McLean, J., and Wolfish, M.: Chronic illness in adolescents. *Pediatric Clinics of North America,* 21, 3, Mar. 1972.
34. Mendelsohn, R.: Broadening the horizons of pediatric practice. *Clinical Pediatrics,* 9, 11, Nov. 1970.
35. Noyes, A., and Kolb, L.: *Modern Clinical Psychiatry. 5th ed.,* Philadelphia: W. B. Saunders

Co., 1958.
36. Oremland, E.K., and Oremland, J.D.: *The Effects of Hospitalization of Children.* Springfield, Il.: Charles C Thomas, 1973.
37. Poznanski, E.O., Miller, E., Salguero, C., and Kelsch, R.: The Quality of Life Following Kidney Transplantation in Children and Adolescents. Unpublished manuscript, 1976.
38. Pless, I.B.: Epidemiology of chronic disease. In Green & Haggerty (Eds.) *Ambulatory Pediatrics.* Philadelphia: W.B. Saunders, 1968, p. 760.
39. Pless, I.B., Satterwhite, B. and VanVechten, D.: Chronic illness in childhood: A regional survey of care. *Pediatrics,* 58, 1, July 1976.
40. Pless, I.B.: The changing face of primary pediatrics. *Pediatric Clinics of North America,* 21(1): 222-224, 1974.
41. Richardson, D.W., and Friedman, S.B.: Psychosocial problems of the adolescent patient with epilepsy. *Clinical Pediatrics,* 13:121-126, 1974.
42. Richman, L.C.: Behavior and achievement of cleft palate children. *Cleft Palate Journal,* 13:4-10, 1976.
43. Rodgers, B., Ferholt, J., and Cooper, C.: A screening tool to detect psychosocial adjustment of children with cystic fibrosis. *Nursing Research,* 23, 5, Sept.-Oct. 1974.
44. Rothenberg, M.B., and Vincent, H.B. Jr.: Comprehensive of an 8-year old following traumatic amputation of the glans penis. *Pediatrics,* 44:271-273, 1969.
45. Rozansky, G.: Psychiatric study of parents of children with cyanotic congenital heart disease. *Pediatrics,* 48:450-451. 1971.
46. Schilder, P.: *The Image and Appearance of the Human Body.* New York: International Universities Press, Inc., 1950.
47. Selye, H.: *The Stress of Life.* New York: McGraw-Hill, 1956.
48. Senn, M., and Solnit, A.: *Problems in Child Behavior and Development.* Philadelphia: Lea and Febiger, 1968.
49. Shah, C.: Rehabilitation of handicapped children: Hospital day-care unit or residential center? *Canadian Journal of Public Health,* Vol. 64, May-June 1973.
50. Social and Rehabilitation Service. Medical Services, Department of H.E.W., Mimeo. Aug. 1974.
51. Spitz, R.: Hospitalism *Psychoanalytic Study of the Child.* New York: International Universities Press, 1:53-74, 1945.
52. Stocking, M., Rothney, W., Grosser, G., and Goodwin, R.: Psychopathology in pediatric hospital. *American Journal of Public Health,* 62:551-556, 1972.
53. Sultz, H., Schlesinger, E., Mosher, W., and Feldman, J.: *Long-Term Childhood Illness.* Pittsburgh: University of Pittsburgh Press, 1972.
54. Tew, B.J., and Laurence, K.M.: Mothers, brothers and sisters of patients with spina bifida. *Developmental Medicine and Child Neurology* (supplement) 29:69-76, 1973.
55. The New York Times. Sunday, Feb. 13, 1977. Sect. E. Pg. 8. *The Handicapped, A Minority Demandings Its Rights.*
56. Tisza, V.B., Irwine, E., and Scheide, E.: Children with oral-facial clefts: A study of psychological development of handicapped children. *Journal of the American Academy of Child Psychiatry,* 12:292-313, 1973.
57. Travis, G.: *Chronic Illness in Children.* Stanford: Stanford University Press, 1976.
58. Voeller, K.K.S., and Rothenberg, M.B.: Psychosocial aspects of the management of seizures in children. *Pediatrics,* 51:1072-1082, 1973.
59. Walker-Smith, J., Porteous, N., and Gardiner, A.: The effects of coeliac disease on the mother-child relationship. *Australian Paediatric Journal.,* Vol. 8: 39-43, 1972.
60. *Webster's 3rd New International Dictionary of the English Language,* 2nd ed. unabridged, Springfield, Mass.: Merriam.
61. Wilbur, B.: *Community Health Services,* Philadelphia: W.B. Saunders & Co., p. 200. 1965.
62. Yamamoto, K., and Thomas, E.: School-related perceptions in handicapped children. *Journal of Psychology,* 77:101-117, 1971.

12

Sociocultural Deprivation and Its Effect on the Development of the Child

Nina R. Lief, M.D. and Judith Zarin-Ackerman, Ph.D.

INTRODUCTION

This chapter describes the major types of child rearing deprivation found in lower socioeconomic families and the effects of such deprivation on the child's growth and development. We will describe: 1) the behavioral symptoms in the child arising from such deprivation, 2) their far-reaching consequences for the individual, his/her family and society, and 3) the variety of treatment approaches we have utilized. Several case studies will be presented which illustrate these points. Although we are aware that any one particular deficit early in life may have more than a maturational effect and that early deficits tend to be interrelated, for the sake of discussion, we have artificially extracted and focused on one particular deficit— i.e., deviant child rearing skills—in order to demonstrate the considerable damage that this specific deficit may cause. We would like to emphasize at the very beginning of our discussion that the general milieu in which this deficit occurs is always multifaceted and multicausal and, in reality, it is impossible to tease out the various differential effects of each identified deficit.

Since the impact of organic deficits on the child will be discussed in other chapters of this volume, we will not emphasize this aspect of deprivation. We will also not engage in the familiar discussion of "nature vs. nurture." Suffice it to say, we believe that the personality develops as a result of the impact of the environment upon the given endowment of the individual; the resulting personality depends upon the interaction

362

of these two forces. Thus, we shall consider the interplay of these two factors in the deprived sociocultural milieu from which our cases are drawn.

Before we embark on the discussion of specific case studies, we have to define our terms. The term "deprived" as well as common synonyms such as "disadvantaged," "high-risk," "culturally poor," "disorganized," "crisis oriented," tend to be used when referring to families who are economically categorized as lower class. Most scales of socioeconomic determination are based on the two variables of father's occupation and amount of annual income (13). As such, they are not really expressive of deviant family dynamics—the phenomenon with which health professionals are most frequently concerned. Although studies have repeatedly shown that there can be significant differences in family dynamics even within a group of lower-class families, the stereotype linking family dysfunction with economic poverty still persists (22).

It persists, perhaps, because our research techniques are not refined enough to measure so-called "soft" phenomena. For example, if an investigator entered a household and was interested in whether the family valued reading and education, s/he might objectively count the number of books and other reading materials found in the home. If there were few or none, s/he would conclude that this family valued reading and education less than a family who had an abundance of reading materials around. However, if s/he had sat down and spoken with the family, s/he might have discovered that one of the family's frequent activities is going to the public library; in fact, each member of the family, including the children, has his or her own library card. So, although they could not afford to own books of their own, they had found a way of exposing their children to books and, in addition, making reading a family event. The point is that "deprived" and "disadvantaged" are terms that are relative in meaning; they presume an implicit superior vantage point. Thus, not only must these terms be explicitly defined for both cause and effect but the criteria for definition must be articulated.

Several efforts at such explication have appeared in the literature. Theodore Shapiro, in a new text in infant psychiatry sets up a trichotomous dimension of viability ranging from "failure" to "survive" to "thrive" (24). Hartmann, on the other hand, found it easier to define the opposite of deprivation—i.e., as an average expectable environment which allows opportunities for normal growth (11). Professionals are still struggling to define what the elements of this "average" environment are, or should be.

Recently, the struggle has taken on a less academic and more practical focus with the recent emphasis on children and the law. Goldstein, Freud and Solnit, for example, report on the legal profession's longtime struggle to define the "best interests of the child" and suggests that perhaps a better approach would be to define the "least detrimental alternatives" for the child (10). In both the Hartmann and Goldstein et al. examples, the existence of a certain set of minimal needs which must be filled in order for normal growth and development to take place is acknowledged. However, neither they nor others have successfully defined that set of needs to the point where explicit establishment of criteria for both research studies and practical legal decisions concerning child rearing deprivation is possible.

For the purposes of this chapter, we are concerned with that particular deprivation which results in the lack of consistent and loving caregiving, thus depriving the child of an adequate level of physical comfort and emotional support. Not only does this deficit cause real physical and emotional dangers for the child, but it also creates a cognitive deficit as the predictability of events is severely limited. Thus, primary motivational systems which affect future accomplishments in every realm of adult life are directly related to the quality of caregiving.

REVIEW OF LITERATURE

The effect of membership in a particular socioeconomic group on behavior has been the subject of thorough investigation. In particular, the late '60s and early '70s saw a burgeoning of an extensive literature on the sociocultural effects of class on the development of the child. Indices for both parent (including parental attitudes and child rearing skills) and child were commonly reported.

In a major review of the literature, Hess reports the significant findings in this area (12). In an attempt to organize the vast number of studies into a conceptual framework, Hess emphasizes a major thesis, i.e., that there exists a functional and influential relationship between social structure and individual behavior and that the acquisition of behavior in childhood, as well as the child rearing techniques of parents, is shaped by social and cultural realities. More specifically, Hess states that the economic realities of lower-class life directly affect how the child fits into the family structure and his worth vis-à-vis both his particular family unit and society as a whole. For example, Barry, Child and Bacon found that child rearing practices in agrarian societies differ in significant and related ways from those of industrial, urbanized societies (1). Most recently, Keniston in a report on the changing structure of the American family demonstrated how child rearing techniques changed with the liberalization of child labor practices and the institution of mandatory school attendance (14).

In a general sense, there are several significant differences between lower- and middle-class members which can be seen as related to their resultant child rearing practices. Cohen and Hodges have delineated the following characteristics among lower-class groups: 1) greater preference for the familiar and tendency for simplification of world experiences; 2) rejection of intellectuality; 3) restriction of language and modes of communication; 4) reliance upon nonwork related friendships and kinships contacts; and 5) a lower level of skills and experience in obtaining and evaluating information about events and resources. More specific to child rearing, findings have been reported which indicate significant differences between classes in areas of toilet training, breastfeeding, tolerance for aggression and sexual behavior, physical vs. verbal punishment, responsivity time to distress, use of the verbal mode of communication, level of aspiration for the child, stereotyped expectations of male vs. female children, and attitudes toward school and education (2, 3, 5,6,7,8,15,16).

In a chapter on the effects of child rearing patterns, Marans and Lourie provide the most cogent account to date of specific child rearing deprivations that occur in what they term the "culture of poverty" (17). They hypothesize that the lowest classes of our society have specific child rearing patterns which tend to perpetuate their way of life. Their observation is that this phenomenon is generalized across all ethnic groups and that these patterns provide ready-made sets of solutions for ongoing generations which allow the individuals to remain unresponsive to new environments, new educational attainments, and/or new trends in society.

Child rearing patterns are determined in part by 1) the child's physical endowment,* 2) the variation of parenting demands at each age and 3) the variations in the external conditions of the family's space. Specifi-

---

*The level of physical deprivation that occurs in lower-class families is most cleearly illustrated by the elevated incidence rates of perinatal, maternal, and infant traumata, e.g., prematurity, anemia, and toxemia (18,19,20,23,25,26).

cally, Marans and Lourie talk about three characteristics of lower-class child rearing which they believe lead to deprivation in the child. These characteristics will be briefly discussed here.

First, they report that these families display an inordinate amount of "magical thinking," i.e., primitive mental processes which are age-inappropriate and that manifest themselves primarily as a disavowal of facts and/or circumstances which are responsible for reality. For example, pregnancies are rarely planned and few parents demonstrate even a preliminary understanding of the use of birth control as it relates to pregnancy. Adults in the families interviewed by Marans and Lourie tended to reconstruct reality on a purely subjective basis rather than finding a way to act on the circumstances in a way which would create change in their lives.

Admittedly, learning to accept change is difficult—it takes an ability to adapt to varying circumstances. The authors point out that "magical thinking" serves to contribute to feelings of vulnerability in the child, i.e., feelings of lack of control and beliefs that the world is arbitrary in nature.

Second, deficits in child rearing skills may stem from the fact that the dependency needs of the primary caregivers in these families (almost always the mothers) have very frequently gone unmet and are still actively seeking gratification. Thus, the caregiver has difficulty filling the child's needs when her own have been so flagrantly ignored. Add to this deficit a realistic amount of anxiety about her family's financial and physical well-being and, in addition, no available extended family for support, the result is a parent-infant dyad that is contingently responding to each one's own internal needs only, and not the needs of each other. This, of course, is appropriate for the infant but not for the parent. Not only will the child be unable to satisfy the parent's needs in any consistent way, but as the child's needs continue to go unfulfilled, s/he will become more difficult and more unpleasant to deal with. The manifestation of this deficit frequently is a general overdependence on the bottle—the bottle being used as a substitute for parental attention and affection. This, in turn, may be a preliminary step toward malnourishment and even later alcoholism.

A third major child rearing deficit noted in these families is a consistent lack of adequate perceptual stimulation during the first year of life. Not only does perceptual stimulation relay sensory information about the world to the infant but it provides him/her with the opportunity to differentiate him/herself from his/her environment. This differentiation is essential for later successful social interactions and for healthy ego functioning. Stimulation in lower-class disorganized families tends to be delivered in an arbitrary manner—sometimes too often, sometimes not often enough. Research has shown that stimulation, in order to be effective, should be contingent on the infant's behavior and not on parental whim. Continuous overstimulation can result in children who will use withdrawal as a means of protecting themselves over time.

All of these deficits in and of themselves may or may not have specific consequences for the child. However, experienced as a pattern of deviant child rearing, they can be insidious in their effect on the emotional and social development of the child. The major result frequently is a child who is emotionally over or understimulated and who has developed an armament of "survival techniques." These "techniques" constitute a premature consolidation of reaction patterns that tend to preclude modification by later experience. That is, the child, prematurely pressed into situations which are beyond his coping capacities, develops defensive skills which allow him to survive the immediate situation but prevent him from integrating, processing and learning from it. Creativity in gleaning "rules of living" from one situation and applying them to the next slightly different situation is a luxury these children cannot afford. And, of course, the cycle completes itself when the child applies the same set pattern of responses to raising his own children.

Thus, we can conclude that sociocultural deprivation is extremely potent in its effect on the development of the child, particularly when the deprivation is of a psychological nature. Moreover, the effect is often repetitive, affecting generation after generation. When children are forced to compete with their own caregivers for the fulfillment of basic ego needs such as feelings of trust, self-respect, and confidence, they miss out on shared emotional experiences of mutual intimacy and affection resulting in a level of functional deprivation that can be all encompassing.

CHARACTERISTICS OF OUR POPULATION

The cases to be reported in the following section come from the records of a community health center where both authors work. The Center offers comprehensive health care—i.e., medical, counseling, and child development services—to families in the Manhattan areas of East Harlem and Yorkville. We believe this catchment area is representative of the problems and stresses of lower-class life encountered in most urban areas.

As of August 1, 1977, 246 families were receiving care at the Center.

The median size of these families was three and the mean was 2.96. The ethnic distribution of the families was as follows: 45% white; 35% Hispanic; 15% black; and 5% other. Many of our families were single parent families and families in which both adults worked. Over two-thirds of this population had incomes of less than $11,000 per year (68.7% or 169 families). Of these, 24% were on public assistance.

The largest age group of our total Center population is the "under 20" category. Close to half (44.9%; 27 individuals) of the active families fall into this category. The age range of the children seen at the Center for counseling services is from two years to 19 years; the majority are between four and 12 years of age.

Usually, the problems presented at time of entry to the Center are in a critical stage of development and necessitate an immediate and concrete response. Thus, developing a preventive ongoing non-crisis-oriented program in this population, while obviously the most economical in the long run, is difficult.

Acting out at home with symptoms of temper tantrums, depressions, and hyperactivity represented 23% of our cases.

Hyperactivity was almost a byword represented by 28% of our population. We discovered that it was not so often associated with organicity but rather with inhibition of motion because of crowding, lack of facilities for gross motor movements, the child's anxiety and/or the parents' instability and need for quiet, and their intolerance for normal age-appropriate activity.

Disrupted families with concomitant feelings of anger and confusion and separation anxiety as well as sibling rivalry were represented by another 20%.

School problems were represented by 20% and these broke down into 1) placement problems, 20%, 2) school behavior problems, 11%, 3) learning disabilities, 14%, and 4) poor performance, 9%. Interestingly, the largest school problem was not the child's behavior in school, but the difficulty in finding a facility to meet his/her needs (46%). This is just another indication of the burgeoning gap between the educational system and the parent.

Excretory problems were another category—enuresis and/or encopresis or constipation, 9%.

Although we have placed the problems into categories, no family or child presented a single problem. The difficulties encountered in any one family were usually multifaceted, including physical, financial, social, cultural, and educational factors in various combinations, so that all cases were extremely complicated. We discovered that categorization of problems was difficult for two reasons. First, very rarely does a problem exist solely for the child without any contributing problem involving the parents existing as well. Secondly, children's problems almost always ended up being *family* problems. In addition, discovery of a child's behavior did not always occur at the initial interview but often took several sessions to be uncovered by the primary case manager. Parents often clung to a stereotyped phrase to describe what they perceived as the child's problems (e.g., hyperactivity) and only through working with them over time were we able to redefine the issues involved. Because of this, no single type of intervention was decided on in an "a priori" fashion. Instead, we felt intervention had to be multifaceted, comprehensive, and adapted to each family's needs and the family's individual ability to make use of the available services. No particular school of therapy was favored; the approach was eclectic. Whatever seemed best for the patient after careful consideration by the staff members concerned in the family's care was instituted and carried out by the staff member best equipped to render the service.

Direct environmental manipulation was instituted in almost all cases. Help in the areas of housing, school intervention, Welfare assistance, finding suitable play centers and dental and medical health care was needed to some degree in most cases.

Supportive therapy in the form of counseling was a very common need and followed the usual time-honored patterns. Group therapy for parents dealing with developmental issues of childhood as well as individual sessions with parents concerning specific individual problems were utilized. Parenting classes for parents with newborn infants beginning at four weeks of age and continuing weekly for the first crucial three years are also part of the program. The leaders of these classes taught appropriate developmental expectations and need. Individual therapy and group therapy as well as art therapy were used as the needs arose in each case.

Special facilities for learning disabilities were also provided individually and carried out in close cooperation with the child's school. Regular case conferences with appropriate staff members to discuss the goals of therapy and specific interventions were an integral part of management.

CASE STUDIES

We have included five cases from our clinic. The first four cases describe specific child rearing deficits in the families, their various effects on the behavioral outcome of the children, and the particular nature of our intervention. These children range in age from 12 months to six years. The fifth case provides what we feel to be a perfect example of the cyclical nature of this deficit. This case describes a young woman who was poorly parented as a young child and who, in turn, repeated those parenting techniques with her own child. Discussion of the case follows after each presentation.

CASE ONE: UNDERSTIMULATION

Presenting Problem

R.M. was a 13-month-old girl of Costa Rican and Black American lineage who was referred by her aunt who lived in close proximity to the family and, having children of her own, felt there was something wrong with R. M.'s rate of development. She persuaded the parents to have her "checked out."

Family Composition

R.M. was the youngest of three children. She had two older half-brothers born to her mother by the husband of her first marriage in Costa Rica. R.M. was the daughter born of her mother's liaison to a Mr. M.— an American Black. The mother's sister and her family and Mrs. M's mother live close by and have close contact and influence in this family's life.

Background

Mrs. M. migrated from Costa Rica within the past three years with her two sons, now eight and eleven. She is a subdued and remote person who, at the first visit, dressed in ethnic garb with her hair plaited. In subsequent visits, she had changed her hairstyle and her way of dress-ing—her hair was short and she wore a neat blouse and skirt. However, she was never very animated nor did she show much concern for her daughter. The father was also seen on the first visit. He was a tall handsome black man wearing ethnic attire. The father did not live in the same household with his child and her mother.

The home consists of three rooms. Financial support comes from Welfare; they receive $140 every two weeks. The family sleeps in the same room, mother and R.M. in one bed, the boys in another.

The mother spends most of her time in a job-training program so she leaves R.M. with her mother. The grandmother takes care of her reluctantly and leaves her to her own devices most of the day, giving minimal physical care. However, on her visits to the Center for Comprehensive Health Practice she was always neatly dressed and seemed adequately cared for.

R.M. seemed normally developed physically. There was no history of difficulty in delivery, or of physical illness, nor was there any evidence on examination of physical abnormality to account for her level of development.

Action: Developmental Assessment: 13 months

At the first visit, a Bayley assessment of motor and mental development was done. R.M. achieved a Mental Index of 100, being able to do all age-appropriate perceptual and fine motor tasks. The Motor Scale, which measures gross motor coordination, yielded a borderline score of 76 due to the fact that she could neither crawl, stand by herself, or pull herself to standing.

Both parents observed the testing. The mother was remote and seemed to pay little attention. The father was interested and curious about the testing materials. He asked many questions about appropriate toys and revealed that R.M. had no such little toys. In addition, he indicated that little attention was paid to playing with her, nor was she ever allowed on the floor in the house as the floor was "too cold." So she was kept on the lap or in a carriage most of the time. They had not been aware that what they considered good care was inhibiting the child's motor development. It was suggested that they could put a blanket or quilt on the floor and allow R.M. to move about as much as she was able to, and to stimulate her with a bright toy such as a red ball, so she would be tempted to try to reach for it.

Appointments were made for nutritional guidance, inoculations and general family care. The boys, who were born of a different father and brought up under different circumstances in Costa Rica, were reported to be doing well and had no presenting problems, but appointments were made to see them also which the mother did not keep. Four months after the initial visit she did return to report that R.M. had learned to walk "yesterday"—at 17 months. She also reported that Mr. M. was no longer a part of the family, that she still had no job and was still on Welfare.

Developmental Assessment: 25 Months

When R.M. was 25 months old the mother returned with her. Testing at this visit revealed that her motor development had progressed to normal levels. However, her mental development had not kept pace with her chronological age. She gained a number of points, having increased her receptive vocabulary and refined her recognition of shapes and eye-hand coordination, but she still had no expressive language. Pencil manipulation was inadequate, as well as her ability to carry out simple requests such as pointing to parts of her own body or her mother's face or to parts of a doll. She showed definite signs of understimulation and a lack of desire to respond. Her behavior was marked by both indifference and anger, a behavior seen frequently in young children whose needs are not met to their satisfaction, and who have also learned that their behavior does not serve as a signal for the desired response. Her mental development score fell within the retarded range at 62, as measured on the Bayley Scales.

A Denver Developmental Evaluation, a few weeks later, confirmed the slow development in social, gross and fine motor coordination as well as the very poor language development. When this was pointed out to the mother she said, "I guess I'll have to pay a little more attention to her." This was said in an offhand disinterested manner—her main concern was obviously with herself.

As the mother did not follow any of the advice given by the counselors, arrangements were made to place her in a Day Care Center where the staff would be informed of her special need for stimulation. The mother would be given assistance in evaluating her own potential and forming realistic work and social goals.

Discussion

This case illustrates the effects of understimulation at any early age on motor and language development: The difficulty was not in assessing the problem or in finding the appropriate services as is usually the case. The problem here was that the parents were carrying out their role by protecting the baby from exposure to cold.

The middle-class value of giving room for exploration was not feasible in this case, as it may not be in many poor families, so that adaptations had to be made. They did not understand the need for play. They had to be advised how to compensate for this in their milieu by placing blankets or quilts on the floor to allow play. The toys middle-class families always provide for children were considered unnecessary—particularly small manipulative toys. When parents such as these do purchase toys they are usually big, sometimes expensive, break easily and do little to enhance the infant's manipulaive ability.

The poor family often misses appointments for a variety of reasons. Often they have no phone to use to call, cancel or change appointments. In addition, clinic health care does not encourage appointment keeping behavior. They do not yet understand how to use services in an ongoing manner to prevent problems but only for the crises of a severe illness or injury. In addition, the breakup of the family and the loss of the father who seemed to be the only one interested enough in R.M.'s development added to the difficulty of establishing a responsive environment for her. Actual physical involvement in altering the environment had to be instituted. If need be, a staff member may need to take mother and child to the Day Care Center until the pattern of taking the child there becomes integrated into the family's life-style. This is a painstaking, expensive service but without it no break in the cycle of poverty can be achieved.

CASE TWO: MOTOR INHIBITION
AND SENSORY DEPRIVATION

Many of our patients came to us not seeking help primarily for the child but rather seeking help for themselves. The child's problems are often uncovered in the course of developing an understanding of the family as a whole. This was the case with M.S., a seven-year-old boy whose mother came for care of sciatica and obesity.

Presenting Problem

M.'s presenting symptoms included an inability to concentrate well enough to learn to read, "hyperactivity" in the classroom, sleeplessness and nightmares. He was put to bed at nine o'clock every night but was unable to fall asleep until three in the morning. This condition had existed from birth and had not responded to usual medications or procedures the family attempted. By the time he was seen by us there was a sense of resignation to this situation.

From birth until he was three years old, M. had eczema over his entire body. This required a great deal of medical attention including diets, local application and baths. This caused the family to incur large medical bills. This family's limited income comes from the father's occupation as an elevator operator in an apartment house.

Children were kept from playing with M. by their parents because they were afraid his rash was contagious. He also was not allowed to play with other children or go into a pool because of his condition. He wanted desperately to play with the children. Treatment for the eczema involved wearing plastic gloves, having his arm strapped to his body, and having to wear black patches over his eyes at night. The eczema cleared up by the time he was three; however, unfortunately, his sleeping problem was by then well-established and the freedom for developing motor skills inhibited, as well as critical opportunities for socialization and establishing identity. The family had no awareness of the effects of this early trauma on the present problems of the child.

Family Composition

The family consisted of the parents and three children. The eldest, aged 13, was a product of the mother's first marriage; our patient and a sister, aged three, were of her second marriage. During the last pregnancy, the mother developed phlebitis and bursitis. The treatment caused another onslaught of medical expenses which resulted in a garnishment of the father's meagre income. Although the skin lesions are no longer prominent, it is still necessary for the child to use ointments and cream regularly which add additional expense.

Background

The mother, aged 32, is a nonpracticing Irish Catholic. She is the fourth of nine children. Mrs. S. had to assume the role of surrogate mother to all. Her father was an alcoholic who beat them and she remembers how this terrified her. At five years of age, the mother was in an automobile accident and hospitalized for two months. As a result, she lost the ability to speak for several weeks and when speech returned, she stuttered. At the time, her mother refused therapy for her but she has since had extensive therapy. However, she still stutters and this is intensified under stress. She attended school through the ninth grade. She is unable to read; this, too, may be the result of her accident. Interestingly, however, she is very verbal and one would not suspect this deficit which she revealed only after many sessions when her confidence in her case worker had been established.

At age 21, she married to escape from her family. The marriage lasted three years. Her eldest son was born of this marriage. She terminated the marriage because her husband became a "hippie" and she could not cope with his way of life. She worked and supported her baby alone until she met her present husband who is of Italian/Jewish ancestry. He, too, came from a difficult background. His father had also been an alcoholic. Mr. S. had been considered a delinquent and when his mother died, he was placed in a state school from which he ran away. He managed to attend school until the twelfth grade. He works as an elevator operator and has been a steady worker, but in a low paying job for eight years.

M. was the first child of this marriage, and his sister, Diane, now three years old, was the second.

They all lived in a five-room, fifth-floor walk-up apartment. The boys share a room. The sister has her room and the parents have their own bedroom.

In addition to the care of her own family, the mother has to clean and maintain the neighboring apartment of her mother who recently underwent surgery for a malignancy of the colon, and her two older retarded sisters. The sisters formerly had been taken care of in a state institution but, with diminution in care at the institution, were brought home to live with their mother. They are adults—both very obese and needing a great deal of attention.

In spite of all of these difficulties, there seemed to be good family relations. Both parents were concerned and affectionate toward the children. There was no outstanding sibling rivalry between the children. They communicated well with each other. The older boy was doing well in school and presented no specific problems.

Shortly after contact with this family began, the father and mother separated because the father could no longer carry the financial burden. They decided that if he left the home, the mother and children could then be supported by Welfare and he could clear up the debts they had incurred. He moved to a nearby building where in exchange for a room he became the superintendent in addition to his regular job. He hooked up a CB radio to the family apartment so he could be in frequent communication with them. In addition, with assistance from our staff, he was enrolled in a mechanic's course to train as a maintenance engineer so that his prospects of attaining a better job and supporting his family would increase. After a period during which he was missed very much by his wife and children, he began to visit. There is a possibility that the family will be reunited in the near future.

The family required coordination between medical, social, psychiatric and child-oriented services.

Action

The mother's sciatica was felt to be related to her obesity. She was maintained on a diet and, as a result, lost 25 lbs. Her sciatica improved. She began to take an interest in her appearance and began to enjoy going out with her husband.

She was relieved of the greater part of her responsibility of caring for her mother and retarded sisters when a social agency was found to care for them. This gave her more time to care for her own children and home. She also was placed in a group therapy program where she could discuss with other women problems of child rearing and this proved very beneficial. Her daughter, Diane, needed dental care and this was arranged for. Her oldest son was doing well and needed only routine medical checkups and treatment for minor illnesses.

M. required the most extensive planning and care. He still needed to be seen by the allergist periodically because of his skin condition. He had some difficulty in breathing. This needed to be evaluated as it was not clear whether it was due to adenoids or an allergy and may have had some relation to his sleep difficulty, although it was felt that psychological issues were the main factor. We postulated that fright, caused by the covering of his eyes at night, was the primary basis for his sleep pattern as well as having a role in his inability to read. There was nothing in his birth history or in his physical examination to support the diagnosis of hyperactivity, as a result of organic damage. His learning difficulty was investigated and it was found that he was not retarded but that his development was delayed, probably related to the early motor, exploratory and play restriction.

Contact was made with his school. The situation was discussed with the teacher. She came to understand M.'s need for movement and became less upset by his inability to sit still; she assigned him tasks which allowed him more activity. His reading deficits were taken care of by a member of our staff trained to deal with learning problems. He was assigned for individual psychiatric therapy to deal with his feelings. In addition, he was enrolled in an activity group at a neighborhood children's center where he engaged in athletics and became especially proficient in swimming.

Initial work in psychotherapy was aimed at building up his concentration span and self-mastery. When it was found that he could not handle too many stimuli, only a minimum amount of play material was supplied. He was helped to focus on one project until completed. For example, the therapist held the crayons for him and gave him each one when asked for until he completed the picture himself. Then, his achievement was recognized and he was able to say, "I did it all by myself." The focus was to get him to establish self-reliance and at the same time achieve mutuality in the therapeutic relationship.

Much of his play centered around the issue of power. "Who is stronger, a man or a woman?" He was helped to rework this question so that he could consider ways of using his power to exercise his own conscious controls and not depend on parental or teacher control. This also enhanced his sense of masculinity, and helped support feelings and identification with his father.

M. felt comfortable enough to voice his fears of being eaten up, a fear that he was responsible for his father's leaving, and a fear that he might harm his mother. The relief from these fears was followed by a release of energy, allowing M. to attend more to his reading. He not only learned to read but achieved a Grade 2 level while he was still in Grade 1. His school behavior improved. He finally began to fall asleep at nine o'clock without nightmares. Throughout the therapeutic sessions conferences were held with the mother to help her understand how M.'s problems had developed and how she could help. She was very perceptive and able to utilize this awareness, especially after she was freed of the care of her mother and retarded sisters and able to devote more time to her own children.

These results were achieved by the cooperative efforts of the medical, educational, psychiatric, social work, recreational, and vocationsl staffs of several agencies who were monitored and directed by the Center's staff. Needless to say, this family is functioning significantly better than ever before. This case is not closed since such families require continued regular care to insure continued progress.

Discussion

The major deprivation which distinguished this case was the inability of this family to make use of public services offered in the city. With the breakup of the family, they forced society to help financially. The disruption of the mother's care of her own family came as a result of her caring for her needy parental family because she could not afford help and did not know what social agencies to approach. The lack of knowledge of the factors in her son's development and the inability to obtain a proper assessment of his condition contributed to his problems. Inadequate as our social agencies may be, such as they are, they do offer some significant aid. However, most of the families we have encountered do not know how to utilize the existing health care and social service systems to help them minimize their deprivation.

CASE THREE: ATTACHMENT AND SEPARATION

Presenting Problem

K.C. is a six-year-old black boy. He was referred by his school because he was not learning to read, was considered hyperactive and had poor peer relations. The school was concerned that he might be retarded and wanted an evaluation as they were not planning to promote him. K. is one of twins. His twin sister was not presenting any problem. He also had an older brother, age eight and a half, who was doing well in school.

Family Composition

All of the children were of the same father but the parents were not married and did not live together. The children live with their mother who is age 25 years old, and a devout member of the Church of Islam.

Background

K.'s mother had been using drugs intermittently from the age of 19. She is the younger of two sisters who had always lived with their mother. Their mother married a second time and had five additional children by her second marriage. The two sisters of the first marriage were always in conflict with the children of the second marriage. Comsequently, they developed a closeness which has continued as adults. The grandmother had been alternately attached to and rejecting of the patient's mother. When the grandmother found that her daughter, K.'s mother, used drugs she contacted an agency and had the twins taken from their home during the first year of their lives and placed in foster care where they remained until four and a half years of age.

During the placement in foster care, the twins were moved to several homes. Although they were always kept together, they were never in any one foster home long enough to make any firm attachments to others. They remained the longest time in the last home where the foster mother was a very strict, rigid disciplinarian who favored K.'s twin sister. K. was often tied in a chair as punishment. This technique was continued by K.'s mother when she took over the children's care.

The children have been with their mother for the past year and a half, living in a very dilapidated roach and rat infested apartment which is kept neat and clean and well furnished. K.'s room has curtains and a canopy bed.

The father does not live with the family but sees the children from time to time, gives little support and never brings the children any gifts. The mother is very resentful of this. She also feels that both her family of origin and her husband's family do not pay sufficient attention to her children. When attempts to move to better quarters were made, she refused and frankly confessed the reason was that she did not want to be in the same neighborhood as her family since frequent encounters were painful. The family is supported by Welfare. Inadequacies in income are made up by occasional shoplifting and presents from the mother's boyfriends.

All three children were seen at the Clinic. They are all well-dressed and polite. Our patient is excessively soft spoken, tends to whine, but can be understood. There is no speech pathology. His general health and physical development are normal. He was born at term by breech delivery and no resuscitation was needed. Although the mother took heroin during her first four months of pregnancy, and occasionally later, there was no evidence of withdrawal and the infants left the hospital on the third day. The mother cared for the twins for the first six months and reported him to be a cranky baby. When the twins were six months old, all her children were taken into foster care. She does not know their developmental milestones. The children were returned to their mother because she petitioned for them. At this time, K.C. was four and a half years old.

At home, the mother has continued the same harsh discipline as utilized in the foster home. She takes good physical care of the children. She takes them to school, calls for them, cooks and cleans for them and takes them to the playground and the park until seven in the evening. She puts them to bed at 9:30 p.m. She is very impatient with K. and considers him stupid. She also complained that K. screamed and became very upset on the few occasions when she went out and left the children. She perceived his behavior as "bad" and lacking in gratitude after she had taken the children back to live with her.

Educational Evaluation

An educational evaluation consisting of a Bender, Gates reading test and a Goodenough picture test revealed that K. has no word recognition.

He can write letters that he can recognize. His auditory discrimination is good but his visual discrimination is fair to poor. He is right-handed and footed, but left-eyed. On the Bender his productions were extremely immature. The motor component appeared to be affected by a poor body image with undifferentiated boundaries which were revealed in his drawings. His thinking and memory functions were inhibited. He was unable to retain simple memorization tasks or any ordered thinking. However, he responded well to instruction and practice. The impression of his test behavior was that he was very compliant, bewildered by tasks of the early reading readiness stage and had many developmental gaps. It was felt that he had a developmental lag. It was speculated that it might be due to severe neglect, harsh punishment, inconsistency in handling, and possibly "scapegoating" as the sister was the preferred child. The role of organicity was never substantiated by neurological investigation. The psychological factors of lack of attachment, poor self-image and excessive inhibition were considered the more important issues that could be therapeutically dealt with.

Action

The program developed for the care of this family involved many staff members and agencies. The mother was helped to find a suitable apartment in an area she accepted. In addition, the mother had had a high school education and was anxious to have additional training so she could earn a living. She was registered in a class for clerical work and received job training with payment of $69 weekly. Her longstanding but erratic drug abuse is being dealt with by special staff of the unit and she is cooperating.

The children were all seen and given appropriate preventive inoculations and medical care. K.'s twin sister was doing well and needed no special assistance. The older brother was doing well in school but cried frequently and seemed insecure. Playgroups and a therapist were arranged for him. A special program was set up for K., consisting of sessions with a therapist. At these sessions, the mother was present because it was felt that she needed a model of how to deal with K. and his special needs. In addition, other staff members saw K. to help improve his reading skills. A school visit was made and the staff was advised not to expect him to work at grade level and not to emphasize his failures. They gave full cooperation but felt that he needed to be transferred to a Special Education class as he might not be promoted.

The mother was also seen by K.'s therapist at parenting sessions to improve her understanding of K.'s needs— his separation anxiety, his need to be aware of his own identity, to have small achievements recognized so that he could be motivated to work and improve his self-image. While Miss C. was in parenting session, K. was seen in play therapy.

In the play session, K. did some drawings that suggested some perseveration which might have been due to organicity. His body movements while drawing gave the impression that he was trying very hard to focus on his task. The figure in his drawing changed identity several times and gave the impression of poor differentiation between himself and other family members, especially his twin sister. Therefore, some of the work centered around helping him organize his mental imagery well enough to get it on paper. He needed a great deal of reassurance. For instance, he would draw a snowman and ask, "if one of the feet is orange, the other should be orange, right?" He would draw a triangle and need to have its shape verified. When he drew his family, labels were put under each figure to stabilize their identity. When he said he did not know how to spell his mother's name, it was suggested that he put "mommy." This delighted him and helped affirm his relationship to her.

Then he drew many pictures of himself naming the body parts. He seemed to be sure of only one thing about himself, that he was black. So, great care was taken in coloring to use black to color the skin. This also pleased him.

There were many instances of telephone play in which he would call the therapist and seem confused. He would say, "Hello," saying he was his brother, or his sister or the therapist. His true identity was always pointed out and was received with satisfaction when the therapist said she would rather talk to him.

After initial difficulty in keeping appointments, the usual pattern in this population, the therapy progressed well for about 12 sessions when the staff member conducting the parenting session had to be changed. Then many sessions were missed but family contact, good rapport, and regularity of attendance were established again and progress was made. K. was promoted at school and did not need special placement. Miss C. continued her training. A new apartment worked out well. Miss C. made a liaison with a more suitable man who was supportive of her and the children. Contact with this family is being maintained. The mother's drug problem requires long-term treatment.

Discussion

This case shows the effects of the trauma of early separation and inconsistent caretaking on development and the effect of harsh inhibiting punishment on body image and boundaries of twinning. In addition, some of the learning problems were related to the harsh punishment which inhibited body movement and restricted exploratory activity needed to stimulate learning. The case also demonstrates what can be accomplished even in the face of a drug problem with continued social, psychiatric, and educational therapy. It also raises the doubt regarding the manner in which foster parenting is sometimes carried out with its minimal regard for the importance of early attachment and the personality requirements for adequate foster parents. This is not an uncommon situation in this population and is one which needs to be considered more fully and sensitively by agencies trained to understand the special developmental needs of infancy and early childhood.

In the recounting, it sounds as though this case went easily and well and, in the long run, it did. But it is important to be aware of the number of missed appointments and late arrivals for appointments. Great tact and understanding on the part of the staff was needed to overcome lifelong patterns of distrust. A tremendous amount of effort was necessary to establish a sense of relatedness among the family members with the therapists.

CASE FOUR: ENCOPRESIS AND ENURESIS

Presenting Problem

E. was a six-year-old male who had suffered encopresis for two years. This, however, was not the main reason the family began attending the Center for Comprehensive Health Practice. They came because of the mother's obesity and hypertension. The problem of encopresis was revealed in the family history and was not a pressing issue for the family although they were disturbed about it.

Family Composition

The father is aged 32, mother 31, two sons, W. aged ten, and our patient, E. was six years old.

Background

The family is Puerto Rican in origin but has lived in New York for most of their lives and had lived in a housing project for six years. They have four rooms—one bedroom for the boys and one for the parents, a living room, kitchen and bath.

The father completed his H.S. equivalency one year ago, the mother dropped out of school in the eleventh grade. The father has two jobs—he works as a porter in an office building and also has a part-time job in a book store. The rent is $186 and the net take-home pay is $760 monthly. They just manage on this unless there are extra expenses. At present, they owe money for furniture. The mother is preparing to take her H.S. equivalency exam and finds it very difficult. On the days she attends classes, she finds she eats more than on others. She has difficulty keeping on a diet. It is essential for her to lose weight because of her hypertension. She also fears a pregnancy because of a hospitalization for a "nervous breakdown" following the birth of her first child. Because of her obesity she cannot use a diaphragm nor has she been successful with an I.U.D. An abortion was performed a year ago. She spends most of her day at the public school helping volunteers raise money for special projects. She also assists in after-school activities for the children. She returns home after this with her children and prepares dinner. The family eats together, then the father leaves for work. A good deal of the housework is done by the father when he is home during the day. The older brother helps with some chores but E. does not, and his brother does E.'s share, too.

Both sets of grandparents live in the city, but they are not close and do not help with babysitting. The M. family always goes out together. The parents do not have time alone.

The father, except for needing glasses, was in good health. The older brother wears glasses and has asthma. E.'s problem began two years ago following an illness in which he had a swollen ankle which was diagnosed as arthritis. A medical investigation at this time included a rectal examination and, following this, the encopresis heightened. He has had only one accident in school. All other incidents of soiling and wetting occur at home and mostly during the day. When asked how he felt about his soiling he replied, "not so bad." At first, the parental attitude was stern and punitive. Then they became less punitive and appeared unconcerned, thinking that this would be more successful. Now, they vacillate between punishment and neglect depending on their mood and the extent of the soiling. The father expressed the view that E. was too interested in play to attend to his toilet needs. So, there is much ambivalence and inconsistency in dealing with the problem.

Action

The mother was given a thorough medical evaluation, placed on a diet and assigned an individual therapist so the relation of her emotions to her overeating could be understood.

The brother was seen and the cause of his asthma investigated and treated.

E.'s physical examination revealed no organic reason for the encopresis or enuresis. He was seen by a child therapist to explore the dynamics of his problem. It soon became apparent that the general policy of the family was to suppress anger at all costs. A display of anger of any kind was considered bad manners and not to be tolerated. No shouting, talking back or physical scuffles were allowed between the brothers. The parents never permitted themselves to express angry feelings to each other. It was speculated that W.'s asthma and E.'s wetting and soiling were avenues for displacing their anger. E. also resisted doing his assigned household chores which his older brother often did for him, because E. was designated as the baby of the family and forgiven for not completing his tasks. The boys were not allowed to play outside unsupervised as the neighborhood was bad; this meant confinement at home after school. The housing project was surrounded by dilapidated housing and vacant lots used by many drug addicts. The area was considered generally unsafe.

During the mother's sessions, it became apparent that she was angry at her husband because she felt he did not take her seriously, would placate her as though she were a child and then do as he pleased. She was also angry because she permitted him to go out alone and he accepted this and went occasionally to the opera or a movie alone. She said she "spoiled" him by allowing this. She felt she had no way to deal with her anger and often overate at these times as well as when she was frustrated by her inability to complete all of the requirements for her high school equivalency tests.

After understanding her own feelings, it became easier for the mother to understand E.'s symptoms as the only outlet he had for his anger. Less stress was then put on holding back feelings and open communication of feelings was allowed more and more.

Concrete steps were taken to enroll E. in an activity program so that he is no longer confined at home after school. Nor is he infantilized by accepting his omission of his tasks but he is expected to do them, and recognized for accomplishment in this area and in toileting. He now has only occasional "accidents" but usually gets to the bathroom in time.

The concern over the mother's obesity and hypertension continue. The insights she has obtained are taking a long time to produce results. The father is having difficulty overcoming his image of his role as a husband who treats his wife more as a child than an equal. This is a cultural pattern not limited to this culture but often encountered in our patients.

Discussion

This family maintained at all costs the facade of a "happy" well-integrated family with heavy investment in school and community projects. In this area, they served as an example for the community and kept concealed the issues that were problems for them. The encopresis and enuresis did not fit in with those classified or caused by early coercive toilet training as described by Bemporad et al. although that came later when failure ensued (4). There was inconsistency in the training and some infantilization, but the main need seemed to be an outlet for anger. The suppressed anger seemed to be one of the particular characteristics of this family's sociocultural pattern.

CASE FIVE: LACK OF GOOD PARENT MODEL

Presenting Problem

Many of our cases do not respond even with the most comprehensive and dedicated care, because of the irreversible result of one of the major deprivations of children in the lower class, which is the disorganization of the family, resulting in a lack of consistent, concerned parenting—so there is never a good model to follow. Parenting is performed in a haphazard, impulsive manner, often by multiple disinterested caregivers such as relatives, neighbors, slightly older children than the child in need who are enlisted unwillingly to perform the task of parenting.

Family Composition

Such was the case of C.C., a 21-year-old caucasian female, who became known to our Center when she presented herself for detoxification from heroin. She was unmarried and in the sixth month of her pregnancy, complicated by hepatitis. She was hospitalized immediately and was followed in the hospital by our staff through delivery, and back at our Center when hospitalization was no longer necessary.

Background

C.C. was the daughter of an alcoholic mother who cared for her by doing domestic work when she was capable of working. She had many other caretakers and lived in many different homes during her growing years, which she reported as "rough." She never knew her father. She had no siblings. The father of her child was in prison. She had known him for some time before he was jailed and had some attachment to him as she visited him in prison.

She was still theoretically living with her mother and had no home of her own. She was not on Welfare. She had managed to finish ninth grade and had been able to maintain herself with odd tedious clerical jobs for six years prior to her pregnancy, although "high" most of the time on heroin which she began using at age 15.

Her baby, a girl, was a breech delivery at 35 weeks gestation. She weighted 4 lbs. 5 ozs. and was placed in an isolette where she was kept for a week. The baby was born in relatively good condition. She had no respiratory distress or other neonatal illness and no symptoms of addiction. Oxygen therapy was not needed. A supra pubic tap was performed to determine evidence of infection from the mother's hepatitis—the results were negative. The baby remained in the nursery 26 days.

The mother was not allowed to touch the infant at first because of her hepatitis, but by the twenty-second day of their stay, she was encouraged to visit the baby in the nursery. She did this fairly regularly but frequently missed opportunities to feed her.

The mother and baby were discharged before an apartment could be obtained for them and went to live with C.'s mother. Eventually, an apartment was found and mother and baby moved into it. During the stay with grandmother there was constant conflict about the care of the infant.

Action

Attendance at the Center was erratic for physical care, counseling and parenting classes; many home visits had to be made. The baby was examined at 18 days and was seen again at five months. Good weight gain and normal neurological development were found.

When C. found a new boyfriend, her attendance became even less frequent. She returned to the use of drugs and was then entered in the methadone program. This did not last long as she got a job babysitting and so could not come for her medication daily. The paternal grandmother took the infant. The patient left her apartment and went back to her own mother's. She left the baby with the paternal grandparent for extended periods. Finally, it was necessary to involve the Bureau of Child Welfare (BCW) who placed the infant in foster care. The mother did not make the foster care visits allowed, but after three months, she finally obtained her own apartment on DSS benefits and received probationary custody of the child. Drug use continued. The infant was finally left with the paternal grandmother and the patient lost contact with the baby. She was known to have continued on drugs and maintained herself by prostitution.

Discussion

This grim story is a frequent one in this population. Many individual workers and agencies were involved in an attempt to rehabilitate and save the parent-child relationship. In this case, as in so many others where the mother-child bond is not established early, it is hard to effect one later. An additional barrier, in this case, was the hepatitis which kept mother and baby apart when a bond might have been initiated by a mother who had herself never experienced good parenting—a situation that is difficult to overcome even under the best of conditions. This particular case has its own unique additional barrier to establishing the essential bond.

In this case, we saw developing inadequate parenting repeated in the third generation. The repetition of this pattern is one of the basic problems and most difficult to overcome in this population.

DISCUSSION

In this chapter, we have described some of the major behavioral disorders which we have found in deprived children, some of their long-term effects, and the types of treatment approach we utilized.

The cases cited were characteristic of our entire population as they all involved complex family problems which required a large staff and an integrated approach utilizing a variety of therapeutic techniques. These families have so many problems that a solo-practitioner using a single therapeutic approach would probably not be able to accomplish all that is needed in a single case. The combination of therapies under the continued guidance of a relatively constant staff is better able to alleviate an appreciable degree of malfunctioning and improve the lot of the child.

We also tried to indicate that, although in some cases it is possible to achieve good results, in spite of the multitudes of difficulties, improvement does not go steadily forward. It takes a long time to develop a rapport with these families, to get them involved and to develop trust in the staff so that they will keep appointments in a quasi-dependable manner and missed appointments can be kept to a minimum. We needed to establish in the parents a basic trust in the staff that they as children had not established with their own parents.

It is difficult also to detail in each case the hours spent, sometimes fruitlessly, in trying to effect interagency cooperation and continued operation of this interagency relationship in a given case. It can and must be done although it adds to the time needed for good case management and hence to the financial cost of service. To maintain an interdisciplinary staff in order to effect the type of major changes discussed here is a considerable financial strain. Once our patients began to recognize that they saw the same staff members each time and that the staff kept appointments, they then began to keep appointments. A minimum of time was spent in waiting so a patient did not have to spend a whole day waiting to be seen, nor did they have to go to different buildings or floors for care. As many needs as possible were attended to in one place but by different members of the staff.

Most patients had difficulty in using existing agencies by themselves, as demonstrated most clearly in Case Two. Others had tried many agencies. This caused increased expense to society because services were often duplicated, definitive procedures were not effected and so the patient tried again in another agency, with a repetition of the intake process, only to find no resolution to his/her problems.

While, in some of our cases, the sociocultural aspects played some role, as in Case One where the parents inhibited motion because of the fear of allowing the freedom of movement on a cold floor, or Case Four where the family withheld its anger at any cost, most of the difficulties were not produced by sociocultural deprivation per se, but by a general lack of understanding of the developmental needs of a child—in short, inadequate parenting. This lack of understanding of the needs of a developing child operated in all our cases.

In Case One—Understimulation—the parents were not aware of the need for motor and language stimulation of their child. The mother was not able to show affection and interest in her little girl or understand the need for consistent, involved care. There was some concern about but no understanding of the role of parenting and too much emphasis on the mother's own fulfillment.

In Case Two—Motor Inhibition and Sensory Deprivation—the devastating effects of medical treatment were not understood by either physicans or parents from the point of view of the child's emotional development and its potentially aversive effects on his ability to read, to attend for extended periods of time, and to enjoy a relatively undisturbed sleep pattern. This was all exacerbated when his mother had to divide her caretaking time between her own family and her parental family. The mother was not aware of the effect of this on her children. The father was aware of his need to keep in contact with his family. His heroic efforts might not have been necessary in a society mindful of the needs of the child to have two parents. The procedure of having the father without a job as a secret visitor in order to insure Welfare payment to the mother and children is a common situation in our population.

In Case Three—Attachment and Separation—the twin infants were separated from their mother and put in foster care. However, they were frequently moved from one placement to another so that they had difficulty in forming attachments to any one person (the boy more so than the girl because for some reason she was the favored child). The effect of punitive discipline and the fear of separation were not understood by the mother when she did take the children back. She, herself, had experienced harshness as a child and she accepted this as the proper model to follow in child rearing. In this case, a lack of awareness of the developmental needs of a child was displayed by the social agencies as well as the parent. The child's need to develop attachments, the effect of premature separation, harsh punishment in place of discipline and their effect on identity, learning ability, and continued separation anxiety were not recognized.

In Case Four—Encopresis and Enuresis—it was demonstrated how a sociocultural attitude—the need to inhibit expression of anger as well as physical outlets in play—caused symptoms in a mother and her two children. The earlier understanding of this in the children made it easier for them to respond to therapy. The mother was less responsive to therapy although she did make progress. The father had great difficulty.

Case Five—Good Parent Model—illustrated the effects of poor maternal care, and inconsistent, unresponsive caretaking and how this pattern often repeats itself across generations. Our patient's mother was an alcoholic. She gave inconsistent care to our patient and her substitutes were, in come cases, less than adequate. Our patient was unable to establish, for reasons both physical and emotional, a bond with her child and soon entirely abandoned her. It can be expected that the effects on this baby may be similar so that the process will be continued in the following generations. This is an unfortunately extreme case, even though we saw it in varying degrees in a great many of our cases.

SUMMARY AND IMPLICATIONS

In all of our cases, the main or contributing deprivations were an inadequate understanding of the developmental needs of the infant and growing child and an inability to respond appropriately to these needs.

Our society is willing to train parents to do all kinds of things, e.g., hairdressing, carpentry, computer programming, garage mechanics, anything but parenting. Appropriate parenting, however, is not something that one knows instinctively. It has always been taught by the elders of the culture to the younger generation. In our society, the extended family is disappearing. Instead, we have a society with few good parental models, and social and economic stresses which it cannot meet. The result is the spawning of an ever increasing caseload of parents who cannot cope. The financial burdens alone are beyond our society's means—no matter how rich. It seems obvious that there is a need for prevention not remediation, yet, our institutions seem to be primarily geared for the latter. There is lip service given to the idea of prevention, but no substantial backing on a large scale. Not until the effects of early sociocultural deprivation become well-publicized and integrated into the understanding and thinking of established governmental agencies who allocate funds can we expect a change in this attitude. Surely, after reading *Every Child's Birthright: In Defense of Mothering*, few could not heed the call to a reordering of priorities (9).

If we, as a society, are really sincere in our desire to reduce learning problems, school dropouts, deliquency, crime, drug addiction and maladaptive emotional defenses, then we must address our attention to early parental deprivation and, in our society, this usually means maternal deprivation. We need to teach parents what they want and need to know about child rearing, and provide them with the financial support during their children's first three crucial years so they can do their job with knowledge and affection and feel that society regards their job as important. Parenting is the most important of all professions. There is a large body of pertinent knowledge which has been accumulated, but not made readily available to parents. To be sure, more information can be amassed, but this will not solve our problem. Current knowledge must be circulated so that parents can utilize it. Some beginnings have been made but this dissemination of information must be encouraged and enlarged so that appropriate child rearing techniques can become as much a part of a child's health care as inoculation.

REFERENCES

1. Barry, H., Child, L., and Bacon, M.K.: Relation of child training to subsistence economy. *Am. Anthrop.*, 1959, 61, 51-63.
2. Battle, E.S. and Rotter, J.B.: Children's feeling of personal control as related to social class and ethnic groups. *J. Personality*, 1963, 31, 482-490.
3. Bayley, N. and Schaefer, E.S.: Relationships between socioeconomic variables and behavior of mothers toward young children. *J. Genet. Psychol.*, 1960, 96, 61-77.
4. Bemporad, J.R., Pfeifer, C.M., Gibbs, L., Cortner, R. H. & Bloom, W.: Characteristics of encopretic patients and their families. *Journal of the American Academy of Child Psychiatry*, 1971, 10, 272-292.
5. Cohen, A., and Hodges, M.: Characteristics of the lower blue-collar class. *Social Prob.*, 1963, 10 (4).
6. Davis, A. and Havighurst, R.J.: Social class and color differences in childrearing. *Am. Sociol. Rev.*, 1946, 11, 698-710.
7. Deutsch, M.: The role of social class in language development and cognition. *Am. J. Orthopsychiatr.*, 1965, 25, 78-88.
8. Eron, L.D., Walder, L.O., Toigo, R. and Lefkowitz, M.M.: Social class, parental punishment for aggression and child aggression. *Child Dev.*, 1963, 34, 849-867.
9. Fraiberg, S.: *Every Child's Birthright: In Defense of Mothering.* New York: Basic Books, Inc., 1977.
10. Goldstein, J., Freud, A., and Solnit, A.J.: *Beyond the Best Interests of the Child.* New York: Free Press, 1973.
11. Hartmann, H.: *Ego Psychology and the Problem of Adaptation.* New York: International Univ. Press, 1958.
12. Hess, R.D.: Social class and ethnic influences upon socialization. In L. Carmichael, (Ed.) *Mussen's Manual of Child Psychology.* New York: Wiley, 1970, Vol. 2.
13. Hollingshead, A.B.: *Two-factor index of social position.* US: Author, 1957.
14. Keniston, K.: *All Our Children.* New York & London: Harcourt Brace Jovanovich, 1977.
15. Klatskin, E.M.: Shifts in child-care practices in three social classes under an infant care program of flexible methodology. *Am J. Orthopsychiat.*, 1952, 52-61.

16. Maccoby, E.E. and Gibbs, P.K.: Methods of childrearing in two social classes. In W.E. Martin and C.B. Stendler (Eds.), *Readings in Child Development*, New York: Harcourt, Brace, 1954, 380-396.
17. Marans, A.E., and Lourie, R.: Hypotheses regarding the effect of childrearing patterns on the disadvantaged child. In J. Hellmuth (Ed.), *The Disadvantaged Child*, Vol. I. New York: Brunner/Mazel, 1967, 17-41.
18. Morrison, S.L., Heady, J.A. and Morris, J.N. Social and biological factors in infant mortality. VIII Mortality in the post-neonatal period. *Arch. Dis. Child.*, 34:101-114, 1959.
19. Naeye, R.L., Diener, M.M., Dellinger, W.S., and Blanc, W.A.: Urban poverty: effects on prenatal nutrition. *Science*, 166:1026, 1969.
20. Osofsky, M.J.: Poverty, pregnancy outcome and child development. In D. Bergsma (Ed.), *The Infant at Risk. Birth Defects* Original Articles Series, Vol. 2, 1974.
21. Osofsky, M.J., Rizk, P.T., Fox, M.R., and Mondanaro, J.: Nutritional status of low income pregnant teenagers. *J. Repord Med.*, 5:18-24, 1970.
22. Pavenstedt, E.: A comparison of childrearing environments of upper-lower and very low-lower class families. *Amer. J. Orthopsychiat.*, 1965, 35, 89.
23. Rider, R.V., Tayback, J. and Knoblock, M.: Associations between premature birth and socioeconomic status. *Amer. J. Public Health*, 45:1022-1028, 1955.
24. Shapiro, T.: A psychiatrist for infants? Chapter in E.N. Rexford, L.W. Sander, and T. Shapiro (Eds.) *Infant Psychiatry, A New Synthesis*, New Haven: Yale Univ. Press, 1976.
25. Thompson, A.M.: Prematurity: Socio-economic and nutritional factors. *Bibl. Paediat.*, 8:197-206, 1963.
26. Wallace, H.M.: Factors associated with perinatal mortality and morbidity. *Clin. Obstet, Gynec.* 13:13-43, 1970.

Part IV

ASSESSMENT OF NORMALITY AND PATHOLOGY

13

A Conceptual Model for the Assessment of Developmental Normality

ROBERT D. MEHLMAN, M.D.

The aim of this paper is to elaborate a conceptual model of growth and development which is clinically derived and which can adequately synthesize empathic and empirical data, while leaving room for any possible additions, discoveries and speculations. If this is effective, it means that the successful interplay of the cognitive and intuitive approaches can potentiate rather than inhibit each approach in its usefulness. *It is against the background of this model that an assessment of normality, if one is to call it that, can be made.*

THE OEDIPUS COMPLEX AS AN EMPATHIC BEGINNING

It makes sense, in attempting to understand and develop a sense of expectable developmental process, to begin in an area in which one can empathize *most* readily with processes, dilemmas, imperatives and conflicts of development. It is not surprising, when one thinks about it from this point of view, that the place where Freud's earliest preoccupations took him clinically would lie, then, in the area of the so-called Oedipus complex, its sequel and its complications (7, 9, 10). Although this is only the last filter and complication of childhood, it sets the stage for adult functioning and represents the playground upon which adult life is experienced. It is far easier to begin here and work in both chronological directions, since we by and large approach life from the perspective of an essentially genital character structure.

If we are to elaborate a working model, it is probably easiest to initially oversimplify the description and make the distinction between the oedipal situation which is a sociological experience, the oedipal phase which is a developmental period, and the Oedipus complex which is a dynamic phenomenon or emotional configuration. We consider first a relatively static model.

The Static Model: The Oedipal Game

The oedipal situation concerns itself with the family configuration. It is a sociologic situation in which the child lives from somewhere after the second to third year until about the fourth or fifth year and sometimes slightly later. It has particular ingredients to it (7, 9, 10). Mother, father and child are the traditional components that are included, but since we are trying to create a model to include *all* possibilities or to remind us of all situations and which is as flexible as possible, it is important in the situational diagram not simply to limit ourselves to the notion of the three-person or triadic configuration. The triadic configuration that we will talk about a bit later is pertinent to the oedipal *stage* and certain higher level abstractions or conceptualizations referring to the nature of one's object relationships, rather than to the *actual* situation.

For our purposes, it makes sense to add in our simplistic schema a fourth position that represents siblings. That would mean that the oedipal framework includes fundamentally four positions: the subject child, the two parents and a sibling position (Figure 1). By putting in the sibling position we are reminded that if there were *no* sibling position in *actuality*, the nature of the interaction among people in these positions would be quite different from that of a four-position oedipal situation. We will give little consideration at this juncture to the details of what goes on among the various people, since this is described elsewhere and is well known (7, 9, 10). It is pertinent simply to remind ourselves that among mother, father, child and sibling there are a wide variety of possible interactions.

Since we are trying to consider what is needed to play what now looks like a baseball game, the metaphor could perhaps be carried forward a bit. For instance, if one had a game minus one of the players, such as the first or second baseman, representing mother or father or sibling, it is clear that one could have a ballgame that would go on but it would be quite a different sort of enterprise. Certainly, in evaluating children

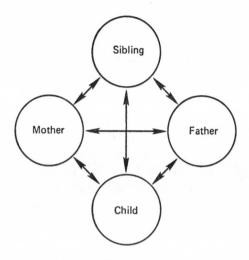

Figure 1

as they present themselves in a child guidance clinic, the experience of their having grown up without an *actual* father has presented numerous examples of the differences. For example, in the presence of rampant oedipal fantasies and with the father actually absent, the young boy whose oedipal strivings in the direction of his mother at that time flood him with aggressive impulses directed toward a fantasied father, inevitably projects onto this image the aggression he experiences in himself, making the father into a frightening man. This cannot be adequately reality-tested if father is absent and does not return home after work to be experienced as a reality. It may well frighten the player off the field entirely, to quit the game or sit on the bench.

The same is true in the absence of a mother but with somewhat different configurations involved. The absence of a sibling again alters the situation drastically, with very serious consequences centering usually upon the intensity of the relationship of the three remaining players. There is little leavening of the oedipal intensity.

Necessary Ingredients

There are many other elements that need to be considered. Certainly, one must have *place*. In other words, just as the team needs a ball park or empty field to play in, so the oedipal situation needs a place. A game that takes place in a formal ball park is significantly different from one that takes place on a street. The analogues involved in the metaphor can be diagrammed by drawing a complete circle around the quadratic figure we have already constructed (Figure 2). The *place* of the oedipus. in this metaphor or the stadium situation has an integrity whose importance we oftentimes fail to recognize. The line we have drawn around this figure represents a barrier between the exigencies of the outside world and the imperatives of the oedipal world or the game which we are considering. The artificial or contrived imperatives of the game itself merge with the pressing exigencies of the real world, such as survival, avoiding the traffic, thievery, and, if allowed, becloud the imperatives of the oedipal "game." The more basic emergencies of human life become more pressing and disrupt the nature of the game. The player at bat has to worry about what the pitcher is going to do and at the same time wonder whether he is going to get run over on the way to first base. These considerations are reflected in the oedipal situation, and we could say at this juncture that the oedipal situation cannot run its course in

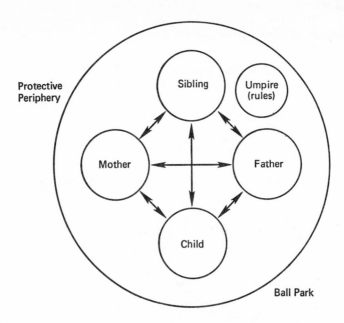

Figure 2

the absence of a very significant barrier between its microcosmic imperatives and the external world with its more realistic incursions.

A third ingredient necessary for a game is a system of rules and regulations and a certain amount of social structure. Certainly, the position of the umpire, or at least what he represents, which has been drawn as a small circle in Figure 2, is an important ingredient in any ball game. Some general agreement about the rules and regulations is necessary lest there be chaos in the field. The ingredients of the static model, including the individuals involved, the variety of interactions that can go on among them, the place in which it occurs with its preservation of its internal imperatives by relative exclusion of the outside, and some internal stabilization and structure, are all vital to the flourishing oedipal situation.

The Dual Function of Parent

There is something quite peculiar about the nature of the participants in the game described in the sense that the parents in the oedipal situation essentially wear two hats. They are obviously participants in the internal game itself; at the same time they represent the umpire and are responsible for the maintenance and provision of the field upon which the whole thing takes place and the protective wall around the field.

If, for example, the parents' financial worries are such that they cannot contain this within their own management systems, so that their worry it externalized onto the children, then *some* of the burden for providing the barrier between the outside the world and the inside world is shifted to the children. This inevitably alters the nature of their participation in the ball game. In essence, the *child* may be asked to wear two hats.

In assessing the nature of the developmental process at this particular time, the presence or absence of these various ingredients becomes essential in the understanding of the nature of the process which the child is experiencing. The need to be a pseudo-adult, while participating in the fantasy of infantile life so active in the oedipal phase, distorts to a considerable degree the nature of the oedipal experience itself.

The Ghost Oedipus Complex

Along with the peculiar dual role of the parents, one must also remember their subjectivity. Not only are parents the repository of interest in participating in this particular game for their own reasons as parents and as lovers of the objects involved, but also they are the containers of the residue of their own situations when they were children. In other words, along with each of these participants there exists more or less of the remnants of what we might call a ghost oedipus. We could thus draw dotted lines for each of the parents representing ghost ball games in which they may or may not still be very actively participating with their own parents and their own siblings, which is not pertinent to the actuality of *this* game but is nonetheless very important to the parents and very seriously colors their behavior (Figure 3)*.

The mother, for example, may see in her young daughter the same incestuous inclinations and rivalry for husband that she herself experienced vis-à-vis her own mother as a child. She may experience this unconsciously as wickedness, rivalry, threat or whatever, depending on her character structure, and respond accordingly rather than as a *parent*. One would hope, according to the principle of wearing two hats, that the mother would participate in the ball game but at the same time could *remain a parent* and allow the child the space to play the game, to live it out, to work it out, and to struggle with it without this being such a threat to the mother that she would have to excoriate the child for it.

Protection of the Microcosm

The oedipal situation being described is isolated from the real world, except through the interpolations and interventions of the parents, such as through their ghost oedipus and through their notion of structure, which is also a function of the resolution of their own oedipus complex. There is no reality for children of this age other than the reality wihin this context, which beclouds external reality in any ordinary expectable circumstances.

If external reality does crowd this situation, it is remarkable how insistent oedipal inclinations can be. The distorted ball game, which will take place nonetheless, will take place within narrower, distorted or perhaps impossible-to-reality-test confines. The rival may become fused with enemies or dangers of the real world, rather than remaining separate from them within the context of a fantasy life, which has the possibility of some resolution and restoration.

---

*The first baseman may be responding to the last big game instead of the current one.

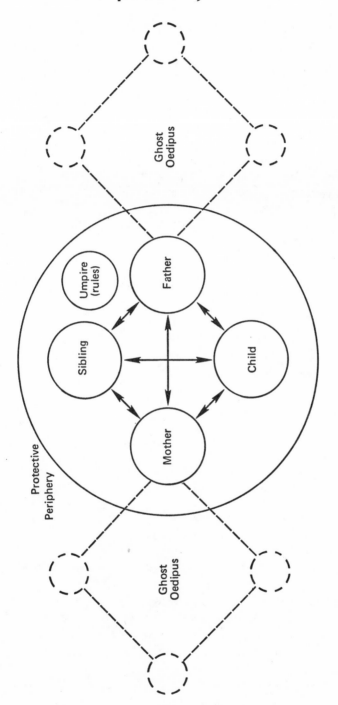

Figure 3

Time

One more ingredient is needed—a certain amount of *time* must go by. In the model, this is represented by movement from left to right (Figure 4). A ball game that stops after the first inning, one that stops in the middle, one that runs its course, and one that goes on forever, are all quite different. The unresolved oedipal situation which continues pretty much as is, with subsequent objects being relatively simplistic displacements or substitutions for primary oedipal figures, becomes a chronic, somewhat dissociated distortion of the real world. This is evident in forms of neurotic characters, some of whom defy pathologic description but are variants of hysterial character formation. The reality of their life is chronically distorted by the superimposition of oedipal imperatives.

Before moving forward and trying to understand the dynamics or the process of the oedipus complex, we are now forced by dint of the metaphor to ask further questions. What more do we need for this ball game? How does the player get into the ball park? Why, and under what circumstances? What is needed for the individual to participate? One cannot have a game unless the participants are able to distinguish one player from another. Certainly one must be able to distinguish male from female or must at least be concerned about this in this particular venture. Furthermore, one would have to say that, to be able to distinguish oneself from others, one would have to be reasonably solidified.

Antecedent Developmental Sequences

What we have come upon are certain *developmental sequences* that are prerequisite antecedents of the kind of game we expect. For example, a child who is overly possessive of mother and poorly separated from her will have a great deal of difficulty allowing mother to be at bat and go to first base without running along with her. Struggling with the problem of possession of the mother versus allowing her, albeit ambivalently, to have a relationship with father that is quite separate from the child is a relatively sophisticated development in a child's life.

The problem of children getting into bed with their parents regularly and systematically in the oedipal period, either wanting to break up the parental couple or to participate in some way, it is to be expected. If the issue of primary separation is involved, the fusion of these two issues loads the imperatives in the pregenital direction and makes for distortion of the flexible capacity to allow some kind of working-through and reality-testing on the child's part.

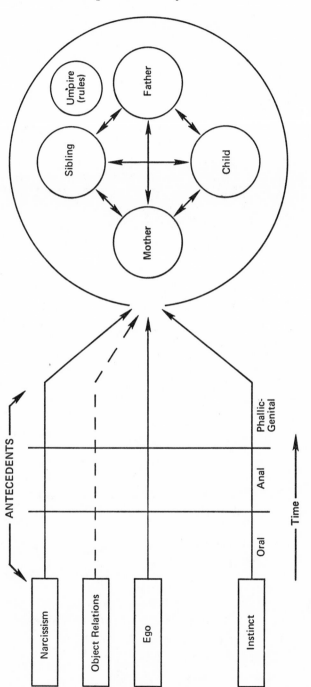

Figure 4

DEVELOPMENTAL LINES

What emerges from this is the concept of evolution along various development lines (5). The two lines that are pertinent to what has just been described would be an *ego developmental line* and an *object relations line*. A line up to the entrance of the ball park labeled ego development, as in the Figure 4, could represent the fact that there is a sequence of events that must have taken place in order for the complicated event of the ball game to proceed. In addition to self-object determination and the ability to distinguish between the sexes, the child needs the ability to bind affects or to wait in the face of pressing affective needs. I will not go into detail at this juncture, but only refer to the extraordinary amount of research that has been done in understanding innate development, learned capacities, and various inputs from the social situation. These fit within the context of expected levels of ego development.

The child also has to *want* to play the ball game. This involves motivation and involves another line of development. Following Freud's model with the phallic inclination or the phallic-genital interest he described in terms of instinctual process, the importance of considering some antecedent line of input that takes cognizance of instinctual or drive processes becomes obvious.

In addition, this thrusts upon us the notion of what is *at stake* in the shaping of these imperatives. In other words, the wish to win, the urge to victory, or the wish to hit a home run has content in itself, but beyond this imperative one is now forced further to wonder what is at stake. Why is a home run so important? Here we must add another ingredient—some consideration of the nature of the narcissistic processes. In other words, what is in this situation in terms of self-worth, self-value or experience of self that participates with the instinctual drives to make the development move? These processes have intensity, urgency, and self-centered imperative.

Summary Lines of Development

The model has roughly taken all possible lines of development and summarized them in three or four basic lines (Figure 4). Interestingly enough, each of these lines of development is pertinent to certain schools or preoccupations in psychoanalytic thought and literature which have both historical and present importance. Freud's early preoccupation with instinctual drive processes and his earliest and central preoccupation with the unconscious identify the biological line as the significant concern of the early psychoanalytic writers (20). The development of ego psychology, as well as the non-psychoanalytic inputs of Piaget and others, has colored the second phase of psychoanalytic development with a concern with the *ego*, its processes, its distortions and, more recently, its growth and development, both innate and experientially induced (20). The child psychiatry movement is, in many ways, a product of these efforts; further, through research efforts and para-analytic investigations, it has enhanced and enriched the understanding of the nature of developing egos. This process still goes on and in many ways is still very much a frontier.

The nature and central importance of object relations, demonstrated by the work of Melanie Klein (13), of Fairbairn (4), Jacobson (12), Modell (16) and others, represent another line of study in development whose richness and stimulus have lent a great deal of excitement and at times a refreshing counterweight to some of the ego psychological preoccupation.

The concept of narcissism, as well as the notion of self, which at times in the literature seems to be more important than the instinctual processes that Freud was so concerned with, making aggression, for instance, at times appear to be secondary to narcissistic injury or narcissistic threat to the self, is a currently fascinating and clinically very relevant concern (21). Kohut and others have conceptualized a line of development or process which appears in some ways so large that nobody has heretofore been able to encompass it (14).

This diversion is not without purpose in that it is important to recognize that the precursors to the oedipal situations are now roughly divided into a variety of psychoanalytic and para-analytic preoccupations, *all* of which have an importance. It is essential to reconize that no individual can adequately make reference to all of these processes at once.

We have now elaborated a series of general lines of development, summarizing other lines and generally considering all phases of development. Freud's developmental schema, however, is elaborated as pertinent to the instinctual processes. His discovery of the sequential centrality of particular body zones and the preoccupations centering around them resulted in the delineation of the oral, anal, phallic or genital stages (7). These stages are delineated in Figure 4 by vertical lines crossing all lines of development.

Freud's notion of an oral phase need not•be elaborated here, other than to say that the child is hungry, has needs for temperature regulation and a certain amount of protection from physical stimuli such as cold, heat and too much light. The child arrives with these needs and a certain physiologically built-in schedule of requirements that need to be met by the genital-stage mother.

Parental Regression

What happens that enables a genital-stage person to become so conversant and communicative with the oral-stage child? Observation would suggest that a partial *regression* has ensued that enables this kind of communication to take place. The barriers of communication have been lowered and the empathic awareness has been heightened. Some vaguely remembered or unconsciously carried memory of one's own dependent needs, wishes, longings, or subjective bodily contentment can resonate with that of the child such that the mother knows when the child is hungry, cold, excited, or overstimulated. This openness, readiness to mother, and availability to the child are the parental side of a kind of alliance that is established between mother and child that allows the parent to respond empathically to the particular needs of the child at any given moment.

Maternal Narcissism

Since the mother has carried the child within her over a period of time, has been in tune with movements and bodily communications of one kind or another, and has been enormously preoccupied with the subtlest shifts in her own bodily economy during the relatively long gestation period, it is not surprising that the feeding mother, even in the face of considerable inexperience, can become an effective participant in the process of infantile empathic communication. She is no longer a neophyte. The process in the mother started even earlier in her decision to have the child, the transformation of her narcissism to include the concept of another individual, and the readiness to expect, look for, and invest first in her body and then in the body within her body.

The Maternal Function: The Child's Narcissism

In many ways, the mother's function for the child is to help maintain its *narcissistic integrity*, while at the same time maintaining her own in the face of the partial openness and regression that have enabled her to be so intimately connected with the child's needs. There is separateness and yet togetherness, such that the combination results in adequate nurturing and care within a range that does not leave the child hurting too much, experiencing too much or wanting too much over too long a period of time. At the same time, the maternal empathy is dependent upon the capacity of her ego strength to allow this *partial* regression without a more across-the-board, global regression, which would result in a gross distortion of her reality sense. Clearly, the cadence of the communication, the ego elaborations of needs, the child's progressive ability to bind affect and to wait a bit or to live on expectation are all involved in the interaction. Thus a child whose capacity to effectively communicate with its mother is somehow impaired has put the situation in serious jeopardy. The mother's resultant inability to respond, unless in one way or another she can make up for the child's inadequacy, may exceed the child's innate capacities to tolerate a lack of gratification. As a consequence, the feeding situation may very seriously jeopardize a child's sense of well-being and injure the child's *receptive* or *dependent narcissism* (23). The same would be pertinent to a mother whose regressive processes had been too much of a threat to her, so that she had to flee the maternal situation. Similarly, one could consider the relative intensity of the child's drive endowment, an area of speculation and research, as a possible disruption of the economy of this microcosm (15).

Relationship Among Developmental Lines

It is apparent, then, that there is an intimate relationship at any given time among the instinctual processes, ego development, object relations and the narcissistic economy of the child. This is the phase-specific model of each phase of development which we must have in mind if we are to understand and make some assessment of the developmental process at hand. Action on one line of development clearly requires response and action on another line, which in turn affects all the others. It is this interdependency which creates forward developmental motion. As ego development, for instance, stimulated by instinctual process, proceeds and the object relations become more complex, so do narcissistic issues. As efforts to manage the narcissistic issues become more elaborate, the nature of the object relationships becomes more complex and as such complements the narcissistic need. This, in turn, adds new burdens to the ego, new instinctual stimuli, and new narcissistic issues.

Increasing perceptual capacities, such as the distinction between self and object, for example, which have an innate or biological component as well as a component of learning in object relationships, thrust new problems to the fore; these must be mastered in order to maintain the narcissistic equilibrium. All kinds of problems have to be mastered once the illusion of oneness with an object has been dissipated. The problem of the absence of the object, for example, must be integrated in one way or another, lest the child feel narcissistically threatened and ultimately damaged, In this way, we can see that there is a *circular interaction* among the lines of development, proceeding from earliest to later processes, with an inevitable push to elaboration and complexity, since action on one line of development will ordinarily impel change on the other lines. This, which is seen as an innate growth process, is an adaptive necessity. The "impetus to growth" described in the literature, referring to curative processes in analysis, probably harks back to this process, which occurs in treatment if we are successful in removing the impediments to its ordinary workings (1). As in other fields of medicine, the physican can faciliate, but the healing or changing process ultimately comes from within the patient.

Forward Developmental Movement

One could now ask: Why does a child move into Freud's second phase of development? For example, we could say that on an instinctual level there is a shifting interest from the oral to the anal zones. Freud suggested that there was something biological and innate in this. Again, how much or how little is a matter of research or dispute but need not trouble us as long as we make sure that we allow it space in the conceptual model as a continuing instinctual line. Contemporaneous with this are certain ego developmental processes, such that the child is able to direct its attention to its feces, do things with its urine, and do a variety of other things in a more deliberate fashion than the more random kind of activities that have occurred earlier. The ability of the mother to control this becomes more limited; indeed, the child is beginning to eat different kinds of foods and the nature of the excrement begins to approach much more that of the adult. The forgiveness for producing such smells, as an aspect of the partial regression that the mother experiences with the youngest infants, is more progressively threatened as the nature of what the child is doing begins to break through this envelope of infancy. It will more-or-less threaten the mother's integrity if it goes on too long. This becomes an imperative on the object line of development. In addition, certain pressures, such as taking care of other children, pressures from the birth of other siblings or social pressures from husband or relatives, add complexities to this development.

It must also be remembered that there are intrinsic factors that contribute to the necessity of some kind of coming to terms with one's excrement. The object relations component of this need not be elaborated further at this point, except for the fact that the alliance between the parent and the child can be thrown into jeopardy as new issues begin to press forward with new imperatives which simply can't be ignored as a child grows and develops. Sooner or later there is a requirement that the child manage its own excrement.

The Narcissism of the Anal Phase

If one considers the regression to orality that the mother experiences, it is clear that successful negotiation of these later issues on the part of the mother is dependent on her partial regression to the anality her child is experiencing. Despite the triteness and universality of this situation, at stake are certain vital narcissistic issues. Intrinsically, the issue of the integrity and value of the child's body, its products, it ability to keep itself intact, i.e., not vomit, not make a mess, and not lose control of a body function, becomes the playground of narcissistic integrity. A major component of the toilet game is an issue of body control and body integrity. One could say that *cohesive anxiety* is the narcissistic affect in this and is the predominant narcissistic issue in this phase (23). Corollary to this, who is in control becomes imperative, and, resonant to the child's narcissism, the sense of humiliation becomes a narcissistically moral schema of great importance and enormous impact.

We have touched here on object relations, ego capacities, narcissistic imperatives and instinctual processes once again. The very same sequence of events that we have alluded to in the previous phase is still going on in a circular motion in which internal processes and pressures resonate to object related issues and are intimately connected with narcissistic imperatives at any given time. The net result again is the forward progress we call development. This is not a magical process that occurs on its own, but is a comprehensible interaction among these various lines of development such that the only thing that can happen if all systems are reasonably intact is developmental progress.

The opportunities for pathology in this process, of course, are obvious, as we begin to elaborate the complexity of the interactions and the various things they are dependent upon. Indeed, it becomes a wonder that all of this can move forward without something going awry. The complexity is such that nobody could plan all these things or, for our purposes, even remember they exist. The extraordinary capacities of intuition and empathic sensitivities, however, do a remarkable job of keeping us out of trouble both as parents and as clinicians.

The Progression to Genitality

Freud felt there is a biological progression toward focus on the genital area on the part of the child (7). Others have felt that this is not primary but secondary. For our purposes, the debate is irrelevant. The erotic or genital preoccupation seems now to move center-stage in the child's instinctual life. On the ego line of development, the difference between the sexes becomes a much more real issue, and whether this occurs first is, again, of little matter. It suffices to acknowledge that the curiosity is there, as well as the capacity to integrate previously observed phenomena, such as the presence or absence of a penis or differences in the anatomy. This changes the nature of the relationships with the particular objects involved.

By this time, on an ego line of development, the differences between objects have been solidified and the differences between sexual objects are now added or become available for integration. A re-exploration of parental body configuration takes place and again new narcissistic issues are thrust upon the child. The child, who discovers it has or does not have a piece of equipment or decides it is or is not like one parent or another, now has a problem, depending upon what those particular things may or may not mean. In some way or another the child has to come to terms with this.

Receptive and Cohesive Narcissism

On the narcissistic line of development we would presume that the oral or receptive narcissistic imperative has been sufficiently processed, so that the needs remain but without central preoccupation with their gratification. The oral economy is taken relatively for granted. The receptive narcissistic issue, which is always a potential on a regressive basis, is now secondary to other imperatives. In a sense, the narcissism of orality has been bound in expectation and transformed in a variety of ways from an immediate and constant imperative to higher, more elaborate levels of intermittent and symbolized or substitute gratifications, as well as to various forms of binding and waiting. Narcissistic nutriment can be obtained through those processes, as well as through

the primary ones of immediate gratification. The notion of the hallu-
cinated breast as the first form of this is well known (6, 8, 11).

The imperatives of the anal stage, including the initial mastering of
one's body and of narcissistic cohesive anxieties, and the mastery of
certain aspects of one's body as separate from the parent, presumably
have taken place. The child survives the anal phase, having integrated
a cohesive anxiety with certain transformations of narcissism, such that
the privilege of defecating and urinating "where and when I want" is
substituted for by the pleasures of defecating "where and when I choose
to," with an internalization of the parental request and an enhanced
sense of self on the basis of a now partially internalized parent.

The sense of self and its enhancement, with the added elaboration of
an internalized object as a product of these processes, are part and parcel
of narcissistic transformation. One thing makes up for another. Narcissism does not disappear but takes different forms and is stabilized
through enhanced ego processes. The child who presents his feces is
first proud of *them,* and then is proud of *dealing* with them; he is anxious
narcissistically if this is thrown into jeopardy. In this sense, any smart
nursery school teacher with a group of three year olds is going to recognize that these children's narcissistic frontier is to a large extent in
their pants and only precariously maintained. On the first day of school
she has a bunch of cohesively very anxious children. A walk to the
washroom, with an introduction to the toilet and reassurance of its
proximity, is usually all that is needed to allay this anxiety and allow the
children to move forward from their initial trauma of being blocks or
miles away from the familiar source of their narcissistic integrity, in the
form of the home-base toilet.

The Phallic Narcissistic Imperatives

Having survived the anal phase with an intact narcissism transformed
enough to be ready to be preoccupied with issues other than bodily
cohesion, power, and self-will, the child now faces a new round of imperatives and anxieties. These are thrust upon him by *new* perceptions
and *new* awarenesses that are themselves a product of successful dealing
with prior issues, out of which they grow. The narcissism is *again* in
jeopardy with these new perceptions, awarenesses, preoccupations and
urgencies.

What we have described, then, is a linear development which has
brought the child to the entrance of the oedipal ball park. The child

now has a phallic narcissistic investment in genital issues, is hyper-aware of the difference between the sexes, has a need to compete and strive in the service of its narcissism, has stabilized oral issues by internalizations and transformations, and has, in general, a reasonably well organized sense of cohesion as a capacity to delay, wait, schedule, and regulate. He is now capable of and interested in participating in relationships with objects other than on a one-to-one basis. The mother-child or parent-child dyad has inevitably become more complex and there are no longer just two people in any relationship. There are the two people and their relationships with each of the other individuals in the oedipal situation.

In this way, all lines of development have interacted in a mutually stimulating way to result in the ingredients that constitute the oedipal phase. The oedipal *situation* affords the opportunity for a *narcissistic processing* in the oedipal *phase*, just as has taken place in the oral and anal phases of development. This three-year processing of the child's infantile narcissism results in an accommodation to *new* perceptions and *new* imperatives, both from within and from without, allowing for the continuation of a sense of intactness and undamaged narcissism via certain transformations.

The Oedipal Phase and its Progressive Processing

The details of the oedipal phase itself are well elucidated elsewhere and are not the subject of this particular paper (7, 9, 10). It is important to remember, however, that there are various differences that have been described in the oedipal experience pertinent to girls versus boys, and that the oedipal phase is not simply one issue, one process, or one item. These processes represent a whole *sequence* on several lines of development (9, 10). They involve complex narcissistic expectations, reality-testing, transformations, reinvestments, and reprocessing that go on over a *long period of time.*

The notion of a *sequence* emphasizes the time element we have described, which is analogous to the working-through process seen in adult psychotherapy. In many ways, the sequence of the therapeutic process of confrontation, clarification, interpretation and working-through is pertinent to normal development, since it seems to describe the elements of a process that stimulates integration and transformation of various primary or antecedent narcissistic and instinctual imperatives.

What is fascinating and somewhat paradoxical about the oedipal situation is that, taken at a distance and in a very condensed fashion, the whole thing would appear to be an enormous narcissistic blow to children, who don't get what they erroneously feel entitled to get or expect to have. This would seem like a devastating experience. Seen only in this light, one would expect a profound depression and a suicidal child seriously in need of help. This is, of course, not the case and, by and large, little children of age five or six are not profoundly depressed, except in very special circumstances.

In actuality, the oedipal processing goes on continuously, with reality-testing, injury and repair intimately interconnected from the first to the last. The confrontations and working-through take place over mini-events and in mini-fashion continuously. At any given time, it is not *all* loss that is being experienced, nor is it *all* restitution. They go on simultaneously and repeatedly in small doses. The effective substitution of "My father and I add up to the strong man I fantasized I was," or one victorious winner replacing the illusion of "me the entitled winner," represents the compensatory dyad setting up a successful latency process. This does not come about suddenly but is fostered every day in the successful oedipal phase processing.

Narcissistic Imperatives

More must be said in reference to narcissistic imperatives. It is helpful in considering each of the phases to have a sentence or a phrase which characterizes in summary form the *narcissistic imperative of the age* and the nature of the sense of well-being and later self-esteem processes that are in jeopardy. The *receptive* narcissistic imperative of the oral child in the earliest months is one of gratification at an oral and sensual level. The intactness and success of this can be characterized by saying "I *feel* good," with a bodily, sensual quality of total involvement. The anal child, who is caught up with a *cohesive* narcissistic imperative, is dealing with "I need a sense of control and relative power over my own body processes in order to feel safe, intact and feel good about myself as well as be valued at all by others." Self-esteem in the sense of object gratifications begins to appear at this level; however, it is not as well organized as the self-esteem that emerges at the end of the oedipal phase. Self-esteem depends upon a measuring and observing capacity.

The child at the oedipal phase feels the need to win, to compete and, more specifically, to be the primary one in the eye of the parent of the opposite sex. The triangular configuration keeps emerging; jealousy, rather than the envy of earlier phases, becomes very prominent (22). During this period the child achieves a sense of what it is to win or lose. The child must emerge from the oedipal phase and the process of narcissistic transformation that takes place during this era with a still intact, albeit transformed, narcissism that is compatible with his new reality-testing sense and the particular demands and exigencies of the social situation. The final acceptance of the oedipal defeat is perceived as a comfortable experience only if it is commensurate with a progressive identification with the parent of the same sex and a self and socially-nurtured illusion of the availability of the resources of that parent to the child's narcissistic services: "My father and I add up to one strong man."

There is, then, a sequence of development of narcissistic imperatives in cadence with Freud's sequence of instinctive preoccupation. This is represented in Figure 4 by the vertical lines crossing all lines of development to remind us of separate, but related, age-specific sequence on all lines of development.

The Fate of the Antecedent Lines

In order to add linear depth to understanding of oedipal phase processing, it is important to pay attention to each of these lines of development and to attempt to understand their vicissitudes through the oedipal situation, as well as their fate and locus as the oedipal situation comes to a close (Figure 5).

It is the formation of *new structure* that is the most significant outcome of the oedipal phase. It becomes evident that this structure, which results from the identification with the parents in the restitution component of the oedipal phase, has ingredients of *many* lines of development. This is a new product of the transformation of the narcissism, which has nonetheless retained its intensity in the imperatives connected with it. In the place of self-preservative impulses and inclinations, a structure which supersedes the values of simplistic reality-based self-preservation has come into being. That one would die in the service of maintaining one's ideals intact is a remarkable and new complication resulting from adequate oedipal processing. On a group basis, wars have been fought and the most outrageous acts have been perpetuated in the service of one system of ideals or another. This is the new narcissism of latency. In addition, a certain amount of the narcissism of the oedipal phase continues to find gratification and value in the increasing ego *capacities*

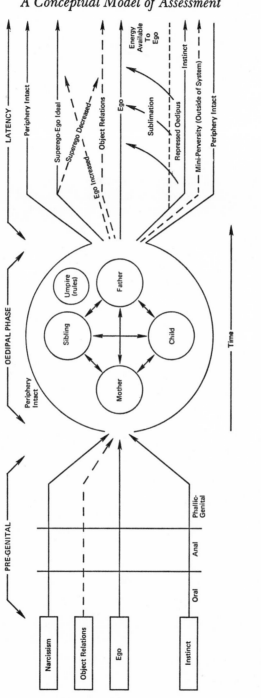

Figure 5

to live up to the requirements of the superego. A great deal of the narcissism of the younger child finds its locus in a successful ego operation.

Latency, Its Evolution, and Its Processing

It is important to note that the superego and its ideal that have been formed at this time are infantile, rigid and fraught with the pregenital or primary process qualities of the projective infantile mind. The amount that is repressed at this time is relatively significant and requires a considerable amount of energy to maintain. The ego is relatively small or weak, although certainly enormously enhanced from its state prior to the oedipal processing. With the waning of the oedipal preoccupation, the child is now able to attend school and pay attention to its ego growth without turning everything into an oedipal conflict. We would expect that, by the end of the relatively long period of time of about six years that comprises latency, one would have a very significantly enhanced ego capacity. At the same time, the severity and intensity of the superego, as well as the unreality of the idealizations, will have diminished almost proportionately. These processes are represented by the sloping lines in Figure 5. Simultaneously, the energies and the content of the repressed oedipal conflict are allowed partial slow emergence, fueling ego functions, capacities, and tasks in the form of various kinds of sublimations or aim-inhibited activities, such that the content of the residual repressed conflict is diminished to a considerable extent. Each of these processes needs to be taken up individually.

Sublimations

The process of sublimation can be partial, inadequate, or complete, depending upon how removed the ultimate oedipal object becomes from the process itself. A sublimation is not lasting or invulnerable unless it develops autonomy from the original object, with a transformation taking place such that the gratification is essentially in the doing rather than in the doing for a recoverable, internalized object. In other words, the pleasure has to become autonomous of the superego object, which becomes subsumed into an ego function.

For example, one certainly sees a lot of intense physical or intellectual activity in the service of pleasing a superego parent, whose thinly disguised or aim-inhibited form is present in external or internal representation during these activities. If this is the case when adolescence comes or the various adolescent processes become active, the sublimation often no longer persists or changes very drastically. Children interested in athletics primarily in the service of their incompletely sublimated oedipal and pregenital activities will often lose interest in these altogether despite enormous skill and capacity, once their adolescent genital activity takes form.

Idealizations

The idealization of the parent must be able to stand the slow reality-testing enhancement of the expanding ego capacities. For example, the arbitrariness of how much monetary allowance one gets or doesn't get as a function of parental personality is slowly and partially replaced during latency by the awareness of the realities of economic life. From a narcissistic point of view, this probably cannot be relinquished entirely until about age 15, but nonetheless the idealization of the parent as all-encompassing has to undergo a slow transformation in the face of the realities. The father, who, as instructor in some athletic endeavor, is the greatest person in the child's life, is slowly supplanted, often by the child himself, and the idealization of the father either collapses totally in the face of his defeat or is transformed slowly to more abstract forms. The father as the *teacher* and the father who *was* the greatest are examples of this. The enhanced narcissism of the ego at the expense of the superego and ego ideal represents a healthy development of capacities, flexibilities and functions, including successful sublimations.

It becomes evident from this that a successful latency involves the diminution of the intensity of the obligation of repression on the instinctual line, of the urgency of the ego ideal, and of the severity and import of the structure provided by the superego. The result is an enhanced ego capacity, which is the central structure emerging from the enormous and lengthy process of latency. Latency seen in this context is anything but quiet. It is a surging, developing, although highly regularized, interaction among various lines of development, with changes taking place on all of them simultaneously. This process is a product of a satisfactory management of the oedipal imperatives and is an extension and outgrowth of the oedipal phase. It makes sense in thinking of the oedipal phase to not exclude latency but to recognize the latency as a stabilization of the oedipal processes so that continuing growth and development can take place. It makes sense to view the processing of oedipal issues as continuing through latency and adolescence.

Narcissistic Autonomy

The increased worldliness of the latency child is, in general, a pseudo-worldliness which is dependent upon the presence of an intact preliminary of the child's life—a home. Latency children have inordinate capacities in many relatively two-dimensional areas, as long as other areas are present, intact, or taken care of in one way or another. The prodigious musical, artistic, or athletic accomplishments of these children which would seem to take them into a worldly context are nonetheless enormously dependent upon the relatively simplistic structure of the containing household. This is the pseudo-precocity of latency children who can rise to the occasion when necessary. The ego capacity to function at an adult level is there, but the readiness to maintain autonomy is not. The child who crosses the street on his own very well, alert to the dangers confronting him, so often will give that as yet unwanted responsibility back to his parents when crossing the street with them. He will then blithely fail to pay any attention to the traffic, causing parents to wonder how he survives at all on his own.

We have attempted to delineate an ever-expanding and increasingly encompassing ego process that occurs via maturational and integrative forces during the course of latency. With the diminishing rigidity and severity of the relatively more external parental representations of superego and ego ideal structure, as well as the successful diminution and some of the intensity of the repressed instinctual processes via forms of sublimation and neutralization, an optimal situation exists for adolescence.

From the developmental push point of view, if there is a reasonable latency phase which progresses along the lines delineated above, inevitably one *must* have an adolescence; conversely, if one is to have a reasonable adolescence, there must have been a considerable amount of latency processing. Corollary to this, if a satisfactory adult adaptation is to take place, something resembling an adolescence must occur sooner or later.

In the face of an evolving process, there is now a strong ego, a relatively more integrated superego and a relatively more available source of energy via the processes of sublimation (Figure 5).

Adolescence, Its Evolution and Inevitability

At this point, age 12 or 13, new things begin to appear. Why an adolescence occurs has been attributed to many factors. The classical formulation of the burgeoning of physiologic development, with the increase of physiologic inputs in terms of libido and aggression, is the easiest for most people to accept, since the manifest aspects of this are so self-evident. This push from below and within means that the instinctual processes that have been relatively tamed by the process of sublimation take on a new intensity, at the same time as their access to consciousness through various channels has been enhanced by the successful latency. The conscious awareness of impulse would be very great at this point.

It is equally important in this consideration to pay attention to other aspects of these developments and their interplay on various lines of development. A developing body, for instance, is put into a different position vis-à-vis the experience of self than a relatively stable body configuration. In other words, the child, whose body image is subjectively organized and relatively stable, in discovering changes such as pubic hair or the massive changes of female development that occur so early, has thrust upon it a new integrative imperative. What starts as an alien experience has to return to a former status of being taken for granted.

Reality-Testing the Residual Oedipus Complex

Body changes and the need to integrate these bring into awareness a latent and continuing interest in the erotic life of grownups, which in part has been aim-inhibited by complete or partial sublimations during latency. Again, it is not sufficient to say that from a teleologic point of view there is no room in the home for the grownup child who becomes a sexual threat and who must therefore find a life of his or her own. The increased awareness and preoccupation with these sexual matters seriously test the child's capacity to maintain in repression those residual aspects of the oedipus complex. Increased stimulation and participation with other children that occur during this phase further burden those functions. The erosion of certain aspects of the latency superego rigidity also conspires in this process so that there now ensues a lengthy period of breaking into consciousness of oedipal residuals, which often occurs surprisingly and unexpectedly. The residual ball game transiently reappears center stage (Figure 6). Interestingly enough, some of these issues have not been barred from consciousness, but, rather, separated by a barrier of something that looks like dissociation, in the sense that conscious awareness is feasible in certain circumstances while in other circumstances it is not.

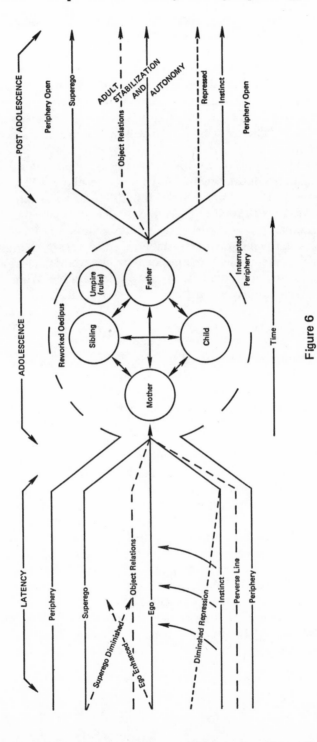

Figure 6

For example, a 17-year-old boy, while listening to an argument between mother and father which was not unlike many previous ones,
found himself increasingly involved, first in listening and then in participation. Initially, he clearly sided with his mother, feeling that father
was a bit of a tyrant. This was his traditional view of the angry father
who made mother cry. As the argument went on, he became increasingly
aware of the thought that if the argument went on long enough his
parents might get separated and divorced, and that if this did come to
pass it would probably be best for his mother. He found himself aware
of his wish for this to happen, as if this would bring relief to the family.
Behind this was the fantasy that if father was gone he and mother could
live happily and comfortably without tension and anxiety. This was
reminiscent to him of the earlier experiences of the comfort in the home
while father was away and the tension that returned when father came
home. What the child became aware of, now for the first time in full
consciousness, was the presumption he had had all through latency that
this would actually happen. He remembered this presumption now as
something that he had been conscious of under certain limited circumstances. He was shocked by this awareness in the midst of the family
argument and realized for the first time in consciousness that his presumption of his mother really wanting to leave his father was erroneous.
On the contrary, mother and father were married to each other, and
when the chips were down she clearly would stay with father irrespective
of any sympathy, empathy or understanding that she might have for
her son. This was a piece of reality-testing of a residual oedipal fantasy
that had been separated from other good reality-testing functions by
dissociation and repression so that the fantasy could be maintained. It
was only under pressure of the adolescent situation that the ego function
that had been long since capable of doing the job could come into
juxtaposition with the oedipal fantasy, which could then be reality-tested.
The result was a transient but meaningful experience of shock, dismay,
minor upset and grief work, which was noticed by the adolescent only
subjectively in terms of a transient feeling of minor disorganization, a
need to be by himself, a special dream or two, a bit of moodiness, a wish
to do some thinking, and then a changed view of his parents in which
they seemed to be more like whole people. There was a sense of growing
detachment from his parents.

This example describes an aspect of the stabilization of the oedipus
complex during the beginning of latency, which represented a residual
fantasy that had been maintained for narcissistic reasons. The adolescent

was now through with his fantasy and was able to grieve and to work through its loss. He was clearly finishing part of the oedipal work that had to be done. If this had not been done, the unconscious or dissociated fantasy would have colored his ongoing relationship with his parents and also the nature of his later heterosexual relationships. By having undergone this process, he was now more autonomous of the parental situation, and his developing sexual life could emerge more on its own and less as a mirror or reflection of the unconsciously maintained illusions and wishes.

The move to a more complete reality-testing of the oedipus complex has added a whole segment of reality to this boy's experience of his parents that had been covered by an illusion in the service of this childhood narcissism. In the process of making this shift, something happened that allowed him to experience this new reality, in the face of his need, without suffering permanent narcissistic damage. He was able to substitute one thing for another and maintain his narcissistic integrity. On the ego and object line of development, he has added a dimension to his perception and experience of his parents. In the process of this, although he has given up or lost an aspect of the illusory parent, the enhanced capacity for complete and fulfilling object relationships and an accompanying enhanced sense of self represent a narcissistic gain.

The Adolescent Perimeter

The perimeter of the child's life until latency has been represented by the solid line in the diagram, which in many ways represents the wall of the house or the intactness of the barrier between the world of exterior realities and the internal oedipal world. The adolescent's world would probably most accurately be surrounded by a broken line representing both encompassment and its failure (Figure 6). The adolescent's world is no longer containable by the illusion of parental totality. The sense that the parents make the rules and provide all the substance and that they are totally capable is seriously eroded by the end of latency. The burgeoning ego will have punctured many holes in this illusory periphery. Also, from the sociologic point of view, it now becomes increasingly impossible for the parents *actually* to maintain the periphery or contain their children. During latency, for example, although the children do have access to the outside and are exposed to many bits of data, whether from school or television, the ability of the child to synthesize and maintain illusion is great. The parents are also able to maintain a microcosmic world of the family. As we have seen, it is only this containment that can give validity and narcissistic importance to the details of such a microcosmic thing as the oedipus complex, which would otherwise be globalized onto the external world and run an entirely different course.

In adolescence the interaction among the lines of development conspires to make the periphery look much more intermittent. The fact that the parents themselves, for the reasons of incestuous taboos, can no longer provide within the context of the household the equivalent of actual sexual gratification has been alluded to in the psychoanalytic literature (2). The reality-testing of oedipal fantasies means that partially sublimated forms of gratification are no longer as entirely satisfactory and the reality of the outside world and the adult world is no longer maintainable only as illusion.

The front door of a household where adolescents live is a swinging door. The child goes out into the outside world, but he also has access to come home. The ability to be a child and to be an adult transiently is the exclusive privilege of adolescence and characterizes it as much as anything else. It is this situation which provides the space for adolescent processing to take place.

An interesting sidelight to these issues lies in the problem of when one can expect a child to be able to accept parents as they are in their totality. For example, when can the child of a psychotic parent genuinely experience the mother's disablement or problem as a human problem of her own, as her illness or misfortune, without the sense of simply having been deprived by mother? From a clinical point of view, one seldom sees this genuinely occur before the age of 15 and then only under special circumstances. It probably has something to do with the maturational possibilities of separation and is a function of the involvement of various lines of development, such that the child's narcissism can be genuinely autonomous of its parents. Adolescence is an interim phase where the child is still able to be connected and to return to dependency and narcissistic attachment to parents other than simply as beloved objects. Autonomy is not complete.

The Subdivision of Adolescent Chronology

It should be evident by now that adolescence, like latency, cannot be talked about without further subdividing these phases of development. Certainly, early, mid, and late adolescence are rather natural divisions in terms of one's expectations of the issues of the moment. The early preoccupations with body issues and intensity of drive organization, followed by mid-adolescent reality-testing processes, particularly with respect to the oedipus complex, and the later adolescent issues, which have to do with the orientation to the real world and one's place autonomous of the supplies, nutriment and an encompassment, as well as protection, of the parents, are sequentially shifting preoccupations of an as yet unconsolidated personality structure. There is always the active interaction among the lines of development to promote a forward motion, as well as inability to hold still.

In summary, adolescence involves an ongoing risk to the intactness of the child's narcissism, a burgeoning and developing ego, a pressing sociologic reality validated in many ways by a developing ego, a pressing instinctual life which puts pressure on the other lines of development, and an evolving and progressively more elaborate object relationship which now begins to include in a far more three-dimensional way the total awareness of primary objects and in consequence of others as well. There is no way of separating these various lines of development, since action on one necessitates action on another, and reciprocally, reasonable progress on one without consonant progress on the others could result in severe distortion of the processing of adolescence.

If one looks at the issues of autonomy, coming to terms with one's own body, the elaboration of object relationships, broadening ego perceptions and capabilities to deal with reality, the vital nature of the processing of adolescence for the quality of subsequent life processes becomes self-evident. Sooner or later, the issues of adolescence *must* be confronted.

THE USE OF THE MODEL

What has been outlined and represented in the model thus far is a developmental framework or operating model predicated upon an evolving, *internally generated* developmental progress, including movement along significant lines of development, with each successive and perhaps artificially delineated stage resulting in significant transformations of narcissism, increased binding and integrative capacities, a more complex, realistically valid and consequently flexibly useful object relationship potential, and a greater adaptive capacity with the passing of integrative time. Efforts to understand an individual of any age require an appreciation of the *processes* that are taking place.

Byways and Detours

For example, a latency child regularly withdraws to his room and, while staring into space in a dreamy state, with his hands between his legs, is clearly experiencing a mastubatory process. While this is not terribly disturbing if it is not too extensive or does not get in the way of other activities, it does reflect to us that a considerable amount of what might be included in the centrally integrating process of latency is for the time being left out. In other words, the energies, efforts, gratifications and push that would result in sublimations or at times even some untoward direct pursuits in the service of residual oedipal consciousness or thinly disguised displacements of oedipal involvement are going into mastubatory activity and in all likelihood feeding a dissociated fantasy experience. The extent of the fantasy life varies from child to child and certainly cannot be called pathological in any sense of the word. Of importance, however, is the extent to which the energies are stalled in a byway or a sidetrack outside the central system and to the extent to which they sequentially migrate from isolated and isolating fantasy systems into productive and creative activities which move into the central stream of the child's life. In some ways, this alternative to integration is to be seen as a "fingers-crossed" or "it's all right except" behavior, which in excess hangs as a threat over an otherwise reasonable development. It tells us that the development is not as yet adequately synthesizing some of the ongoing processes.

Developmentally Crossed Fingers

A residue of this sort of thing in adult character structure is reflected by an individual lying on the couch, manifestly cooperating with the analyst and apparently participating actively in an effective analytic involvement, but nonetheless secretly crossing his fingers. Other examples of this are represented by this individual who whole-heartedly goes about life with the notion that if things are *really* bad, he can always kill himself. There have been notable clinical examples of people who have routinely carried poison pills as a means of self-destruction, despite the fact that in the manifest and current aspects of their life, things are going well and comfortably. The narcissistic *reservation* that is involved in retaining the means for self-destruction is an extreme example of a failure of a narcissistic transformation at earlier phases carried forward to the now age-specific analogue of exactly the same thing.

Perversity and Mini-Perversity

From this perspective, perversions represent a short circuiting or fingers-crossed component of the developmental process. In this context one might go back and look at the earlier times of life and recognize, for example, that the enuretic who is never dry has not experienced the normal global processing of the narcissistic imperatives involved in the negotiation between parent and child over these issues. In this sense, the child might go on to an apparently reasonable development but always retain insistence on the infantile prerogative of bedwetting thoughout the oedipal phase, which to that extent represents a counterweight to putting all one's narcissistic and instinctual eggs in one basket. The child who still wets through the oedipal phase can always obtain gratification in regressive fantasy in the face of oedipal frustrations, thus reserving a major component of its instinctual and narcissistic processes for its own mini-perverse devices. This may continue all through latency and represent the equivalent of either a symptom formation or what would otherwise be an enhanced repression or repressive capacity. With these children, almost nothing is terribly reliable in attempting to reverse these processes (although the regressive enuresis of a child who has already been trained or processed does seem eminently treatable). Rather than being amenable to treatment in its classical sense, these children seem to wait for the later integrating process of their developing adolescent sexuality. With the emergence of adolescent sexuality and the onset of adolescent masturbation, for example, these symptoms seem more than usually to disappear entirely and reliably as the burgeoning adolescent sexuality evolves. What would appear to be happening in these cases is the final *re-integration* of a split-off or a dissociated line of development which has been imperative as a counterweight to things happening on other lines (Figure 6).

Another example of a separation from the main schema would be a child who regularly cheats and steals through latency, despite otherwise good and reasonable functioning development. On close examination, the cheating and stealing represent a form of entitlement, serving an important narcissistic need.

It is reasonable to expect this kind of activity to occur transiently in most children at various times, but its persistence and degree of secrecy, which may become more and more elaborated as time goes on, mean that it then amounts to another form of private mini-perversity. The striking aspect of this is that one sees it in those individuals who in the rest of their life are rigorously moral and perhaps coping with an unmodified and overly rigid version of a latency superego. This is common, for example, in adult obsessionals who, despite the rigidity and regularity of their morality, under various private and special circumstances can be found to cheat on their own with a feeling of total justification, as long as the rest of the observing superego is adequately subverted (in other words, if it is maintained secretly). Once it becomes public, there is humiliation, shame and enormous guilt. What is striking in such moral individuals is that the secrecy from the outside world would seem to serve the same function as a dissociation from one's internal observer and in this way represents a form of chronic acting-out.

Morality and Social Misbehavior

An interesting side note to this kind of activity appears in attempting to understand the relationship between morality, superego formation, and various forms of social misbehavior. Ordinarily, from a developmental point of view, we find child psychiatrists and others heaving a sigh of relief both sociologically and clinically with the advent of superego formation, with a sense that there is an element of control, predictability and the usual sense of guilt and restraint connected with it. This is certainly correct as far as it goes. However, in accompaniment with this one must recognize the possibility that with the sanction of behavior as moral, morally sadistic behavior or behavior that is sanctioned by this internalization can be far more destructive than otherwise would be the case.

It is also noteworthy that if one looks at children prior to the formation of the reliable superego, it is very difficult to find genuine malicious murder of younger siblings. This is in contrast to the regularity of murderous wishes directed towards new siblings. In addition, many of these children are large, well coordinated and certainly have access to weapons such as hammers. Also in the millions of the households that we are talking about, it is inconceivable that every young child is adequately protected from this sort of thing by an ever-present adult. No matter how one thinks this through, it is very difficult to come to any conclusion other than that prior to the adequate formation of the superego the narcissistic threats involved in actually perpetrating such an act are far greater and far more reliable a limit to such activities than we would otherwise think. On the other hand, there are numerous examples of sadistic murder, malicious intent and so on on the part of latency children.

What this suggests is that, alongside the prohibiting aspects of the superego formation and the internalization process that has taken place, there also is a sanctioning or *permission-giving* function that in some ways is more dangerous to others than its absence. At times, when working with young children, one can see specific progress in the elaboration of these internal structures. The relief that children experience by this maneuver is manifest and is certainly one aspect of the motivation involved in the developmental process of internalization and the formation of the structures we call superego. One might even venture to postulate that a more reliable and internally structuralized superego would result in far more vicious, frightening and perversely organized infancy than the one we ordinarily know.

These individuals have another "perverse" line of development that must be taken into consideration in the model (Figure 5). The child who gives up the bedwetting in adolescence would be represented by having this mini-perverse, always available activity rejoin the main line of development and become subsumed into various other processes, such as active sexual life and the evolving ego and object lines of development, with the consequent narcissistic transformation taking place. The child who steals all through latency may have an integrative crisis of some kind during adolescence along the lines of the previously described adolescent who becomes aware of his residual oedipal fantasies. These crises represent integrative nodal points and, although they may appear to be symptomatic at the moment, we would be grossly mistaken in our assessment if we did not recognize that these symptoms, although transiently troublesome, were part of developmental progress.

POST ADOLESCENT DEVELOPMENT

We have elaborated so far a model of development that has taken us through adolescence. From this point onward, our model in some ways gets into a lot of philosophical difficulties. This is not surprising in view of the fact that we are talking about adult development and to that extent we are talking about ourselves and about things that concern the quality of life in general as one or another group of people may see it. With respect to this, when one begins to discuss what is normal, what is abnormal, or what is expectable, we begin to run into everybody's investment in his own way of life and philosophy and the preoccupation with the correctness of his own existence.

Erickson's concept of life stages extending beyond the infancy is certainly pertinent to this; also, the ideas of life crisis at one time or another have contributed significantly to making us aware of the fact that development does not stop once one is grown up (3). The study of the geriatric patients and the increasing interest in them on the part of psychoanalysts and others make as much of a contribution as child psychiatry in introducing a parameter of new data vitally needed in understanding developmental processes.

The End of Adolescence

Some notion of what ends adolescence or what we mean by an ending of adolescence is not easy to come by. At this point it is worthwhile to remind ourselves again of the distinctions among process, subjective experience, and sociologic situation that we have made in each of the prior phases of development.

Optimally, the sense of self that emerges from the adolescent experience is in tune with one's inner and outer realities in the same Janus-faced way that Rapaport describes (19). If one now had to describe what is the residue of an adolescence or the new result of the adolescent processing, we would have to say that it involves the integration of a sense of self with very significant portions of one's superego and id, such that there are now ego-syntonic portions of each of these structures which are experienced as part of self. In addition, there is a core sense of self which is autonomous of each of these structures. There are aspects of each of these structures that remain ego-alien or ego-threatening. One would hope of an adequate adolescence that those ego-alien aspects or portions of the psychic apparatus are relatively minimal compared to the more integrated portions.

Individuals should by this time be experienced as much as possible as individuals of totality, including the 360 degress around them. Instinctual processes should be available for reasonable gratification and ego processes should be developed to an extent of reasonable fulfillment. At the same time, superego processes should be available but not unduly tyrannizing and social connectedness should be reasonably balanced by an inner involvement. We are talking about a sense of self-autonomy comparable to Rapaport's ego-autonomy, which involves an autonomy from within, supported by a connectedness from without, and an autonomy from external tyrannization, supported by an availability and gratification of instinctual process from within.

Marriage and Love

Successful marriage depends to a large extent on the relative completion of the adolescent process. The so-called neurotic marriage that we see is probably more appropriately called a developmentally immature marriage. For example, the young boy marries a figment of his mother in the appearance, attitude, or character style of a wife who marries him because of *her* needs to be dependent upon somebody. They are investing in a relationship for mutually diverse purposes, which for the moment may be gratified by the situation the couple find themselves in. As one or another of the individuals progresses and decides he or she wants a child, for instance, the man in this situation may experience enormous oedipal rivalry or the woman's sense that she is valued for herself and not for what she can produce may be seriously jeopardized. To progress to the complexity of a genuine marriage, there is *another* narcissistic transformation that must take place beyond the sense of integrity of self. This involves an ability to partially open one's narcissistic closure to include another individual, without at the same time failing to recognize that individual's autonomy. This would be as close to a description of being in love or loving an object as we could delineate in terms of our model; at face value it represents an enormous risk.

The Narcissistic Problem of Having Children

Having a child again represents a narcissistic transformation which takes us to our earliest descriptions in attempting to delineate the nature of our model. Where the child fits in the economy of the adult individual's life varies and requires a considerable understanding of the linear development of the mother's narcissism. If there has been a sufficient mutuality and narcissistic openness with respect to her spouse, it is clear that the wish for a child is not only a wish for *my* child, my extension of me, but represents a wish for my child and *his* child. The woman who says "I want a child" as she comes into treatment and therefore wants a man is, to a large extent, putting the narcissistic cart before the horse. Needless to say, there are many marriages where just this process is occurring and the children are experienced only as extensions of the mother's narcissistic self, with a husband only as a convenience. This also occurs when the husband experiences his wife only as a means by which he can "have a family." His child becomes an idealized self of some sort, oftentimes signaling the relative affective abandonment of his spouse, who at that point may become depressed and feel deprived of an ingredient that she has come to depend upon narcissistically.

Old Age

I will not attempt to carry a model forward in all of the details of the vicissitudes of adult life, but one should be aware that the same lines of development and processing that we have described continue throughout life, including old age and old age of parents. Also, as various functions are lost or various upholsterings of the structure of one's character are lost in old age, the basic character roots and the developmental issues that remain pertinent to the individual are thrust forward into center stage. It is not surprising that the grown children who have to deal with ancient parents in these situations make the mistake of failing to recognize the processes with which they are dealing. So many children responsible for their elderly parents deal with them as if they themselves were the children still and the parents were the parents they once were. They attempt to revise the parents' character in a way that they would have always wanted to revise it. In some ways, this represents filing a last complaint of childhood about the actual nature of one's parents. While some of these are residues of projective experiences, as often as not these are unintegrated pieces of recognition of the reality of parental character structure and are residues of an as yet uncompleted task of adolescence.

SUMMARY

In summary, then, the developmental model continues as a scaffolding that embodies the history, structure and dynamic process of each individual. An instance of clinical observation represents a coronal section through an ongoing continuum whose ingreaients have an invisible past, a confusing cross-section of present ingredients, and a hypothetical future. The model elaborated here is an attempt to integrate a knowledge of the past such that the cross-sectional present is comprehensible and the future can at least be postulated from its inputs. The model is a linear or saggital section which exists only in our mind's eye and is never seen clinically as such. It is made up of the myriads of cross-sectional views we obtain clinically and personally and represents a synthesis of clinical experience, life experience, and empathic processes. In essence, it is a graphic representation of a philsophy of these processes and is presented as a philosophy of normality as a continuing process. It is provided as an outgrowth of and a background for daily clinical work.

432   *Child Development in Normality and Psychopathology*

REFERENCES

1. Bibring, E.: Contribution to the symposium on the theory of therapeutic results of psychoanalysis. *Int. J. Psychoanal.*, 18, 1937.
2. Blos, P.: *On Adolescence.* New York: The Free Press, 1962.
3. Erikson, E.: Identity and the life cycle: Selected papers. In *Psychological Issues.* Vol. 1. New York: International Universities Press, 1959.
4. Fairbairn, W.R.: *An Object-Relations Theory of the Personality.* New York: Basic Books, 1954.
5. Freud, A.: The concept of developmental lines. In *Normality and Pathology in Childhood.* New York: International Universities Press, 1965, pp. 62-92.
6. Freud, S. (1895): Project for a scientific psychology. *Standard Edition*, Sect. 16., Vol. 1, pp. 327-331, London: Hogarth.
7. Freud, S. (1905): Three essays on the theory of sexuality. *Standard Edition*, Vol. 7, pp. 125-243.
8. Freud, S. (1911): Two principles of mental functioning. *Standard Edition*, Vol. 12, p. 219 and Footnote 4.
9. Freud, S. (1924): The dissolution of the oedipus complex. *Standard Edition*, Vol. 19, pp. 173-182.
10. Freud, S. (1931): Female sexuality. *Standard Edition*, Vol. 21, pp. 223-243.
11. Freud, S. (1940): An outline of psychoanalysis. *Standard Edition*, Vol. 23, pp. 188-189.
12. Jacobson, E.: *The Self and the Object World.* New York: International Universities Press, 1964.
13. Klein, M.: *Contributions to Psycho-Analysis.* London: Hogarth Press, 1948.
14. Kohut, H. *The Restoration of the Self.* New York: International Universities Press, 1977.
15. Korner, A.F.: Some hypotheses on the role of the congenital activity types in personality development. *Psychoanalytic Study of the Child*, 19:58-72, 1964. New York: International Universities Press.
16. Modell, A.: *Object Love and Reality.* New York: International Universities Press, 1968.
17. Nagera, H.: Early childhood disturbances, the infantile neurosis and the adulthood disturbances: Problems of a developmental psychoanalytical psychology. *Monograph Series of the Psychoanalytic Study of the Child*, No. 2. New York: International Universities Press, Ch. 4 p. 41-47, 1966.
18. Pulaski, M.A.: *Understanding Piaget: An Introduction to Children's Cognitive Development.* New York: Harper and Row, 1971.
19. Rapaport, D.: The theory of ego autonomy: A generalization. *Bull. Menninger Clinic*, 22: 13-35, 1958.
20. Rapaport, D.: A historical survey of psychoanalytic ego psychology. In G.S. Klein (Ed.) *Psychological Issues*, Vol. 1, No. 1 pp. 8-17. New York: International Universities Press, 1959.
21. Rochlin, G.: *Man's Aggression: The Defense of the Self.* Boston: Gambit, 1973.
22. Segal, H.: *Introduction to the Work of Melanie Klein.* New York: Basic Books, 1964, Ch. 3, pp. 26-40.
23. Waelder, R.: Some Reflections on the Role and the Manifestations of Narcissism in Ordinary Life and in Psychopathology. Presented at Boston Psychoanalytic Society and Institute Scientific Meeting, April 21, 1962.

14

The Assessment of Emotional Maturity in the Young Child—A Guide to Maturation and Development

BRUCE HAUPTMAN, M.D.

INTRODUCTION

Purpose of Assessment of Emotional Maturity

The assessment of the emotional maturity of a young child is done for the same reasons as the assessment of physical maturity, i.e., to see how the child is getting on. Is the child generally well and fit for what we as parents, educators, and professionals see in store for him as he grows up and moves through school, trades, vocations, professions, relationships, or, is there an impediment in the way, a block in the child's path, which precludes or impairs the child's getting on with life?

If we can agree on the existence of a block or obstacle, and if we possess the tools and techniques for diagnosing the block, then we must account for why the child is the way he is at the present time, at this moment of our assessment. This is the major organizing principle behind our work. If we can agree that there is a block, and then diagnose or study it, and in the process account for why it exists, then and only then can we compose a rational plan of therapy. This is essentially no different from examining the child physically.

Let us say the child is bowlegged, and our sensitivity to that particular phenomenon is distorted. We may not notice it, or, we may notice it only in its most severe forms. Even at worst, we may shrug our collective shoulders and say "so what" for any number of reasons. If it hampers

433

the child, and it might if it is sufficiently severe, and if it is related to other physical factors which hamper life in general, we may study it at length and discover that it is related to vitamin D deficiency. As we begin to learn why the child is bowlegged, we can offer a rational course of action (milk fortified with vitamin D in this case), as a public health measure.

There are any number of examples, the most vivid of which are related to nutritional issues. I bring these to mind here because they form the overlap between the average child's physical and emotional well-being. One cannot study emotional maturity without constantly looking over one's shoulder at the physical child. (It works the other way too.) Major examples of those problems include severe emotional deprivation, protein deficiency states, and cretinism or thyroid dysfunction. The overlap between physical and emotional maturity in these conditions is well-known(2). Severely emotionally deprived children fail to thrive, often have periods of poor physical growth, as well as a plethora of emotional ailments(10,19,21). The process goes back and forth, telling us that the separation of physical and emotional events in young children is a difficult one.

Need to Assess Children at an Early Age

Emotional maturity needs to be assessed at an early age. Why not wait, as is the current general practice, until the child shows signs of failure in grade school or until he reaches adolescence? Perhaps because of what seems to be a greater difficulty in the identification of children in trouble at a young age (clinic statistics regarding incidence of children coming to clinics at various ages bear this out), relatively few preschool children are brought to psychiatric facilities (11). The number of children brought to psychiatric facilities rises rapidly by the time they have reached seven to eight years of age, although the problems have been with the children for years.

There seem to be a number of good reasons why earlier identification is better than later. For one, major decisions concerning the child's education are made at the very start of his/her schooling. Specialized programs have a greater chance of being effective if the child becomes involved at an early age, before he experiences major school failure and becomes totally disillusioned with school as a place of any value. Identification of children at risk at an early stage can lead to the prevention of more serious disorders later. This is seen with autistic(5), deaf(9) and blind children(4,8). A good question is whether all of our efforts might not be better spent studying infants. After all, if we are advocating the earlier the better, then why not? No doubt, there are disorders related to growth and development that must be diagnosed immediately after birth, although these are not, strictly speaking, disorders of emotional maturity. The physical/emotional separation which takes place with maturation is not strictly applicable here. One can talk of temperament in newborns or "syndrome of reactivity" but scarcely of emotional maturity and issues of adaptation and dysfunction. By six to eight months of age, however, delineation starts to be practicable. In the context of this work, overall emotional maturity will be considered at various ages. Emotional maturity will be regarded as an overall adaptive capacity of the individual child, in respect to the life situations he finds himself in, as well as the capacity to respond to new, expected, and unexpected stress.

Another major reason for early identification of problems in young children is related to the ease or lack of ease of remediation. An adult with a bent back may have to live with his crippled condition, although major surgery might give some relief. The younger person with problems of an incipient nature might be helped completely and with relative ease. Another example is in the early identification of either thyroid dysfunction or phenylketonuria. By diagnosing these problems at birth, or in the first year, much distress and suffering on the part of the individual and his/her family could be ameliorated or prevented. Later is too late.

In the study of emotional maturity, programs for working with very young children tend to yield more rapid, complete results. Parents' notions of who the child is are less fixed, and they are more responsive to treatment plans. When the child's difficulty constitutes a *basic lack* within the child, the earlier we can assist the child in recognizing the lack and compensating for it in some way, as with a prosthetic device, the more it becomes integrated into the child's general state of self.

In the overall assessment of emotional maturity of the child, I will take a wide range of areas into account and attempt to encompass substantial bodies of theoretical material. The clinical impression in working with young children is that there is by no means a *substantial* general theory of human development, which adequately describes the entire human condition, especially when one is dealing with the multi-potentialities inherent in human development. In fact, the focus of this work, for that reason, is geared heavily to issues of emotional maturity, i.e., *the complexity and organization of the self, as measured descriptively in a largely observational context of adaptation, and maladaptation or dysfunction.* It constitutes what appears to me to be a pragmatic rather than a theoretical approach.

In physical development, we possess enough knowledge that with relatively simple measures, done by a wide range of people, we can agree on which children are blocked in the process of physical growth, (i.e., where there is an impediment to the attainment of physical maturity). The assessment of emotional maturity is somewhat more complex. It too is done by a wide range of professionals, equipped with some knowledge of the various areas within which one can measure emotional maturity.

GENERAL CATEGORIES OF DYSFUNCTION

It is useful here to pose a very broad categorization of levels of maturation and dysfunction(25). These levels have a developmental cast, as the elements of the first seem earliest in date of onset, and the elements of the third and last assume a complexity of organization which must come later. Rather than seeing these three broad categories in any time sequence, it is, I believe, useful to see them as a means of organizing information and observations about the child. The major importance of these categories is, thus, as *organizers of information* and, by definition, they will dictate the work which must then be done to help the child overcome dysfunctional states, and improve its adaptive capacities.

Fundamental Lack or Incapacity

The first order of categorization involves maturational or developmental impediments that have as their basis *a fundamental lack or incapacity on the part of the child.* The child's basic equipment is lacking, damaged, or impaired, and the child for want of this machinery never had the opportunity to experience life in a more complete manner. The child does not understand us as we believe he should. This inability to understand is implied when we consider primary organic factors such as perceptual or integrative or manipulative defects. These defects can come in many areas, some as obvious as blindness, deafness, and primary defects in the communicative areas of the brain. Some elements that appear to fall in this category, such as language delays, often have complex processes involving both a fundamental lack or incapacity and attributes falling within other categories. The earliest states of severe deprivation can lead to growth failures mediated through the hypo-thalamus and anterior pituitary growth, affecting hormone production. When the child is placed in a supportive environment, the growth hor-mone level goes up, and the child experiences a physical growth spurt. In a similar manner, the child with a serious hearing impairment is greatly helped by a hearing aid.

A blind child, however, is unable to become sighted with a prosthesis. The normal development of locomotion, which is heavily dependent from the earliest on visual tracking, and then on reaching, and then on crawling and walking toward the object, does not ordinarily happen in blind children. The "prosthesis," if one may use that word in a different manner, is the special educative work involving moving the child's arms and body in the direction of a sound cue, to aid the integration of locomotion with sound, instead of sight, reaching for an object and ultimately locomotion(8). The blind child has a fundamental lack which hampers not just the obvious area (i.e., seeing), but also locomotion. For example, a child fails to develop speech. The child cannot verbally ex-press his/her desires, whether for obvious physical reasons related to the oral musculature, as in a super bulbar paralysis, or for some more mys-terious and as yet incompletely understood integrative brain processing problem. Language does not just communicate basic needs; it forms the basis for the development of the capacity for relationships. Assessment of the elements of the langauge disturbance will lead to possibilities for general improved communication and for improvement in relationships which, while not dependent on linguistic functions in a one-to-one way, are as interrelated as seeing and locomotion.

Examples of this sort are the rule rather than the exception and actually defy more than the most general classification. A defect in thyroid hormone, such as underproduction of the hormone, which is seen in many children in iodine-poor areas of the world, leads to a wide range of states of emotional responsiveness. Other factors in hypothy-roidism lead to actual defects in brain growth itself, possibly in the area of complexity of neuronal networks. The end results produce a range of dysfunctions, some fixed, permanent, in lack of actual central nervous system (CNS) function, some relative to general responsiveness, to the environment. Replacement of iodine or thyroid hormone has different effects depending on actual time of replacement. The more formed the nervous system is, the poorer the end result. Thus, the time of replace-ment is related to the overall effectiveness of the therapy(12). Fixed intellectual development, relatively fixed reactive patterns, and a range of accompanying disturbances play a part in taking an increasing toll on the child's overall emotional maturity. Thus, this very broad and general category of a fundamental lack or incapacity on the part of the child plays a critical role in the child's overall maturity.

Before proceeding on to the second of the three categories, a discussion of the term "maturity" would seem in order here. It was chosen in distinction to such terms as maturation and development for specific reasons. It carries with it "structural" implications, that is to say, factors which either are initially or gradually become, for a range of genetic, organic, internal or environmental reasons, over a period of time in a sequence related to the development within the central nervous system itself, fixed, unalterable (relatively or absolutely) and in themselves influence in major ways the way the individual will deal with the world in the future. Call it if you like a creation of systems of filters, a system of learned, but not unlearnable, responses. It is the creation of a way of viewing the world outside and the world inside which is peculiar to each individual. This reaches toward the maturity of each individual. The notion of structure implies a certain fixed frame of reference. It is generally unalterable, and it forms the basis of interaction and processing of events. Perhaps arbitrarily, one might consider the existence of several orders of structures. The ones described above are most rigid. There is virtually no experiential basis outside of the one in which the child is born. Let me clarify that. The child born blind has no more notion of what sight is than we can imagine what it would be like to be a fish or bird. One can approach the concept intellectually. One can simulate it (fly an airplane, "see" words through Braille, "hear" voices and music through vibratory sense), but the experience is limited and we do not operate as if they were there.

The greater the discrepancy between the particular child with his lack of basic capacities and the rest of the world, the more serious the potential for systematic distortion. I do not mean to imply that distortions are inevitable in children with these defects; rather, they develop more easily since the child must keep some account of his or her difference from the rest of the world. The problem is compounded by the difficulty that the outside world has in keeping some account of the damaged child. Examples of compounded problems are placing a child with a partial hearing loss in the back of the class, or treating a child with a primary language disturbance as if the child comprehends language on a level equal to other children of the same age. The factor being brought in here is the environmental one. A child with the sort of "flaws" described above will have a much more difficult time integrating experience (internal as well as external) than will an intact child. This difficulty is complicated by the well-described problem of being parents to such children. Parenting is geared to certain cues and expectations, the child's siblings, the parents' families, friends and neighbors' children. Through these factors one learns, at least in part, one's response to a child. There is no need here to get into the controversy about how much of mothering is instinctual and how much is learned. Neither one's instincts nor one's learning serves one well in dealing with these sorts of problems. The children described here are therefore either over- or under-cared for, i.e., the timing of acknowledgment of the children's needs is off for a range of reasons, and this compounds the child's already difficult time integrating experiences. The blind or retarded child deals with a mother who wishes to be free of her defective child or, through guilt, overindulges the child. The quality of parenting is also unreliable. I am not suggesting inevitable events, but rather predispositions to them, and events which have in clinical situations complicated the lives of such children and their families.

Because of the above, these children seem more at risk for the other two categories of disturbance—deprivation and neurotic conflict. Further, they are children who have a heightened chance, because of misperception and poor adaptation to reality, objectively perceived, to be considered to have varieties of psychotic disorders. A psychotic child with obsessional symptoms suggestive of additional neurotic or conflictual disorders of internal variety is primarily considered a psychotic child. The same child with an extremely rigid character style is also still seen as a psychotic child, and the character dysfunction is subsumed under the other, apparently more serious one. Children in this group form the major proportion of children considered seriously disturbed (atypical, autistic, psychotic, etc.). (As Chess has noted in her studies of rubella children, those children are at heightened risk for developing a wide range of severe and mild emotional disorders(6).

Deprivation Experience

Leaving children with basic impairments, the second group is as follows: Children whose basic disabling condition is seen as a result of deprivation experience. These children are fundamentally biologically intact. Their earliest experience was good. They had adequate parenting and achieved a state of early integration of self. They were capable of entering into a relationship at its earliest stages as basically whole or intact children, with competent enough care given. Their capacity to perceive and to integrate reality, and their motility and manipulation of external things were competent. However, there was (as Winnicott describes) an environmental failure which was too great and too rapid to be coped with. The timing, the extent and the manner of this failure, and the speed of its recovery, the adequacy or not of future mothering, are all factors affecting the severity of the child's disturbance. They all relate to the type of disturbance which may arise in the child, and the general manifestations it will take. The basis of the disturbance is linked to an early, too rapid, withdrawal of mothering. The child cannot cope or sustain the image or internalized notion of the maternal presence and, because of this failure, defenses arise which are precociously mature or distorted in their functioning.

When the primitive self needs to survive on its *own* without the maternal illusion supported by the frequent maternal presence(24), a second order of structures appears in the child. If the first order has its basis completely rooted in the biology of the individual, in the individual's primitive perceptual, integrating manipulative state, then the second order óf structures which gives a further sense of the concept of psychobiologic self, is rooted in the individual's survival as a person, a whole, functioning being, distinct from any other. Structural distortions that creep in here seem to have their genesis in the earliest relationships, and can be likened to, and perhaps are rudimentary forms of, character defenses or personality styles of later life. They determine the manner in which one individual can make use of another to further his or her own complexity and emotional maturity.

This process is akin to an "imprinting process." The individual has some awareness of a time when it was better taken care of. Winnicott describes some of these "adaptive styles," in reference to the development of false self. This process is also seen in reference to development of an obsessional style in early childhood in response to maternal depression, and the beginnings of an hysterical and an emotionally unstable style in response to particular forms of maternal withdrawal. Each of these "entities" ranges from what we consider "normal" emotional development to dysfunctional forms(15). At the pathological end of the spectrum we have full-blown delinquency, obsessional character disorders and as-if characters, as well as certain severe "borderline" states where the dysfunction of the self in an apparently normally endowed individual begins to approach the distorted innate perceptual capacities of the first group.

To repeat, this category of dysfunction occurs when an event—maternal illness, death of a parent, a protracted or poorly handled separation in a family with already shaky emotional resources—leads to the actuality of, *and* subjective perception of, a maternal withdrawal at a rate too great for the child's fragile, unstructured or malleable "ego." The capacity to trust blindly in the well-developed maternal "ego" is to some degree shattered. The form of the shattering and the return or not of that maternal ego will determine the form that the child's defensive organization will take and the extent to which the premature structuring will be organized.

The precocious or premature ego state comes at a price to the individual, a price which will be discussed at length. Worse examples of this process are seen when antisocial tendencies develop into delinquency. The precocious ghetto preschooler who goes through dangerous streets to shop for his mother and navigates his way home, by mid-adulthood rarely ventures much further afield, confined to his ghetto habitat by fears and enormously rigid, precociously conceived character defenses. From these two categories come the vast majority of children whom we see, who present as being ill to schools and social institutions.

Conflict Within Child

Assuming that the child has an adequate endowment and is adequately looked after, the developing personality becomes increasingly complex. As the child moves from dyadic to triadic relationships, various internalizations take place which do not easily blend with others. Just as one sees warring between members of a child's family, the warring can take place within the child as his models collide in their prohibitions and license for instinctual gratification. The "conflict" is *within* the child himself, independent of the real world. These "neuroses" have their roots in the earliest points of stress to the child(18), points which were experienced, but bridged for the moment. When new crises arise in the child's life, the foundations of these bridges are shaken, and the child experiences distress as though from an earlier time. This is not the massive form of anxiety or distress that forces the development of precocious defenses. To some extent, as in early, brief separations, the symptomatic distress leads the child on the route to forming new supporting relationships outside the family. This would be at the normal end of the continuum. At the pathologic end, the anxiety or distress is so severe that self-recovery is not a feature and a new order of structuring takes place—the development of a neurotic defense, a symptom, which serves as a higher level developmental block because it deters the process of evolution of emotional maturity, a process which seems dependent on continuity of relationships, initially inside the family, but then outside with other adults and peers of both sexes. This third order structure, the neurotic symptom or defense, therefore also colors the individual's assimilation and interaction with the inside and outside world. A depressed affect could be confused with hunger, leading to overeating or anorexia. A subtle, unintended environmental signal from another person could be taken to alert the child to danger, precluding or limiting the relationship and further growth.

Implications for Treatment

As was previously stated, for each individual child, these groupings overlap different orders of structuring, complicate the diagnostic picture, and often confuse attempts at therapy. Treatment of the first category, which Winnicott calls "privation," is essentially substitutive. One must try to make up for that which is not there, or at least provide a physical environment which will not further compromise the child. The child needs to be educated with his or her lacks in mind, via enrichment programs which compensate for what is absent. In the second group, where there has been maternal failure, maternal replacement or its counterpart is in order. Often in children described as seriously ill, both categories overlap, and provision of both elements is essential to the child's development of self. Psychotherapy is the choice for the third category, for it is through the psychotherapeutic relationship that the child's conflicts can be explored and some chance exists for altering these third order structures.

It is important to keep in mind that these broad categorizations do not imply diagnosis. They deal with forms of predisposition or risk. Diagnosis, as currently used, usually suggests *intensity* of illness. An adjustment reaction of childhood is less of a manifest disturbance than a neurosis or psychosis. Current nosologies deal in terms of intensity and intransigence of illness. The categorizations described above are broad groupings with etiologic bases. Obviously, the greater the perceptual-cognitive impairment, the greater the predisposition to disturbance. The greater the maternal factor, the greater the predisposition to compromise of emotional maturity based on factors related to integration of self in the context of a facilitating environment. It is important to remember that work with the child must include attention to each area, since treatment for each is different— with different intentions and, it is hoped, different results.

The issue of multiple factors in the development of the child is strongly stated here. A child usually experiences dysfunction because of an accumulation of factors rather than just one. An ulcer or colitis develops because of stress, plus a physiologic weakness in the organ due to genetically-linked enzyme disturbance. The stress may be there today and not yesterday because a particular teacher presents work which the child has always found difficult but tolerable with a different sort of teacher and the child is experiencing distress at home because a sibling is dealing with a new developmental task and mother is preoccupied—and so it goes.

The above groupings suggest a means of accounting for and organizing why the child is the way he is now. They set the stage for organization of treatment plans. In practice, diagnosis seems to be of little general use in suggesting treatment plans. This is most obvious in two respects. When one surveys clinics treating children, one finds psychotherapy clinics whose therapists see children a few times and counsel parents, clinics that do long-term psychotherapy, clinics that work with entire families with relatively little attention to the child, behaviorist clinics, clinics that deal with educational failure, clinics that prescribe drugs as their major mode of work, and clinics that work with children primarily in groups. Each clinic espouses a standard approach to everyone and has a great deal of difficulty in offering a child or family anything but the standard clinic fare. (See A. Freud (8a) on "separation clinics," etc.)

A more glaring example of this comes from my own experience consulting to a school which works with the most seriously dysfunctional or defective children. At this particular school, I began to study the records of each child. As one might expect, most of these children had been seen at multiple institutions for elaborate examinations of all sorts. Diagnostic labels had been given to each child at various points in his life as a result of one of these examinations (which were often so extensive as to necessitate placement in a hospital for days or weeks to facilitate the exam). I became aware that the label the child had been given did not correspond to any clinical set of phenomena, but was most strongly correlated with the institution which had done the examination, There was an insitution for autistic children, another for schizophrenic children, another diagnosed retardation; "cerebral encephalopathy—etiology unknown," aphasia, and atypical child were the labels in other institutions. Here was a group of children very ill indeed by almost any standard—no debate over that—yet there was such wide discord in diagnosis. Further, without doubt, each diagnostic label carried with it strong etiologic connotations, as well as implied therapeutic regimens which were to affect the child and family for years. After a while, I could look at the label and predict not the child's symptomatology or the cause of the child's dysfunction, but the institutions at which the child had been seen. Listening to debates among experienced clinicians on lesser ailments of childhood and how to diagnose them can become even more confusing, although the clinical accounts of the child's ailments are remarkably consistent, in terms of collection of historical data and description of the behavior in the office. Diagnosis should be revealing of etiology and anticipate and proffer treatment; however, this is generally not now the case with emotional disorders of childhood.

We now move from the problem of classification to the next step which is the rationale behind this approach to assessing the emotional maturity in young children, that is to say, an approach focusing on emotional maturity as judged by the capacity for adaptation.

Problems in Assessment of Young Children

The problems of evaluating emotional maturity in young children are considerable. As with any form of preventive medicine, one wishes to seek out and deal with those factors which in later life will present the individual with overwhelming burdens and hardships in the form of emotional crippling. Emotional crippling can mean "neurotic" symptoms such as fears, depressions, anxieties, psychosomatic symptoms, limitations implicit in the term character disorder, or psychoses of various sorts. From the standpoint of the individual, careful assessment is essential. From the standpoint of society in general, it is imperative because, as with physical illness, the constrictions of emotional illness afflict not just the immediate sufferer, but those around him as well.

Numerous attempts have been made to study the roots of various forms of mental illness, i.e., to study its epidemiology[20]. In terms of the amount of effort, the actual results have been rather small. This is true even when one surveys quite diverse fields of endeavor. One can study young children and begin to make actuarial predictions, i.e., statistically valid but not inevitable predictions on extremes in intelligence, the course of observable infantile autism and childhood psychosis, certain temperamental characteristics, certain biochemical defects, and severe states of emotional deprivation. An example of predictability concerns the group of seriously deprived, institutionalized children. It is in this group that we seem to anticipate our group of sociopaths and delinquents. These are the lessons learned from such diverse fields as linguistics, ethology, anthropology, psychometrics, experimental psychology, biochemistry, psychoanalysis, genetics, epistemology, and from the relatively new series of longitudinal studies which have grown up alongside child psychiatry.

The biochemists have been immensely helpful when they isolate rare specific enzyme defects, or when they explore endocrine disorders and relate the developmental aspects of thyroid chemistry to explain which children are susceptible and how the susceptibility varies. When they move into explanations for autism or serious emotional disturbances in children on the basis of a vitamin deficiency, they move away from the firm base of the narrowly defined, neatly circumscribed syndromes. If children with thyroid deficiencies have serious emotional ailments, that does not mean that children with serious emotional ailments have thyroid disease (logical fallacy). The same sort of thing is seen in genetics, where geneticists are able to show fragmented or reduplicated genes in chromosomes in Down's syndrome and several rare clinical syndromes. They then move into areas such as schizophrenia and manic depressive illnesses, character disorders, and homosexuality—and attempt to explain *all* on the basis of the genetic model.

Clinical pathologists attempt to explain behavior on the basis of defects in rare minerals such as lead. Certainly, there is a relationship in certain children between heightened levels of lead in the blood and tissues and certain behavioral abnormalities. In other cases, an increase or decrease of minerals (e.g., copper) has been found responsible for delirious and demented states. Hyperactivity, a familiar label these days, has been seen at times as related to certain post-encephalitic states, also believed related to food additives; does that explain most of the etiology of disturbance of the large numbers of children who are restless and "overactive"? Very unlikely. Other disturbances in emotional maturity have been found to be related to various endocrine dysfunctional states such as adrenal corticosteroid, or thyroid, or anterior pituitary (growth hormone) malfunctions. However, the pituitary gland scarcely explains a fraction of emotional disturbances or dysfunctions.

Each explanation is inadequate, but as we begin to piece together information from these many fields of endeavor, we see multiple causes, or multiple possible etiologies, for what may look quite similar clinically at first glance. In fields of endeavor which have as their principal interest the study of mental dysfunction, we find similar phenomena. From divergent schools of psychoanalysis, dynamic formulations are offered in the study and intensive exploration of individual cases. In terms of those individual cases, the formulations may offer both an approximation of the dynamics of the disturbance and a rational basis for treatment. Of course, different analytic schools have different explanations for what appear to be similar clinical events. There seem to be specific cases which fit better with one or another school of thought. As a specific formulation is extended from a single case or small group of cases to larger groups and entire cultures, i.e., as it moves from the specific to the general, it suffers from the same faults and fallacies as do logical arguments in general which move in that direction, i.e., acute logical failure. The formulations or explanations begin to sound increasingly forced and hollow, the scientific basis for them, when and if it was there in the beginning, begins to be lost, and often what is obscured is the fact that the theory was *very useful* in explaining a few cases and did in fact offer very compelling clues to etiology and therapy.

What is the nature of the problems that increasingly seem inherent in studying the assessment of emotional maturity in children? Each of the varied disciplines mentioned above has defined its field along very specific lines (biological, physical, chemical, etc.). This is true, in different ways, with each developmental or analytic school of thought. One defines normality and abnormality in terms of the discrepancy which appears in the tests devised to define and identify normality and abnormality of a given system of thought. Hence, lead toxicity leads to emotional disturbance. Lead toxicity is defined in terms of abnormal blood lead levels. Emotional disturbance is thus deemed more likely with elevated levels of lead in the blood. Another example: A child is very motorically active. The level of the child's motor activity and restlessness becomes equated with emotional disturbance; the more active the child is, the greater must be the child's emotional problems.

These examples are perhaps simplistic; yet the same tautologic reasoning is apparent in the analysis of each of the predominant systems of thought. This process is particularly evident in longitudinal studies. The misfortune of such studies is that they each enter into a study of the human condition on the basis of narrowly-defined ideas about development and then attempt to draw increasingly complex hypotheses and formulations on increasingly slender points of observation which take place in the study, in respect to the theoretical underpinnings of the study and the observations permitted within the structures of the theories underlying the studies. The results of the studies would hence be obvious. Manifestly disturbed children were identified, and could be identifiable through the criteria of the most diverse studies. They stood head and shoulders above the theoretical bias of each study. As Michael Rutter and others point out, seriously deprived small children ended up at high risk for delinquency(20). The autistic children end up at high risk for institutionalization(14). But what of the vast majority? We should pursue the problems inherent in studies of this sort.

The Nature of the Development of the Self

We seem, then, in the assessment of the emotional maturity of the young child to be studying *the nature of the development of the self* or the nature of character formation. This statement should then throw many other factors into a general context. Factors such as perception, cognition, object relations, language, thought, play, education, social, emotional and physical development *all enter in and cluster around the central focus of the development of the self, the issue of emotional maturity, which is measured and assessed here, section by section, in its adaptive capacities—ultimately, we are concerned with the child's capacity for adaptation and secondarily with the family's and society's capacities for adaptation.*

At this point, I will examine a wide range of factors, in the child and the mothering person, as well as in various other members of the family and the outside world, as they relate to the child's development. I will demonstrate how a study of these factors explains or answers the question of *why the child is the way he or she is at this time.* We will study the interplay of these factors and how they seem to influence or distort the developmental process—ultimately, how these factors are subsumed by or seem to measure the child's capacity to adapt to his life situation.

I will initially present the factors organized in two broad categories: first, descriptive factors; then, observational ones. The first are gained largely through history, taken from people close to the child. The next comes through direct observation and work with the child, including actual observation of the child alone, with mother, with strangers, with other children, at home, and in school, over a given period of time. The period of time varies, depending on the ease with which the basic question of accounting for *why the child is the way he is now* is answered. It can take a brief period of history-taking and observation in some, or, when the factors are highly complex or mysteriously concealed, literally months of intensive work. The following is an attempt, on the basis of current accumulated knowledge, to focus on what seem to be the significant factors contributing to the child's *adaptability, his/her developmental progress*, or lack of it, or potential for it, all subsumed under the broad general label of *the child's emotional maturity*. With a focusing of this knowledge, keeping account of some of the problems and historical conflicts discussed above, it seems possible to describe, assess and anticipate a variety of disturbances, some inevitable and some hinging on predictable and at times not always foreseeable circumstances. On the basis of the assessments, it also seems possible, keeping in mind the etiologic framework broadly presented before, to offer a rational basis for work with a child, and in a fairly quantitative way to keep track of the child's progress, and ultimately reevaluate the treatment given. Was it proper and sufficient, or useless? On the basis of the efficacy or failure of treatment, we can support or invalidate the constructed hypothesis regarding the child's emotional maturity?

The procedure suggested here is one which should lend itself to a step-by-step assessment of the young child. When material is not available at any given juncture, then one must account for its lack. Often the unavailability of material in a particular area helps provide clues as to the child's difficulties. The basic work may involve a search or exploration for that bit of information, as a microbiologist or chemist seeks to find the bacteria or enzyme defect, which will finally explain why the child is ailing and suggest a cure. For certain children, sections may seem unnecessary, where meticulous attention seems warranted in other cases. One should be able to account for why there is a particular interest in one section or a lack of need for another section. The guide starts off with a section of general questions regarding the identification of the particular child, and a statement of initial concerns regarding the child.

I. GENERAL INFORMATION FOR IDENTIFICATION PURPOSES

A. Child

Name, sex, age and birthdate, natural or adopted, (twin).
Size of child in relation to age (height, weight, head circumference).
Child's dress.
Gross physical disabilities (obvious handicaps and deformities, clumsiness, gait, hearing, speech and vision).
Significant medical or psychiatric illnesses identified to date.

Statement of initial general concerns about the child in the following categories:

1) *emotional* (erratic, labile mood, restlessness, irritability, relatedness, anxiety, fearfulness, overabundant sadness or affection, difficulty concentrating);

2) *social* (capacity for relationships, disturbance between individual and his or her environment, with distortion in attention to environmental factors, i.e., too preoccupied or oblivious);

3) *intellectual* (general alertness and capacity to grasp thoughts and ideas, distortions in thought, child is precociously "adept" at intellectual things, or dull, or frankly retarded);

4) *educational* (capacity to be taught, level of schooling, level of enrichment, child is too involved in educational process or not educable);

5) *physical* (general size and stature, illnesses, handicaps, physical peculiarities);

6) *language* (peculiarities of language, precocities, lags, idiosyncrasies).

Note that these categories are by no means "pure"; they overlap. It is in this overlap between categorizations that one begins to learn the primary, or multiple, determinants of a specific problem. The need to review this categorization recurs in each section, with the aim of an increasingly sophisticated appreciation of the nature of the concerns about the child being made at each step.

B. Parents

Name, age, occupation, education, natural or adopted, (twin).
Initial appearance (dress, manner).
Significant medical or psychiatric illnesses.
General cultural factors (e.g., country of origin).

C. Other children

Name, sex, age.
Medical or psychiatric illnesses.
Education.

D. Additional members of the household or significant relatives

Name, age, occupation.

Relationship to child.

Significant medical or psychiatric illness (significant people who have died in the course of the child's lifetime should be included in this category).

Significant pets.

E. Grandparents (when not included as part of household)

Age, general health.

Occupation and education.

Availability to child and parents (e.g., babysitter, lives far away, doesn't have anything to do with child or parent).

II. HISTORICAL INFORMATION

A. The Inception of the Child

1) Prenatal Attitudes

This section deals with circumstances surrounding the conception and birth of the child. Was the child wanted, planned, accidental? How long was the mother pregnant before realizing it? Was an abortion contemplated or planned? What were the grandparents' attitudes to the pregnancy? What was the father's position? In addition to these fairly specific questions, one should also account for such things as prenatal care, how the mother felt during pregnancy, sex of the child wished for, as well as accidents, injuries and illness during each trimester. (List actual illness, especially maternal hypertension, bleeding, toxemia during pregnancy, drugs taken, actual length of pregnancy.) Also take note of serious emotional upheavals during pregnancy. If pertinent, compare the pregnancy with this child with other pregnancies as to ease, comfort, activity of fetus. Is mother currently pregnant again or planning another pregnancy?

2) Perinatal Disturbance

This section treats the period of time around the birth of the child as a particularly critical one. Note particular family conflicts at that time, including marital conflicts, economic distress, problems with the extended family (especially siblings and grandparents). (Describe the birth of the child in physical and emotional terms: difficulties in labor, birth weight, number of days mother and child remained in the hospital, help available to mother after leaving hospital, fetal distress if noted especially in labor and immediately post-delivery.) What was mother's reaction to her new infant? What was her interest in him or her both in the hospital and once home? How did grandparents and father fit into this picture? How soon after mother returned home did she feel fit to take on the care of the child? Was there a change in her general emotional state from before delivery to after the baby was born? Was she particularly elated or depressed? Could she function with her new charge? These are all factors which will set a general stage for the environment into which the child is born. They are also factors which affect the child at a point prior to child's having any previous experience with the world; some of the factors are physical ones, others are critical caretaking ones, but all are there at the beginning and therefore experienced by the child as basic givens. In this section, note any particular concerns that mother, family members, or physicians had regarding peculiarities of the baby (specific defects, handicaps, illnesses), and mother's response to the peculiarities.

3) Early Infant Behavior

Ask the parents, as much as possible, the temperament of the new child during his/her earliest days. What characterized this newborn as special or different from any other baby? All babies are far from alike and all have certain qualities recognized by those closest to them as unique, even prior to extensive handling or possible environmental intrusion. Note, in particular, patterns of feeding, toileting, and sleep(7). How easy was it for the infant to establish convenient schedules? How generally active was the newborn? How adaptable was he to change; what was his response to external stimuli and internal distress (such as fatigue and hunger? Was he easily distracted; did he persist at something (such as feeding) or did the child need to be constantly reminded that he was feeding? Did the child startle easily, respond intensely to any sound, cry all the time, never seem comforted, or was this a placid, inert baby who needed to be stimulated, whom mother aroused to feed and play with? Was the infant accommodating, did he change his earliest "habits" (especially sleep) to those of the civilized world or did he persist in a fixed and unchanging manner in spite of attempts to modify his day to fit in with everyone else's? (Of course, the parent's "style" of living is a factor here, too; certainly more rigid parents will have greater need of flexibility in their infant and perhaps make greater demands on the child's "adaptability.") Was the child easily comforted or was his general irritability and reactivity so great that almost nothing quieted or satisfied him?

B. The Development of the Child

In this general section, we will focus on the history of the child. At various general times, we should account for the increasing complexity and organization of the child in a number of areas in an orderly manner, so that quirks or idiosyncrasies in the child's life course can be delineated further and specific failures or retrogressions will become obvious. Note that this is an historical account, and not meant to fully describe a peculiarity as it exists now. That will come later as particular issues are elaborated in terms of the child as he or she appears now, and how he or she has adapted to life as he or she stands in the present.

1) *Infancy*

(a) *physical growth and maturation,* including height, weight, and head circumference, and especially, periods of lack of change in these factors, or actual weight loss.

(b) *illness:* frequency, severity, hospitalizations (length of, and reason for), injuries, accidents. In particular, note respiratory, gastrointestinal, and dermatologic problems, and seizures or "spells" of various sorts.

(c) *sleep:* What are the child's general sleep patterns, length of time of sleep, and changes in sleep habits? Has there been some alteration of sleep patterns described in the section on early infant behavior?

(d) *feeding:* Describe feeding habits, breast or bottle feeding, weaning, food idiosyncrasies, reaction to solid foods, particular bowel problems. Response to any effort at training, if any, by this time.

(e) *social:* Milestones in respect to communication and contact with others. This should include onset of smiling, reaction to being held, earliest interest in parts of himself such as thumb or fingers, hair, genitals, and parts of the outside world such as pillow, blanket, hard or soft familiar toy to be comforted by or played with, bottle, pacifier (transitional phenomena—Winnicott(24)). What were the infant's reactions to parents, siblings, familiar people and strangers? At what point did the infant discriminate mother from others; at what point did the infant become upset at being left with a stranger?

In this part, one should particularly note hyperalertness, differential responsiveness to different people, placidity and unresponsiveness. The notation of these responses also continues from the section on early infant behavior, only now the infant has had a chance to experience his environment and to be affected by it. In general, one should account for the infant's general interest in his environment, his periods of playfulness, and the rudiments of a sense of who the child is, which should appear increasingly through this first year of life in response to himself and to his surroundings. The actual period of time under discussion should be through approximately 18 months. The term "infancy" literally means "no speech," and is followed by another general period of accelerated language acquisition which, while having roots in "infancy," flourishes in the "toddler" period here defined arbitrarily as 18 to 36 months. The toddler period, as that term applies, also carries with it accelerated locomotion maturation (which also has roots in infancy).

2)*Toddler*

  (a) *general physical health:* Include accidents, injuries, specific illnesses, hospitalizations if these have occurred, the child's general response to them. As above, note the developing child's size and weight gain in respect to other children his age and in the particular family. Illnesses include chronic physical symptoms.

  (b) *development of motor skills:* At what age did the child walk, skip, run? Can the child manipulate small objects easily; is the child physically adept both in terms of gross movements and fine manipulation? Is there a sense of handedness yet? Have there been periods of time of backslide in motor development, for example, did the child for any period of time lose an acquired skill or ability? Is the child accident-prone?

  (c) *sense of self:* Is the child generally cautious or fearless? Is there a difference when the child is aware that adults, especially mother, are watching? Does the child overextend his abilities to get into trouble or actual danger?

  (d) *social development:* Does the child play with other children? How does the child react to strangers, to mother's leaving and returning? In general, can you characterize the toddler's reaction to separations?

  (e) *sleep patterns:* Where and with whom does the child sleep? Have there been periods of sleep difficulties, wanting to sleep with parents, nightmares? Is the difficulty in response to any external event?

  (f) *feeding patterns:*Has there been a progression in the toddler's food preference, an increase in variety, willingness to try new food? How rigid is the child in this regard? Have there been overt feeding problems in terms of eating too much or too little?

(g) *toileting:* Is the child bowel and bladder trained? Can you characterize the experience in terms of ease, difficulty, completeness, regressions?

(h) *special problems:* Has the child developed specific fears or behaviors that the parents find disturbing? What are they? Can you account for their development?

(i) *general adaptability:* One should begin to account here for how the child is getting on with the imposed tasks of life; dealing with a change in the intensity of mother's interest, with new people, such as peers, strangers, babysitters, other family members; the development of relationships with older, and possibly, younger siblings. The discussion which started in reference to these issues in early infant behavior should increasingly be carried on—to account for the impact of environmental factors on the child and the child's interest in and capacity to adapt to his or her environment, in order to increase his or her range of experience and interests and his or her knowledge. Note the waxing and waning of various "temperament" characteristics. Have any family crises occurred in this time span? How has the child coped? We should see possibilities of the development of early specific disturbances, in the form of behavioral aberrations, fears, excess activity, restlessness, excess placidity and/or withdrawal, and very specific behavior reactions. We should also begin to see an emergent "style" of coping, both with instinctual needs and with external events and crises. The child's emergent "personality," in terms of how we could predictably expect the child to handle himself or others in a particular crisis, becomes increasingly marked. How utilitarian that style of coping is and how well or poorly it serves the child as he moves through increasingly complex experiences, through situations where the child is increasingly treated as an independent entity, begins to tell us about what we have termed emotional maturity, the capacity to take on life experiences in a way which facilitates integration and development of the self, in respect to both the individual's basic instinctual needs and the facts and vicissitudes of the outside world.

(j) *communicative ability:* Does the child understand and is the child understood? Is language proceeding in a way that we see with other toddlers? This particular area will be dealt with separately and at length later.

(k) *play:* Does the child have some rudiments of the ability to play? Are toys used in an organized way to express the child's interests? Are they used as parts of communication with others, especially other children? Elaborate in terms of particular types of play, noting that the roots of this ability are seen in infancy, with the child's interest in earlier possessions and the beginning use of these possessions to master anxiety-producing situations, such as separations. Note things such as scribbling, drawing, use of dolls, fantasy in play. Note also play with self in front of a mirror and awareness of parts of self. In this section, note basic interests of child expressed through play or communication (verbal, etc.) in terms of fantasy. This would include play themes, dreams, nightmares, and interest in specific stories which the child might tell or wish to be told. Try to include interest in themes of specific fears, wishes, concerns about sexuality, bodily integrity, death, themes relating to the child's evolving self-experience and perception.

3) *Preschool Child (three to six years of age)*

Critical issues for the preschool child are as follows: To some extent, the child is assumed to have achieved some control or mastery over his basic instinctual needs. The preschool child can manage his basic needs, feed himself, and toilet himself, with occasional help. The basic questions have to do with the child's beginning ability to move from a primary maternal person and with the vicissitudes of relationships in the outside world. Is the child prepared to share things with other people? Can the child acknowledge that people in the world have interests which do not include the child, i.e., the beginning of movement from dyadic to triadic relationships? Starting early in the toddler period (or before), there is a recognition that other members of the family have relationships with each other that do not include the child. This now moves to the outside world. The child plays with other children and needs to experience and accept that the other children at a given moment may not want to include him or her. The child needs the teacher and at that moment the teacher is occupied with someone else. How urgent is the child's need? Can the child begin to accept the teacher's word that the child does not appear to be in danger and can wait for just a moment until the teacher has finished up with something? Does the child have some capacity to be alone? I do not mean here the sort of child who has never developed the capacity to be with another person, who has never clearly separated from its mother, who is, in fact, too frightened to do so and thus builds huge walls to keep everybody away and is always alone, but the child who has had a reasonable earliest relationship, has a sense of himself as a separate individual, and at times can and likes to be by himself as a separate individual to learn and explore. Does the child seem to be able to be involved with other children in his fantasy life and tolerate their needs too? The basic question here is how the earlier structures (incorporations or identification if you like) have prepared the child for the increasing complexity of life as he moves increasingly away from the mother, into increasingly complex cognitive, social and emotional issues, into an increasing plethora of relationships of different sorts with both sexual and aggressive aspects. A particular point of reference here is how the child copes with the beginnings of school(13). The child's response to these new stresses should be noted. The parents' ability to respond to their changing child and the child's new needs should be noted, in terms of their ability to give the child support in this developmental step.

(a) *development of language and communication:* Have these closely related factors progressed in some orderly fashion now that the child is increasingly away from mother, or has there been a cessation in change, a lack of further development, or actual regression indicating the child's lack of preparation for the next step?

(b) *eating and toileting habits:* Here too, the emphasis is on orderly progression toward independence or behavior that reflects a block.

(c) *physical health:* Height, weight, specific illnesses, accidents, and injuries should be described here, as well as special events such as prolonged separations and/or hospitalizations.

(d) *development of symptoms or behavioral disturbance:* Do the parents or teachers or day care workers note specific fears, sleep disturbances, or behavioral problems, or other "symptoms"? These could be characterized by increased fighting and negativism or increased compliance and lack of self-assertion. Now that the child is in groups, is there a profound difference between how the child is in a group and how the child is alone or with one other person? Is the child particularly impulsive or destructive?

(e) *social skills:* Characterize in general the child's ability to develop relationships with people other than parents, such as peers, teachers, and strangers. Does the child prefer older or younger children or even adults to peers? What is the preference in terms of sex of peers and adults?

(f) *child's play habits:* How does play serve the child—as an expression of fantasy, as a means of communication? What is the nature of the child's fantasy preoccupations at this point? Note, as before, the child's expression of fears and wishes regarding own body, others, death and sexuality, as well as attempts to master complex (abstract) notions or concepts. Also note issues present in dreaming as related by child, as well as interest in telling or being told specific stories. Capacity or interest in non-formed (art) materials and types of expression vs. use of formed toys in play should be noted.

(g) *intellectual development:* Begin to note the child's interest in and capacity to make use of that which later will be formally called school. Interest in and abilities to make use of pre-academic things should be noted. Do academic pursuits seem to be an escape from relationships? Do materials continue to be used as primary expressions of the child's fantasy, with disregard for their formal educative use? Try to note these in various pre-academic areas such as pre-reading interest and pre-math skills' acquisition. Is there some constriction in the child's ability to use these materials? Is the child preoccupied with other things all the time? Is the child fearful of exposing itself to possible failure? In this section, these issues are noted in terms of general development of interests and abilities or as notations of general blockages and failures and/or regressions, supporting a general notion of a child in some difficulty in dealing with his own basic needs or with the outside world.

(h) *environmental factors:* Mention should be made here as to whether the child's general environment is supporting his growth or in some manner impeding it. For example, is the mother confused about her role in letting go of the child at this point?

C. The Environmental Factor

1) Parental History

In this section, give an account of the life of the mothering person (the actual individual could be the mother, father, a relative or another person). Here we are specifically interested in an account of the mother's life, an account of her experience as a child within her family and her relationship with her parents. Often a conflict between parent and child in one generation is rekindled when the child reaches that stage of development which troubled the parent. A similar account of the father's experience with his family, assuming a traditional mother-child-father family unit, should be determined. An account might be given of what each parent thought of his/her own childhood, and what he or she sees as similarities and differences in his/her experience with the child.

Specific mention should be made of whether the parents had relatives (their own parents or siblings) who were psychiatrically or neurologically ill, with dyslexia, retardation or seizures. If there are two parents, can we characterize the status of the marriage? Does the child (or children) constitute a burden or aid to the family's stability? Does the child (or others in the family) threaten to tear it apart, or is this child uniquely responsible for the survival of the family unit? Can the parents characterize their ideas of child rearing in terms of permissiveness, restrictiveness, punishment and rewards? Do the parents (and grandparents) generally agree on the handling of the child?

2) *General Social Status*

Is this a nuclear or extended family? Are there significant friends involved? Is this a traditional family unit, a commune, a fragment of a family unit? Describe special cultural issues (e.g., Haitian, Puerto Rican, Irish, Indian). Who lives at home in the daytime, who takes care of the child, and who works? Describe pertinent racial or religious factors (e.g., reliance on a clergyman or medicine man, etc.) as well as socioeconomic status: poor, on welfare, higher or lower status than parents, i.e., upwardly or downwardly mobile. In general, this section should begin to develop a picture of the child's environment.

III. OBSERVATIONAL INFORMATION

A. *The Interaction of the Parent with the Observer (Teacher, Therapist, etc.)*

Characterize each parent's appearance in terms of appropriateness with respect to the format chosen for the interview (office, classroom, home, etc.). It is more useful if a standard or set interview is adhered to in order to provide a standard with which to view typical versus atypical behavior. An interview done at home will have certain attributes that an interview done at a school or hospital office will not, and the appropriateness of an individual action must be related to the context in which it occurs. Certain types of behavior will seem extraordinary in any setting and should be described as such. Is the parent open or guarded? Does she (he) tend to give a reasonable account of the child or reassure us that everything is, or was, fine or bad? Does the parent see specific problems in him/herself? Does the parent constantly compare herself with the child? Does he or she see him/herself as being emotionally ill; does he or she see problems in his/her past? Does the parent seem to be presenting as the one with the problems; does the child seem left out?

In summary, characterize the following: unusual behavior in respect to the parent's relating to you; unusual treatment regarding the child as the parent interacts with you.

B. Mother-Child Interaction

Can the child leave mother (or father) to play while mother speaks to the observer? Note the child's independence at this time. In effect, can the mother *allow* the child to play alone? This would be seen in an initial interview. It could be further observed at the beginning of school, over the first few weeks of the school year, and returning to school after each holiday. How easy is it for a child to leave mother and enter into an increasingly familiar situation? Can we see the child play alone in the presence of mother and in the context of mother being involved with the observer? Can the mother let the observer play with her child?

It is important to note here the time needed to secure the desired observations. Do we need one hour, a day, a series of interviews, or observations over the course of a year to secure the necessary information? The time needed will, no doubt, depend on the context within which the observations are taking place (school, day care, clinic, hospital). It is important to remember that a series of observations may be needed; if questions cannot be readily answered, one needs to explain why not, as a factor of the overall study of the child.

In the initial interview, what was the child's reaction to mother leaving the room and returning (with observer in the room with the child) and later, if possible, the child's reaction to being left alone(1)? These observations should be noted and considered in the context of a history of significant separations for the child (mother's illness, hospitalization, new baby, etc.). Also note the child's initial reaction to verbal and physical encounters by a stranger (observer). Does the child respond to movement, but not to speech?

A discussion of issues involved in separation will be noted here. The vicissitudes of what has been termed attachment behavior are related to a number of factors. Age, for example, is most important. In an initial interview, most three-year-olds would not tolerate mother's leaving the room, while most four-year-olds would, once assured of the general security of the situation. Culture is also important; certain foreign-born children behave differently from the norms for their age, and certain differences in child rearing practices seem consistent with this behavioral difference. In general, variations in attachment behavior form a bimodal curve or graph, i.e., the same behavior could have diametrically opposite roots in the mother-child relationship and should not in itself be considered a significant factor in isolation. Additional notes should be made here on the mother's actual handling of her child, e.g. her response to her child's crying, to special situations like putting toys away—if the observer asks the child to put toys away, does mother help or distance herself? A child may cling tenaciously to mother or may totally ignore mother; both extremes are noteworthy.

A discussion of the various types of problems implicit in the vicissitudes of the mother-child relationship follows. Mother's awareness of her own child's peculiarities and idiosyncrasies should be characterized as they are observed in an initial interview and throughout the course of subsequent contact in different settings. Discrepancies between the historical information (reported by the mother) and the observational data (what you saw) will begin to become apparent. Also increasingly apparent will be the mother's awareness or lack of awareness of her child through the vicissitudes of a series of predictable stresses. In general, it is important to note if mother appears to be stable and static or erratic and unstable. Also, is any noted instability temporary (as might be caused by a temporary illness or a death in the family) or permanent (evidence of an unstable individual or instability in a relatively chronic form caused by a maladaptive marital or family situation)? Or is the instability a result of the existence of this particular child and why? A very rough classification of these phenomena follows:

1) Is the mother in question generally aware of her child's needs and demands? Is she selective in gratifying them, i.e., can she set limits, does she have reasonable priorities?

2) Is the mother generally aware of the child's needs and does she always gratify them, i.e., she can't or doesn't let her child be frustrated or suffer distress?

3) Is mother erratic in her awareness or response to her child's needs and demands and is unable, therefore, to meet or gratify them, and thus appears highly arbitrary in her responses?

4) Is mother erratic in her awareness or responses to her child's needs and demands, i.e., sometimes aware and responsive, and sometimes arbitrary?

In each of these, is the behavior on the mother's part related to the particular developmental level of the child or to this particular child (versus others in the family), or is her response unrelated to a specific developmental level in her child (or to this particular "difficult" child versus her other ones), but somehow most related to mother's overall personality style (or personality disorder if such is the case)? Does mother generally comprehend what is going on or is she confused, or retarded, or preoccupied? Examples of permanent states of erratic mothering are seen in some cases of child abuse or when the mother has a schizoaffective or manic depressive illness. Temporary maladaptive behavior (from the child's viewpoint) could be the result of mourning a death in the family, the birth of a new child with concomitant postpartum reaction, or a serious acute physical illness. Temporary maladaptive behavior in an erratic or relatively constant form could be related to the mother's inability to deal with a specific developmental problem that her child is experiencing, as a result of her own inability to deal with this problem within herself (and perhaps *her own* mother's inability, etc.). If the mother's inability to deal with her child is temporary, once she and her child muddle through this problem, they can resume a more consistent mother-child interaction; if she turns the child over to someone else at that time, she should resume her maternal role at a later time.

At times we see a particular mother who is unable to handle a particular child. Note here that a mother with recurrent psychiatric or medical illness might at the time of her illness seem unable to function with her child. There must be a number of qualifying points here. For one, was the child him or herself in reality (or in the mother's fantasy) responsible for the mother's disturbance? Is another child or family member responsible? An example can be as follows: At the time of birth of the child, the mother suffers a serious loss of someone (a parent or close friend). The mother's loss and grief are inextricably bound up in the person of the new child, and her mothering of this child is strongly colored by her grief and management of the grief in its myriad forms. Is the mother capable and clever enough to comprehend the difficulty and fortunate enough to find a substitute to care for the child at the time of crisis? Also pertinent here is the issue of what part the child plays in the overall character structure of the parent (such as in incest, child abuse, and agoraphobia).

In general, then, can we describe mother's perception of her child—her delight and acceptance or her misery and rejection? Can we evaluate her ability to regress, empathize and identify with her child and still maintain her own identity as mother and parent? Can we describe the appropriateness of mother's interaction with her child and the effectiveness of her responses to the child as they impede or facilitate development? Or can we predict that, because of specific developmental problems in the mother or primary deficits or peculiarities of temperament in the child, that development will become skewed? Is the child a participant in his upbringing in a useful sense (or harmful, when there is a parent-child reversal around specific issues, or globally, i.e., the young child takes care of the parent in some major way)? Does the child develop a sense of being able to participate in or influence what happens to him or her, or is the child a passive partner, or is the child totally walled off? Does the child need to be exceptionally aware of his or her parents in order to survive, hence, developing precociously a sense of self that is distant from instinctual life and services an ill parent (a false self)?

C. Father-Child Interaction

Observations concerning the father should begin to explore issues in two areas:

1) Does the father facilitate or impede the development of the child's more aggressive needs? Does the father experience difficulties in setting limits for the child; does he over- or underreact when the child does things which could be construed as playful, provocative, risky or outright dangerous? Is there some permission for the child to explore and experiment with what must be seen as more aggressive and even destructive fantasies and wishes, in the context of a facilitating environment as constructed by the father in respect to the child's aggression?

2) The imposition of the father places the child in a triadic relationship. In observations of the family unit, can the child tolerate the parents' involvement with each other (or with the observer), which may exclude the child for bits of time? Does the child demand attention, provoke, or withdraw and isolate himself? Do parents respond to the child's particular behavior and in what way? Is the response consistent and supportive or does it lead to further confusion and chaos?

D. Observations of the Child

This section attempts to assess the child through specific observations of the child, i.e., through the eyes of the observer, who, although notably biased, has a basis for bias (or a system of bias) outside the world of the specific child, hence his or her own reference point. It is the position of this author that the individual observer's bias is preferred to the bias implicit in any one particular system of thought or philosophy, because it is more completely knowable and manageable by the observer. The observer's self-knowledge, thus, is the only "filter" that the observer needs to contend with; the filters of other people or systems can be, to a large extent, excluded, except so far as the observer has been educated in them. In this sense, one tends to rely most heavily on what one sees directly of the subject, and only secondarily on what one has been told (by the parents or other examiners). Thus, the issue of some ideal theoretical objectivity, implicit in the total adoption of a system of thought or complex theory, is in question when one is dealing with the complexities of an individual child.

The study of child observation is a complex one and, as a study itself, is beyond the scope of this work. One need only to say that the tradition is a substantial one, drawing on Darwin but excluding Freud, who did not observe children to a great degree (his grandson was an exception) in developing his theory of early development. More recent contributors to the field of child observation include Anna Freud and the Kleinians.

I will state a few points in reference to observation:

1) At this point the issue is the child, rather than self-aggrandizement or justification of some theory. Therefore, descriptions ought to minimize terminology which implies a theory or theoretical position.

2) If any standard must be set, and there must be one, it should be a descriptive one, preferably one which refers to other children in similar socioeconomic and cultural groups. That is not to say that an entire neighborhood or culture or country cannot run amok, or be peculiar in certain areas of child rearing or development, but at least that group serves as a point of departure from which to study deviation (in a positive or negative sense) and adaptability.

3) The observer ought to define his or her position in reference to the subject under observation; the observer must note his tools, his space and equipment, paraphernalia, and inclinations toward activity and passivity in any particular observation session. The time of day and length of session need to be noted. This is particularly important with younger children in respect to fatigue and restlessness and with older ones who are taken out of their habitat (school).

4) A system of observation needs to be adopted, especially in respect to recording information. The one suggested in this work implies a starting point external to the child (its environment), moving gradually inside to an actual description of the child himself, his gestures, movements and attempts at communication, and then his play and fantasy, which reveal his conceptions of himself and his instincts and overall integration of self.

A basic question here is: To what extent can one describe the child exclusive of the world around or using the environment as a means of reflection of the child, devoid of momentary contribution. This would seem to bring together the following bits and pieces: the state of the "psychosoma" (i.e., the relationship within the child of physical state and mind or psyche); more directly, the state of mind of the child, his capacity to think, organize, abstract and relate those thoughts and abstractions to him/herself and others in communication; the child's play and dream space (as the place where fantasy as expression of instinctual processes has an arena of expression, as well as a point of union with the objective world). Also included are the issues of the child's complexity and his overall capacity versus deviant, bizarre, preoccupation with internal problems or with his own state of cohesion. Self-monitoring functions should be noted in this section. In this regard, capacities to play and to dream are seen as signs of health and emotional maturity, in that they give evidence of potential for sustained and continued maturational flow and integration; also, this gets to the more basic issue of the relationship of the mind to these integrative processes in the overall development of self, i.e., those attributes of self which lead to growth, integration, and protection.

1) *Describe the Child*

(a) *Physical appearance:* The appearance of the child should be noted, starting with such gross observations as that of gross physical handicaps, mannerisms, gait, posture, and coordination, to increasingly finer detail of facial expression (fear, anxiety, grief, apathy, joy, sadness) and eye contact. Is the child's general activity level high or low; does your approach or withdrawal make a difference? Is there a difference between verbal and nonverbal approach to or withdrawal from the child? Does the child seem generally interested in the inanimate parts of the environment or in people (yourself)? Is the child active or passive in his interest? Does the child seem generally bright and alert or dull and listless? What is the complexity of the child's interests? Note, in particular, the child's facial expression in response to your interest, both physical and verbal.

(b) *Language:* Does the child seem to possess language? Does the child attempt to communicate? At what general level?

(c) *Social skills:* Is the child particularly sociable; does he seek you out eagerly, try to ignore you, run away, or is there a more complex process involving several distinct mechanisms, for example, at first the child moves away and then, when apparently trapped, the child seems to permit you to approach, but is now ignoring you in an almost oblivious fashion? Is the child's mood stable or does it fluctuate rapidly?

(d) *Ability to deal with people:* In a more complex way now, characterize the child's ability to deal with people, initially with you in an encounter, but later on in more complex and varied situations. Can the child differentiate people, for example, mother and teacher? Does the child see them as distinct people or is everyone treated in the same way? Can the child share adults with others, i.e., can the child tolerate the observer (teacher, for example) turning to another child? Does the child relate differently to adults of different sex? What is the child's ability to deal with strangers (children and adults)? Can the child take part in groups; what is the influence of the group on the child and of the child on the group? Is the group of a mixed sex one, or of the same or opposite sex? Does the child need an adult present to take part in interaction with another child? Does the child have the ability to work alone or in the presence of an adult or another child? Can the child wait its turn? Does the child seem distracted easily (note particularly why one can or cannot explain the cause of the distraction)? To what extent does the adult's presence keep the child focused on an activity? What is the nature of the child's relationship to others (adults, peers, siblings, parents, classmates): empathetic, manipulative, teasing and provocative, passive, shy, mechanical, accommodating, assertive or submissive, non-existent, or clinging? Note differences between reactions to familiar people and to strangers. How long is a person a stranger? Is there a carryover in relationship from one observation session or class to another, one week to the next? The variability or consistency of what has been described should be noted. This may bear on the capacity for regression under stress or, for some children, when they sense that they are safe. (Note highest and lowest functioning; note times of improvement and deterioration.) Does the child do dangerous things when alone? What about when with others, especially parents? This gets at the state of self-surveillance (superego). How has the child changed over the period of time you have known him? What have you done to foster the change? How much effort does it take?

2) *Child at Play*

The observer needs to pay careful attention to the child's capacity and interest in play. Various types of play will be described; some or all (or none) may be present in any one child. Play forms the arena, like language in the adult, where the child explores himself and the world around him. This section deals with various types or levels of complexity of play, as a general means through which the observer may study the child. The actual content, i.e., thematic material, of the play will be dealt with in the following section. In this part, note the shifting from one type of play to another and, if possible, just what happens to facilitate the shift. What causes disruptions of the play, i.e., what makes the play break down? It might be an external event, such as the arrival of someone new, or a threat of some sort; or the explanation may come from the actual content of the play. What follows here is a description of various forms of "play."

(a) *elements of austistic objects* (22): These include parts of the body, such as fingers, hair, and parts of the outside world experienced by the child literally as parts of the body. The child's distress when a bit of straw or paper is removed is literally like giving up a part of itself. When this type of play interest predominates, to the exclusion of much else, then the extent of disturbance of the child is severe. Humming or vocalizing could be included (perhaps the preoccupation or certain autistic children with music fits into this category; they must experience the external music as of themselves). This all differs from the next category which is seen in certain respects in most children.

(b) *elements of transitional objects* (24): Infants use the thumb and fist and older infants babble before dropping off to sleep. Older children sing while preparing to sleep. Interest or preoccupation with parts of the body, hair, hands, feet, genitals; interest and preoccupation with bits of wool or cloth, initially often sucked in conjunction with part of the hand or tongue; special interest in pictures, or faces, or parts of another person are all common. More formed objects such as toys serve a comforting purpose and, unlike autistic objects, satisfy the need for the maternal presence. When mother is truly lacking or inadequate, the transitional objects lose their meaning and power to comfort; autistic objects remain and even assume more desperate proportions. When the mother is nearby, the transitional object can be even more comforting than the mother herself, for it remains totally within the infant's control. In the transitional object, there is implicit some aspect of "not me." There is the beginning of play, the beginning of a merger of the infant's fantasy with something of the outside world. The toy, stuffed animal or blanket serves (as Winnicott describes) a purpose partway between the subjectivity of the infant's fantasy, the illusion of the maternal presence, and the reality of the toy which is objectively perceived, i.e., the "not me." When the infant's instinctual needs increase, the comforter or toy is recognized as being, in fact, quite external and inadequate to fulfill certain needs (food, diaper changes); it is then attacked and/or discarded for the moment. Mother is now more important. When the needs are fulfilled, transitional objects can be used again, having survived the infant's rage, and remained a familiar and comforting thing, residing outside the omnipotent power of the infant. As noted previously, to "play" in this manner requires the presence of a good enough mother in her own right to sustain the infant's image of a caring person.

(c) *individual play:* The child plays alone with blocks, cars, cups, wheels, stuffed animals, not necessarily with regard for the toys' apparent (to us) function, but also not with a primary comforting function. There would seem here to be a more active use of the toy to express fantasy, without the formal design of the toy greatly impinging on the fantasy of the child, for here he has no one to challenge him (only the fabric of the toy itself). He spontaneously applies fantasy to the toy, as the painter colors his canvas—there is little formal restraint.

Subsequently, the toy begins to be used with some recognition of the objective sense of it. Thus, the child allows the physical reality of the toy to further impinge on his fantasy; in fact, the physical state of the object now helps to shape and organize the fantasy and the play enjoys greater complexity. As toys of increasing elements and complexity of materials are chosen, the child learns to accept the boundaries of their physical presence and design. A car is a car, not a building; a teddy bear is an animal, not a breast or comforter, etc.

In this section, one should pay attention to such aspects as the child's ability to persist, distractability, and ability to combine several toys in more extensive and elaborate applications of fantasy to the real world. Here, too, could be described innovative versus perserverant forms of play (somewhat suggestive of the child's intellectual ability in terms of his elaboration of themes in the play) or frustrated repetition in play suggestive of overbearing anxiety or some unconscious search through the play for themes representing needs as yet unintegrated or obscured. The repetition may serve a comforting function; it may suggest mastery of a task the child needs to learn for any one of a hundred reasons. There are other possibilities in play of this sort, namely, does it serve to ignore others (deliberately or more accidentally)? Does the play actively exclude others—anyone or everyone? Does the play seem to assist the child in integrating himself? Note how easily the play breaks down into direct instinctual expression—fear, love, anger, hunger—and how easily it becomes changed and breaks down into a general increase in motor activity and restlessness. Again, note if the play takes place in the presence of, but not directly involving, the mother or teacher. Also if the child requires the presence and actual participation of the adult.

(d) *parallel play:* The child now allows another child (or adult) to play alongside; if it is to be another child, then it is often at least in the presence of an adult. There is even an exchange or perhaps a sharing of materials and toys, while ignoring what the other child is actually doing in play. Parallel play in the playground is most dramatically seen in the playground seesaw when two children seem occupied in tandem until suddenly, with no regard to basic laws of physics (or no regard for one's partner), one child has had enough and abruptly gets off, sending the other hurtling to the ground in tears.

(e) *overlapping play:* The seesaw leads into notions of overlapping play. This is where two children share in a notion or fantasy or song; they share a toy. Note here the duration of play and what makes one or the other child withdraw. Certain sports are included here. There is a beginning opportunity for children to become aware of each other through or in the context of each other's fantasy life. This is initially in the presence of an adult, but later can take place for extended periods of time without an adult actually being present or with an adult in the form of a coach or referee. Initially, there are two children; when there is a confrontation, the play breaks down and each child goes his own way or a coach or teacher breaks up a dispute. This would seem to offer the roots or beginnings of peer relationships, and a necessary condition for moving out of the "nursery," as depicted in James Barrie's *Peter Pan,* and into latency. Special problems which would be considered elaborations of this level of play would focus on relationships between close-aged siblings, especially the intense relationship which develops between twins, which probably has its origins in earlier forms of play, at times before the individual conceives of himself as a whole individual, so that the twins fulfill elements of transitional (and perhaps even autistic) phenomena for each other.

(f) *play in group:* Groups of small children play together, initially with an adult and later without. We begin in nursery school, for example, to see the beginnings of small "gangs" initially needing an adult present, but later functioning for brief periods of time without the physical presence of an adult. These early groups function partially on shared fantasy interests, partly to exclude others. They offer the opportunity for sustained interaction of a stable nature, outside the family. Initially, the relationships are based on common interests related to the expression of instincts or needs through fantasy. This is seen more clearly in older groups (latency age children express instinctual matter directly through games, songs and rhythms). The basis here becomes increasingly one related to the development of relationships, with the momentary instinctual needs taking on more ephemeral and subservient roles (but never entirely done away with).

By this point, the structures developed within the child have achieved a basic stability. Structural elaboration and modification will take place, but the child is no longer dependent on and at the mercy of the primary relationship; changes will take place, but the stability of the play space, supported by a network of relationships, needs only modest alterations as the child ages. It is now, more than ever, that we can see the evidence of the integration of the internal world of the child, experimenting with increasingly new routes of expression and seeking out the outside world and what it has to offer in increasingly mature and self-gratifying ways. The child is now not subject to each momentary instinctual whim, fantasy, or need; he or she has achieved an increasingly cohesive and directed means of self-expression. One may speak here of the development of complex structures which will look like stylized expressions of self. Further elaboration as the child moves toward increasing self-sufficiency and independence can also be conceptualized in classical structural psychoanalytic terms such as ego, ego ideal, and superego. Factors such as self-censorship and modulation are pertinent here. Various over- or underelaborations of these structures or anxieties brought on by conflicts within the structures are seen and attributable to the third etiologic category or disturbance. The fantasy itself is modified through increased capacities for gratification of instincts though increased opportunities for involvement in the outside world.

(g) *creative play:* This is one of a group of specialized forms of play. The child here has made use of play material in particularly novel or imaginative ways. The relationship between this form of play and works of art is intended. In this form, the work itself remains of primary importance; instinctual gratification and/or the development of relationships remain secondary. Interesting art forms on the border of this phenomenon are seen in little children's use of finger paints or chocolate syrup as artistic media: One sees a delicate balance between the smearing and the mouthing of the syrup or the rubbing and smearing of the finger paint and the desire to make an artistic production. The instinctual pull and immediate gratification from the media are difficult to escape, and one can see a child struggle, often pulled back and forth over and over, creating a picture and then destroying it for the sheer pleasure of eating the syrup or smearing the paint. At other times, through other media, opportunities for shared experiences and relationships predominate as in a musical group or choir, where the instinctual gratification and development of relationships are both secondary to a shared experience through creation of music.

(h) *pretend play* is another specialized form of play which should be discussed here. Children frequently acknowledge, when pressed, that what they are playing is, in fact, not real, but "pretend." For the observer to insist to the child that the play is "pretend" seems as ludicrous as to insist that the adult's verbalization is not real, i.e., is not related to possible action.

Aspects of pretend are seen in such diverse phenomena as "playing house," playing with imaginary companions, and various types of role playing. There are particular types of pretend play which seem to dominate the child's entire range or scope of playing. In these forms of play one sees readily the reflected preoccupations of poorly integrated or potentially fragmenting sense of self.

(1) The child is constantly stating that what he or she is doing is "pretending," i.e., not real, as if needing a constant reminder of the fact. The child seems to need this cushion of safety, lacking in the healthier child's ability to play without active and constant attention to issues of fantasy and reality. The assumption here is that one is dealing with a child who experiences difficulty maintaining his or her boundaries of what is fantasy, what is internal and subjective, and what is of the real world. The child, however, maintains an awareness of the bizarreness of the fantasy and of his struggle with sustaining the barrier, and verbalizes a reminder for himself and the person he is playing with. The reminder also stresses the compelling nature of the fantasy, i.e., that the child desperately needs to play this out, needs the adult presence to support the play, yet states his awareness of the potential danger of being lost in the fantasy, as in Peter Pan's moving in and out of the fantasy field of Lost Island.

(2) The child is preoccupied with multiple roles, costumes, needing the costume in order to participate, lacking a firm enough grasp on him/herself to submerge him/herself in play with others without the constant reminder of the costume. An example of this is a four-year-old boy who came to school each day fully dressed as someone else, the costuming reflective of difficulties he was having in separating, in that it would permit him to move from his mother into some form of dramatic play which he would organize. A teacher, out of some frustration and recognition and of this need, asked one day, "When is he going to wear a little boy costume?"

(3) *mirror:* Another specialized form involves interest in mirrors. This is a preoccupation of "classical" proportions, as in Narcissus, whose extreme interest in his own vision is cited through his name as evidence of rather serious disturbance. The key here, as with the other specialized forms, is a preoccupation with the forms of play, as distinct from the particular fantasy content; hence, interest in mirroring can be seen as reflecting disturbance in the child, through the persistence of the form of the communication, rather than the content. An example of this is a latency girl who was totaly engrossed and preoccupied with mirrors, in which she saw her good self in one and her bad self in the other. The younger child looks

behind the mirror to see who is there; the older child who still does this offers a clue of lack of recognition of his/her own person. Lacan (16) writes of a normal stage of "mirroring"—"le stad du miroir"—in which, from six to 18 months, the child uses the mirror as a means of integrating various parts of itself. Winnicott (23) extends that concept and uses the metaphor of the mirror to describe how the child "sees" himself through the mother's response or lack of response. A pathological form of this is the child who constantly imitates another child or adult motorically, in play or in speech. Either the child uses the other person as an organizing force in a repetitive way, suggesting a seriously disorganized internal state, or the child hides his own "true" self, his own basic needs, by totally following another child or adult, thus gaining something from the relationship without the danger implicit in exposing his own needs more directly.

3) The Fantasy World of the Child (Observations of the Internal World of the Child)

The various expressions of fantasy bring us closest to a study of instinctual needs and the success or failure of their interplay with the world. The study of the child's fantasy in its many forms provides another parameter within which to learn about emotional maturity, as the child reveals his or her grasp of his basic needs and how they might be met; it tells about overall awareness of completeness and/or complexity of the needs and the reality of their being met or gratified—or the likelihood of failure and disappointment and even disaster. Fantasy must change as one's needs change, and as the mental representation or awareness of those needs fits them into place, and as one's opportunities for fulfillment, expression, and gratification change through time and different experiences, aging, etc. The complexity and richness of fantasy also tell about the extent to which the mind has integrated the parts of the body and the varied needs of these parts. It also gives clues as to the overall intelligence of the child, i.e., the sophistication with which the integration has taken place (or the sophistication of its failure to take place), and the expressions of the child's general mood or emotional tone.

Increased manual dexterity is indicative of increasing mastery over more and more muscle groups and coordination of those groups under control of a central organizing process. Likewise, increasing complexity of fantasy implies a coordination or organization of instinctual processes arising from various organs and parts of the body under a central proc-

essing and organizing entity, where the changes of fulfillment and gratification are greater than if these needs compete independently at lower
levels of integration, often resulting in a state of internal anarchy and
perceived distress.

  (a) *Fantasy in play:* Recurrent themes in play should be noted, es-
      pecially ones which seem self-initiated or self-motivated. Lack
      of original themes in play should also be noted, as in a child
      who never seems to express his own needs, but always those
      of parents or peers. In this manner, one needs to describe how
      external events are incorporated within the themes of the play
      or how they are systematically distorted. What is the nature of
      the distortion (crisis of various sorts such as separations, tra-
      gedies, disappointments)? Do the themes in the play reflect the
      child's life interests or developmentally appropriate interests
      at this time, or are they more generally those of concern to a
      younger (or older) child? Are they systematically or uniquely
      "distorted"? What is the nature of the distortion and how do
      you account for it? General themes that need to be accounted
      for can be listed as those reflecting the child's current life
      situation at home, in school, in the interveiw, with some interest
      in various important people in the child's life, in respect to
      interests reflecting satisfaction and/or disappointment. These
      themes may be taken up aggressively in the form of attacks of
      destruction, or affectionately in respect to sexual feelings at
      different levels. The provision of appropriate materials or toys
      at home, in an interview situation or in class will facilitate this.
  (b) *Fantasy in art:* Using art materials, the fantasy can be studied
      most systematically. The child may be given standard instruc-
      tions, such as "draw a person" or "draw a family," or he may
      be given an impressionistic suggestion, as in a squiggle game,
      or total freedom, as with a blank piece of paper. All of these
      forms have their place and permit the study of various levels
      or aspects of fantasy; they also take into account the child's
      comfort or discomfort with the setting of the observation and
      the observer.
  (c) *Fantasy in storytelling:* A child's interest in or preoccupation with
      various stories should be noted; what stories does the child like
      to tell and which ones does the child like to be told?
  (d) *Further into fantasy world:* As one moves further into the fantasy
      world of the child, one deals at some level with dreams, either
      told spontaneously or given upon request to the observer. De-
      scribe the content of the dream, the child's general apprehen-
      sion or interest in the dream (was it pleasurable or frightening),
      the awareness of a terrifying experience at night (nightmare)
      without recall of the fantasy itself, the repetitive nature of the
      dreams, i.e., was it unique, or is the child preoccupied or fixed
      on this issue? Note that there is a progression in the devel-

opment of the form of dreams, that initially in toddlers, dreams are experienced in the room, i.e., as occurring outside the child. "They came from without, from the air and sky"(17). Sooner or later they still take place outside, but originate within (the child will say "I dreamed with my mouth"). Then, the dream is experienced in the head or the eyes or the mouth; finally, in late preschool children, the more "adult" experience is noted. One important concern is the child's ability to distinguish that the dream took place in sleep, does not continue long after waking, and does not, in fact, begin to dominate a large part of the child's waking life. As Winnicott once said of a child describing his problems, "It's not that at night I have bad dreams and nightmares, it's that all day I live them." A boy who told me about having nightmares about murdering his family needed to check the locks in his room several times a day to make sure that he had not wandered in their direction at night and needed to actually see them to be reasured he had not done it—hence the power of fantasy.

In describing fantasy of different sorts, make careful note of the child's special interests and concerns, themes of self-aggrandizement, self-deprivation, suicide and murder, sexual concerns, magical interests such as superheroes and imaginary companions and the roles they play and their endurance over a period of time, and if they facilitate or impede growth.

IV. CONCLUSION

At this time, a list of concerns about the child should be stated, accounting for, in your judgment, what is special about this child and the space in which he lives. The concerns need to be sorted into the following headings:

A. Intelligence
B. Education
C. Physical
D. Linguistic
E. Social
F. Emotional

A concluding statement describing the child should now be made. List significant factors that have already been explored in the general categories of social, emotional, physical, intellectual, educational, and linguistic patterns. One needs to account for all information—historical, observational, and educational—that seems *deviant, unusual* or *atypical.* On the basis of the above we should account for why the child is the way he or she is at this time, organizing conclusions around the broad etiologic groupings of: 1) factors structurally *intrinsic* to the *child*, 2) factors resulting from *environmental failure,* and 3) factors related to *conflicts within the child.*

It is important to keep in mind that, when problems are instrinsic to the child, therapy will need to support or replace what is not there, to aid the child's general assimilation and integration. When factors are a result of environmental failure, then one needs to address the issue of environmental restructuring or even replacement or, perhaps, therapies to the environment. Issues related to conflicts within the child are best dealt with through psychotherapies of various sorts.

TREATMENT PLAN

In writing a treatment plan, one should make a statement of what one plans to do for the child and family at this time, as well as further information that would be deemed essential by the next review of the child.

Return to the listing of general factors: educational, social, emotional, physical, linguistic, intellectual, and under each heading state what your plan is for the child.

A. *Educational plan:* List under each academic area what your specific goals are for the next academic three-month period. What do you hope to accomplish in self-help areas, language, sensorimotor, art, etc.? There should be a rationale to this plan, based on your study of casual factors; if the child reads poorly because of needing eyeglasses, then the therapies are both physical (obtaining eyeglasses) and having to do with enrichment, or now offering the child what the child was unable to take advantage of in the past because of visual impairment. Note specific special educational techniques to be employed.

B. *Physical:* State what physical therapies need to be done, ranging from improvement of coordination and muscle tone to review of seizure status or medication for a specific physical ailment, hearing aid, etc.

C. *Specific Language Program:* A specific language program should be outlined here, too, in reference to the underlying cause of the language disturbance. If problems are multiple, then multiple therapies may be needed, such as psychotherapy and specific forms of speech therapy.

D. *Social:* To deal with social factors, family therapies or counseling, education of a parent, removal of child to a new environment, etc. may be necessary.

E. *Emotional:* Specific therapies recommended for the child's emotional disturbance should be stated, whether some form of psychotherapy, group therapy, or drug therapy. The rationale for the therapy, based on underlying etiology of the emotional disturbance, should be stated, as well as the specific goals of therapy, i.e., what you are treating, what you do hope to do, and how long you expect it should take. This, too, as with each section, should be reviewed at periodic intervals.

F. *Intellectual:* A statement concerning overall intellectual development and distortions should be made, with general reference to the nature of the disturbance, and what the treatment of the intellectual factors will be. If the aim is to improve intellectual levels through enrichment programs, environmental manipulation, or psychotherapies, or drug therapies, or treatment of a specific medical disorder, then this should be stated.

REFERENCES

1. Ainsworth, M.D.S. and Wittig, B.A.: Attachment and exploratory behavior in one year olds in a strange situation. In B.M. Foss (Ed.), *Determinants of Infant Behavior*. London: Methuen, 1969.
2. Bakwin, H. *Journal of Pediatrics*, 35:512, 1949.
3. Bruch, H.: Psychogenic malnutrition and atypical anorexic neuroses, In H. Bruch (Ed.), *Eating Disorders*. New York: Basic Books, 1973.
4. Burlingham, D.: Special problems of blind infants, *The Psychoanalytic Study of the Child*, Vol. 30, pp. 3-13. New York: International Universities Press, 1975.
5. Call, J.:Follow-up of young treated autistic children. Paper presented at 2nd Infant Psychiatry Institute, American Academy of Child Psychiatry. June 1978.
6. Chess, S., Korn, S., and Fernandez, P.: *Psychiatric Disorders of Children with Congenital Rubella*. New York: Brunner/Mazel, Inc., 1971.
7. Chess, S., Thomas, A., and Birch, H.: *Behavioral Individuality in Early Childhood*. New York: New York University Press, 1963.
8. Fraiberg, S.: Parallel and divergent patterns in blind and sighted infants. *The Psychoanalytic Study of the Child*. Vol. 23, pp. 264-299. New York: International Universities Press, 1968.
8a. Freud, A.: The symptomatology of childhood: A preliminary attempt at classification. *The Psychoanalytic Study of the Child*, 25:19-41. New York: International Universities Press, 1970.
9. Galenson, E., Miller, R., Kaplan, E., and Rothstein, A.: *Assessment of Development in the Deaf Child*. In Press.
10. Gesell, A. and Amatruda, C.: *Developmental Diagnosis: Normal and Abnormal Child Development*. Clinical Methods and Pediatrics Applications, 2nd Edition, New York, 1947.
11. Hauptman, B.: Review of children seen at Mass. Mental Health Center Children's Unit by age from 1970-1973. (Unpublished manuscript).
12. Illingworth, R.S.: *The Development of the Infant and Young Child* (5th Ed.). London: Churchill Livingstone, 1972, p. 319.
13. Isaacs, S.: *Social Development in Young Children*. London: Routeledge and Kegan Paul, 1967.

14. Kanner, L.: *Childhood Psychosis, Initial Studies and New Insights.* New York: Winston/Wiley, 1973.
15. Khan, M.M: *The Concept of Cumulative Trauma in the Privacy of the Self.* London: Hogarth Press/The International Psychoanalytic Library, 1974.
16. Lacan, J.: *Le Stude du Miroir Comme Formateur de la Function de Ju,* in Ecrits I. Paris: Editions du Seuil, 1966.
17. Lewin, B.D.: *The Image and the Past.* New York: International Universities Press, 1968.
18. Nagera, H.: *Early Childhood Disturbances, the Infantile Neurosis and the Adulthood Disturbances.* The Monograph Series of the Psychoanalytic Study of the Child, No. 2, New York: International Universities Press, 1966.
19. Provence, S. and Lipton, R.C.: *Infants in Institutions,* New York: International Universites Press, 1963.
20. Rutter, M.: *Maternal Deprivation Reassessed.* Maryland: Penguin Books, 1972.
21. Spitz, R.A. and Wolf, K.M. Anaclitic depression: an inquiry into the genesis of psychiatric conditions in early childhood, *Psychoanalytic Study of the Child,* 2:313. New York: International Universities Press, 1946.
22. Tustin, F.: *Autism and Childhood Psychosis.* New York: Science House, 1972.
23. Winnicott, D.W.: Mirror role of mother and family. In P. Lomas (Ed.), *The Predicament of the Family,* New York: International Universities Press, 1967.
24. Winnicott, D.W.: *Transitional Object and Transitional Phenomena in Playing and Reality.* London: Tavistock, 1971.
25. Winnicott, D.W.: *Through Pediatrics to Psycho-analysis, The Anti-Social Tendency.* New York: Basic Books, 1975, pp. 306-315.

15

Psychological Testing in Childhood

LETTY J. POGUL, Ph.D.

INTRODUCTION

Is Johnny ready for kindergarten? An infant is being considered for adoption; is he developing on schedule? A five-year-old has impaired articulation; another does not speak at all. An adolescent girl refuses to go to school, a boy has no friends, another child seems bright but is not performing well at school, a degenerative disease has been identified in another child—what level is the child performing at now? A boy has a sensory handicap—should he be in a special or regular school? Is this child retarded or aphasic? These and a multitude of other presenting statements and questions have been brought to pediatric psychological test situations by parents, educators, and physicians with the expectation of receiving information to aid in a decision making process.

There are those, however, who bring other kinds of statements to the psychological test situation: "If he could hear or see better his score would be higher; he's bored by tests and doesn't try; he's afraid you'll ask him something he doesn't know and then he'll stutter; he's clumsy and can't do puzzles well; he has no brothers and sisters to teach him to read; he's only three years old and he hasn't had much experience." These statements reflect legitimate areas of concern about the psychological testing of children, and by inference raise issues about the establishment of rapport, test selection, testing to a handicap or around a handicap (sometimes referred to as deficit and non-deficit testing), and the notion of the "qualitative" as opposed to the "quantitative" aspects of assessment, the second Q in I.Q. testing.

In general, the psychological test offers essential uniformity of administration and scoring procedures. When tests are given under conditions which are relatively equal, then differences in responses suggest individual differences in the children tested. The performance of a given child can be compared with the performance of another child, or comparisons can be made with his own performances at different time periods, regardless of whether the test was administered by different examiners in different places. While no two testing situations are precisely the same, in so far as test conditions, instructions, and scoring can be specified, it is possible to make comparisons (28). Moreover, the child's test responses can be compared against some known criteria namely, normative data obtained from standardization samples. The standardized test permits investigation of such varied problems as age changes within a child, the effects of education, the effects of psychotherapy, and changes as a result of drugs or trauma (4).

The process of psychological testing and behavioral assessment of children is complex. It is by no means infallible. The instruments are not equally effective for all children, and the instruments are clearly not so exquisitely refined that they accomplish all that they are purported to do. Additionally, neither the interplay between intellectual factors and emotional factors, nor the multiple interactions produced by the environment are completely understood. Although tests have been derived from observation and research in child development (7, 13), and extensive use has been made of factor-analytic research (18), it is only in recent years that attention has been given to tests based on major developmental theories (16, 20, 21). Nevertheless, with recognition of the limitations of the concepts of personality, intelligence, and I.Q. (23, 24), and related problems such as validity difficulties with atypical child populations, the psychological testing of children by an experienced child clinician can significantly contribute to the understanding of the child.

RAPPORT

One of the single most important aspects underlying child testing is the establishment of rapport. Unless one can make certain assumptions about the child's willingness to perform, and that his performance represents his "best effort," then the usefulness of the testing procedure is obviously curtailed. The idea is to elicit and sustain interest by creating an atmosphere that is relaxed and friendly without being overwhelming—in effect a nonthreatening environment. Dependent upon the setting (in a hospital outpatient clinic, children are sometimes concerned that psychological testing involves infringement on the body or the application of painful stimuli), and the particular child, some explanation is usually given about the nature of the procedure. Where applicable, some discussion is reserved for why the child thinks he has come for testing, and that while he is a unique child, the chances are that his problems are not unique, and that they are shared by some community of children.

The age of the child, his language, his level of relatedness, and his comfort are just a few of the variables that make a difference with regard to being able to "read" some of the child's behavioral cues. For the infant, discomfort or anxiety comes primarily from internal needs that are not met. There has to be concern with such things as temperature, noise levels, sudden movement, how one holds a baby, the involvement of the mother if she is present, and a general willingness to "communicate" on both vocal and nonvocal levels. For the preschooler, the mother's presence may or may not be necessary, and is often dependent upon how much separation anxiety and stranger anxiety is generated. The preschooler, whether he be timid and quiet or friendly and outgoing is very much directed by his need to move and to explore and manipulate objects. He cannot be hurried and yet his attention span is limited. Approaches which are novel and game-like help to sustain curiosity. Flexibility of the procedure itself is necessary if refusals or other examples of negativistic behavior are to be held to a minimum.

Children who do not speak or cannot be spoken to, require much longer periods of time to adapt to the testing situation. There is more physical contact (particularly with the young child), in the form of holding or touching and there is greater use of gestural language combined with vocalization. Drawing is often useful as a communicative adjunct. Occasionally siblings are brought to the test room and exposed to similar materials to show the child what is to come. And sometimes a brief session is set aside for the single purpose of having the child meet the examiner and allowing him to get a sense of the surroundings and the materials.

Eleven-year-old Maria spoke just a little English. Moreover, when she did speak she held her hand over her mouth because she was embarrassed about her repaired hare lip and residual cleft palate speech. Maria had been considered untestable on prior evaluations because she would not speak at all and was otherwise minimally responsive. It was decided that she should meet the examiner before any testing was undertaken. She allowed the examiner to take her hand and lead her on a tour of the clinic, where she was able to observe rooms and materials, and other children, one of whom was in a wheelchair. Brought into the particular test room, she casually fingered the leaves of a plant. The examiner explained something about the plant and invited Maria to help with the watering of all the plants in the room. This led to a certain amount of water play which in turn caused Maria to giggle. Busy with the plants and the water and the helping (her hands were in use, of course), Maria "forgot" about covering her mouth and withholding speech. She began to comment about one thing or another, partly in English, partly in Spanish. Her hypernasality interfered only minimally. Maria moved quickly towards direct verbal exchange with the examiner. She was ready to be examined.

An imaginative five-year-old girl played "dress up" and "school" with the examiner before she considered the test situation to be "safe."

An eight-year-old boy told "knock knock" jokes and explained how T.V.'s Mr. Spock could be beamed up out of any place he didn't want to be in. He was reassured about beaming out procedures in the event he felt anxious in the test situation.

An immature 13-year-old girl with psychomotor seizures refused any part of testing until she displayed a series of gymnastic positions. Poses were very important to this girl who used them as "cover" behavior for the psychomotor episodes.

TYPES OF PSYCHOLOGICAL TESTS

There are an incredibly large number of more or less objective test instruments available to the psychologist for the assessment of child behavior. It is unlikely that any one examiner can be familiar with all of the published materials, but the pediatric psychologist must be prepared to deal with a variety of tests, covering the age range from infancy to adolescence.

The following is a broad classification of types of instruments used to assess child behavior. The few specific examples given within the various types are commonly used instruments.

A. Developmental Tests
B. Intelligence Tests
   a. Global
   b. Picture Vocabulary
   c. Performance
C. Perceptual Tests (visual-motor)

D. Readiness Tests
E. Academic Achievement Tests
F. Projective Tests
G. Social Competence Tests

Developmental Tests

Gesell Developmental Schedules, 1947

The schedules evaluate development in the four areas of motor, adaptive, language, and personal-social behavior, and cover an age range from four weeks to three years. The four areas are considered to reflect ongoing processes, with specific skills and associated behaviors occurring at particular ages. Testing includes presentation of objects, direct observation of responses and a parent interview. Many of the Gesell items have been included in other infant scales.

Bayley Scales of Infant Development, 1969

The scales are divided into the mental scale, the motor scale, and the infant behavior record, and cover an age range from two months to two and a half years. Precautions by Bayley have been noted (5), to the effect that these scales like most of the infant scales, evaluate current development and possible deficits and do not predict future ability levels.

Intelligence Tests-Global

Wechseler Intelligence Scale for Children-Revised (WISC-R), 1974

The WISC-R is an individually administered test of intelligence which provides separate verbal and performance I.Q.s as well as a full scale I.Q., and which covers an age range from six years to 16 years 11 months. Factors measured by the WISC-R are considered to correspond to factors of verbal comprehension, perceptual organization, and freedom from distractibility (6). Detailed analyses of what the 12 individual subtests are said to measure are available for the WISC, the predecessor of the WISC-R (11, 14).

Revised Stanford-Binet Intelligence Scale, Form L-M, (S-B, L-M) 1960, renormed, 1972*

The S-B, L-M is an individually administered test of intelligence, with tests grouped into age levels which extend from two years of age to superior adult. The scale yields a mental age (M.A.) and I.Q. The sub-

---

*Minority ethnic groups have been included in the standardization population of the WISC-R and the 1972 standardization population of the S-B, L-M.

tests cover a wide variety of tasks and include such skills as matching geometric forms, perceptual discrimination, practical judgment and common sense, vocabulary, recall of digits and sentences, interpretation of pictures or verbal situations, analogous reasoning etc. S-B subtests can be grouped according to constructs like general comprehension, visual-motor ability, arithmetic reasoning, memory and concentration, vocabulary and verbal fluency, and judgment and reasoning (32). The 1937 edition of the S-B has been adapted for use with blind children, the Hayes-Binet.

Merrill-Palmer Scale of Mental Tests, (M-P), 1931

The M-P is an individually adminstered test of general intelligence for young children, 18 months to 71 months. It is considered a preschool test.* The scale includes language tests, formboards, puzzles, picture tests and tests of motor coordination. Although it is an essentially timed test, it is highly appealing to young children. Many of the nonverbal items may be administered by pantomime, and can be used for the deaf** and bilingual children. The scoring makes allowances for refusals and omissions.

Intelligence Tests—Picture Vocabulary

Pictorial Test of Intelligence, 1964

The Pictorial Test of Intelligence is an individually administered test for three to eight year olds. The test is divided into six subtests: picture vocabulary, form discrimination, information and comprehension, similarities, size and number, and immediate recall. There are 54 stimulus cards, and the child chooses his answer from among 137 response cards. The test is especially useful for the physically handicapped seeing and hearing child.

*Intelligence Tests—Performance****

Leiter International Performance Scale, (LIPS), 1948

The LIPS is an individually adminstered nonverbal test of intelligence

---

*Other well known tests for preschoolers include: The Wechsler Preschool and Primary Scale of Intelligence (WPPSI), the Minnesota Preschool Scale, the Cattell Infant Intelligence Scale, and the McCarthy Scales of Children's Abilities.

**The Nebraska Test of Learning Aptitude has been standardized on deaf and hard-of-hearing children.

***Other well known tests of global intelligence of the Performance type include: The Progressive Matrices of Raven, the Columbia Mental Maturity Scale, the Porteus Maze Test, and the Arthur Point Scale of Performance Tests, Revised form II.

with items arranged in an age scale format from age two to age 18. Very little motor activity is required, and speech and hearing are not necessary. The test calls for matching color, shapes, and objects at the younger levels. At the higher levels the matching is according to a principle which may involve analogy or function, or classification. The items become more complex as the scale progresses from one age level to the next.

Perceptual Tests* (visual-motor)

Bender Gestalt Test for young children, 1964
The Bender Gestalt Test for young children is an adaptation of the Bender Gestalt Test. It is an individually administered test involving copying designs for children ages five through 10. Developmental norms are available. The test requires visual-spatial perception, visual-motor coordination, and grapho-motor control.

Benton Revised Visual-Retention Test, 1974
The Benton Visual-Retention Test is an individually administered test with procedural variations for the age range from eight years of age through adult. The number of correct reproductions of the designs and number of errors, can be compared with the expected normal score for each age and intellectual level. Visual-spatial perception, grapho-motor and visual-motor coordination, and immediate recall are required.

Readiness Tests**

Metropolitan Readiness Tests, 1976
The Metropolitan is an orally administed test for Kindergartners which permits a practice procedure so the child knows how to take the test. The child is tested for such things as: vocabulary, listening comprehension, sound discrimination, visual matching, quantitative concepts, and sound-letter correspondences.

---

*Other well known perceptual tests for children include: the Frostig Developmental Tests of Visual-Perception, the Beery-Buktenica Visual—Motor Integration Test, the Ayres Space Test, and the Purdue Perceptual-Motor Survey. There are also perceptual tests of the auditory type for children: the Auditory Discrimination Test, the Basic Concept Inventory, and the Illinois Test of Psycholinguistic Abilities.

**Other well known readiness tests include: The Kindergarten Evaluation of Learning Potential, the Boehm Test of Basic Concepts, and the Valett Developmental Survey of Basic Learning Abilities.

Academic Achievement Tests*

Wide Range Achievement Test, Revised edition, 1978

The Wide Range is an achievement test which can be administered individually or in groups. There are norms from Kindergarten through College. The achievement areas of reading (word recognition), spelling, and arithmetic are measured.

Projective Tests**

The Rorschach Technique, 1921

The Rorschach consists of 10 inkblots which are symmetrical in shape. Half of the stimuli have color and the other half are achromatic. The child is presented with one card at a time and is asked to report what he sees. He is subsequently asked about the location of his perceptions, the determinants (form, color, shading, and vista and movement), and the content of his perceptions. Each component reflects a different aspect of personality, and various combinations with varying emphases determine the individual's personality structure. It was Herman Rorschach's hypothesis that the subject's verbal responses to an ambiguous visual stimulus would reflect particular ways of perceiving his world and provide a picture of his personality (29). Ames et al. (2, 3), published sets of Rorschach norms for children between two and 16 years of age.

The Children's Apperception Test, (C.A.T.), 1949

The C.A.T. is an individually administered projective technique*** for children from three to 10 years of age. The technique is based on the Thematic Apperception Test. There are 10 C.A.T. cards which show animals in different human situations, and are designed to elicit fantasies related to oral activity, aggression, sleeping, sibling rivalry, toilet training, parent nurturance, and other aspects of the child's relationship to his family. There is also a human modification of the C.A.T. (C.A.T.-H). The Thematic Apperception Test may be used with some children.

---

*Other well known achievement tests include: the Stanford Achievement Test, the California Achievement Tests, Tests of Academic Progress, McGraw-Hill Basic Skills System, and the Peabody Individual Achievement Test.

**Although the word "test" is used, projective instruments should more properly be called techniques, devices or methods; they are not tests in the usual psychometric sense of the word.

***Other kinds of projective techniques employ sentence completions, drawings, and word associations.

Figure Drawings

Figure drawings of children have been used as a projective technique, as an index for conceptual development, and as an adjunct measure of intellectual functioning.

When used as a projective technique, there is minimal structuring and little limitation with respect to age. The examiner may use an inquiry procedure which involves questions with regard to siblings, parents, peers, schooling, attitude towards the body etc. The set of drawings obtained (male and female) are subject to an analysis of drawing traits such as: line quality, symmetry, sequence of drawing, size of drawings, emphasis on particular details, and incongruities. Interpretations of figure drawings used projectively often have a basis in psychoanalytic theory, but have developed from the study of the drawing traits in relation to the clinical background of the child, and other test data.

Koppitz (19) suggests that the child's figure drawings represent a current stage of mental development, subject to change in time as a result of maturation and experience. Using Sullivanian theory as a reference point, she presents developmental norms, as well as emotional "signs" which she considers to be reflections of the child's anxieties.

The well known Draw A Man Test, updated as the Goodenough-Harris Drawing Test represents the use of figure drawings (instructions call for drawings of a man, a woman, and the self) as an instrument for assessing intellectual maturity. There are norms for children from five years to 15 years of age, and separate norms for boys and girls (6).

Social Competence Tests*

The Vineland Social Maturity Scale, 1965

The Vineland Scale is a developmental schedule in questionnaire form which covers the age range from birth to over 25 years, but which in practice is most useful for younger children and mental retardates. In an interview with the parent or child himself, the scale provides information about such things as: general self-help skills, self-help in eating and dressing, self-direction, occupation, communication, locomotion and socialization. A social age can be computed. There is an adaptation of the Vineland Social Maturity Scale for preschool blind children.

---

*Other examples of Social Competence Tests include: the Adaptive Behavior Scale, for age three and upward, designed for mental retardates but useful as well for children with emotional disorders, the Preschool Attainment Record, for ages six months to seven years, and the Cain-Levine Social Competency Scale for mentally retarded children.

FIGURE 1. Drawing of a late adolescent boy. The diagnosis under consideration was paranoid schizophrenia. The boy was subsequently hospitalized following an assault on his mother.

FIGURE 2. Drawing by the same boy who did Figure 1.

FIGURE 3. Drawing of a pre-adolescent girl. The diagnosis under consideration was hysterical neurosis.

FIGURE 4. Drawing of an early adolescent girl. The diagnosis under consideration was obsessive-compulsive neurosis.

THE I.Q.: THE QUALITATIVE ASPECTS OF INTELLIGENCE TESTING, AND DEFICIT AND NON-DEFICIT TESTING

If, as Anastasi (4) has pointed out, we could accept that the I.Q. is a particular score on a particular test and that it is an expression of an individual's ability level at a given point in time in relation to his age norms, we would not be caught in the reasoning that inadequate test performance is the same as inadequate intelligence.

The I.Q. is a useful index of current mental functioning, and the discrepancy between the I.Q. and school achievement has continued to be considered one of the most important indicators of disturbance in the child (26). However, it is clear that such a simple index could not be expected to reflect all aspects of complex development.

Currently used intelligence tests generally indicate "what" a child can do, whether he solves something correctly or not, but provide little in the way of "how" and "why" a child performs as he does. While this state of affairs will change with the emergence of new tests, present tests and the testing situation offer rich opportunities to gain behavioral information about the child, apart from numerical score values. A simple example may be found in the "Cutting with scissors" item (located at the 24-29 month level on the Merrill-Palmer Scale). One three year old may approach the task eagerly and immediately. He seems to know the function of the scissors and their relationship to the paper. He tries to cut the paper, persisting for a long time with little visible frustration, but his manipulatory skills are such that he cannot successfully complete the task. Another three year old also approaches the task quickly. He grabs the scissors and the examiner's pencil as well, and proceeds to cast the scissors on the floor and mouth the pencil, while paying little attention to the paper. He too fails the item. Yet another three year old wants "Mommy do it." He appears intimidated by the scissors. The third child fails as well. These three children might conceivably produce similar numbers of task successes and failures. But how much would be lost about these children if only the numerical scores were recorded and acknowledged.

Verbal responses to standard test questions or stimuli can also provide abundant sources of behavioral information, and are particularly helpful where differential diagnositc impressions are concerned. Consider the example of the child who is asked "what is this?" as he is shown a pencil. The child says "pencil." The very next question is "what is it for?" (the pencil is, however, no longer in sight). The child hesitates and finally says "five." He does not seem to understand that the question "what is it for" refers to the antecedent, pencil. The words contained in "what is it for" have no meaning without the antecedent referent. But the child does make a response. In a sense, he copes. He appears to respond to the only word he can give meaning to, namely "for" or really "four", and supplies the next word in a natural sequence "five." Given the question "what is it for?" with the pencil in sight, the child can say "writing." The example is simplistic, but the point is that what may seem like a bizarre response or a non sequitur, may in fact represent a facet of a specific disorder of language.

Vocabulary subtests offer much information in addition to whether a child knows what a given word means. Consider the child who manages reasonably well with a series of definitions and then gives the response "milk" to the stimulus question "what is a gown?" Asked for some elaboration, the child says: "You know, a gow-won of milk." Similarly the word "skill' is defined as "weight 50" (probably received as 'scale'). The examiner is alerted to the possibility of poor auditory discrimination and how meaning becomes distorted for this child. Responses on the basis of phonological similarity are not uncommon in children with auditory perceptual disorders.

> An 11½ year old boy with chronic adjustment difficulties responded to the vocabulary subtest of the WISC in the following manner: "nitroglycerine, it means, nitro means not paying attention, and glycerine means not listening (note clang association, glycerine-listenin (g)) . . . umbrella, umbrella you carry it around with you so you won't get too hot when it's raining and you won't get cold when the sun is shining, . . . stanza, that's a poem chair, . . .join, it means leave me alone, I hate you (said with little affect), it means climb, (and finally), it means I'm doing something, why don't you join me." Other definitions were of immediate good quality and did not elicit the thinking disorder.

Although standardized I.Q. tests are not designed to assess personality as such, there are many parts of these tests which permit informal evaluation of personality. The comprehension subtest of the WISC-R lends itself to such evaluation.

> A 13-year-old boy with long-standing medical problems, some aspects of which were considered functional in nature, was absent from school much of the year. He was referred for testing because of poor grades and difficulties with peer relationships. On the WISC-R, he achieved a Full Scale I.Q. of 100 with a Verbal Scale I.Q. of 97, and a Performance Scale I.Q. of 104 placing him within

the Average range. The poorest functioning occurred on the comphrension subtest, where a scaled score of 7 was obtained ... 10 is an average scaled score. While most children of Bill's age have long since overlearned the "right answers" to the given practical-social judgment situations, and give those answers whether or not they would in fact behave that way. Bill did not. He could not deal at all with the question having to do with "why we need policemen" because he became so preoccupied and sidetracked with his idea that all policemen have larceny in their hearts. His philosophy of "finders-keepers" prevailed in the situation having to do with the question about a lost wallet, even though he added "you are supposed to give it to the lost and found." Why a house of stone or brick would be better than one built of wood became very problematic for Bill who got caught up in such unnecessary details as whether "wood" meant "planks or boards or thick wood." While he could see that it wasn't the thing to do to fight with a much smaller child, he again engaged in such reasoning as: "Well how small is the kid, if he's not so small, I'd hit him, well I guess I would hit him, you can't be sure." He saw the need for "secret ballots" as protection against being "killed" for voting the wrong way. He saw no reason "why a promise should be kept." And when asked: "what is the thing to do when you cut your finger?", he said, "clean it with peroxide, wash it, put a bandage on it, and if it's still bleeding go to a doctor before *I* get gangrene." (In addition to the obsessive detailing around bodily hurt, note the self reference.)

The Information subtest (on the Wechsler series) can also elicit material which can be helpful in the diagnostic process.

Joe, an 11-year-old boy considered to have superior intelligence was referred for testing because of failing grades in his sixth grade class. On the information subtest of the WISC, failure began to occur almost immediately at relatively "easy" levels. He said that "sugar" could be gotten "in a drug store," and that "one dozen made a dozen, 100 things make a dozen." At one point, he listed the four seasons of the year as "September and October," and at another point he was correct. Some responses were accurate and succinct "the stomach digests food," whereas he ascribed the authorship of *Romeo and Juliet* to "a man named Princess Queen." Some responses were perseverations on a single theme, some were concrete, and others bore no apparent relationship to the stimulus. There were also examples of confabulated reasoning. Thus, unable to deal with the question, "why does oil float on water?", and after having responded that "Abraham Lincoln" was celebrated on the 4th of July, he then said that "C.O.D." meant "the cross." When asked about "the cross" he said, "the cross, he died ... Abraham Lincoln died near the water on the cross."

Because the I.Q. test generally covers a variety of areas and requires an hour or more to administer, the examiner, is given the opportunity to observe responses which may constitute clinically important signs, such signs as: articulation defects, syntactically disordered speech, anomic difficulties, cluttering and the various types of dysfluencies, difficulties with serial ordering, confusion around left-right orientation, the dyspraxias, minor motor difficulties, and when they are elicited, rigidity of thinking, tangential thinking, stimulus-bound reactions, catastrophic reactions and others. Omnibus I.Q. tests like the Stanford-Binet are considered useful in the assessment of brain damaged children for example, because they lend themselves to the construction of profiles. Rather than speak of a generalized impairment in memory, one can describe difficulties with memory for words as opposed to memory for objects, pictures, or ideas. And since brain damaged children often show task-specific performance, descriptions of this nature are helpful in assessment and could have implications for practical educational techniques (10).

Related to the qualitative aspects of I.Q. testing, and attending to areas of strengths and weakness within a test performance is the notion of testing "to the deficit" and testing "around the deficit." Approaches with exceptional children usually involve testing "around the deficit," an avoidance of the handicap or difficulty. Dependent on the various types of exceptional children, modifications and adaptations of existing tests have occurred (1, 25). Taylor (30) has made extensive use of adaptation in assessing brain damaged children. She has maintained that using the standard form of a test plus variations, the examiner can elicit what the child knows, how he knows it, and approximately at what level his reasoning is taking place. Thus, on a "similarities" task via a questioning technique, one might learn that a given child tries to think of a common category for two items even though he may be incorrect. Such a response is more mature than the response of a child who is still thinking in terms of specifics and does not even attempt a categorization (30). Excerpts from the test protocols of minimally brain damaged children (MBD) with language disorders examined for a research study (25), illustrate some of the difficulties as well as some of the changes in response which can occur as a result of modification of standard instruments.*

---

*In actual clinical practice, the standard test is used for scoring purposes according to precise instructions for administration of that test. If a modification is used for a specific purpose for a particular child, it is used after the fact.

A standard "similarities" item using the stimulus "wood and coal" elicited the responses: "Cold is wind and a tree is wood," and, "Wood is hard and I don't know what cold is." The modified item "wood and charcoal"* (which negated difficulties caused by poor auditory discrimination) elicited from the same children: "Wood is hard and charcoal is hard" and "You make fire with wood and charcoal." The standard item using the stimulus "iron and silver" elicited variants of "iron" as an appliance, and "silver" as silverware or money. The essence of the "similarities" task, namely to induce a commonality, was restored to the children when the stimulus was modified to "a piece of iron" and "a piece of silver." A standard "verbal absurdities" item stated: "A man had the flu twice. The first time it killed him, but the second time he got well quickly" (31, p. 90). Confusion was mirrored in the child's response: "How can you get sick when you fly?" When the item was modified, and "a terrible cold" was substituted for "flu," the child's response was declarative and correct . . . "after you die, you don't get better."

Testing "to the deficit" is an obvious penalty. But, in fact, a given child is required to function with his deficit, or even to compete in spite of his deficit, with nonimpaired children. Accordingly, one might administer a formboard test (or any other test where manipulation is a factor) to a child with infantile hemiplegia to see how he differs from "normals," how he responds as compared with other hemiplegics and, most importantly, how he adapts to his handicap. Phrased another way . . . . . how handicapping is his handicap. Using the verbally saturated Stanford-Binet with a language impaired child can be very illuminating.

An approach with more merit however, is one which involves both testing "to the deficit" and testing "around the deficit." Information is gained from discrepancies between the two in terms of global scores, in terms of subtest clusters, and in terms of behaviors and attitudes elicited. Moreover, such assessment more closely approximates the "real world" in which the child must operate. Few learning situations cater only to that which a child can do.

Tests for the Cognitive Dysfunctions

Tests which concern themselves with intellectual impairment deal primarily with deficiencies or deficits in such functions as spatial per-

---

*The modification "wood and charcoal" was used prior to the publication of the 1972 norms for the S-B, L-M, which employed the same wording.

ception, memory, abstraction or concept formation, attention, and language. The instruments are used as one of the approaches for making an inference about "organicity" or brain damage, and some are used as indices for the presence of learning disabilities. The adequacy of normative samples for some of the tests has been questioned (6).

A general intelligence test is almost always a part of any testing procedure for the cognitive dysfunctions. "A relatively low level of general intelligence is probably the most constant behavioral result of brain damage in children. The failure in intellectual development may or may not be severe enough to place the child in the category of mental retardation. When it does not, his intelligence level still tends to be below expectations based on the intelligence levels of his parents and siblings ... " (9, p. 765). Information relative to specific dysfunction in language can be elicited through the use of such tests as: the Auditory Discrimination Test, the Illinois Test of Psycholinguistic Abilities, and Screening Tests for Identifying Children with Specific Language Disability. Performance on visuoperceptive and visual-motor tests like the Bender Visual-Motor Gestalt Test for Children, the Beery-Buktenica Visual-Motor Integration Test, the Revised Visual Retention Test, the Ayres Space Test and the Purdue Perceptual Motor Survey can be useful indicators of dysfunction particularly when compared with the child's performance on language and reasoning tests. The Reitan-Indiana Neuropsychological Test Battery for children five years through eight years of age explores brain-behavior relationships through such areas as: tactile form recognition, tactual performance, finger tapping, categorization, screening for aphasia, lateral dominance, etc.(27).

THE PROJECTIVE TECHNIQUE: RORSCHACH AND THE
THEMATIC APPERCEPTION TEST (T.A.T.)

The projective tool provides another means of observing a child under relatively controlled conditions. It is an unstructured task where the stimuli are vague and where the child perceives, interprets, and projects the ideas which reflect his "personality." Some psychologists have advocated the use of projective devices to assess intelligence. Such an approach has had some basis in the observation that I.Q. tests and schoolwork are more nearly adapted to middle class values, and consequently prejudicial to the values of others. The position is also taken by those who consider that mental retardation is a consequence of personality disturbance. However, these are minority positions. By and large, the projective device is not used as a substitute for an assessment of intelligence, but is used as a very important adjunct. A given child may respond in one way to an unstructured projective situation, and in a very different way to the objective I.Q. test situation, but it is the very fact of the differences which when compared can give a more complete picture of the child.

The Rorschach is one of the most popular of the projective techniques. Normative data (2, 3, 22) have increased the use of the technique with children. Interpretation of the Rorschach is based on a series of indicators and their relationships to one another. R is the total number of responses to all 10 cards, and the location symbols W,D,d, and S denote what part of the inkblot has been used in the percept (W = whole, D = large usual detail, d = small detail, S = white space). The determinant symbols F (form responses), C (color), M (human movement), FM (animal movement), m (inanimate movement), Kc (shading) denote how the child sees the inkblot and what made it look a particular way. And finally there are the indicators which denote content, H (human), A (animal), At (anatomy), Obj (inanimate objects) and so on. Percepts which are commonly perceived are denoted by the indicator P (popular), while rarely perceived percepts are denoted by the indicator O (original). The test is complex however by virtue of the general significance of each test factor, the interrelationships of the test factors, and the overall relationships to the developmental process.

The W or whole response, the ability to use the whole inkblot in giving a percept is seen as an ability to organize, synthesize and abstract. Given the overall interpretation of the use of W, one is then interested for example, in the quality of the W. Is it based on a crude outline of the inkblot (lesser mental performance), or is it based on elaborate integrative constructions (superior mental performance)? However, the developmental aspect must be considered. The undifferentiated whole response is characteristic of the two and a half to four year old. The well structured whole response which requires synthesizing is most uncommon in children under five years old, and is usually not much present until seven years (17).

M or the projection of human movement onto the inkblot, is said to reflect emotional adjustment, empathy, the ability to delay gratification, self-awareness, the ability to use fantasy productively, and so on. According to Levitt and Truumaa (22), there is a consensus among experts that little or no M is to be expected in the preschool and primary school years, and that its first appearance is likely in the latency or early adolescent period, and that it tends to increase in frequency through adolescence. FM or the projection of animal movement onto the inkblot reflects a more infantile, more primitive level of personality. M and FM bear a relationship to one another (as do other Rorschach factors or indicators). "Where FM>2M the individual is ruled by immediate needs for gratification rather than by long range goals . . . Where M>FM the impulse life is subordinate to the value system of the individual . . . Where M equals FM . . . the impulse life is not in conflict with the value system" (22, p. 51). With respect to the child, the FM response closely identifies his feelings. The M response signifies the beginning of the child's identification with adult ideas, and this identification does not usually make its appearance until prepuberty (17).

With respect to the few Rorschach factors mentioned, consider the following response given to Card III by a four and a half-year-old boy:

> "This is a butterfly (center D), but I can't tell what the rest of the picture is. Now I know, I think it is two people trying to catch the butterfly with nets."

Although he began with a usual detail (D), this child stayed with the situation and reorganized and synthesized his percept into an elaborate schema using almost the entire inkblot (W). Moreover he used human movement (M) which is unusual for his age, as well as the more spontaneous FM (the animal movement was further clarified during the inquiry portion of the test) which is appropriate for his age. Just the one response suggests that at the very least, this child has very superior intelligence. Whether his precocity is fostered by an overconformity to adult standards could not be known without inspection of all the responses.

The Rorschach can aid in statements relative to development, cognitive modes and perceptual organization. It can also be used as a basis for a structured interview (15). However, the use of the Rorschach to differentiate conditions of psychosis and organic brain damage in children is of doubtful reliability because both groups may produce overlapping kinds of responses and behaviors, such as: perseveration, regressed or primitive responses, fragmented responses, color naming (12). But since no single test or device is used as the sole criteria for a diagnostic impression, the problem is attentuated. Thus when perceptual distortion due to possible organic brain damage is suspected (as opposed to distortions based on bizarre fantasy), then tests for the cognitive dysfunctions can be included.

The Thematic Apperception Test (T.A.T.) consists of a series of pictures to which children (generally 10 years or older) tell stories following the outline: Say what is going on in the picture, what led up to it, and what the outcome will be. An inquiry is often used when the stories are completed. The stories are considered as "projections" or as being tantamount to placing the child's feelings, needs, and drives onto people or things in the outside environment. The T.A.T. pictures are best viewed as a group of social and interpersonal situations which the child imagines (8). Since he is not bound by a reality situation, there is less constraint on verbal responses. The interpretation of the stories requires finding common denominators, or themes or patterns in the stories. This is usually accomplished through organizing the stories according to such categories as: the main theme, the main hero, attitudes towards the parents and society, major conflicts, attitudes about love, aggression, punishment and so on (8).

> An 11½-year-old boy was brought in for evaluation because of his concern about his small size. He told the following story to Card 1 (boy looking at a violin) of the T.A.T. "This boy he wanted to play the violin so bad because all his friends play it. Then his mother said, 'If you want it so bad I'll buy it for your birthday but you have to practice it and not give it up.' Then his mother bought him the violin, and after a few weeks of play, he didn't want to play and his mother forced it on him, and then he had to sit there and not go out and play." (Examiner Question "Q.") "His mother got mad at him and hit him." Q. "He played it even though he didn't want to, and when he grew up he became a great violinist."

A brief restatement of the story serves to delineate the main theme on a descriptive level: A boy wants to do or be like his peers. The means to this end is provided by the mother as a gift, but a gift with restrictions. The boy accepts but then rejects the gift, and the mother becomes coercive and the boy performs and conforms against his wishes.

If one summarizes the story, one can identify the main hero as a boy who experiences difficulty with respect to peer behavior, and whose attitude toward the parental figure, the mother, is both dependent and compliant and resistant. The mother figure is introduced as a dubious supporter and punitive agent. There is conflict around achievement and pleasure. The defense mechanisms of negativism "he didn't want to play," and reaction formation "he became a great violinist," are noted. (Very prominent in other themes was the mechanism of identification with the enemy "then the man and the dinosaur were great friends.")

That the boy believes that he must relinquish his wishes in order to avoid maternal rejection is one possible interpretation which follows from the initial restatement of the story. Other themes emerged from others stories. In real life, the boy was concerned with his size (which was in fact not especially small for his age) as a consequence of his lack of power in relation to more aggressive males. He was also overly attached to his mother.

In addition to the descriptive and interpretive levels, the main theme can also be understood in terms of other levels which employ psychoanalytic concepts (8). When the main data from each story are summarized, repetitive patterns usually become apparent. As with all projective devices or tests, the material is most sensibly used in conjunction with factual behavioral information.

OBSERVATIONS AND INTERVIEW

The evaluation of a child implies more than applying a stimulus to an organism in order to elicit a response, as one might find in an experimental laboratory. The I.Q. test, the developmental scale, the projective device, the specialized tests, suggest a variety of assessment approaches for children, but the tests—particularly in the area of personality assessment—cannot meet the entire task. "Other sources of information are needed to follow up or supplement the leads provided by test scores, to assess traits for which no adequate tests are available, and to obtain criterion data for developing and validating personality tests" (6, p. 606). The techniques of observation and interview (including a parent interview), permit more differentiation of the particular child, and the particular nature of his presenting problems, as well as providing information about the history of events which may have contributed to the problem.

Young children cannot be interviewed as such. Naturalistic observation at home or with familiar people, is to be perferred, but is not always feasible. The following is an observation carried on in the home, prior to formal testing, of a two-year-old girl, an only child of college educated parents, who was being considered for nursery school as an early entrant.

Amy is an attractive child with dark hair and eyes. Handedness as expected is not yet established, but there is right hand consistency for some skills. Body build is sturdy and well proportioned. She is taller (about 36 inches) and heavier (30 pounds) than the average two year old. One wonders whether her larger size may invoke greater expectations from others as they may infer that she is older than she is. Gait is surefooted and devoid of the toddler's broad-based stance. Climbing is well-established and there is good navigation on stairs going up and down. Fine finger grasp is well-developed in terms of small things picked up from the floor, turning on light switches and the T.V. knob, and turning the pages of a book one at a time. A finger grasp is used with a pencil to make elliptical type scribbles.

Gaze is direct and intent for people and things. Tonal quality of voice is pleasant, and a variety of inflections are used. Telegraphic or condensed speech is still present, and there are a smattering of words which are "anybody's guess." But three and four word sentences with the use of pronouns like "I" and "mine" are heard. For the most part, the Mother's interpretation and translation are required only occasionally.

(The following sequence of behavior was observed.)

Amy approached the examiner almost immediately with the command "books," the condensed form for "read me books" or an equivalent thereof. A Dr. Seuss picture vocabulary book was used, and Amy accepted the examiner's lead and echoed "see the bear." She soon began to spontaneously name and gave qualifying explanations "hat, it's a party hat." She did not name indiscriminately. If she did not know the name, she did not say anything. She did not classify all animals as "horsie" or "doggie." As attention wore thin Amy caught sight of her mother's purse, "money" and decided to explore. She settled on some pennies which she turned into a counting game, "one." She waited expectantly for the Examiner to say "two," so she could squeal "three" with delight.

At this point a two-and-a-half-year-old boy and his three-and-a-half-year-old sister entered. (These children will not be described in detail since the focus of the incident is on Amy). Briefly, the boy is a sturdy, round-faced child whose presence is immediately felt. He is a definite character, aggressive, demanding, boisterous, and totally unable to "wait a minute." The sister by contrast is petite, not as vibrant, but in good command of herself, verbal and social in a conforming way. She is sometimes quite harassed by her brother.

The brother and sister worked initially as a team, taking over Amy's toys, squealing and playing a verbal repetitive game they seemed to know "moo, goo, goo, schoo you schmoo, you you . . . " Their noise seemed to aid in their takeover. Amy remained on the periphery, a little startled even though she knew the two. She watched as they manipulated her toys and finally said: "das my doll, das Amy's doll." She apparently made the decision to enter the fray and tried to retrieve her doll. The boy shoved her and ran from the room. As he left he took the frenzied atmosphere with him and the two girls quieted down and began to interact with one another. The girl assumed the lead with "let's play" and directed Amy to the bathroom where she submitted to being the "baby." The girl went through the whole grooming process berating Amy at every step: "Wash your dirty face, ooh your hands are dirty, mommy combs your hair, don't cry." There was active role playing on the part of the three-and-a-half-year-old but Amy clearly cooperated, that is until she was pushed towards the toilet seat with the command "make pee pee." "No pee pee," protested Amy (who was not willing to be toilet trained). Amy became less enchanted with the game, and seemed rather relieved as the two children left. A period of listlessness ensued, but gradually she resumed her spirits and once more approached the examiner with "books."

Amy is an engaging child who appears advanced for her age both in terms of physical and mental development. She shows examples of the two year old's sense of developing autonomy, some of the ritualistic behavior of the two and a half year old, and some isolated behavior of the three year old—the ability to be controlled to some extent by language and beginning attempts at social conformity. Her play is beyond the expected play level of the two year old and is interactive. She was outmaneuvered by the older child and the more aggressive child, but she "took a stand" and did well for her age.

Gloria, a four-year-and-nine-month-old girl was observed for purposes of possible inclusion in a study of normal child development.

Gloria is the older of two female children. She is dark haired and has large luminous eyes. By contrast, her skin appears pale and sallow. Body build is slender but height appears average for almost five years of age (about 40 inches), and general proportion is good. Stride is as expected smooth and rhythmical. Hand preference is right. Speech however, is marked by a nasal quality e.g.: "url" for girl, and contains a variety of infantile sound substitutions, "widdle" for little, and omissions, "gove" for glove. Intelligibility is nevertheless intact, particularly if the listener is familiar with the speech of young children (one is also aided by the context of the immediate situation).

Gloria is meticulously dressed, down to the smallest matching detail. The clothing is clearly "little girl" and meant for display. However the little girl appears quite opposed to "show" of any kind. The following incident was observed.

Gloria was invited into the playroom by the examiner. She held on to her mother's dress attempting to hide her face. She did not permit separation. Her facial expression was strained and frightened. She did not speak, but shook her head in response to her mother's queries. She gestured her wants. Her mother appeared ineffectual and helpless, almost in direct proportion to the child's anxiety. They did not seem to get comfort from one another.

The examiner decided not to focus on Gloria and directed talk to the mother. Once out of the limelight, Gloria began to move cautiously about the room, glancing every now and then at the examiner stranger. She seemed more interested in knowing about the examiner than in touching the toys. Did she first have to ascertain the relative safety and acceptance of the environment before she could permit herself any freedoms? It then became quite apparent that Gloria had "tuned in" on the conversation between the mother and the examiner, and she began to gesture towards herself when her name was mentioned. Finally when the mother was fully engrossed and appeared relaxed herself, Gloria approached the examiner and began whispering softly. Was it now clear to her that her mother was relaxed and so that must be a sign that the examiner was a friend and not a foe?

The whispering became louder, and it was apparent that Gloria was pointing out things about people and things that were wrong in some way: "The doyee's (dolly) foot is broken, mommy has a hole in her sock." One got the impression that she was "telling on them," as she may have felt that her mommy was "telling on her." The mother went right on talking, she did not seem sensitive to the child's cues. The examiner adjusted her full attention to Gloria whose face appeared more relaxed too. Her general activity had taken on more spontaneity. The "ice was broken" when Gloria seemed to forget herself and the whisper turned into an unexpected shout: "I'm telling you about the doyee." The surprise caused everyone to laugh, and at that point she allowed her mother to leave the room.

Gloria's animation increased and she made sounds of delight "ooh, eee" as some game-like tasks were presented. She was eager to the point of impulsivity, grabbing at the materials as if they would be taken away if she didn't hurry. She responded to the structuring of the examiner and happily repeated "we have yots of games to pway." But perhaps she had to hurry lest the anxiety return, because at that moment she expressed some concerns about her mother's whereabouts and whether or not the door was locked. Was this situation really safe after all? Gloria was told that it was time to go. She freely kissed the examiner as she left, announcing "I'll come back."

Gloria is an almost five-year-old girl who has achieved adequate skeletal and other physical attributes of maturation for her age, but whose speech articulation and development are below par, and whose social and emotional development are also below expectation for her age. Instead of the more stable, reliable, secure behavior frequently associated with four and a half to five year olds, one sees the insecurity, and emotional extremes of the three and a half to four year old. Gloria was not considered eligible for the study of normal child development.

Michael, a two year, seven-month-old boy, an only child, was observed prior to a general developmental evaluation. His parents considered themselves to be "progressive" and had tried to rear their child according to "psychological principles." The father explained that Michael was accustomed to "straightforward" words such as "bowel movements" and "pee pee" (note the two levels, "pee pee" seems a little less sophisticated but perhaps more straightforward than "bowel movement," in any event the two terms did not seem comparable), and that he knew all about puzzles, and that he was not permitted to handle certain books in the house "he knows which are his and which are ours," and that he liked water and had tried experimenting with the water in the toilet, but that practice had been stopped by simply telling Michael not to (remarkable restraint for little Michael). The parents characterized their child as one who "takes things philosophically and is not very reactive—but he has a mind of his own."

Michael appears on the small side for age, but his body is nevertheless well-proportioned. Hair is fair and eyes are blue. Hand preference is not yet established. Gait is smoothly coordinated, but deliberate and slow moving. Hand functions appear well-developed for age. Speech is composed of short sentences of good intelligibility "me go bye bye," but just as Michael moves slowly and deliberately as though he measures carefully, so his speech seems metered, and verbalizations are few and far between.

Michael is dressed in a pale blue and white outfit, more usually seen on the infant or early toddler. The baby clothing reinforces the small size and creates an infantile picture. An extraordinary neatness is noticeable about this little boy. Everything about him is exactly in place, not a speck of dirt is to be seen on his clothing, nor is much "sticky" from the left-over lollypop to be found on mouth or hands. The following incident was observed:

Michael looked a little anxious as his parents left, but he did not cry or say much. He seemed to study the examiner and watched from a short distance. The examiner sat on the floor and surrounded herself with a few toys. Michael moved in slowly. He looked interested in the possibilities inherent in the situation. He seated himself in a small chair next to the examiner and patiently awaited events to come. All of this time, he remained quiet, but alert to everything. Michael's momentum built up very slowly. He was invited to knock down a tower of blocks. He appeared to deliberate the problem. Was he afraid to be untidy, or unruly, or to lose control? Finally he pushed gently, carefully controlling the fall of the blocks with his other hand.

Gradually he became a little more animated and said: "all fall down, some more." Despite the fact that he was pleased and a little excited, he did not move much. He continued in an unhurried fashion, but experimented with a little wilder play and pushed the blocks so that one spun across the room. "Hit the chair" was repeated as a chant. Was he surprised to find that a little aggressive play could be fun? For the first time Michael got out of his chair and moved about to retrieve the scattered blocks. As he did so, he spotted a toy T.V. set and began to half hum and half say the words to the Ajax commercial. Was he feeling more buoyant, or did the toy T.V. set off the association? He approached the chair and it became apparent to him that he had to crawl underneath to get the blocks. He hesitated. It was not known if he was considering the possibility of getting dirty, or the mere exertion of the act, or whatever. After a moment, he said: "London Bridges" and crawled under the chair to get the blocks. Maybe the comment had something to with "London Bridge is falling down," like the blocks fell down? In any event, he was quite smiley as he emerged with the blocks. He was a little mussed looking, but "I get it" (the blocks) seemed more important.

In some ways Michael demonstrated the disequilibrium of the two and a half year old in that he did not adapt easily to the new situation, and that he tended to be ritualistic. But at the same time he showed evidence of the acculturation of the 3 year old (keeping himself within proper bounds). It is suspected that some of his controls were excessive and were built in early by parental demands, possibly at the expense of some of this child's spontaneity.

Interview procedures with the older child are less fortuitous and more structured, and some older children can directly corroborate certain observations.

Charles, almost 15-years-old, was brought for evaluation because of poor peer relationships, a sudden drop in grades at school (ninth grade), and the fact that he recently seemed excessively concerned with certain sounds and word combinations. A tall, thin, blond boy, Charles wears corrective lenses. Facial skin is marked by a touch of adolescent acne and there is an accumulation of fuzz in the moustache area. Nails and fingertips are bitten "I chew them when I get nervous." Speech is rapid, tonal quality soft, and there is the suggestion of a residual lisp. Gaze was usually averted.

Charles viewed the testing procedure as "treatment." He said he was "worried" about being changed, that he liked things the way they were, and that he didn't want "to remove the bad things—if

you're changed it's no good, like when you're afraid of things, like being scared of a test in school, it's partly exciting, it's like loving and hating, you should have both."

In a manner that seemed flat and automatic, Charles recited in detail the nature of his ever-increasing difficulties. He said that the p sound bothered him "as far back as I can remember—the feeling comes over me, a wave of anger and disgust." Q. "Yes, words like 'disrespectful' give me a creepy feeling." More often than not the boy's father played a prominent part in a complicated system of sounds and sights, with the boy taking the position that he father's behavior was deliberate. "He makes a lot of sounds I don't like, he has a way of sniffing and snorting just before he says something negative, his face is flat, his eyes look mad." Q. "Yes, soft tapping of a pencil on paper bothers me. I have a feeling of annoyance about certain round bottles, it takes a certain combination of moods, I pick it up and put it down again, I can't stand it if the desks in school rock back and forth and make a noise." Q. "I'm scared of mirrors." Q. "I don't like my face." Q. "It's the darkness of the brows." Q. "People tease me about these habits but I have to do them."

There were fears around falling asleep, about being away from home, fear of making a mistake, fear of crowds, and fear of being approached by stange men. Almost any line of questioning elicited fears which were part of this boy's thinking disorder, and marked personality disorder.

Clinical Illustration: Excerpts from a psychological evaluation—The "Acting Out" Child

Reason for Referral: George is an almost 11-year-old boy referred for evaluation because of aggressive and rebellious behavior. He is currently hospitalized for surgery for bilateral femoral anteversion.

Developmental milestones were reported as within normal limits. Beginning at age four, George sustained a number of injuries which were said to be "accidents," and which included a penetrating injury to the right eye. There have been many hospitalizations, always at different hospitals. The family history is positive for psycho-social pathology.

General Observations: George is a tall boy for his age. He wears corrective lenses. Gait is clumsy, presumably by virtue of the anteversion of the feet, and there is a tendency to pitch forward. He is noted to have chipped front teeth, a burn scar on the left forearm and on the left cheek. There are also numerous small, round marks on the legs.

Speech is readily intelligible despite some sound substitutions, and difficulty with the organization of language. Discounting the sub-voice mumblings George used when he didn't wish to answer, it was otherwise amazing to see how adroit he could be when it came to avoiding giving information. Although cooperative for testing, he remained selective and evasive about his home life and the various "accidents."

Test findings: George obtained I.Q. ratings within the Average range (WISC-R), with some unevenness of functioning reflected in verbal areas. No particular discrepancies were noted with regard to visual-spatial perception and/or synthesis. Achievement skills measured fell below expectation for grade placement. However, George's school attendance has been erratic, and he has "run away" from home several times.

Although evasive in direct interview, Geroge was able to "say" a little more via the projective device. George's stories revolved about a mother and son, wherein the son employed the theme "you'll be sorry when I'm dead." Invariably, the boy would mysteriously disappear (George has run away), with the hope that his mother's attention and sympathy would be aroused. However, little satisfaction was derived because when the boy returned "the mother doesn't even think it's her son."

Adult figures were otherwise perceived as being engaged in some form of unusual exhibitionistic behavior.

> "She's an actor and the form of her dress is a pumpkin." (The choice of "pumpkin" was considered idiosyncratic. It was subsequently associated with the nursery rhyme "Peter, Peter pumpkin eater" which in turn raised a variety of associations of a sexual nature.) "She is a flying actor (flying is a term often used in connection with the use of drugs and/or alcohol). "When she comes from one show, she practices the next show." Q. "She's going to do a flying act." Q. "She does it with a man." Q. "I don't know who the man is." Q. "We put a net under them and if anything goes wrong, they can fall in the net." Q. "She's a mother, she got kids, she makes beds and washes dishes." Q. "She likes to do the flying act cause she gets paid."

Sentence completions included:
> One's closest friend can, "harm another." Behind one's back, "he has been stabbed." The best of mother's may forget that, "they have children."

While implications for a learning disability are present and should be additionally investigated, the immediate problem is that of an "acting out" child responding to what the history suggests is chronic deprivation by significant adults. Whether George is still capable of forming attachments to people on other than an infantile level remains to be seen.

Child abuse charges were subsequently lodged, and George was placed in a residential school and treatment setting.

SUMMARY

The psychological testing of a child represents an integrative effort by a trained and experienced pediatric psychologist for the purpose of contibuting to a decision making process and treatment plan for that child. The evaluation procedure is a clinical procedure, but it does not constitute a diagnosis in the traditional medical model with implications for exact etiology and prognosis. It is rather, as Anastasi (6) suggests, a gathering of multiple kinds of information from multiple sources which are subject to hypothesis testing, and confirmation for each individual child. For the most part, the information obtained is "here and now" just as the problems are "here and now." Some inferences can be made about expectations for performance on the basis of departure from developmental norms.

The methodology and instrumentation of the psychological assessment process do not meet the laboratory criteria for precision, but perhaps that is because of the complexity and elusiveness of human child behavior. That human behavior can even be fully defined, much less codified for prediction purposes, seems a contradiction in terms of the concept "human." However, to want to know and to try to know the multitude of possibilities is also "human."

REFERENCES

1. Alpern, G.D., and Kimberlin, C.G.: Short intelligence test ranging from infancy levels through childhood levels for use with the retarded. *American Journal of Mental Deficiency*, 75:67-71, 1970.
2. Ames, L.B., Metraux, R.W. and Walker, R.N.: *Adolescent Rorschach Responses: Developmental Trends from Ten to Sixteen Years*, 2nd ed. New York: Brunner/Mazel, 1971.
3. Ames, L.B., Metraux, R.W., Rodell, J.L., and Walker, R.N.: *Child Rorschach Responses: Developmental Trends from Two to Ten Years*, rev. ed. New York: Brunner/Mazel, 1974.
4. Anastasi, A.: *Psychological Testing*, 3rd ed. New York: Macmillan, 1968.
5. Anastasi, A.: Psychological testing of children. In A. Freedman, H. Kaplan, and B. Saddock (Eds.), *Comprehensive Textbook of Psychiatry*, 2nd ed. Vol. II, Baltimore: Williams and Wilkins, 1975.
6. Anastasi, A.: *Psychological Testing*, 4th ed. New York: Macmillan, 1976.
7. Bayley, N.: Development of mental abilities. In P.H. Mussen (Ed.), *Manual of Child Psychology*, New York: Wiley, 1970.
8. Bellak, L.: *A Guide to the Interpretation of the Thematic Apperception Test*, New York: The Psychological Corporation, 1947.
9. Benton, A.L.: Psychological tests for brain damage, In A. Freedman, H. Kaplan, and

B. Saddock (Eds.), *Comprehensive Textbook of Psychiatry*, 2nd ed. Vol. I, Baltimore: Williams and Wilkins, 1975.

10. Bortner, M.: *Evaluation and Education of Children with Brain Damage*. Springfield: Charles C. Thomas, 1968.

11. Ferinden, W.E., and Jacobson, S.: *Educational Interpretation of the WISC*. Linden, New Jersey: Remediation Associates, 1969.

12. Francis-Williams, J.: Rorschach With Children. London: Pergamon Press, 1968.

13. Gesell, A., and Amatruda, C.S.: *Developmental Diagnosis*. 2nd ed. New York: Hoeber-Harper, 1947.

14. Glasser, A.J., and Zimmerman, I.L.: *Clinical Interpretation of The Wechsler Intelligence Scale for Children*. New York: Grune and Stratton, 1967.

15. Goldfried, M.R., Stricker, G., and Weiner, I.R.: *Rorschach Handbook of Clinical and Research Applications*. Englewood Cliffs. N.J.: Prentice-Hall, 1971.

16. Goldschmid, M.L., and Bentler. P.M.: *Manual: Concept Assessment Kit—Conservation*, San Diego, California: Educational and Industrial Testing Service, 1968.

17. Halpern, F.: *A Clinical Approach to Children's Rorschachs*, New York: Grune and Stratton, 1953.

18. Kaufman, A.S., and Hollenbeck, G.P.: Factor analysis of the standardization edition of the McCarthy scales. *Journal of Clinical Psychology*, 29:358-362, 1973.

19. Koppitz, E.M.: *Psychological Evaluation of Children's Human Figure Drawings*, New York: Grune and Stratton, 1968.

20. Laurendeau, M., and Pinard, A.: *Causal Thinking in The Child: A Genetic and Experimental Approach*. New York: International Universities Press, 1962.

21. Laurendeau, M., and Pinard, A.: *The Development of the Concept of Space in The Child*. New York: International Universities Press, 1970.

22. Levitt, E.E., and Truumaa, A.: *The Rorschach Technique with Children and Adolescents: Application and Norms*, New York: Grune and Stratton, 1972.

23. Liverant, S.: Intelligence: A concept in need of reexamination. *Journal of Consulting Psychology*, 24:101-110, 1960.

24. Maher, B.A.: Intelligence and brain damage. In N.R. Ellis (Ed.), *Handbook of Mental Deficiency*, New York: McGraw-Hill, 1963.

25. Pogul, L.J.: The effects of reduced linguistic complexity on intelligence test performance in children with minimal brain dysfunction and associated language disorders, Unpublished doctoral dissertation, Columbia University, 1974.

26. Rabin, A.J.: Diagnostic use of intelligence tests, In B.B. Wolman (Ed.), *Handbook of Clinical Psychology*, New York: McGraw-Hill, 1965.

27. Reitan, R.M. and Davison, L.S.: *Clinical Neuropsychology: Current Status and Applications*. Washington, D.C.: Winston Wiley, 1974.

28. Robinson, H.B. and Robinson, N.M.: *The Mentally Retarded Child*. New York: McGraw-Hill, 1965.

29. Schneidman, E.S.: Projective techniques. In B.B. Wolman (Ed.), *Handbook of Clinical Psychology*, New York: McGraw-Hill, 1965.

30. Taylor, E.M.: *Psychological Appraisal of Children with Cerebral Defects*. Cambridge, Mass.: Harvard University Press, 1961.

31. Terman, L.M. and Merrill, M.A.: *Stanford-Binet Intelligence Scale Manual for the Third Revision Form L-M*. Boston: Houghton-Mifflin, 1960.

32. Valett, R.E.: *A Profile for The Stanford-Binet L-M*. Palo Alto, California: Consulting Psychologists Press, 1965.

16

Approaches to the Dying Child

RODMAN GILDER, M.D.
and
PENELOPE BUSCHMAN, R.N., C.S., M.S.

INTRODUCTION

Painful and debilitating illness, hospitalization with its strange environment, and the threat of losing the mother's care, put unusual emotional stress on the child. This has been described in vivid detail in the literature. Here we are emphasing the emotional stresses which are added when the child's illness is likely or sure to be terminal.

In this chapter, the focus is on children who have a fatal illness which continues beyond the acute phase, necessitating repeated tests, drugs, and hospitalizations. These children and their families endure great emotional stress for long periods of time. Their care often requires special team efforts.

Since approaches to the child depend to some extent on the child's age, we shall begin by discussing the kinds of problems encountered at various ages. Then, we shall discuss more general approaches to the dying child which we and others have found helpful.

DEVELOPMENTAL STAGES WITH CLINICAL EXAMPLES

Infancy: Birth to Three Years

The infant, dependent totally on mothering for survival, is vulnerable

The authors wish to thank: Dr. James A. Wolff, Professor of Pediatrics, Attending Pediatrician, and Director of Pediatric Hematology-Onocology, Babies Hospital and Dr. Thomas V. Santulli, Professor of Surgery, Chief of Pediatric Surgery, Babies Hospital and Attending Surgeon, Presbyterian Hospital for their ideas and suggestions in the preparation of this chapter.

to abandonment. From about six months on, he* apparently fears abandonment above all, and in the second year, dismemberment as well.

The infant lives in the present. He has no clear sense of time, and as far as we know has no concept of death looming in the future. Such a concept, however, threatens those on whom he is completely dependent for care. They are operating under a cloud, with the knowledge of impending death.

Robert:

Robert, the only child of a couple in their mid 30s, was diagnosed as having infantile chronic granulocytic leukemia at the age of seven months. From the age of one month on, he had been sickly and his mother sensed that he was indeed seriously ill. He was hospitalized between eight months and one year for a course of chemotherapy complicated by infection, nausea and vomiting, and severe weight loss. His mother remained with him day and night during the early months of this hospitalization, caring for and nurturing him. Father visited each day.

At nine months, Robert had a bone marrow remission. Because of extreme malnutrition, he had to be moved to the Metabolic Unit for hyperalimentation. While the parents were elated at the news of the remission, mother commented, "But the longer we have him, the more difficult it will be."

The mother was unable to remain with Robert in the unit. And coinciding with the separation, the mother became markedly anxious, complaining of palpitations, weakness, shortness of breath, and a light-headed sensation. She developed a phobic reponse to riding the subway, her only means of transportation to see Robert. After an illness of a week's duration, she was able to visit daily for a few hours in the evening with the father. Robert, who had been responsive to his mother, father, and a few select nurses, now became irritable and withdrawn. His babbling stopped. He turned to the wall, pulling his blanket over his head. However, a primary nurse began to work with Robert, and he responded to her overtures.

At the referral of the staff, both mother and father were seen for several sessions by the nurse therapist. Each parent was isolated in his own grief and had not been able to help the other. The father, who had continued to teach and attend law school at night, felt that he had kept a "stiff upper lip" and that his wife simply needed to get hold of herself. As the sessions progressed, he cried and spoke of his own feelings for his son. He also disclosed that he had used work and school to escape emotionally. The mother

---

*In this chapter, we use the generic "he" for male or female child.

spoke of her sense of failure in having produced a sickly infant, as well as her need for her husband's comfort, understanding and support. The therapist pointed out that the mother's somatic complaints were in response to extreme stress and were precipitated by the unplanned separation from Robert. Father accepted this, and he and his wife moved closer together, agreeing to help each other.

Robert went home to his family on his first birthday. He was in remission and able to tolerate feedings well. Mother and father acknowledged sadly that this was a bittersweet time. They felt their attachment to Robert deepening, but knew that in time he would die.

It is the job of the staff to support and encourage the mother, to emphasize and clarify her importance in the care of the child, to understand her stress and unending feeling of exhaustion, and to substitute for her when necessary. A primary care nurse may be assigned to child and mother. The mother needs to be able to express her feelings and questions regarding the role of her husband and how the siblings should be cared for. The staff should make sure that the mother is made as comfortable as possible at night, and encourage her to room in, if feasible. She should know that her role in the care of the child remains invaluable. Mothers, especially, may be acutely sensitive to any implied criticism. Their helplessness and frustration increase as the illness progresses, and they live with a deep sense of failure, failure in their primary duty: protection and survival of their children. Thus, the pain and stress are so great that families of terminally ill infants (and for that matter, children of any age) may need special supportive therapy.

Early Childhood: Three to Six Years

This is a time for the internalization of parental admonitions and standards and the appearance of true guilt reactions. Children from this age on may see the illness as punishment. Schowalter gives a vivid example (9).

In this period, it seems that many children have a concept of death as not living anymore and not functioning. The living person has gone and is not coming back. Freud and Burlingham write of four-year-old Bertie who refused to admit that his father had been killed in the war. But after six months, during which he repeatedly involved himself in play which denied the reality of his father's death, he was able to tell this story: "My father has been killed and my mother has gone to the hospital. She will come back at the end of the war, but he will not return" (4). The way in which the concept of death is introduced to the child depends on the parents' attitudes and experiences. How the child defends against these ideas depends very much on the parents' defenses and what they will allow. At this age, children apparently do not have a clear sense of time. What does permanent or eternity mean to them? These are difficult terms even for the adult.

Can seriously ill children conceive of their own demise? Very likely they can, although adults would like to deny this. Children, like adults, use whatever defenses they may have at their disposal to deny such a dreaded possibility. Rarely do children at this age state directly that they are afraid that they are going to die. See Morrissey (7), however, for one example of a child who directly confronted death. More often one has to infer this anxiety from the child's actions and from what he says.

Edward:

At the age of four years and two months, Edward was diagnosed as having lymphosarcoma. During his first hospital admission, he was a difficult patient, aggressive toward other children, uncooperative and unfriendly with the staff. His mother visited occasionally in the evening and was erratic in her support of the child.

Edward was seen by the nurse therapist for several sessions in which he vigorously played out his feelings. One fragment of the play follows:

Edward, playing roughly with a doll (representing a boy patient): "Mothers bring babies into the hospital and they die."

Pointing to the outline of a boy figure, Edward smears paint and says, "No more boy; all gone!"

Nurse: "Can we get him back?"

Edward: "No!" He gives the doll an injection. "This boy is going to die. He can't see, can't talk, can't cry!" He tapes doll to desk.

Nurse: "Is he scared?"

Edward: "Yes." As he marches out of the office, "Now this boy (i.e. Edward) is coming back tomorrow!"

Thus Edward saw illness, treatment, hospitalization and death as aggression upon him. The defense in play was to turn the tables and take on the aggressive role himself against a defenseless patient who died. But he clearly identified with the doll who could not see, hear, talk or cry, and who was going to die. All gone. There was no reversibility.

Billy:

Billy, the fourth of eight children, was diagnosed as having acute lymphocytic leukemia at three years and three months of age. He remained in remission after the first hospitalization until he was five years and two months old when he suffered central nervous system involvement. At five years and seven months, he had a bone marrow relapse and died three months later.

During remission, he asked more about death than did any of his siblings at comparable ages. When an aunt died (Billy was four years and nine months old at the time), he asked about the box and about putting it in the ground. He said, "Not me, Mom. I'm not going to die!" Half-joking with his mother, he said, "I won't die. Doctors won't die; firemen won't die; policemen won't die. Will you die, Mommy?"

She answered, "Yes."

He said, "I won't die!" Mother said that he would, sometime—like everybody else and Billy answered with laughter, "Not me!"

The parents took Billy and his siblings to the cemetery several times. They talked about death and burial and how the soul goes to heaven. They made the trips to the cemetery into a warm family affair. Billy described the place as " . . . pretty. It's the place with the ducks." On the other hand, the parents made strong effort is to keep the fact that Billy would die from his siblings. They vigorously denied that the other children were aware of Billy's impending death. This was in spite of their recounting in a parent group meeting that the 10-year-old brother had said when Billy was at home and vomiting, "Don't die, Billy, I'd be the only brother left."

This balance of facing death and denying death with both Billy and his siblings seemed to work out well in this family.

These two examples suggest the child's dawning understanding of his situation. His adaptation depends to a large extent on parental attitudes and support.

Late Childhood: Six Years to Puberty

During this period, the character structure becomes more stabilized with strong defenses against guilt and shame. Ideals develop, and the conscience gradually becomes less rigid and more adapted to social customs. The relationship with parents is loosened and interest is diverted more toward other adults and peers.

By this age, most children who have had a fatal illness for some time sense the seriousness of their situation. Just how they cope depends on their own defenses and on the way the adults, especially their parents, cope with their own feelings.

Four examples are presented to show different kinds of reactions in children of this age.

Carlie: Perfect Control

At six years, nine months of age, Carlie, the oldest of four children of a Catholic family, was diagnosed as having acute lymphocytic leukemia. After the first hospitalization of about four weeks she was in remission to the age of 10 years and three months.

Her parents told her that she had a blood problem. To protect her, they avoided telling her the diagnosis or prognosis. She was a well-behaved, sensitive, responsive child, interested in girlish things, including dolls. The parents played an active role in parent group meetings. Although they argued that she did not understand the seriousness of her illness, they were able to report what Carlie was saying which suggested that she was indeed concerned with the idea of separation from mother and of dying.

For instance, she remarked how adults liked her better since she got sick. At another time she said, "I don't want to grow up . . . I don't like how boney I look . . . I might die before long . . . Am I going to die today? . . . Will you be happy or sad? . . . Why does Daddy look so sad?" While Christmas shopping for her mother, she confided to her aunt that she wanted to avoid buying something perishable like underwear, but rather " . . . something mother will remember me by till she's 100 years old—if she lives that long."

Both parents, though inwardly distressed, were always supportive of Carlie; they denied that she would die soon and said they hoped that everything would be all right.

Carlie's illness relapsed when she was 10 years and three months. She said, "Daddy, you look as if it's serious." He said, "Yes." She asked if she would die from it. He blurted out, "Yes." She was terrified. However, when she realized she would not die right away, she calmed down. Later she said, "Then I won't be able to have babies."

When she was 10 years and seven months old, during the second relapse of the illness, her mother brought her to a psychotherapist because she seemed more anxious than usual. He saw her four times. During the interviews, she appeared pale but comfortable and in no pain. She was friendly, responsive, polite and in perfect control. She ostensibly accepted her situation. She rationalized smoothly and used denial when it seemed plausible.

However, in her responses to her drawings and the TAT cards (8), in her telling of a dream, and in talking of her family and pets, she was able to communicate her hidden feelings.

She drew a neat controlled figure of a girl. "The girl is happy just being there and going someplace she likes." To the drawing of the boy, she said. "He looks lost, bewildered . . . wonders where he should go . . . feels blah . . . wishes he knew what to do."

To the TAT card #1 she explained, "He's just given up the

violin. He's tried hard. No one can help him with it. I play the flute!"

To card #2: "A high school girl going to school in the country. Sort of wishes she doesn't have to go. Looking back to her mother, brother, or father doing their jobs. She wishes she could stay home and help. Mother looks helpless and tired . . . "

She was critical of her brother, two years younger, who was now stronger than she. He teased her. He did not take care of his animal pets. His turtle died and he stepped on a pet bird.

Carlie talked long about the various pets who had died. When the therapist suggested that the deaths were very upsetting, she said, "I think God knows best. "He's doing what's right. He wouldn't [have me die] if it wasn't right."

She recounted a dream: "On a train to a big pool . . we were measuring water where it came up to us. My little cousin went down and down. She said, bubbly 'It's coming up to my nose'."

She explained that her cousin, seven months old, had recently been baptized. Baptism had been delayed because as a newborn the infant was not expected to live.

It is evident that Carlie lived in apprehension of impending death. This was true even in the early years of the illness (ages six through 10 years) when the parents had tried to protect her from the knowledge of the disease. She had asked questions about dying, but being sensitive to their apprehensions, as well as her own, went along with their denials and reassurances. This balance was maintained until she was 10 years old when her father in his anguish blurted out the truth. After her initial panic, the parents could be freer and more frank with her and more responsive to her anxiety.

She had more than ordinary resources with which to cope. She had the ability to repress her anger and put a good, almost goody goody, covering over her main concerns. Still, death was near for her. It was associated in her mind with the feeling of being lost, bewildered, and helpless, with anxiety over separation from home, and with drowning and the restitutive wish for baptism and rebirth.

As for blame, she displaced it from her parents and from God, who " . . . is doing what's right," to her brother who killed animals by his thoughtlessness, his clumsy aggressiveness, and his lack of maternal care.

Juanita: Hypochondriacal

Juanita's illness was diagnosed as acute lymphocytic leukemia when she was almost 10 years old. Initial treatment was successful inducing a remission. She was home for four months during which she had a school phobia, not an uncommon occurrence in children with terminal illness. She then suffered a bone marrow relapse and so returned for her second admission.

While in the hospital and she was anxious about her body and had many hypochondriacal complaints of pain in her stomach, back and legs. Juanita was lonely and missed her mother who was unable to visit frequently.

In interviews with a nurse therapist, Juanita told the following dream: She was given a baby to hold. She needed a bath and Juanita placed the baby under running water. Mother entered and said, "Oh, Juanita, do you know what you've done?" Juanita responded, "I drowned the baby dead! The baby is dead."

In a later interview while the nurse therapist was giving her a back rub for back and leg pains, she was able to ask the question, "Will I ever get better?" (Not quite the question, "Am I going to die?" But very close.) The nurse explained that the disease would not go away, but she would sometimes have good days. The child was relieved temporarily. She said the pain was gone and she asked to get out of bed and walk around.

A few days later, she related a second dream to the nurse therapist: "I wanted a pizza to eat. And who do you think went out for it? It was you!"

In subsequent interviews, she avoided discussions of the seriousness of her illness or death or drowning. Two weeks later, when asked to recount the first dream, she did so but eliminated any reference to drowning. Apparently she had repressed the memory of "drowning the baby dead."

This condensed material gives us a glimpse into the hidden thoughts of the child. There is evidently the idea of death by passively drowning which Juanita handles in the dream by taking the active role (and perhaps invoking her early murderous wishes against her brother, two years younger than she). To wish to drown someone is certainly a guilt-producing idea. Her hypochondriacal complaints may be evidence of her deserved suffering. On the other hand, to be suffering does have a positive value. It stands against the fear of dying: To be suffering is to be alive.

Why was the child relieved when the nurse gave her a back rub and explained that the illness would not go away? It seems the child was able to get closer to the nurse with whom she could identify. The nurse accepted the child's expressions. This diminished guilt. The patient was less alone. Trust was fostered.

The second dream suggests the child's wish to be helped and fed by the nurse. And during subsequent days and in the context of her relationship with the nurse therapist, she was better able to repress her fears of death and maintain a more comfortable state.

Catherine: Moody and Difficult

Catherine's illness was diagnosed to be acute lymphocytic leukemia at nine years and three months. Five months previously, she had experienced generalized fatigue and night terrors on several occasions. Two months later, on her ninth birthday, she began spiking fevers and complained of joint pains.

She was the fourth of five children. She had always been somewhat demanding, stubborn, and moody. She was aggressive with peers and loved gym and biking.

The mother insisted that the child not be told she had leukemia; and the father agreed. Discussions with the parents alone and in the parent group failed to loosen their resolve that the child be kept from knowing the seriousness of her disease.

On being interviewed by a psychotherapist in the hospital, however, the child spontaneously remarked that her dog died at the age of nine years and that she herself got sick on her ninth birthday. Later she remarked that John (a boy near death with leukemia two doors away) had the same disease as she.

Still, she maintained, as the mother had to her, that she had the same disease as her mother who was taking vitamin B-12 for anemia.

Thus, while insisting that her disease was not serious, she unconsciously revealed how anxious she was about her possible impending death. She was moody and complaining, taking out her anger especially on her mother who, in vain, tried to appease her.

Malcom: Phobic, Oppositional, and Sullen

Malcom was 11 years old when the diagnosis of actue lymphocytic leukemia was made. The parents, both professionals, came to one group meeting of parents of children with leukemia. They felt overwhelmed by the thought of their child's illness. So they stayed away from further group meetings in at attempt to avoid thinking about the illness as much as possible.

Malcolm had always been a somewhat oppositional child; but with some sensitive flexibility on the mother's part, he had functioned fairly well and was popular with his peers. Since the onset of his illness he tended to be sullen and morose with his parents and his doctor. When he lost his hair because of medication, he began withdrawing from his friends. He avoided contact sports as he feared his wig might be knocked off.

About one year after the diagnosis was made, the illness relapsed. He became especially angry and complaining to his doctor. A crisis developed in treatment because he refused to swallow 6 mercaptopurine, a tastless anti-leukemic drug. Even when the capsule would approach his mouth, he would retch and vomit. His mother tried to fool him by dissolving the drug in potato or pancake. He usually discovered what she had done and would promptly vomit.

The hematologist pursuaded the parents to have a psychiatric

evaluation. In an interview with a psychotherapist the parents
brought out how their child had lately been especially difficult to
deal with and how against parental pressure, he managed to maintain a remarkably messy room. It was clear that their child was
angry and depressed. When the therapist suggested that they open
up a discussion with the child about the question of his diagnosis
and the seriousness of his disease, they answered that they felt
unable to handle it. And besides, they had been afraid to tell him
he had leukemia because he might then stop taking all medication
and become completely uncooperative. The father suggested that
Malcom be hypnotized and then pursuaded to take the drug.

In the first interview, Malcom was wearing a wig. He smiled
stiffly, and was initially guarded and angry. He was angry at his
doctor, the hematologist, who he said would not give him a straight
answer about his blood, and he was furious that the doctor had
said a year ago that the disease would be over in one year. "Now
it's a year and I think it will be one more year, at least." Actually
the doctor had only implied one year by saying euphemistically,
"Let's see in one year." So the patient felt he had a grievance against
the doctor—a grievance which shifted the focus away from his real
anxiety and frustration, the fact that he had an incurable disease.
This issue was hidden behind Malcom's struggle with his doctor
over the procedures and medications.

In the second interview, he explained that he didn't want to talk
to his doctor about the disease. "He's too busy," Malcom rationalized. But in the interviews with the therapist he was becoming
more spontaneous and flexible. He told of a dream: "Three fire
engines get smashed up ... I'm yelling, where's the fire? But no
one answers ... " The therapist suggested that the dream was like
his illness, no one answered his questions.

In the third interview, he described a complicated dream in
which he was being chased and cornered. The therapist suggested
that the patient himself felt cornered with his illness. Then Malcom
asked why he had to take all the medicine.

Therapist: Your mother says it's a matter of life and death. That's
very dramatic; but it is important to take the medicines. The illness
goes on. There are good times and bad times. The drugs are getting
better with more research. But still they do not cure the illness.

Malcom: Mother said it's like her anemia. She has some of it. It
goes on and she takes iron pills.

Therapist: No. It's different. It's more serious.

Malcom: What's it called?

Therapist: It's like leukemia.

Malcom: Was I born with it?

Therapist: No. You got it. But we don't know how or why. You
know about leukemia?

Malcom: No ... but I've heard the name.

Therapist: You are in very good hands. Your doctor is one of the
best in the country. So it's important to take the drug so we can

help you when the illness kicks up.

The therapist then suggested counterphobic measures to conquer his problem, and with some enthusiasm the father, son and therapist worked out a plan.

After this interview, Malcom returned home whistling and immediately went to his room and straightened it up. To the parents, he looked immensely relieved. That evening as he and his parents were crossing a busy city thoroughfare, he said to his mother, "Why didn't you tell me it was incurable? . . . It's about time a fellow gets answers."

In succeeding visits to his doctor, he was markedly more open and friendly. He teased his mother with a story of a man who suddenly died of " . . . asthma, heart attack and (pause) leukemia!" But less sadistically, he and his mother were able to have a long talk about heaven. They both hoped there was one. Meanwhile in interviews with the therapist Malcom worked on counterphobic games so that he was soon able to swallow the capsules without vomiting.

Why should there be such a positive reaction in a boy to receiving such bad tidings? In the first place, the tidings were not news to him. He strongly suspected, and may have been already convinced that he had a life-threatening and incurable disease. But now he was allowed to express his anger concerning his situation toward his doctor and his parents, whom he felt should have been frank with him. He had been afraid his parents were not strong enough to discuss the seriousness of his disease. And he had been anxious and guilty about his anger against them. From the third interview on, he was able to combine forces with father and therapist to master the phobia. He could gain strength from them, feel less isolated, take an active role and feel better about himself. Also, verbalizing his feelings gave him a sense of mastery. Meanwhile, he and his mother could be closer and could talk about dying and the possibility of heaven.

So his feelings were not all wrong. On the contrary, they made sense. He did not feel so guilty and ashamed. By explaining that doctors are working on the disease and that drugs do help, the therapist suggested that there was hope.

Reviewing some of the themes from the children of latency age, it appears that they have strong defenses against the threat of terminal illness. Still they frequently have a clearer and more precise knowledge of their illness, including its seriousness, chronicity, incurability and the threat of death, than their parents would like to admit. These children often feel not only anxious but also angry, ashamed, and guilty. They may be able to hide these emotions (much better than younger children) in line with the parents' defenses against their own similar emotions. They are likely to have to have a sharp awareness of their parents' stressful reactions. And they often do their best to avoid increasing their parents' distress or in any way threatening them further, for to do so would threaten the children's own security.

After a few months experience with a terminal illness, children of this age usually grasp the basic facts of the illness. They observe other children in wards or clinics with similar diseases, they peek at medical charts, they overhear conversations between parents and staff, they watch TV, read newspapers, magazines and the comics. It's difficult to fool these children about their illness. They have a hard time dealing with parents who attempt to fool them.

Adolescence

Just as the child is struggling to enter the adult world, it is tragic that he should be weakened and debilitated and finally cut down. He can now not only grasp the fact of death but its universality. It is particularly ineffectual to try to fool the adolescent about the nature of the illness. He has one advantage over younger children: He may be able to express his feelings with the help of abstract concepts and with more subtlety and power. Besides, being less dependent on his parents, he may find it less dangerous to express his disturbing thoughts and to confide in others.

Benjamin:

When Benjamin was nine, Hodgkins disease was diagnosed. From then on, he had repeated hospitalizations, courses of radiotherapy and chemotherapy. The doctors, nurses, and his mother conspired to keep the knowledge of the diagnosis from him. At 12 and 13, he looked up diseases in the library and appraised other children in the hospital who were getting similar treatments. His mother and the hospital staff deflected his questions concerning the diagnosis. They maintained he had anemia. Depressed and demeaned, he felt he was getting nowhere. He later explained, "I felt they didn't have confidence in me ... I wasn't mature enough for them."

When he was 13 years old, plans for his Bar Mitzvah were moved up several months. He was very ill at the time, and his mother wanted to be sure he would have the party before he died. She told her son, however, that many of his friends would not be able to attend unless the occasion was made earlier. Benjamin went along with his mother. However, he confided to his pediatrician that he knew that the date was changed " ... for other reasons."

At camp when he was 14, Benjamin was able to sneak a look at his medical chart. He found that the diagnosis was Hodgkins disease; but he told no one. He kept harassing his mother and staff with questions about his illness and angrily objected to all the treatments. He was trying to get revenge.

When he was 18 years old, his mother told him that he had Hodgkins. "It was a calm after the storm," he later said. "We all took a deep breath." Then he began to cooperate with all the treaments, and a therapeutic alliance was established which carried through to the end. He died at the age of 20 years and nine months.

In college he was extraverted and boisterous. "My point is to get known around campus. I'm always around someone all the time. I can't be alone for some reason. I don't know why. The more people I know the more I learn about life." Thus, he fought for his existence against its threatened termination and for closeness to peers against the threatened separation.

At the same time he built strong attachments to the hospital and the nurses who knew him well. "I enjoy the hospital. It's a home away from home . . . the hospital is a crutch . . . I'm with my own." The hospital and nurses, like a good mother, protected him. He suffered from insomnia based in part on a fear of dying in his sleep. But he was able to enjoy the long nights chatting with the nurses.

In some families, the parents may absolutely forbid being frank with their children regarding the diagnosis and the seriousness of his illness. The child may go along with the parents' denial to protect them. Meanwhile, he may make it fairly clear to the staff that he knows what his situation is. As the adolescent gets older, he is more and more independent of his parents and may insist on privacy from them, so that the doctor or nurse may be able to deal with him as a separate person, not only as a child of his parents. Thus, the adolescent may wish to talk of death but not involve his parents.

During these years, the adolescent's feelings may shift very rapidly from rage to grief, to guilt, to shame, to denial and elation to complaining and spitefulness, to extreme compliance, to withdrawal.

Peers, though they are important to the patient, often fail to give support because they themselves are so upset regarding the debility and threatened demise of a friend with whom they can only too easily identify.

CARE OF THE DYING CHILD

Care During the Last Days

In the last days or hours, ministering to the young patient and watching as he succubs is extremely painful to all concerned. Little has been written of this in the professional literature. We have found the work of Evans (2), however, to be most helpful.

As they become weaker, children of any age generally withdraw energy and interest from the external world and regress to a more primitive level. Their behavior suggests a return to symbiotic relationship with mother (or nurse). What is important is the presence of the mother figure to hold, comfort, and feed. And we could theorize that by means of a primitive identification and fusion with the mother, these children feel relief from tension and gain a feeling of support that defends against the anxieties of sickness, debilitation, and separation. Holding his hand, rubbing his back, singing, and talking quietly to a child in this state are more important than what is said. The child may be content to be nursed in the most infantile manner. Gone are the guilt and shame for having the illness. The child's needs are simple: He may ask for his favorite toy or blanket or a favorite food. He may be frightened and tearful and ask the mother to hold his hand or just be there.

He may be able to express his disappointment and say how angry he is at his parents or the staff. One seven-year-old boy shook his fist in the face of his special nurse but said nothing. The nurse suggested that he must feel very angry. He nodded but remained silent.

What can be offered the child at this time before death? When feasible the best comfort for the child is the mother's active and close care, day and night.

A five-year-old boy was dying of acute lymphocytic leukemia. His parents had worked hard during the two years since the diagnosis was made to help him understand his "blood sickness" and to reassure him by their comforting presence through his good and bad days. At the same time, they expected that he would die and, accordingly, months before made funeral and burial arrangements so that when the time came they would be free to be responsive to their other children. They actively participated in the parent-staff group meetings. They worked to arrive at a comprehensive understanding of the disease and treatment, and frequently met with the hematologist and the nurses so that they would be kept up to date on his day-to-day progress.

On the last admission, the mother slept in with her child and arranged with the father to have the other children boarded with friends. The parents made it clear to the hematologist that their child's suffering should not be unnecessarily prolonged. When, in fact, they were willing to stop active treatment, the hematologist felt it was still not yet time. Two days later the hematologist agreed that he had nothing more to offer in anti-leukemic treatment. He cancelled all medication (except for analgesics), reverse precautions and the orders for frequent vital signs. He continued to visit regularly. Several days later, the child died quietly in his mother's arms.

The staff's role is extremely important in supporting the parents who are living in with the child and carrying much of the care of the child. The mother needs support; she should be looked after, encouraged, and given occasional relief from her duties. In her difficult situation, a mother may be particularly sensitive to criticism. One mother became enraged because an intern asked her to leave the room while he was starting an infusion. She felt he failed to appreciate the importance of her role with her child.

It may be important for siblings to visit before the child dies. They need careful preparation and a warm welcome from the hospital staff as well as some opportunity after the visit to discuss their feelings and impressions.

Some parents in their anticipatory grieving, particularly if their children have been ill for a long time, begin to detach themselves from them as if they were already dead. They may find it too difficult to remain in the room with their children.

> One mother of a five-year-old boy who was comatose and dying of an inoperable brain tumor, could not bring herself to visit her child. Instead she called the nurses on the unit several times a day. When he actually died, she experienced relief.
>
> The mother of a 16-year-old girl, dying of cystic fibrosis, commented after her daughter had rallied, "I can't stand it. I've already said good-bye."

Easson (1) notes that parents often see their dying child as a reminder of their own vulnerability. If their identification with the child is strong, they may not be able to remain with the child while he dies. In such cases, it is essential that a nurse or other figure close to the child take the place of the mother by the bedside.

Most parents start grieving as soon as they begin to accept the idea that their child will probably die. Nevertheless, with staff help, many are able to carry on ministering to their children, lending them the closest care and support. One has the impression that these parents may be working hard to detach themselves from their children when they are away even for a few minutes. Yet when they return, they are intensely involved with them and experience the very opposite of detachment.

Near the end, further regression and withdrawal are not uncommon. Some children want to be left alone and to exist in what appears to be an objectless, autistic world. They want to reduce all stimuli from the outside world. A 10-year-old boy pulled the sheet over his head and insisted that everyone leave. Shortly afterwards he became comatose and died.

As the time of death approaches, careful consideration of medication for relief of pain and anxiety is necessary. The children may not complain; but irritability, restlessness, and crying signal their distress and discomfort. Repositioning and touching or rubbing the painful areas may be helpful. For severe pain, radiotherapy and medication may be necessary.

There is a great deal that can and should be done for the dying child. From both parents and staff, the child needs emotional support, sensitive and tender care, and adequate medication.

Interference with Good Care

From our observations and those of colleagues in several hospitals, difficulties may frustrate the smooth functioning of sensitive care. Some examples follows: 1) The doctor, at the request of parents, leaves orders not to tell the child the nature of his illness. The child, however, senses the seriousness of his illness and tries to engage the nurse in a discussion of the subject. The nurse is caught between following orders and responding directly and truthfully to the child. 2) The child and hospital staff are in a running conflict over how much analgesia he should have. The staff tends to delay the narcotic administration because the child seems to be "acting like a baby and pretending the pain is severe." 3) Doctors and nurses delay or withhold narcotics because of the fear of promoting addiction in the child. 4) A night nurse is hesitant to wake up a resident when a child needs pain medication because the resident who needs sleep might get angry. 5) A resident avoids challenging an attending doctor's management because the child is the attending's private patient. 6) Intravenous narcotic administration is delayed because the doctor is not immediately available and the hospital rule is that only a physician may administer a narcotic intravenously. 7) All standing orders for narcotics are automatically cancelled after two days. All standing orders are cancelled when the child goes to the operating room. The doctor forgets to renew orders, and the nurse fails to remind him. 8) In the last days of the illness when the child needs peace, comfort and relief from pain, he is subjected to repeated venopunctures, x-rays, and a succession of diagnostic procedures. The doctors want to be sure that nothing is missed that might save the child's life. 9) In contrast to such heroics, the staff on rounds quietly passes by the room with the dying child and waiting mother. The child's life cannot be saved; so "there is nothing to be done."

Underlying Causes

All these examples of interferences with giving the child and family full support have their own partial explanations and rationalizations. However, they all suggest some underlying theme, some unconscious motivations—unconscious because they are generally unacceptable.

The pediatric literature contains repeated admonitions not to avoid dying patients. And there seems to be a broad consensus that we should deal with children's concerns about their illness, give sufficient medication to relieve pain and anxiety, minister closely to make them more comfortable and less alone, and allow them to die in peace.

What interferes with these sensible aims? The answer lies in the unpleasant emotions generated in the doctors and nurses. We identify with the dying patient—or more accurately, we identify the child of our own childhood with the dying patient—and so, we are threatened by thoughts of separation and death. Also, we have a sense of failure for not being able to successfully oppose the forces that are inevitably moving the child to his death. Meanwhile, we may unconsciously feel angry at the child for making us feel failure. The child is more powerful in dying than we are in saving. Solnit and Green (10) suggest that those of us who have chosen our careers in part to combat the destructive forces in ourselves may feel particularly frustrated. At the same time we may feel guilty for being angry and for failing in the battle to save the child.

It is particularly difficult to face a child's direct questions about his fatal illness if we have trouble facing our own anxious identifications with the child, our anger, guilt and frustration.

Why should medication for anxiety and pain be withheld or delayed? It seems that the staff is unconsciously under pressure to avoid being a party to the child's death. There is the anxiety that the staff be blamed for doing more harm than good, or worse, for being partially responsible for the child's death.

The unnecessary ordering of tests near the end suggests that the doctors are leaning on their old patterns of medicine to protect against facing the awesome fact that "death will have its day." The avoidance of the dying child and the remarks to the effect that nothing can be done imply a denial of the importance of relieving suffering—a denial which serves to protect the doctor and nurse from their own discomfort, their own feelings of failure.

What Can Be Done to Mitigate Interference with Good Care?

Considering the feelings aroused in the staff, it is not surprising that there are difficulties in carrying out full care. These difficulties can begin with the diagnosis and extend more or less through the whole illness, often intensifying in the last days. At the time of initial diagnosis, the parents feel devastated. They need time to ask and re-ask the same questions as they gradually learn to accept the facts. The doctor has to spend time explaining the illness and his plans for treatment and in the following days he will have to repeat what he has already explained. The doctor should try to convey to the parents that they and he must work together for a single objective, that is to render the best care, make the child as comfortable as possible, and give all necessary support. In these first days and weeks after the diagnosis has been made, other parents, who have lived for some time with children having similar illnesses, may be able to offer more emotional support than the staff. The latter can systematically bring compatible "old" and "new" parents together.

Still, the relationship of staff to parents is crucial. An open and trusting therapeutic alliance needs to be developed. Questions and issues should be discussed. For instance: How much time should the mother spend with the child in the hospital? How are the siblings being taken care of? How can the father help the child and support the mother? How are the costs of care being handled and what resources are there to help with these costs? Are the parents anxious that their child is not getting the very best care? Is there the apprehension that research will take precedence over the best care possible? Is the mother angry at the doctor or the nurse but afraid to say so for fear that her child will be made to suffer?

Many of these questions might arise with the family of any ill child. But they are made more intense by the severity and the incurability of the illness and the expectation of death at the end. So the professional staff has to make special efforts.

Perhaps, the most important goal is to listen to these children and find out what their concerns are. Most children do not explain directly just what is upsetting them. Toddlers or preschoolers have difficulty putting their feelings into words because of their immaturity. But for all ages from toddler up, the concerns are so fraught with anxiety that one cannot count on children to communicate directly with doctors, nurses, or even with their parents. Some time is needed to sit down with the children and, in a way appropriate to their age, talk and play with them. Without such special efforts, the staff may miss the children's main concerns: For instance, children feel angry and feel they shouldn't be; they fear they will be left alone and be allowed to suffer; they have the idea that somehow they deserve or have caused their illness; and worst of all, they sense they will soon die.

What should children be told about their illness? They should be told what they need to know to maintain their self-esteem and trust in the important people in their lives and to cooperate fully with the treatment. A healthy respect for the truth generally promotes close cooperative and loving relationships and a feeling of mutual trust. In the long run, it seems wiser to explain that the illness is chronic, that it may not be cured or that no cure has been found yet. But should children be told that they are going to die? This is the most painful question of all—and lurks unsaid in most of these children over four years of age and in all the adults who are taking care of them.

Sometimes a child will ask directly, "Am I going to die?" A respect for the child and a regard for truth call for an affirmative answer. On the other hand a regard for the vulnerability of the child, and the awful fear connected with the idea of his own death, suggest that we do our best to respond in a way that emphasizes hope, love, comfort and protection, while minimizing the threat of death. Kliman (6) suggests "a pediatric dose of bitter truth contained in a sweetened syrup of hope" (p. 38). Some parents say, "Yes, you're going to die and so are we all . . . . sometime." They imply that death is not so near and that we are doing it together. But this fails to reassure the child who knows he is dying. The idea of heaven where all will join may assuage some of the anxiety of separation. But the reunion is for future, and children object to leaving their family now. Some parents say, "Yes, you are going to die. And we are so sad.' Thus, parents and child experience closeness, love and comfort as they mourn together.

Most adults are not comfortable with such direct communication; and many children and adults, at least at this time in this culture, tend to lean heavily on suppression of thoughts of death. Parents say they are able to carry on by "forgetting" the future and focusing their attention on the details of day-to-day care. This position can help control their own fears and the children's as well.

The doctor, nurse, and social worker can help by being as open with the parents and child as possible, encouraging them to express their concerns, and helping each family find its own way of coping with the illness.

For the child who has months and even years to live with an illness such as leukemia, we have found that group meetings with the parents and staff are very useful (5). In the supportive setting of the group, parents feel less isolated and helpless and dare to bring up questions with their doctor which they would otherwise suppress for fear of antagonizing him. Meanwhile, the staff can learn what the parents' concerns are and gather information about the child and the siblings.

Those who are closest to the child and involved in long hours of care, usually the mother and one or two of the nurses, need special support. The mother should feel wanted and needed as part of the team. The nurses, who are involved in the day-to-day care of the child when he is very ill, need special consideration as well. Their professional training and experience help protect them from an uncontrolled emotional involvement. But if they are working closely with the child, they are bound to feel the strain, suffer an important loss at the end, and have to live through a period of mourning.

We have found various kinds of group meetings to be most useful. They involve the individuals who are chiefly responsible for the child's care. Staff meetings are necessary so that all will work together and be supportive of the nurse who is closest to the child. No one individual should try to bear the main emotional burden alone. The anxiety and guilt reactions can be mitigated through a general discussion of the realities of the situation. When one member of the staff is especially upset, this can be aired freely. And sometimes a staff member should be relieved of some duties.

At some time there is a shift of emphasis in treatment goals from lifesaving, death defying activity to relief of suffering. When should this time be? The decision cannot be made by the doctor alone. It involves consultations, staff meetings, and meetings with the parents, so that if possible a reasonable consensus can be established.

With some families, the hospital chaplain's role of understanding and support may be very helpful. In his acceptance of death, the chaplain may be an important solace to the family. He may be able to give a special meaning to life and death that the medical staff cannot give.

Finally, care should not cease with the death of the child. The doctor may suggest that the parents return after one month to go over any questions, including those regarding the postmortem examination. Parents have other questions also: They want to talk over their concerns about how much the child suffered, their responsibility for the illness or death, good feelings and bad feelings toward the hospital and staff, the reactions of their other children, and the stresses threatening the marital relationship. Many parents are eager to discuss these questions in follow-up group meetings. (Fischhoff and O'Brien (3) recently have reported this.) One main theme in these meetings is the terrible loneliness they feel in their grief. Some worry about their sanity because their grief persists; even after a year or two it may not be attenuated.

SUMMARY AND CONCLUSION

Developing approaches to dying children is difficult work because of the strong emotional forces involved. However, it is also rewarding work because it is possible with team effort to be helpful and effective.

In this chapter, we have discussed reactions in children at different age levels and general reactions which may apply to children of all ages. Our experience suggests that children as young as four years of age often understand death as an irreversible process and fear death for themselves.

The team should be in close touch with the child's concerns and the concerns of the parents. This can help them to accept the reality of their situation when they must and, at the same time, allow them their defenses, such as repression, avoidance and denial, when these work well for them.

The parents' mourning reactions begin with the first partial acceptance of the idea that their child will probably die. When away from the child, some parents work to detach themselves emotionally from the child as if he were already dead. Yet when they are with their child they can minister to him with an acute sensitivity that appears to be the very opposite of acceptance of loss and detachment.

We have described some of the emotional reactions experienced by the hospital staff which can interfere with treatment. And we have suggested maneuvers, especially group meetings at various levels, which can be useful in diminishing the interference and in strengthening the staff's therapeutic and supportive role.

We are working in the shadow of death; and while we cannot win in the end, there is a great deal we can do in the meantime to understand and help.

REFERENCES

1. Easson, W.M.: *The Dying Child: The Management of the Child or Adolescent Who is Dying,* Springfield: Charles C Thomas, 1970.
2. Evans, A.: If a child must die . . . *The New England Journal of Medicine,* 278: 138-142, 1968.
3. Fischhoff, J. and O'Brien, N.: After the child dies. *Journal of Pediatrics,* 88:140-146, 1976.
4. Freud, A. and Burlingham, D.: *War and Children.* New York: International Universities Press, pp. 68-69, 1944.
5. Gilder, R., Buschman, P., Sitarz, A. and Wolff, J.A.: Group therapy with parents of children with leukemia. *Amer. J. of Psychotherapy,* 32:276-287, April, 1978.
6. Kliman, G.: *Psychological Emergencies of Childhood.* New York and London: Grune and Stratton, pp. 30 - 43, 1968.
7. Morrissey, J., R.: Death anxiety in children with a fatal illness, *American Journal of Psychotherapy,* 18: 606 - 615, 1964.
8. Murray, H., A.: *Thematic Apperception Test.* Cambridge: Harvard University Press, 1943.
9. Schowalter, J. E.: The child's reaction to his own terminal illness. In *Loss and Grief: Psychological Management in Medical Practice.* B. Schoenberg, A. Carr, D. Peretz, and A. Kutscher, (Eds.) New York: Columbia University Press, pp. 51-69, 1970.
10. Solnit, A.J. and Green, M.: Psychological considerations in the management of deaths on pediatric hospital services 1. The doctor and the child's family, *Pediatrics* 24: 106-112, 1959.

APPENDIX
SUGGESTED READINGS

Chodoff, P., Friedman, S.B., and Hamburg D.A.: Stress, Defenses and Coping Behavior: Observation in Parents of Children with Malignant Disease. *American Journal of Psychiatry,* 120:743-749, 1964.
Freud, A.: The Role of Bodily Illness in the Mental Life of Children. *Psychoanalytic Study of the Child,* 7: 69-81, New York: International Universities Press, 1962.
Friedman, S.B., Chodoff, P., Mason, J.W., and Hamburg, D.A.: Behavioral observations of Parents Anticipating the Death of a Child. *Pediatrics,* 32: 610-625, 1963.
Furman, Erna: *A Child's Parent Dies.* New Haven and London: Yale University Press, 1974.
Furman, R.A.: Death and the Young Child. *Psychoanalytic Study of the Child,* 19:321-333. New York: International Universities Press, 1964.
Hamovitch, M.B.: *The Parent and Fatally Ill Child.* Duarte, California: City of Hope Medical Center, 1964.
Heffron, W.A., Bommelaire, K., and Masters, R.: Group Discussions with the Parents of Leukemic Children. *Pediatrics,* 52: 831-840, 1973.
Hoffman, J. and Futterman, E.H.: Coping with Waiting: Psychiatric Intervention and Study in the Waiting Room of a Pediatric Onocology Clinic. *Comprehensive Psychiatry,* 12: 67-81, 1971.
Karon, M. and Vernick, J.: An Approach to the Emotional Support of Fatally Ill Children. *Clinical Pediatrics,* 7: 274-280, 1968.
Martinson, J.M. et al., Home care for children dying of cancer. *Pediatrics,* 62:106-113, 1978.
Solnit, A.J. and Green, H.: The Pediatric Management of the Dying Child: Part II. The Child's Reactions to the Fear of Dying. In: *Modern Perspectives in Child Development,*

A.J. Solnit and S.A. Provence (Eds.) New York: International Universities Press, pp. 217-228, 1963.

Spinetta, J.J. The dying child's awareness of death: A review. *Psychological Bulletin,* 81:256-260, 1974.

Vernick, J.P., and Karon, M.: Who's Afraid of Death on a Leukemia Ward? *Am. Journal Dis. Child,* 109: 393-397, 1965.

Waechter, E.H.: Children's Awareness of Fatal Illness. *American J. of Nursing,* 71: 1168-1172, 1971.

Name Index

Subject Index

537